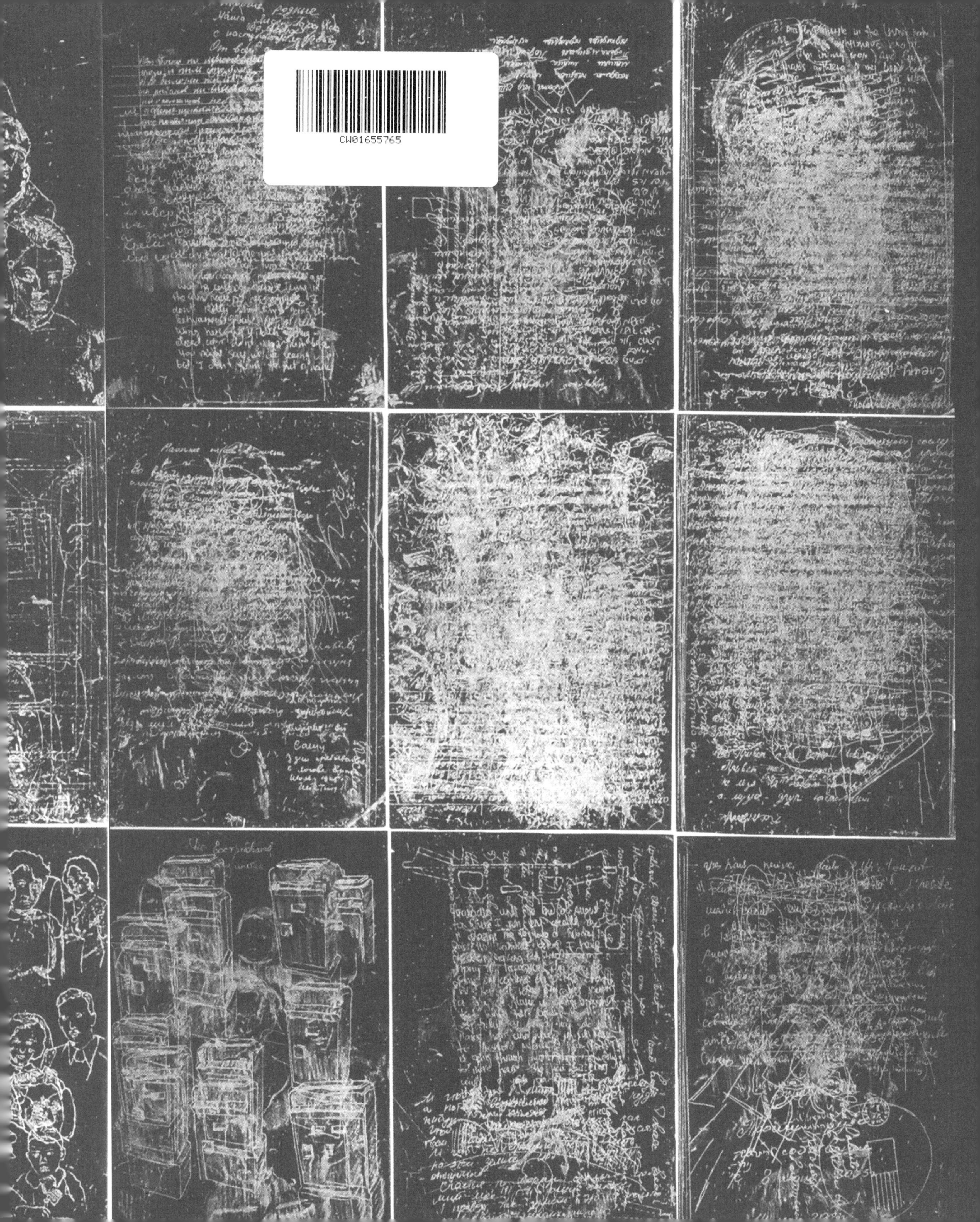

frozen dreams

Contemporary Art from Russia

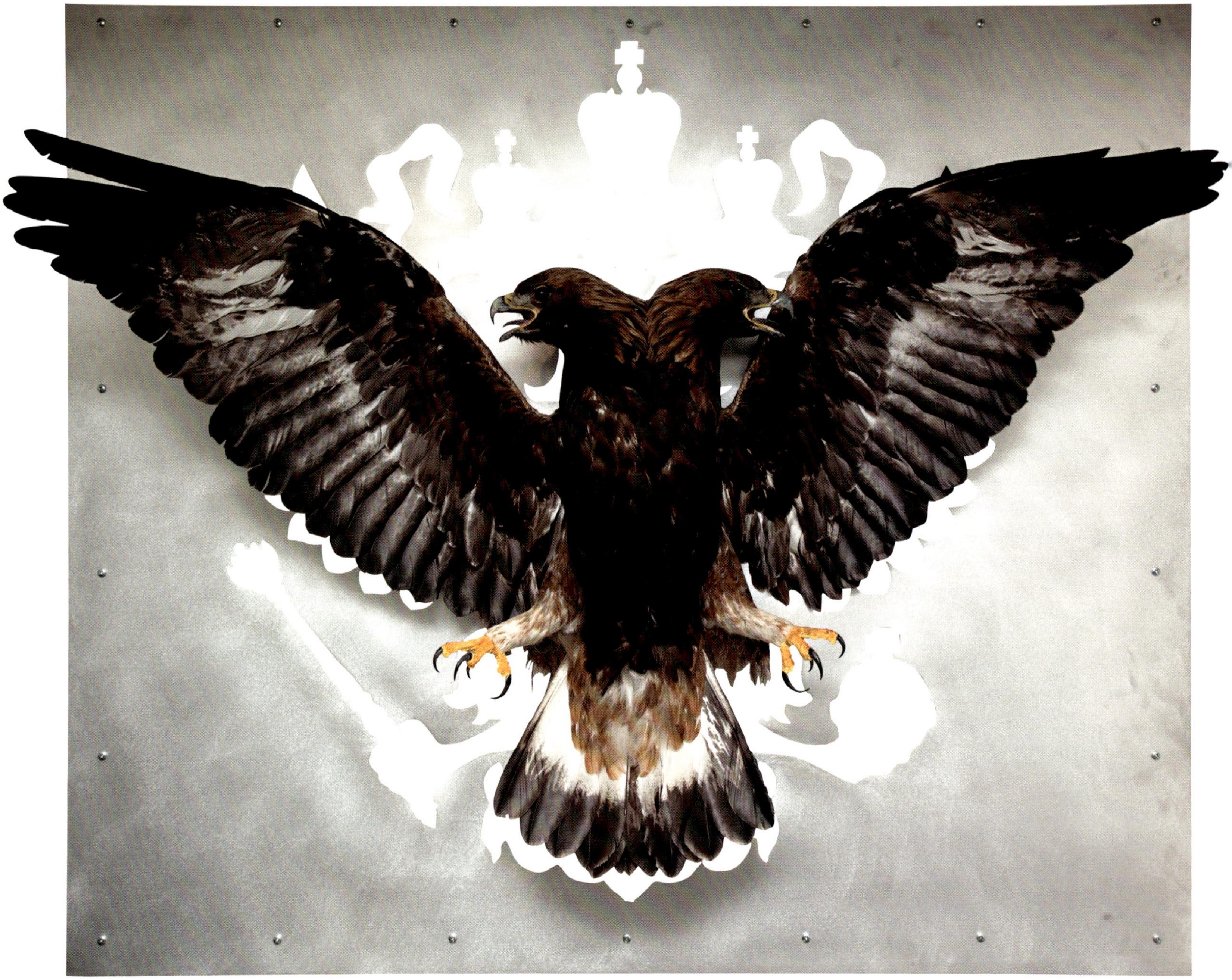

Yuri Shabelnikov
Coat of Arms, 2010
Two stuffed eagles, taxidermy, aluminium
135 x 165 x 43 cm

Courtesy Guelman Gallery, Moscow

frozen dreams

Contemporary Art from Russia

Editor
Hossein Amirsadeghi
Executive editor
Joanna Vickery

Essays
Ekaterina Bobrinskaia
Alexandra Danilova
Eleanor Heartney

TransGlobe Publishing

TransGlobe Publishing Limited
6 New Street Square
London EC4A 3LX
United Kingdom

info@tgpublishingltd.com

First published by
Thames & Hudson in association with
TransGlobe Publishing Limited

Distributed worldwide
(except in the United States and Canada) by
Thames & Hudson Ltd.
181A High Holborn
London, WC1V 7QX
United Kingdom

www.thamesandhudson.com

ISBN: 978-0-9567942-0-8

A CIP catalogue for this book is available from
the British Library.

Designed by Struktur Design Limited
Printed in Singapore

Contents

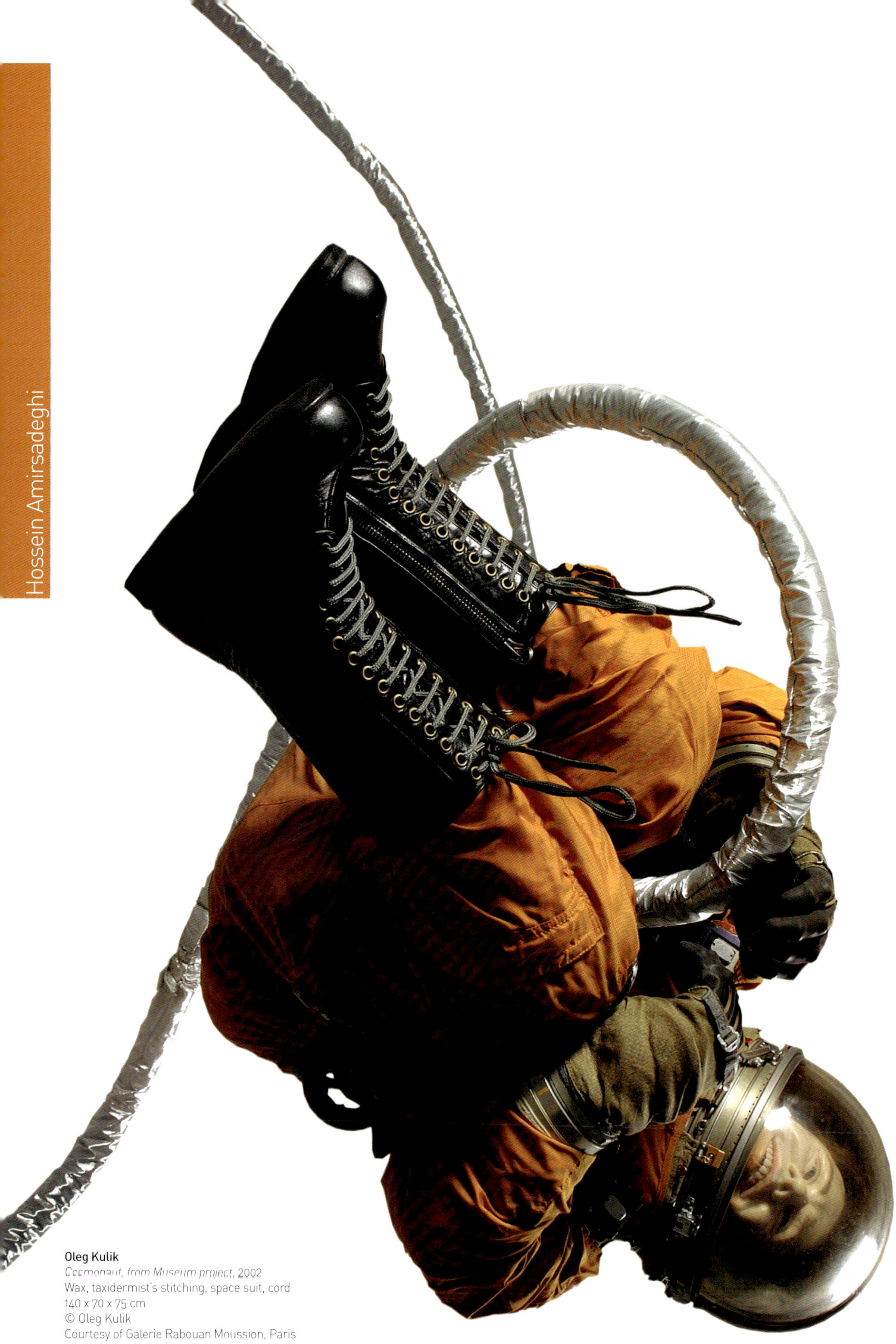

Oleg Kulik
Cosmonaut, from Museum project, 2002
Wax, taxidermist's stitching, space suit, cord
140 x 70 x 75 cm
© Oleg Kulik
Courtesy of Galerie Rabouan Moussion, Paris

Foreword

Painting is not even a picture of the world, but a striving beyond its boundaries.
Eric Bulatov

Hossein Amirsadeghi

Frozen Dreams: Contemporary Art from Russia is the fourth book in my series attempting to bring the periphery to the centre, and vice versa, in the world of contemporary art. Despite the increasing numbers of books, catalogues, exhibitions and monographs published in recent years on contemporary art from outside of Europe and America, surprisingly little is available on the subject of Russia.

The idea for *Frozen Dreams* came to mind two years ago, but the general consensus was that the time wasn't yet right for such an enterprise. Like a bull facing a red rag, I was all the more intrigued. How could a culture of enormous international importance, a major player on the world stage for much of the twentieth century, lack artistic cogency? The names of Kazimir Malevich, Vassily Kandinsky, Natalia Goncharova, Mikhail Larionov, Alexander Rodchenko, Ilya and Emilia Kabakov and Boris Mikhailov are common currency. But what about their contemporaries and successors, as yet known only to the cognoscenti? Enabling an informed closer look at Russian modern and contemporary art came to seem imperative. Visiting with such powerful Moscow advocates of the contemporary scene as Joseph Backstein, Olga Sviblova and Aidan Salakhova only served to reinforce my initial instinct that this was a book crying out to be made.

While twentieth-century Russian art was an instrument of propaganda, artists today are gazing largely in the opposite direction. Shielded for so long from the world outside of their country, the new wave employs a mix of aesthetic languages to create a distinctly Russian oeuvre. Whether or not they are all successful is a matter of opinion; the jury is still out. This is exactly what makes the subject such a fascinating one. Modern Russia has been a paradox in the making. The fight for the land's heart and soul is as old as the myth of *Rus*. A state with the world's largest land mass, blessed with fabulous natural resources and an extremely well-educated citizenry, continues to struggle to find its rightful place in the hierarchy of nations. Russian contemporary art faces similar challenges. The transformation of artistic language since perestroika has utilised the language of Soviet ideology to produce new art with unbounded creative license.

Frozen Dreams brings all of these differing expressions together while referencing, often for the first time, focused analysis of this intensely complex scene. Forces pushing and pulling Russia closer to and farther away from Eurocentric culture have made for interesting juxtapositions, while a natural predisposition towards conceptual forms has its roots in the Russian deference to literature. Many leading artists have experimented with art as a literal interpretation of history, striving to create approaches totally uninfluenced by Western models. A preoccupation with the Communist past is overladen with an icon-busting present, leaving the observer to marvel at the multilayered nature of new art as it reflects a new social order. While Soviet artists were condemned to produce work that would change social conscience, contemporary practitioners are turning everything on its head.

Art in the Soviet era was without a doubt a contributing factor in undermining younger generations' beliefs in the Communist system. This factor alone – the mediation of visual arts in the unfolding of social and political transformation – ensures the validity of an interest in Russia's cultural archaeology. But Russia is not alone in this. There is no doubting the transformative power of culture through the application of unusual thinking in the contemporary world. The rise of contemporary Russian art has resulted in the creation of an infrastructure of museums, galleries, exhibitions and art fairs. Once isolated from the rest of the world, the country's artists now beat world records – Ilya Kabakov's *Beetle* was sold for the staggering price of £2.9 million in 2008. Moscow alone is home to numerous public and private museums of contemporary art, not counting the art centres, galleries and exhibition halls. And the audience for contemporary art continues to grow.

Collecting habits and demographics have also changed beyond recognition over the past fifty years. The collecting of Russian contemporary art has dramatically shifted from having been a semi-illicit occupation during the Soviet period. Then, its marketplace was international while it was itself 'underground'. Collectors came from all over the world, and some of the most important holdings of late twentieth-century Russian art today are in the West, a notable example being Norton Dodge's collection housed at the Jane Voorhees Zimmerli Art Museum in New Jersey. Understandably, many of these collectors were motivated by the predicament in which the underground artists found themselves.

Today it is mainly Russian collectors who are buying Russian contemporary art. Western observers are not so familiar with the subject since many artists are actively pursuing their careers in Moscow, taking advantage of its burgeoning cultural infrastructure. Artists who emigrated in the 1980s are returning to their country with its buzzing art scene. These collectors are buying everything from abstract paintings by Vladimir Nemukhin and Lydia Masterkova to Conceptual drawings by Pavel Pepperstein.

Many of those involved in the art scene speak about the need for more support, whether private or governmental; these debates are inevitable when one takes recent history into account. At the same time, the preoccupation with market forces and their influence, positive or negative, on art production is a relevant debate in Russia as it is in any nation today. Alongside questions about what path educational establishments and cultural institutions can take in the future, there seems to be a strong mood for change, which does not necessarily mean following the same path that arts education has taken in the West over the past fifty years.

For an outsider in both the artistic and the historical senses, the contrasts in Russia can seem somewhat overwhelming. So were some of the challenges we encountered in making this book, which involved bringing disparate strands of contemporary art practice together, housing artists and cultural elites under one roof while maintaining a dispassionate, neutral stance. The selection of artists in *Frozen Dreams* is based on merit; it does not follow a particular logic or bias. What it does do is demonstrate the diversity of artistic production in Russia today. To the extent that we have succeeded, the plaudits go to my editorial and production teams, but mostly to Joanna Vickery, supported by a troop of young Russian Amazons taken on board this risky voyage of discovery.

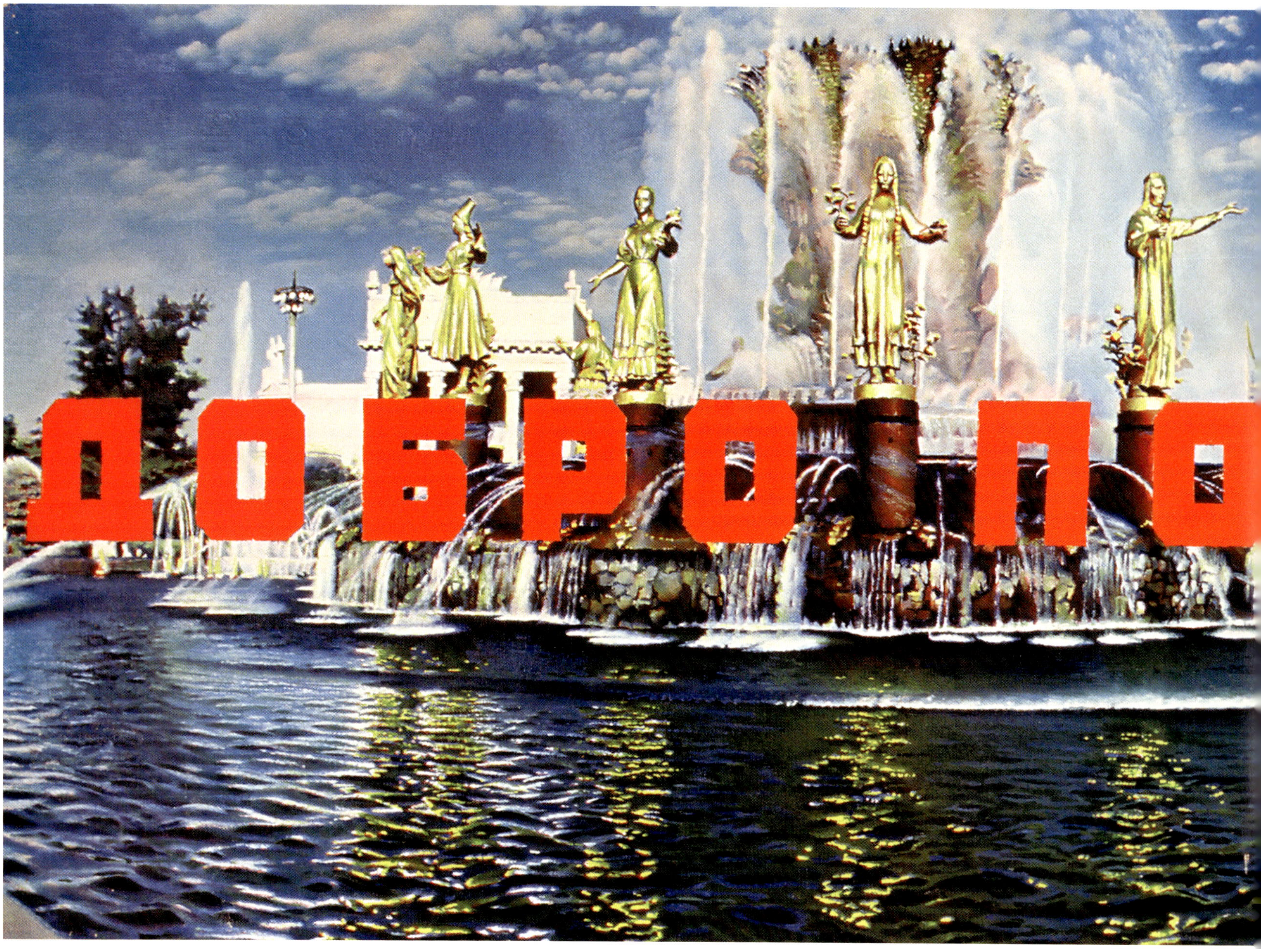
ДОБРО ПО

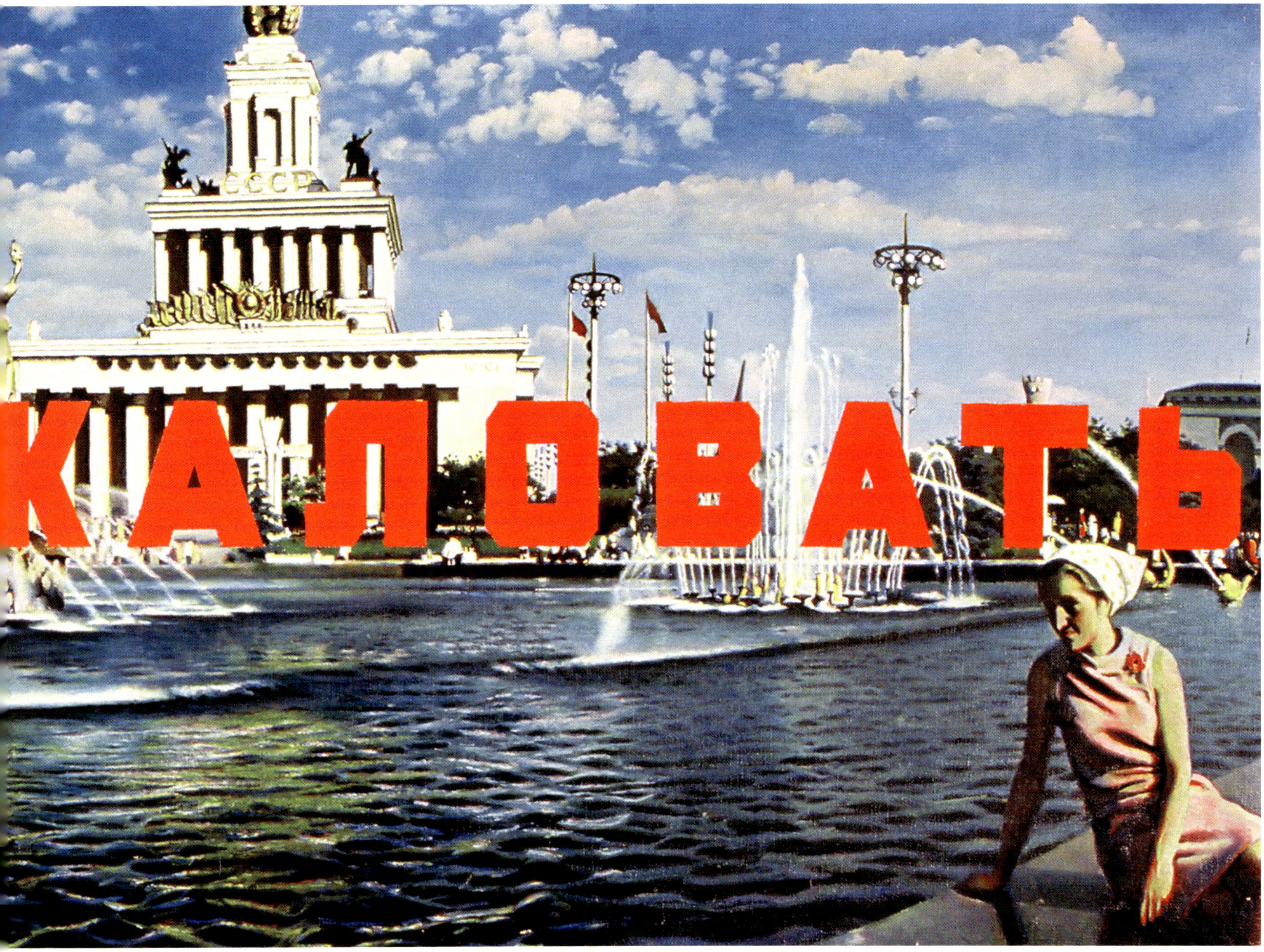

Eric Bulatov
Welcome, 1973–4
Oil on canvas
80 x 230 cm

Courtesy of Alex Lachmann

Russian Modernism & Contemporary Art

Ekaterina Bobrinskaia

Nowadays Russian twentieth-century art is well known to the Western public. The names of Kazimir Malevich, Vassily Kandinsky, Natalia Goncharova, Mikhail Larionov, Vladimir Tatlin and Alexander Rodchenko have become integral to the global history of modern art. At the same time, Russian art is not fully understood and remains somehow 'other'. This is not merely a result of the country's lengthy insulated existence behind the Iron Curtain. Filippo Tommaso Marinetti, one of the founders of Italian Futurism, was struck by the unfamiliar form of the movement's eastern counterpart during a trip he made to Russia in 1914 to deliver a series of lectures. Both bewilderment and disappointment are apparent in his address to the Russian Futurists, whom he accused of not living in the future but in some 'super-past' time. Indeed, Russian Futurism paralleled the Italian movement while simultaneously contradicting it and followed its own developmental logic – behaviour characteristic of Russian modern and avant-garde art in general. Russian artists of the early twentieth century absorbed a great deal from European modernism. But while they saw themselves within the context of European culture, they often rejected it, striving to create their own concepts and strategies.

Russian artists of the 1900s were attracted to extremes. Their work combined the ultra-modern with the traditional, metaphysics with utilitarianism, social utopias with an 'art for art's sake' mentality, natural (organic) with man-made (mechanical) aesthetics. One of the most important characteristics of Russian modern art in general is its multilayered nature, the ready intertwining of contradictions. It can best be described as a collage possessing the qualities of a glimmering conceptual field, a torn space, a mix of languages, the unification of high and low culture.

Russian art went through many stages over the course of the last century. Early twentieth-century modernism and the work of Soviet unofficial artists, which is to say contemporary Russian art, are dissimilar, of course, and in many ways the traditions are antagonistic. Nevertheless, there remains a kind of internal tradition, not always obvious, sometimes even hidden, as well as dialogues and polemics which unite artists of the 1910s and '20s with of those of the post-war period. An understanding of the unique characteristics of Russian modernism is essential before one can sensibly explore the reciprocity between unofficial and contemporary Russian art, on the one hand, and Russian modernism and the avant-garde, on the other.

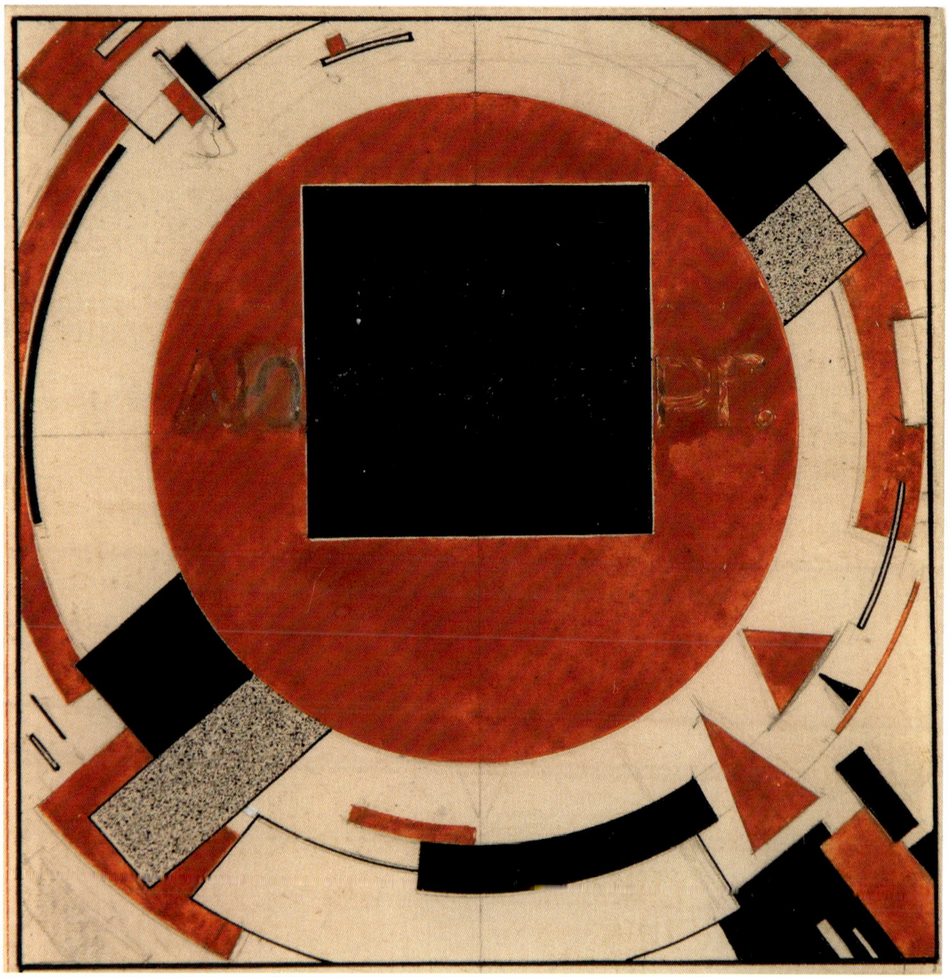

El Lissitzky
Monument to Roza Luxemburg, 1919–1921
Gouache, ink and pencil on paper
9.7 x 9.7 cm
© Greek State Museum of Contemporary Art
Courtesy of Greek State Museum of Contemporary Art – Costakis Collection

Histories of Russian modern art usually begin in 1907 with the opening of the *Blue Rose* exhibition in Moscow,[1] a prologue to the stormy onslaught of the Russian avant-garde. The exhibition included paintings by Pavel Kuznetsov, Martiros Saryan, Nikolai Sapunov and Sergei Sudeikin, whose work combined Symbolist and Neo-Primitivist characteristics. Many early twentieth-century trends in Russia share elements from new developments in European painting, such as Symbolism, Fauvism and Expressionism, as well as a fascination for Russian folklore, icon painting and Eastern art. This can best be seen in the work of Kuzma Petrov-Vodkin, which is based on a fusion of Symbolism and Old Russian art. His most famous painting, *Red Horse Bathing* (1912), presents a fantastical world of his own creation, not a well-known mythological subject. Many have seen this painting as a vision of the impending catastrophes of World War I and the Revolution, a metaphorical illustration of the period's charged atmosphere, riddled with anxiety and dreams of the future. The Old Russian icon tradition fuses naturally in Petrov-Vodkin's paintings with the search for a new formal language capable of capturing modernity's steely dynamism. The turn to the icon-painting tradition as a means of creating pertinent contemporary works became a strong thread within Russian modernism. During the 1920s and '30s, an interest in Old Russian art could be observed in the work of Alexander Samokhvalov; Victor Popkov and Dmitry Zhilinsky are notable proponents of this trend from the second half of the century. The desire to create an alternative mythological reality marks the work of much unofficial art. For example, in the 1960s Boris Sveshnikov and Alexander Kharitonov united Symbolist and early modernist aesthetics and gave them new forms.

The famous *Jack of Diamonds* exhibition opened in Moscow in 1910.[2] Both the group's name and its early exhibitions possessed a distinctly shocking character. The subject matter and style of their paintings, as well as the atmosphere generated during their shows, were reminiscent of fairground entertainment. Risk, youthful fervour, energy and impudence were brought to artistic life by the Jack

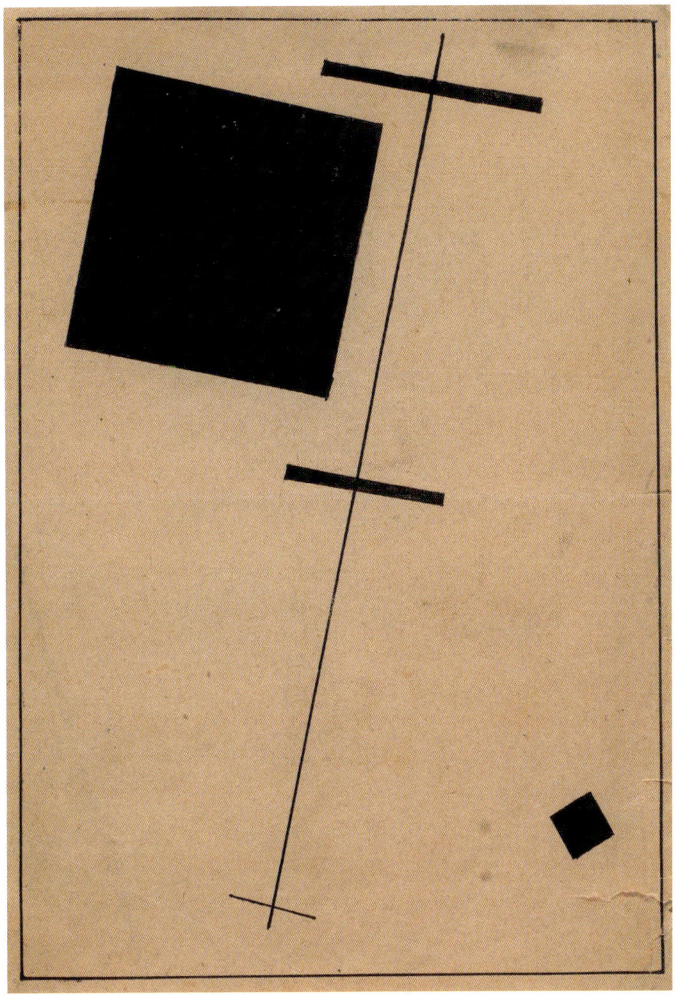

Kazimir Malevich (attributed)
Untitled, c. 1920
Lithograph
22.5 x 15.5 cm

Courtesy of Greek State Museum of Contemporary Art – G. Costakis Archive

of Diamonds artists. Their first exhibition heralded the colourful, provocative appearance of the avant-garde.

A blurring and juxtaposition of many different styles – a consistent feature of Russian culture – found full expression in the art of the Jack of Diamonds group. Admirers of Cézanne (some critics even called them the 'Moscow Cézannistes') and of Cubism in general, they blended their innovations with forms from traditional low culture – signs, *luboks* (popular prints), folk toys – thus turning Analytic Cubism into a decorative feature. They began what was to become a long tradition (extending into the 1970s) marked by a primary concern with the painting's surface, rejecting literary subject matter and narrative. Instead, they discovered the beauty of the canvas itself, of its material texture, through paint and rhythmical brushstrokes. In the 1920s this approach would be developed by the artists of the OMKh group and in the late works of Robert Falk, who had a strong influence on many unofficial artists of the 1960s and '70s.

Neo-Primitivism was one of the most colourful and original movements in Russian art of the 1910s. Although it reflects French Fauvism and Expressionism, as a whole it represents an autonomous Russian school whose approach is characteristic of the Blue Rose and Jack of Diamonds painters Vassily Kandinsky, Pavel Filonov, Mikhail Larionov and Natalia Goncharova, as well as their colleagues Mikhail Ledantu, Alexander Shevchenko, Kirill Zdanevich, Kazimir Malevich, David Burliuk, Marc Chagall and Olga Rozanova. Neo-Primitivism was one of the most powerful forces in the Russian avant-garde up until 1913. One of its main characteristics was a return to national artistic traditions, not only icon painting but a wide range of folk crafts: *luboks* and embroidery, old shop signs and the applied arts. These artists were also interested in traditional Eastern and pre-modern art, from cave paintings to ancient Scythian artefacts.

Neo-Primitivism was usually mixed with other styles. For example, Larionov's *Promenade (Venus on the Boulevard)* (1913) combines Neo-Primitivist images of simple provincial life with the dynamic motion typical of Futurism. In fact, it was Larionov and his colleagues who succeeded in imbuing Neo-Primitivism with a sense of movement; his works are sophisticated yet at the same time the most radical and extreme variants of that style. In the series Seasons of the Year (1912), he turned to the most ancient modes of art for inspiration.

Neo-Primitivism possesses another important characteristic of the avant-garde: self-conscious eclecticism. This and other trends acquired a formulaic style known as 'everythingism', described by Larionov and Ilya Zdanevich in 1913. 'We recognise all styles, old and new, as suitable for our art', proclaimed one of their manifestos. This freedom from formal constraints provided Russian art of the 1910s with liveliness and energy embodied in a ceaseless 'state of becoming'. A programme of eclecticism fusing diverse styles was a dominant characteristic of the late twentieth-century New Artists group heralded by Timur Novikov and centred in St Petersburg.

Looking closer at Futurism itself, in Russia it was a crucial movement in the history of the Russian avant-garde, whose artists and writers created their own form of it, as we have seen. Futurism took on the ideological burden of creating art for the country's future, aiming to transform human life along the way. Numerous artistic and literary groups were linked to this ideology, and its presence is apparent in the work of diverse artists. One of the particularities of Russian Futurism is its deep link to a Neo-primitivist, sometimes expressionistic, aesthetic, which gave it the 'archaic' palette that Marinetti found so surprising. In 1913, the Larionov-led group Donkey's Tail published a daring and paradoxical manifesto, 'Rayonism and Futurism', calling for a return to national traditions and an emphasis on Eastern culture while sounding a monumental hymn to the forms of contemporary life typical in other European countries.

The history of Russian Futurism is connected not just to the field of painting but, perhaps even more, to different forms of socio-cultural engagement. The whole of artistic life in the 1910s was transformed by Futurist discourse, including artist- and writer-led public debates and lectures, the famous tour of Russian cities by Futurist poets, and the publication of poetry anthologies, manifestos and statements of theory. These manifestations were energetic, occasionally aggressive, always spectacular and, at times, even farcical.

In the field of painting, Futurist dynamism was often combined with aspects of Cubism. Cubo-Futurism, built on the foundations of this unification of aesthetics, is apparent in works by Malevich (*The Organ Grinder*, 1912–13), Rozanova (*Factory and Bridge*, 1913–14) and Liubov Popova (*Italian Still Life*, 1914).

The year 1915 was a crucial turning point in the history of the Russian avant-garde, with Malevich formulating his idea of non-objective art. During the *0,10* exhibition, which opened at the end of 1915, he showed his famous *Black Square* and a series of Suprematist paintings. Elementary geometric forms floating in white 'cosmic' space embodied Malevich's breakthrough towards a new artistic language as well as the key to a new conception of the world. Non-objective art became the leading trend in Russia, with his ideas finding individualised interpretations in the work of Rozanova, Kliun, Popova, Alexandra Exter and Ivan Puni. Malevich's own art went through several stages during which he worked in black, in colour and, at the end of the 1910s, in white. He described Suprematism as an all-inclusive idea – aesthetic and philosophical, socially minded, even religious. Kliun recorded a memorable comment that Malevich made in conversation: 'Malevich always harboured a tendency towards mysticism. One time ... he answered my questions with, "Maybe, I will become the patriarch of a new religion?"'[3] This statement does not just summarise the artist's personal ambitions and outlook. The avant-garde was characterised by a lack of clear aesthetics, a constant intrusion into the sphere of politics, pretensions to revolution, an insistence on its own philosophy and a search for the tools with which art could create new life rather than just mimic it.

Victor Pivovarov
Composition with Red Square, 1974
Enamel on plywood
170 x 130 cm
© Victor Pivovarov
Courtesy of the Ekaterina and Vladimir Semenikhin Collection

At the end of the 1910s, Malevich established UNOVIS in Vitebsk. Together with his students Ilya Chashnik, Nikolai Suetin, Lazar Khidekel and others, he and El Lissitzky created a commune as the basis for an art school. Its activity became the most colourful manifestation of Suprematism's life-building capabilities. Together with their students, Malevich and Lissitzky addressed projects concerned with the creation of a new sphere of objects and architectural forms.

Another proponent of non-objective art was Vladimir Tatlin, who, from 1914, stopped painting, turning instead to the creation of 'counter-reliefs' out of ready-made materials; along with his conception of non-objectivity, these works are usually seen as the forerunners of Constructivism. Tatlin's idiosyncratic form of construction combined natural, organic forms with artificial, mechanical ones. Most importantly, his counter-reliefs foreground the qualities of each material – its mass, weight, hardness, potential malleability and resistance. Working with materials in this way was a prologue to entering the sphere of production, the projection of a new blueprint for human existence, a new physical world. These strands were fully developed in the 1920s through the Constructivists' focus on the production of furniture, kitchen utensils, clothing and so on.

The Constructivists, who came together as a group in the early 1920s, included Alexander Rodchenko, Varvara Stepanova, the brothers Vladimir and Georgy Steinberg, Gustav Klutsis and others. Their ideological programme was based on a novel interpretation of artistic creativity, now viewed from the perspective of engineering and industrial and laboratory work. In their 'constructions', these artists attempted to create a new version of the world through novel forms of artistic production and thinking. Their constructions, of course, correlated with the world of technology and machines. Sometimes they simply aestheticised ready-made machines; more often, they adapted machines' inner workings, evoking functionality and a wilful subordination to problem-solving.

These Constructivist ideas were highly influential during the second half of the twentieth century, most prominently on the Dvizheniye group of kinetic artists, which was founded in 1962 by Lev Nussberg; the other influential member was Francisco Infante. The group's utopianism and formalism, its desire to dissolve the boundary between art and life, and its use of new scientific and technological developments stood in the way of its existing on a completely unofficial basis. Many works by Dvizheniye were responses to official commissions, for example the civic decorations for the fiftieth anniversary of the October Revolution. Meanwhile they carried out radical experiments with artistic language, their spatial constructions attempted to overstep the boundaries of traditional art forms, and their theatrical actions represented first steps in the areas of performance art and happenings. Many of the avant-garde's utopian ideas were taken up and developed by them, but, unlike their Constructivist predecessors, their works are more meditative and lack ostentation and aggressive calls to recreate the world. Occasionally, they display elements of irony or play which are unfamiliar in the Constructivist context.

Artistic freedom, which was to become a critical issue, was already a problem in Russia in the early twentieth century. A constant search for autonomous art free from established aesthetic and social norms characterised the history of the avant-garde. After the Revolution of 1917, the notion of autonomous art acquired new meaning. Many people believed that the avant-garde's explosive energy correlated somehow with the Revolution itself, and, subsequently, the very real opposition between the new art and social pressures was pushed to the background. Creative autonomy seemed to acquire a universal status and to concern the totality of culture, and began to control a range of social spaces.

In the second half of the twentieth century, the notion of autonomous art was an important stimulus for the formation of unofficial art in Russia. The avant-gardist art at the beginning of the century took on a romantic flavour and was perceived as a heroic vehicle for artistic freedom. Simultaneously, the ideas of revolutionary art were rethought and debated within Moscow Conceptualism, while the works of some avant-garde artists – predominantly Malevich and his followers – were interpreted as being excessively authoritarian.

Avant-gardism was only one strand in Russian art of the first half of the twentieth century, and in fact it did not occupy a central position in the artistic life of the time. Alongside it were trends as diverse as Symbolism, a wide range of modernist styles and a nascent Neoclassicism. Realism continued to develop, in the mid-1920s acquiring a new force, enriched as it was by modernist innovations.

The year 1925 can tentatively be considered as the end of the history of the avant-garde and a return to figurative easel painting. Unions such as OST and the Circle were formed around this time to promote the new principles of figurative art. This does not mean that the avant-garde completely ceased to exist. It was no longer a major, vital force, however, even though some artists in the 1930s and '40s continued to work with similar ideas.

By the 1930s, the general atmosphere of Soviet culture was becoming increasingly politicised. Art addressed popular taste and, under the strict control of the State, was seen, first and foremost, as a propaganda, educational and agit-prop tool. The year 1932 saw the establishment of the Union of Artists, which became the one official creative organisation. Socialist Realism was confirmed as the new doctrine and the only permissible creative style; all deviations were termed 'formalism' and heavily persecuted. Russian art came to be isolated from the rest of the world for several decades. In many ways because of this isolation, the country's modern and avant-garde art took on mythic status and was transformed into a symbol of artistic autonomy.

It is difficult to see the art of the 1910s and '20s seriously influencing Soviet artists of the 1950s and '60s. The majority of avant-garde works were simply not known to them or to the public. Information about Western art was difficult to come by and fragmentary. Nevertheless, during the Thaw, Soviet artists evidenced a new interest in the heritage of the 1920s, especially the figurative language associated with OST. This influence fed the so-called 'Severe Style' within the framework of the Union of Artists. Artists such as Pavel Nikonov, Victor Popkov, Nikolai Andronov, Geli Korzhev and others did not break with the official Soviet aesthetic but tried to renew it. During the 1970s, among artists associated with the 'Leftist' wing of the Union of Artists, Surrealism became popular. Alexander Sitnikov, Olga Bulgakova and their colleagues created effective theatrical, enigmatic paintings. Overall, however, the interaction with the modernist tradition had a superficial, incidental character and was likely just a fashionable means of giving work a commercial look.

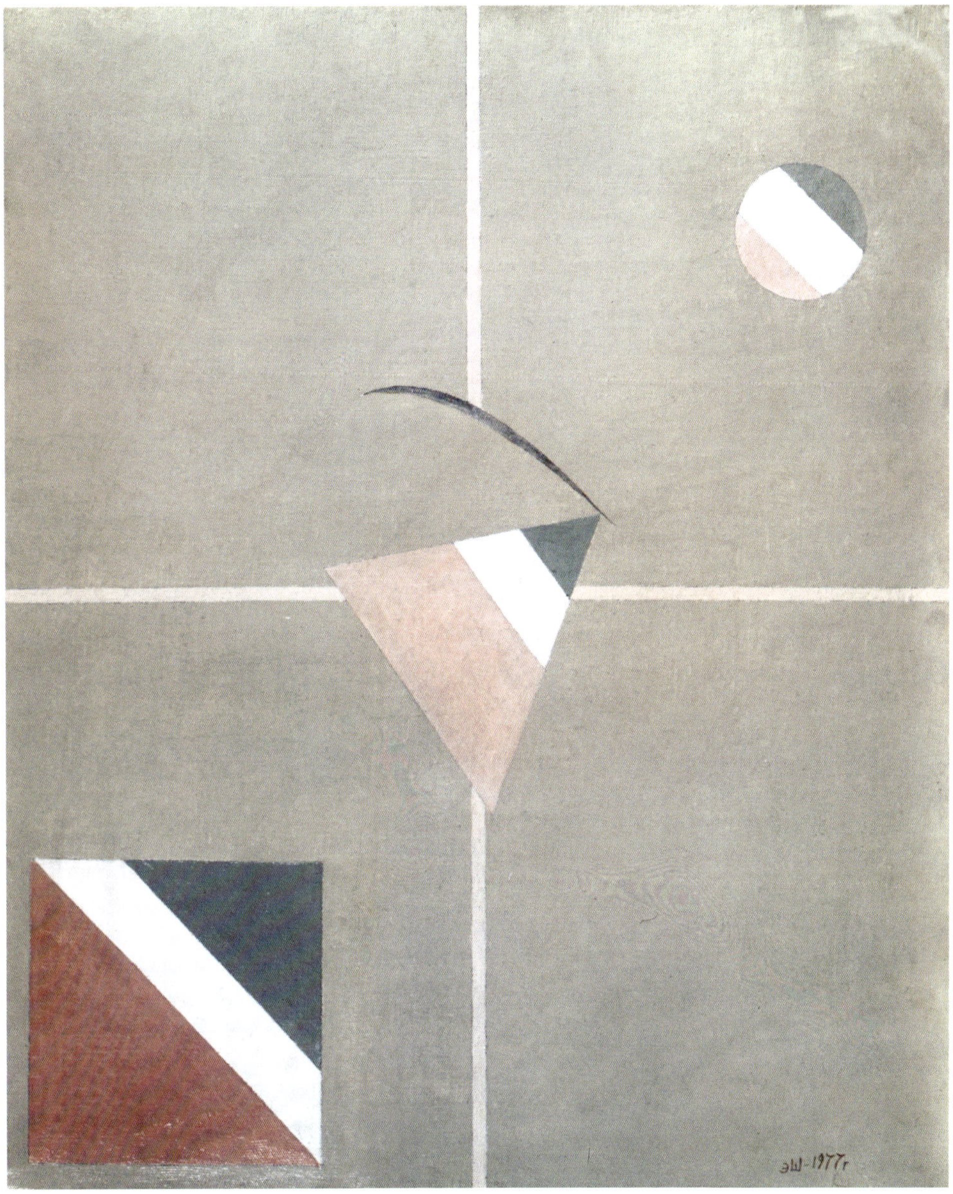

Eduard Steinberg
Composition, 1977
Oil on canvas
59.5 x 49.5 cm
© Kolodzei Art Foundation
Courtesy of Kolodzei Collection of Russian and Eastern European Art, Kolodzei Art Foundation

Meanwhile the relationship between the modernist tradition and non-official art took a different turn. Modernism and the art of the avant-garde were traditions upon which many artists began to depend in their own artistic searches and with which they polemicised. Unofficial art was born in the mid-1950s, its appearance linked to changes in Soviet society following Stalin's death in 1953.

A private, semi-underground artistic life had existed between the 1930s and the early 1950s. Many artists, both famous and forgotten, who had lived through the era of modernism continued to work into the 1960s. However, this more passive layer of unofficial culture never claimed an autonomous, active role for itself. A new generation, appearing from the mid-1950s, consciously chose their underground status. The unofficial circle was formed mainly of those who were banned from participating in exhibitions of the Union of Artists because of their 'formalist' tendencies, who hadn't graduated from official institutions or who led a double life – an official and an underground one. The unofficial community tried to organise its own exhibitions, a number of which took place in educational establishments, cinemas, clubs and private apartments. As a rule, these were short-lived, often banned and closed by force. Unofficial artists of the 1950s and '60s were not interested in avant-garde experiments per se. The dominant desire was to assimilate and master the numerous artistic forms banned by official culture in order to reconstruct and understand the history of modern art, of which whole chunks were 'missing' due to official bans.

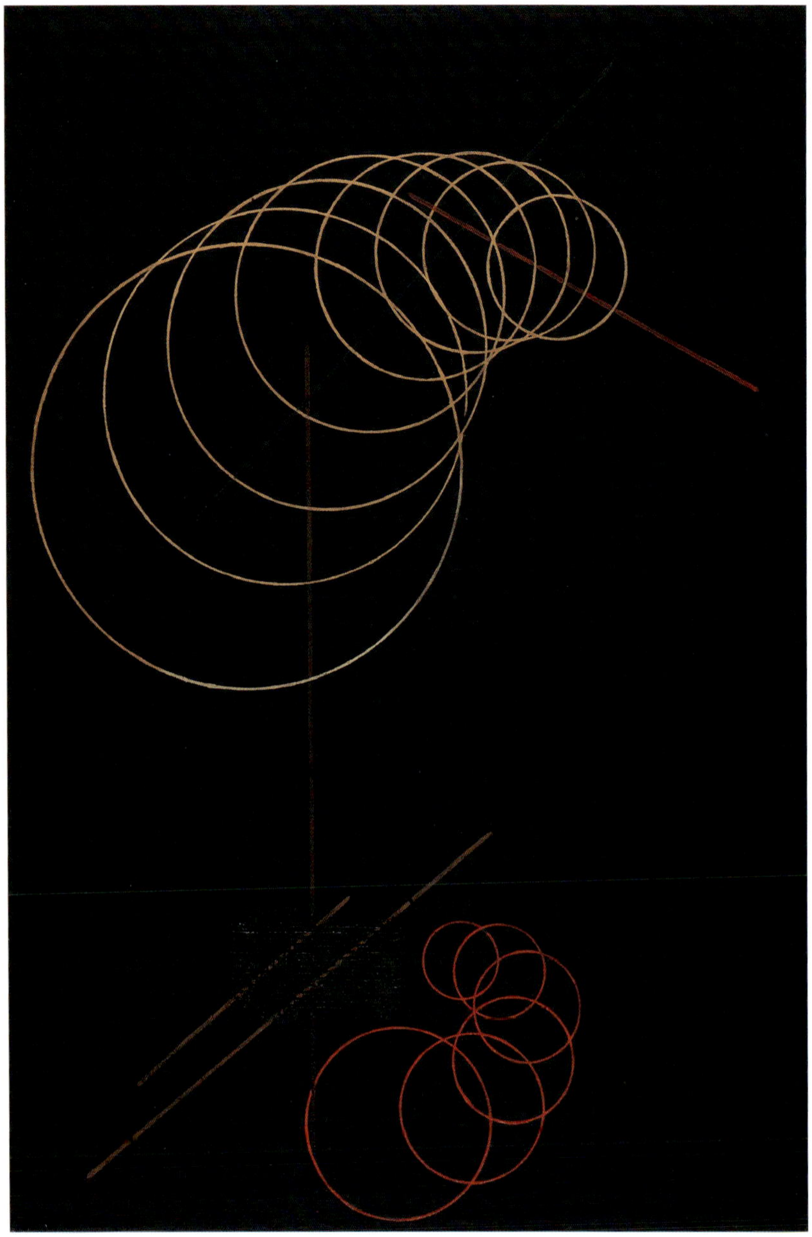

Alexander Rodchenko
Linearism, 1920
Oil on canvas
102.9 x 69.6 cm
© Copyright Greek State Museum of Contemporary Art
Courtesy of Greek State Museum of Contemporary Art – Costakis Collection

The avant-garde of the early twentieth century had never been particularly stable, nor did it comprise long-lasting artistic groups. It also had never fit specific stylistic definitions, as artists would constantly add, unite and superimpose multiple tendencies. What did define the avant-garde was a disdain towards schools and stable associations. In this connection Varvara Stepanova noted a revealing statement by Alexander Rodchenko in 1919: 'The main characteristic of Russian painters is individuality and the absence of a "school".'[4] Unofficial culture in the second half of the twentieth century was organised along the lines of private acquaintance, dominated by personal ties rather than shared concepts.

One typical example is the Lianozovo Group, formed in the mid-1950s around the artist and poet Evgeny Kropivnitsky and comprising Lev Kropivnitsky, Valentina Kropivnitskaya, Oscar Rabin, Lydia Masterkova, Vladimir Nemukhin, Olga Potapova, and Nikolai Vechtomov. Membership was based on personal friendships, not on a shared aesthetic. Rabin occupied a distinct position in the group during the 1960s and early '70s; his apartment-studio became one of the first artists' salons, open to anyone interested in unofficial culture. It is not an exaggeration to say that nearly all of underground Moscow visited Rabin's apartment during this period. His art had a direct or indirect influence on many artists of the time.

Expressionist artists occupied a central place in unofficial culture. The term *Expressionist* can, of course, only be applied in the sense of an artistic style centred not on the representation of an inner world but on the communication of the emotionally charged qualities of objects, people and situations. Expressionism in mid-century unofficial culture took the form of both figurative and abstract painting. When figurative, it often co-existed with Primitivism, as seen in the works of Anatoly Zverev and Vladimir Yakovlev, as well as Lev Kropivnitsky, Oscar Rabin, Mikhail Roginsky, Boris Koshelokhov and Mikhail Kulakov. Each of these artists created their own unique language, thus rendering connections between them tangential and tentative.

One of the most colourful versions of Expressionism was created by Rabin, whose realistic reconstructions of Moscow's streets or suburbs are in fact metaphysical landscapes of life, representations of the spirit. This explains his predilection for strict iconography, distortion and straightforward metaphors which enforce a particular mood. Instead of choosing lofty subject matter that was tragic, romantic, fantastical or mythological, he favoured everyday reality, often grotesque or parodic but never ostentatious. The objects in his paintings are frequently devoid of domestic roles, having become signs or metaphors. He chose objects that had already attained symbolic value: money, newspapers, official documents, road signs and stickers. Uninterested in everyday existence, Rabin explored the metaphysics of non-existence, exhaustion, and the extinction of life and its substitution by empty symbols, signs and markers.

Non-objective art also played an important role in the unofficial art of the 1950s and '60s, with abstraction being central to many artists' practice in part because it made possible the most obvious, direct rejection of the language of Socialist Realism. The turn to non-objectivity allowed artists to understand anew the inherent value of pictorial space, to rediscover its autonomous existence and renounce

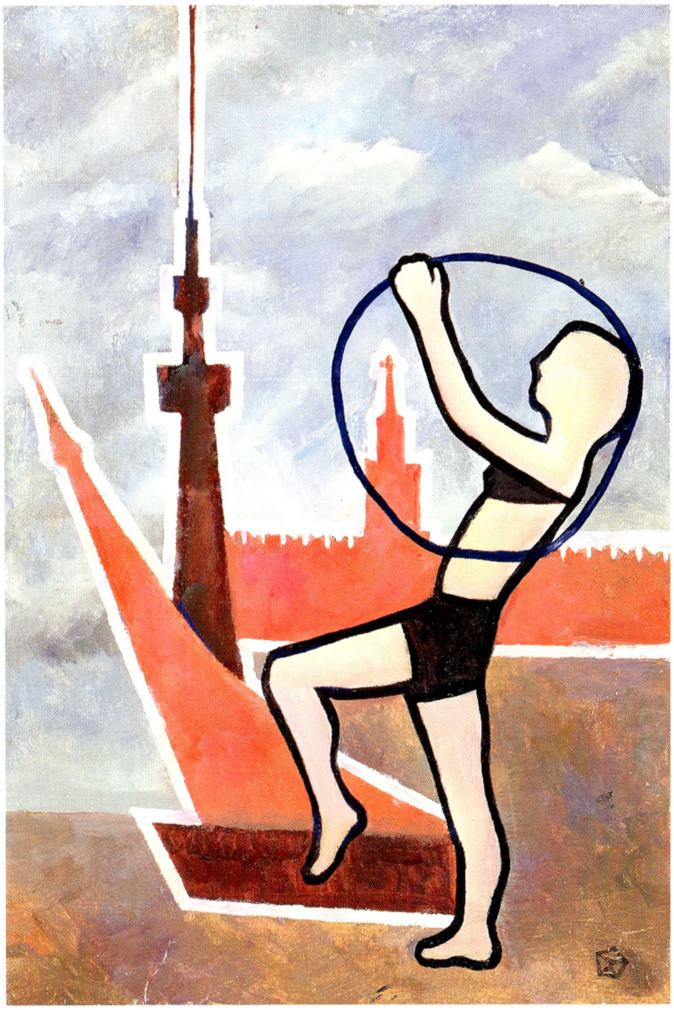

Alexander Melamid
Portrait of Wife Katya with Hula Hoop, 1972
Oil on canvas
65 x 45 cm
© Alexander Melamid
Collection of Shalva Breus

a utilitarian understanding of art. Expressive abstraction, which formed one of the main strands of non-objective art, found its longest-lasting manifestations in the work of Lev Kropivnitsky, Boris Turetsky, Vladimir Yakovlev, Vladimir Nemukhin, Lydia Masterkova, Mikhail Kulakov and Evgeny Mikhnov-Voytenko. These artists were of course sensitive to American Abstract Expressionism and Art Informel, which offered not only an effective visual form for painting but also a particular concept of the artist's role. Abstract Expressionism carried with it a myth of heroic individualism, an image of the artist-creator as capable of immediate, raw self-expression. This myth was crucial to the appearance of a certain aura around the expressive abstraction of Soviet unofficial culture. Many artists were attracted to Abstract Expressionism because of its myth of freedom and the subjectivity behind its sweeping, explosive brushwork. Early abstract art associated with Kandinsky also played a role, however, often determining the originality of Russian expressive abstraction through an interest in metaphysics and philosophy, an appeal to self-reflexion rather than to formal aesthetics.

Artists working abstractly often relied on deep meditation, creating independent painterly environments and a fully formed world outlook. Eduard Steinberg, for example, developed a unique dialogue not only with non-objective painting as formulated by Malevich but with the Russian icon tradition. Steinberg created an artistic system in which space and form came together in configurations which resonated with the inner rhythms of artist and spectator alike. Vladimir Weisberg, on the other hand, while offering his own contemplative outlook, continued to develop the 'white on white' theme, which had made its first appearance in Malevich's work. Finally, Mikhail Shvartsman's personality and presence at the heart of artistic life were no less meaningful than his paintings. Shvartsman created a unique artistic language, a type of non-objective painting that he termed 'hieraturae'.

The work of Francisco Infante opened up a dialogue with the avant-garde on several levels. For one thing, he reframed the legacies of Malevich and Constructivism. At the same time, he explored geometric forms without limiting himself to the pictorial space of the canvas, often carrying his compositions over into the real space of nature. Like his predecessors in the early twentieth century, his projects are utopian models of the world. Unlike them, however, they do not try to re-create the world by using strength of will. On the contrary, the artist harmoniously reconciled artificial, man-made constructions and forms with the natural environment and its rhythms.

Both the myth and the atmosphere of unofficial culture changed substantially in the 1970s and '80s. If previously it had concerned itself with questions of metaphysics and ahistoricism, the movement became more interested in day-to-day Soviet existence. A decisive moment was the turn away from expressive, metaphorical, emotive styles towards the analytical, distanced position of the artist-as-researcher occupied with a 'scientific' or ironic representation of society. Sots Art and Moscow Conceptualism best reflected this new position.

The term 'Sots Art', used to describe a movement that united many different painters and sculptors, was thought up in the early 1970s by Vitaly Komar and Alexander Melamid. Each artist created his own Sots Art style. The group's members included Leonid Sokov, Alexander Kosolapov and the Gnezdo group, comprising Viktor Skersis, Gennady Donskoy and Michel Roshal. Others whose work demonstrated Sots Art characteristics included Boris Orlov, Rostislav Lebedev, Grisha Bruskin, Eric Bulatov and Boris Mikhailov. As a rule, Sots artists were mainly interested in elements of life and culture directly linked to Soviet ideology and politics. Diverse emblems and symbols, as well as characters ranging from famous Party leaders to anonymous Pioneers and model workers, became protagonists in the majority of Sots Art work.

The Sots artists were the first members of unofficial culture to rethink and consciously explore and engage in dialogue with the polemics of the Russian avant-garde and modernism instead of simply rebuilding their traditions. Their focus was primarily on agit art. Certain works engage directly with the propaganda aesthetic of the early Soviet avant-garde, for instance Melamid's *Portrait of Wife, Katya, with a Hula Hoop* (1972). Artists placed popular icons or signs of Soviet propaganda in surprising contexts, thus defusing their seriousness and aggression.

Early Sots Art also resurrected the ideas of everythingism and eclecticism developed by the avant-garde during the 1910s. Works by Komar and Melamid like *Meeting between Solzhenitsyn and Heinrich Böll at Rostropovich's Dacha* (1972) unite diverse historical styles ranging from Old Russian icon painting to Cubism in a playful manner. This can also be seen in works like Viktor Skersis's *Young Girl with a Gun* (1973–4).

Boris Orlov created a distinctive interpretation of modernism, becoming one of the first figures within unofficial culture to work with its legacy and myth in a continuous fashion. Instead of aping the modernist experience, he used it as one of a number of languages with whose help he constructed his own mythological world. The citing of modernist traditions in Orlov's sculptures is based on a conscious, recognisable distancing from them. Modernism is remembered and reborn as an exhausted language that has become the precedent of contemporaneity. The style and formal language of Russian modern and avant-garde art are apparent in his representations of sailors, sportsmen or celebratory busts, which can be compared with Malevich's costume-sculptures for the opera *Victory over the Sun: Female Torso, Torso and Peasant's Head* (1928–9). Both are characterised by flat, coloured planes and light geometric precision. However, his use of modernism consists merely of another module, another mythological code, making up his formal language.

The liberation from ideology as a system of conceptual constructions standing in for the real world became one of the key motifs for artists working within Sots Art or Moscow Conceptualism. Many of their works were based on the disruption of the logic and wholeness of Soviet culture's visual language. For example, they would take the shape of paradoxical intrusions of the personal and private into the strict structure of official production, as in Komar and Melamid's *Double Self-portrait as Young Pioneers* (1982–3), or of works which defied interpretation by creating conceptual breaks and empty spaces, as in Monastyrsky's *Finger* (1978). Grisha Bruskin offered yet another method for the reduction of ideology in *Fundamental Lexicon* (1986), in which the protagonists, settings and stereotypes of Soviet myth become isolated, disjointed letters, the 'text' dissolving back to its foetal stage as the alphabet.

The artists who are usually spoken of in relation to Moscow Conceptualism shared few formal concerns. Instead, the common denominator was artistic method or the relationship with the different contexts in which art exists – historical, social or existential. In discussions about Moscow Conceptualism, it is often noted that Russian culture itself has an inherent and natural predisposition towards a conceptual form of art. This is thought to manifest itself in the interest expressed by artists in the investigation of non-aesthetic problems (including social or moral ones), a process that is naturally accompanied by the reduced significance of purely formal language and a deference to text. The latter aspect promoted literature and writers to cult status. Soviet propaganda also aided the appearance of Conceptualism, with artists interpreting the ideology surrounding everyday social space as an important factor in the formation of a new type of art privileging ideas and texts and their functionalities.

Although the experiments of the 1910s and '20s remained little known, during the second half of the twentieth century, up until perestroika, the Moscow Conceptualists created an important interpretation of Soviet culture whereby life was 'conceptual' in the sense that language and ideology were substitutions for, and hid behind, the material world of objects. To an extent, this was a type of myth-making, another picture of the world. At the same time, paradoxically, it found points of agreement with Soviet culture's mode of self-presentation.

The dematerialisation of art had first been explored in the early 1920s as a result of the intersection of pure art and industrial manufacturing. At the time, the transformation of social and domestic environments was seen as crucial to the reformation of humanity and the world. Such ideas came to the fore among many practitioners: Constructivists, productionists, projectionists and LEF (Left Front of the Arts) members. In 1924 the projectionists voiced their position as follows: 'An artist is not a producer of commercial things (such as wardrobes, paintings), but the (projected) method is the organisation of materials.' Unlike the supporters of manufactured artworks, they insisted on their autonomy, claiming that 'painters should remain where they are, i.e. they should not enter manufacture. Their work should be exclusively planar and methodical as a foundation for the construction of thousands of schools and laboratories which are to teach new forms of knowledge and mass consciousness.'[5] In other words, the artist had to create concepts and ways of thinking, which would determine conscience, production and a way of life. These radical ideas of the 1920s have much in common with Conceptual art.

One of the most 'conceptual' pieces of Russian avant-garde art is a series of drawings by Malevich done in 1915–16, in which framed words and phrases act as substitutes for images (*A Purse Stolen in the Tramway, A Fight on the Boulevard, Village*). Malevich provided the following comment on one of these drawings: 'Instead of drawing realistic huts, it is much better to write "Village"; everyone will visualise it in greater detail and with a larger concept of the whole village.' His text-drawings are a theoretical project, a musical score for the viewer's conscience and imagination. Unlike normal paintings, they open up a field of freedom and pure inner contemplation.

At first glance, Ilya Kabakov's text-painting *Guilty?* (1982) recreates the same principles. Word replaces image, leaving the viewer with the task of conceptually recreating and seeing the 'picture'. There is a fundamental difference, however. Malevich's 'conceptualism' was utopian in nature. Words for him were vehicles providing access to an alternative meditative and, crucially, authentic space of freedom. In Kabakov's work, words do not replace dead pictorial stereotypes but emphasise them. His text-paintings uncover the image's unavoidable reliance on language and question the human capacity to see without textual, linguistic support.

Many formal characteristics of Moscow Conceptualism of the 1970s and '80s were tied in with its relationship with literature. Members of this movement did not concern themselves with artistic forms but with different types of consciousness and ways of thinking, which were simply mirrored by physical objects. It is perhaps for this reason that it became the most 'literary' movement within Russian art of the last few decades. The Moscow Conceptualists explored literature's centrality within Russian culture, the latter's specifically literary way of thinking and conceiving the world.

Many of Kabakov's albums, paintings and installations centre on literary themes, including text and narrative as critical features for the telling of a story. His stories are redolent of ready-mades;

Ilya and Emilia Kabakov
Taking Out the Garbage Can, 1980
Oil and enamel on masonite
150 x 210 cm
© Ilya and Emilia Kabakov
Courtesy of Ilya and
Emilia Kabakov

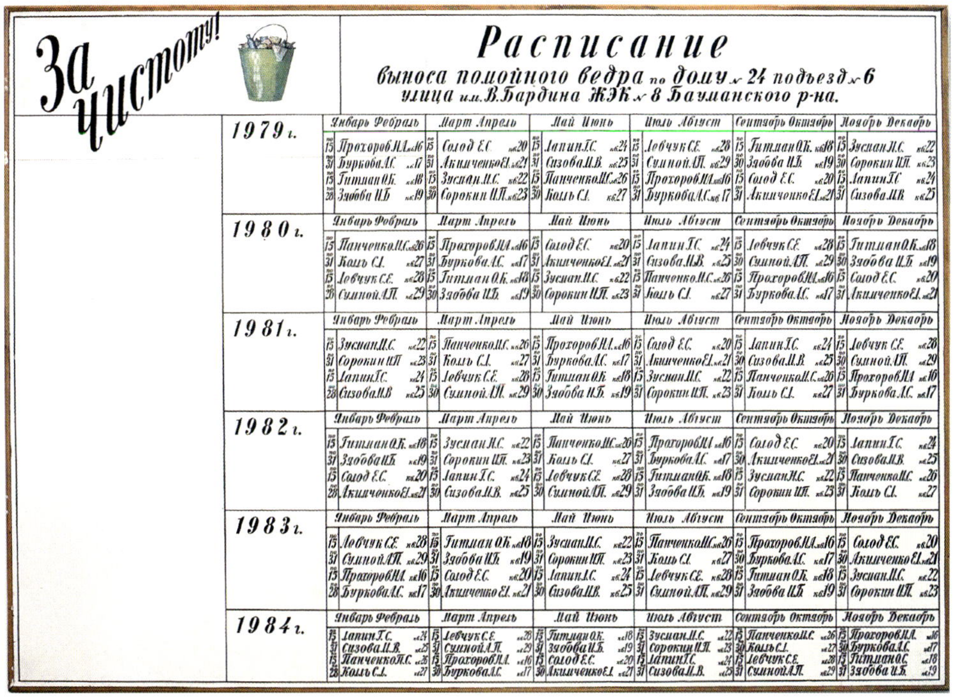

he forms his texts out of stylistic clichés and a compilation of commonplaces. These he uses only as tools, however. He is not interested in the stories themselves but in the tradition of storytelling and description. In essence, the artist repeats the same narrative over and over again: the ways in which 'reality' is constructed and visualised out of a myriad of voices, tales and comments, and in which it recognises its own ephemeral nature and falls apart, having come across its own shadow – text and ideology.

The Moscow Conceptualists' literariness is in many ways antithetical to the modernist desire to create an autonomous visual language. For them, this tradition is foreign, and they often argue with and reject it. Art, they believe, is not formal experimentation but a way of being.

Another turning point in unofficial culture occurred in the late 1970s–'80s, when a new generation of artists appeared in both Moscow and St Petersburg. In Moscow, these were primarily younger Conceptualists like Yuri Albert, Vadim Zakharov, Andrei Filippov, the Mukhomor (Toadstools) group (Konstantin Zvezdochetov, Sven Gundlach, Vladimir and Sergei Mironenko, Alexei Kamensky), Inspection Medical Hermeneutics (Pavel Pepperstein, Sergei Anufriev, Yuri Leiderman) and Champions of the World (Gia Abramishvili, Andrei Yakhnin, Boris Matrosov, Konstantin Latyshev). In St Petersburg, there were the New Artists (Timur Novikov, Oleg Kotelnikov, Ivan Sotnikov, Sergei Bugaev [Afrika] and others) and the Necrorealists (Evgeny Yufit, Andrei Myortvy, Evgeny [Debil] Kondratyev, Igor Bezrukov and their colleagues). For all of these practitioners, whose works had affinities with the so-called 'New Wave', the traditions of the 1950s–'70s were subjects of reflection, irony, mockery and provocation. Their credo was to create an all-encompassing project for life and art, one that was playful, provocative, and free of official dogma and the exclusive snobbery of unofficial culture. Demonstrating a renewed interest in Primitivism and Expressionism, they had active recourse to forms of popular culture. The traditions of the avant-garde were important to them as an embodiment of creative life-energy and a symbol of art's autonomy. In St Petersburg, the New Artists looked back directly to the avant-garde and strove to recreate the same experimental, playful and provocative atmosphere.

Timur Novikov offered one of the most original interpretations of the avant-garde tradition, his canvas pieces combining classical art and 1920s avant-garde practice. His compositions are not direct quotations, although they take into account both Suprematism and Constructivist experimental design. Rather than a destructive gesture, Novikov saw in the work of the avant-garde a burgeoning new classicism notable for its rhythm, clear and simple compositions, lightness, clarity and balance. In the 1990s, he developed these themes within the framework of a project that went on to take the form of the New Academy. The New Academicians' search was for a stylistic formula capable of communicating life's nuances, filled with Baudelaire's 'enthusiasm of beauty' and close to classicism but at the same time deeply contemporary. Each of the Neo-Academic artists developed their own artistic language. Members included Olga Tobreluts, Oleg Maslov, Victor Kuznetsov and George Gurianov. Gurianov, for example, created a synthetic form of classicism in which the legacy of Soviet culture was 'antiquated'.

The 1990s were a time of attempting to understand the Western art world, the rules of the art game and the logic behind its institutions. There were victories and disappointments, triumphs and failures. The decade heralded the establishment of new arts institutions, the arrival of new artists on the scene, and the acquisition of new strategies and visual ideas. It is difficult to draw a direct connection between Russian modernism and contemporary art. In a globalised context, with free access to information, modern art was no longer seen as pertinent. Despite this, artists today are turning anew to their avant-garde heritage and to the legacies of Russian modernism as a whole.

During the past century, Russian art changed its appearance several times. It was radically avant-garde, it was archaic, and it looked to folk traditions for inspiration. During the Soviet period, the avant-garde was denied while unofficial artists persevered in reconstructing or reinvigorating the modernist tradition. Art in twentieth-century Russia was an instrument of ideological propaganda, yet its practitioners never forsook the notions of freedom and autonomy. In the twenty-first century, Russian art is finding its place within the context of global culture, striving to preserve the radicalism and drama characteristic of Russian culture while looking resolutely outwards.

Notes

1 The title of the exhibition became the name of an artistic group that included Kuznetsov, V. and N. Milioti, Saryan, Sapunov, Sudeikin, N. Krymov, P. Utkin and others.

2 The exhibition featured work by Pavel Konchalovsky, Ilya Mashkov, Aristarkh Lentulov, Robert Falk, Mikhail Larionov, Natalia Goncharova and Alexander Kuprin. The group was formed in 1911. Larionov and Goncharova, who took part in organising the first exhibition, were not members.

3 I. Kliun, *My Artistic Journey* (Moscow, 1999), p. 138.

4 A. Rodchenko and V. Stepanova, *The Future Is Our Only Goal* (Munich, 1991), p. 136.

5 I. Lebedeva, 'The Lyrical Science "Electro-organism" and "Projectionism"', in *The Great Utopia, Russian and Soviet Avant-garde, 1915–1932*, exh. cat., Berne and Moscow, 1993, p. 188.

Art & Politics in Russia since 1953

Alexandra Danilova

The last fifty years have been a complex and contradictory period for Russian art, history and culture. Throughout this period systems of shared reference points and values were re-evaluated several times. The Thaw, the Cold War and the stagnation that followed were succeeded by perestroika and Russia's reappearance on the international stage. However, the euphoric rediscovery of the West evaporated quickly, to be replaced by a painful search for a new position in the context of globalisation. These difficult, often contradictory processes had their effects on the development of Russian art.

A critical moment in this process was the Thaw, a short-lived period of liberalisation in the mid-1950s that followed the death of Stalin. One of the most important events of the time was the 1957 International Festival of Youth, whose broad cultural programme introduced Moscow to the latest innovations in global culture and showcased alternative artistic outlooks. Although Realism, which had been promoted by the Soviet government, did not lose its credibility during those years (even today, it remains one of the most influential styles in Russia), this was the period when Russian modernism evolved further from its origins in the first decade of the twentieth century.

A major step forward was the move towards abstraction. Many artists, inspired by the work of leading international post-war artists exhibited in Russia for the first time at the International Festival of Youth in 1957, as well as in exhibitions of American Expressionism at Sokolniki in Moscow in 1959, saw abstract art as a symbol of freedom synonymous with the new youth culture. Mikhail Kulakov painted spontaneous, large-format, expressionistic signs; Vladimir Slepyan developed a Russian version of Tachisme; and members of the Elia Belyutin school created an entire theory of abstraction. After Khrushchev's crackdown on the latter group's exhibition at the Manege in 1962, the term 'abstract art' fell into disgrace. Many members went into self-imposed seclusion in order to safeguard their styles and philosophies.

Photo of the Bulldozer Exhibition, 15 September 1974
© Komar and Melamid
Courtesy of Former Komar and Melamid Art Studio Archive

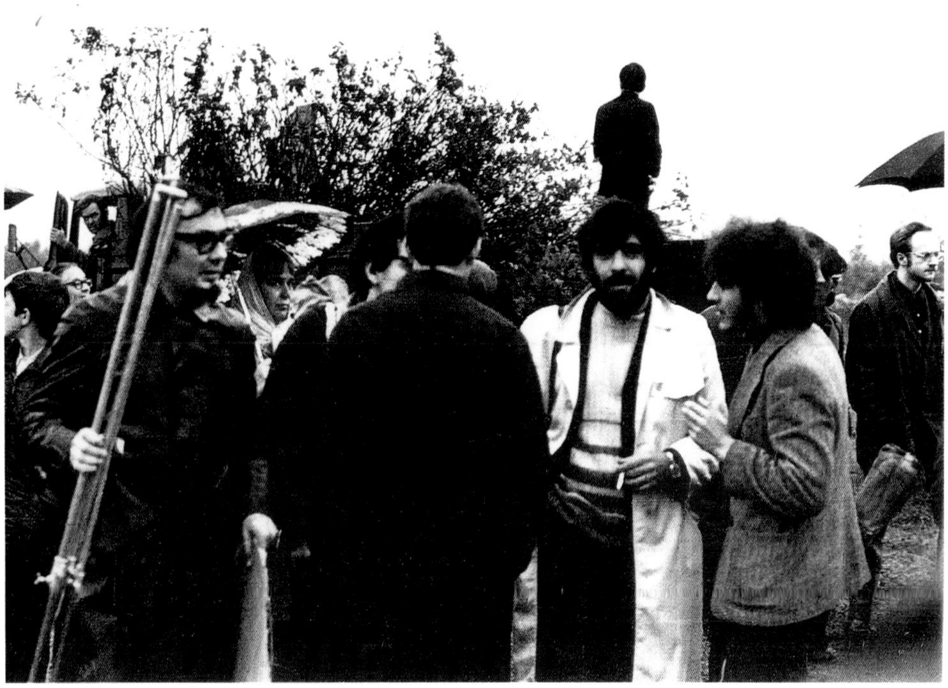

Another strand in the development of Russian post-war abstraction involved utopian attempts to marry art to scientific and technological progress. In this context, formlessness became associated with 'scientific' creativity. In Yuri Zlotnikov's series Signal Systems, an interest in mathematics and semiotics was transformed into a systematic study of geometry and the structure of visual signs. This trend continued into the 1960s in the work of Dvizheniye, a group led by Lev Nussberg and whose members included Francisco Infante and Vyacheslav Koleychuk, who developed ideas about the transfiguration of space throughout their careers. They were particularly interested in the collision between nature and geometry, and in the artistic presentation of different optical effects.

The fate of abstract painting and its followers changed following the exhibition *Thirty Years of the Moscow Society of Artists* in 1962 and, to a greater extent, as a result of Khrushchev's famous dictum stigmatising non-figurative art. Calling modernism 'anti-Soviet', he forced a large segment of contemporary art practice into an illegal, underground existence.

The Lianozovo Group, which met at the house of the poet and artist Evgeny Kropivnitsky, became one of the first and most significant circles of non-official, contemporary art; its name derived from the suburban railway station near which most of its members lived. Kropivnitsky's diverse talents made it a prerequisite that participants included not just artists but poets, including Vsevolod Nekrasov. Their philosophical mood found expression in the paradoxical forms of Kropivnitsky's work, in the semi-abstract compositions of Lydia Masterkova and Vladimir Nemukhin, and in the bitter social irony of Oscar Rabin. The works of the Leningrad artist Evgeny Rukhin, who combined an interest in formal experimentation with prosaic, everyday motifs, approached the spirit of the Lianozovo circle's poetics and aesthetics.

These artists looked back at the experience of the Russian avant-garde in the early twentieth century, inspired by the notion of the work of art as an epitome of the universe. Using realistic motifs, they sought to discover a 'higher order' and, by overcoming chance and accident, to attain a level of metaphysical meaning. These traits are found in the frozen still lifes of Dmitry Krasnopevtsev, in which ordinary studio objects are elevated to the status of universal signs, or in painter Vladimir Weisberg's geometrical compositions, constructed with fine tonal variations of white and in which objects dissolve into light.

One of the other key characteristics of 1960s non-official practice was the tendency to transform art into a magical or religious ritual, as in the insular, enclosed 'hieraturae' of Mikhail Shvartsman, which resemble ancient totems, or the quasi-religious letters and texts written on Dmitry Plavinsky's canvases. Art's mystical nature is embodied in a slightly different way in the free, painterly forms of Vladimir Yakovlev or the improvised canvases of Anatoly Zverev, who turned both the artistic process and his own life into an idiosyncratic performance.

By the end of the 1960s, then, there had been a fusion of many different styles and forms and it had all happened relatively quickly.

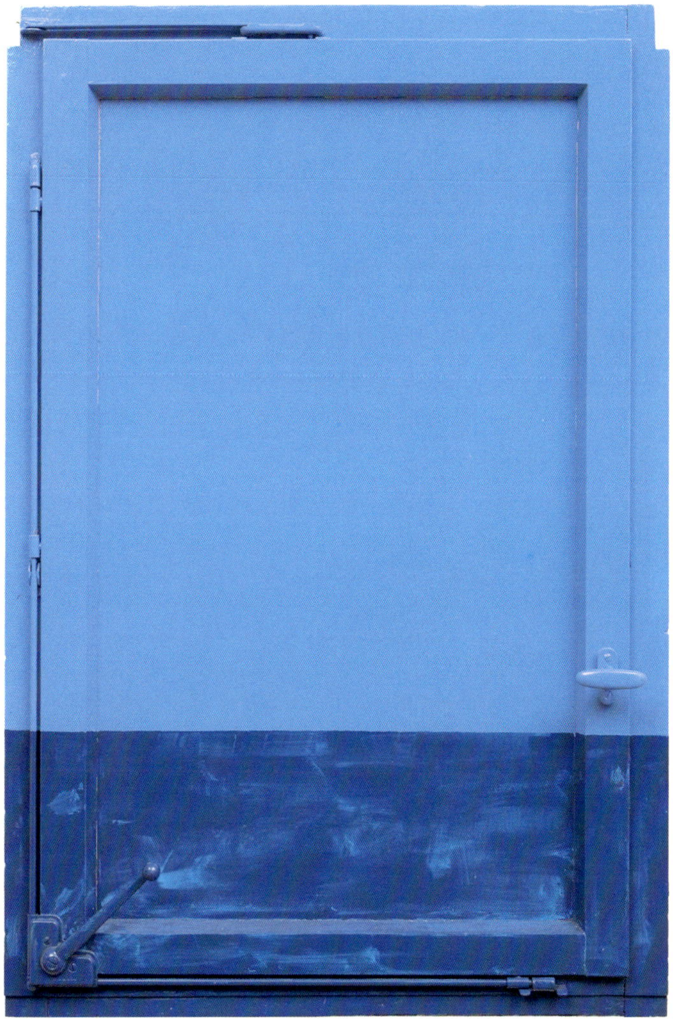

Ivan Chuikov
Window LXIX, 2005
Oil on wooden panel
with metal hardware
120 x 81 cm
© Ivan Chuikov
Courtesy of Phillips de Pury

It can be said that from behind the Iron Curtain, Russia absorbed nearly fifty years of European artistic innovation and development in just a decade. Russian Modernism and avant-garde European art of the 1920s and '30s, American Expressionism and the latest developments in global culture all had significance for artists of this generation. It would be a mistake, however, to define 1960s Russia as culturally provincial, as a place of rapid assimilation of Western artistic practices. Russian art chronicling a new way of life appeared at nearly the same time as new realist trends in Europe and American Pop art. Where Western artists were attracted by novelty and the power of consumerism, the extreme modesty of Soviet interiors provided inspiration for Russian underground artists, as can be seen in Mikhail Chernyshev's ascetic framed pieces of wallpaper and Mikhail Roginsky's minimalistic 'portraits' of kerosene stoves and ceramic tiles.

The underground artists, having inherited a kind of modernist utopianism from their avant-garde predecessors, craved universal recognition, having been forced to survive, from 1962 on, in tiny studio apartments among a small circle of devotees. The 'Bulldozer Exhibition', organised by Rabin, Nemukhin, Rukhin and others, saw a drastic turn of events. The destruction of this small, free, plein-air show of paintings caused a huge reaction in the Western press. From that time on, it became impossible to deny the existence of 'other' art in Russia. As Vladimir Yankilevsky put it, 'From this moment it was no longer dangerous to be an unofficial artist – we were legalized. It became prestigious – people started talking about the exhibitions. The whole of Moscow saw them ... I believe that the history of "unofficial" art ends after the "Bulldozer Exhibition" thanks to this.'[1]

Although the chronological development of modernism was quite different in Russia than it was in the West, the first post-war Conceptual works appeared in Russia in the late 1960s and early '70s at almost the same time as in Europe and America. Just like its international counterpart, Moscow Conceptualism was a reaction to the sudden 'cooling' following the failure of 1960s liberalism and the dissolution of youth movements. In Russia, politics turned more conservative following the Prague Spring in Czechoslovakia. Increased ideological and political prohibitions resulted in the appearance of a dissident movement. The impossibility of unquestioningly accepting the uncompromising situation in which they found themselves forced artists to adopt a detached point of view. 'Talking about the 1970s ... one remembers a small, energetic ghetto, whose inhabitants didn't quite belong to this world but who floated over and observed its goings-on,' remembers Ilya Kabakov, one of the founders of Moscow Conceptualism.[2] The role of outsider and foreign commentator was characteristic of the movement and underpinned the metaphysical interpretations of time and space found in Kabakov's oeuvre and those of Victor Pivovarov, Eric Bulatov, Ivan Chuikov and Oleg Vassiliev. These artists destroyed the previous generation's notion of a painting as a flat surface for artistic experimentation. Instead, metaphorical emptiness prevailed, a utopian space of absolute freedom precisely described by Bulatov when he said that a painting 'is not even a picture of the world, but a striving beyond its boundaries'.[3] By conceiving the picture surface as a means of penetrating space rather than an end in itself, as the modernists had done, the Moscow Conceptualists were able to explore and question many different visual stereotypes. The Renaissance notion of the painting as a window onto the world helped these artists to complete the act of inversion by turning the view out of the window into a conceptual space. Good examples are the Zen-like emptiness of Kabakov's works on paper, Vassiliev's flashes of light or spectrum paintings, and the silent backdrops of Chuikov's Window paintings.

On the one hand, the Moscow Conceptualists wished to perceive the world as a single universe devoid of detail, like an invisible space, and on the other, they did the opposite, recording minute existential details. In doing this, they strove to turn everyday, banal objects and words into universal signs and symbols. Many art historians have noticed the relationship between Moscow Conceptualism and Russian literature. Evocations of characters from nineteenth-century novels by Gogol or Chekhov, and of the tradition of the 'little man', are to be found in the paintings and graphics of Kabakov and Pivovarov, who poeticised the dreams of ordinary Soviet citizens. Russian Conceptualism inclined towards the creation of new forms of art ranging from Kabakov's now famous albums and word paintings to Pivovarov's drawing manuals, Bulatov's slogan paintings, Lev Rubinstein's library cards and the concrete poetry of Dmitry Prigov.

This 'visual literariness' intensified after 1975. Unofficial art's public recognition following the 'Bulldozer Exhibition' resulted in the creation of the Gorkom for graphic artists and of the first sanctioned exhibition space for unofficial art. However, this attempt to create an official organisation for underground art ended in failure; there were

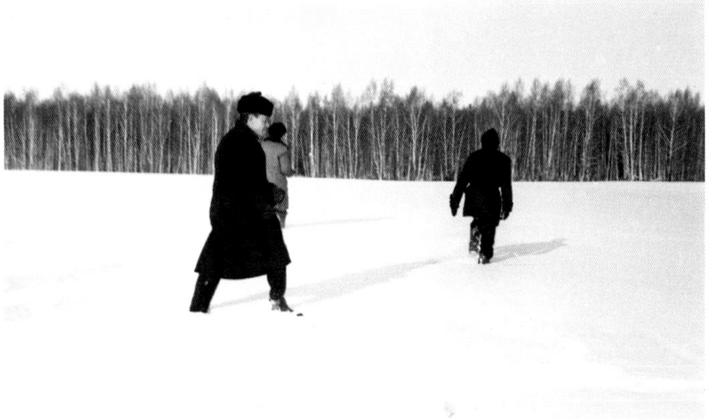

Collective Actions
Photo-documentation of the group's action Ten Appearances, 1 February 1981
Kievogorskoye field, Moscow Region
© Igor Makarevich
Courtesy of E.K.ArtBureau

practitioners whose work could not be described as either painting or graphics. These were the poets and artists who were creating objects and staged actions. It was during this period – the mid-1970s – that a generation of Conceptual artists appeared whose practice presented the new aesthetic in the 'purest' of forms.

The work of Valery and Rimma Gerlovin, Andrei Monastyrsky and Lev Rubinstein, and the performances of Collective Actions appeared on the surface to be uninteresting and lacking in expressiveness. The main focus shifted from the aesthetic to the intellectual. Scientific experiments which took as their point of departure not only the usual artistic questions but also the particularities of human perception became popular. This attempt to give visual form to abstract categories manifested itself most prominently in the practice of Collective Actions, founded in 1976 by Monastyrsky, Nikolai Panitkov, Nikita Alekseev and George Kisevalter. The group's actions and the post-mortem discussions by its members and participants created an environment of constant reflection and reflexivity. For example, during the performance *The Time of Action* (1978), participants unwound a 7-kilometre piece of string from within a forest. This 'non-event' evoked time passing, transforming the string into a visual metaphor for its flow. As one of the participants remembers, 'The day was beautiful. The string just kept unwinding ... an analogy was formed subconsciously between the string and the passage of time – we live our lives while the string stretches and unwinds and, despite its seeming endlessness, it, sooner or later, comes to an end.'[4] Viewers' and participants' comments, thoughts and opinions were thoroughly documented and became part of the artistic whole. The documentary and archival material of Collective Actions, consisting of descriptions of performances and participants' statements, exists in several volumes entitled *Trips Out of Town*.

Many works of Moscow Conceptualism were by their very nature collaborative; they required not only the presence but also the active participation of the viewer. Works like Monastyrsky's *Cannon* (1975) and *Finger* (1978) offered spectators a chance to perform simple experiments on their own sensory organs. It was typical of Conceptualism that these works moved away from the visual towards the cerebral.

By definition, any composition within this framework presupposed a subtle game with systems of signification. Signifier and signified could exchange places freely since artists took as their point of orientation the system of abstract meanings and commonplaces through which a work could acquire significance.

This style was used by the Sots artists as a foundation for their conceptual experiments. Created by Vitaly Komar and Alexander Melamid, Sots Art's origin can be dated to 1972; its name hints at an analogy with American Pop art. Komar and Melamid used to joke, 'If there was an over-production of things in America, in the USSR there was an over-production of ideas.'[5] Using the exhausted language of Soviet propaganda, the artists turned it into a form of artistic expression with the help of conceptual transformation: 'We imagined an eccentric artist, who finds genuine pleasure in visual, graphic propaganda. We imagined this person painting "idealistic slogans" and "ideological quotations" on red bunting, identified by their deeply personal, individual emotions and thoughts.'[6] Taking on the role of a hapless imaginary painter, Komar and Melamid created a series of works which translated 'personal' forms into the language of posters and slogans. This analytical approach to a 'foreign' language created an unarguable affinity between early Sots Art and Moscow Conceptualism.

However, this playfulness and irony did not have long-term significance. The followers of 'conceptual Sots Art' included the group The Nest, whose name came from their first performance at VDNKh in 1975 during which members hatched eggs in a giant nest, parodying the style of Soviet agricultural shows. The term 'Sots Art' subsequently became associated with a different artistic strategy. In the work of Alexander Kosolapov, Rostislav Lebedev, Boris Orlov and Leonid Sokov, forms of Soviet ideology surrendered their conceptual meaning and become visual metaphors. These artists married up Soviet, European and American visual clichés, turning the 'over-production of ideas' into a synonym for mass culture. Their strategy, which attained wide circulation in the 1980s and '90s, was developed by young artists such as Andrei Filippov, Nikolai Kozlov and Dmitry Vrubel. At the same time, in the work of this younger generation the use of myths often became part of a more complex conceptual, Postmodern game.

The 1980s were the era of the *Neue Wilde*. A new interest in painting, bright colours, urban folklore and youthful forms of opposition superseded the intellectual rigour of Conceptualism and the visual asceticism of Minimalism. This burst of energy gave a new lease of life to artistic circles in New York, Paris, Rome and Berlin, and also took hold in Russia. The late 1970s had already seen the coming of age of young, daring artists who challenged the idea of generational continuity rather than simply distancing themselves from tradition.

The art associated with youth culture in Russia, as elsewhere, was witty, scintillating, mischievous and punkish; ignoring rules and laws, it challenged and mocked everything in its path. The artistic strategy of the Toadstools (Mukhomor) group – Konstantin Zvezdochetov, Sven Gundlach, Vladimir and Sergei Mironenko, and Alexei Kamensky – can be characterised in precisely these terms. The group made itself known in 1978 through outrageous performances which shocked the Moscow Conceptualist elite. For the Toadstools, art was neither a profession nor a sphere of research but a way of life. Their art was lightweight, entertaining and constructed along the lines (as Orlov put it) of 'a carnivalesque abandonment and freedom'.[7] Examples included the performance *Excavations* (1979), during which, in a surprise gesture, one of the group's members was dug out of the ground instead of the buried treasure participants had been expecting, and the fantastical plan to steal and sell a painting from the State Tretyakov Gallery with the aim of establishing Russia's first prize for Conceptual art. These works' paradoxical nature attracted equally bizarre events. The group's only 'musical' production, 'The Golden Disc', in which their absurdist poems are heard to the accompaniment of popular Soviet songs, was banned by the authorities along with albums by famous Western rock bands such as Kiss, Led Zeppelin and the Rolling Stones. The beginning of the group's persecution in 1983–4 did not spell an end for the New Wave, however. The tone set by the Toadstools was taken up by many young artists, not only 'students' of the group like Champions of the World (established in 1986 by Gia Abramishvili, Boris Matrosov, Konstantin Latyshev and Andrei Yakhnin) but the 'third generation' of Moscow Conceptualists, whose works were formally very different. While the visual richness, energy and carnival spirit of the New Wave exploded as a complete contradiction of the strict asceticism of the 1970s, the art of the following decade maintained this New Wave spirit and built on the tradition.

'The feeling was that, if two years ago the combination of two words together in a sentence was achieved with a great, heroic effort, now everything spoke in rhymes,' remembers a member of The Nest, Viktor Skersis.[8] As a continuation of this 'playful' strategy, Skersis himself performed a series of actions with Vadim Zakharov in the 1980s (the SZ group), in the course of which they parodied Soviet society (*Self-defence against Things*, 1981–2) and the phenomenon of illegal exhibitions (*The 4th Personal SZ Exhibition: Portable*, 1984). In this instance, the punk daredevilry of the New Wave turned into a conceptual gesture of simulation and simulacra. As Andrei Monastyrsky astutely remarked, however, in the 1980s structure was 'exchanged for surface'.[9] New Wave works were striking in their brightness, colourfulness, and interest in texture and mark-making. Examples include SZ's 'gold' advertisement poster and Konstantin Zvezdochetov's famous *Fridge Novel* (1982), an old fridge covered inside and out with text and bright, funny drawings. Like their immediate predecessors, these artists explored the margins of culture. An informal, youthful aesthetic and backstreet atmosphere captured their attention, not the official, bureaucratic style of social and political posters.

Another characteristic of the Russian art scene in the 1980s was the interest in collective, group actions and collaboration, which became a prerequisite for many artists. As Vadim Zakharov, a member of SZ, has said, 'We believed it was possible to fundamentally change the understanding of the terms "artist" and "artistic work". This was our reaction to the artists of the previous generation who had chosen the status of "God in the sky" for themselves.'[10] It is not surprising that this youthful vision, which challenged art itself, resulted in the appearance of a huge number of artists' groups and collectives. The tone was set by the legendary gallery APTART, created in 1982 in the apartment of one of the founding members of Collective Actions, Nikita Alekseev; the term 'apartment art' also originated there. Taking a conscious decision to distance himself from 'seriousness', one of the key figures of Moscow Conceptualism suddenly proclaimed himself to be a New Waver and turned his studio apartment into a space for artistic experimentation. Over the course of its existence, APTART established the foundations of Russian contemporary art, albeit in a jokey, playful manner. It regularly hosted exhibitions, performances and actions, thus becoming a testing ground for new strategies. For many artists outside of Moscow, APTART exhibitions were a means by which to propel themselves onto the scene there. It is in part thanks to the well-known exhibition *Moscow–Odessa* (1984) that, for the first time in the history of Russian art, there appeared the names of new artists who suddenly became famous overnight, including Sergei Anufriev, Yuri Liederman, Olga Petrenko and Ludmila Skripkina (the Pertsy group), and Larissa Rezun-Zvezdochetova. In this way, APTART reflected yet another important trend: the inclusion of new cities in the mapping of contemporary art.

Leningrad (St Petersburg) became one of the most important centres of culture during the 1980s, the early years of the decade giving rise to several influential artists' collectives. Timur Novikov's New Academy of Fine Arts, with its attempt to resurrect the original avant-garde, was one of the main sites exerting a gravitational pull in Russia's northern capital. The other significant figure there was the artist and film director Evgeny Yufit, who surrounded himself with like-minded sympathisers and followers. Yufit termed his creative practice 'Necrorealism'. Despite this dark-sounding label, the movement's poetics were founded on absurdist subject matter and a total lack of cause and effect. Yufit's minimalist works radically reduced their visual attractiveness, making them unappealing to the general public. The films were ugly, distant and absurd, but at the same time had a markedly individual, easily recognisable style.

The direct opposite of Necrorealism's northern coldness was Mitki, another St Petersburg subculture formed in the 1980s. This group, which united more than twenty artists, poets and musicians, derived its name from one its founders, Dmitry Shagin. Like the artists of the Moscow New Wave, Mitki chose urban folklore as one of their main themes. With their boundless love for the world around

Pertsy group
Drain, 1987
Object
73.5 × 46 × 20 cm
© Pertsy group
Collection MANI Museum
Courtesy of E.K.ArtBureau

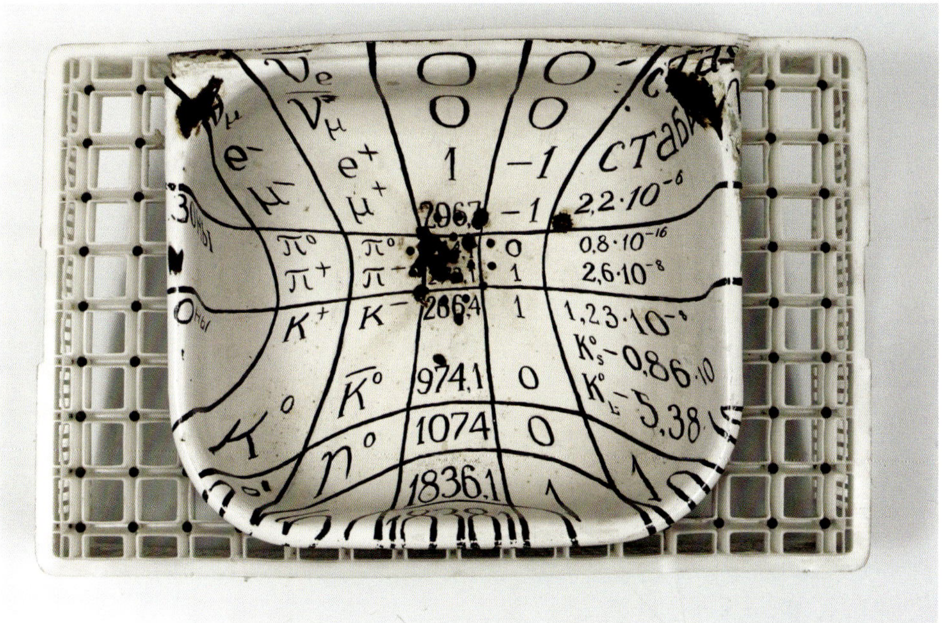

them and their bubbly humour, they gained popularity by poeticising the everyday. By the 1990s, Mitki had won fame not only in Russia but also in the West.

St Petersburg, which had become home to several influential movements and subcultures, was an exception on the artistic map of the time, as centripetal forces were still strong, enriching Moscow with an influx of new life. Odessa's artists, for example, were quickly assimilated into the circle of Moscow Conceptualism, although Conceptualism's 'immateriality' and its orientation around intellectual games received a distinctly alternative interpretation. Minimalism became a formal characteristic of the work of Inspection Medical Hermeneutics (Pavel Pepperstein, Yuri Liederman, Sergei Anufriev) and the Pertsy group, while the 'symbol-sign' was stripped of its previous spectacular form and turned into an idiosyncratic, absurdist figure. It is noteworthy that the collective spirit of the '80s seems to have impregnated even Moscow Conceptualism, with much work being executed through collective effort.

The history begun by the Toadstools and APTART was continued by other experimental communities of the New Wave such as Kindergarden (Nikolai Filatov, Andrei Roiter, German Vinogradov) and the studios on Moscow's Furmanny Lane. 'The House on Furmanny', which came into being in 1987, became a symbol of the commercial success of Russian unofficial art of the '80s. The West's desire for all things Russian at the time meant that paintings were bought in large quantities by international buyers, mainly Western diplomats and businessmen. The multicoloured brightness of the New Wave served as a catalyst for the development of multifaceted trends and turned the Moscow art scene into something of a boiling cauldron. Everything and everyone were striving for recognition, and this energy spilled over in the form of exhibitions, performances, concerts and alternative fashion shows. Perestroika determined the state of mind of an entire decade, uncovering the absurdity of the Soviet myth and opening a window onto freedom.

The 1990s were the 'happiness epoch', a short-lived but surprisingly productive period. Post-perestroika, all bans and limitations came crashing down, and it became possible to acquire art materials without being a member of the Union of Artists. The 1988 Sotheby's auction in Moscow gave some idea of the real 'value' of unofficial art, and artists began trying to embody their creative ideas on a monumental scale with barely a thought for political regimes or market movements. However, this golden age was destined to be superseded by disillusionment and a painful search for self-positioning in the new sphere of globalisation. The Western fashion for all things Russian and Soviet was fleeting, and artists came face to face with the everyday, hard-hitting side of the international market. The situation was worsened by the country's lack of institutions specialising in contemporary art. There were no galleries, museums or art fairs, and a regular art press practically did not exist. Or, to be more precise, all of this existed in a specifically Russian samizdat, communal form whereby artists, critics and viewers were all old friends. Contemporary art, which had been defined over a period of thirty years as 'art for oneself', aspired for public recognition and social status throughout the 1990s.

That same decade witnessed the creation of a functional infrastructure for contemporary art and the birth of an active art market and gallery system, foundations and schools. Galleries and institutions specialising in the questions posed by contemporary practice appeared with incredible rapidity. In 1989, Andrei Erofeev started the first collection of contemporary art in the Tsaritsino Museum, which was handed over to the State Tretyakov Gallery in 2001. It was on this foundation that the latter's Department of New Trends would be based. The Centre for Contemporary Arts was triumphantly opened on Yakimanka in 1991 with its own exhibition space and a diverse cultural programme. The First Gallery opened in 1989; the following year saw the opening of the influential Regina and Guelman galleries, followed by the respected Aidan (1992) and the experimental XL (1993). More than twenty-five galleries from across the country were registered at Art Moscow, Russia's first contemporary art fair, in 1996.

The 1990s also witnessed a significant geographical expansion of contemporary art. In previous decades, unofficial artists had been largely Moscow-based. The capital turned out to be a centre of attraction, a place that accumulated creative energy and to which artists from different cities gravitated. At the beginning of the 1990s, new 'minor' art capitals began to appear – Ekaterinburg, Krasnoyarsk, Kaliningrad, Novosibirsk, Nizhniy Novgorod. Quite often, these centres not only did not want to copy Moscow but made a concerted effort to differentiate themselves from Muscovite taste and fashions. One of the best examples is Timur Novikov's New Academy of Fine Arts in St Petersburg, which opposed Moscow's eclecticism with an orchestrated return to ancient Greek order and mythology, and to compositional discipline and clarity. The New Academy declared the old Russian imperial capital to be the guardian of classical beauty and the academic tradition. Novikov, the movement's theoretician as well as its founder, was supported by George Gurianov, Denis Egelsky, Yulia Strausova, Olga Tobreluts and the critics Ekaterina Andreeva and Olesya Turkina. The conservation of the canons of 'eternal beauty' coincided in many ways with a new global interest in Neoclassicism and glamour. It is not difficult to find resemblances between the

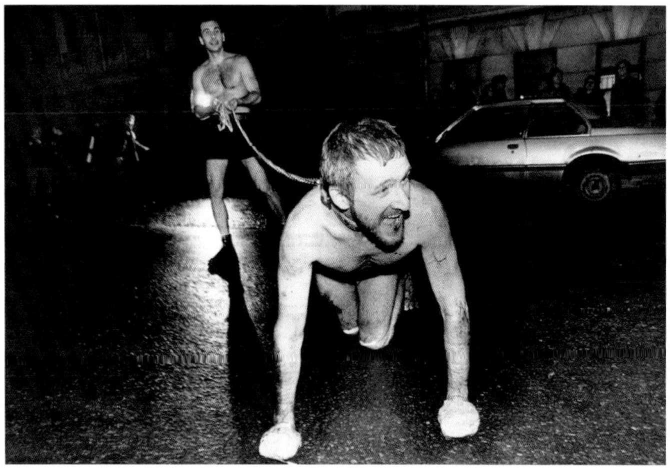

Oleg Kulik and Alexander Brener
Mad Dog, or The Last Taboo Guarded by Lone Cerberus. Moscow, Yakimanka street in front of the Guelman Gallery,
November 23, 1994
Black and white photograph
Variable dimensions
© Oleg Kulik
Courtesy of Oleg Kulik

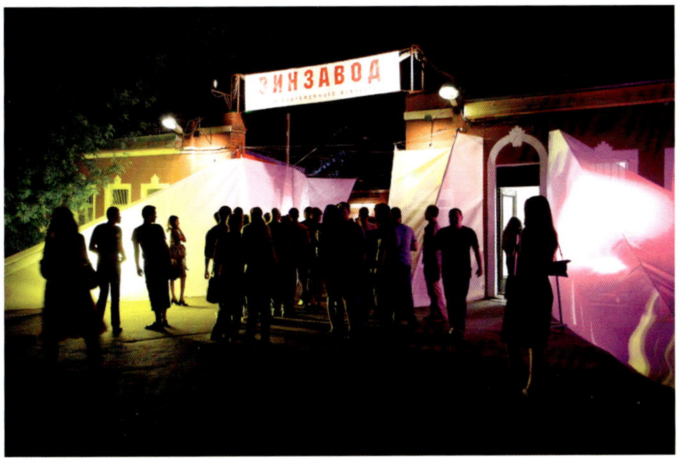

Night of Galleries at Vinzavod,
15 May 2010
© Vinzavod
Courtesy of Vinzavod PR
Department

art of the New Academicians and that of the French duo Pierre et Gilles. Having spread quickly outside the confines of St Petersburg, Neo-Academicism found adherents in Moscow and elsewhere, as in the majestic porticoes of Valery Koshlyakov's cardboard paintings or the monumental compositions executed in biro by Alexei Belyaev-Guintovt. Aidan Salakhova became one of the main supporters of the Neoclassical style in Moscow, developing it not only in her own work but also in the Aidan Gallery's exhibition programme. In many ways this anticipated the leading trend of the next decade, when Russian artists would find themselves searching for compromises between socio-cultural relevance and commercial success, the avant-garde and classical 'beauty', high art and design.

This split identity was intrinsic to Postmodernism and 'new consumerism', the appearance of which was noted by critics everywhere. Large numbers of works bordering on pastiche were created in response to the notion of the world as a field of free-floating quotations, the need to scrutinise every gesture within the context of the old and the new, the freedom to use 'foreign' languages as easily as one's own, and the comprehension of the potential for appropriation and of art as a playground of cultural codes and clichés. Examples include Tatiana Antoshina's comic paraphrases of international art, and Dubossarsky and Vinogradov's monumental canvases depicting illustrations from school textbooks.

With the acceptance of images as if chosen from a stockpile becoming second nature to artists and with the growing interest in new technological possibilities, many practitioners turned to photography, which had become one of the most popular media by the mid-1990s. Photography's increasing interest was no doubt due to the many exhibitions that took place regularly under the umbrella of the Moscow Photography Biennale from 1996 onwards. Many artists were attracted by the dual nature of the photographic image, which allowed for the convergence of diverse temporal and social contexts, as can be seen in the work of Vladimir Kuprianov, Olga Chernysheva and Igor Moukhin. The union of documentary-style photography with digital technology in the work of AES+F lends their highly fake, surreal images a strange credibility.

Enthusiasm for alternative technologies can be seen in the multimedia art created by Vladislav Efimov and Aristarkh Chernyshev. Joining forces in 2004 with Alexei Shulgin, they organised the Electroboutique project. Their interactive installations and objects, consisting of LCD screens, neon lights and other technological innovations, not only gave the nod to the games and entertainment industries but were also a powerful critique of contemporary society, in which technology had become part of the fashion industry.

For Russia, the 1990s were not only a period of entry into the global context but a time of difficulty accompanied by the demolition of social and political infrastructure. It is not surprising that this latter process inspired a marked interest in the exploration of taboos, most notably through the well-known antics of the Moscow Actionists. Theirs was an art of harsh, often violent performances joining the radicalism of Body Art with social criticism. These included Oleg Kulik's shocking transformation into a man-dog; Vladislav Mamyshev-Monroe's transvestite self-re-imaginings; the exhibitionist actions of Alexander Brener; and the anarchic freedom of Anatoly Osmolovsky's early works. Much art of the 1990s was dedicated not to the exploration of the possibilities and limitations of the human body but to a rejection of social, moral and ethical norms, even challenging the notion of art itself. It is not by accident that the end of Actionism was marked by a queuing up of court cases, starting with the 1997 conviction of Alexander Brener for vandalism in Holland. This was followed by criminal investigations in Russia into the performances of Avdei Ter-Oganyan and Oleg Mavromati, both of whom were accused of inciting national and religious hatred.

The very fact that a work of art may be a cause for discussion and contention not only between artists, critics and art historians but also among lawyers and political analysts has heralded a new stage in the evolution and development of contemporary art in Russia. The probing of art's limits is no longer regulated by the revolutionary audacity of artists, by their courage and unexpected decisions, but by existing legal, moral, ethical and aesthetic frameworks. Contemporary art has firmly secured its place in the social fabric, even becoming an integral part of it. It has stopped being 'different', 'other' and elitist, focusing now on a large audience rather than a small, initiated circle. And it has found its patrons, collectors, researchers and, most importantly, its public, whose number is constantly growing. The interest in questions posed by contemporary art has resulted in the creation of multiple foundations and new platforms for exhibitions. The art scene has not been immune to globalisation. Galleries, salons and design studios have started to coalesce into large cultural centres, for example Art Strelka and Vinzavod. In emulation of Western trends, there is a fashion for rehabilitating old industrial sites to create spaces for contemporary art, with the tone being set by PROEKT_FABRIKA and continued by Vinzavod, Garage Centre for Contemporary Culture and Red October. The recent significant increase in the number of devotees of contemporary art has, first and foremost, changed its character, pre-empting an interest in public taste and popular culture. Aiming for recognition and success, contemporary artists have often needed to appropriate the resources and approaches of commercial advertising and show business. Often their productions verge on design, sometimes merging with it completely.

The rise of contemporary art has created an infrastructure of museums, galleries, exhibitions and art fairs. Russia, once isolated from the rest of the world, now has a vibrant domestic scene – Moscow alone is home to several public and private museums of contemporary art, art centres and exhibition halls. In fact, the relatively large number of museums accurately reflects the complex history of Russian art over the last fifty years, the consistent cherishing of the human gaze and of individual interpretation.

Notes

1 Interview with Ilya Kabakov, in Vadim Zakharov and Georgy Kisewalter, *Album on Workshops. First Part. 1982–1983* (cardboard folder containing twenty-two pamphlets).

2 Georgy Kisewalter, ed., *The Strange Seventies, or The Loss of Innocence: Essay, Interview, Memoirs* (Moscow, 2010), p. 358.

3 Ibid., p. 93.

4 From Eric Bulatov, *'Poverkhnost' – Tsvet* (Surface –Light), ms article, Collection MANI Museum.

5 From Irina Pivovarova, 'On the Action: Time of Action' (November 1980), reprinted in *Poezdka za Gorod* (Moscow, 1988), p. 29.

6 Vitaly Komar, 'Sots Art and Official Sots', in *Field of Action: The Moscow Conceptual School in Context*, exh. cat. (Moscow, 2010).

7 Interview with Boris Orlov, in Zakharov and Kisewalter (note 1).

8 Kisewalter (note 2), p. 250.

9 Conversation with the author, 2010.

10 Interview with Vadim Zakharov by Fedor Romer, 'Dynamic Pairs' (Moscow, 2002).

Western Perceptions of Russian Contemporary Art

Eleanor Heartney

Coloured by decades of Cold War facts and fantasies, Western perceptions of twentieth-century Russian art owe as much to Hollywood as to art history. Behind the Iron Curtain, this story goes, a band of intrepid artist-insurgents maintained a secret cultural underground. They heroically risked imprisonment and death in the fearsome gulag by slipping their politically unacceptable works to Western collectors and curators willing to smuggle them out of Russia to the Free World. With the dissolution of the Soviet Empire, this narrative continues, some of these rebels achieved acclaim and success, while others were laid low by a capitalist market that prizes spectacle and superficiality over political commitment.

There is some truth in this narrative, but the reality of the evolution and emergence of contemporary Russian art is much more complicated. Courage and danger abounded, but the Soviet establishment's relationship to artists was not as fixed as this Cold War narrative suggests. Post-Stalin, when deviation from the Party line could indeed bring death or exile, there were periods of freeze and thaw. Artists discovered ways in which to work simultaneously inside and outside of the system, and the nature of the work they created was resistant in ways that are often incomprehensible to observers outside the Soviet Union.

Even today, two decades after the fall of the Soviet Empire, it is often difficult for Westerners to see contemporary Russian art clearly. The romance surrounding the notion of unofficial,

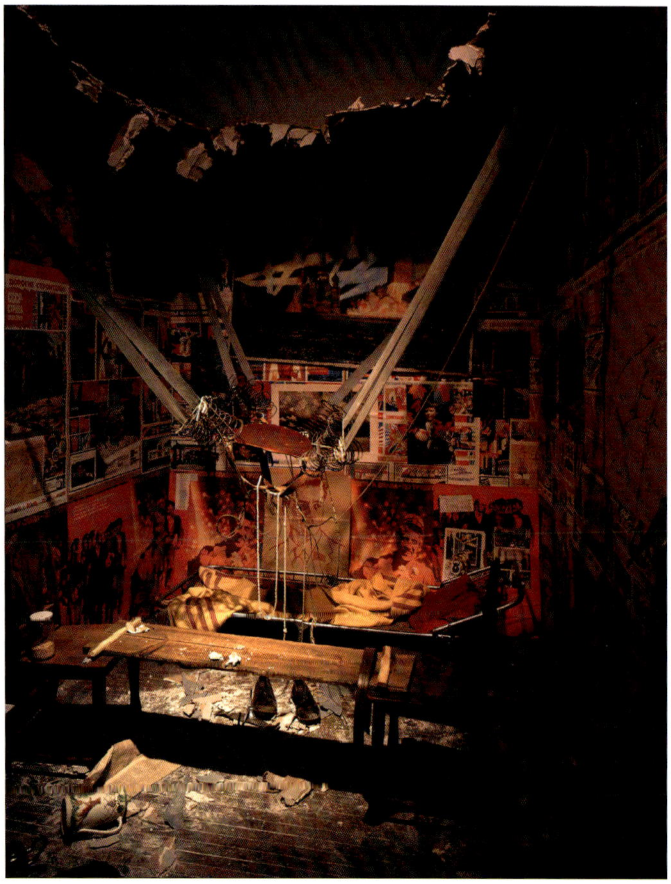

Ilya Kabakov
The Man Who Flew Into Space From His Apartment, 1981-88
Mixed media installation
279.4 x 241.3 x 373.4 cm
Photo: D. James Dee
© Ilya Kabakov
Collection of Musee National d'Art Moderne, Centre Georges Pompidou, Paris
Courtesy Ronald Feldman Fine Arts, New York

nonconformist or dissident artists (the shifting terms themselves suggest how difficult it is to pin this tendency down) continues to get in the way of understandings and assessments. Because images, ideas and even words have different meanings on either side of the former Iron Curtain, much can get lost in translation.

This essay, by an observer who has followed developments in Russian art over the last twenty-five years from the distance of the United States, is an effort to sort out some of these contradictions and paradoxes. Although vaguely aware of Sots Art through exhibitions of the work of various expatriate Russian artists during the 1980s, my most electrifying early encounter with contemporary Russian art occurred in 1988, just three years before the unanticipated dissolution of the Soviet Empire. The exhibition was Ilya Kabakov's *Ten Characters* at Ronald Feldman Gallery, New York. The normally neutral white-box gallery space had been utterly transformed into a dark warren of rooms evoking a Soviet communal apartment. Each space contained the traces of one of the apartment's ten inhabitants, all of whom were consumed with eccentric obsessions at odds with any rational social purpose. These included such improbable characters as The Man Who Never Threw Anything Away, The Man Who Flew Into His Picture and The Man Who Collects the Opinions of Others.

For me, this beguiling installation disclosed the true 'otherness' of Russian art. While it had been possible to assimilate Sots Art, with its satirical appropriation of iconic Soviet personages and symbols, into Western models of political art, it was clear that Kabakov was up to something completely different. The absence of didacticism and the gentle poetry of his characters' fantastical desires warned against a flat-footed reading of his work as a critique of the Soviet system or a documentary report on contemporary living conditions.

Even today, the years of Soviet rule remain an inescapable factor in the evolution of Russian art. For six decades, Soviet artists were cut off both from developments in the West and from the remarkable achievements of their own precursors in the pre-Stalin days. Soviet ideology turned reality upside down, forcing a separation between official declarations about the arrival of the utopian worker's paradise and the more dismal actuality of constant surveillance, shortages, thwarted possibilities and Orwellian rhetoric. At the same time, paradoxically, the State's heavy hand drew artists and writers together into a shared imaginative space quite unlike the art worlds of the capitalist West.

Today, Russian artists travel freely, partaking of the mobility of ideas and movement that characterises the age of globalisation. Like their counterparts elsewhere, they are influenced by new developments in technology and electronic communication, the hybridisation of identity and the international Esperanto of Postmodernism. However, their work remains coloured by the history of art during the Soviet years, and by the realities of the country that has emerged from the wreckage of that unsustainable system. In order to make sense of it, these particularities need to be taken into account.

First and foremost, it is necessary to parse the relationship of art to politics in Russia. Critic Joseph Backstein has noted that in the Soviet era aesthetics were inseparable from ideology.[1] This was contrary to contemporaneous developments in Western art. Just as Stalin was tightening his grip on the cultural apparatus and decreeing that art must serve the Party through representation of the triumphant workers' state, in New York the one-time Marxist Clement Greenberg was formulating his theory of formalism. Greenberg decreed that the only art of value was that which retained its autonomy by escaping from any form of social commentary, narrative or illustration. Thus were created two exactly opposite visions of art. Abstraction came to be seen in the West as an activity inherently free of politics, while in Russia it became a mode of resistance to the official management of consciousness. Members of Greenberg's avant-garde eschewed references to private life, spirituality, erotic fantasy and the dreary reality of working-class life as betrayals of their transcendent vision. The Russian avant-garde embraced these approaches precisely because their particularity flew in the face of the Soviet ideology of undifferentiated collectivity. In the West, women artists struck out against formalism's purported universalism and challenged their marginalisation with the anthem 'The Personal is Political'. In the Soviet Union, that notion encompassed the whole of the unofficial experience while failing to empower women.

Rejection of the party line left a great deal of room for experimentation, as we have seen. Unofficial artistic approaches that emerged in the post-Stalin era included the expressionistic still lifes of Oscar Rabin, the abstract collage paintings of Evgeny Rukhin, the academic nudes of Vladimir Weisberg, the surrealistic assemblages of Vladimir Yankilevsky, the realistic depictions of downtrodden Soviet citizens of Semyon Faibisovich and the lyrical site-specific transformations of nature of Francisco Infante.

Especially in the later Soviet period, developments sometimes paralleled those outside, but always with a difference. Take, for instance, Sots Art, often described as the Russian version of Pop art. But while Pop drew on advertising's glamorisation of the icons of Western consumer capitalism, Sots paid ironic homage to the equally packaged ideology of Soviet Communism. Thus these two movements served simultaneously as celebrations and critiques of what were seen during the Cold War as diametrically opposed political systems.

Sots Art is sometimes folded into Moscow Conceptualism. The use of texts and graphics in the work of artists like Ilya Kabakov, Victor Pivovarov and Eric Bulatov appears to echo the approach of Western Conceptualists like Joseph Kosuth and Lawrence Weiner. Again, however, the difference lay in each variation's relationship to authority. While many of the Western Conceptualists espoused a generalised Marxism, their works tended to steer clear of direct engagement in politics. Instead, they focused on the instability of language as one cultural system among others. The Russians, by contrast, were challenging an oppressive regime seeking total control through the use of language which was not just unstable but deliberately mendacious. As a result, any challenge to that system of meaning had a political edge.

A similar difference can be discerned in the Actionist art of the West and of groups like Andrei Monastyrsky's Collective Actions.

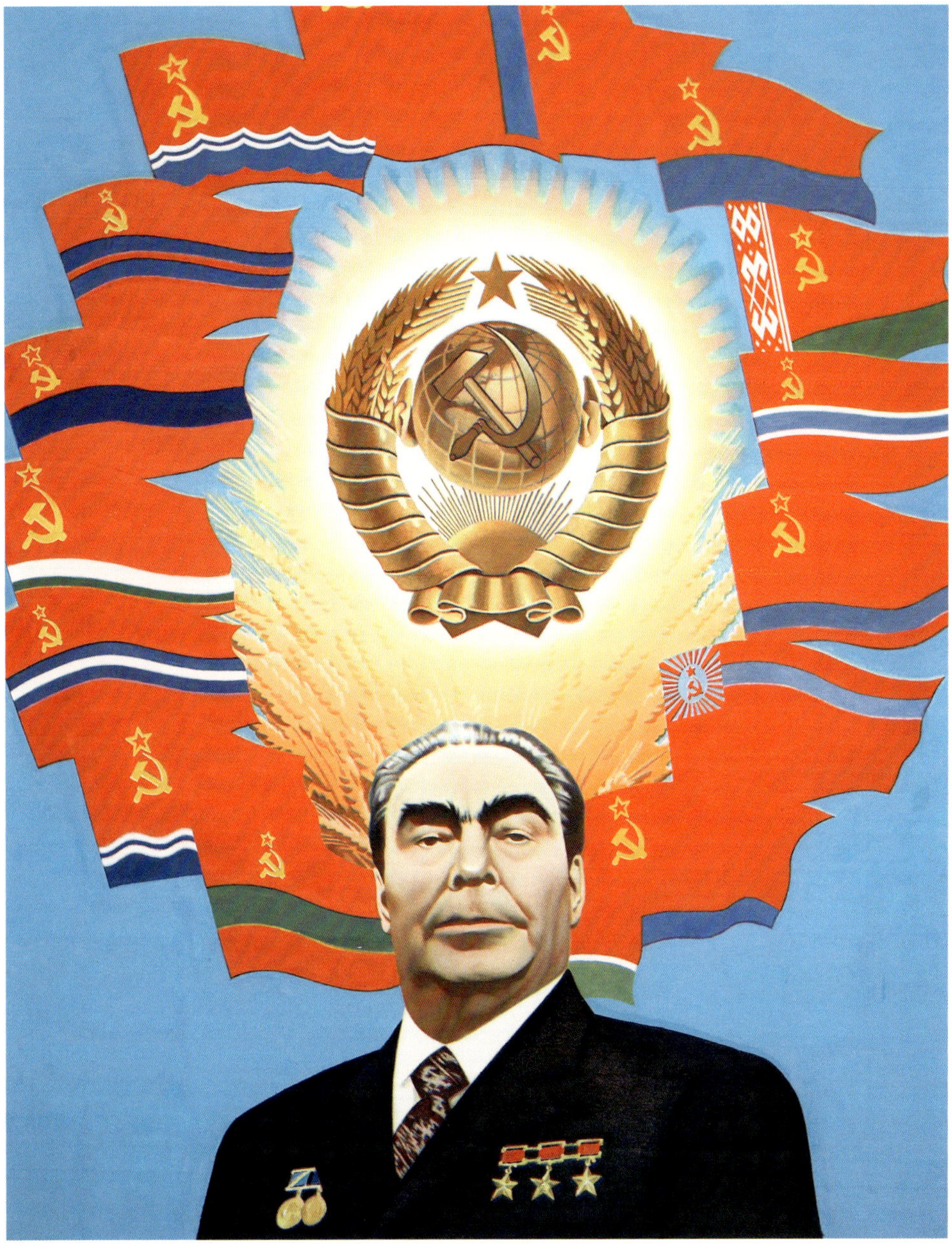

Eric Bulatov
Brezhnev, Soviet Cosmos, 1977
Oil on canvas
260 x 200 cm
© Eric Bulatov
Courtesy of Phillips de Pury

Western performances of the 1970s often took place in public spaces where both art-world insiders and passers-by could be confronted with challenges to their normal modes of social interaction. Performances in Russia were more likely to take place in the remote countryside, attended only by small groups of invited artists who shared in the experience and analysis of enigmatic actions not meant for wider consumption.

The authorities met these approaches with varying degrees of tolerance. The establishment of the Union of Artists in 1932 extended state control over practitioners but also made it possible, through the conferral of studios and stipends, for them to work. Thaws alternated with freezes, at times allowing artists to present their unofficial works in public settings, and at other times forcing them back underground. Landmarks in this dance include the 1957 International Festival of Youth; the 1962 publication in Russia of Alexander Solzhenitsyn's *One Day in the Life Ivan Denisovich* during a brief liberalisation of art and literature; the closing of that window soon after, following Khrushchev's rage at the experimental work presented in the exhibition *Thirty Years of the Moscow Union of Artists*; the hardening of the official stance against dissident intellectuals during the Brezhnev years; and the 1974 'Bulldozer Exhibition', which ended almost before it began.

This latter event having been observed by foreign journalists, their reports forced Moscow City Council to relent and permit an officially sanctioned four-hour outdoor exhibition two weeks later. The presence of these observers was evidence of a growing international interest in Russia's unofficial art scene, stoked by shows in the West of works which had been smuggled out with the help of collectors like Norton Dodge and by the emigration of a number of artists and writers in the 1970s and '80s. This interest came to a head shortly before the demise of the Soviet Union with Sotheby's 1988 auction of modern and contemporary Russian art in Moscow. Open only to foreigners who could pay in British pounds, some of the sale's prices astonished Russians and Westerners alike. Western observers were most drawn to work that appeared to offer a simple narrative of confrontation and dissent; many of the items that sold for the greatest prices were of that nature. However, the American writer Andrew Solomon, who attended the sale, noted that these were not necessarily the most truly political works: 'For Soviet art, an insistence on a multiplicity of truths is as political as the act of painting, while acceptance of a single and easy truth is an old habit of Stalinism.'[2]

Misconceptions went both ways; Soviet artists were equally baffled by the West, which seemed the real utopia, and they longed for its imagined freedom. Monastyrsky has remarked, 'We regarded ourselves as part of a regional (Russian) section of a certain central geographic club located somewhere in the West.'[3] But with the end of the Soviet regime, the flaws as well as the virtues of the capitalist West came into focus. Artists like Komar and Melamid, who had emigrated in 1978, turned their attention to capitalism's false promises in works that spoofed Western rhetoric of democracy and freedom. Artists who remained in Russia retained an investment in provocation; since 1991 they have turned their gaze on the realities of a capitalist structure of which they are now a part. They also discovered the downside of the free market as they lost their state-subsidised studios and discovered that there are losers as well as winners in the competition for a share of the market.

One can see this new attitude in the work of Oleg Kulik. His performances as a snarling dog were read as a comment on the Western desire for Russian artists to play the role of the wild beast. Other artists, such as photographers Sergei Bratkov and Boris Mikhailov, have turned an unsparing eye on the hypocrisies and incquities of Russia's new order. Gosha Ostretsov draws on his fascination with comic-strip culture to envision 'New Government', an anti-utopian story in which the poor and middle class become fodder for powerful elites. Such works are more in keeping with Western notions of political art.

If one Western response to Russian art has been to attempt to assimilate it into a narrative of overt political resistance, another has been to understand it in terms of Postmodernism, a slippery term generally associated with the denial of the possibility of absolute truth and the questioning of artists' claims of independence, authorship and originality. One of Postmodernism's most influential theorists, Frederic Jameson, has tied it to the contradictions of late capitalism. Himself a Marxist, Jameson suggests that the disappearance in the West of a belief in individual freedom and autonomy can be tied to the surrender to corporate capitalism's equation of selfhood and consumption.[4]

While certain features of Postmodern art – among them the cultivation of pastiche, irony and appropriation – certainly are evident in Soviet and post-Soviet art, Western Postmodernism's airy dismissal of meaning and truth are not. In the Soviet world, it was not the individual but the collective that served as a pernicious myth. After struggling for decades against a system built on a cascade of falsehoods, artists were not enamoured of post-structural theories that dismissed 'the Real' as an ideological fiction. Instead, they employed tools such as fiction, irony and satire to expose the distortions that camouflage an underlying truth. As Andrew Solomon put it, 'To tell a truth by way of a lie is as basic to Soviet artists as telling a lie in the vocabulary of truth has historically been to Soviet bureaucrats.'[5] Or, as Joseph Backstein has remarked 'In the Soviet Union, art was doubly real precisely because it had no relation to reality.'[6]

From this perspective, Russian irony in the Soviet era was quite different from its Western counterpart. Pulling aside the curtain of official ideology, artists offered a glimpse of the real conditions of society and underscored the existence of individual beliefs in an officially communal order. Now, with faith in the 'truths' embodied by the West dashed, Russian irony seems to have begun to approximate its Western cousin. The levelling tendencies of Postmodernism are evident in the way that not only Socialist Realism but also once-revered Constructivism have become fodder for younger artists. For instance, the group Blue Noses has recreated the Suprematist forms of Kazimir Malevich with sausages and cheeses. Similarly, Alex Buldakov animates the shapes in El Lissitzky's paintings so that they mime sexual intercourse. Other artists suggest an equivalency between the supposedly conflicting systems of capitalism, Communism and religion. The collective AES+F suggest the convergence of politics, entertainment and corporate profit in elaborately staged videos and photographic tableaux which meld the grandiosity of depictions of war found in eighteenth- and nineteenth-century academic history painting, the élan of edgy fashion photography, and the gleeful gore and mayhem of violent video games. Sots artist Alexander Kosolapov equates the selling of faith, political ideology and consumer goods in works that insert religious and political symbols into Coca-Cola advertisements.

However, it would be a mistake to equate this insouciant attitude towards religious symbols with the blanket rejection of religion often associated with Western art. (Although in fact, even in the West, the opposition between religion and contemporary art is often greatly overstated.) Throughout the overtly atheistic Soviet era, spirituality and mysticism remained powerful undercurrents in much of Russian art. Unofficial artists like Oscar Rabin and Dmitry Plavinksy drew on traditional religious images such as churches, icons and biblical subjects. Eduard Steinberg, Evgeny Rukhin, Lydia Masterkova and others echoed the approach of Kandinsky and Malevich, employing abstract forms to convey spiritual, religious or metaphysical content. A third tactic was to suggest the degree to which Soviet ideology was formulated as a substitute for religion. This is particularly evident in the work of the Jewish artist Grisha Bruskin, who embodies the celebratory clichés of Soviet myth in statues of blank-faced pre-perestroika types, each displaying attributes in the manner of Christian saints. It should not be forgotten that one of the earliest efforts to codify the movement that now goes by the name of Moscow Conceptualism was a 1979 essay by critic Boris Groys, who preferred the term 'Moscow Romantic Conceptualism' because it reflected a penchant for mystical experience at odds with Western scientism.[7]

Today, the Russian Orthodox Church is newly ascendant, frequently aligning itself with the more nationalistic and authoritarian elements in Russian politics. In this climate, many artists have transferred their critique of power from the State to the institutional Church, deliberately provoking confrontations which occasionally have ended in the shuttering of exhibitions, destruction of artworks, and arrests of artists and curators. A parallel development is the genuine or at least less obviously satirical examination of spirituality by other artists. One such manifestation is the New Academy movement, founded in 1989 in Leningrad by Timur Novikov, so during the Soviet Union's last days. The artists working under this aegis express a desire to rekindle art's spiritual essence through a return to classical subjects and styles, as we have seen. Anatoly Osmolovsky's bread icons take spirituality in another direction; perhaps as spiritual are works like Alexander Ponomarev's *Nimbus Generator* (2007), in which an installation of wooden boxes connected by plastic tubing and spotlit from above generate occasional puffs of smoke that rise like spectres, or Sergei Shutov's *Abacus* (2001), an installation involving forty automated figures, all dressed in black robes, reciting prayers from different religions and in different languages.

Such works suggest an ambivalence about religion and faith that is grounded, like so much of contemporary Russian culture, in the double mind produced by the charade of Soviet ideology. Scepticism towards any claim to absolute truth is tempered by a longing for meaning and genuine purpose. If it is a staple of Western intellectual thought that God is dead, in Soviet Russia it was, by contrast, godlessness that failed. The suppression of religion made it more precious while its re-emergence as an ally of the State has made it dangerously powerful.

Feminism offers one final perspective from which to tease out the differences and similarities between the contemporary art of Russia and the West. While women in the West were awakening to feminism in the 1970s, Soviet women already lived in an ostensibly equal society. In effect, however, this often meant a double burden, as they were expected to carry on as before in the domestic sphere while also assuming full-time jobs. This left women artists even less time than men to pursue their creative ideas. The difficulties faced by women artists were philosophical as well. One consequence of Soviet totalising ideology was that private life, domesticity and bodily expression – spheres of experience that Western feminists claimed as their own in their search for non-patriarchal forms to explore – were the province of male unofficial artists in the Soviet Union.

As a result, feminist art was essentially a non-starter in Russia, both during the Soviet era and even in the years after. In a fascinating study of women artists, curators and gallerists in post-Soviet Russia, art historians Matthew and Renee Baigell report that extensive

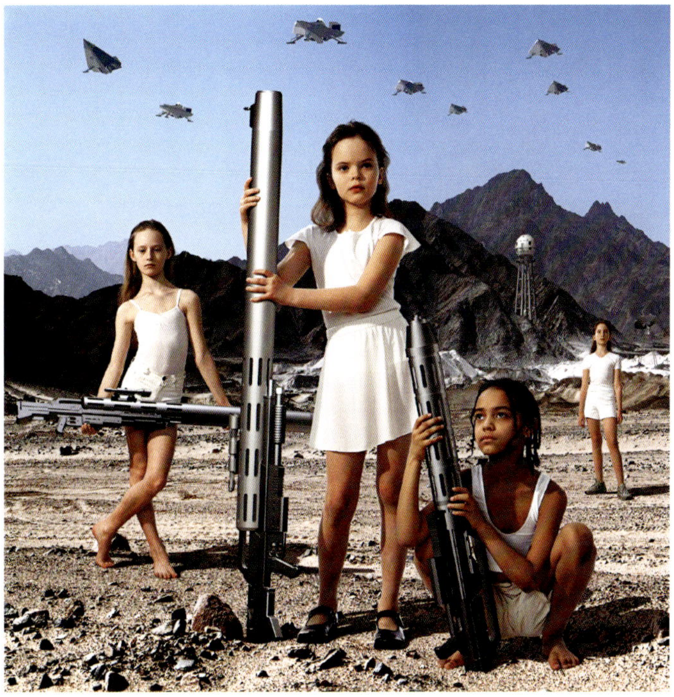

AES+F
Action Half Life. Episode 1 No. 10, 2005
Digital print on canvas
150 x 150 cm
© AES+F
Courtesy of Triumph Gallery, Moscow

interviews reveal a state of consciousness that seems strikingly pre-feminist by Western standards. They note that one residue of the Soviet period is an abhorrence of the idea of the aggressive woman, a figure who conjures up memories of overbearing Stalinist bureaucrats. 'The word *feministka*,' they maintain, 'still carries negative connotations, and although the climate of opinion is changing, all-women shows are still shunned.'[8]

Battling the institutional, practical and psychic odds against them, a small number of women artists did emerge in the unofficial art world. In most cases they were the wives or daughters of artists and often subsumed their careers to their men. Lydia Masterkova, for example, was the wife of painter Vladimir Nemukhin. Her lyrical abstractions were among the few works by women included in the 'Bulldozer Exhibition'. Natalia Nesterova, who was born into a family of artists, has denied that her mysterious allegorical tableaux of Russian life have feminist implications. Among perestroika-era artists, women also appeared as partners in artistic teams. For example, Elena Elagina worked in partnership with her husband Igor Makarevich.

The difficulties faced by women artists in the perestroika era were illustrated by the 1987 *Steam Baths* exhibition, a multimedia extravaganza staged inside Stalin's favourite sauna, which, because of the venue, was inaccessible to female visitors. In an early sign of the changing times, a group of women artists stormed the show a few weeks after its opening and forced the attendants to allow them in. Today, younger women artists like Olga Chernysheva, Aidan Salakhova, Taisia Korotkova and Taus Makhacheva seem to have thrown off some of this baggage and are increasingly visible on both the national and international scenes.

In the matter of feminism, as with other aspects of Russian art, the growing remoteness of the Soviet era seems to be diminishing the distance between Russian artists and their counterparts in the West. For younger Russians, their generation's shared concerns with global politics, science and social issues tend to eclipse Soviet ideology and history. Where once the West and Russia offered distorted reflections of each other, today, increasingly, they are bound together in an exploration of the complexities of the twenty-first century world.

Notes

1 Joseph Backstein, 'Nonconformist Traditions and Contemporary Russian Art', in Alla Rosenfeld and Norton T. Dodge, eds, *From Gulag to Glasnost* (New York, 1995), p. 332.

2 Andrew Solomon, *The Irony Tower* (New York, 1991), p. 39.

3 Quoted in Backstein (note 1), p. 336.

4 Frederic Jameson, 'Postmodernism and Consumer Society', in Hal Foster, ed., *The Anti Aesthetic: Essays on Postmodern Culture* (Port Townsend, WA, 1983).

5 Solomon (note 2), p. 14.

6 Backstein (note 1), p. 332.

7 Boris Groys, 'Moscow Romantic Conceptualism', *A-Ya* (1979), reprinted in Boris Groys, *History Becomes Form: Moscow Conceptualism* (Cambridge, MA, 2010), pp 36–55.

8 Matthew and Renee Baigell, *Peeling Potatoes, Painting Pictures: Women Artists in Post-Soviet Russia, Estonia, and Latvia: The First Decade* (New Brunswick, NJ, 2001), p. 155.

Galleries and Organisations

Artists

Galleries and Organisations

Artists

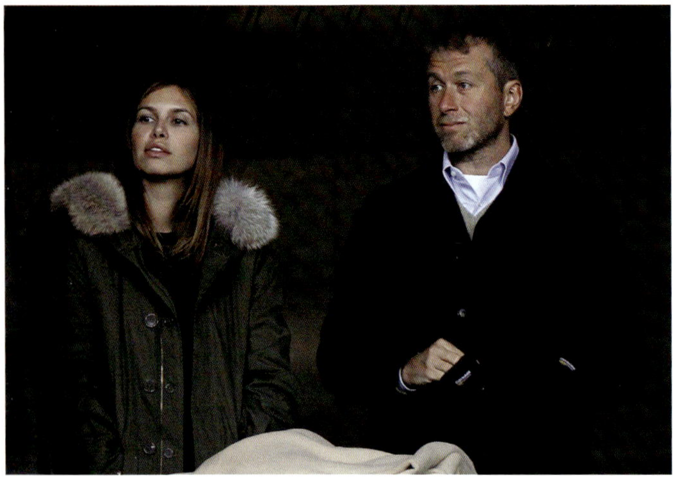

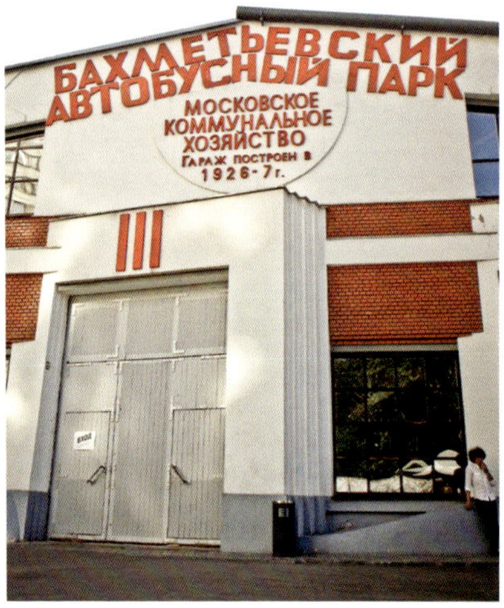

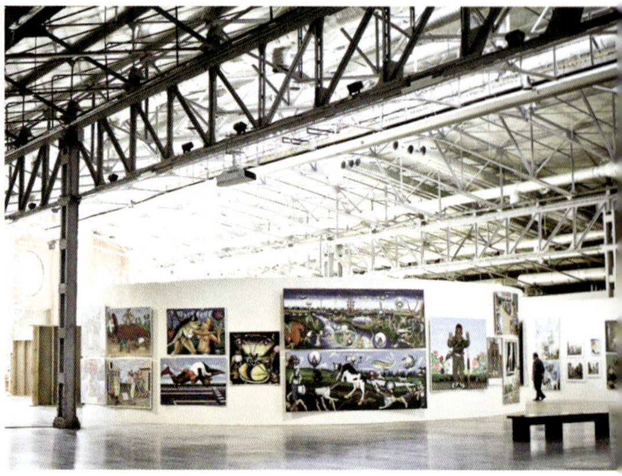

Roman Abramovich and Daria Zhukova are partners in art as in life. Both involved in philanthropy, they are also serious collectors of contemporary art. Abramovich, born in Saratov in 1966, became one of Russia's most successful oil entrepreneurs and is the owner of Chelsea Football Club. Zhukova, born in Moscow in 1981, moved with her mother to California in the 1990s, later graduating with a degree in Slavic Studies and Literature from the University of California. She has a background in fashion, in 2006 co-founding the label Kova and T with her childhood friend Christina Tang. Two years later, Zhukova was appointed editor-in-chief of the fashion magazine *Pop*, a post she held until 2010. She is currently combining her interests in a new magazine, *Garage*, which brings art and fashion together. She also serves as a member of the board of trustees of the Los Angeles County Museum. Abramovich and Zhukova divide their time between Moscow and the UK.

When the couple founded the Garage Centre for Contemporary Culture in the Bakhmetevsky bus depot in Moscow in 2008, they breathed new life into an icon of Constructivist architecture and, at a single stroke, transformed the cultural life of the capital. They set about bringing groundbreaking contemporary shows to Moscow, including, in 2009, the first exhibition of paintings by the American Abstract Expressionist Mark Rothko ever shown in Moscow. As Zhukova has observed, 'Despite his undeniable place in history and the fact that Rothko (Marcus Rothkowitz) was born in the Russian Empire, his work remains largely unknown here [in Moscow]'. As to who thought up the concept of the Garage, Abramovich muses, 'Each of us sees it as our own. I see it as my idea, and Dasha says it was hers.' Today the Garage is mainly run by Zhukova through the Iris Foundation for the Arts, which she established in 2008, with Abramovich taking a back seat, although he does fund some exhibitions with which he then becomes more personally involved.

It was in 2008, the same year that the Garage was founded, that the couple started to collect in earnest, although they had both been surrounded by art before then. As Abramovich explains, most of his friends and acquaintances were collectors and this inspired him to follow suit. His collecting is based on intuition, not on pragmatism, and there is no overarching strategy. He has many experienced advisors and does listen to them, but as a rule will only buy something if he really likes it. The collection has a post-war focus, and the couple buy both Russian and international art, including work by such famous names as Francis Bacon and Lucien Freud as well as by lesser-known younger artists. Purchases must resonate on both an emotional and an aesthetic level, irrespective of value, 'because collecting is a passion'. Although the couple's collection reflects their personal preferences, Abramovich explains that their 'tastes are quite different, although if one of us absolutely does not want to live with something on the wall, we won't buy it'.

Regarding arts sponsorship, Abramovich does not see himself as a patron because he supports many different causes of which art is only one. He usually prefers to fund exhibitions or projects that do not otherwise have any chance of being realised, especially modest community-based initiatives. He has sponsored several photography projects, including the exhibitions *Quiet Resistance: Russian Pictorial Photography 1900s–1930s* (2005) and a show featuring images of Uzbekistan by Soviet photographer Max Penson (2006), both organised by the Moscow House of Photography and shown at Somerset House in London. He is currently funding the New Holland Island project, intended to regenerate a disused 300-year-old military base in St Petersburg to include a new gallery and museum space.

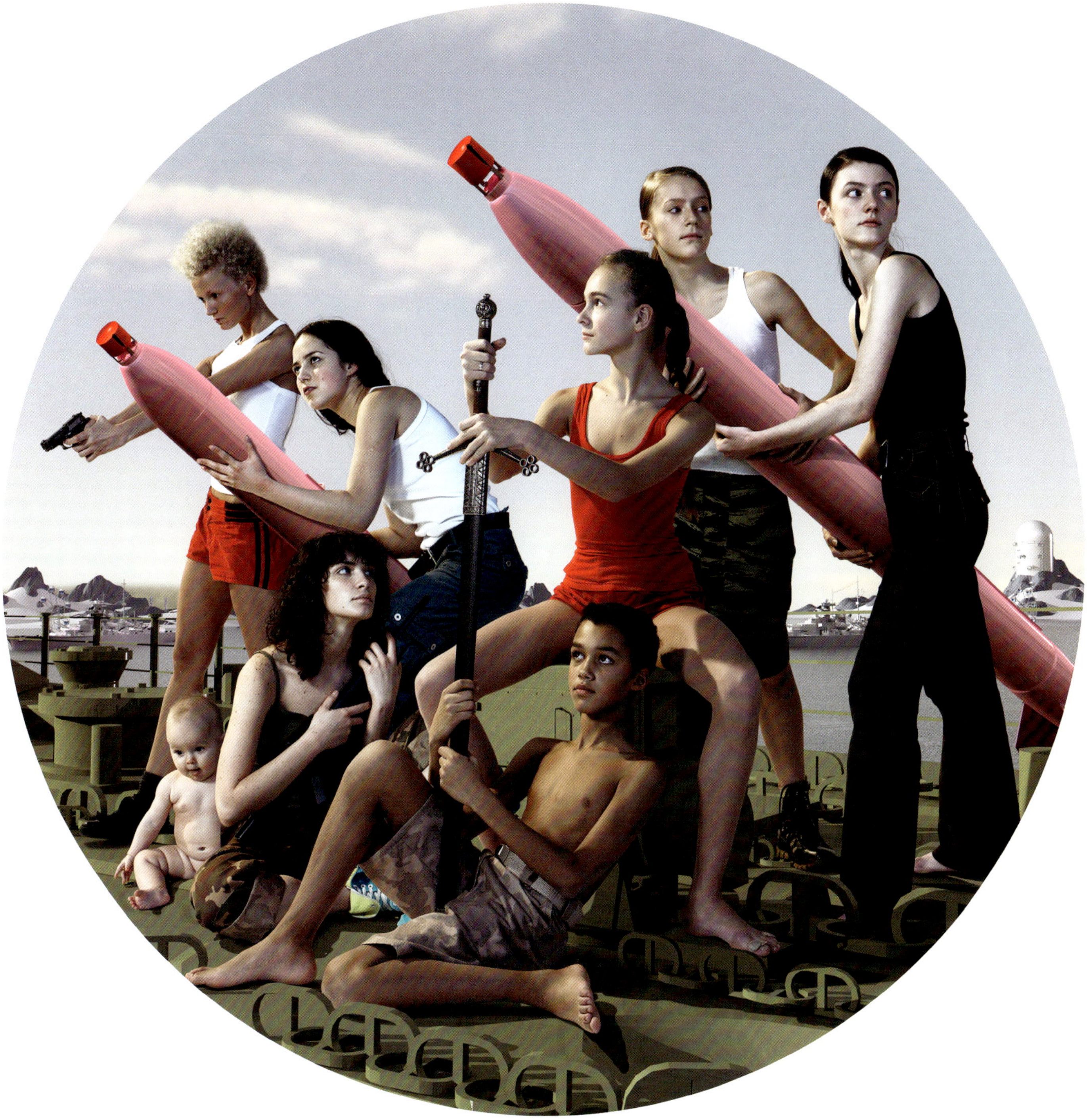

AES was formed in 1987 by Tatiana Arzamasova (born 1955), Lev Evzovich (born 1958) and Evgeny Svyatsky (born 1957); its fourth member, Vladimir Fridkes (born 1956), joined in 1995. Since then, the collective has been known as AES+F. Working with large-scale digital photo- and computer-based art, video and sculpture, the group creates highly intricate, staged, exaggerated compositions and worlds filled with dark humour, sarcasm, irony and a mocking dystopian sensibility. They have participated in numerous exhibitions around the world, and have had their work shown in biennales in Venice, Lyon, Sydney, Gwangju, Moscow and Istanbul, among others.

Speaking about their preference for collective collaboration, Evzovich has said, 'We are one artist, even though there are four of us.' The themes that they explore encompass mass cultural phobias, cultural stereotypes, childhood, war and peace, and the future. Although their subject matter is always topical, their digital collages create seemingly a-temporal, ahistorical universes, in which the boundaries and distinctions between reality, fantasy, history and time are continuously subverted, distorted and collapsed. In the video *Last Riot* (2007), which forms a trilogy with The Feast of Trimalchio (2009) and *Allegoria Sacra* (2011), teenage supermodels inhabit a virtual landscape of snow-capped mountains and desolate beaches. Surrounded by neon dragons resting on oil platforms and planes which collide seamlessly without bursting into flame, the young warriors commit myriad acts of violence against one another. A prime example of AES+F's aesthetics, this is an art that is 'archetypal, figurative [and] very body-oriented ... [based on] the rituals of modern life'.

AES – Witnesses of the Future: Islamic Project (1996–2006) took the form of posters, photo-panels and a makeshift travel agency that publicised a future in which the Taliban had taken over well-known Western monuments, turning them into mosques. The piece achieved infamy for its sardonic digital collages of the Statue of Liberty covered by a burqa and the Guggenheim Museum, Bilbao, bedecked with minarets. Ironically, AES – Witnesses of the Future pre-dates 9/11. Evzovich emphasises that 'even now, when we aren't trying to predict the future, people try to read the future in our works ... We like to work with the theme of mass media. It is exaggerated and distortive, and represents modern paranoia. All of these themes – catastrophes, wars, and so on – are inescapable.'

The irony and humour with which AES+F address heatedly debated topics like Islamic fundamentalism or the exploitation of beauty and childhood by the fashion and advertising industries is explained by the fact that they 'like to remain on the margins and create public misunderstanding, so that it isn't obvious whether it is criticism or admiration. The language is parodying ... We are not interested in political and didactic art'. Intrigued by the hybrid nature of modern culture and the universality of the topics they approach, AES+F's influences are no less disparate, encompassing everything from fashion photography and video games to the Old Masters; The Feast of Trimalchio, for example, modernises a section of the ancient Roman *Satyricon*. Individual gluttony – in the original – is turned into a world of collective wealth and luxury, set in a hotel peopled by archetypal characters: masters, slaves, victims, oppressors, rebels and innocents. The frieze-like compositions are a reminder that the group's inspirations are manifold, encompassing 'exaggeration and the grotesque, a kind of new Baroque ... advertising and fashion photography just as much as Caravaggio'.

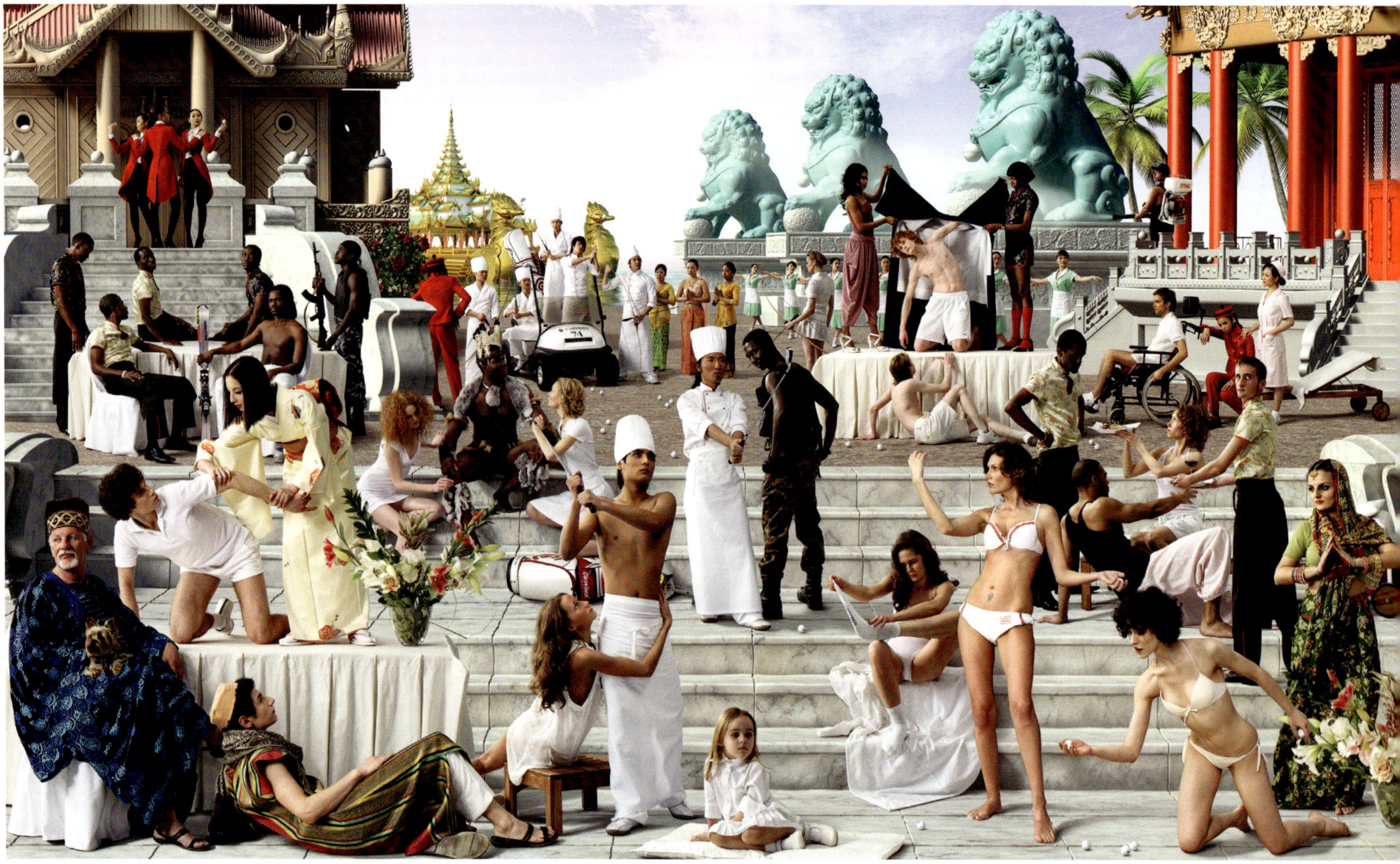

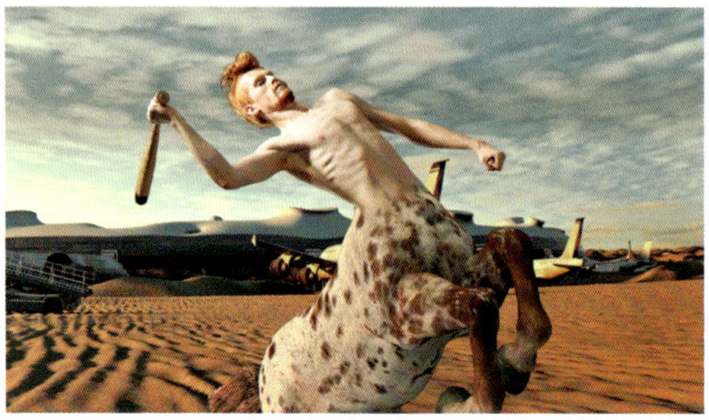

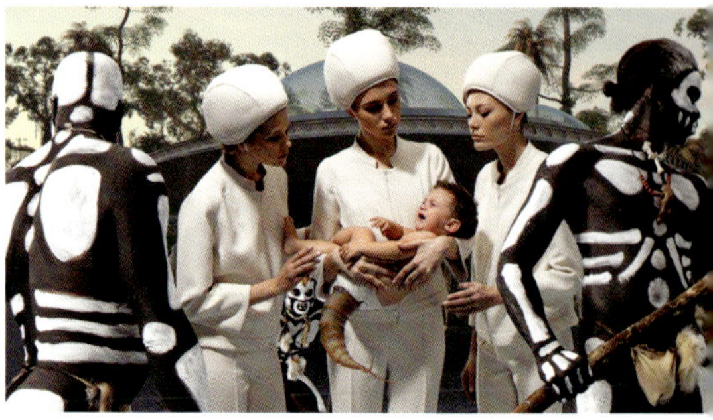

previous page
Tondo No. 16, from the series Last Riot 2, 2007
Digital print on canvas
150 cm (diam.)
© AES+F
Courtesy of Triumph Gallery, Moscow

above
The Arrival of the Golden Boat, from the series The Feast of Trimalchio, 2010
295 x 495 cm
Lambda print on paper
© AES+F
Courtesy of Triumph Gallery, Moscow

right
Stills from Allegoria Sacra, 2011
5-channel full HD video
(work in progress)
© AES+F
Courtesy of Triumph Gallery, Moscow

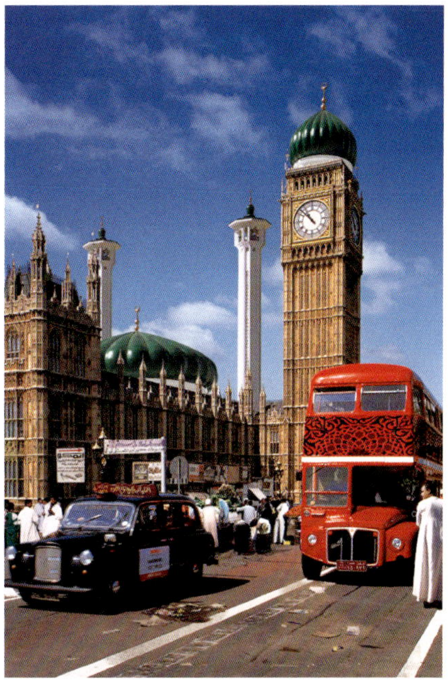

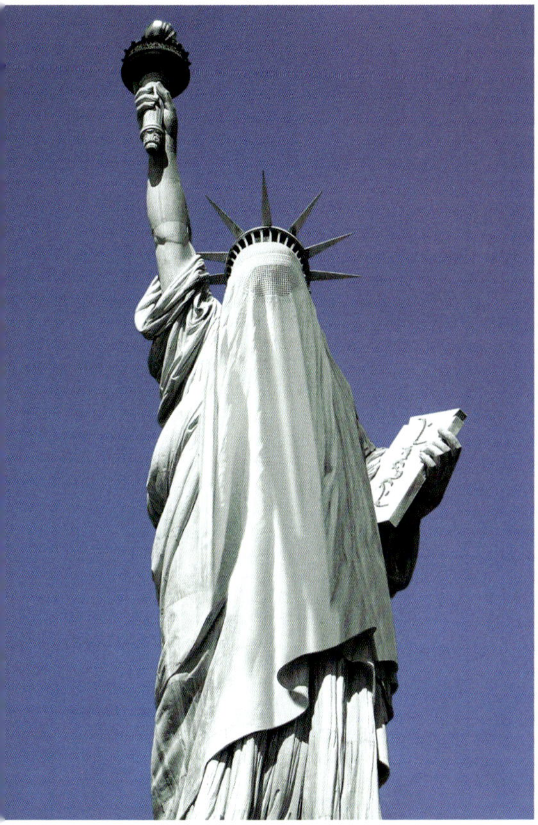

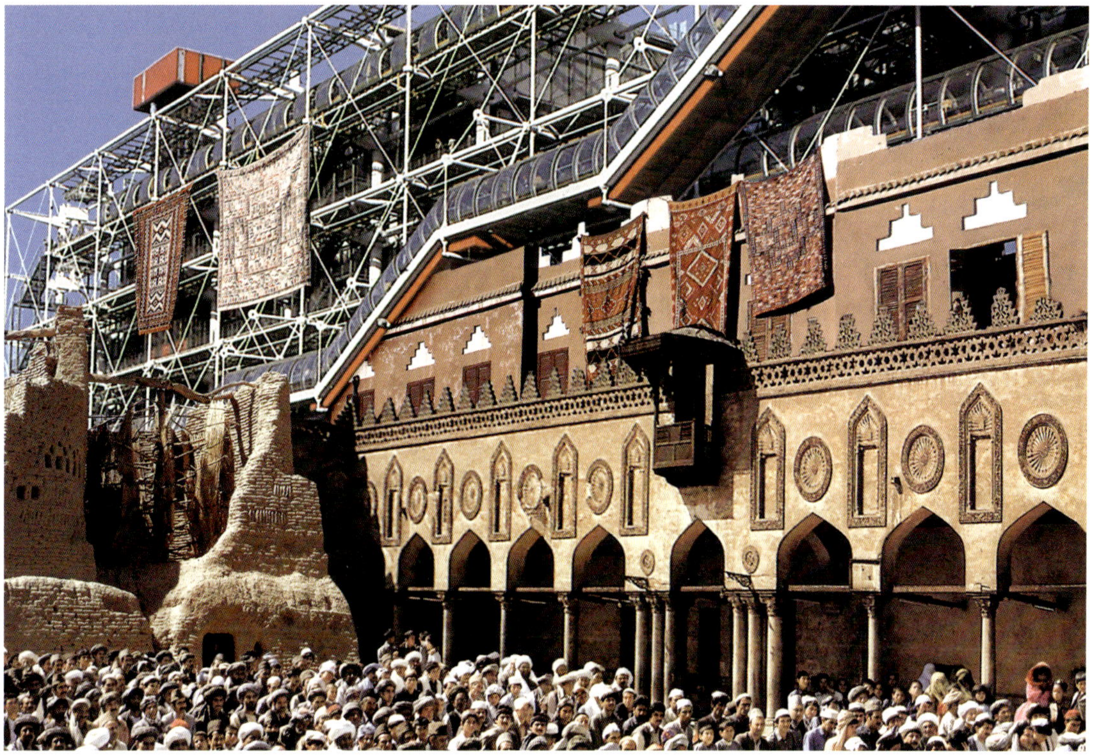

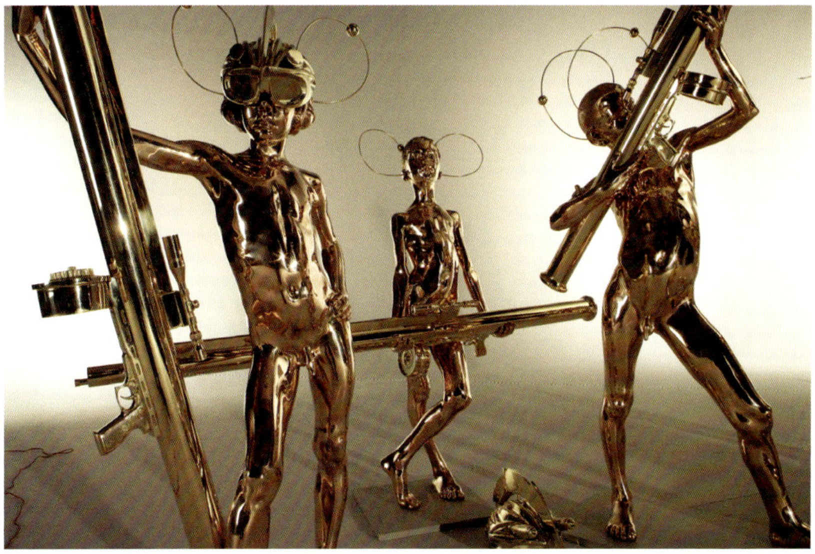

top
London, from the series AES – Witnesses of the Future: Islamic Project, 1996–2003
Digital collage on paper
120 x 80 cm
© AES+F
Courtesy of Triumph Gallery, Moscow

above
New Liberty, from the series AES – Witnesses of the Future: Islamic Project, 1996–2003
Digital collage on paper
120 x 80 cm
© AES+F
Courtesy of Triumph Gallery, Moscow

above
Beaubourg, from the series AES – Witnesses of the Future: Islamic Project, 1996–2003
Digital collage on paper
80 x 120 cm
© AES+F
Courtesy of Triumph Gallery, Moscow

left
Action Half Life, 2007
Series of 5 bronze sculptures (installation view of Warriors nos 1, 4 and 5)
© AES+F
Courtesy of Triumph Gallery, Moscow

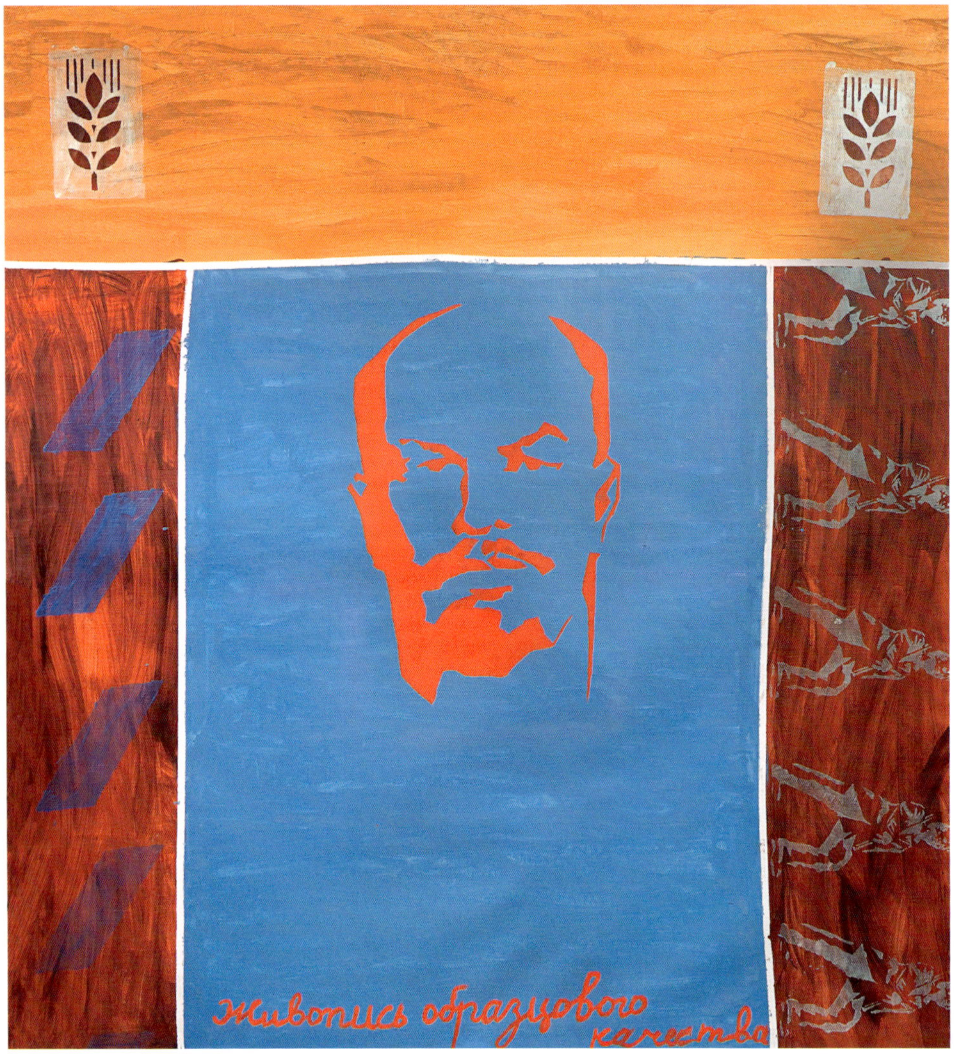

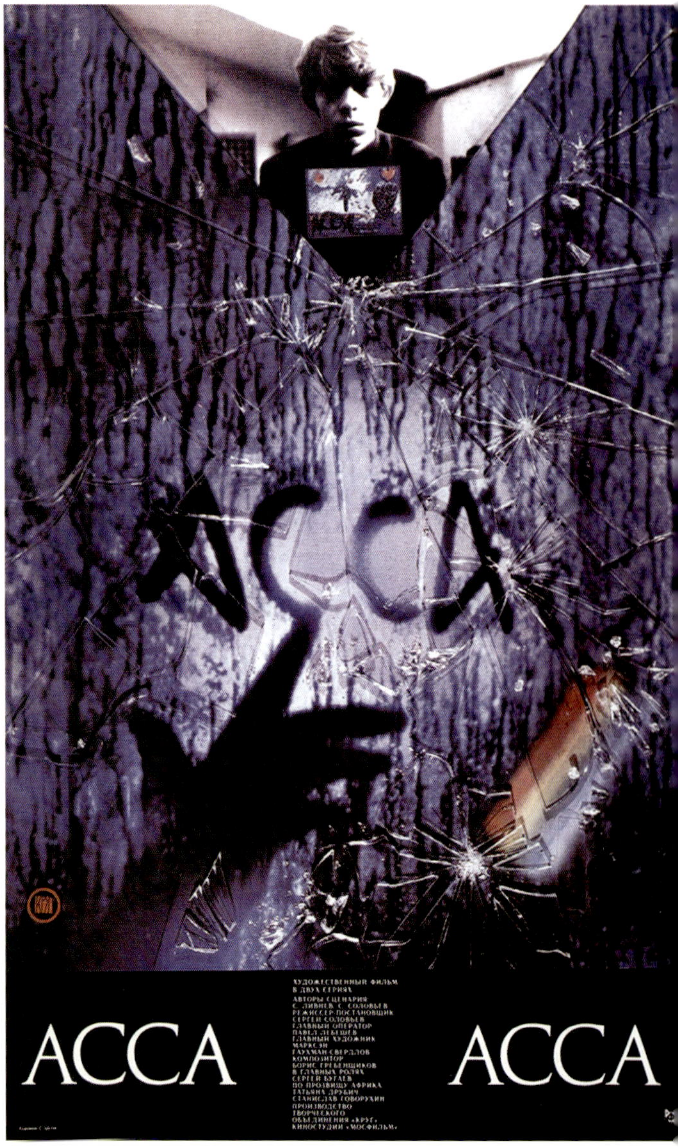

Born in the Black Sea town of Novorossiysk in 1966, Sergei Bugaev was fourteen when he left home for St Petersburg. He quickly became one of the central figures in the underground art and music scene, joining Sergei Kuryokhin's Pop Mekhanika Orchestra. Throughout the 1980s he collaborated with influential rock bands like Kino and Aquarium, counting musicians Viktor Tsoi, Boris Grebenschikov and artist Timur Novikov among his friends.

By 1984, Bugaev had become a leading member of the New Artists group; it was around this time that he adopted the moniker 'Afrika'. He works in many different disciplines, including installation and performance. He took on a starring role as Bananan, the lead character in the cult avant-garde film *Assa*; the film's success led to him directing its sequel and collaborating with John Cage as well as (later on) the Merce Cunningham Dance Company. In 1991 Bugaev began co-editing *Cabinet*, a science-fiction and art journal.

In his artworks Bugaev explores his interest in language from a Structuralist perspective. In his embroidered banners and rebuses, he makes use of Soviet and Western symbols of culture and power to expand on the themes of sign systems, language and psychoanalysis. As an ardent collector of Soviet memorabilia, early avant-garde work, and Russian arts and crafts, Bugaev fits together symbols from different historical periods and styles in order to create palimpsests. The period following the collapse of the Soviet Union was, he has said, a time of 'great aphasia', and this inability to connect signifier to signified is constantly tested and retested in his artistic output.

above
ASSA (poster for the film by Sergey Solovev), 1987
Offset print on paper
60 x 90 cm (approx.)
© Afrika (Sergei Bugaev)
Courtesy of Pierre-Christian Brochet Collection

above left
Art of Exemplary Quality, 1988
Oil on canvas
200 x 200 cm
© Afrika (Sergei Bugaev)
Courtesy of the artist

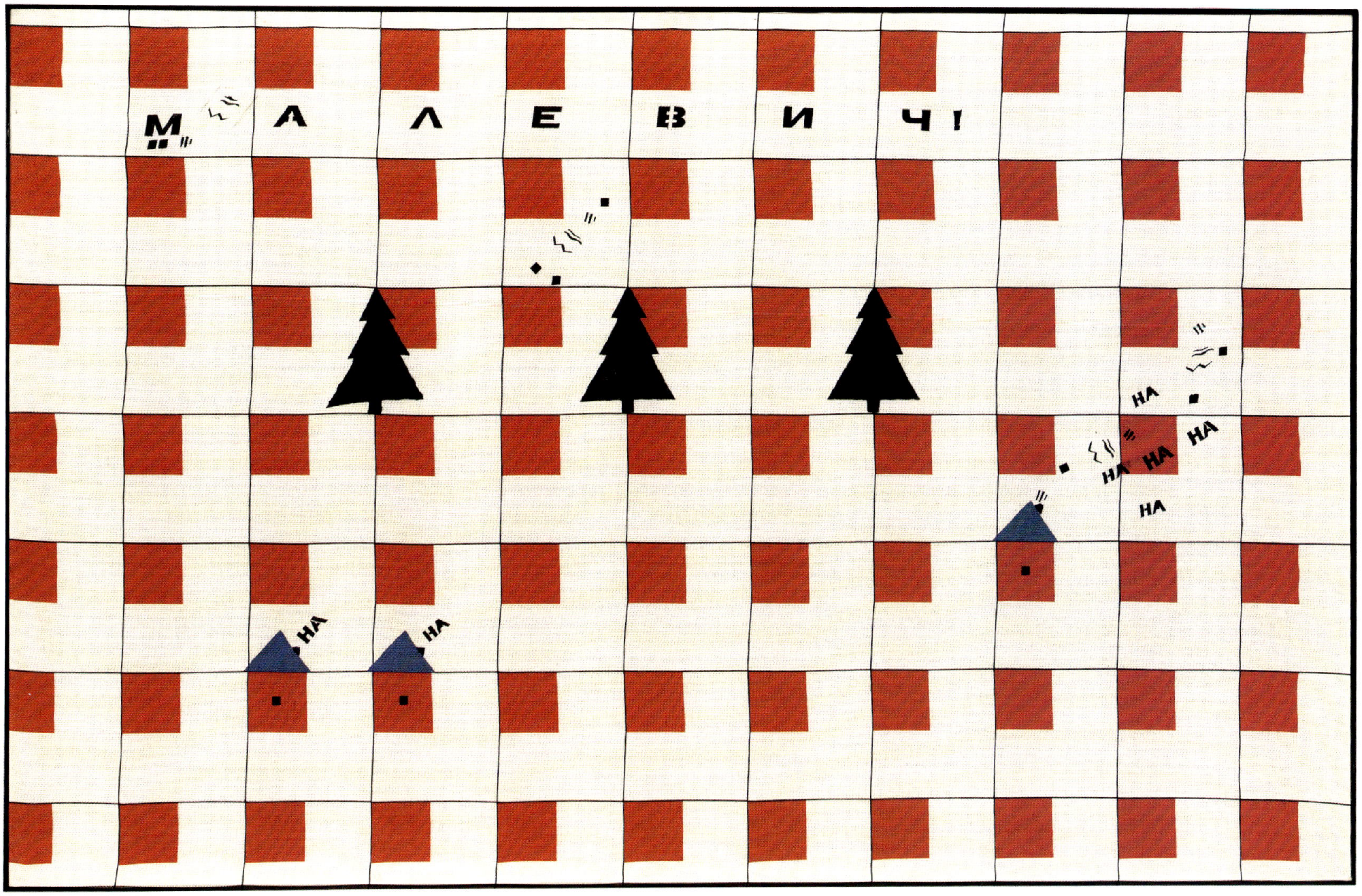

above
Malevich (in collaboration with Timur Novikov), 1988
Tempera on printed cotton
144 cm x 226 cm

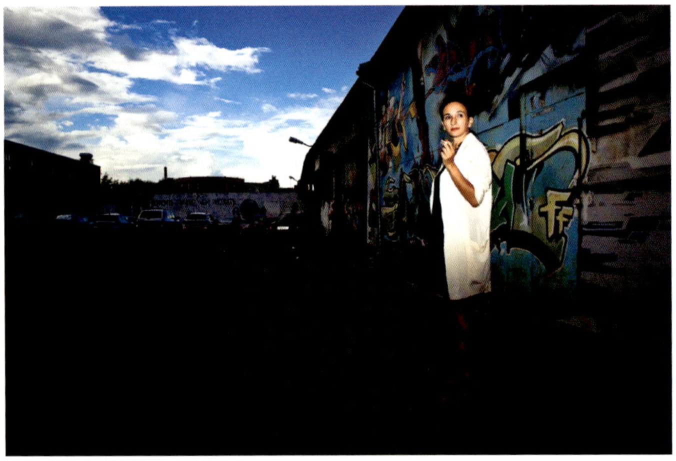

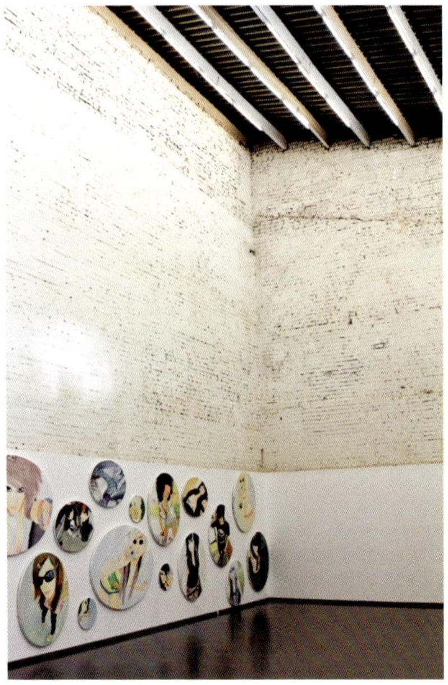

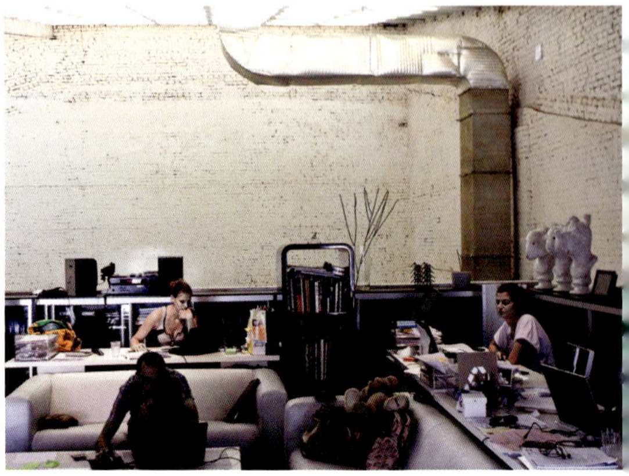

Artist and gallerist Aidan Salakhova was born in Moscow in 1964. She grew up surrounded by art; her mother was an artist, and her father Tair Salakhov is an artist and vice-president of the Russian Academy of Arts. Aidan's first memories of art were seeing her father's paintings in his studio as an infant, and she has said that both his aesthetics and his life were critical formative influences. Aidan never imagined not becoming an artist herself; it was a way of life so normal that she was surprised to discover that other children did not live in the same way: 'My father painted at home, and when he went to work put a suit on, and I was shocked when I found out that in other homes people did not draw.'

Ahead of the wave, in 1989 Aidan co-founded Russia's first private commercial contemporary art gallery, The First Gallery, which held shows of work by Ilya Kabakov, Eric Bulatov and Robert Rauschenberg. In 1992 she opened the Aidan Gallery, which she still runs today from its site in Moscow's Vinzavod cultural complex. She sees one of her roles as educating the public about contemporary art. Since perestroika a new community of art collectors has grown up in Russia who are better informed about classical nineteenth-century art but unfamiliar with the wider scene after the 1970s. Salakhova spends a good deal of her time trying to explain what contemporary art is and foregrounding its virtues and its strengths while also clarifying both its meaning and its importance.

When she is not painting or working in the gallery, Aidan teaches fine art at the Surikov Institute, where she was once a student; she has held this post for a decade. She believes that education is the most important aspect to her work and that outmoded Soviet teaching programmes need to be reformed. She laments the huge numbers of talented artists in Russia who are continuing to paint still lifes and landscapes in an academic realist style.

Aidan is a passionate advocate of art from the post-perestroika period, because, as she says, it does not reflect the local political environment but is 'more pure'. Prior to this time, unofficial artists were simply not considered to be any good, while official ones often held sinecures and have now fallen into obscurity. In terms of freedom of expression in Russia today, Aidan highlights the limits placed on artists, particularly when it comes to their handling of religious issues.

Aidan believes that Russian contemporary art is undervalued on the international market when compared with work from the West. When talking about the Western perspective on Russian artists, she says, 'For them Russian art is either a Russian *matryoshka* doll or a black square. But for merit it does not matter whether a work of art is Russian or made by a man or a woman. It is a work of art which I either like or do not like. That's all.' In terms of being a female artist in a country where few female artists have made stellar careers for themselves, Aidan acknowledges that this is a difficult issue: 'All women in the Soviet Union felt independent, but on the other hand the family duties rested entirely on their shoulders. The women were very strong.'

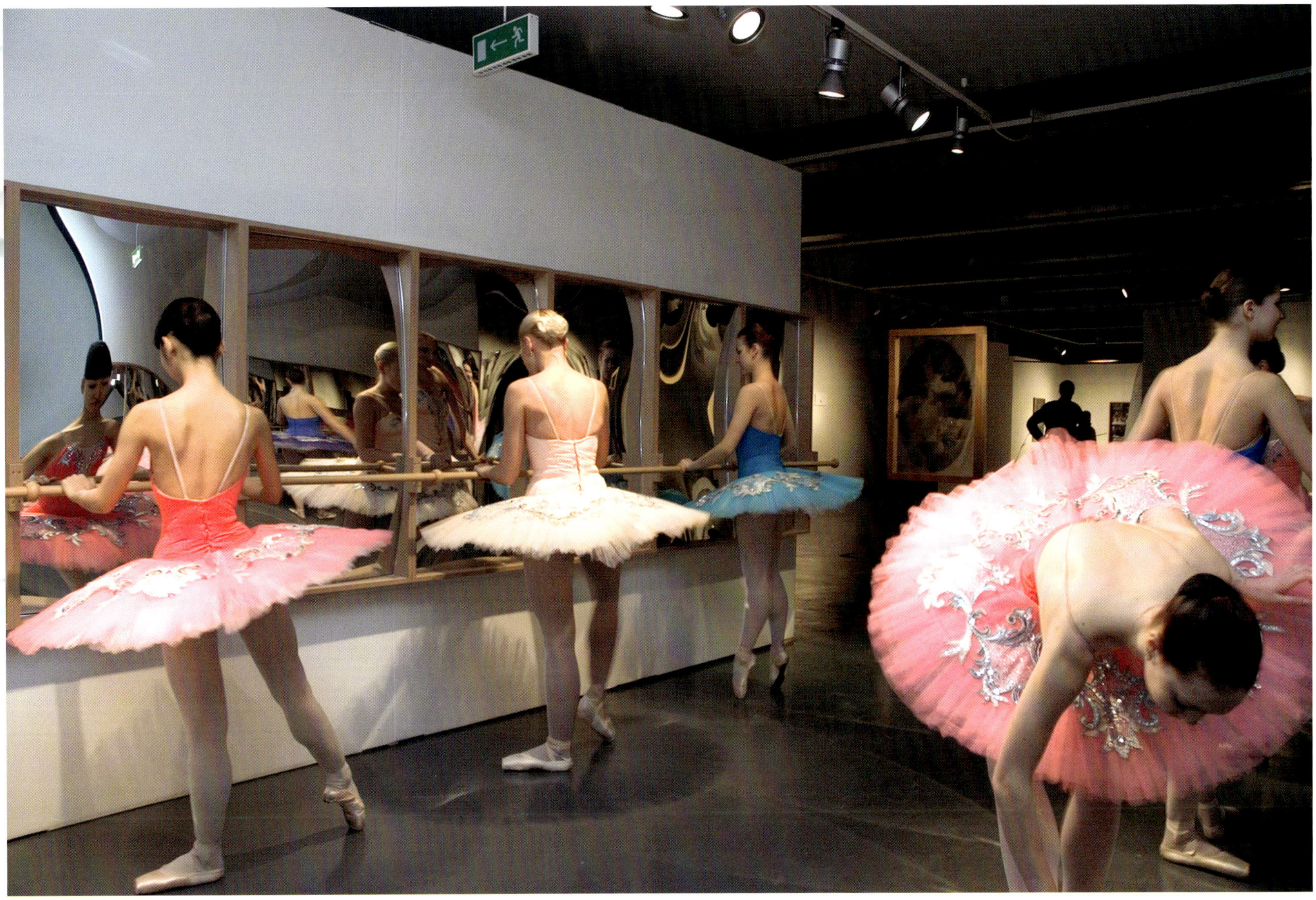

above
Ballet Class with Distorting Mirrors, 2005
Installation and performance at the opening of *Reflexion*, National Centre for Contemporary Art, Moscow
© Yuri Albert
Courtesy of the artist

Yuri Albert was born in Moscow in 1959 and studied in the Art and Graphics Department at the Moscow State Pedagogical University. Between 1974 and 1977, he continued his studies with Ekaterina Arnold, wife of Alexander Melamid, in the studio of the Sots Art duo Komar and Melamid; it was there that Albert first became acquainted with contemporary art. Some of his earliest works were exhibited at unofficial APTART exhibitions in the early 1980s, and he was a founding member of the Avantgardist Club (KLAVA) in 1987.

One of the central problems in his work, says Albert, is the tension between the romantic conception of Art (with a capital A) and Contemporary Art, which seems depleted in comparison, caught up as it is in the institutional concerns of exhibitions, galleries and museums. Despite this seemingly irreconcilable situation, Albert insists on following unlikely paths to remind the viewer of the lost culture that Art once embodied. His projects, inspired by such Conceptual and post-Minimal artists as Joseph Kosuth, Art & Language, Robert Morris and Bruce Nauman, are playful propositions about what form art can take today.

Albert's work frequently operates on the radical principle set out by Duchamp's ready-mades. Taking Duchamp's idea a step further, an early series by Albert offered the artist's services in the realms of house-cleaning, errand-running and childcare as its content. Later projects like *Self-Portrait with Eyes Closed* (1995) and *Excursion with Blindfolded Eyes III* (2005) took a similarly direct approach to the viewer: in the first, gallery visitors were invited to touch the canvases in order to read Braille descriptions of 88 paintings by Van Gogh, while in the second, blindfolded groups invited on tours of Moscow's State Tretyakov Gallery had to make their way through the exhibition halls by holding hands or following the guide's voice. This trust between artist and viewer is what gives Albert's work its meaning. In a recent project at the Paperworks Gallery, Moscow, Albert addressed art's relationship to political and social questions even more directly, asking audiences to express their opinions on issues such as Russia's war with Georgia and the importance of an artist's political convictions. Fascinated by art-historical connections between artists, styles and centres of artistic activity, Albert often humorously thematises his location on the art map with works like *I Am Not Jasper Johns* (1980) or *Direction Signs* (2005). In reality, he divides his time between Cologne and Moscow.

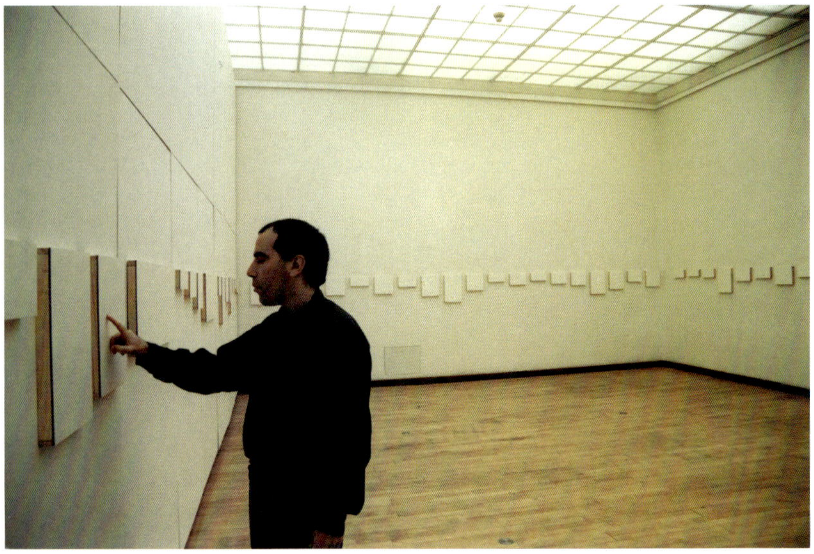

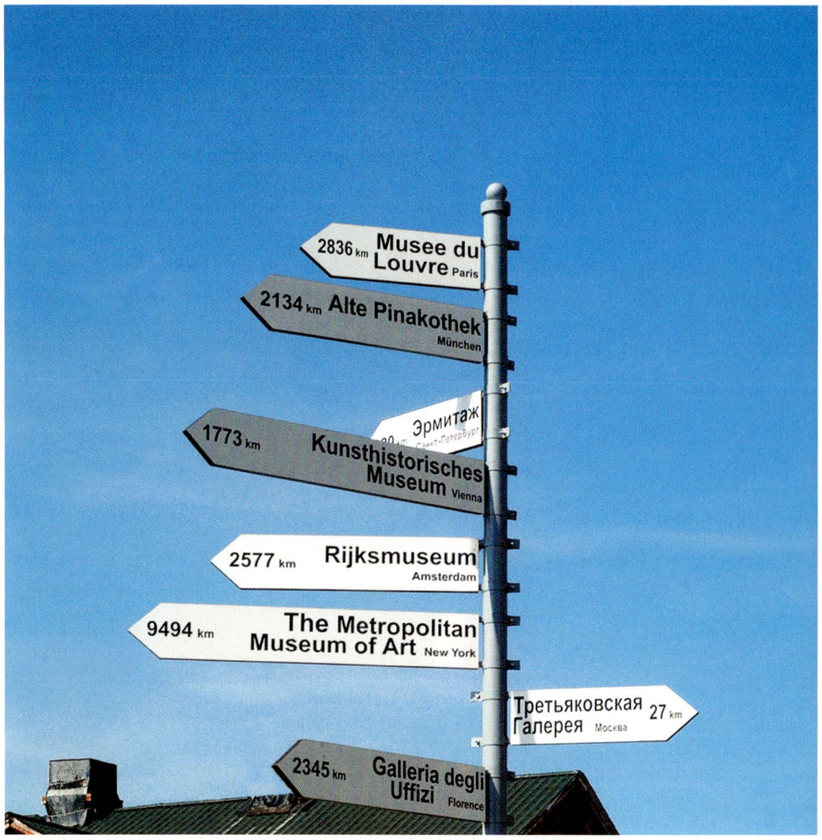

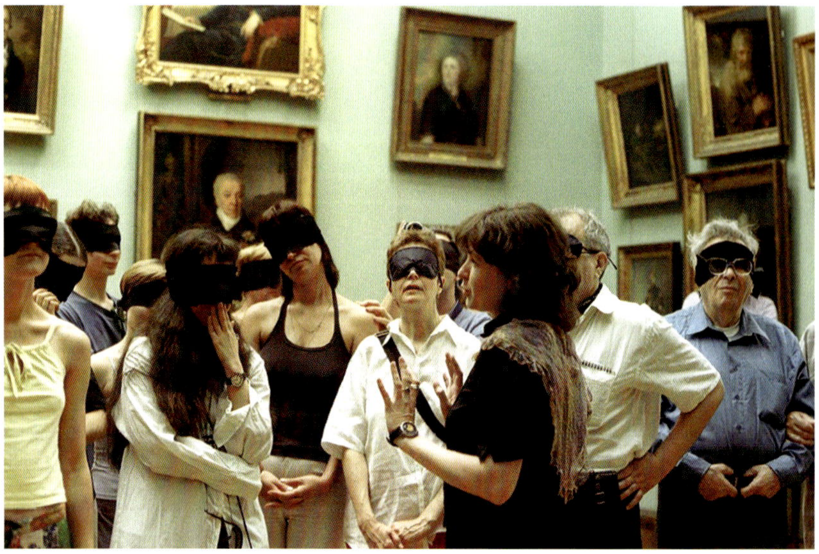

above
Self-Portrait with Eyes Closed (German version),1995
Installation with 88 pictures containing Braille descriptions of paintings by Van Gogh
© Yuri Albert
Private collection
Courtesy of the artist

top
Direction Sign II, Moscow Region, 2005
Metal and enamel
6 m (approx. h)
© Yuri Albert
Collection Marat Guelman
Courtesy of the artist

right
Excursion with Blindfolded Eyes II,
15 July 2002
Performance at the State Tretyakov Gallery, Moscow
© Yuri Albert
Courtesy of the artist

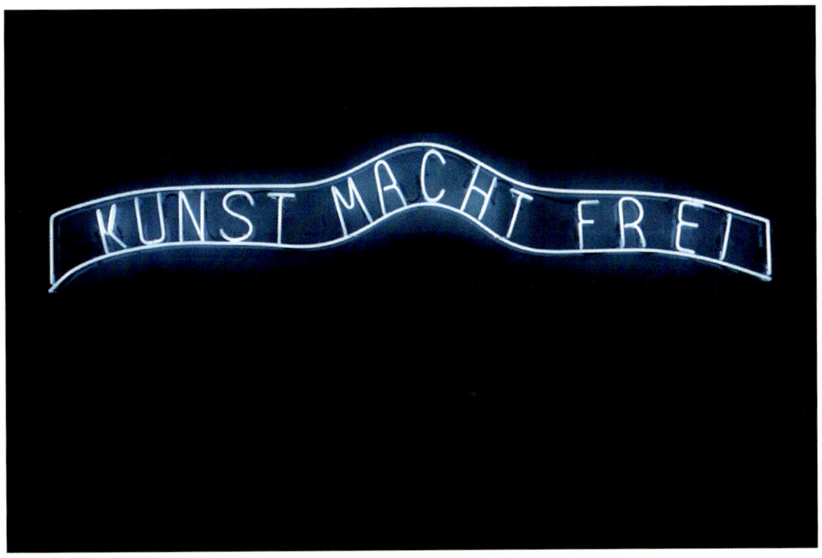

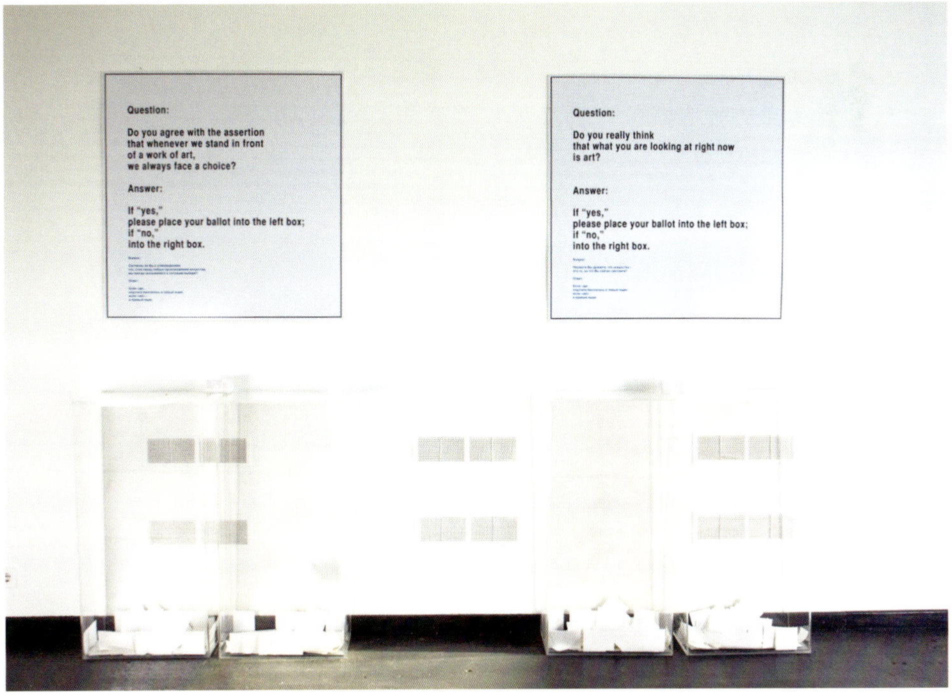

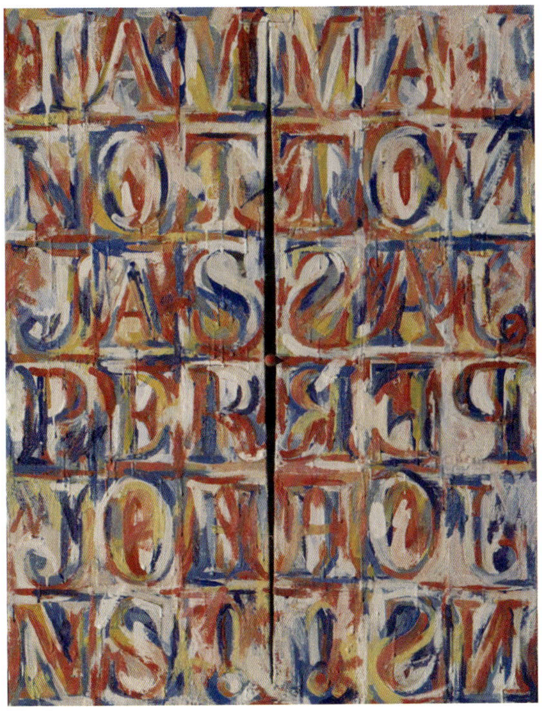

top
Kunst Macht Frei, 2004
Neon tubing with clear acrylic suspension frame
80 x 210 cm
© Yuri Albert
Collection Stella Art Foundation
Courtesy of the artist

left
I'm Not Jasper Johns, 1997
Oil on canvas, mixed media
93 x 73 cm
© Yuri Albert
Courtesy of the Ekaterina and Vladimir Semenikhin Collection

above
Moscow Poll, 2009
Installation and performance based on a work by Hans Haake
© Yuri Albert
Courtesy Paperworks Gallery, Moscow

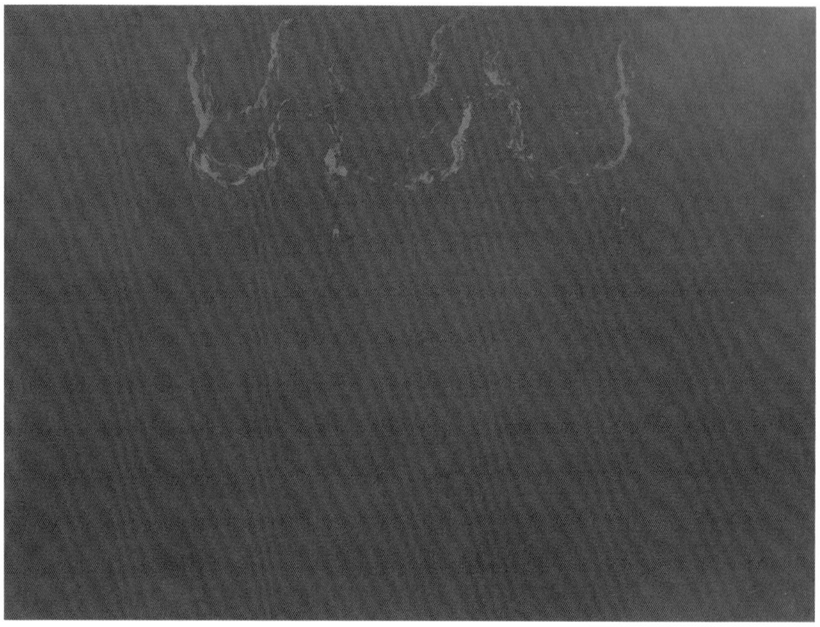

Born in Moscow in 1973, Victor Alimpiev completed his studies at the Institute of Contemporary Art in that city. He works in a variety of media, although the majority of his output since the mid-1990s has focused on video and the moving image.

Alimpiev's videos find formal unity and harmony through the intricate choreographic nature of his approach. Fusing documentary film, performance, music and theatre, he creates works which extend beyond the purely visual to attain musical and poetic meaning. Despite the apparent complexity of his compositions, the richness of their symphonic accompaniments, their opera-like expressiveness and the melodrama evoked by his performers, his works are created with minimal effort. They are a testimony to his sensitivity and intuition, and his ability to discover delicacy and harmony in the banality of the everyday, rather than to a complex programme of post-production editing.

The disciplines of visual art, theatre, dance and music interweave in *Whose Is this Exhalation?* (2008), in which a group of performers representing a mix of ages, genders, races and body shapes form a sculptural unity. Humming a single tone as they exhale, the group remains sensitive to its cohesive wholeness. Mutuality is made evident as each member takes his or her turn to break the monotone chain, to run out of breath and visibly deflate while remaining physically and emotionally supported by the ensemble. Alimpiev's videos focus directly on each character while avoiding a clear narrative structure. The result is a heightened consciousness of the viewer's own body in space and its relationship to a specific context which nevertheless moves beyond pure phenomenology to affect mental and emotional states of awareness.

Sequences of repetitive, minimalist movements accelerate in *Summer Lightnings* (2004), in which close-ups of young schoolchildren tapping their fingers rhythmically on their desks are juxtaposed with dramatic images of an electrical storm. In Alimpiev's work, natural phenomena and the human body and its natural processes such as breathing are brought into close proximity as a metaphor for the universalism and collective nature of even the smallest gesture. Highly abstract and formalist, they are at the same time intensely humanistic.

Alimpiev, who lives and works in Moscow, has exhibited widely in Russia and Europe, including in Moscow, Birmingham, Oxford, Ghent, London and Paris. He also has participated in numerous international biennales.

above left
Two Beautiful Necks, 2010
Acrylic on canvas
200 x 270 cm
© Victor Alimpiev
Courtesy Regina Gallery, London & Moscow

above
Several 1, 2010
Acrylic on canvas
190 x 250 cm
© Victor Alimpiev
Courtesy Regina Gallery, London & Moscow

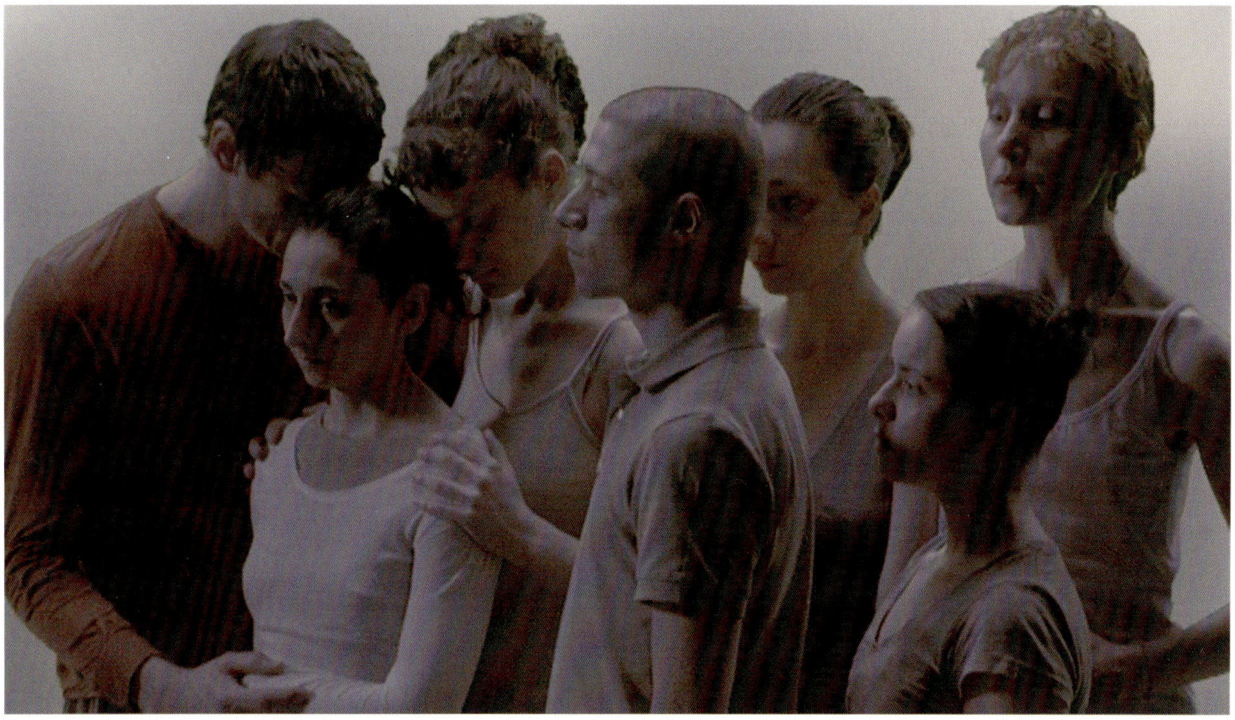

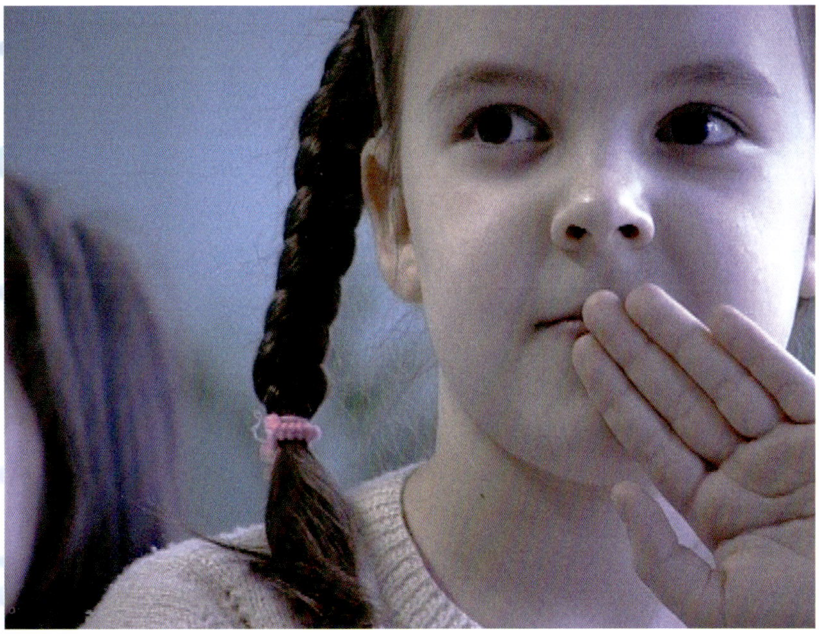

above
Whose Is this Exhalation?, 2008
1-channel video loop
15 minutes 9 seconds
Edition of 5 plus 1 artist's proof
© Victor Alimpiev
Courtesy Regina Gallery, London & Moscow

left
Summer Lightnings, 2004
1-channel video loop
2 minutes 20 seconds
Edition of 5
© Victor Alimpiev
Courtesy Regina Gallery, London & Moscow

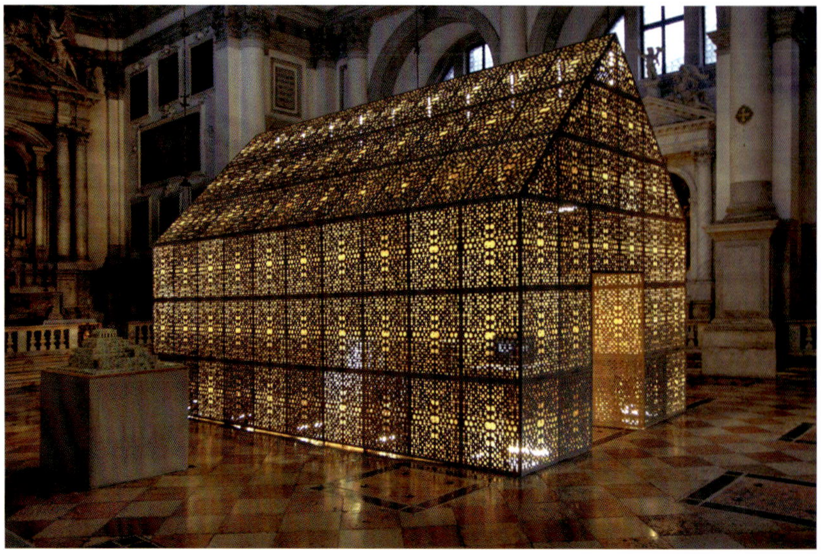

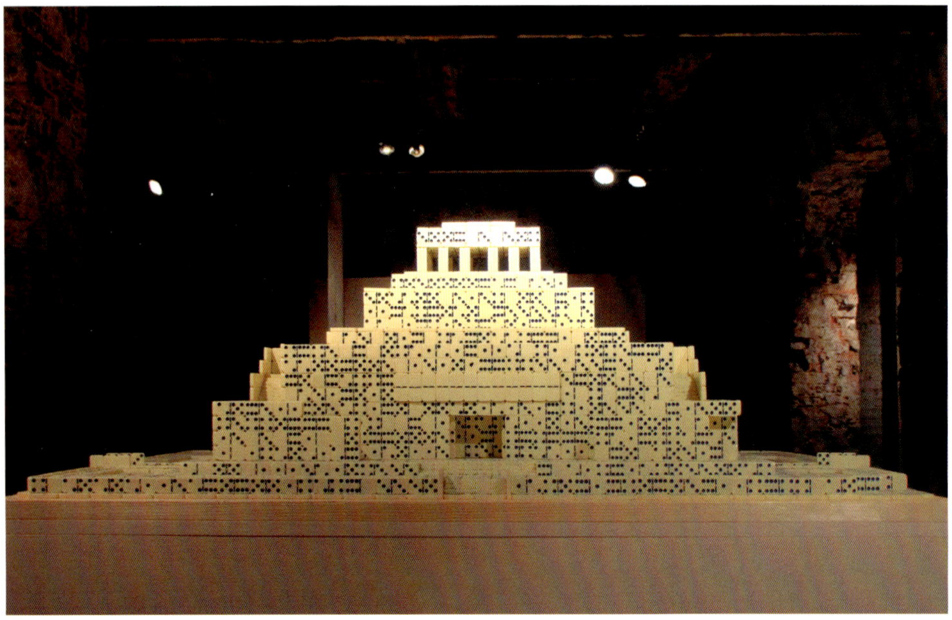

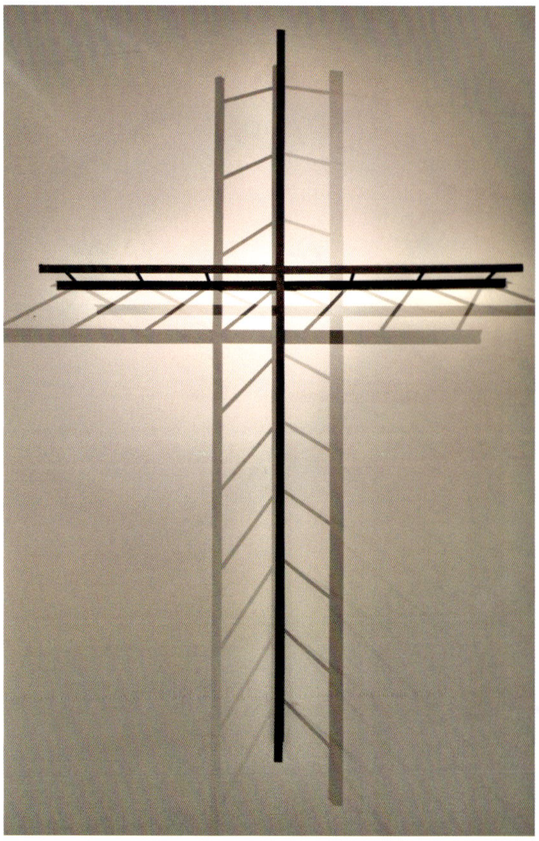

Yuri Avvakumov

Born in Tiraspol in 1957, architect, artist and curator Yuri Avvakumov lives and works in Moscow. Having graduated from the Moscow Institute of Architecture in 1981, he then taught there for five years. In 1988 he set up the independent architectural studio AGITARCH. Together with a group of his contemporaries, he reinvigorated the practice of 'paper architecture', an eighteenth-century European term meant to denote fanciful designs for projects that cannot be realised. Avvakumov's 3-D art combines sculpture and architectural forms to create large-scale gallery models, or installations, which resemble Constructivist urban monuments. Recurring motifs are ladders, bridges and towers symbolic of humankind's ambitious yet often vain endeavours. He often uses game pieces such as playing cards or dominoes as building elements, as in *Bone Mausoleum* (2008), a model of Lenin's tomb.

Central to Avvakumov's curatorial work is a preoccupation with documenting the Constructivist tradition. In 2003 he set up the Utopia Foundation primarily to collect designs for unrealised architectural projects in Russia from the past 300 years. These he exhibits worldwide, often as interactive, multimedia installations, as in the case of *Russian Utopia: A Depository* (1996–2000). Individual designs are displayed in such a way that visitors can pull them out to view them. In 2002 Avvakumov reconstructed Malevich's famous Suprematist architectural models from the early 1920s.

Avvakumov's work is represented in numerous public collections worldwide, including the State Russian Museum, St Petersburg; the State Museum of Architecture, Moscow; the Deutsches Architekturmuseum, Frankfurt-on-Main; the Victoria and Albert Museum, London; and the Museum of Modern and Contemporary Art of Trento and Rovereto. Architectural projects include a commission from the Solomon R. Guggenheim Foundation for the design of a museum complex in Abu Dhabi and designs submitted for the New Holland project, St Petersburg.

top
BornHouse, Chiesa di San Stae, Venice, 2008
Cardboard, wood, lamps
540 x 480 x 800 cm
© Yuri Avvakumov
Courtesy of the artist

above
Bone Mausoleum, 2008
Dominos
62.5 x 170 x 142 cm
© Yuri Avvakumov
Courtesy of the artist

right
Criss-Cross, 1990
Fire ladders
300 x 200 x 40 cm
© Yuri Avvakumov
Courtesy of the artist

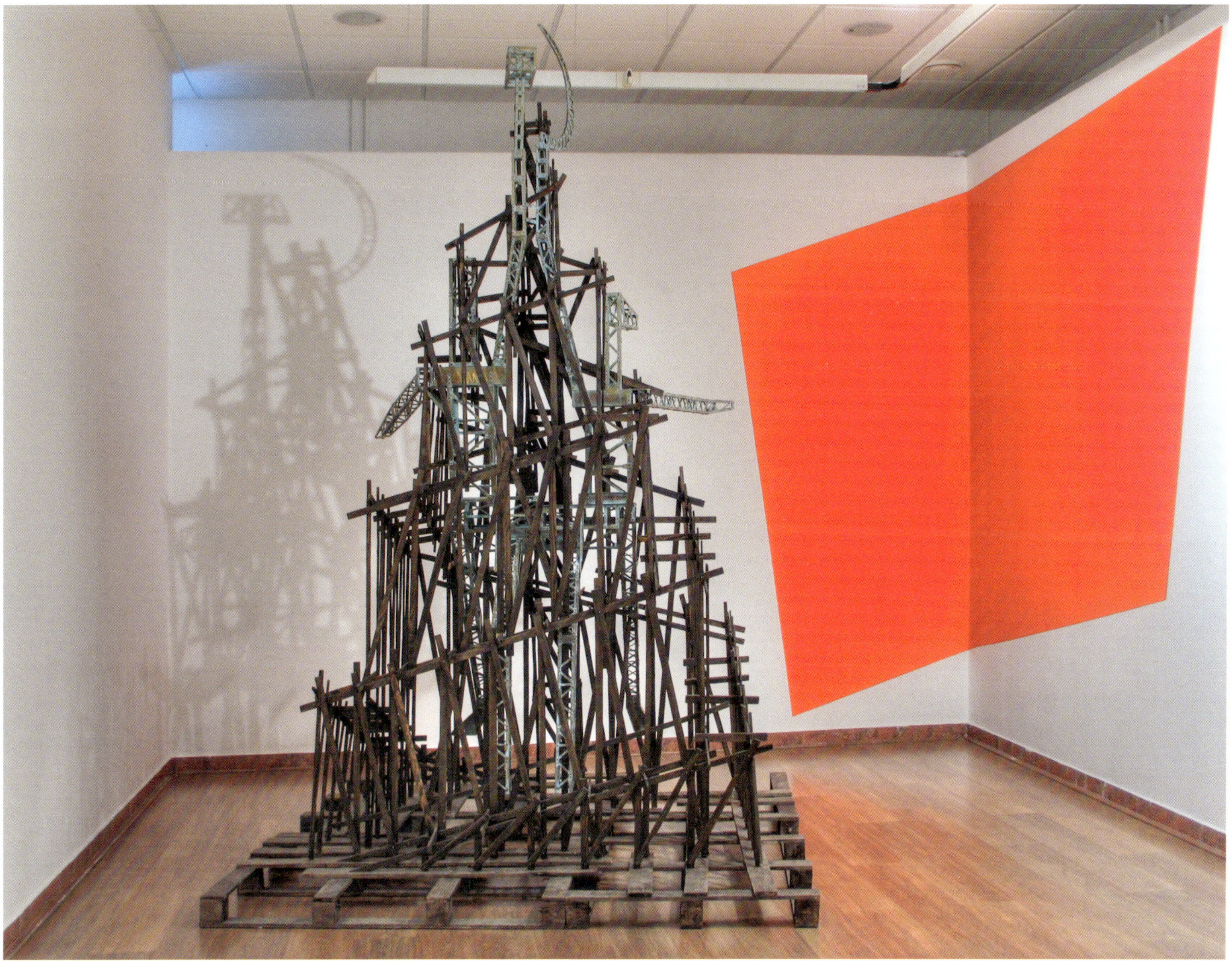

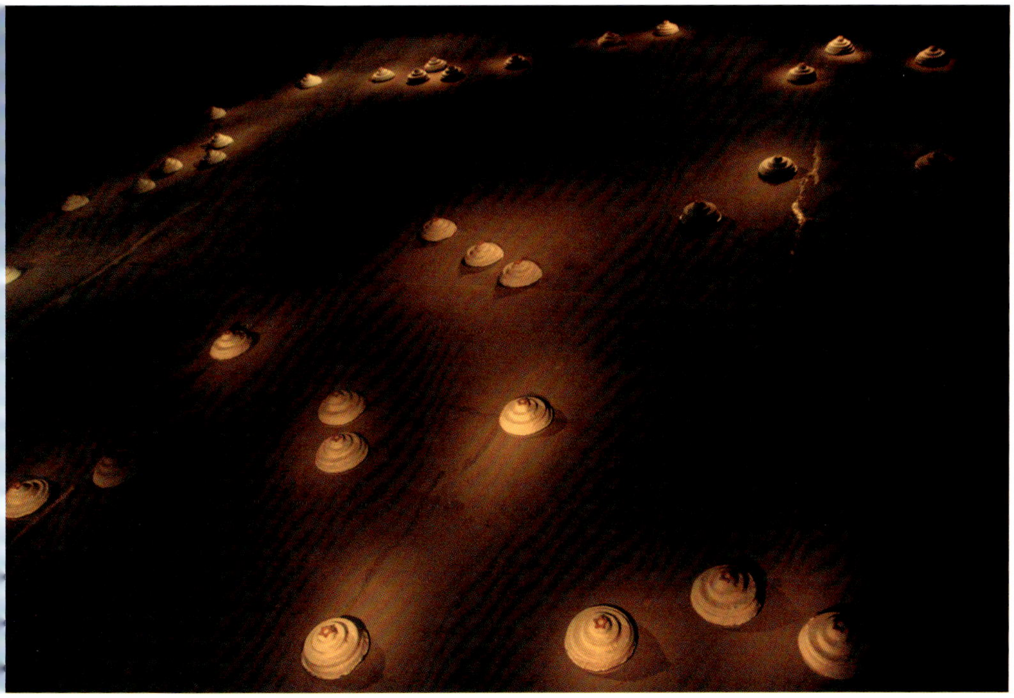

above
Worker and Farmer International, 1990-91
Metal, wood
300 x 200 x 200 cm
© Yuri Avvakumov
Courtesy of the artist

left
Mined Sky, 2011
Installation at Spazio Carbobesi, Bologna
40 cakes
© Yuri Avvakumov
Courtesy of the artist

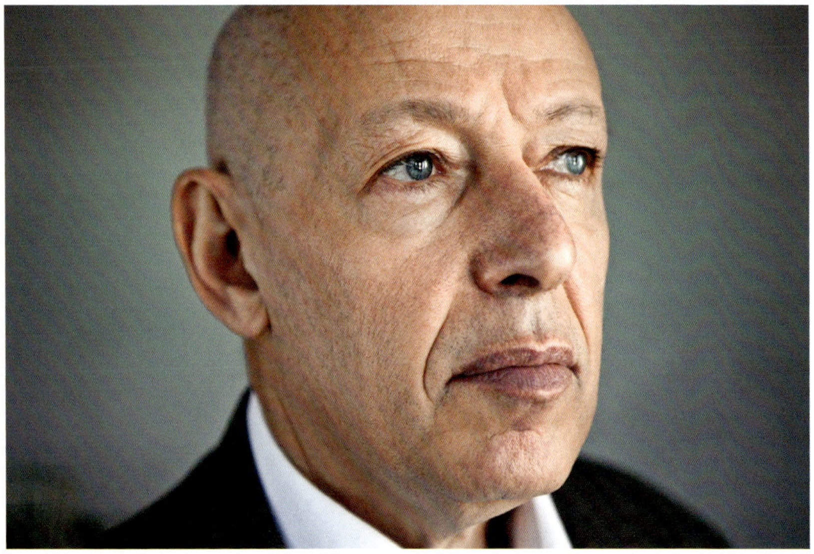

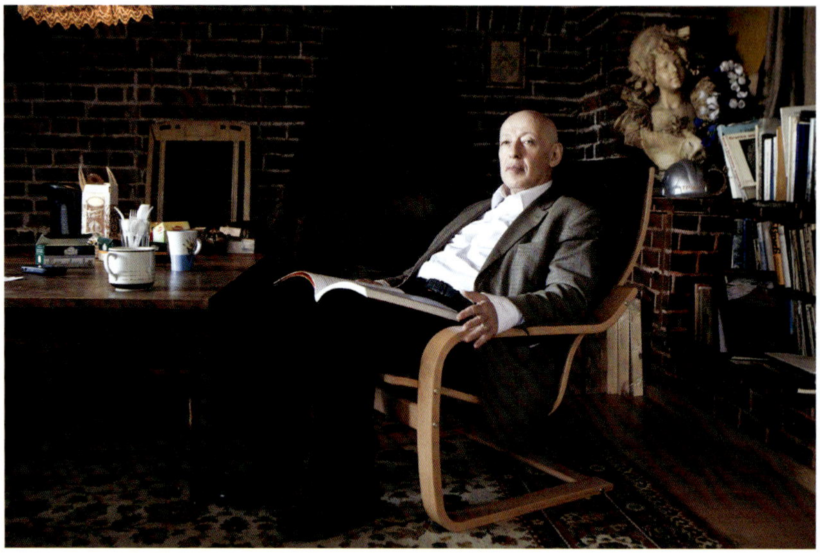

Joseph Backstein

Curator Joseph Backstein was born in Moscow in 1945. He acknowledges that one of the biggest challenges for his generation has been living through a complete transformation of Russia's arts institutions: 'When I started out in the '70s and '80s, we belonged to a very important social milieu which was part of an ideological system; it was the Cold War era.' During perestroika Backstein emerged as one of the first independent curators with his *Steamship* show (1987). His artistic background had been the underground circles centred around Ilya Kabakov's studio on Sretensky Boulevard, a large tenth-floor attic space with panoramic views over Moscow. Today, with much of the interior kept as it was in the '70s, this is the headquarters of the Moscow Biennale, which Backstein helped to establish in 2003.

The early association with Kabakov, whom Backstein considers the most important of Russia's contemporary artists, along with his college friendship with Alexander Melamid were the formative influences on his career as a curator and promoter of Russian contemporary art. Another important influence was the Moscow Conceptual poet and artist Andrei Monastyrsky, who founded Collective Actions in 1976. Backstein became a regular participant in the alternative debates and discussions that raged in Moscow Conceptual circles outside of official Soviet culture, and remembers them as generating a dynamic and creative atmosphere. His earliest curatorial projects date from the late 1980s. In 1990, at the invitation of David Roth, the director of the Institute of Contemporary Art in Boston, he brought the art of his contemporaries to the US, organising the seminal show *Between Spring and Summer: Soviet Conceptual Art*.

Inspired by Roth, in 1991 Backstein founded the ICA in Moscow, of which he is still the director. Since its foundation, the institute has provided a unique platform for arts education, previously dominated by the Soviet Realist school. Backstein's students explore contemporary aesthetics with a strong multidisciplinary approach as part of the curriculum. An important part of his vision for the institute is its focus on Conceptual art, thus continuing the Moscow traditions of the '70s and '80s, and helping to bring such work into the mainstream: 'Contemporary art came back to Russia through the Moscow Conceptual School. In the Soviet Union there was no contemporary art after the avant-garde. It was born again in Kabakov's studio in the 1970s.'

Addressing wider questions of globalism and identity, Backstein believes that art has few barriers: 'We do not have a barrier of language; the tradition of fine art was international from the beginning, and it cannot be closed off. Multiculturalism exists; there is a large and quite complex international scene now.' He believes that the modernising of conservative currents is the way forward, and through his exchange programmes at the ICA he encourages young artists to go abroad in order to assimilate practices and experiences which will help to regenerate the art scene back home. At the same time he feels that Russia's geographical distance from the West plays an ongoing role in determining its cultural identity, while Moscow's centralised position lends it a cultural magnetism that is lacking in other Eastern European capitals. 'Eastern Europeans want to be like Western Europeans, but Russians are different. We are more distant. From Prague you can easily travel to Vienna, but Moscow is far away,' Backstein says.

Backstein's work as director of the Moscow Biennale has raised the city's profile as a lively international centre for the arts. He has attracted a number of Western European curators such as Hans-Ulrich Obrist and Jean-Hubert Martin to work with him. At the same time he has encouraged the integration of Russian contemporary artists with their international brethren. Backstein was appointed commissioner of the 3rd Moscow Biennale in 2008 and, together with Martin, organised a groundbreaking show at the Garage Centre for Contemporary Culture. This exhibition was a major success, attracting over 500,000 visitors each month – unprecedented numbers for a presentation of contemporary art in Moscow.

Alongside the promotion of contemporary art in Russia, Backstein expresses serious concern about the commercial forces that have turned art into an 'entertainment industry'. He recalls that many of his most successful early independent exhibitions were organised and staged for free, in an atmosphere shorn of the pressures of the art market. There is a political dimension to his thinking as well, as he draws parallels between American Pop art, Sots Art and the Conceptual work of Kabakov. Backstein believes that where Andy Warhol found inspiration in transcending post-war capitalism in America, his Russian contemporaries have created their own 'epiphany' in overcoming the limitations of Soviet reality; this is what Backstein believes gives their art its true value. Today, Russia is embracing capitalist market forces, but people still have their own vision. 'In Russia,' Backstein muses, 'people do not fully understand the difference between not-for-profit and commercial enterprise in the arts. They ask me, "Is it not possible to buy something at the biennale?"'

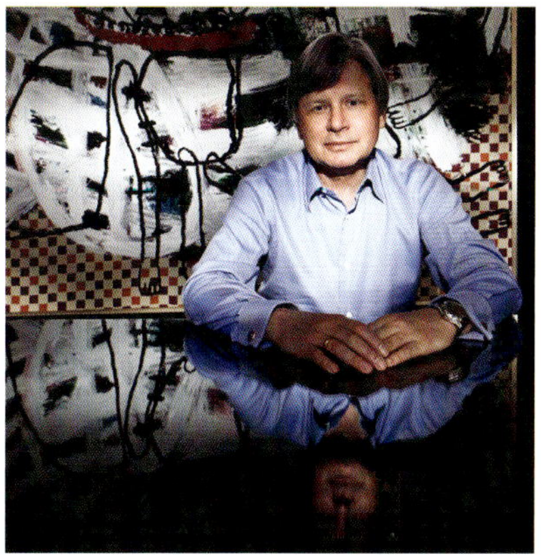

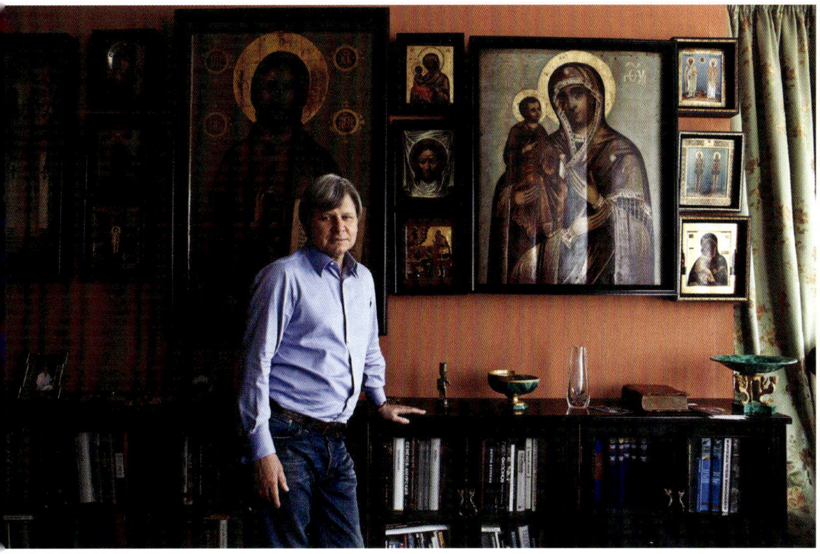

Victor Bondarenko was born in Kharkov, Ukraine, in 1950. He moved to Moscow in 1969 at the age of nineteen following a stint in the army; his father, who worked in a military factory, had ambitions for his son to pursue a military career. However, Bondarenko, who describes himself as a 'figure of protest', did not want to work for the Communist regime, so in the late Soviet period he supported himself by buying and selling antiques and icons on what was then the black market.

Bondarenko left the Soviet Union in 1978 to settle in the US, where he spent some years establishing himself in various businesses, including real estate and insurance, at the same time continuing to deal in art and antiques, attending auctions at Sotheby's and Christies in New York. He also supported the careers of many unofficial artists from the Soviet Union in the 1980s, including the figurative painters Natalia Nesterova, Olga Bulgakova and Alexander Sitnikov, whose works he showed in, and sold from, his Fifth Avenue penthouse in Manhattan. Bondarenko also became friends with Grisha Bruskin and bought several of his works. He organised an exhibition of Russian twentieth-century art at the Nassau County Museum of Art, foregrounding post-war unofficial artists alongside members of the avant-garde.

When the Soviet Union began to collapse in 1989, Bondarenko returned to Moscow to sell imported limousines to the newly rich. During the 1990s he published eleven magazines under the umbrella of his Zig Zag Venture Group. These proved to be hugely popular with Russia's new consumers of the perestroika years and Bondarenko became wealthy. It was during this period that he started to collect more systematically and seriously, first icons – he has one of the most important private collections of icons in the country – and then Russian contemporary art.

Bondarenko looks for marginal, neglected areas and periods, saying, 'I always go against the tide; if no-one is collecting something I have to do it ... I buy marginal artists, outsiders.' Despite the political changes in Russia and the fact that artists are becoming more mainstream, he still views the contemporary scene as marginal, observing regretfully that 'it won't change until this country becomes completely free. Only free people can create truly great art.' His collection of Russian post-war unofficial and contemporary art includes over a hundred works by Eric Bulatov, Vladimir Nemukhin, Ilya Kabakov, Oleg Kulik, Dmitry Gutov and Konstantin Khudiakov, among others. Bondarenko works closely with a number of artists, supporting and commissioning works, most often based on his own projects and ideas. He has a preference for subjects that push boundaries and address Russia's social issues, stimulating controversy and debate, as well as for art as a form of spiritual expression. Describing artists as prophets, he is particularly appreciative of the great avant-garde painters Kazimir Malevich and Vasily Kandinsky, the Dutch abstract artist Piet Mondrian and, among contemporary artists, Anish Kapoor.

Bondarenko is fascinated by the idea of resurrecting Russia's tradition of religious art, which was cut off during the Soviet period. He has commissioned Khudiakov to create a *deisis* for the twenty-first century using digital technology. The project, currently entitled *Deisis: The Coming*, initially met with opposition from the Russian Orthodox Church, so the original title, *Iconostasis 21*, was changed and some inscriptions removed from the work. Gutov's series *Russia Is for All* (2010) was inspired by Bondarenko's concern about forces pushing against multiculturalism within the Russian Federation.

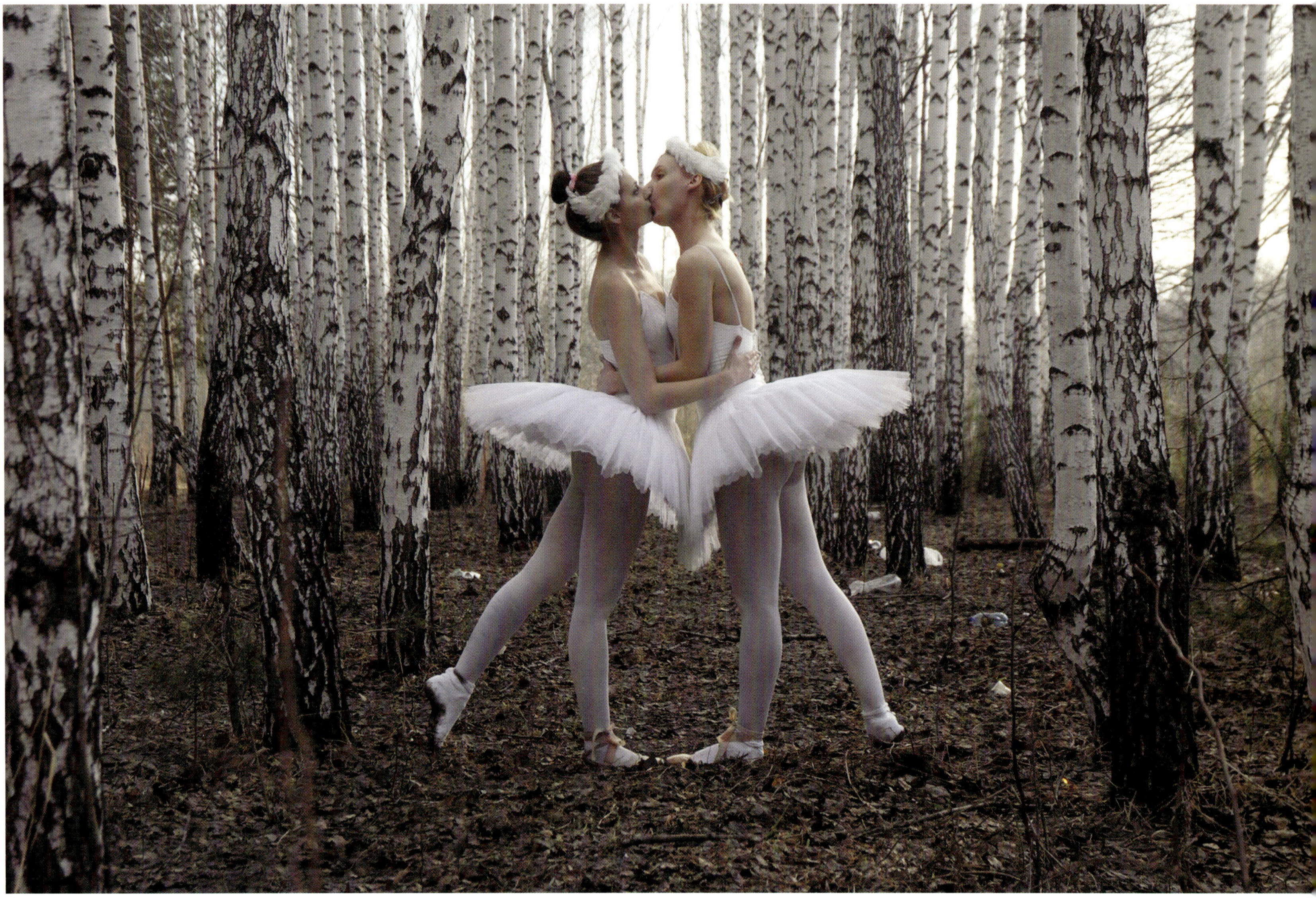

Blue Noses

Blue Noses was established in 1999 by the Siberian artists Alexander Shaburov (born in 1965 near Sverdlovsk) and Viacheslav Mizin (born in 1962 in Novosibirsk). Shaburov graduated from Sverdlovsk College of Arts, Mizin from Novosibirsk Architectural Institute; they live and work in Novosibirsk, Ekaterinburg and Moscow. The group got its name after the two artists put plastic bottle tops on their noses during one of their first performances. Although they remain the driving force, other artists have taken part in Blue Noses presentations. Represented by commercial galleries throughout Europe, the US, China and Russia, their work has been shown at several Venice and Moscow biennales. Using buffoonery, the duo parodies social, political and artistic conventions, reducing human beings to anonymous fornicating consumers subjected to mass-media and political chicanery. Their practice is diverse, embracing video and performance art, action art and photography.

above
Kissing Ballerinas, from the series An Epoch of Clemency, 2005
Colour photograph
100 x 75 cm
© Blue Noses
Courtesy of the artists and Guelman Gallery, Moscow

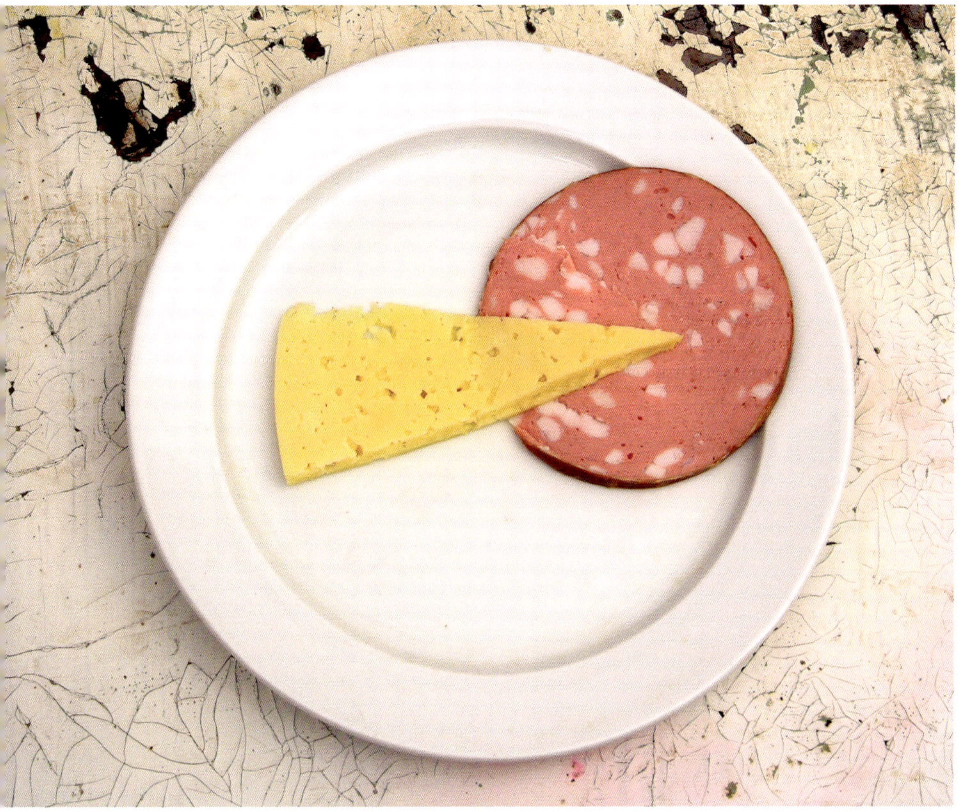

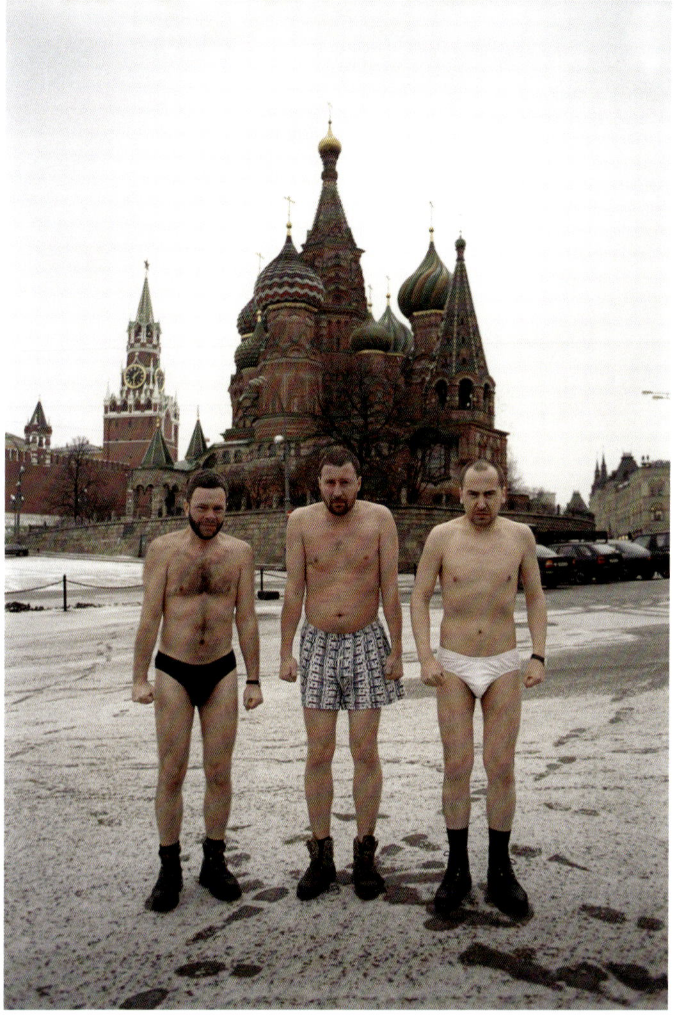

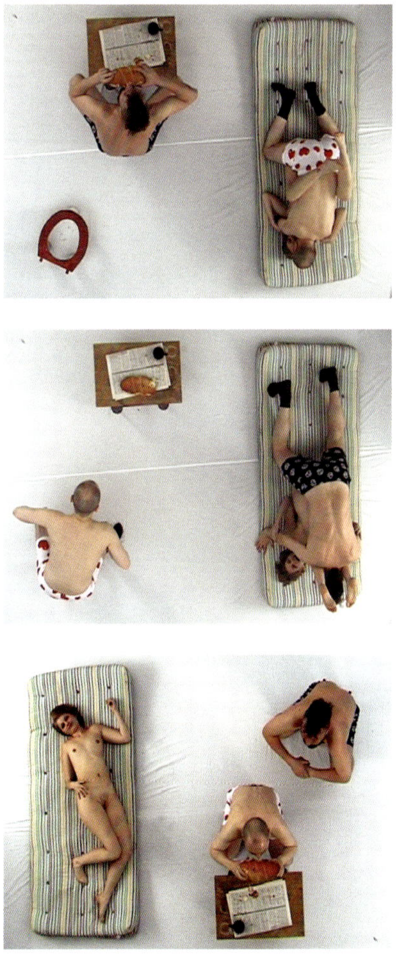

top left
From the series Kitchen Suprematism, 2005–06
Colour photograph
100 x 75 cm
© Blue Noses
Collection of the State Tretyakov Gallery, Moscow
Courtesy of the artists and Guelman Gallery, Moscow

above
From the series The New Holy Fools,1999
Colour photograph
100 x 75 cm
© Blue Noses
Courtesy of the artists and Guelman Gallery, Moscow

left
Stills from Reality Show, 2004
© Blue Noses
Courtesy of the artists and Art4.ru

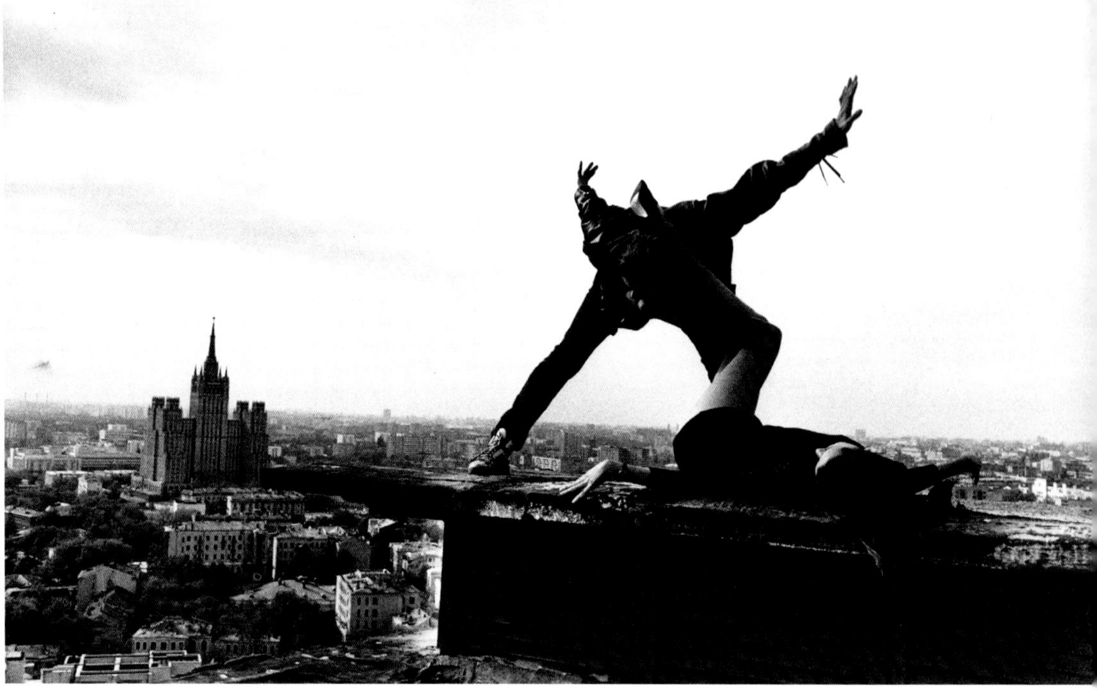

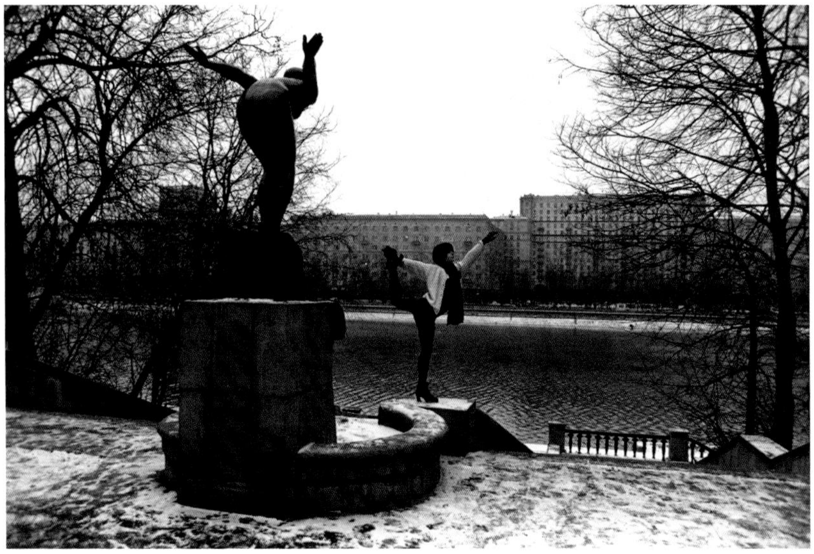

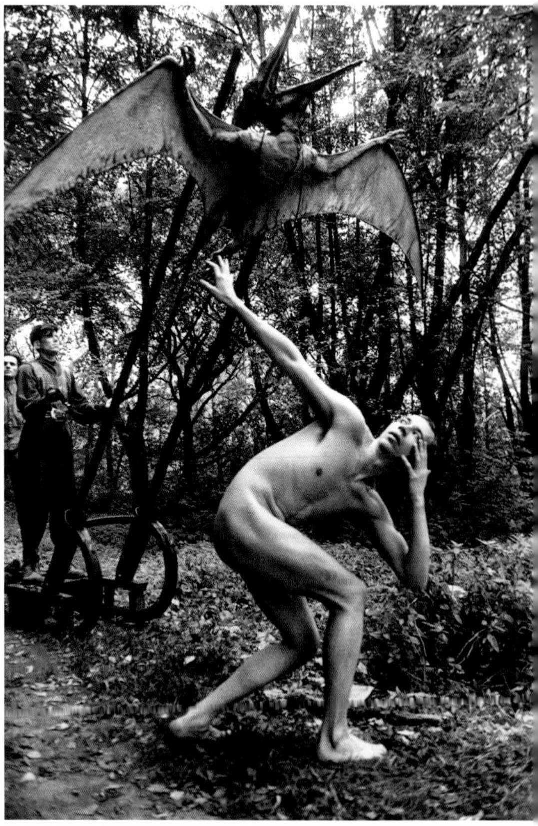

Sergei Borisov

The name of photographer Sergei Borisov is synonymous with perestroika and the anarchic underground youth culture of Moscow and St Petersburg in the 1980s. Born in 1947 in Moscow, where he continues to live and work, Borisov learned the tools of his medium starting at the age of twelve, when he joined the photography club of the Moscow House of Pioneers. Not only do his images of artists, rock musicians, punks and models document a turbulent period in Russian history; they have achieved cult status both in Russia and abroad due to his unerring ability to capture the spirit of the times.

Borisov's meteoric rise began in the late 1970s, when he became a registered member of the Moscow Joint Committee of Graphic Artists (MOGKh) on Malaya Gruzinskaya Street in Moscow – a semi-legal hotbed of nonconformist artists. Having photographed the key personalities of the older generation, Borisov found himself in demand by a foreign press eager for photographs expressing the raw brutality of 1980s Russia.

Working exclusively in black-and-white, Borisov's distinctive style is characterised by his juxtaposition of old and new. The shedding of a painful social and political history is felt in works like *Catwalk* (1987), *Flying* (1988) and *Explanation* (1993), where Soviet urban topography acts as a backdrop for mocking, evanescent poses and gestures. 'I look at photography as something tribal,' he has said. 'I look at the smiles in the portraits – they are different in the 1970s, 1980s and 2000s. In the 1950s there were photographers in Moscow who shot the life of the city – this has so much more value than photos of pretty girls posing in the dunes.' Borisov's images are so brimming with life that they demand complete attention.

top
Conversation, 1993
Gelatin silver print
40 x 60 cm
© Sergei Borisov
Courtesy of the artist

above left
Cloudy Day, 1995
Gelatin silver print
40 x 60 cm
© Sergei Borisov
Courtesy of the artist

right
Dray of the Platinum Age, 1996
Gelatin silver print
60 x 40 cm
© Sergei Borisov
Courtesy of the artist

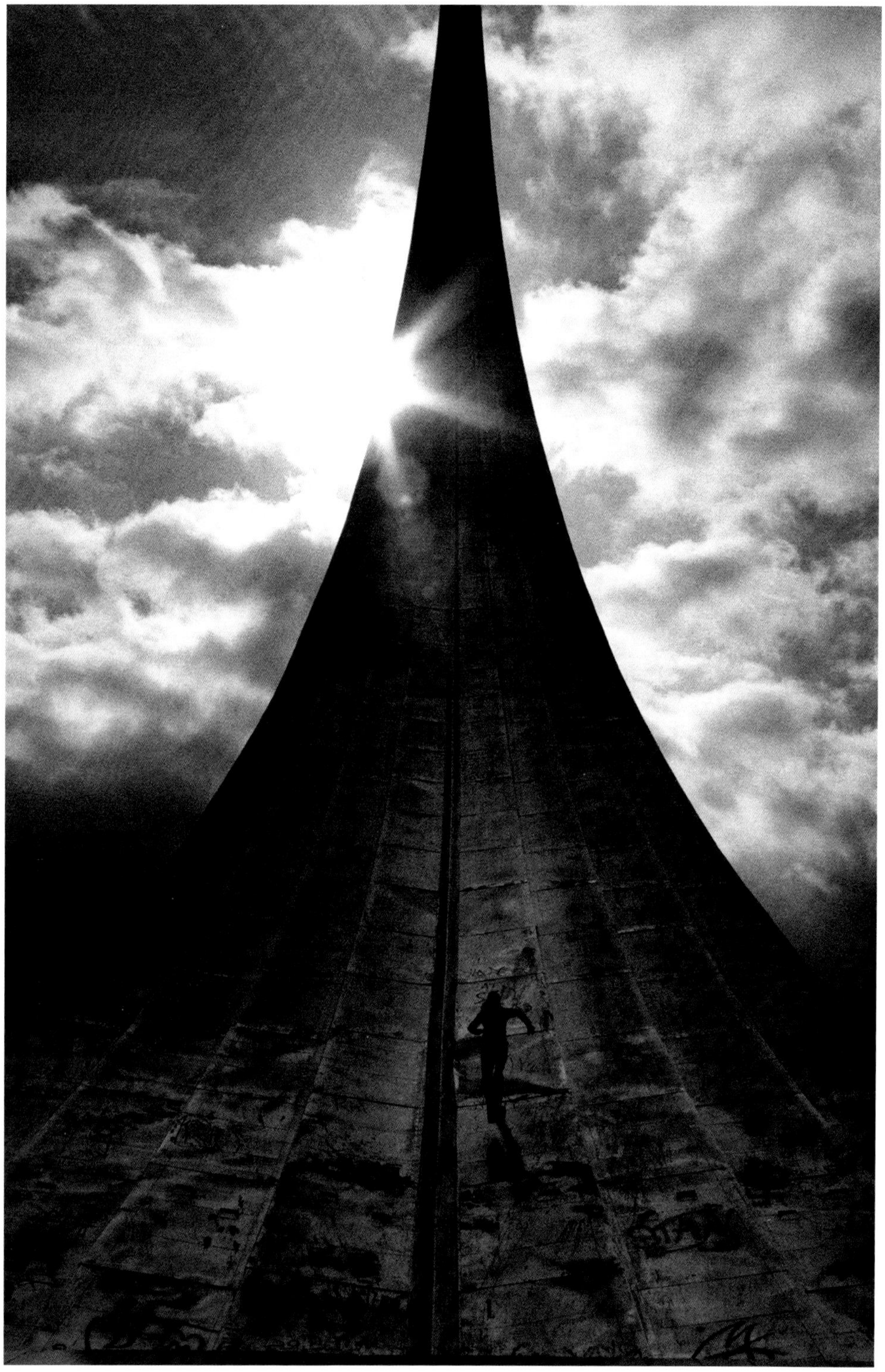

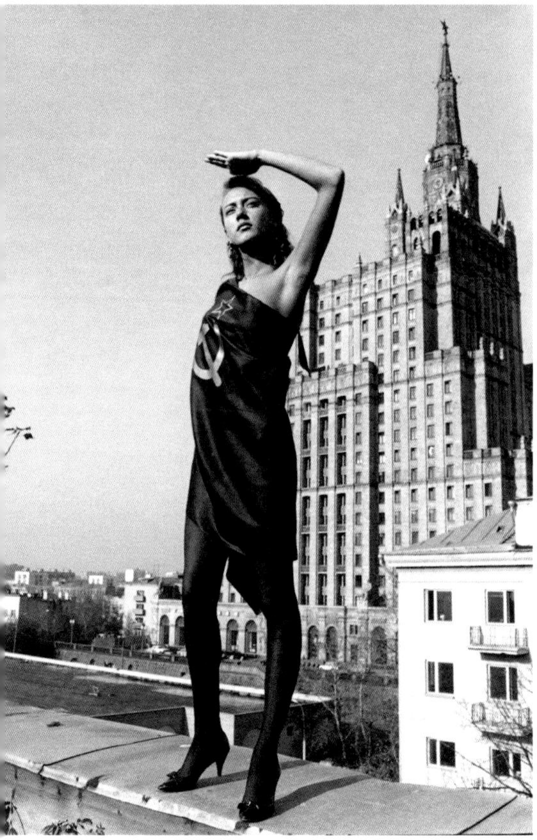

above
Ascent, 2002
Gelatin silver print
60 x 40 cm
© Sergei Borisov
Courtesy of the artist

left
Catwalk, 1987
Gelatin silver print
60 x 40 cm
© Sergei Borisov
Courtesy of the artist

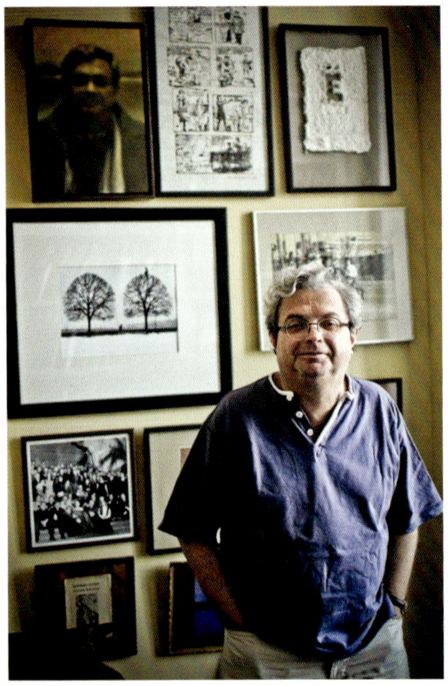

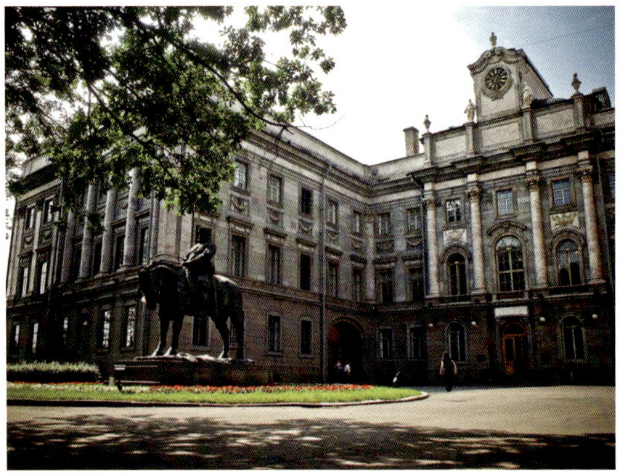

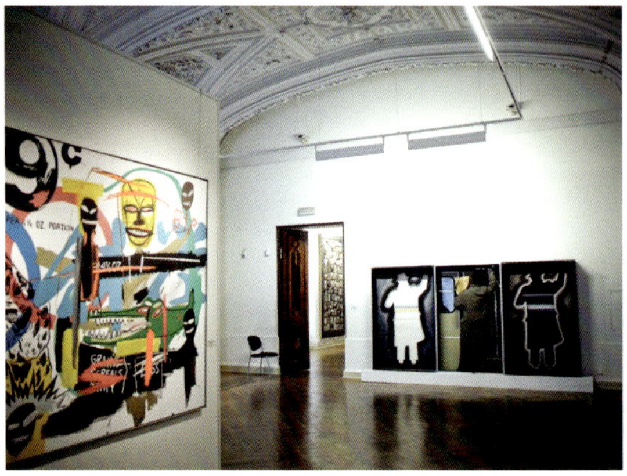

Curator Alexander Borovsky has been at the helm of change in the museum world since perestroika. Aside from working as senior curator of Contemporary Art at the State Russian Museum in St Petersburg, Borovsky was the founder and remains active director of the museum's Department of New Trends. After years of State control of the arts during which public institutions were unable to buy or exhibit unofficial work, Borovsky curated the department's first exhibition in 1990. Titled *The Territory of Art*, the exhibition was organised in collaboration with the Institut des Hautes Etudes in Paris and featured a wide range of Russian and Western artists whose works could not have been viewed previously by a Russian audience: Kazimir Malevich, Marcel Duchamp, Andy Warhol, Claus Oldenburg and Jannis Kounnelis.

Since then, Borovsky has been responsible for creating an exhibitions programme whose tasks it has been to fill historical gaps and take part in the development and evolution of contemporary art. Exhibitions have included installations by Brian Eno (1997) and a focus on international video art, *Along the Frontier: Ann Hamilton, Bruce Nauman, Francesc Torres and Bill Viola* (1996). At the same, there is an emphasis on key figures of Russian contemporary art, from Moscow Conceptualism and Sots Art to a new generation of home-grown talent seen in exhibitions like *Nouveaunovosibirsk Project: Andrei Molodkin, Alexei Belyaev-Gintovt, Gleb Kosorukov and Dmitry Shostakovich Jr* (2001) and *Olga Chernysheva: The Happiness Zone* (2004). Borovsky cites the significance of showing contemporary art in close proximity to older, traditional works in the museum's collection, one example being the partnering of Chernysheva's exhibition with works by the nineteenth-century painter Ilya Repin, thereby creating a dialogue across generations and styles.

Borovsky is keen to state the importance of fostering contemporary art in the context of a long-established, respected museum. Founded in the late 1980s in response to the opportunities offered by perestroika and glasnost, when the confrontation between official and unofficial art and culture were slowly disappearing, the department's main task was to reintegrate Russian art into an international context but to address these questions within the museum setting. On the one hand, Borovsky's initiative follows in the footsteps of tradition; in the late 1920s, the art scholar and writer Nikolai Punin opened a department with the same name devoted to radical and experimental forms of art. On the other hand, Borovsky believes that the museum as a whole remains alive, vital and relevant via the introduction of young talent and new forms of art, media and technology into its spaces, including installations, assemblages, video art, photography and photo-based art. In addition, the museum's permanent collection of contemporary art has been expanding steadily since the founding of the Department of New Trends. The acquisitions policy is closely connected to its exhibition programme, and, since *The Territory of Art*, when it received a large body of work by artists like Sergei Bugaev (Afrika), the Necrorealists, and Olga and Alexander Florensky, it has become accepted practice for works to be purchased following exhibitions.

The task of presenting a varied roster of artists and movements has as its motive public education and the evolution of the museum system itself. Borovsky has spoken about a curator's responsibility to create an objective picture of the current scene, unaffected by questions of personal taste and ideology. With this aim in mind, he is also responsible for the introduction of a large body of work from the Ludwig Collection into the State Russian Museum. Established in 1995, the Ludwig Museum is housed in the Marble Palace of the State Russian Museum. Although it now forms part of the permanent collection, it represents a fitting aspect of Borovsky's strategy as it too exists as an active project, helping to describe a chronology through the art of the second half of the twentieth century. While the Ludwig Museum contains works by internationally recognised names like Michelangelo Pistoletto and Ilya Kabakov, whose work is now too expensive to be purchased by most museums, the Department of New Trends, under Borovsky's guiding hand, has been able to focus on exhibiting and fostering local, regional talent like the New Wave artists and their followers or the Necrorealists.

Thanks to Borovsky's efforts, the State Russian Museum has one of the largest publicly owned collections of contemporary art in the country. At the same time, he can continue exploring and presenting to the public the multiple strands of art history, taking advantage of the museum's decision not to relegate contemporary art to a separate wing, but to actively integrate it into the main Imperial body of the museum. As such, a dialogue has been fostered that keeps both strands of art alive and receptive to ever-changing contexts.

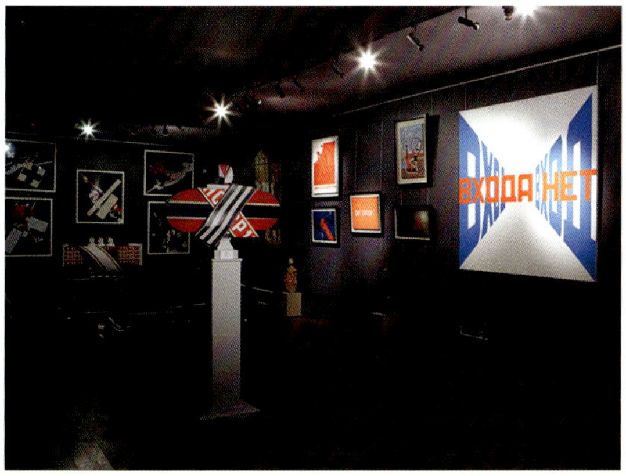

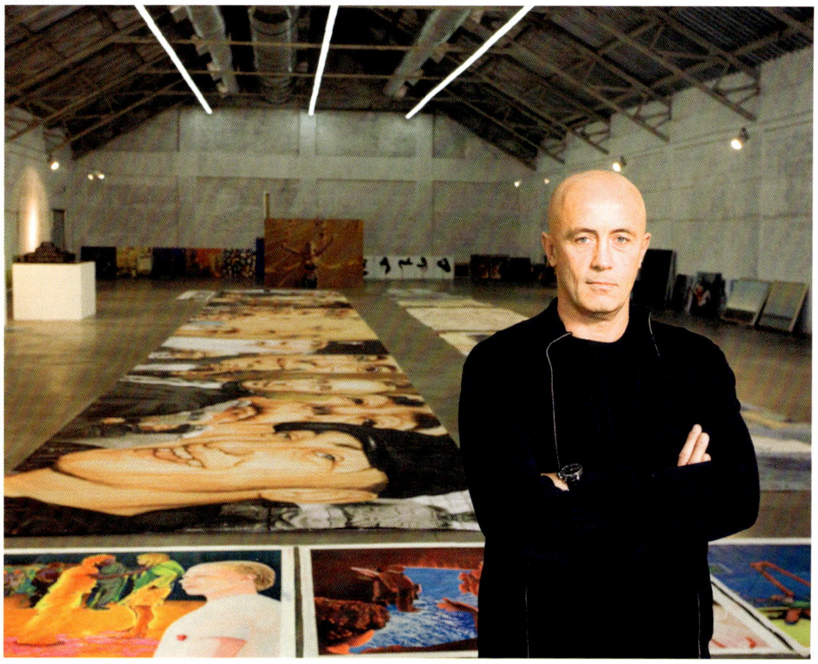

The ArtChronika Cultural Foundation was set up by Shalva Breus in 1999. Since then it has made a considerable contribution to the development of the contemporary arts in Russia, particularly in the field of publishing.

Breus, who was born in Batumi, Georgia, in 1957, lives and works in Moscow. Despite having a passion for journalism, he studied economics, graduating from Moscow State University in 1981 and spending two decades working his way up through the State sector. From 1998 until 2000 he was Vice-Governor of the Krasnoyarsk Region, and from 2000 until 2003 he was Deputy Minister for Property Relations of the Russian Federation. In the early 2000s he became chairman of the board of directors at Ost-West Group and a member of the supervisory board at OJSC Volga.

In 1999 Breus began publishing Russia's first independent, privately owned art magazine, *ArtChronika*. The magazine, one of the country's few art journals, is widely influential. Printed monthly in Russian with special editions in English, its editorial focus is on contemporary Russian and international art, as well as the global auction market. There is also a bilingual website. In 2007 Breus's foundation set up Russia's first independent contemporary-art award, the Kandinsky Prize, named after the great early twentieth-century pioneer in the field of abstraction, a visionary who changed the history of art. One of Breus's initial aims was to assemble an international jury consisting of leading Western curators and critics alongside Russian experts, in order to raise the prize's profile and scope. Central to his policy of openness, the prize welcomes all artists who wish to submit entries, and there are no submission criteria.

Breus's foundation aims to provide accessible resources not only to art-industry insiders, curators and students but also to the wider public. Since the collapse of the Soviet Union, many Russians have continued to be influenced by the outmoded tradition of academic realism, the only officially recognised style until 1989. The public often does not know what to make of contemporary art. The first Kandinsky Prize exhibition brought both glamour and attention to art on a large scale. The show, which was televised, marked a turning point in the perception of contemporary practice and stimulated open debate. Breus is a strong advocate of change in public perceptions, often using the metaphor of 'breaking down walls' to evoke his desire to open people's minds to what art can become as a tool of social change.

Meanwhile his publishing activities have expanded to include several new series of books on art history. Addressing the lack of available information outside of Russia about the country's contemporary art scene, he is planning a series of bilingual monographs on major post-war artists to be distributed internationally. A series of important translations of post-war Western art-historical texts for Russian students and scholars is also planned.

Surveying Russia's growing contemporary scene, Breus sees a need for institutional transformation to generate credibility and a greater degree of professionalism. He explains how the scene grew out of the small, self-contained circle of the Moscow underground, and that this 'rather informal group of people and its informal environment' has led to today's inward-looking, closed culture, making it difficult for aspiring curators and independent critics to build careers and introduce a fresh vision. Breus believes that Russia's art institutions run the risk of becoming too provincial. Even so, he does not believe that this is hindering artists' creativity: 'In the 1920s there was no support at all, but the Russian avant-garde conquered the world ... They were great artists, Malevich and Tatlin; only their friends came to their shows, and the artists themselves were the tour guides; they did not need art institutions.'

An avid collector, Breus has assembled important holdings of German Expressionism and Russian contemporary art over the past decade. He exhibits major works by Eric Bulatov, Komar and Melamid, and Boris Orlov in a dedicated space at his foundation's offices on Neglinnaya Street in the centre of Moscow. Breus sees collecting as an activity that goes hand in hand with social responsibility: 'I do not consider the collection as my own. It has to be in a museum, and I doubt that I will continue to collect long-term. There are two ways to acquire art: you can be like an interior decorator and hang beautiful paintings on your walls, or you can build a museum collection. For me collecting for its own sake does not make sense.' Breus believes that what Moscow needs is a major museum of contemporary art, and his outlook is cautious yet confident. 'Did you know,' he says quizzically, 'that a pessimist is a well-informed optimist? So I am not a pessimist; I am a well-informed optimist.'

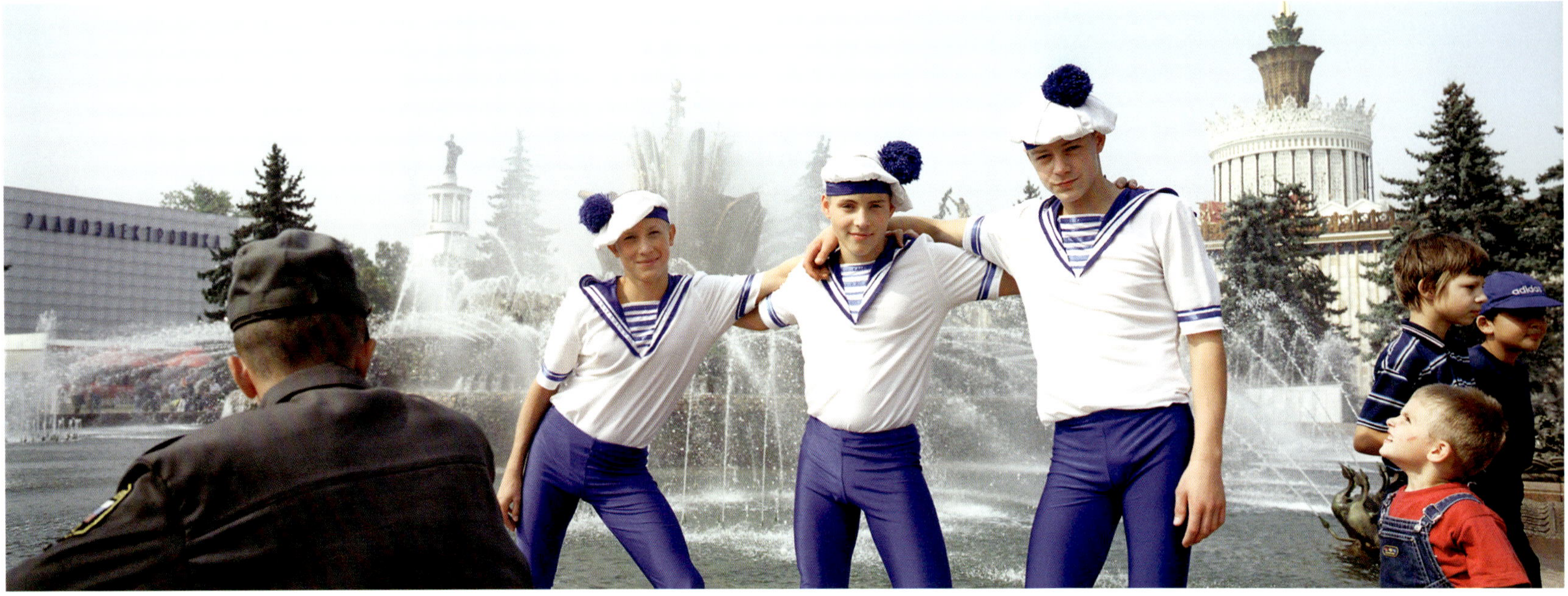

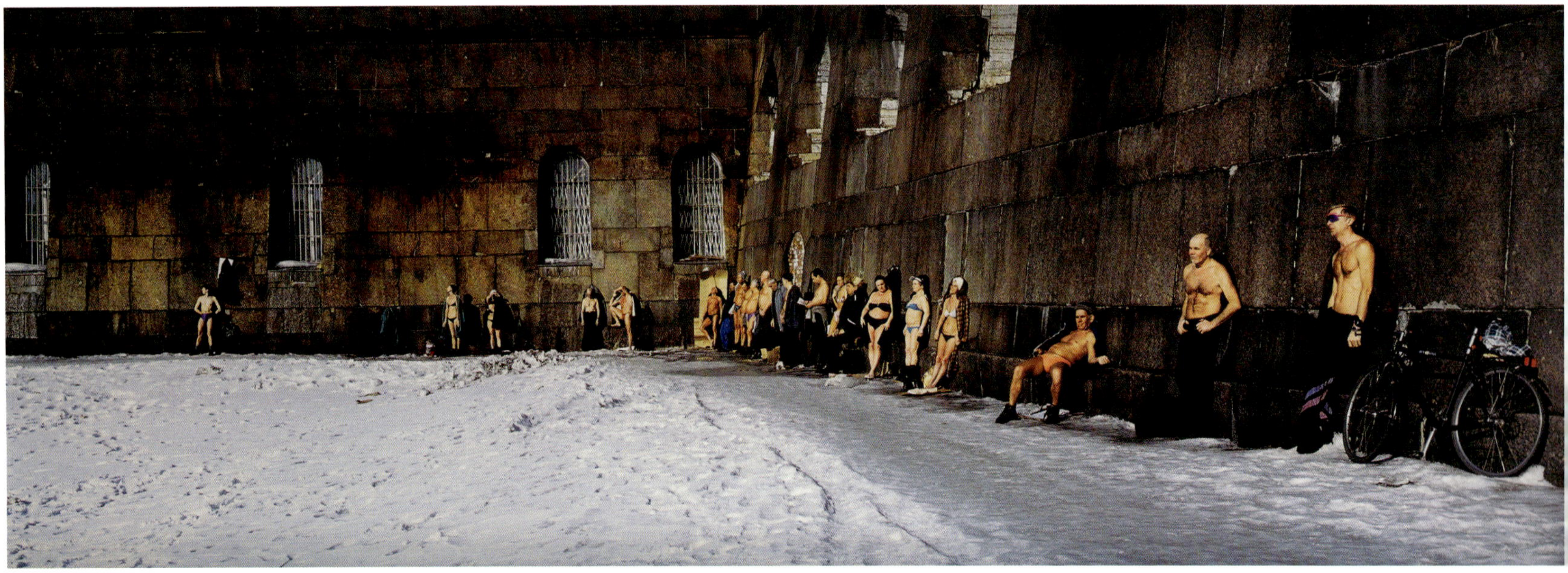

Sergei Bratkov

Artist-photographer Sergei Bratkov was born in Kharkov, Ukraine, in 1960. As a child he took lessons at the Repin Art College in Kharkov; after studying engineering at the Polytechnical Academy (1978–83), he joined an artist's co-operative. His art is predominantly photography-based with some video, and he uses traditional rather than digital film. Bratkov has participated in many major group exhibitions in Russia, Ukraine and Western Europe, including several biennales in Moscow and Venice, and *I Believe* at Vinzavod, Moscow (2007). He has had solo shows at the Moscow Museum of Contemporary Art (2006), the Winterthur Fotomuseum (2008), and the Pinchuk Art Centre, Kiev (2010). In 2010 he was the winner of Russia's Innovation Prize. Bratkov's work can be found in important public collections, including MKHA, Antwerp; the Pinchuk Art Centre; and the Ekaterina Cultural Foundation, Moscow. Since 1999 he has lived and worked in Moscow.

On the surface, Bratkov's work explores the shifting, often uncomfortable social realities and landscapes of post-Soviet Russia and Ukraine. In 1994 the artist collaborated on the *Alchemic Surrender* project in Sebastopol with the Ukrainian-born photographer Boris Mikhailov, whom Bratkov cites as a formative influence. Together they formed the Fast Reaction Group, taking part in and documenting a series of provocative actions aimed at replacing Soviet values with a new, more authentically Ukrainian identity. This period of artistic maturation opened Bratkov's mind to a new, socially engaged practice conducted on the street rather than in the studio.

Bratkov's subjects are typically those most vulnerable in society: orphans, delinquents, pensioners, children exploited by their parents, young women seeking validation and economic survival by selling themselves. On a deeper level, his art addresses the human predicament; what often look like individual portraits are in fact images of subjection to a doubtful human exchange in which the individuals give up their identities for a collective experience. It is not the banality but the spectacle of the everyday in which Bratkov finds his voice. When he moved to Moscow in the early 2000s, finding work as a commercial photographer in a modelling agency inspired his controversial series Kids (2000). In these works the children he encountered at the agency, under pressure from their parents, wear make-up and strike provocative poses. Moving away from the individual portrait, Bratkov has increasingly made use of the panorama to document landscapes both urban and rural.

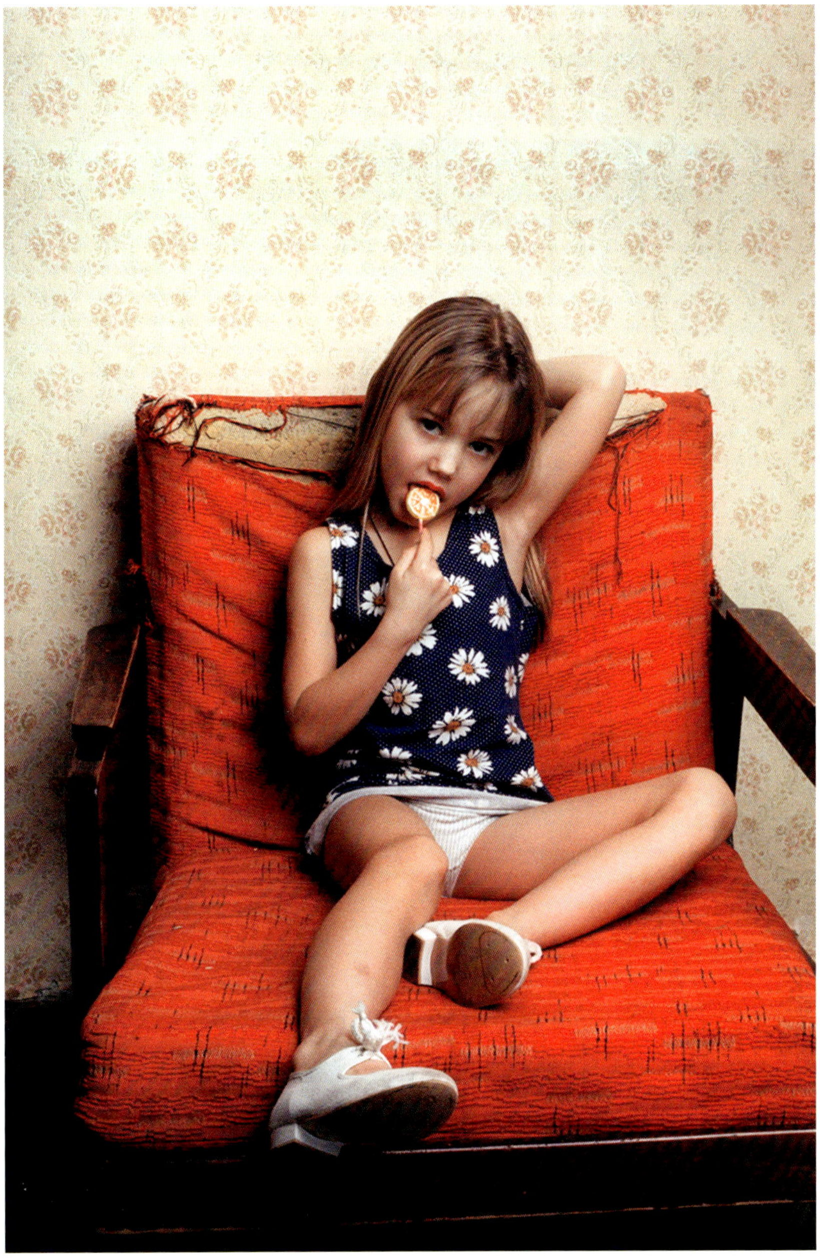

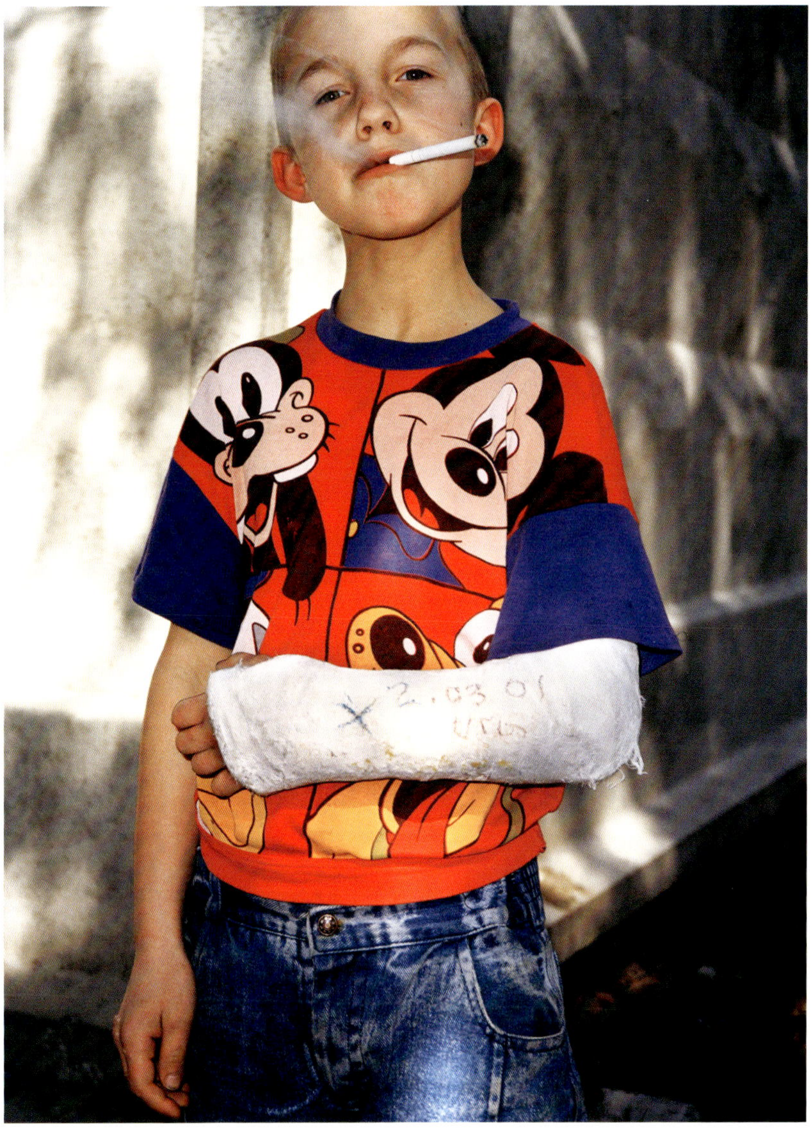

facing page above
No. 42, from the series My Moscow, 2003
C-print
28 x 72 cm
Edition of 5
© Sergei Bratkov
Courtesy Regina Gallery, London & Moscow

facing page below
Untitled, 2006
C-print
70 x 190 cm
Edition of 8 (4/8)
© Sergei Bratkov
Collection of DES

above left
Sonya, from the series Kids, 2000
C-print
40 x 27 cm
Edition of 10
© Sergei Bratkov
Courtesy Regina Gallery, London & Moscow

above
Mickey Mouse, from the series Juvenile Detention, 2001
C-print
120 x 90 cm
Edition of 10
© Sergei Bratkov
Courtesy Regina Gallery, London & Moscow

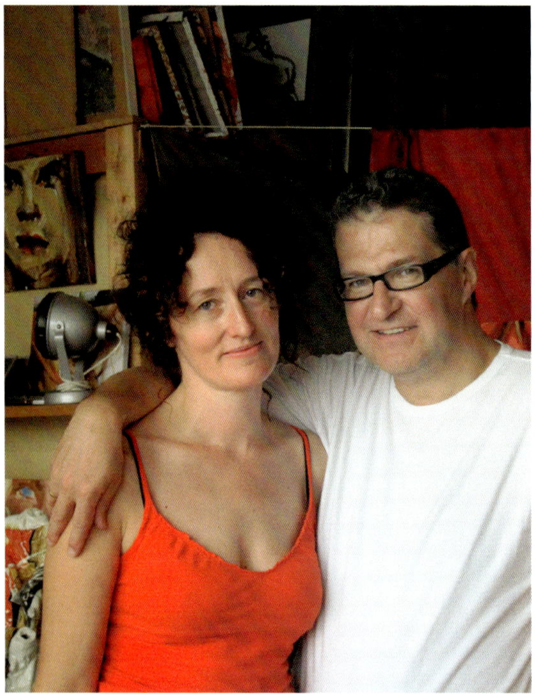

Pierre-Christian Brochet, a French entrepreneur and founder of the publishing house Avant-Garde, has been collecting Russian art since 1989. Having lived in Russia for twenty years, he has since the very beginning specialised in buying the work of young artists. Brochet has a straightforward collecting strategy: he only collects work by artists who live and work in Russia, and who are of the same generation as himself. By supporting his often struggling contemporaries in this way, the publisher of the *Petit Fute* series of travel guides (which covers some of Russia's most far-flung corners) has become a central figure on the Moscow art scene.

The son of a physicist and a schoolteacher, Brochet collected stamps as a child, moving into the visual arts in the early 1980s. His connection with Russia grew out of his father's involvement in Franco-Russian scientific détente during the 1960s. Brochet quickly became aware of the work of Ilya Kabakov, Champions of the World and other artists and groups active in the late 1980s, but at the time he could not afford to pay top prices. So he started to collect work by little-known artists instead. He also began to organise shows of contemporary art and to host lectures and seminars when it was still uncommon for Russian collectors to do so. In 2007, for example, he put together the massive exhibition *New Rules: Future Depends on You*. After opening in Moscow, the show toured many cities in Russia.

Brochet explains his commitment to contemporary work this way: 'The odd thing about collecting is that you can concentrate on a period, on a country. I think I would have collected anything; if I were living in Brazil, I would have collected Brazilian art. It's a matter of being in the country, and I happen to be here. Because of studying not only business but also philosophy, I was always interested in this concept of living in your time ... living what's going on, and being close to people who are creating the period in which you are living. I've been offered works by Corot, whatever. It was not for me.' He is a firm believer is the virtues of popularisation: 'I think very often people do exhibitions and they try to be too intellectual. That's the big point with all the curators. I'm not a curator, I'm just an art lover.' Collecting, he admits, is 'a disease. Either you are ready to spend money on art or you are not ready.' But along with the disease comes a strong sense of responsibility. 'I think seventy years of the Soviet Union just killed the idea of heritage,' Brochet laments. 'Heritage is not a question of giving to your children millions of dollars; it is giving them this awareness of the time they are living in and giving them the opportunity to make the most of it ... When you can really have deep contact with artists, with the world of art, it is the only way.'

Brochet has encouraged others to join his cause. A few years ago, he set up the Contemporary Art Collectors' Club, an association of private citizens who collect the work of Russian artists. In establishing this group, his goal was to educate the country's elite about contemporary art. Ultimately, he hopes to inspire more people to become collectors like himself.

Pierre's wife Anna was born in Moscow. Having graduated in 1988 from the Kalinin Art Academy in the capital, she went on to study Graphic Design at the Polygraphic Institute, receiving her degree in 1995. Since 2005 her work has been included in such important group exhibitions as *I Believe* (2007), the Moscow Biennale (2005 and 2007), the Art-Klyazma festival and *New Rules: Future Depends on You*. Anna Brochet paints eroticised, often nude, female portraits in oil on canvas, as well as on glass and Plexiglas, sometimes incorporating mirrors into her compositions.

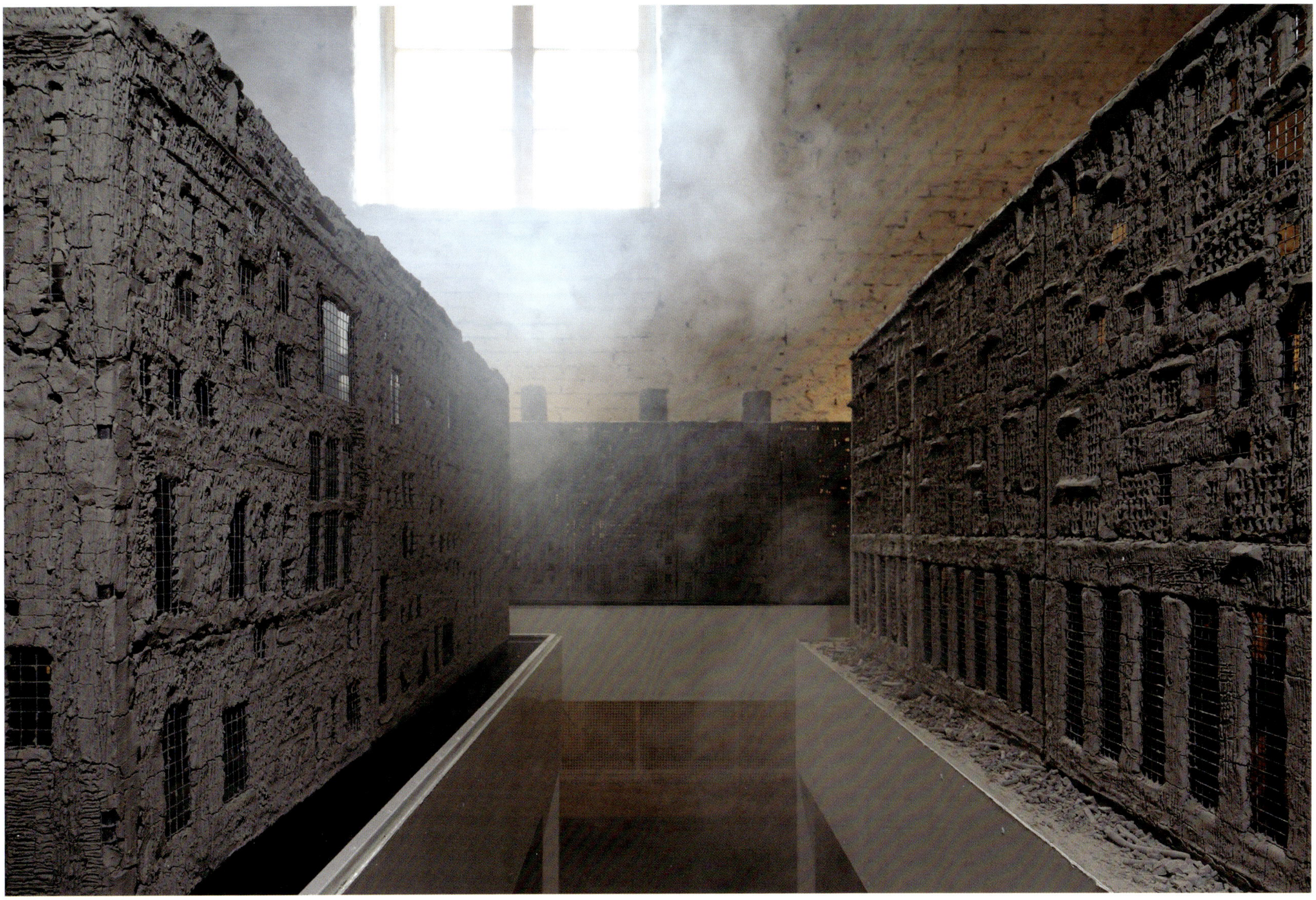

above
Windows and Factories, 2009
Installation view of *Russian Arte Povera*, project for Third Moscow Biennale of Contemporary Art, Perm Museum of Contemporary Art
© Alexander Brodsky
Courtesy of the artist and Guelman Gallery

Artist and architect Alexander Brodsky, born in Moscow in 1955, took art lessons from the age of thirteen, later training to be an architect. From 1972 to 1978 he studied at the Moscow Institute of Architecture, at the same time starting a long-term collaboration with fellow student Ilya Utkin (born 1955). This arrangement lasted until 1992, when Brodsky began to work independently. In 1985 he became a member of the Union of Architects and, from 1986, a member of the Union of Artists. In 2000 he set up his own architectural bureau in Moscow, where he lives and works today. His architectural projects have won numerous international awards; in 2001 he was named Best Artist in Europe at the Milan Triennale. He has exhibited his art projects worldwide for nearly two decades, and his work can be found in numerous public collections, including the Shusev State Architectural Museum, Moscow; the Pushkin Museum of Fine Arts, Moscow; the Institute of Contemporary Art, Boston; the Museum of Modern Art, New York; and the State Russian Museum, St Petersburg. Brodsky won the Kandinsky Prize in 2010.

During the 1980s, Brodsky was a member of the Paper Architects group, which rebelled against the State-sponsored production of low-quality prefabricated, standardised buildings. Eschewing commissions in order to create whimsical, imaginary designs for unrealisable urban structures, their practice had its origins in the utopian movement of Constructivism. Brodsky left Russia in 1996 to live in New York, where he continued to develop his artistic practice. Since returning to Moscow, he has reacted against the unregulated atmosphere of eccentric, lavish building projects which do not respect the city's environment by returning to a reliance on local materials, recycling old windows and bits of timber and glass without reprocessing them. In his art he employs raw or simple, unadorned materials: clay, plaster and glass.

Brodsky's artistic and architectural practices are closely related and blur the boundaries between them. In his art he explores the deep emotional ties between humans and their environment. His man-made urban constructions are metaphors of the past, signs of lives lived and abandoned. These works are far from his idealistic paper constructions of the 1980s. In one of the most moving ones, *Night before the Attack* (2009), hundreds of small plaster figures sit around little lights imitating campfires; in the morning they will go into battle and die. Such works serve as reminders of mortality; the dwellings and lights appear warm and comforting, but the refuge they offer is temporary.

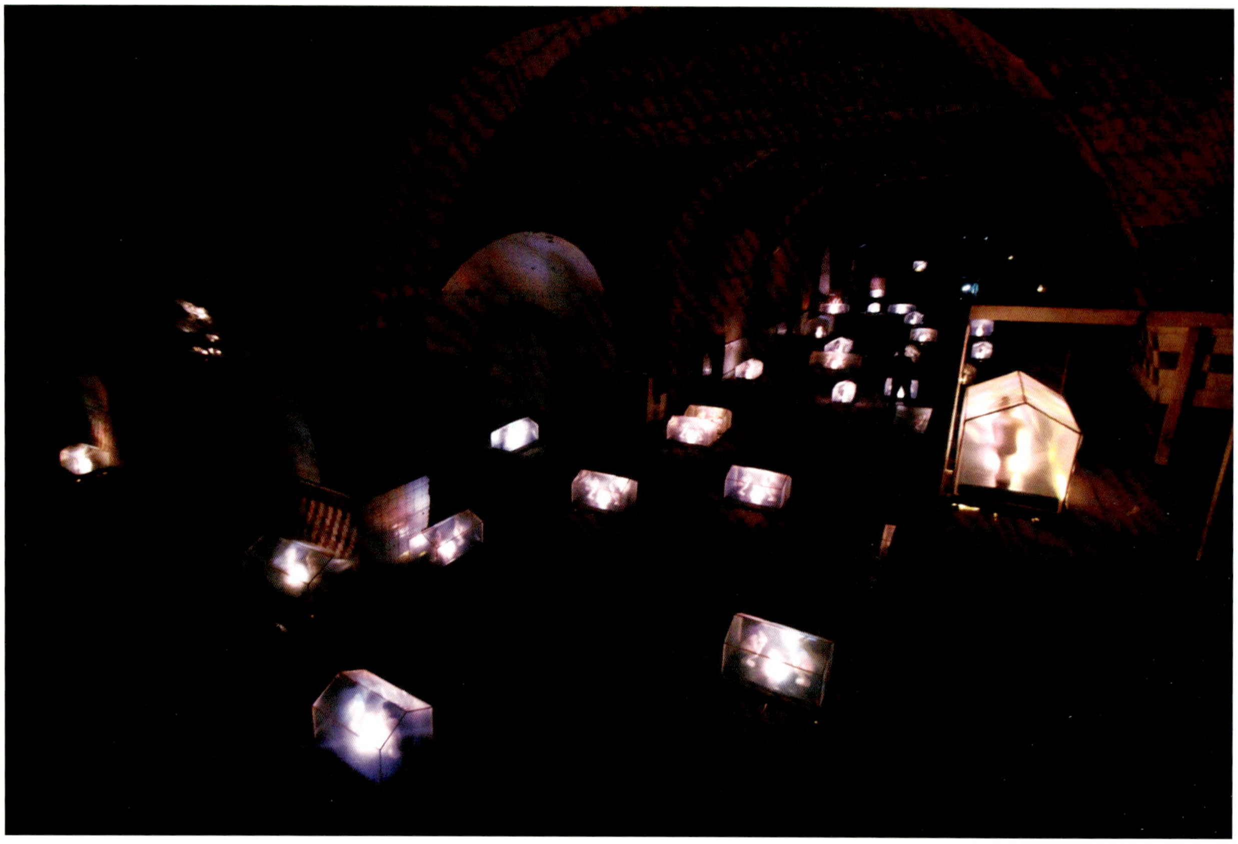

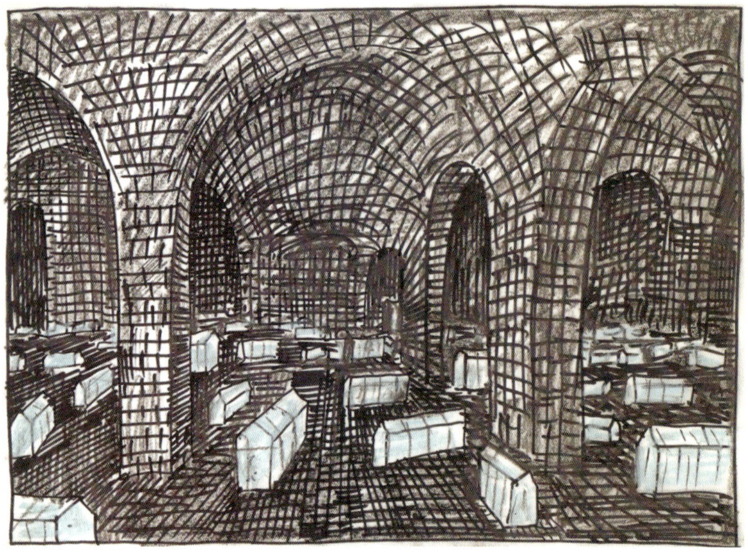

top
Night before the Attack, 2009
Installation view from the Third Moscow
Biennale of Contemporary Art Parallel Project
© Alexander Brodsky
Courtesy of the artist and Guelman Gallery

above
Night before the Attack
(installation sketch), 2009
Biro on paper
Dimensions unknown
© Alexander Brodsky
Courtesy of the artist and Guelman Gallery

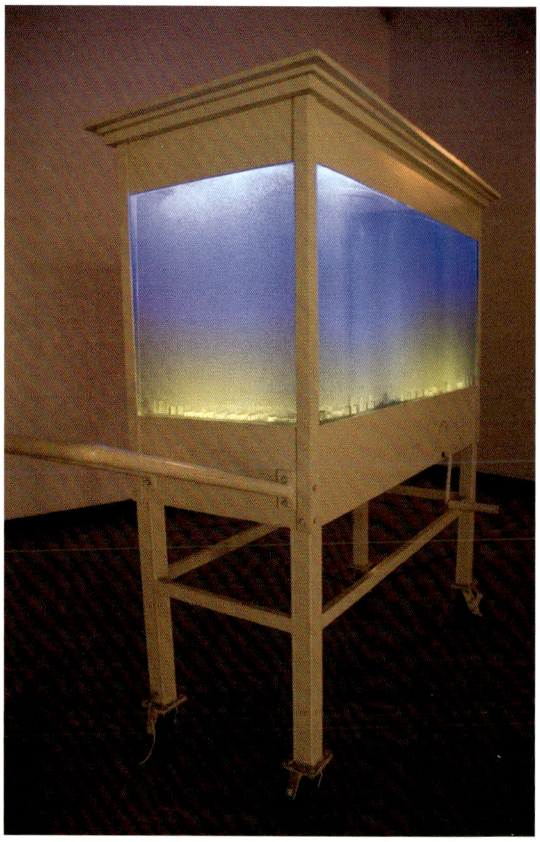

right
Part of the installation
Inhabited Localities, 2009
Mixed media
60 x 150 x 80 cm
10th International Architecture Exhibition,
Russian Pavilion, Venice Biennale, 2009
© Alexander Brodsky
Collection of Perm Museum
of Contemporary Art
Courtesy of the artist and Guelman Gallery

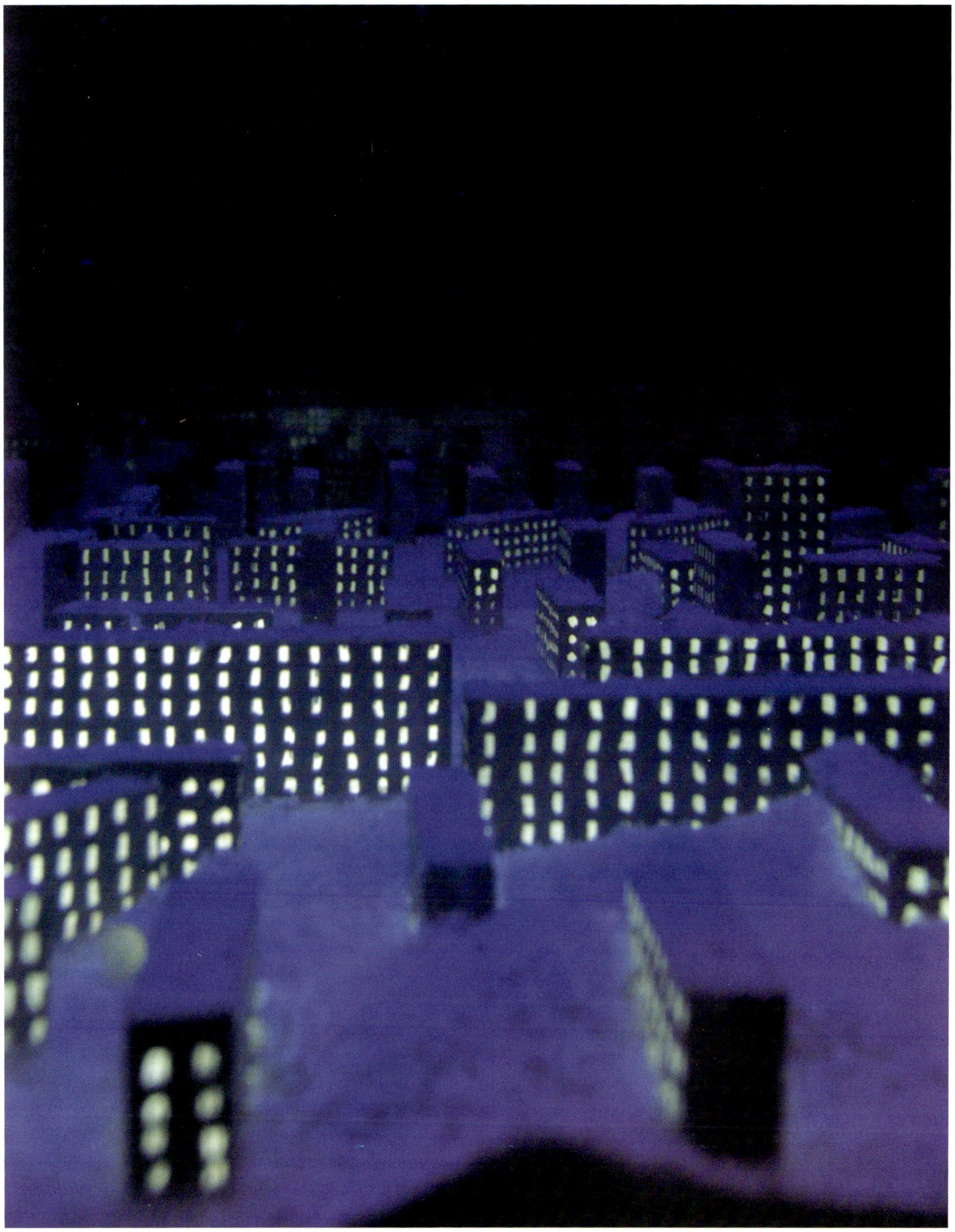

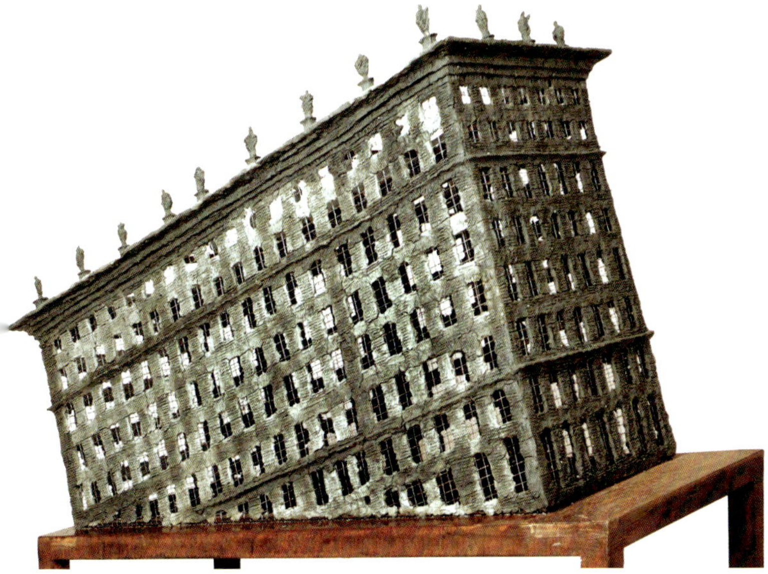

above
The Penultimate Day of Pompeii
(part of the installation Turnoff Points), 1997
Clay, video projection
170 x 60 x 80 cm

Courtesy of the artist and Guelman Gallery

left
Part of the installation
Inhabited Localities, 2009
Mixed media
60 x 150 x 80 cm
10th International Architecture Exhibition,
Russian Pavilion, Venice, 2009

Collection of Perm Museum
of Contemporary Art
Courtesy of the artist and Guelman Gallery

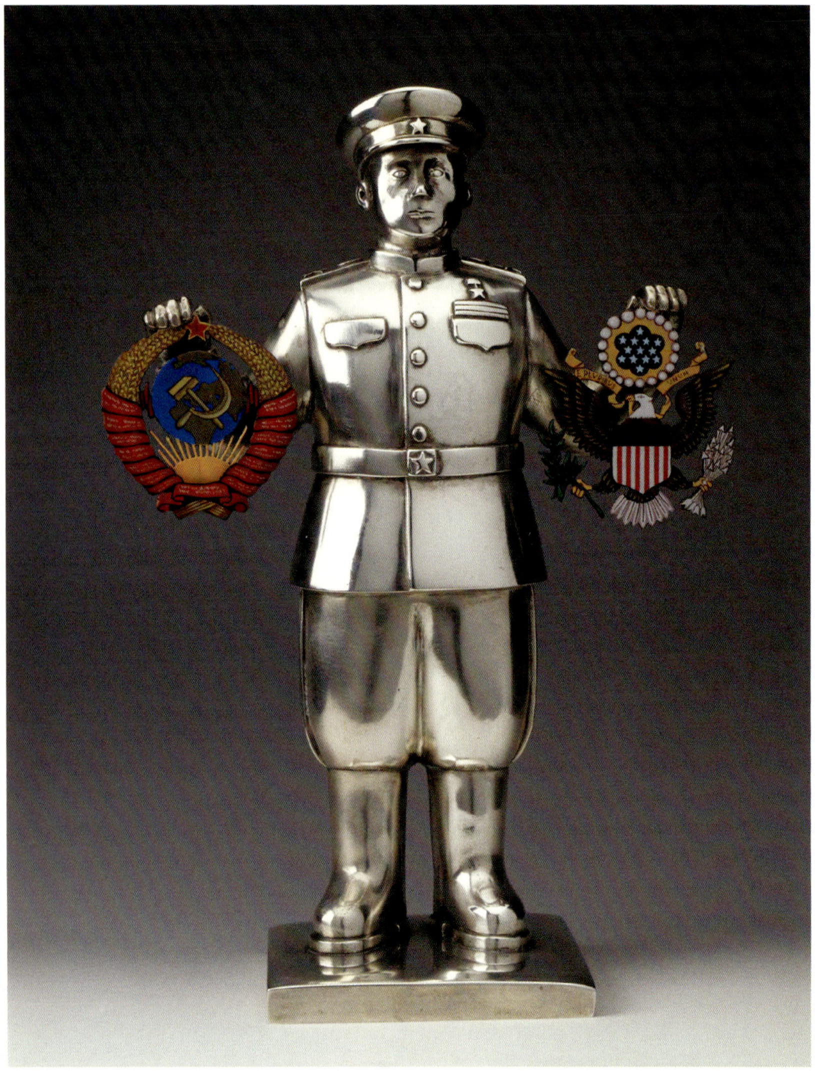

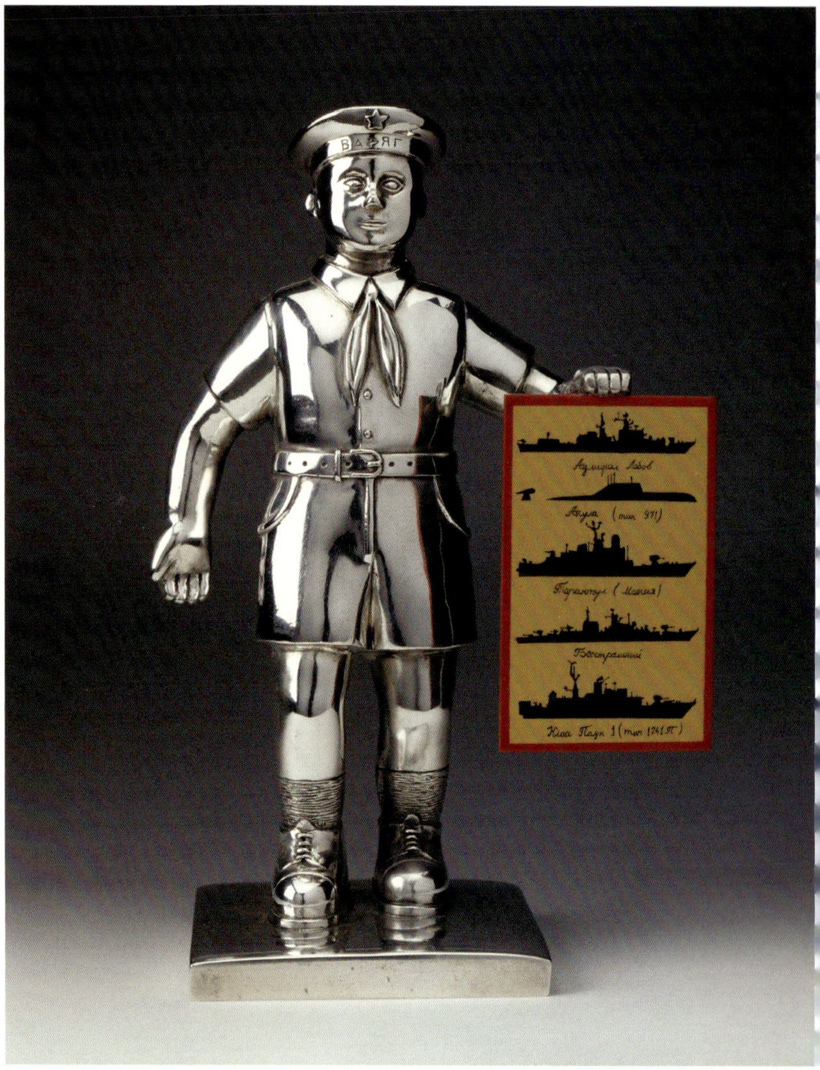

Grisha Bruskin, born in Moscow in 1945, divides his time between New York and Moscow. He exhibited in Soviet underground circles from the late 1960s, achieved sudden notoriety in Sotheby's Contemporary Russian Art auction in Moscow in 1988 and then emigrated to New York the following year. There he started to exhibit with the Marlborough Gallery, sparking off a twenty-year collaboration. Bruskin's work was shown in the Guggenheim Museum's *Russia!* exhibition (2005) and is found in collections both in Russia and abroad, including the State Tretyakov Gallery, Moscow; the Art Institute of Chicago; and the Ludwig Museum, Cologne. Focusing on identity, memory and the need to make sense of the present, his art explores the relationship between self and society, using an iconography that combines Soviet and Jewish imagery. His work is closely connected with Sots Art through its use of official symbols, although it does not share Sots Art's sharp irony and humour; Bruskin's focus is rather on building a personal mythology.

Bruskin works in diverse media, including painting, graphics, sculpture, porcelain, tapestry and performance. Pre-perestroika works typically comprise archetypal Soviet or Jewish figures organised in large groups. The Soviet types in *Fundamental Lexicon* (1986) include Pioneers, heroes of labour, frontier guards and cosmonauts, each figure holding an attribute of his trade. The Alfabet series (1984) shows figures wearing religious dress against a background of illegible Hasidic text. The artist has emphasised that individual figures in these large compositions must be seen as merging with the others to create a community or coherent body.

Bruskin's artwork can be read as a narrative of the breakdown of the Soviet Union and its changing values. Cataloguing and ordering experience, it has shifted from observing the present from outside of Soviet official culture to observing the past through the eyes of the future. His art has become an exploration of memory and the attempt to make sense out of the end of the Soviet era. In his performance *Twilight of the Gods* (2009) he created plaster sculptures of Soviet types from the past, then buried them in the ground before digging them up again. Bruskin likened this process to driving into the future and imagining civilisations coming across cultural artefacts from the Soviet Union: 'I want someone else to see the ruins of this civilisation, the civilisation which I lived in through the eyes of someone in the future.'

above left
General with Insignia of USSR and USA, from the series Life Is Everywhere, 1999
Silver and enamel
23.5 cm (h)
© Grisha Bruskin
Collection of Peter Aven

above
Pioneer with a Scheme of Warships, from the series Life Is Everywhere, 1999
Silver and enamel
20.5 cm (approx. h)
© Grisha Bruskin
Collection of Peter Aven

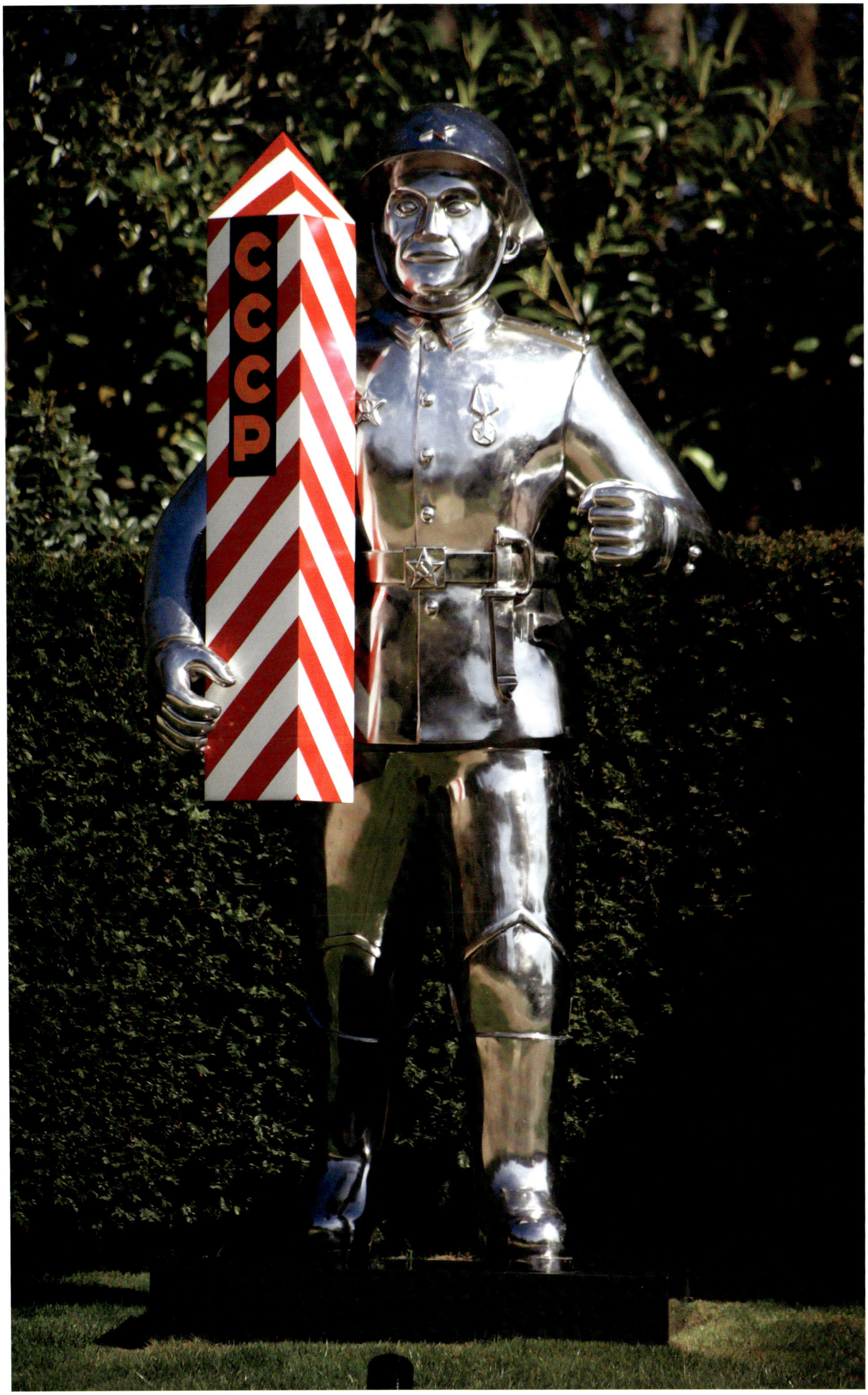

right
Soldier with Boundary Post, 1990
Stainless steel
94.3 x 99.1 x 87.6 cm
© Oliver Bampfylde
Courtesy of Peter Aven

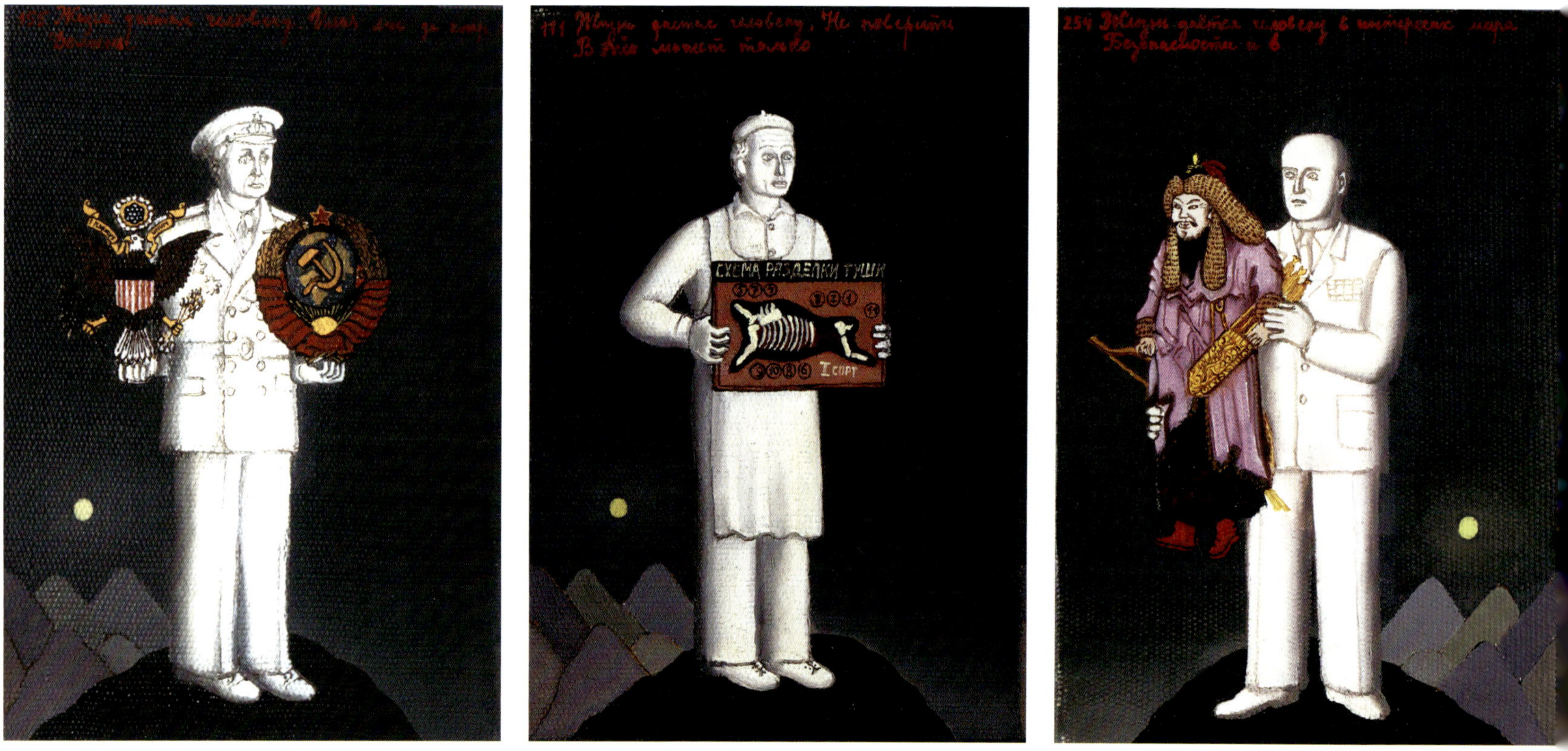

above
Fundamental Lexicon, Part 2, 1985 (details)
Oil on linen
220 x 304 cm
© Grisha Bruskin
Private collection, Germany
Courtesy of the artist

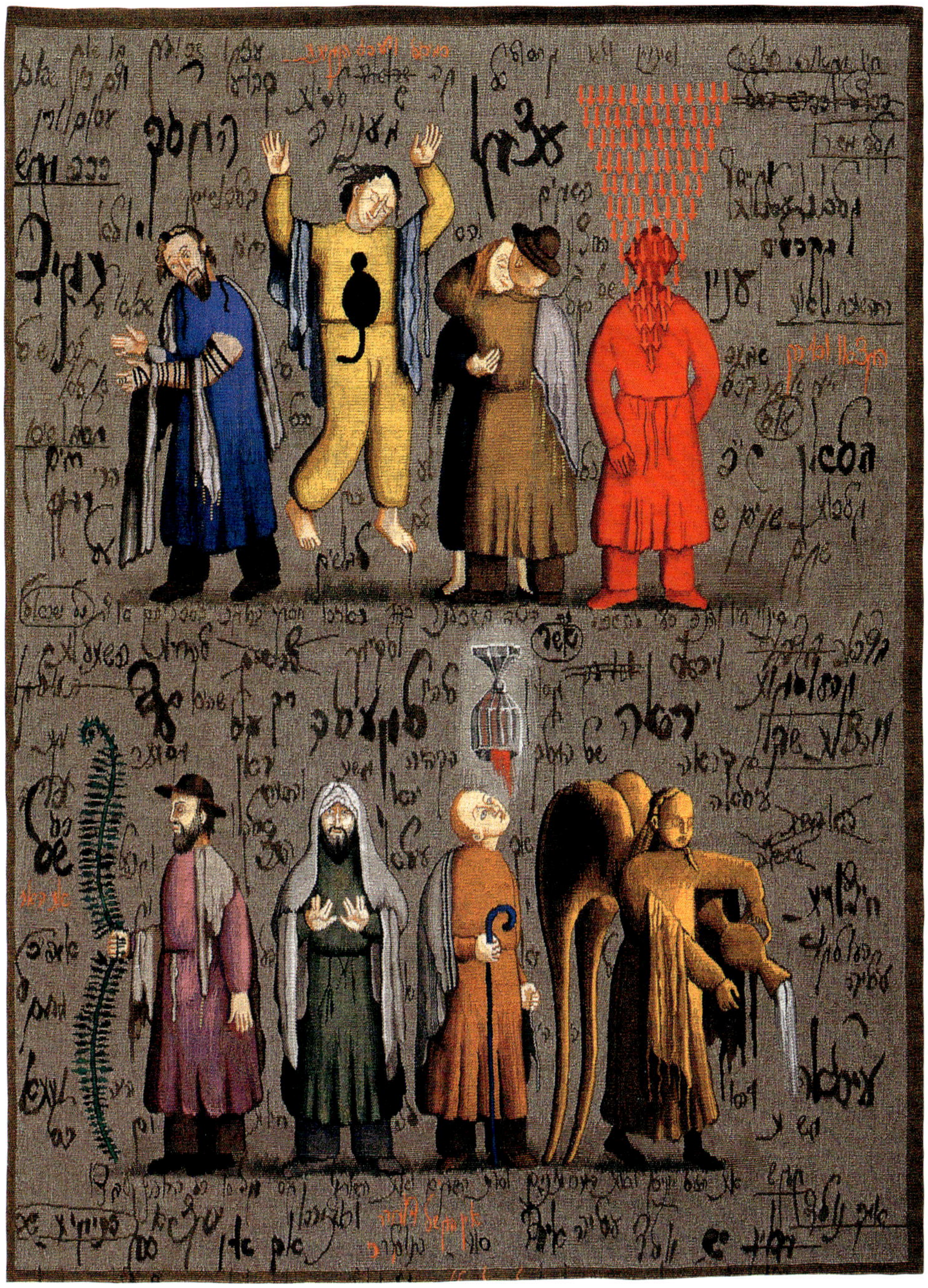

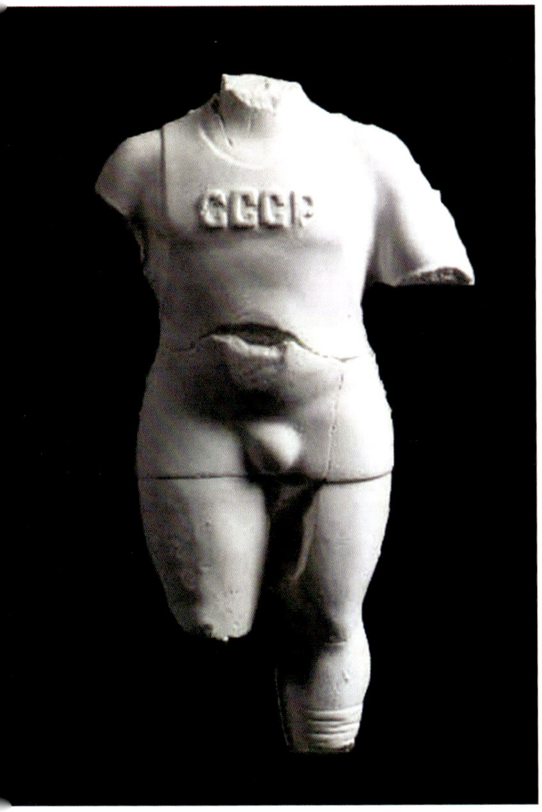

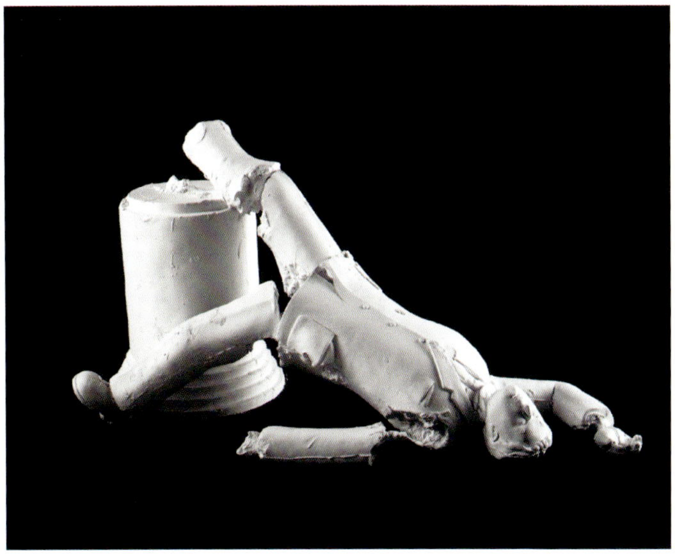

above
Alefbet, 2004–6 (detail)
Wool, silk and linen
208 x 105 cm
© Grisha Bruskin
Courtesy of the artist

far left
Athlete, from the series Archeologist's Collection, 2001–3 (detail)
Painted bronze
15.2 x 91.4 cm
© Grisha Bruskin
Courtesy of the artist

left
Collapse, from the series On the Edge, 2001–3
Painted bronze
48 x 92 x 50 cm
© Grisha Bruskin
Courtesy of the artist

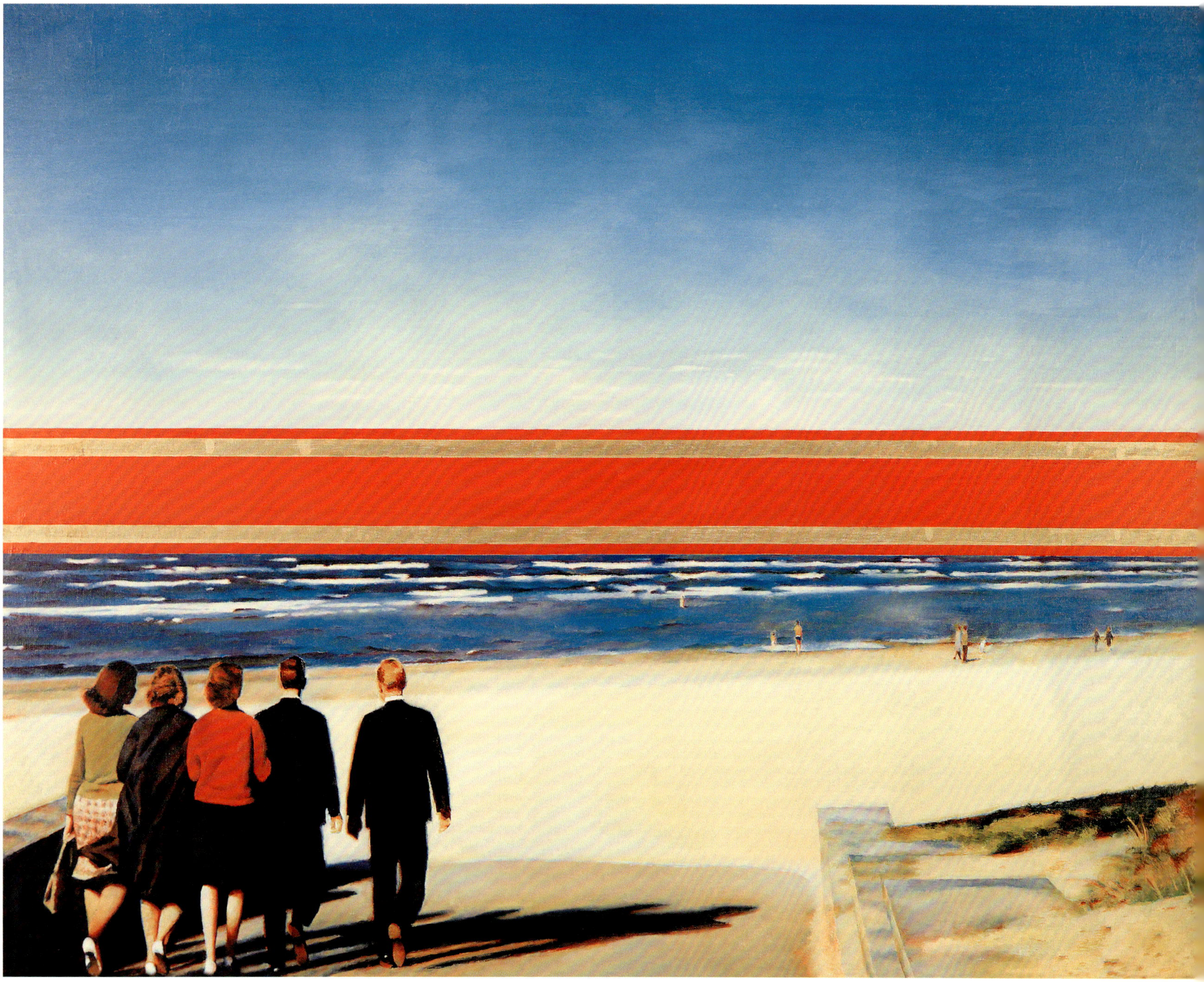

Born in Sverdlovsk in 1933, Eric Bulatov graduated from the Surikov Institute in Moscow, where he was schooled in Soviet realist academicism, in 1958. Like many of his contemporaries, he supported himself as an illustrator of children's books, often working in the company of his friends Oleg Vassiliev and Ilya Kabakov. His idiosyncratic style uses the visual codes and slogans of Soviet art, politics and daily life to explore pictorial and social spaces. In his own words, 'The elements of pictorial space and its ability to transform flatness into space, and space into flatness – this mutual transformation – remain the basis of all my works.' Bulatov, who moved to New York in 1990, has lived and worked in Paris since 1991.

Bulatov's paintings are often characterised by tension between 'a level of social reality, and one of existential reality ... The problem of freedom is exactly the problem of transition from social to existential space'. Using visual tropes and Soviet slogans, the artist aims to express the social context in which he finds himself, and to present the existential freedom that lies beyond the social spectrum. He stresses the sense of movement that arises from the push and pull between the elements in his work: 'It is always very important to me that the image does not function as an illustration of some narrative content ... it is important that the text, the word, functions primarily as a visual form ... My words, as a whole, are always in motion.'

Do Not Lean (1987), a conceptual game between text and painting's creation of spatial illusion, shows a familiar railway sign forbidding leaning against train doors within a landscape with a forest as its backdrop. *Glory to the KPSS* (1975) appropriates a Party slogan and presents it as a vivid red barrier blocking out the blue sky. Playing with notions of the barrier, social prohibition and exaggerated perspective, Bulatov makes a concerted, innovative effort to include the viewer in his field of vision. As he has said, 'Painting consists of three elements: pictorial space ... surface ... and flatness, and on the other side of this flatness, the viewer's own space. I try to include the spectator's space in the pictorial one. From my point of view, this hasn't been done before.' His paintings function as glimmers of openness and freedom beyond social codes and conventions, whether Soviet or Western.

above
Horizon, 1971–2
Oil on canvas
150 x 180 cm
© Eric Bulatov
Courtesy of the Museum of Avant-Garde Mastery (MAGMA)

facing page
Perestroika, 1989
Oil on canvas
270 x 273.5 cm
© Eric Bulatov
Courtesy of Phillips de Pury

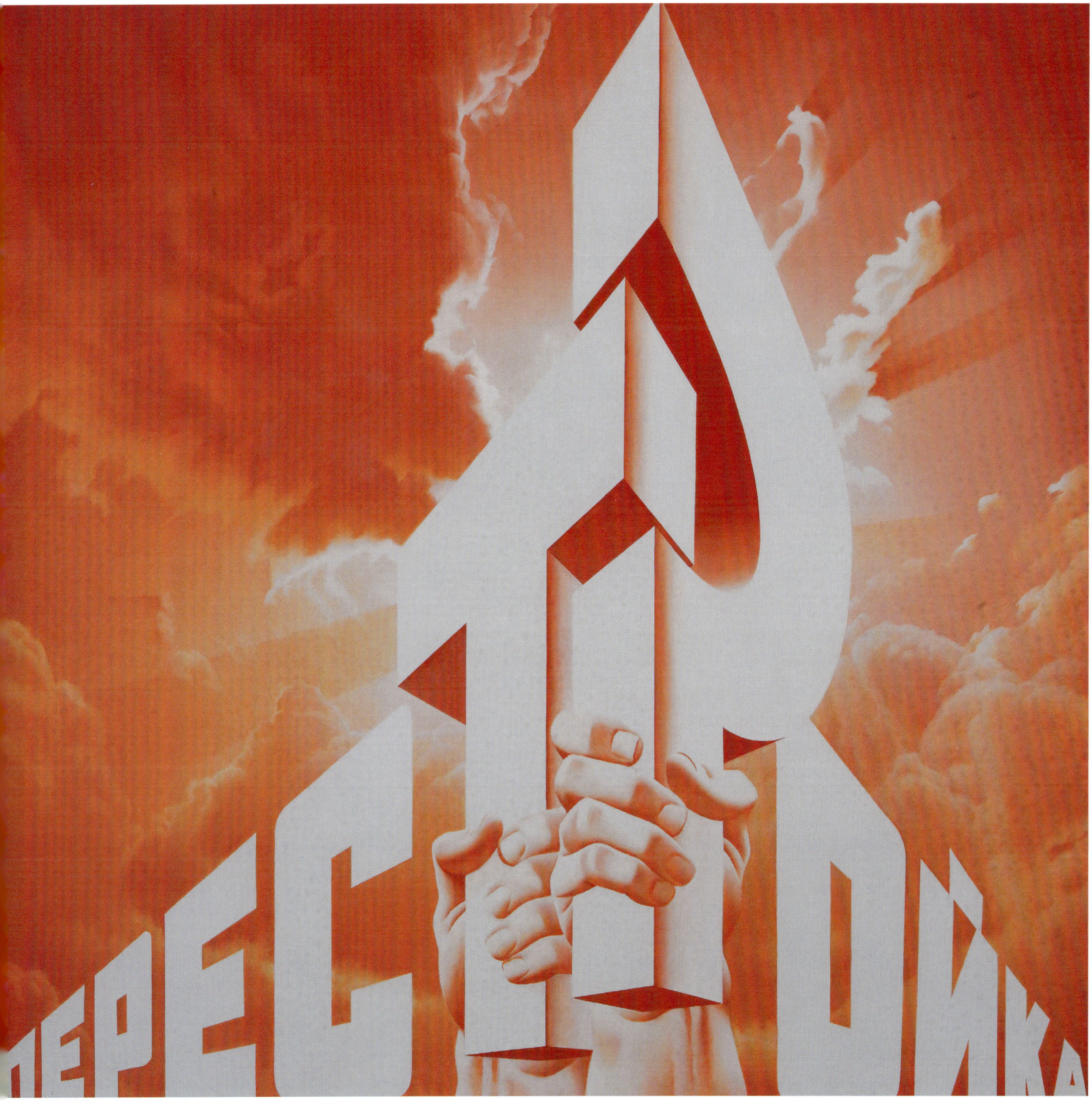
ПЕРЕСТРОЙКА

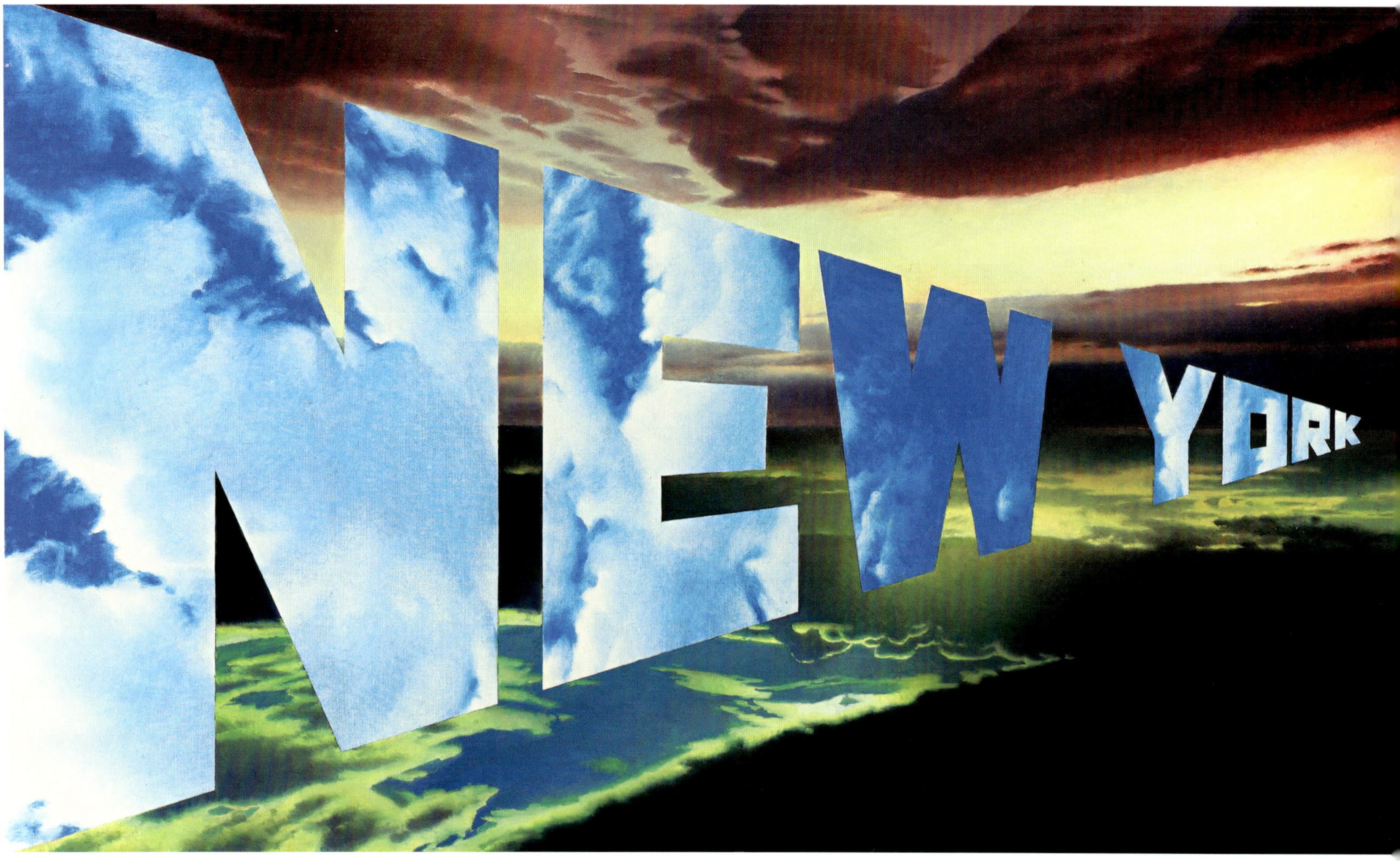
NEW YORK

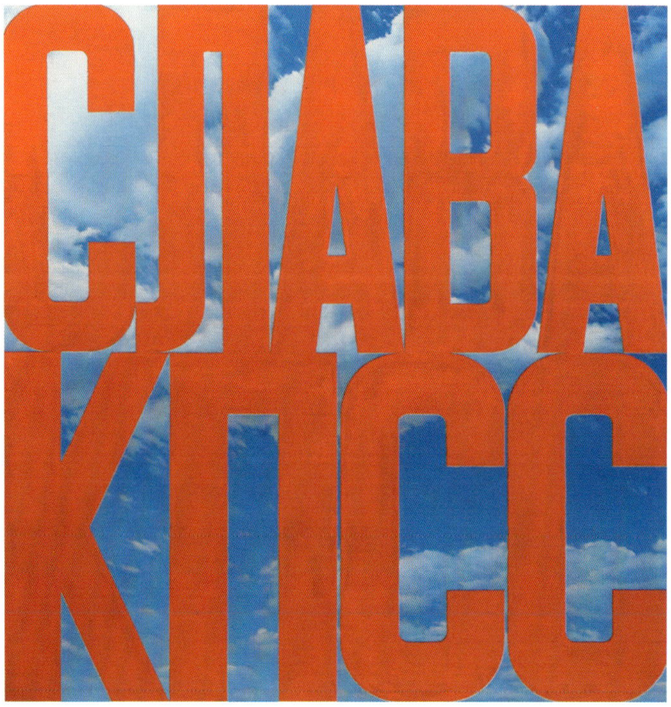
СЛАВА
КПСС

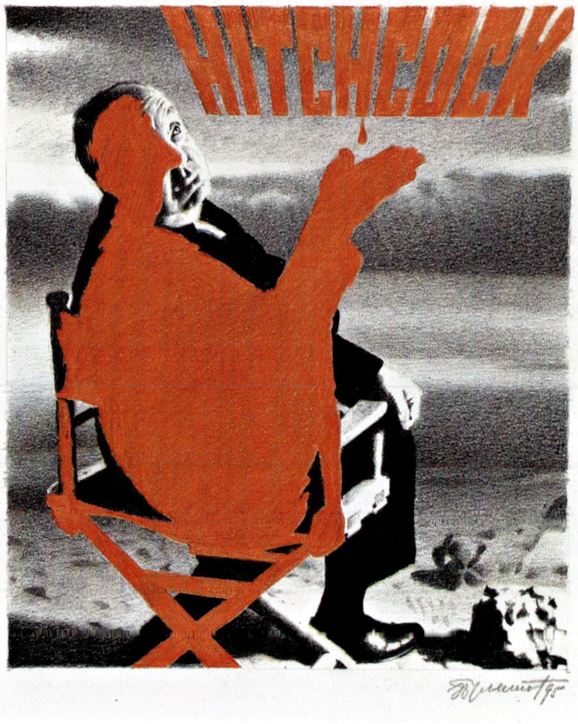
HITCHCOCK

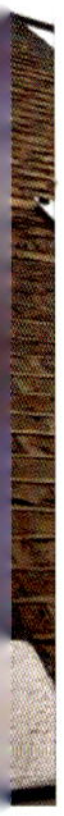

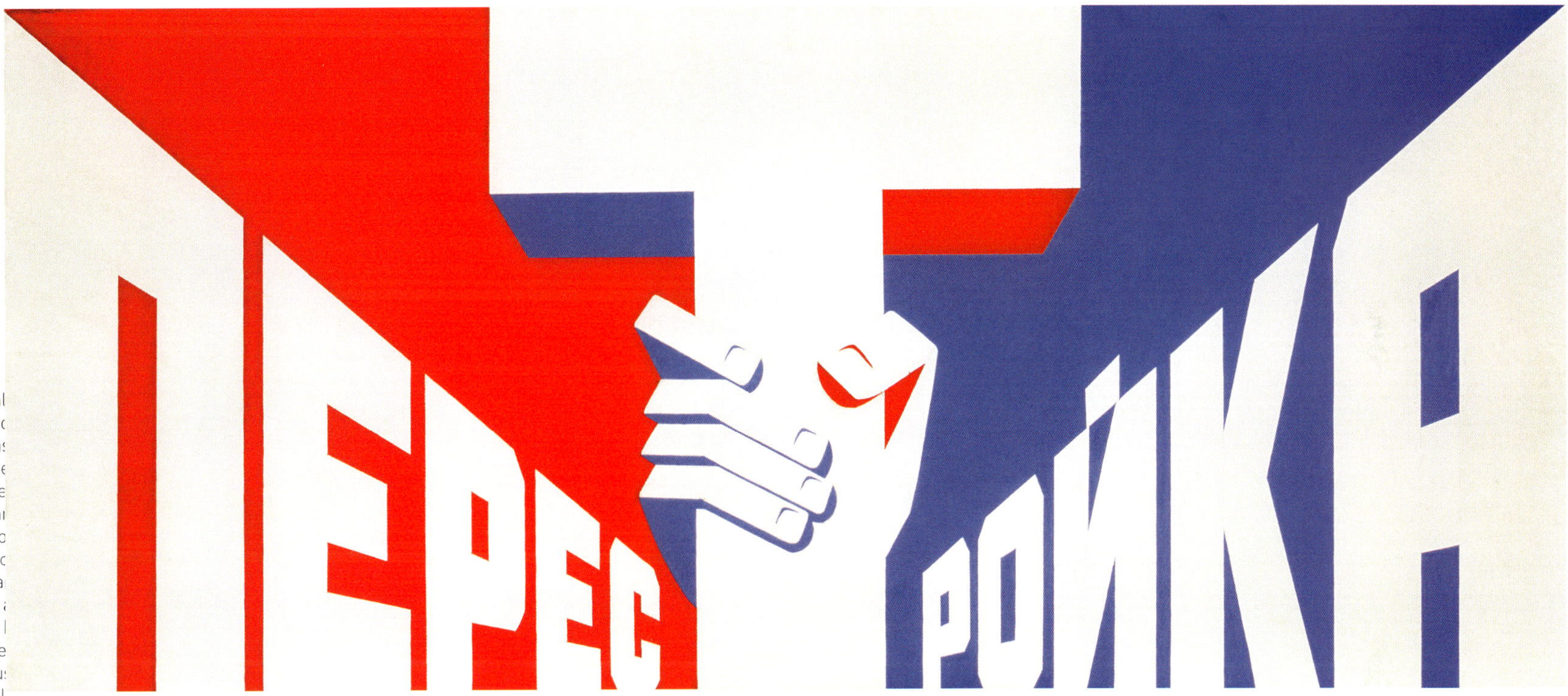

Cal
dec
Eas
ope
are
imi
gro
occ
wa
by
by
the
Ru
bel
cor
pla
I
Uni
Ler
fro

facing page top
New York, 1989
Oil on canvas
105.9 x 177.8 cm
© Eric Bulatov
Courtesy of Sotheby's

facing page far left
Glory to the CPSU II, 2003–5
Copy of the 1975 original painted by the artist
200 x 200 cm
© Eric Bulatov
Courtesy of the Ekaterina and Vladimir Semenikhin Collection

facing page left
Hitchcock, 1995
Coloured pencil on paper
25.7 x 22.9 cm
© Eric Bulatov
Courtesy of Sotheby's

above
Perestroika, 1989
Oil on canvas
89.5 x 210 cm
© Eric Bulatov
Courtesy of Alex Lachmann

following page
Do Not Lean, 1987
Oil on canvas
240 x 169.9 cm
© Eric Bulatov
Courtesy of the Museum of Avant-Garde Mastery (MAGMA)

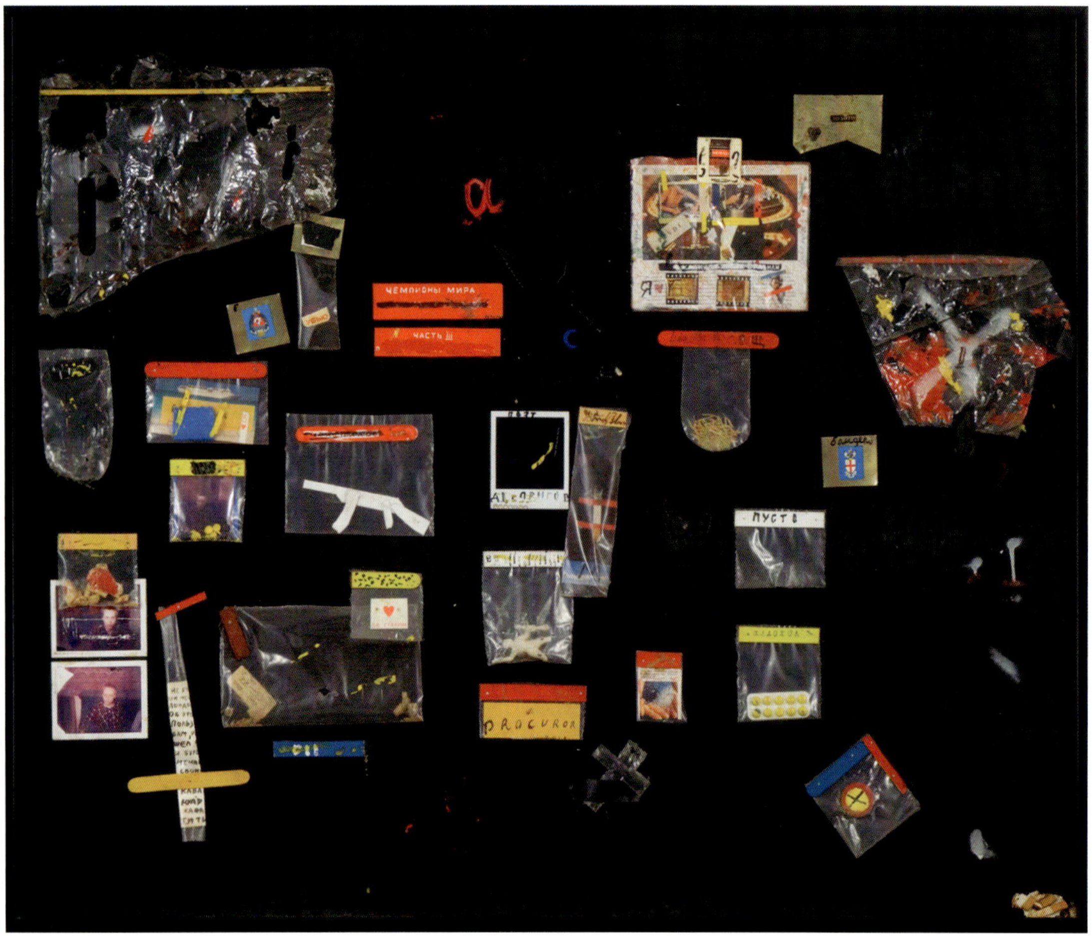

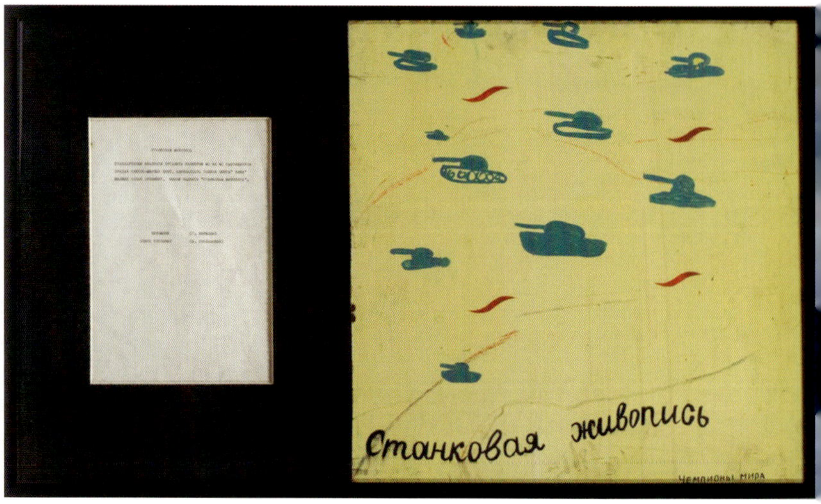

Champions of the World (Gia Abramishvili, Konstantin Latyshev, Boris Matrosov, Igor Vishnyakov, Andrei Yakhnin and Konstantin Zvezdochetov) was a short-lived group active on Moscow's unofficial art scene between 1986 and 1988. The group began as a few friends writing poems together after school and distributing 'angry pamphlets against the school administration'. The band of schoolboys became acquainted with contemporary art through a teacher who was a friend of the Toadstool group and also through *A-Ya*, a journal that circulated in Moscow in the early 1980s.

Like the Toadstools before them, Champions of the World drew no boundary between art and life, and their actions often resembled outright hooliganism. Their neo-Dadaist pranks included picking fights, slitting their wrists, setting fires, dunking their heads in hot soup and playing with homemade explosives. In the more traditional realm, they also made drawings, paintings and works on paper, writing rhapsodic texts to accompany their bizarre actions. Their irreverent attitude ignored customary distinctions between genres and the boundaries of individual authorship, and their works are often decorative, crude or intentionally naïve. Occupying the margins of culture, they saw themselves as 'wandering kamikazes' who, having been sent on a suicide mission, discovered that the war had already been won. With no landing instructions, they assumed a sensibility of perpetual movement and irrational play.

The group first exhibited in the *Art against Commerce* exhibition in Moscow's Bitsa Park in 1986, subsequently showing with the Avantgardist Club, an exhibiting association of artists loosely affiliated with Moscow Conceptualism and the New Wave. Like many other perestroika-era groupings, Champions of the World's collaboration was fleeting, its members going on to develop their own styles and pursue solo careers.

top
Quickwrapped, 1988
Fibreboard, paper, newspaper, magazine clippings, oil, wood, polythene, plastic, Polaroids, cigarette butts, pills, stale bread
100 x 122 cm
© Champions of the World
Courtesy of Pierre-Christian Brochet Collection

above
Easel Painting, 1987
Oil on fibreboard, paper, typescript
51 x 88 cm
© Champions of the World
Courtesy of Pierre-Christian Brochet Collection

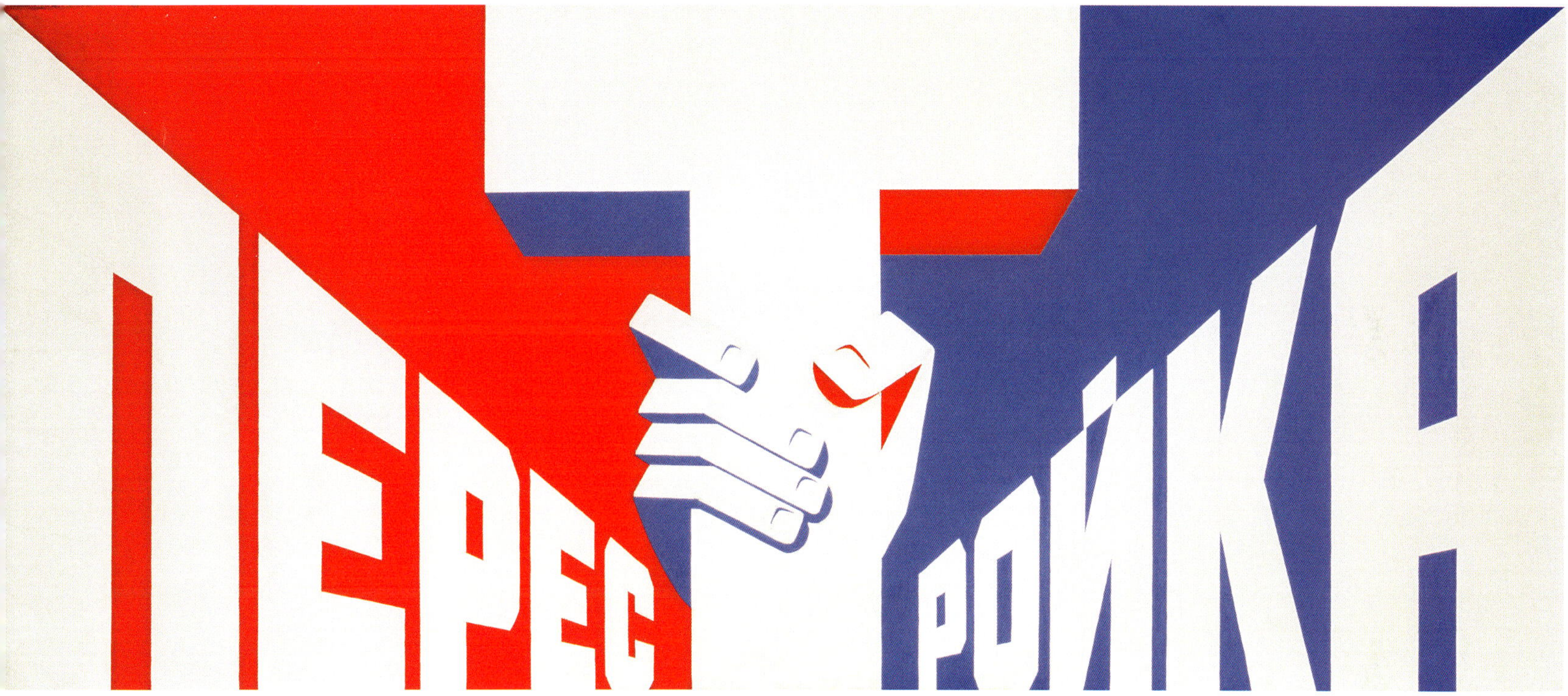

'acing page top
New York, 1989
Oil on canvas
05.9 x 177.8 cm
© Eric Bulatov
Courtesy of Sotheby's

'acing page far left
Glory to the CPSU II, 2003–5
Copy of the 1975 original painted by the artist
200 x 200 cm
© Eric Bulatov
Courtesy of the Ekaterina and Vladimir
Semenikhin Collection

'acing page left
Hitchcock, 1995
Coloured pencil on paper
25.7 x 22.9 cm
© Eric Bulatov
Courtesy of Sotheby's

above
Perestroika, 1989
Oil on canvas
89.5 x 210 cm
© Eric Bulatov
Courtesy of Alex Lachmann

following page
Do Not Lean, 1987
Oil on canvas
240 x 169.9 cm
© Eric Bulatov
Courtesy of the Museum of Avant-Garde
Mastery (MAGMA)

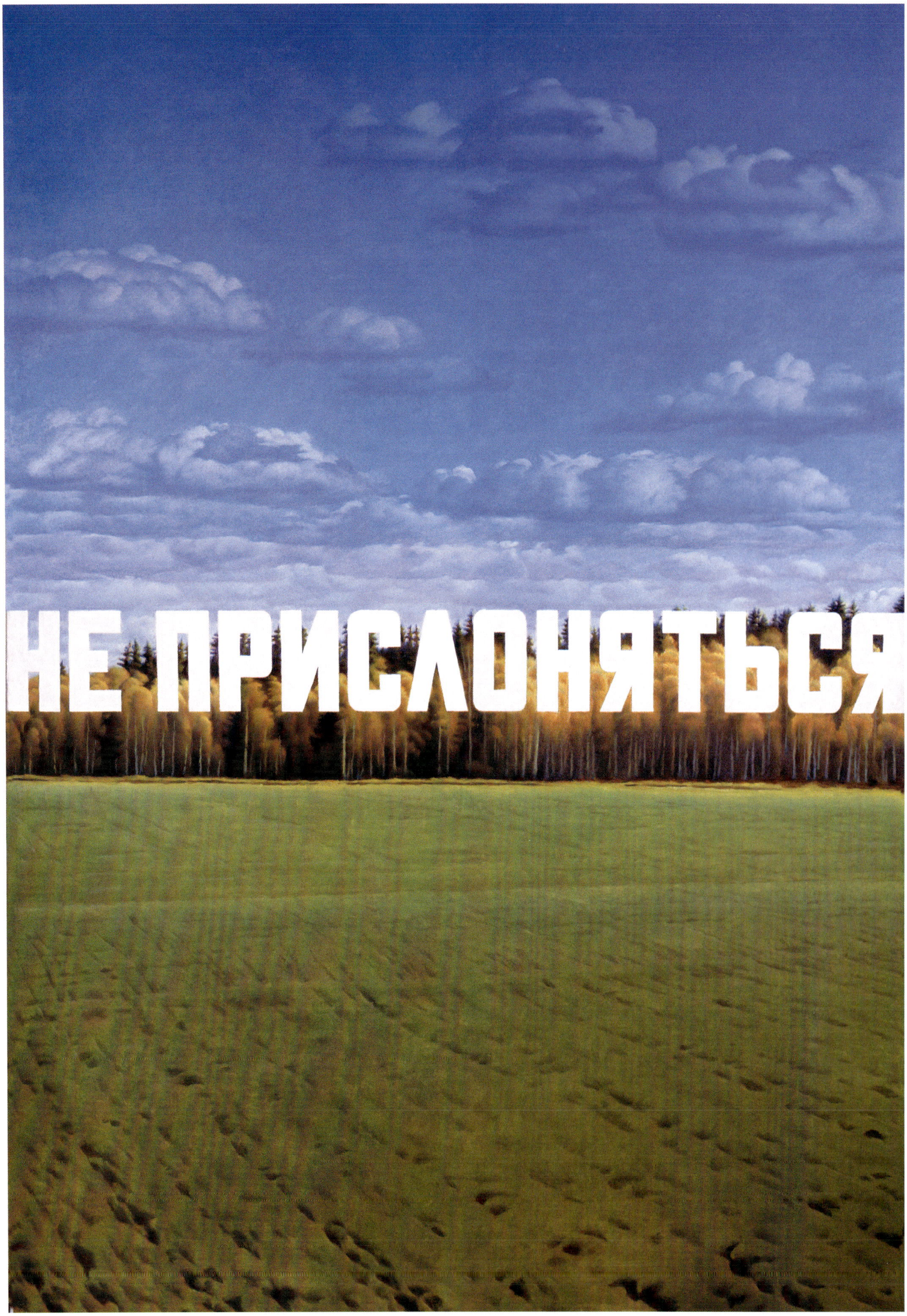
НЕ ПРИСЛОНЯТЬСЯ

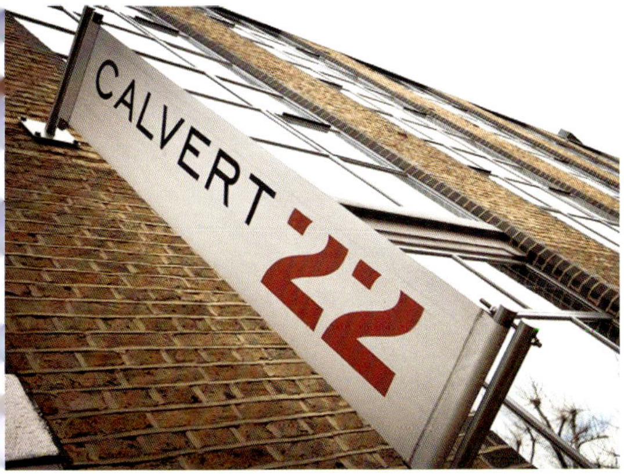

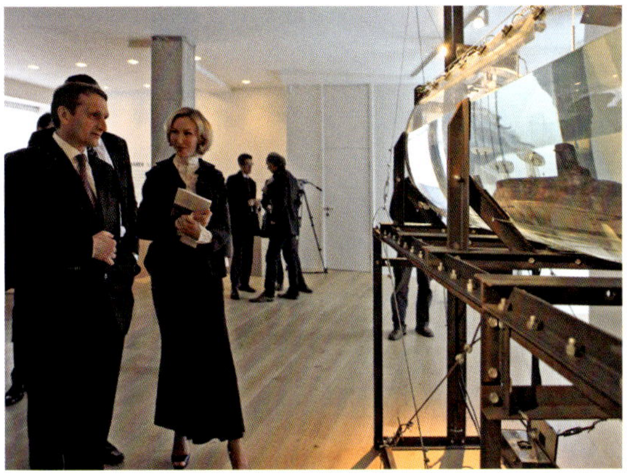

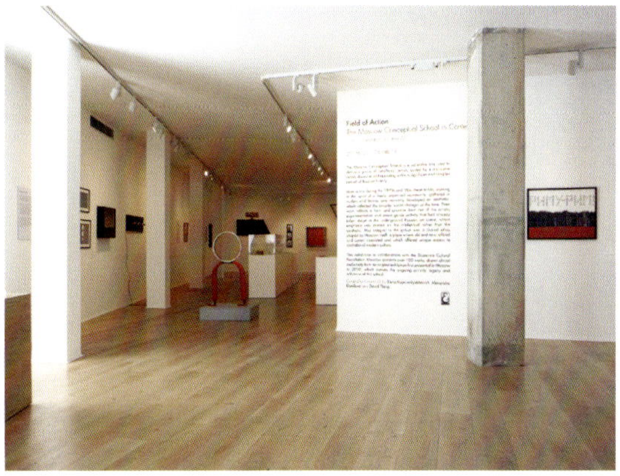

Calvert 22 is a not-for-profit exhibition space dedicated to the promotion of Russian and Eastern European contemporary culture. It opened in 2007 in Shoreditch, London, an area with strong links to Eastern European immigration and today the home of a vibrant, growing contemporary art scene. The gallery occupies a bright, 465-square-metre former warehouse over two floors. Originally designed by architect Sue Minter, it was later developed by Fielden Fowles. The space was funded by the arts philanthropist Nonna Materkova, a Russian-born English-speaking economist who believes that Russian and Eastern European contemporary art needs an international platform to bring it into the cultural mainstream.

Materkova, who graduated from the University of Economics and Finance in Leningrad in 1987, later won a scholarship from the British Council to study at the London School of Economics. She also won a prize during the Yeltsin years as a young leader of Russian businesswomen. The founder-director of Roslink, a London-based corporate-finance consultancy, she keeps business and art completely separate. Despite an interest in the financial side of the art market, she did not want to become a dealer or commercial gallerist herself, and she is not a collector. All of her energies are channelled into her space.

Materkova's interest in art has its origin in her childhood in St Petersburg: 'In the early days I was more interested in the Old Masters. Every child in Leningrad was playing the piano and going to the Hermitage; it gave me a great grounding in culture.' Having gone to London and done a Contemporary Art course at Sotheby's Institute, she recalls a life-changing moment: 'One day we were talking about emerging markets and the tutor said that there was no market for Russian contemporary art. I could see that there was great art; I personally knew many talented artists; I knew galleries in St Petersburg. I was sure this would change, that the market would grow, and it gave me a push to get involved and try to change perceptions.' She sees contemporary culture as a global language spoken by young, creative people.

Calvert 22's exhibitions programme is broad, including solo exhibitions featuring talented, up-and-coming personalities such as video artist and photographer Olga Chernysheva and the Conceptualist Alexander Ponomarov, as well as group shows curated by Western and Russian art historians; one example is *Past Future Perfect* (2009), curated by David Thorp. More recently, Calvert 22 staged a major retrospective of Moscow Conceptualism entitled *Field of Action* (2011), first shown at the Ekaterina Cultural Foundation, Moscow. This show brought major Russian works of the 1980s to the attention of an international audience for the first time. Educational programmes are another important part of the gallery's ethos, with talks, discussions and a growing on-site specialist library.

Materkova has numerous plans to expand Calvert 22's original brief. On the lookout for new international partners, she has plans for a more multidisciplinary focus. While visual art will remain at the core of Calvert 22's activities, they will also feature fashion as well as musical performances from Eastern Europe and Russia. Fired by vision and energy, and with the help of her new in-house curatorial team, Materkova aspires to create an institution with the scope and credibility of London's Whitechapel and Serpentine galleries.

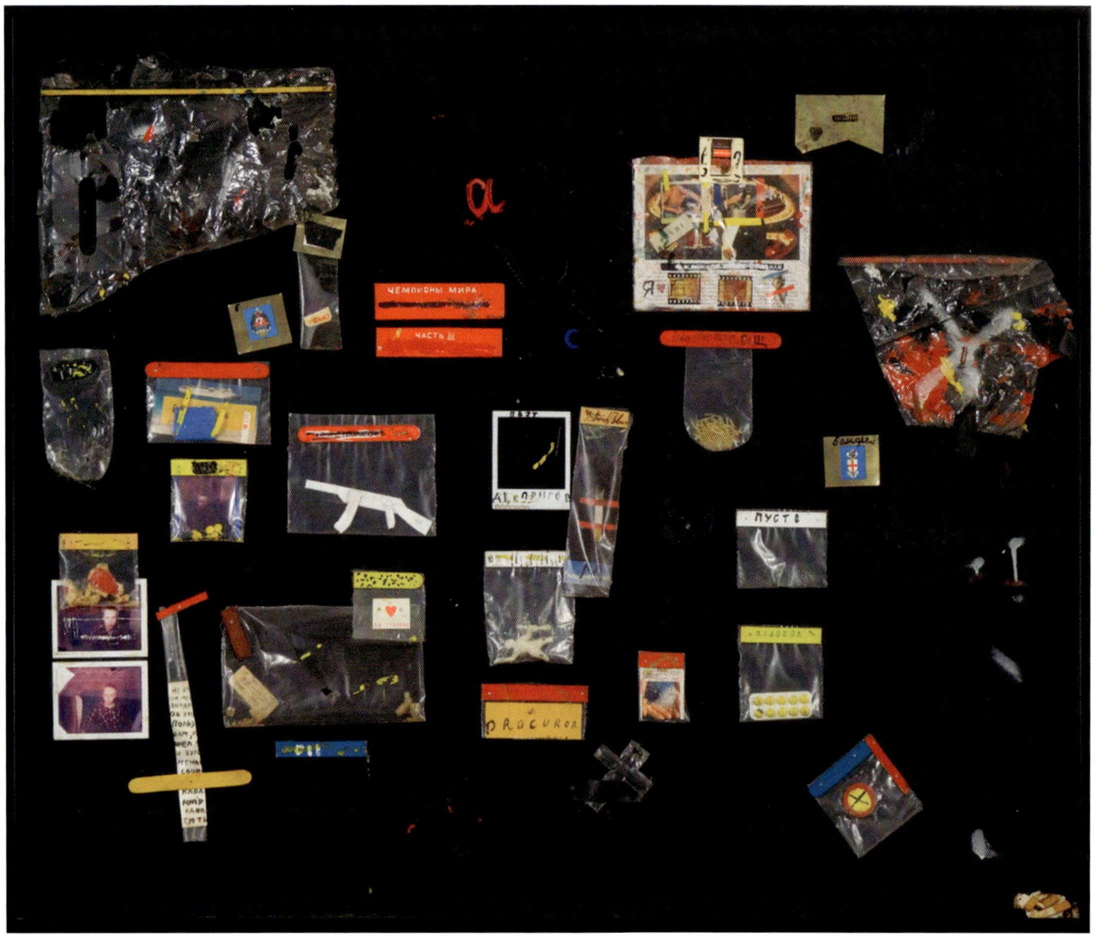

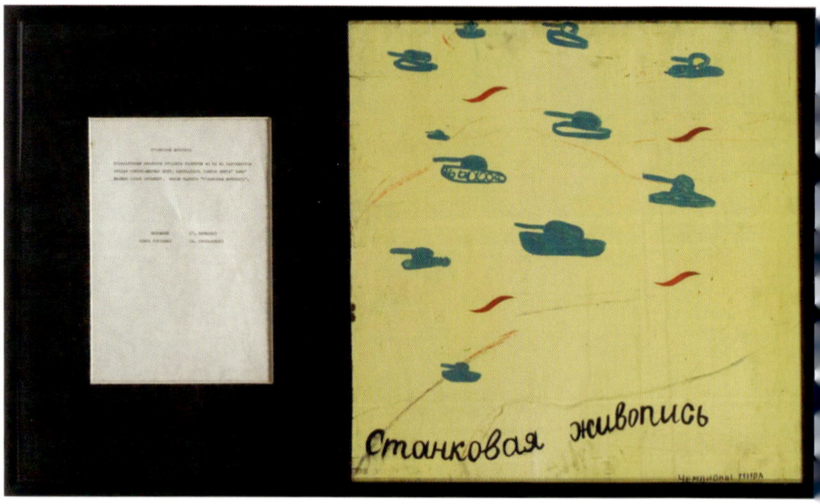

Champions of the World (Gia Abramishvili, Konstantin Latyshev, Boris Matrosov, Igor Vishnyakov, Andrei Yakhnin and Konstantin Zvezdochetov) was a short-lived group active on Moscow's unofficial art scene between 1986 and 1988. The group began as a few friends writing poems together after school and distributing 'angry pamphlets against the school administration'. The band of schoolboys became acquainted with contemporary art through a teacher who was a friend of the Toadstool group and also through *A-Ya*, a journal that circulated in Moscow in the early 1980s.

Like the Toadstools before them, Champions of the World drew no boundary between art and life, and their actions often resembled outright hooliganism. Their neo-Dadaist pranks included picking fights, slitting their wrists, setting fires, dunking their heads in hot soup and playing with homemade explosives. In the more traditional realm, they also made drawings, paintings and works on paper, writing rhapsodic texts to accompany their bizarre actions. Their irreverent attitude ignored customary distinctions between genres and the boundaries of individual authorship, and their works are often decorative, crude or intentionally naïve. Occupying the margins of culture, they saw themselves as 'wandering kamikazes' who, having been sent on a suicide mission, discovered that the war had already been won. With no landing instructions, they assumed a sensibility of perpetual movement and irrational play.

The group first exhibited in the *Art against Commerce* exhibition in Moscow's Bitsa Park in 1986, subsequently showing with the Avantgardist Club, an exhibiting association of artists loosely affiliated with Moscow Conceptualism and the New Wave. Like many other perestroika-era groupings, Champions of the World's collaboration was fleeting, its members going on to develop their own styles and pursue solo careers.

top
Quickwrapped, 1988
Fibreboard, paper, newspaper, magazine clippings, oil, wood, polythene, plastic, Polaroids, cigarette butts, pills, stale bread
100 x 122 cm
© Champions of the World
Courtesy of Pierre-Christian Brochet Collection

above
Easel Painting, 1987
Oil on fibreboard, paper, typescript
51 x 88 cm
© Champions of the World
Courtesy of Pierre-Christian Brochet Collection

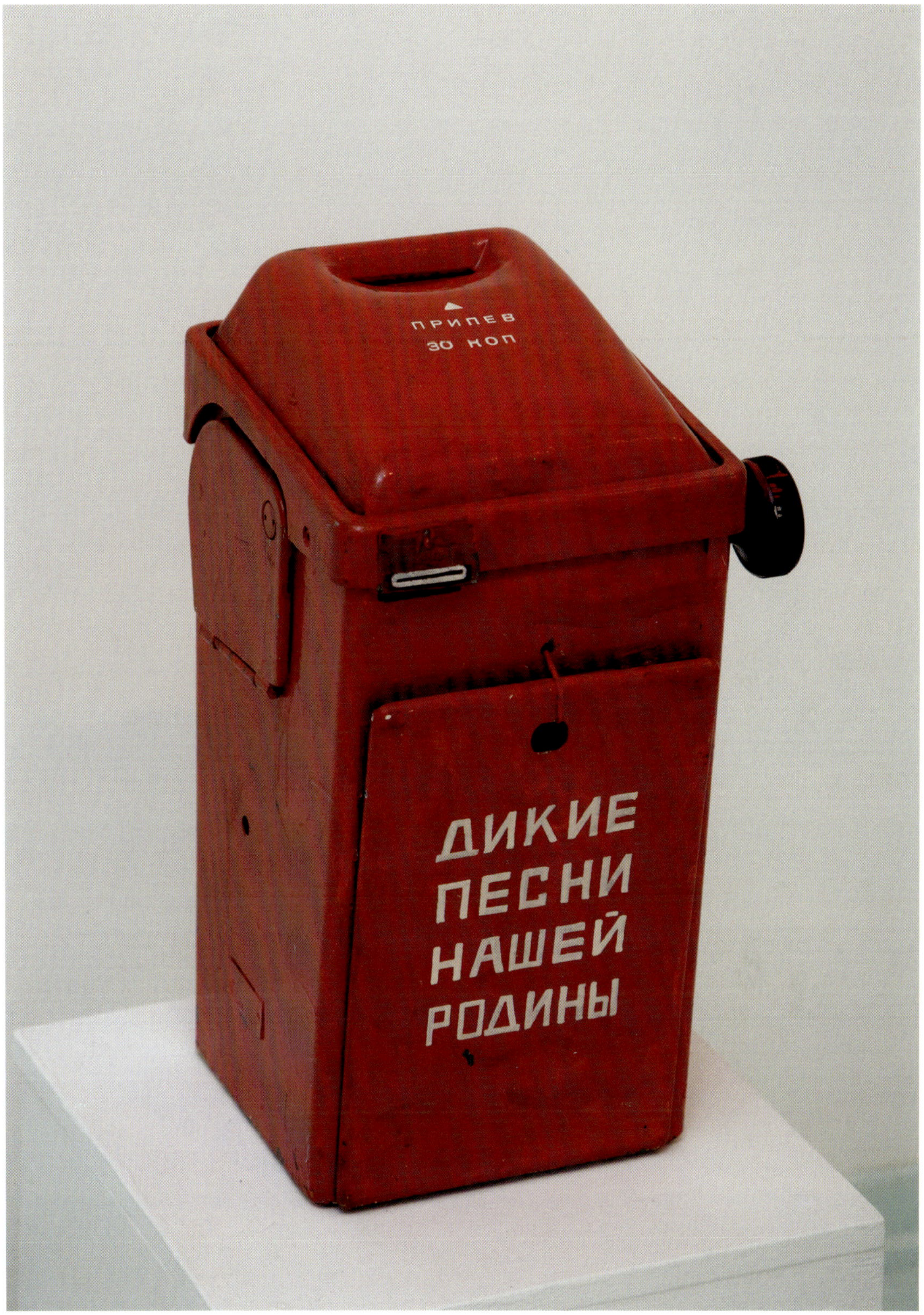

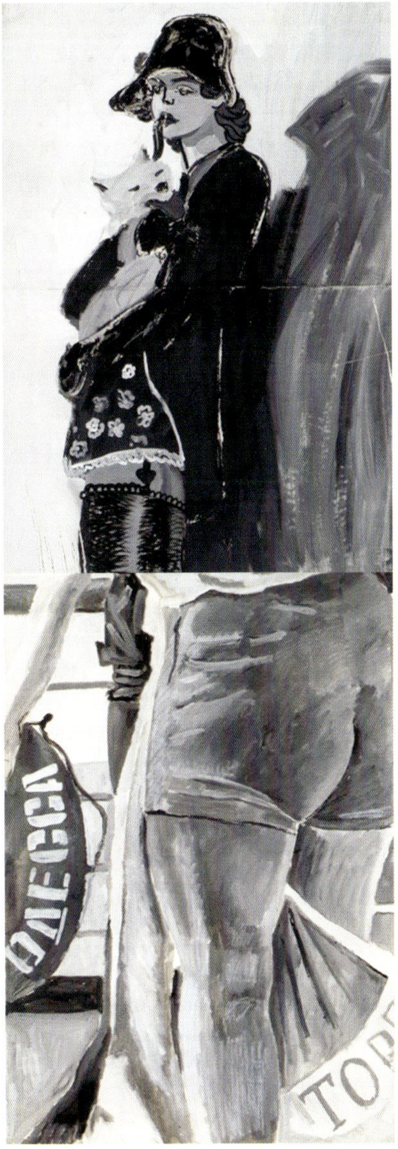

above
Wild Songs of Our Motherland, 1987
Mixed media
45 x 26 x 23 cm
© Champions of the World
Collection MANI Museum
Courtesy E.K.ArtBureau

left
Part of the installation
The Black and White Action, 1987
Gouache on paper
233 x 86 cm
© Champions of the World
Courtesy of Pierre-Christian Brochet Collection

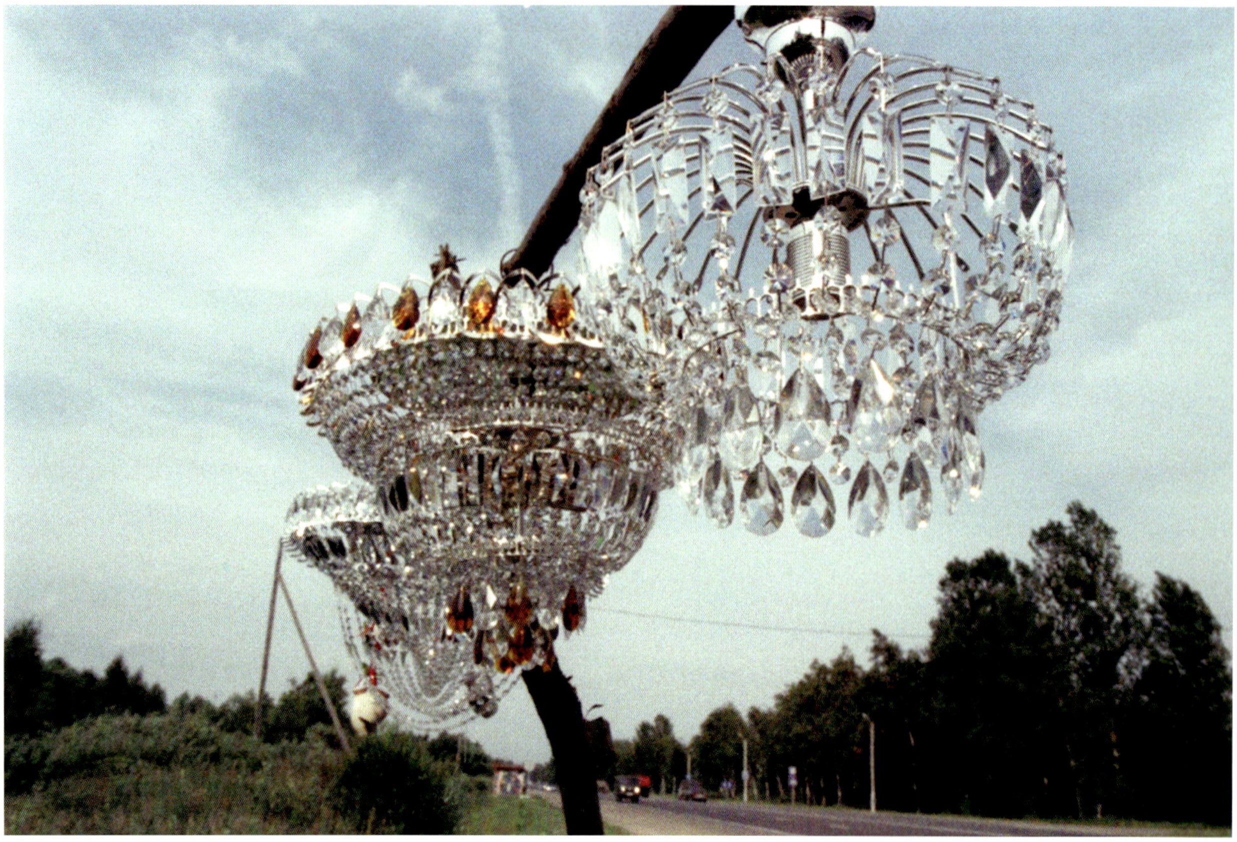

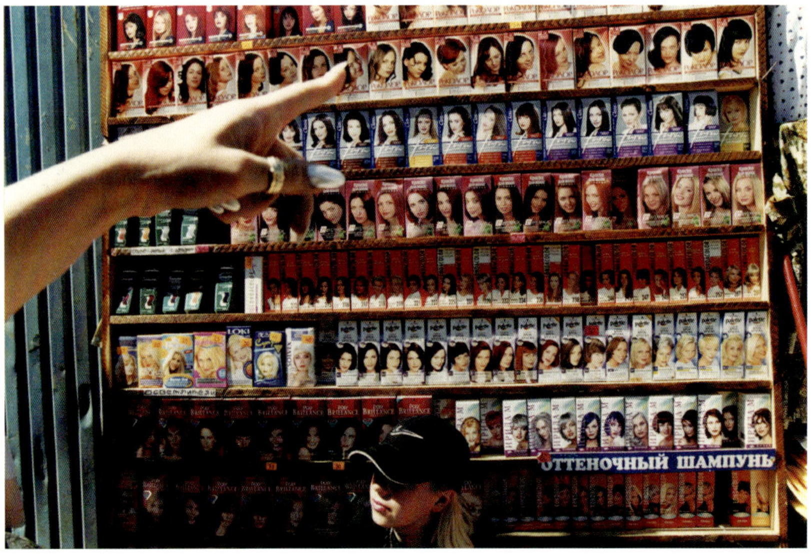

Born in Moscow in 1962, Olga Chernysheva graduated from the animation department of the Moscow Cinema Academy in 1986, before completing her education at the Rijksakademie, Amsterdam. Her practice spans a wide range of media, incorporating drawing, painting, sculpture, photography and video in an attempt to articulate the changing face of Russian society. Having exhibited widely both in Russia and abroad – New York, Paris, London, Utrecht, Moscow, St Petersburg – Chernysheva's solo exhibition *Second Life* was Russia's national entry in the 2001 Venice Biennale.

'I am an animator by training, and judging by the way things stand now, I am [still] an animator,' Chernysheva has observed. Her professional training has meant that her name has become synonymous with injecting life and energy into her chosen subjects. Early works such as the photographic installation *Russian Chocolates or Natural Anti-Depressant* (1996) demonstrate her predilection for visual inspiration from Russian popular, as well as cultural, icons. Working with the all-female employees of the legendary Red October chocolate factory to create *Russian Chocolates*, Chernysheva gave a voice to figures who had fallen off the social radar entirely. It is in her drawings and paintings that her socially aware ethos gathers force; the lineage of Russian Realism can be sensed behind them. One example is Citizens (2009–10), a series that depicts today's Russian populace but which has its formal foundation in the nineteenth-century paintings of the Wanderers and the academicism of Socialist Realism.

It was her first video work, *Marmot* (1999), that won Chernysheva critical acclaim and recognition as a practitioner epitomising Russian art at the beginning of the new millennium. The critic and curator Viktor Misiano declared *Marmot* the first documentary video artwork in Russia. Chernysheva followed it with a range of time-based media pieces.

Video works like *Marmot* and *The Train* (2003) epitomise Chernysheva's thematic thrust. 'I like to discover the sublime in banality,' she has said, meaning that she regards the inconsequential figures on society's margins as 'heroes'. The middle-aged woman wrapped in a fur coat and hat (earning her the comparison with a furry marmot), captured stepping away from a Communist demonstration in Moscow in 1997 to indulge in a private moment and count her measly pension, is the type of individual whom Chernysheva seeks out. Likewise, the procession of her camera through the carriages of a suburban train, mirroring the uninterrupted duration of its rush forward and accompanied by a Mozart andante, is halted by the appearance of a beggar quoting extensively from a little-known work by Russia's national poet, Pushkin.

Succeeding the radicalism and shock tactics of Moscow Actionism, which proliferated in the city in the 1990s directly after the collapse of the USSR, Chernysheva has been seen as signalling a new stage in Russian contemporary art, one that privileges compassion, friendship and community. She is also set apart from another post-Soviet trend which looks to create images and objects that are glamorous, fashionable and highly polished. Instead, she treats her camera like an *avoska*, the 'just-in-case' bag carried by all Soviet citizens on the off-chance that they might find something to buy in the empty State-run shops. However, she does not mourn or romanticise a lost Soviet world: 'If I do harbour nostalgia, it is for ideals ... It is something unattainable that has existed across time. It is eternity ... It is not related to the past or the future. I am not a defender of Soviet-ness; probably I sympathise with particular features, and am interested by the forms that they took in Soviet times.'

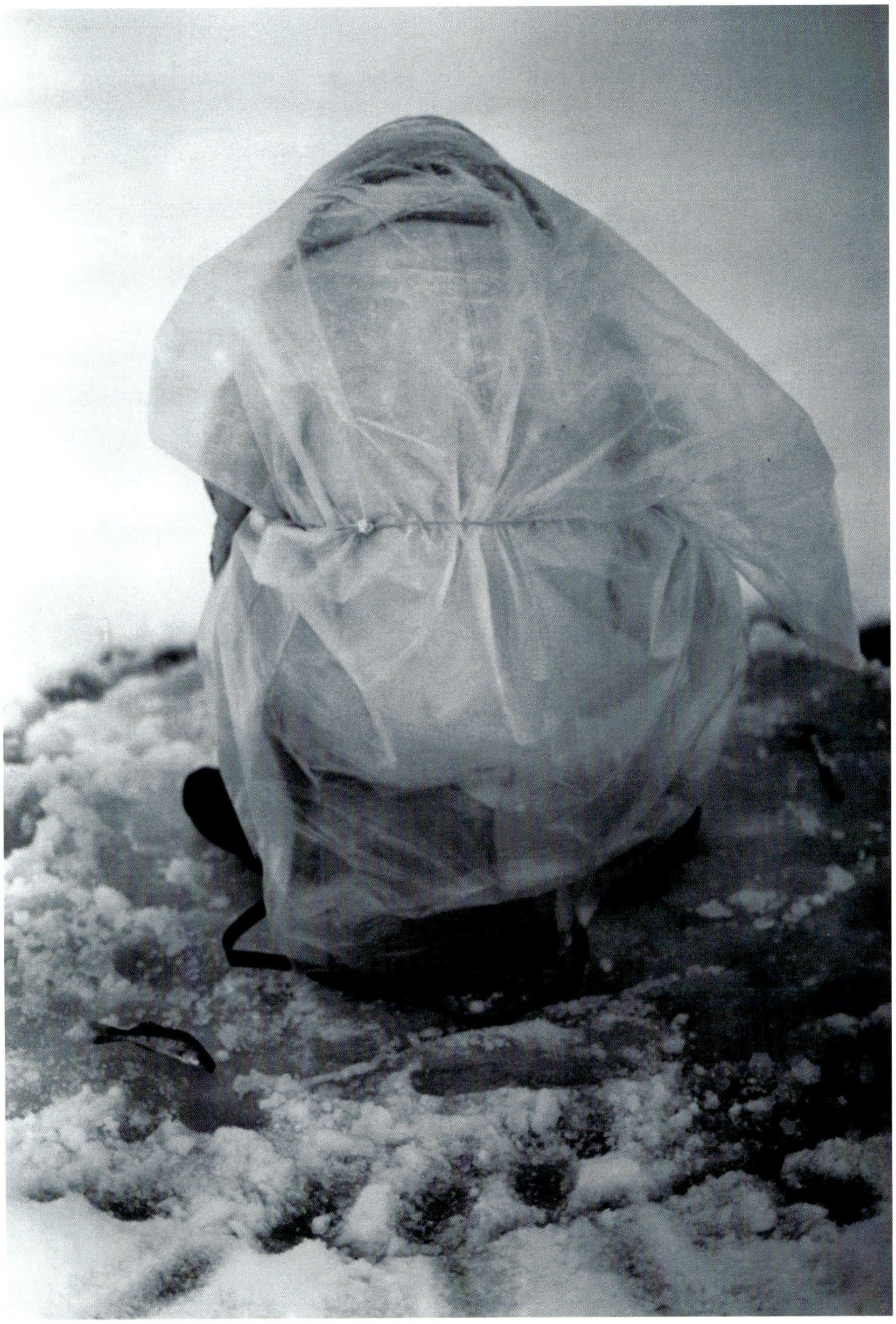

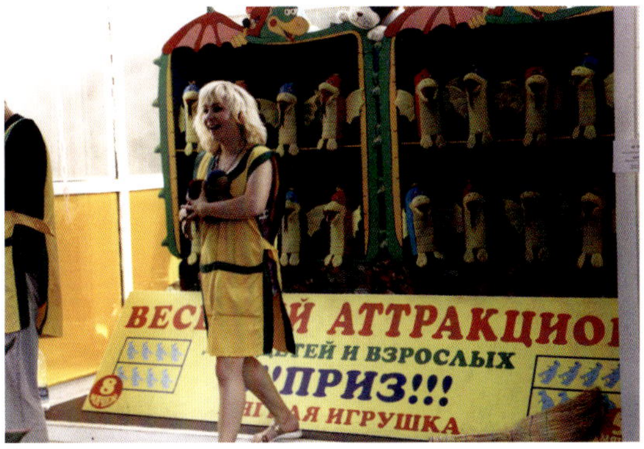

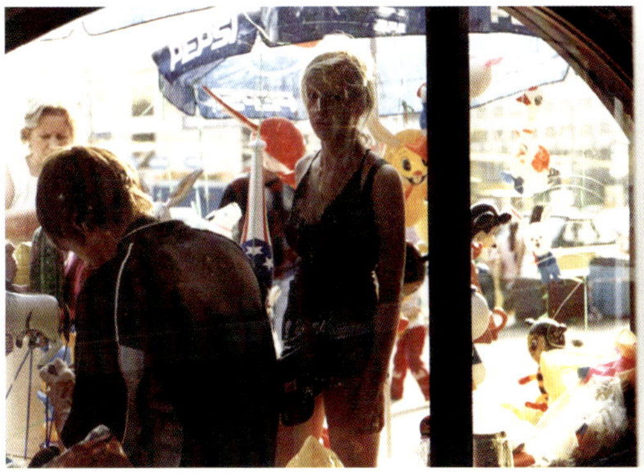

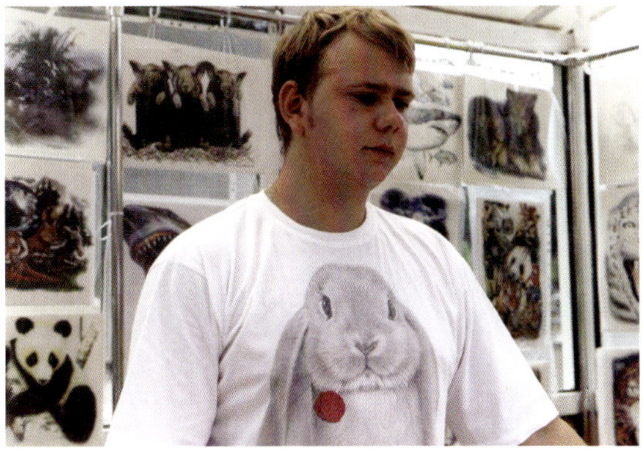

Chernysheva's documentary-style photographs and videos are marked by a distinctly raw quality. Her video work is related aesthetically to that of Soviet avant-garde film makers such as Dziga Vertov and Sergei Eisenstein, and their use of montage. This formal influence is felt in her photographs and drawings as well. Favouring extreme close-ups of her sitters and environments, Chernysheva documents everything from the backs of fur-clad women descending into the metro, in *Second Life* (2001), to brightly coloured knitted hats that metamorphose into cacti, in *Waiting for the Miracle* (2000). Committed to observing the flow of daily life, she explains that 'in a sense, I too am an old-fashioned being. It's not about subjects or about political regimes, but about situations.'

facing page top
Market, 2004
Optical C-print
70 x 105 cm
Edition of 5 + 2AP
© Olga Chernysheva
Courtesy Volker Diehl Gallery and Foxy Production Gallery

facing page left
Market, 2004
Optical C-print
70 x 105 cm
© Olga Chernysheva
Courtesy Volker Diehl Gallery and Foxy Production Gallery

above
Anabiosis: Fishermen-Plants, 2000
Optical C-print
105 x 70 cm
© Olga Chernysheva
Courtesy Volker Diehl Gallery and Foxy Production Gallery

right
Open Hours, 2007
Optical C-prints
101.6 x 152.4 cm (each)
© Olga Chernysheva
Courtesy Volker Diehl Gallery and Foxy Production Gallery

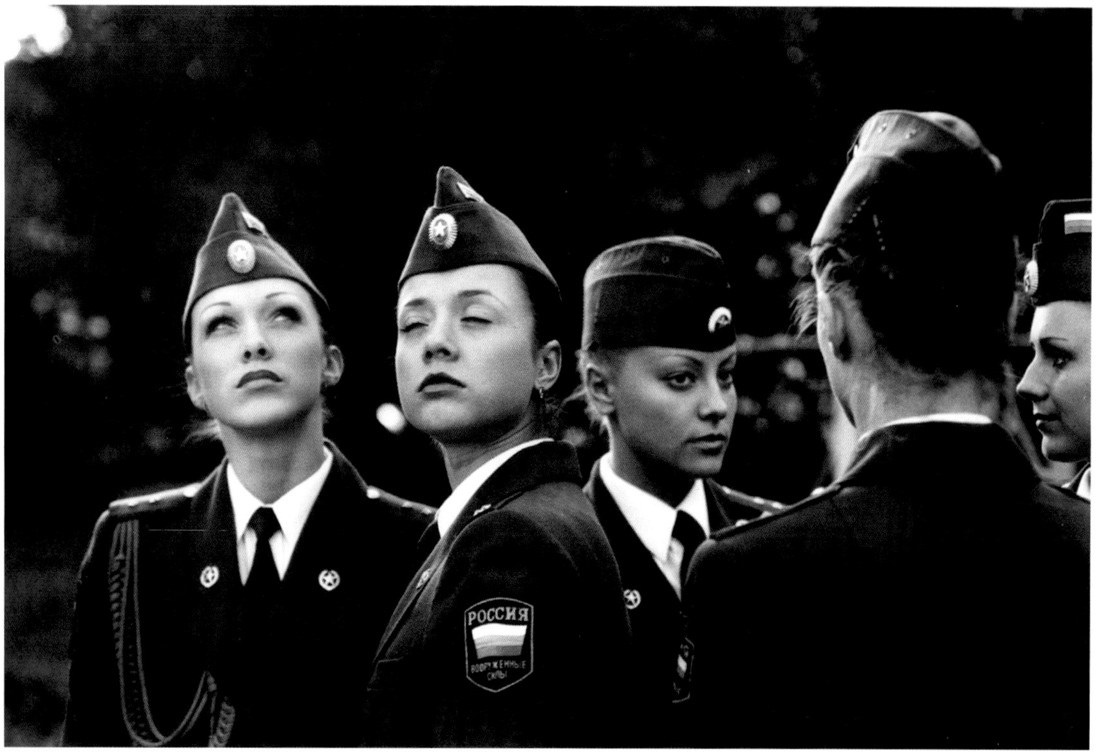

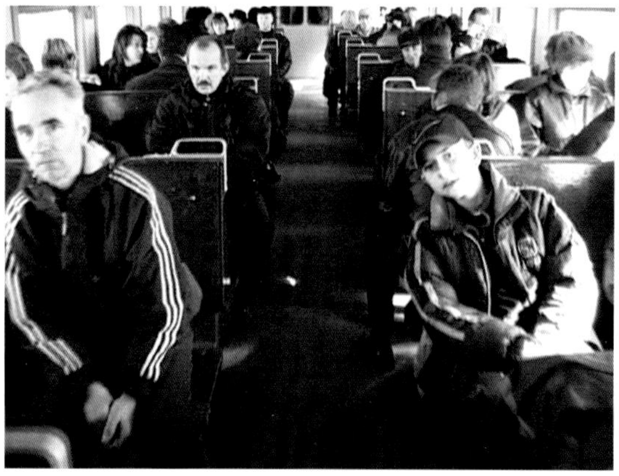

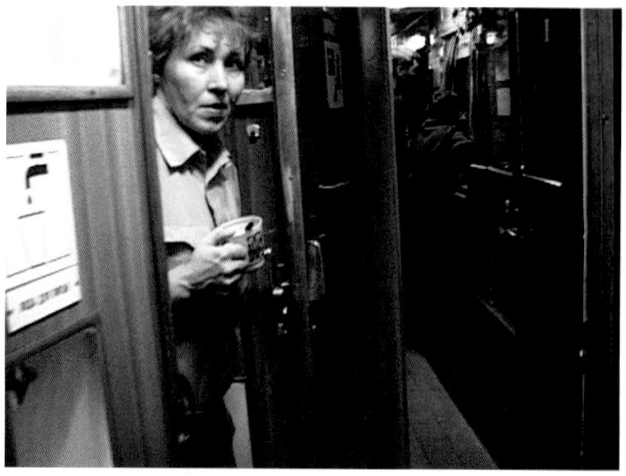

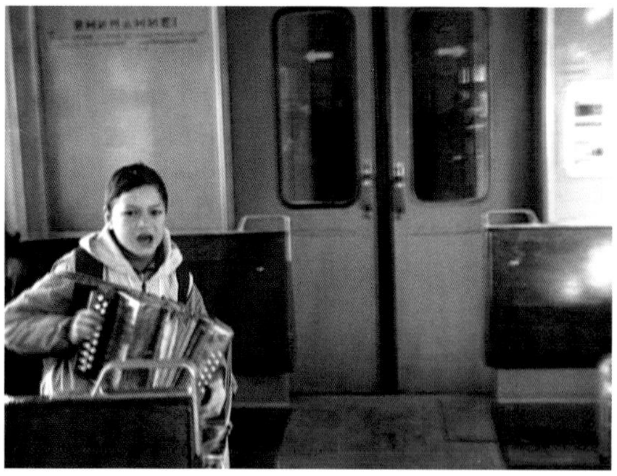

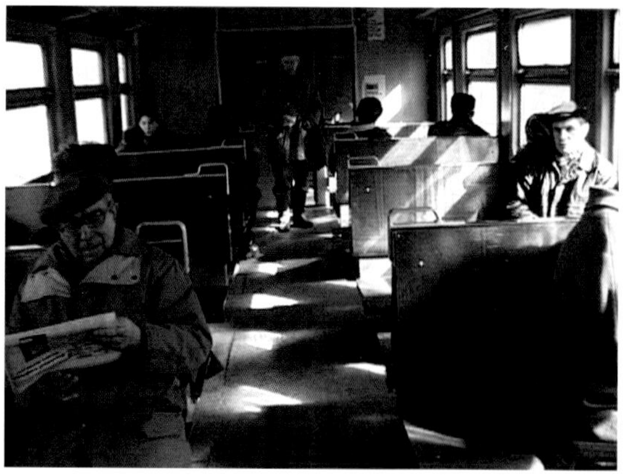

top
Untitled (Park), 2007
Gelatin-silver fibre-based print
60 x 90 cm

Courtesy Volker Diehl Gallery and
Foxy Production Gallery

right
Stills from The Train, 2003
Video
7 minutes 30 seconds

Courtesy Volker Diehl Gallery and
Foxy Production Gallery

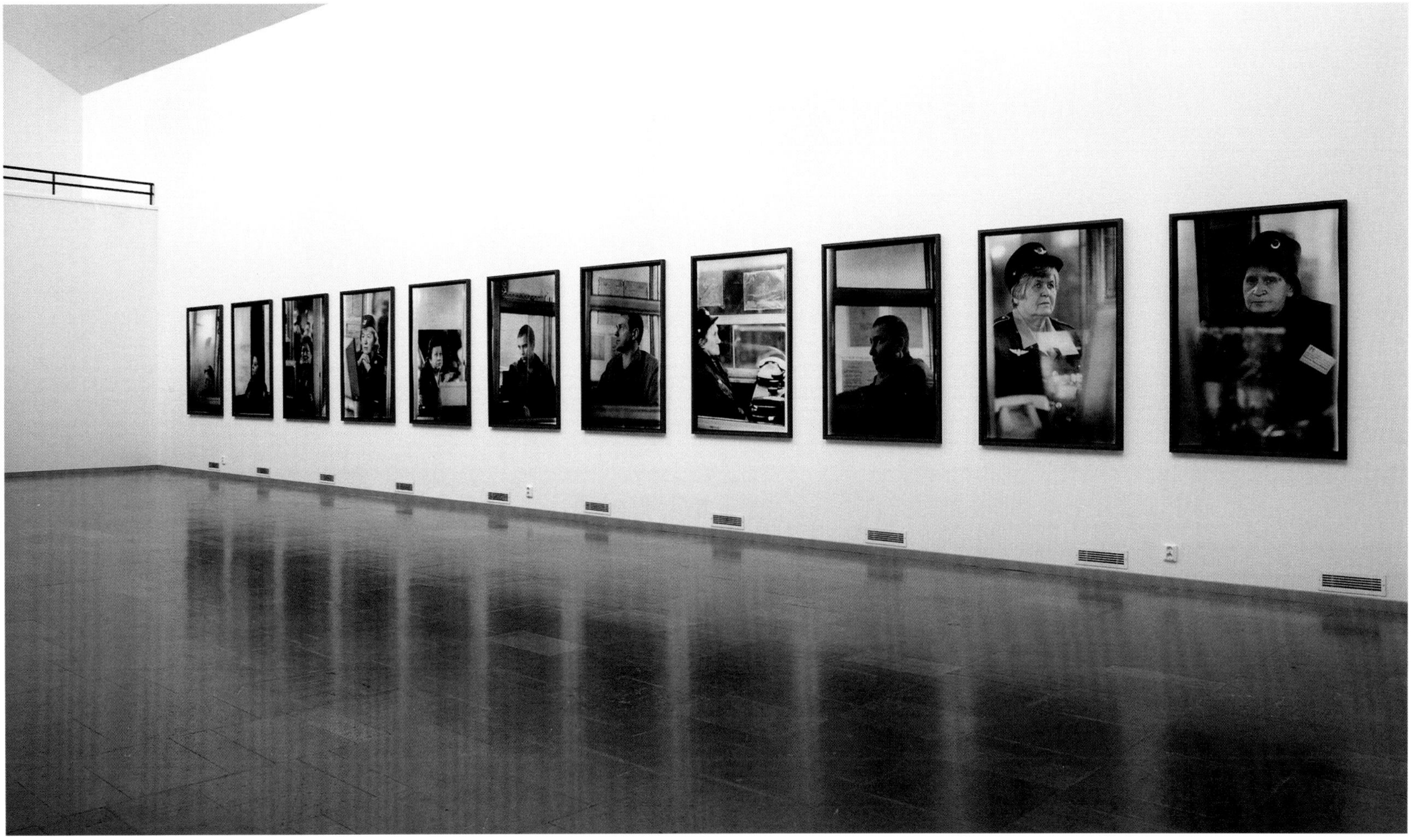

above
On Duty, 2007
View of installation

Courtesy Volker Diehl Gallery and
Foxy Production Gallery

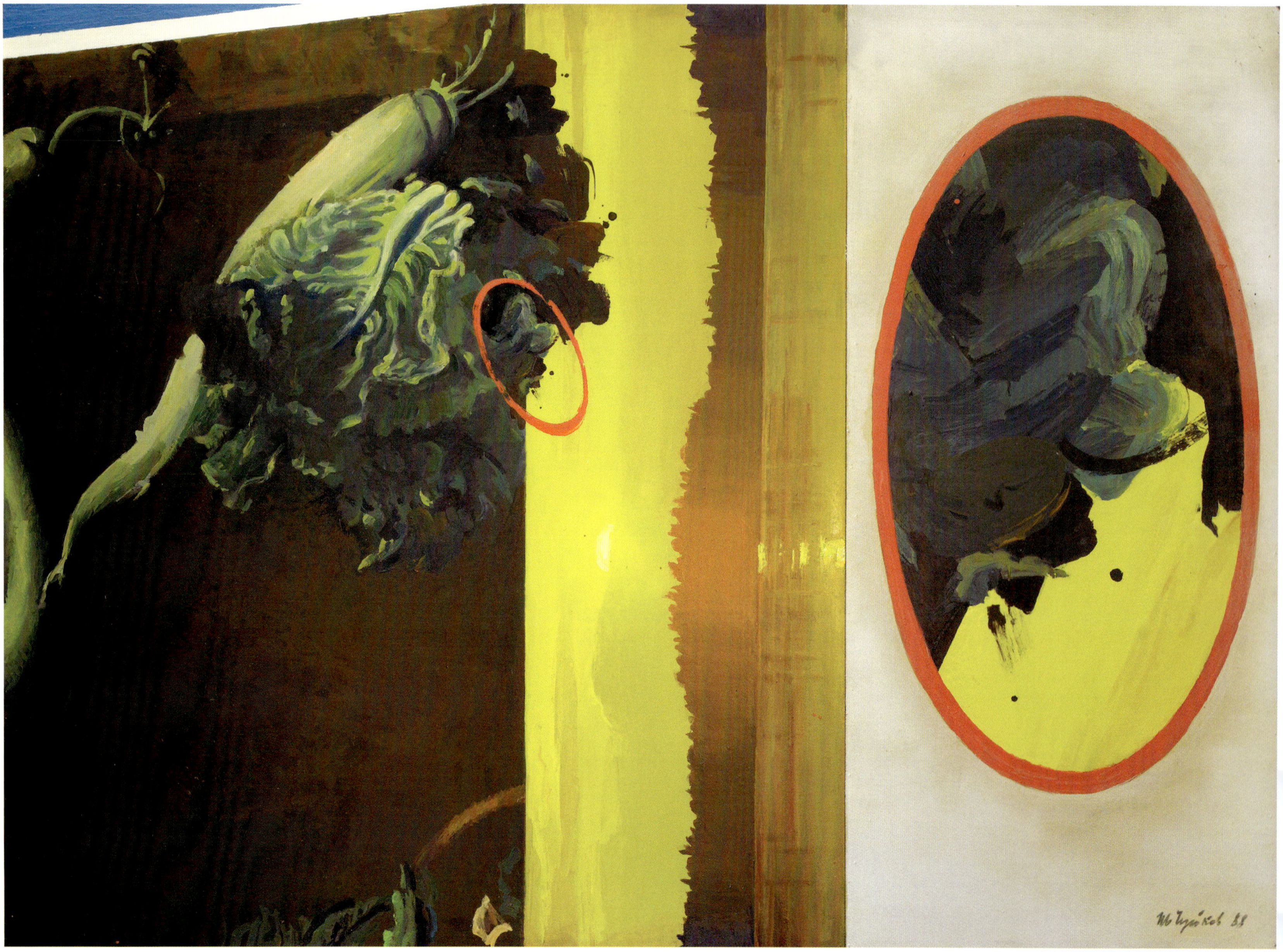

Ivan Chuikov was born in Moscow in 1935 into a family of artists. He first exhibited at the International Festival of Youth in Moscow in 1957 while still studying at the Surikov Institute of Art. It was in the 1960s that Chuikov attained his idiosyncratic style. He began exhibiting abroad in 1977, participating in the infamous Venice Biennale of that year.

Having demonstrated an affinity with Pop art in his early work, Chuikov explores the relationship between reality and simulacra, which he translates into an intricate game between flatness and depth. Despite his signature style, he has stated that 'art is ideological, and when an artist rejects personal style and language, it becomes a form of criticism and an attempt to rise above ideology. This rejection of seriousness and pretence is a play, and playing is freedom.' His approach is evident in *Seascape 1* (1979) and *Window LXIX* (2005), in which he plays conceptual games with the Renaissance metaphor of the picture as a window. Chuikov's panels and ready-made frames offer no openings or perspective, impeding the viewer from seeing through and beyond them. The game is emphasised by the garish palette that he often favours. His graphically defined or blurry skies and landscapes boast of their own artificiality.

Although space is glaringly reduced to flatness – as, for example, in *Panorama III* (1976) – Chuikov's works abound in optimism. 'I have always been astonished by the fact that you can draw everything in any possible way,' he has said. 'Hence my interest in the clash, in the conflict, in the correlations between visual illusion and reality, between different versions of this illusion – different ways of depicting. Essentially it is an issue of language (of visual language in this case). The world can only exist for us in language: change the language and we change the world.'

above
Untitled, 1988
Oil and metallic paint on fibreboard
130.6 x 179.1 cm
© Ivan Chuikov
Collection of DES

facing page
Windows (3 works),
Oil on board
94 x 52.1 cm
© Ivan Chuikov
Private collection, Switzerland

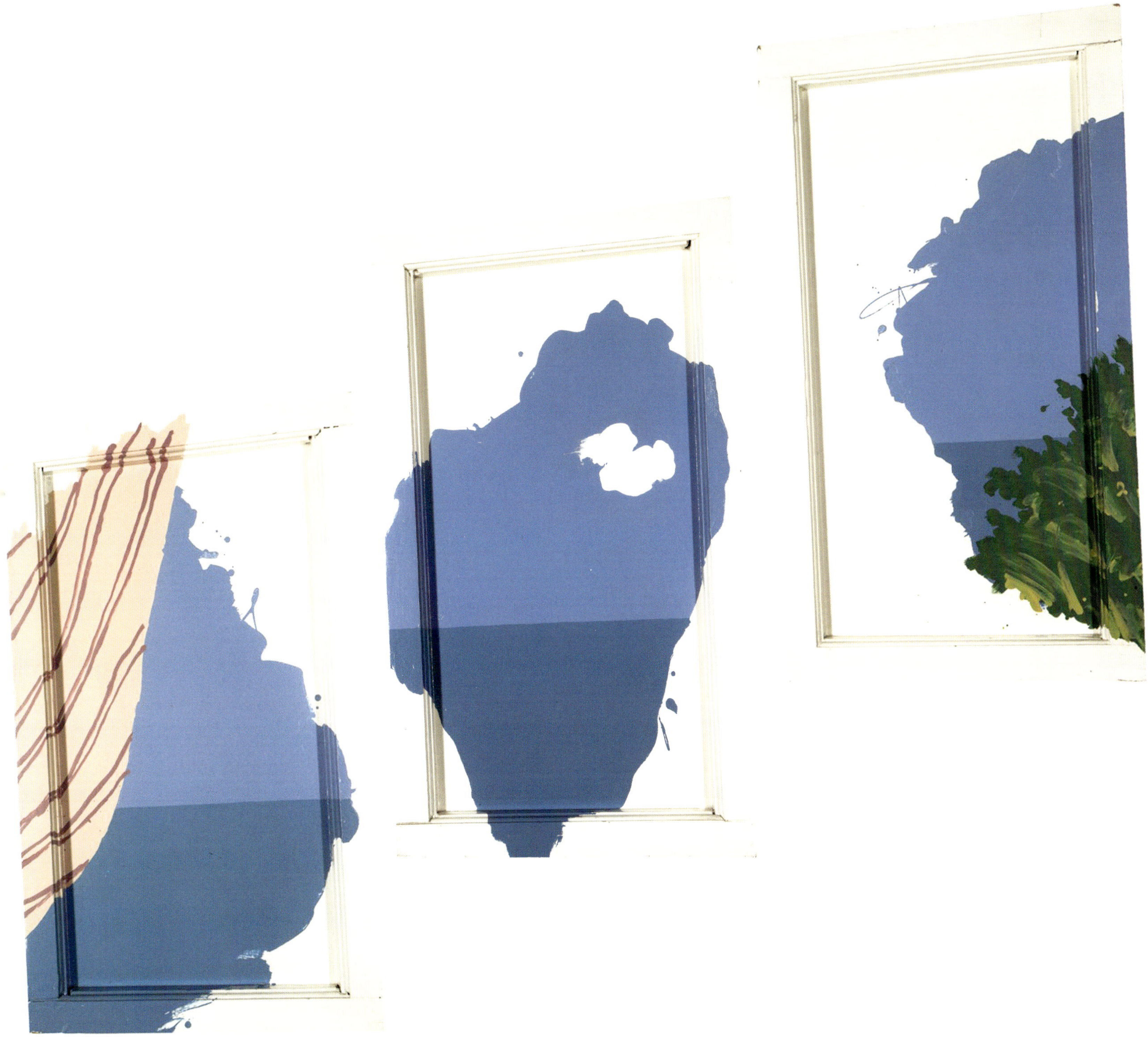

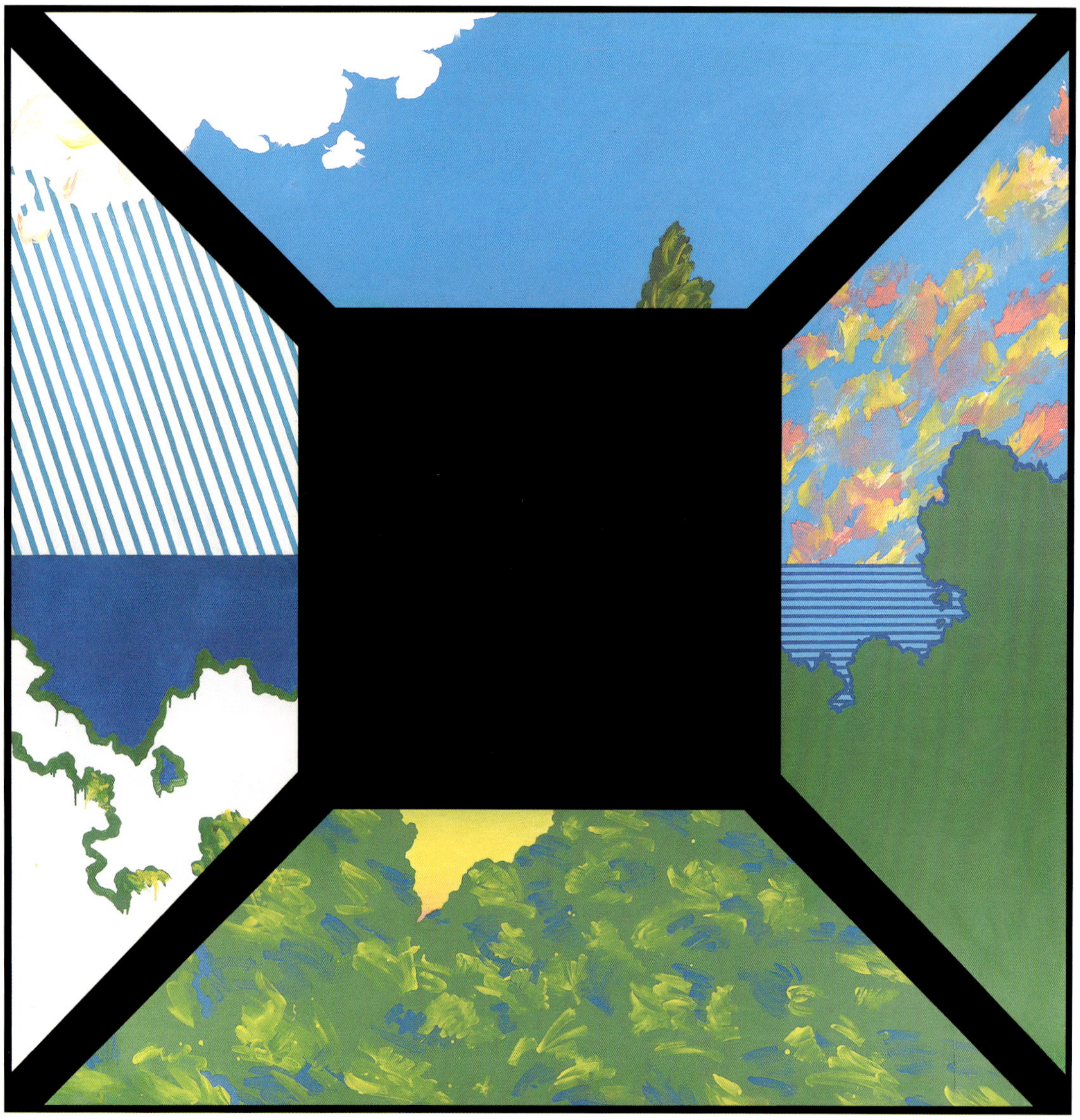

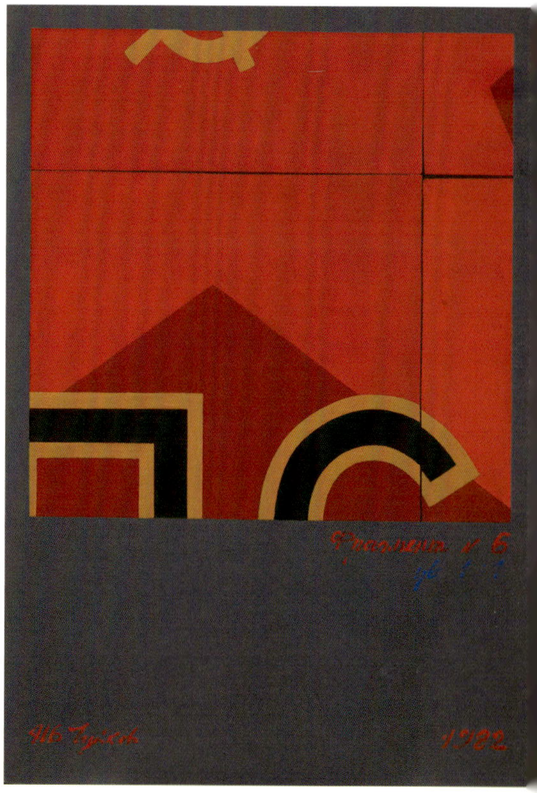

above
Seascape 1, 1979
Enamel on panel
66 x 217.9 cm
© Ivan Chuikov
Private collection
Courtesy of McDougall's Fine
Art Auctions

top right
Fragment No. 3, 1982
Enamel on fibreboard
131 x 180 cm
© Ivan Chuikov
Courtesy of Phillips de Pury

right
Fragment No. 6, 1982
Acrylic enamel on wood
214.4 x 149.9 cm
© Ivan Chuikov
Courtesy of Phillips de Pury

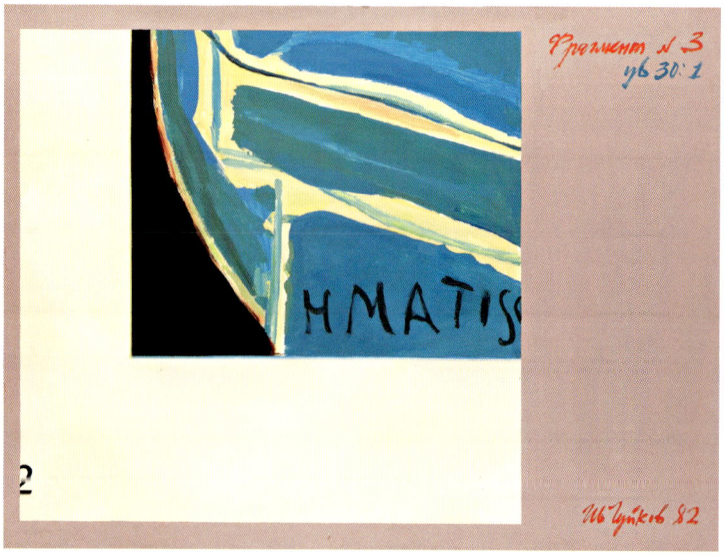

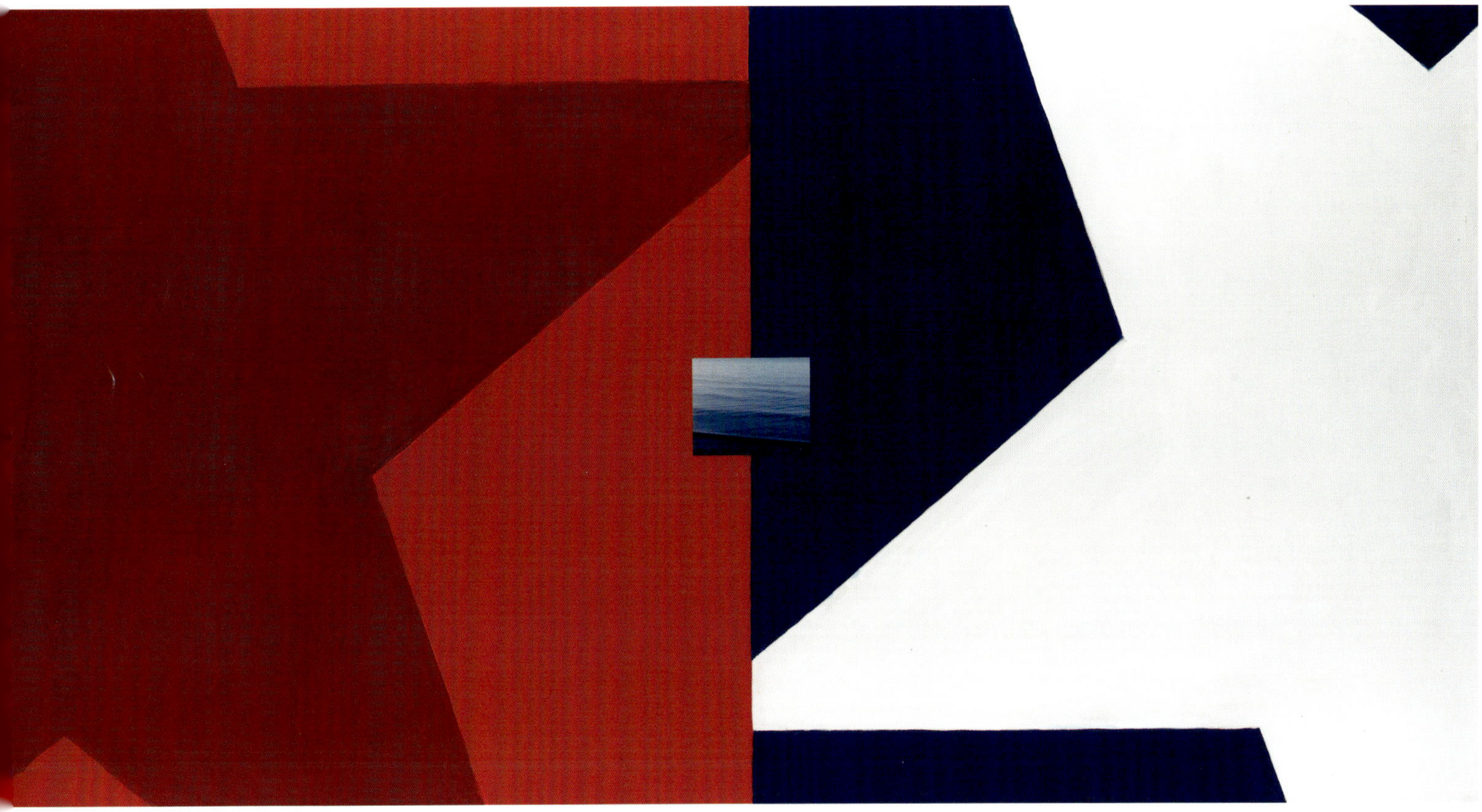

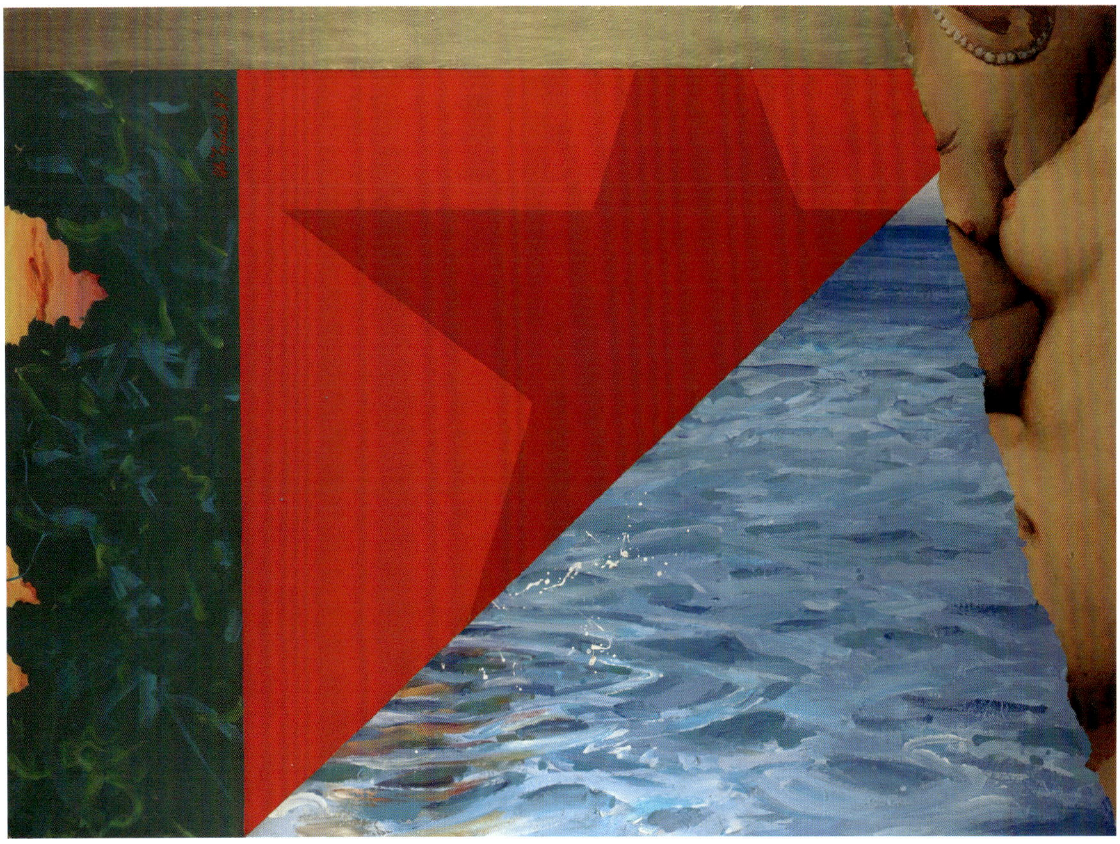

above
Two Stars, 1989
Oil and collage on canvas
96.5 x 173.5 cm
© Ivan Chuikov
Collection of Elizaveta Berezovskaya
Courtesy of MacDougall's Fine Art Auctions

right
Sunset I, 1988
Oil on board
130 x 180.1 cm
© Ivan Chuikov
Courtesy of Sotheby's

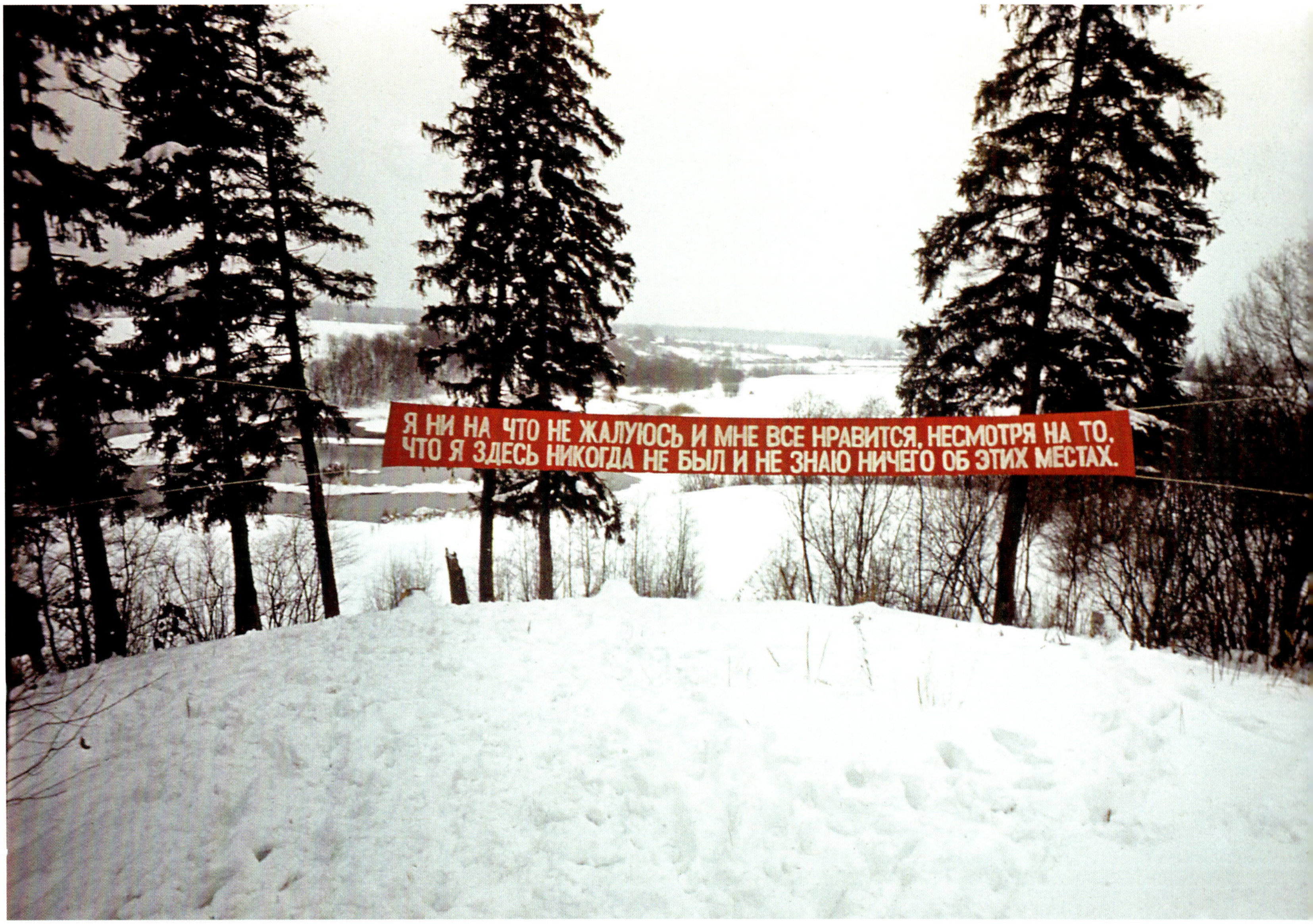

Collective Actions is a group of artists who have collaborated on conceptual performances over more than three decades. Founded in 1976 by Andrei Monastyrsky, Lev Rubinstein, Nikita Alexeev and George Kiesevalter, the group was joined in 1976 by Nikolai Panitkov. Other members have included Igor Makarevich and Elena Elagina, and the philologists Sergei Romashko and Sabine Hansgen. The group's name emphasises the collaborative nature of their work. Early Collective Actions performances took place in a field, Kiovogorskoe Pole, on the outskirts of Moscow, in the artists' apartments or at other open-air, rural locations. In the 1970s and '80s they were a strong artistic force in the Moscow underground, their presentations attracting many viewers and acting as unofficial meeting places where artists could engage with one another.

A central concern of Collective Actions' practice is the attempt to deconstruct the language of art. Art historian Margarita Tupitsyn has noted that Collective Actions artists were determined to 'catapult themselves out of Soviet everyday life and engage in a laboratory procedure of analyzing and theorizing aesthetic practices that would thwart the desire to make commodifiable art objects'. Documenting their performances through photography and video, and collecting and archiving the objects used in their 'actions', are all integral aspects of their practice. Interpretations of, and essays about, their work, as well as transcripts of group discussions, are critical as well.

The group's first performance, *The Appearance* (1976), involved an audience of thirty invited participants who stood and watched as two artists appeared out of a forest and walked across an empty field to hand out certificates to everyone who was present. In *Time of Action* (1978), a large reel of 7 kilometres of white rope was hung between two trees in a forest, and for an hour and a half participants pulled the rope through a field until it came free from the reel. Political slogans, a common form of Soviet propaganda in the form of street banners or billboards, inspired a series of performances. The first, in 1977, called *Slogan*, involved hanging a piece of red cloth with white stencilled words by Andrei Monastyrsky: 'I do not complain about anything and I almost like it here, although I have never been here before and know nothing about this place.'

above
Slogan, 1977
Documentation of an action
Red cloth, stenciled letters
1 x 10 m
Property of Collective Actions Group
Courtesy of Andrei Monastyrsky

facing page
Ring, from Displacement of Spectators, 1989
Rope, metal
130 x 50 x 6 cm
Courtesy E.K.ArtBureau
Collection MANI Museum

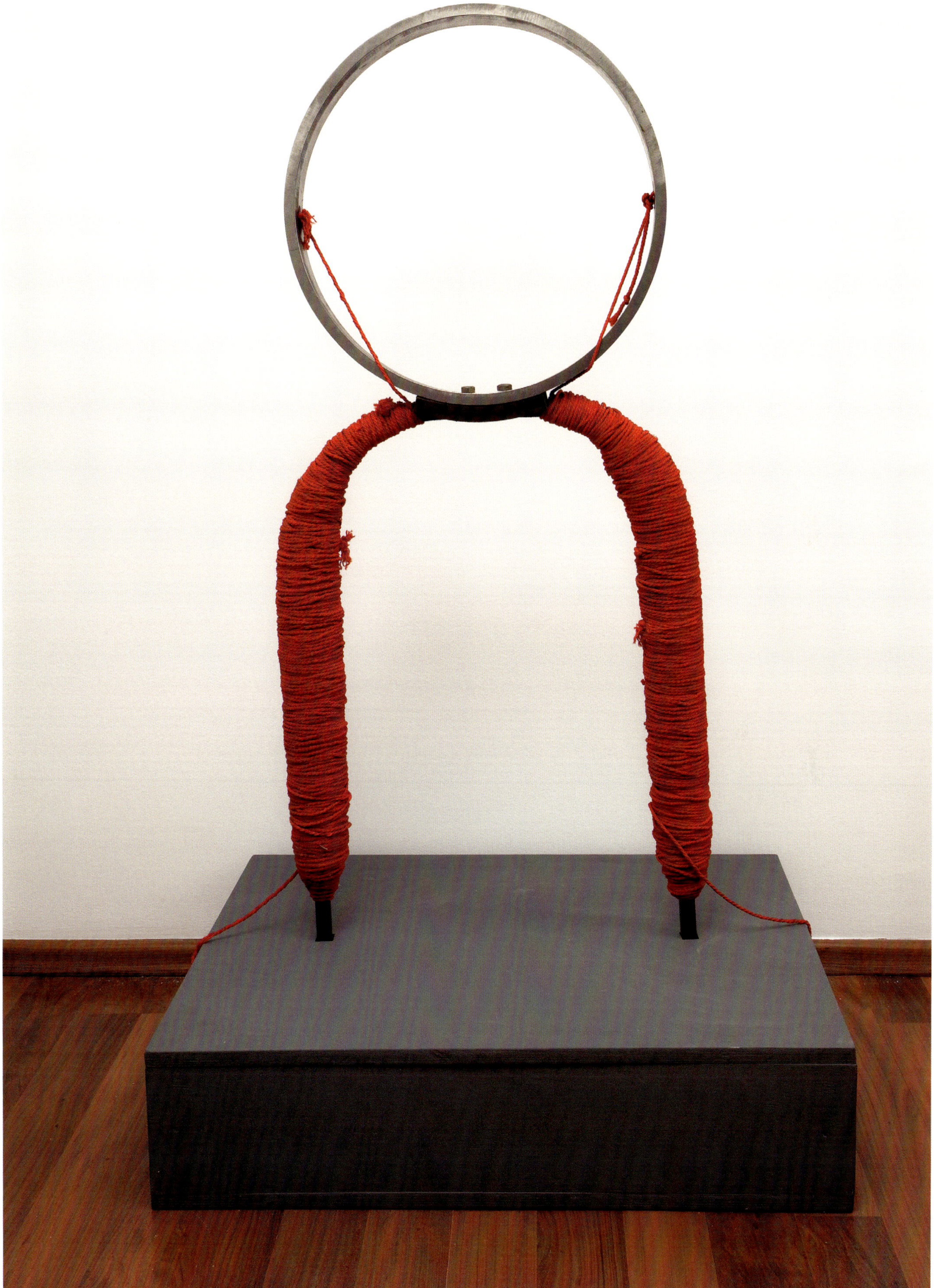

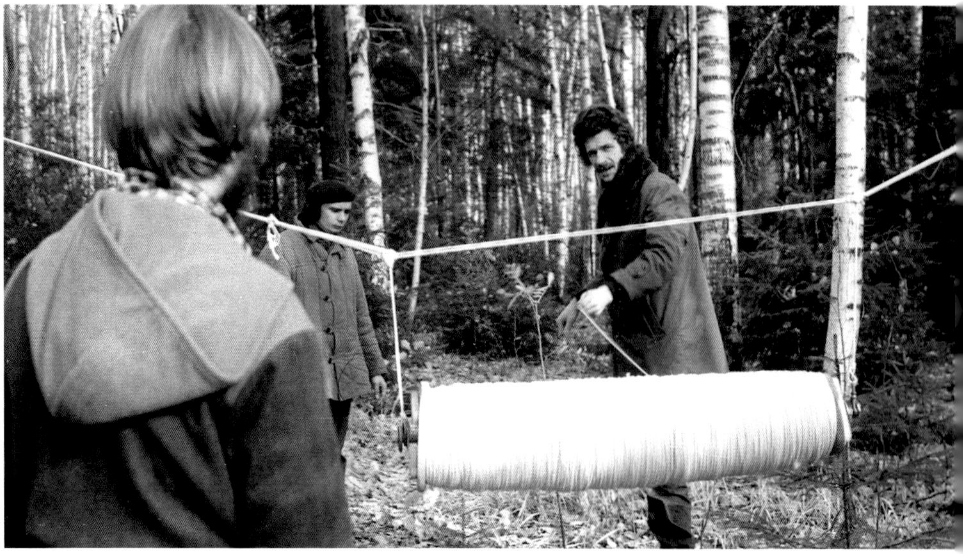

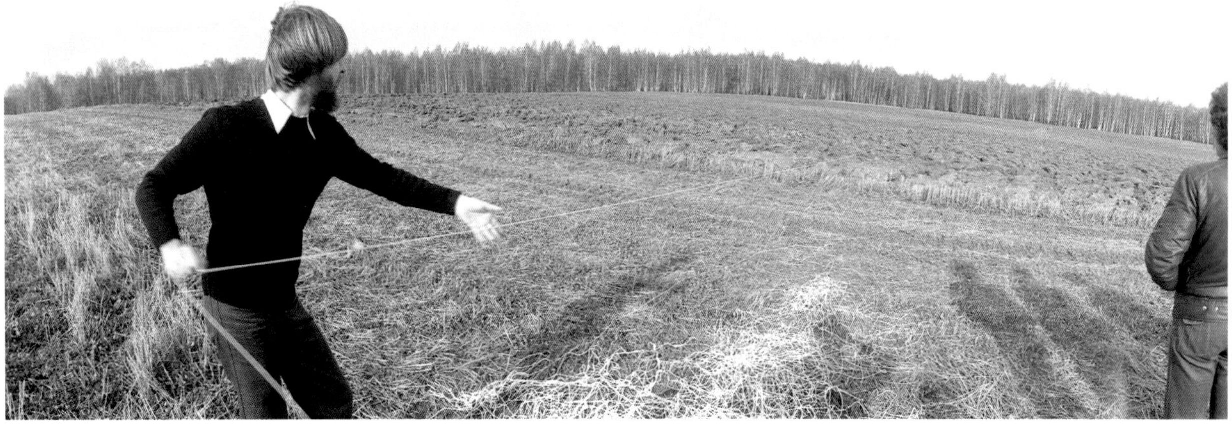

above and left
Photo-documentation of Collective Actions Group, Time of Action, Kievogorskoye field, Moscow Region, 15 October 1978

Photo: Andrei Abramov
Courtesy E.K.ArtBureau

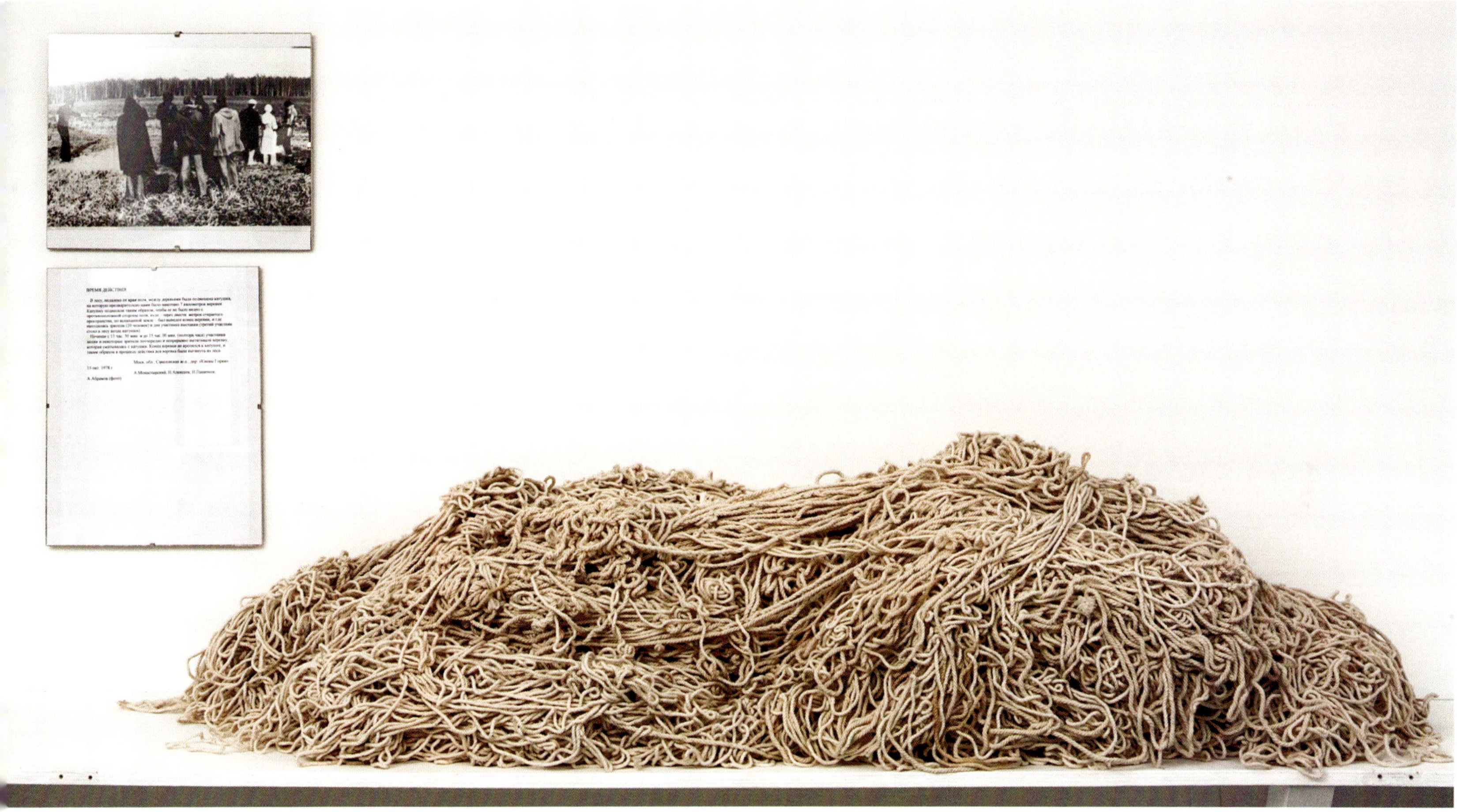

above
Group Rope, 1978
Rope, from Time of Action, 15 October 1978
7 km (l)
Collection MANI Museum
Courtesy E.K.ArtBureau

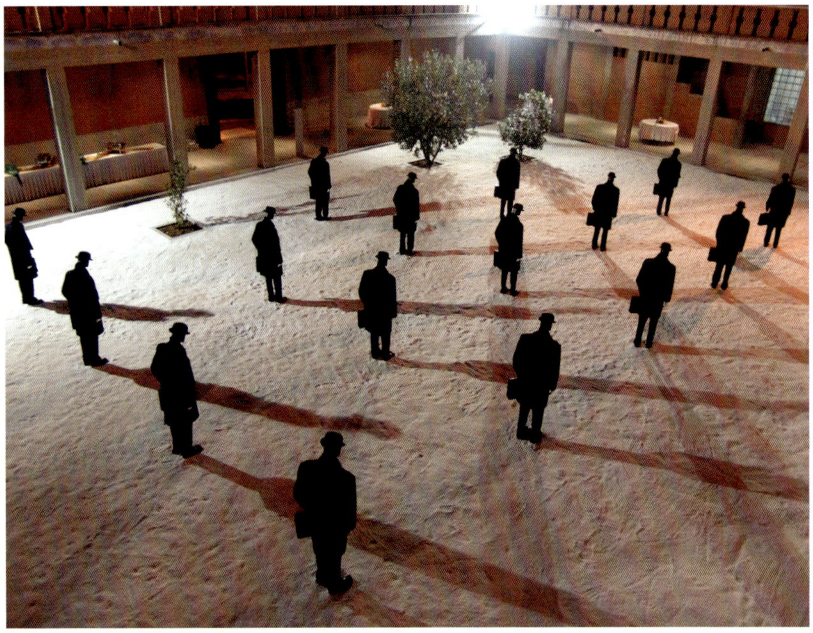

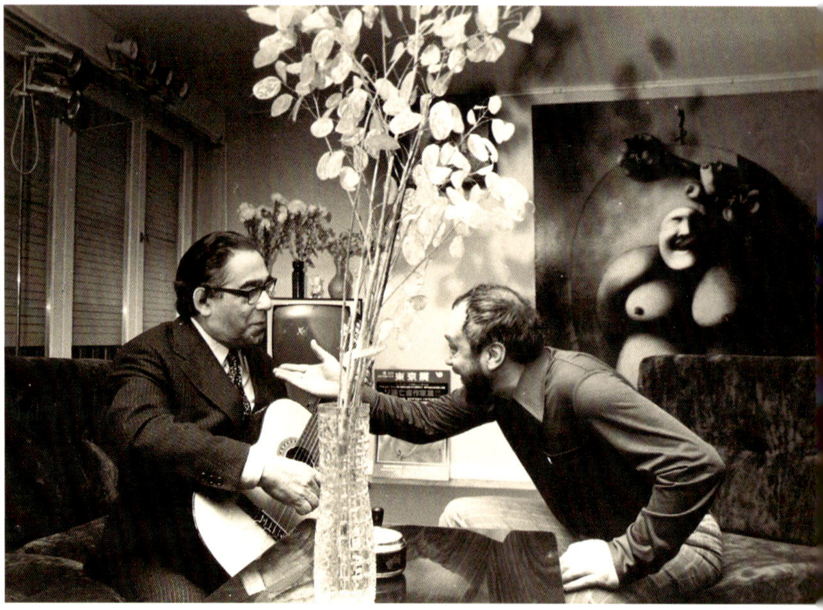

George Costakis, born in Moscow in 1913, was of Greek parentage; his father had gone to Russia before the Revolution as a successful tobacco merchant. The family's fortunes changed quickly during the political upheavals of the 1920s, and they were forced to move from their twelve-room apartment to a small village outside of Moscow. Costakis lost his father and brother during the 1930s, a period when he worked as a driver at the Greek Legation in Moscow. He later took up a position as a clerk at the Canadian Embassy, where he was employed for thirty-five years. In 1978 he emigrated to Greece, where he died in 1990.

Costakis became interested in art and connoisseurship in the course of driving the Greek ambassador to a commission shop in Moscow. Having been inspired to start collecting himself, for ten years he acquired Russian porcelain and Dutch Old Master pictures. It was in the late 1940s that he first encountered work by the Russian avant-garde. By the 1960s he had accumulated a collection of over 2,000 pieces, most of which hung in his small apartment in Moscow. During the 1960s and '70s, he also amassed an important collection of post-war unofficial art. Krasnopevtsev, Plavinsky, Tselkov, Rabin and others were close friends whose works he bought; many others were given by the artists as gifts.

Costakis' home became a hub of underground culture. As curator and art historian Maria Tsantsanoglou has written, 'The influence of the Russian Avant-garde on certain younger artists, such as Lydia Masterkova, Francisco Infante and Eduard Steinberg and others, was largely shaped by their contact with the works in the apartment of George Costakis.' At the time, this art was considered degenerate by the authorities, so Costakis played a role in keeping a creative dialogue with the avant-garde alive. His visitors were scrutinised by the KGB, however, and Costakis himself was eventually pressurised into leaving the Soviet Union.

Costakis' daughter Aliki sees her father's support of Russian artists of the '60s and '70s as having been less a question of patronage and more one of his wanting to help foster their spirit of creative freedom, which was lacking in the Soviet Union. Costakis, she believes, saw himself more as a collector propelled by 'the spirit of adventure'. The camaraderie of the underground community was important to him: 'He appreciated them, loved them personally and tried to help them in every way ... He often bought their works or recommended them to foreign friends.' The art of that generation took time to find a larger audience in Russia following perestroika. In 1994 Costakis' biographer Peter Roberts noted the lack of public exposure of unofficial Russian art and the challenges it was still facing in becoming integrated into mainstream culture: 'Westerners have at least been exposed to a great variety of contemporary art throughout their lives, not so Russians; until recently only those over seventy might have known a world in which existed anything but the boring cliches of Socialist Realism. After such a life in art, to be confronted with the full blown contemporary work now coming from young Russian painters is to be shocked and quite possibly repelled.'

Today Costakis' collection of Russian avant-garde art is divided between the State Tretyakov Gallery, Moscow, and the State Museum of Contemporary Art, Thessaloniki. Works by his contemporaries, inherited by his four children, were brought together for a major retrospective of the period, *Soviet Alternative Art, 1956–1988*, at the Thessaloniki museum in 2006.

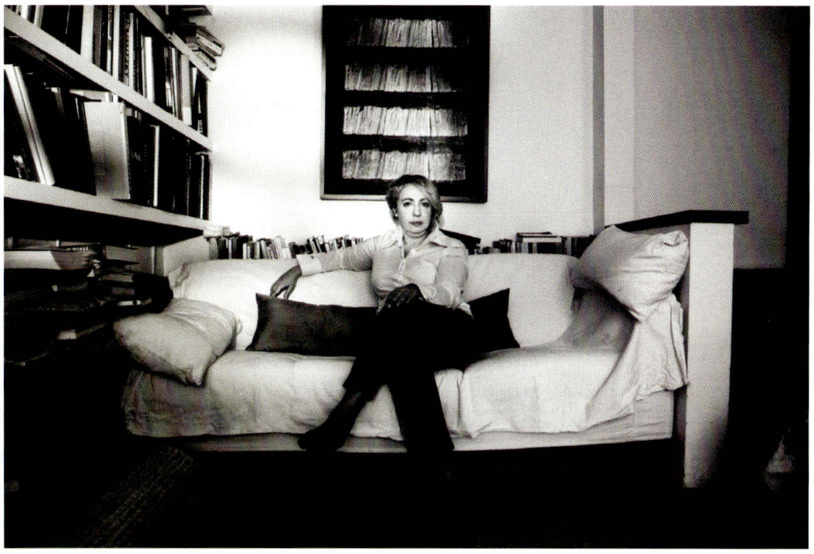

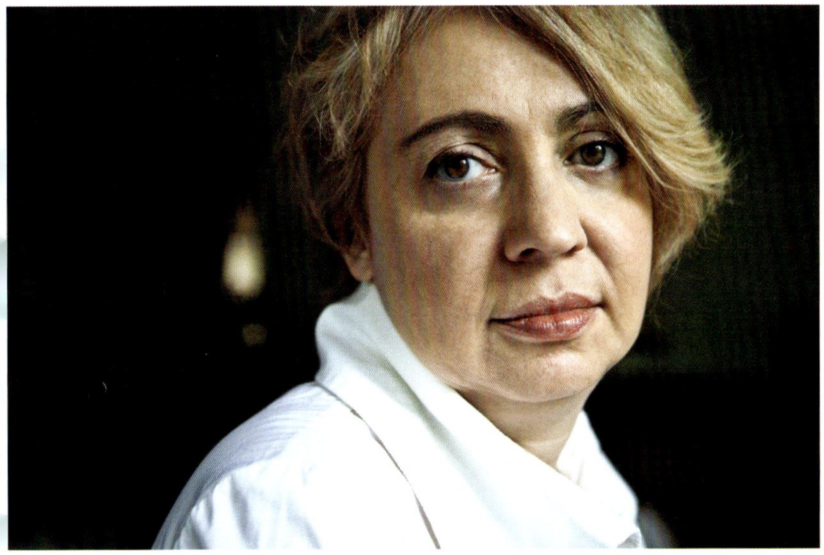

Art historian, writer and curator Ekaterina Degot lives and works in Moscow in a renovated Soviet-era apartment close to Sokolniki Park. She has curated and co-curated numerous shows of Russian contemporary art, including Moscow–Berlin 1950–2000, at the Martin-Gropius-Bau, Berlin, and State Historical Museum, Moscow (2003–4); Struggling for the Banner: Soviet Art Between Trotsky and Stalin, at the New Manege, Moscow (2008); and Kudymkar – Engine for the Future, at PERMM, Perm, and Vinzavod, Moscow (2009). In 2010 she co-curated the First Ural Biennale of Contemporary Art in Ekaterinburg with David Riff and Cosmin Costinas. Since 2008 Degot has been senior editor of www.openspace.ru, a popular independent news site dedicated to the arts. She is also a professor at the Alexander Rodchenko Photography and New Media School in Moscow.

Degot believes that curators and artists alike face many challenges in Russia today, mainly because the former underground art circles have become the powerhouse of the Moscow art scene and because their goals are too capitalistic. Furthermore, she does not see an adequate infrastructure of educational institutions comparable to that in the West that might offer viable alternatives to young artists and art-history students.

As far as current trends are concerned, Degot cites two important ones: a taste for post-Constructivist sculptural formalism, and an aggressive form of anarchic activism, as in the work of the Voina group, who have been pursued by the authorities for their public activities. Degot is not impressed by either trend, observing that 'they both express political, social and intellectual impotence, the result of neo-liberal indoctrination of the last two decades.' She distinguishes Russian contemporary art from Western contemporary art on the basis of its thinking rather than its formalism: 'The most original trait of Russian art is a denial of form, sometimes radical, an identification of art with theoretical, intellectual and literary practices. It questions the professional status of art as object-making, which makes the international prospects of showing this art in a museum setting rather problematic.' Looking back to the early twentieth-century avant-garde, Degot finds it ironic that today Malevich is so highly valued by the art market, given that his paintings, and early Soviet art in general, were not orientated towards the market at all. For such artists their work was not meant to be consumed but to be understood and discussed.

Among contemporary artists, Degot has the highest regard for Ilya Kabakov, Andrei Monastyrsky, Collective Actions and other Conceptual practitioners who have produced original work. Anatoly Osmolovsky is her nominee for 'the most controversial and influential ideologist'. Outside the canon of Conceptualism, she likes the work of artist-photographers Sergei Bratkov, Dmitry Gutov and Olga Chernysheva.

Despite her professional focus on contemporary art, Degot is keenly interested in the sources of modernism, especially nineteenth-century Realism. She prefers figurative to abstract art, with the exception of the Russian avant-gardists, whose abstraction was ideological, not formal. She prefers to see artists trying new things and failing, admiring the process rather than the result. And she likes to mine little-appreciated phases in the careers of artists working outside of mainstream theory – here she cites the late work of Picabia and El Lissitzky: 'I live to exhibit this kind of thing and I often talk with artists who challenge their own practices.'

Degot's professional aim is to see twentieth-century Russian art history – not just the major names, such as Malevich and Kabakov, but the history as a whole – integrated into the international context. She believes that because the most important contemporary artists, like those of the avant-garde, have consistently resisted and worked in critique of the global professional art world, they have the potential to bring about change. Degot puts it this way: 'I hope to challenge the complacency of art.'

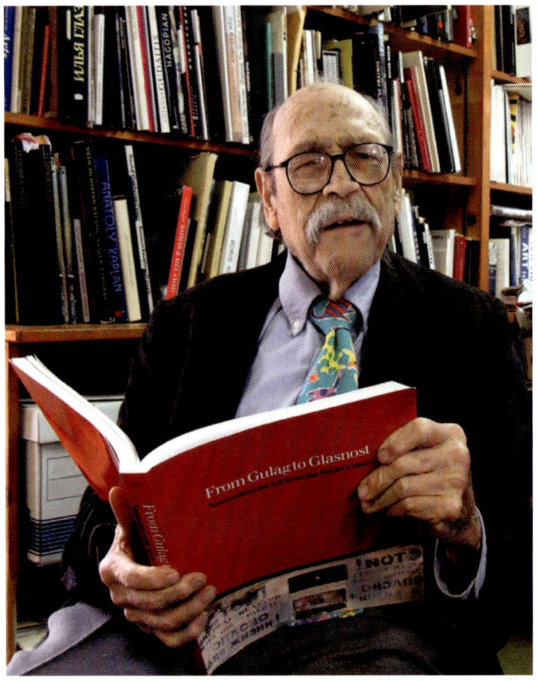

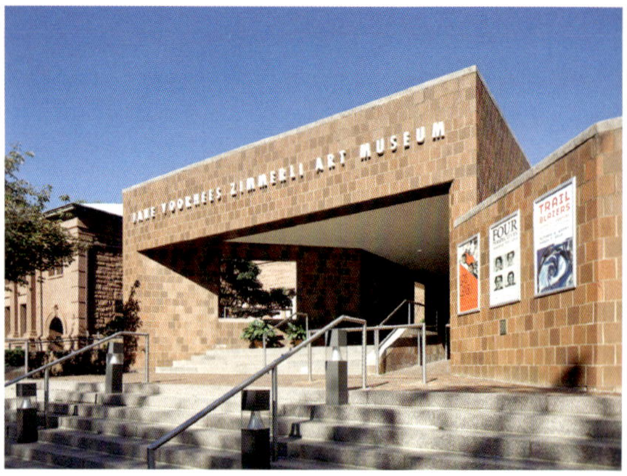

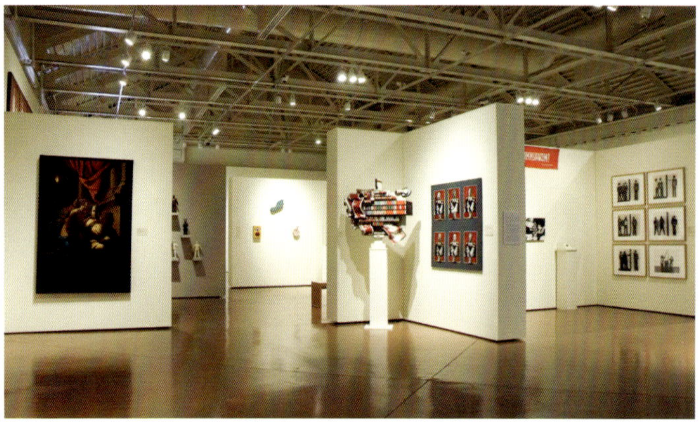

Collector and art philanthropist Norton Dodge was born in 1927 in Oklahoma City. Since 1966 he and his wife Nancy have lived on a 995-hectare farm in southern Maryland. As an American collecting unofficial art during the Cold War, his activities were remarkable for both their scale and their political context. Dodge donated most of the 17,000 works he brought back from the Soviet Union to Rutgers University, New Brunswick, where they are permanently housed in the Jane Voorhees Zimmerli Art Museum. The museum runs an exhibition and education programme promoting Russian underground art of the Soviet period, of which it holds the world's largest and most significant collection.

Dodge's collecting was in part driven by his compassion for the predicament of dissident artists as outsiders in a hostile society and in part by his interest in the Soviet Union through his professional work as an economist and Sovietologist. He first went to the Soviet Union in the mid-1950s with his father, who was a physics professor and diplomat. At the time, Norton was a young graduate student researching tractors for a PhD at Harvard University, but, alongside his academic work, he started to take an interest in dissident artists. He has described how he first read about them in an article in *Life* magazine, an encounter that set him on his future path: 'Contrasting the more pleasant and accessible landscapes of snowy Kremlins and propaganda imagery touting "progress" and "the future good life under Communism," here were abstractions, provocative self-portraits, and spiritually based works that reflected the darker, and the more honest, undertones of a very different Russia than what was being sold as the Party Line.'

As a patron of underground art of the Soviet period, Dodge's mission was two-fold: to materially support artists outside of the system who in many cases had little access to such basic tools as paints and canvas, and to show their art in America. The enormous scale of his efforts and the adventures he experienced are detailed in John McPhee's *The Ransom of Russian Art* (1994), in which Dodge describes how he would travel around Moscow and Leningrad hoping to visit studios, mainly in communal apartments, and how one artist would introduce him to another. He speaks of the remarkable level of trust that built up between him and the artists during the Cold War era, when everyone involved risked very real danger. He also recalls how artists 'would mostly work at great risk facing harassment at best, and loss of any employment, physical injury, or long sentences in mental institutions and prisons at worst'. Dodge believes that artist Evgeny Rukhin's death in a fire in his studio was down to the KGB, and speaks of several others he knew who suffered acute persecution and exile.

In terms of the reception and understanding of this period in Russian art history, particularly outside of Russia, Dodge is of the view that it still suffers from neglect, languishing in the shadow of the art of other nations. He is a strong advocate for the importance of unofficial art and its potential to reflect the history of an era. Dodge also believes that the art he collected possesses a special quality deriving from the dissident status of its makers, telling a timeworn story of the impulse for artistic freedom and the individual's right to self-expression. Politics and scholarship are both aspects of what he describes as a 'private art affair of the heart and soul'. Dodge's advocacy also poses a critical question about the preservation of art produced in an environment in which it is viewed as valueless. As he aptly asks, 'Had I not begun collecting, would these works have survived?'

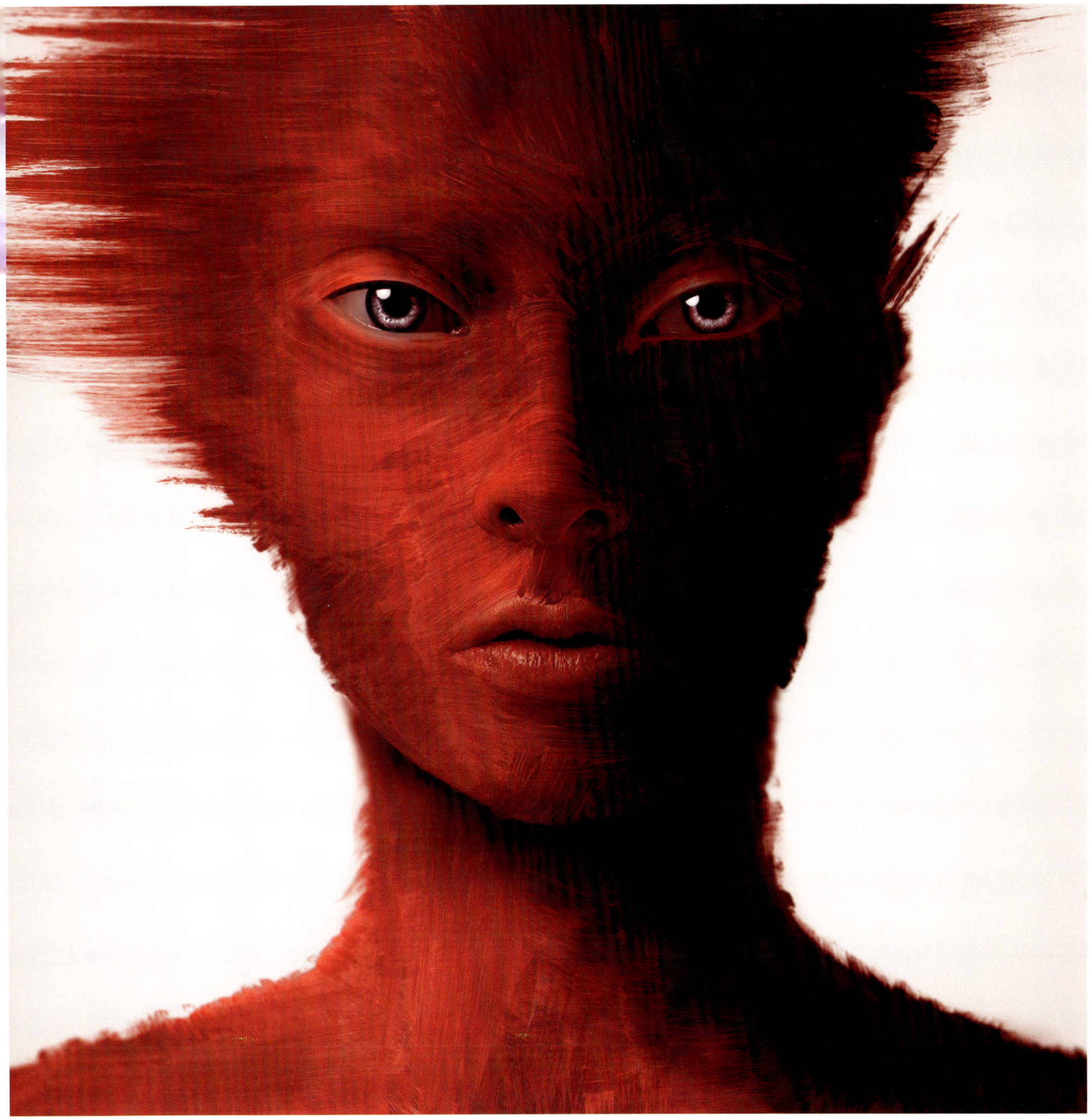

above
Red, 2007
100 x 100 cm
C-print under Diasec
© Oleg Dou
Courtesy of the artist

The photographer Oleg Dou (an acronym for his name, Duryagin Oleg Urievich) was born in Moscow in 1983, where he lives and works. Drawn to art after graduating in 2006 as a computer programmer, he developed the highly finished signature look of his portraits by chance. While editing the portrait of a pale-skinned friend, Dou accidentally exaggerated the lightness of the tone, thus producing a polished effect similar to that of glazed porcelain. On the strength of these beautiful yet eerie portraits, he has been dubbed the 'plastic surgeon of contemporary art'.

Since 2006 Dou has participated in several group shows in Europe and Asia, including the Kandinsky Prize exhibition at the Central House of Artists, Moscow (2007). He has also had solo shows at galleries in Paris, Brussels, Barcelona, Los Angeles and Seoul. Dou's fascination with subjects that appear uncomfortable and strange, and his exploration of human psychology, provoke an emotional reaction in the viewer: 'Art has to resonate with our consciousness ... I love to play with contrasts.' Using a highly manipulated, artificial aesthetic, his portraits nevertheless effect empathy and a recognition of human states and experiences.

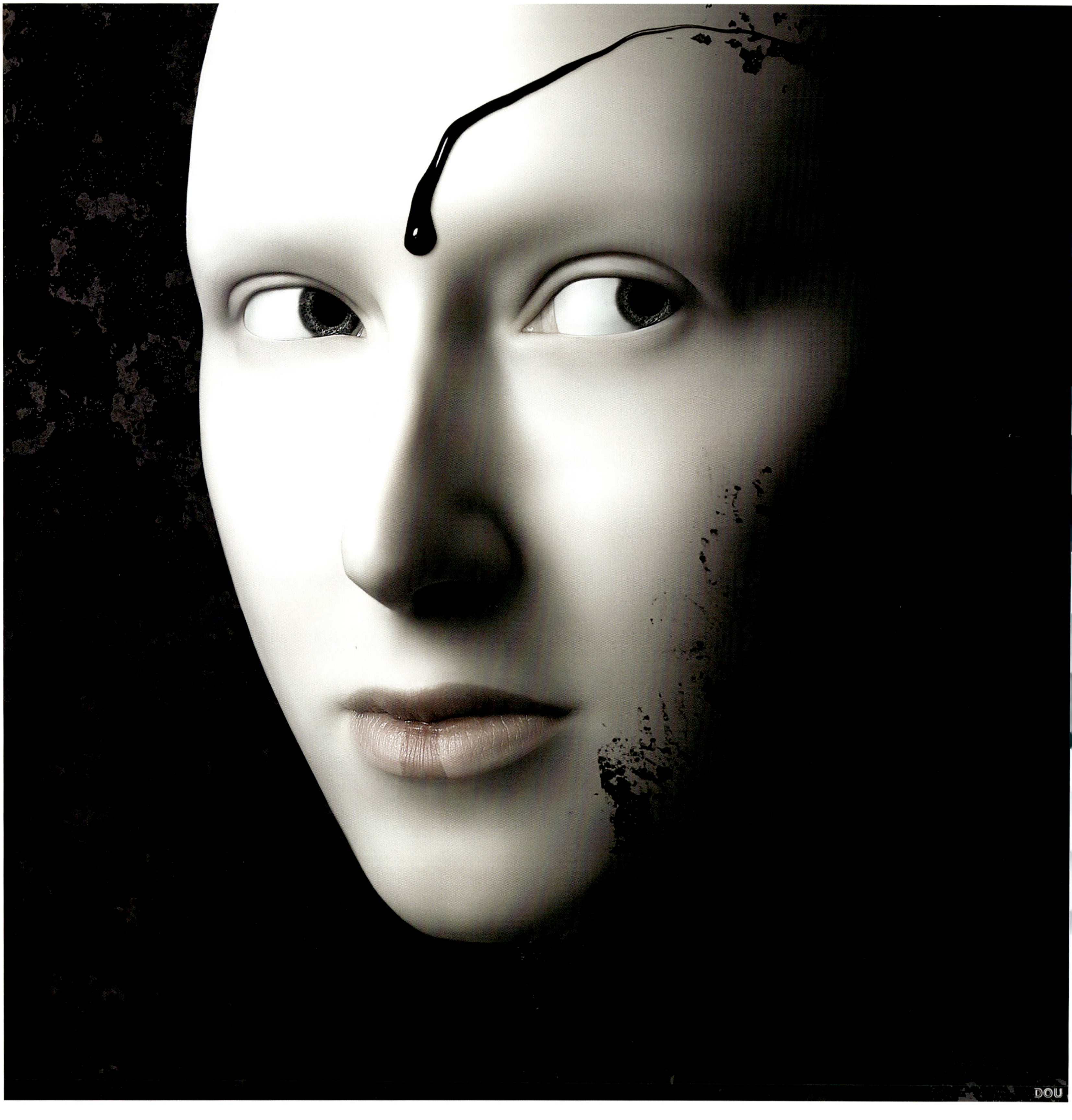
DOU

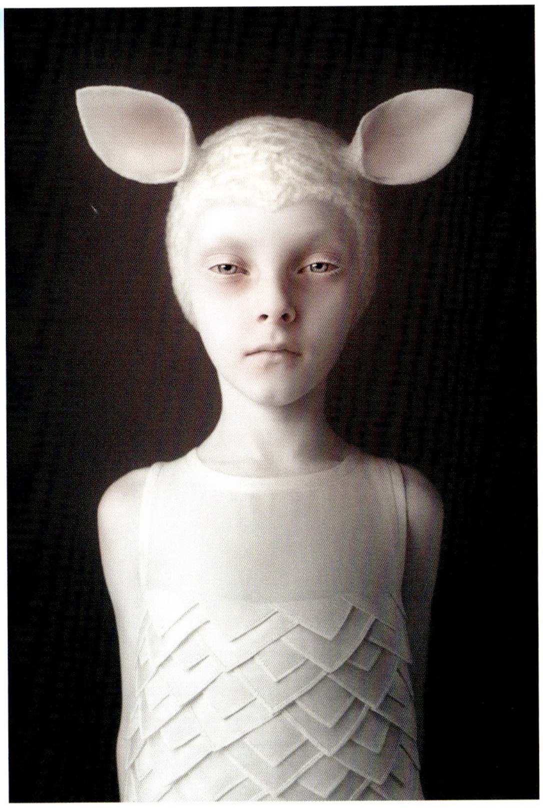

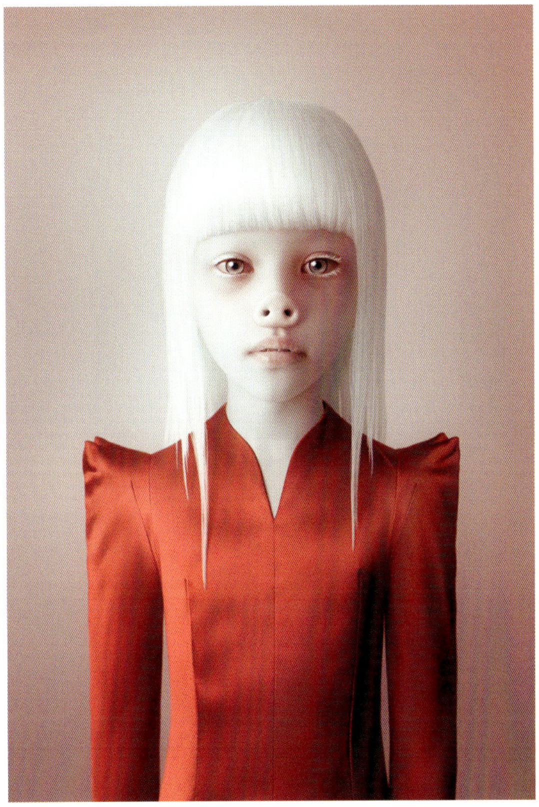

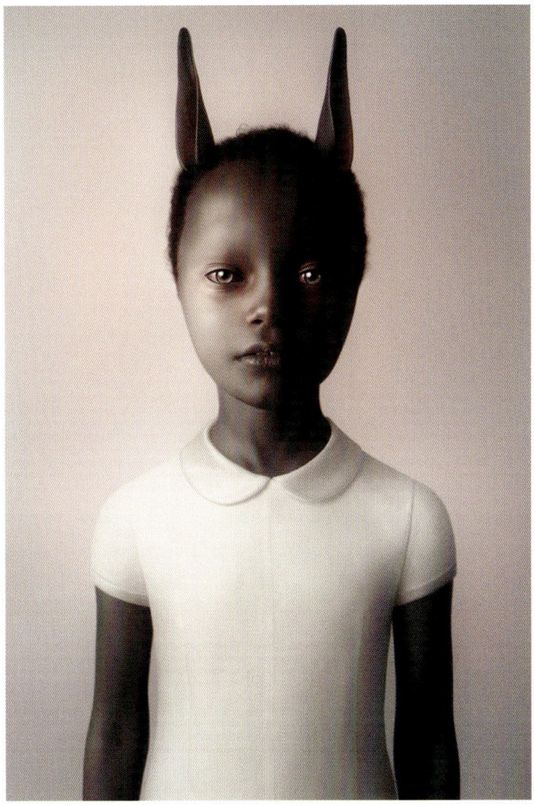

above
Goat, 2009
Variable sizes
C-print mounted on acrylic
© Oleg Dou
Courtesy of the artist

facing page
We Are Made Of, 2006
100 x 100 cm
C-print under Diasec
© Oleg Dou
Courtesy of the artist

above
Pig, 2010
Variable sizes
C-print mounted on acrylic
© Oleg Dou
Courtesy of the artist

above
Rabbit, 2010
Variable sizes
C-print mounted on acrylic
© Oleg Dou
Courtesy of the artist

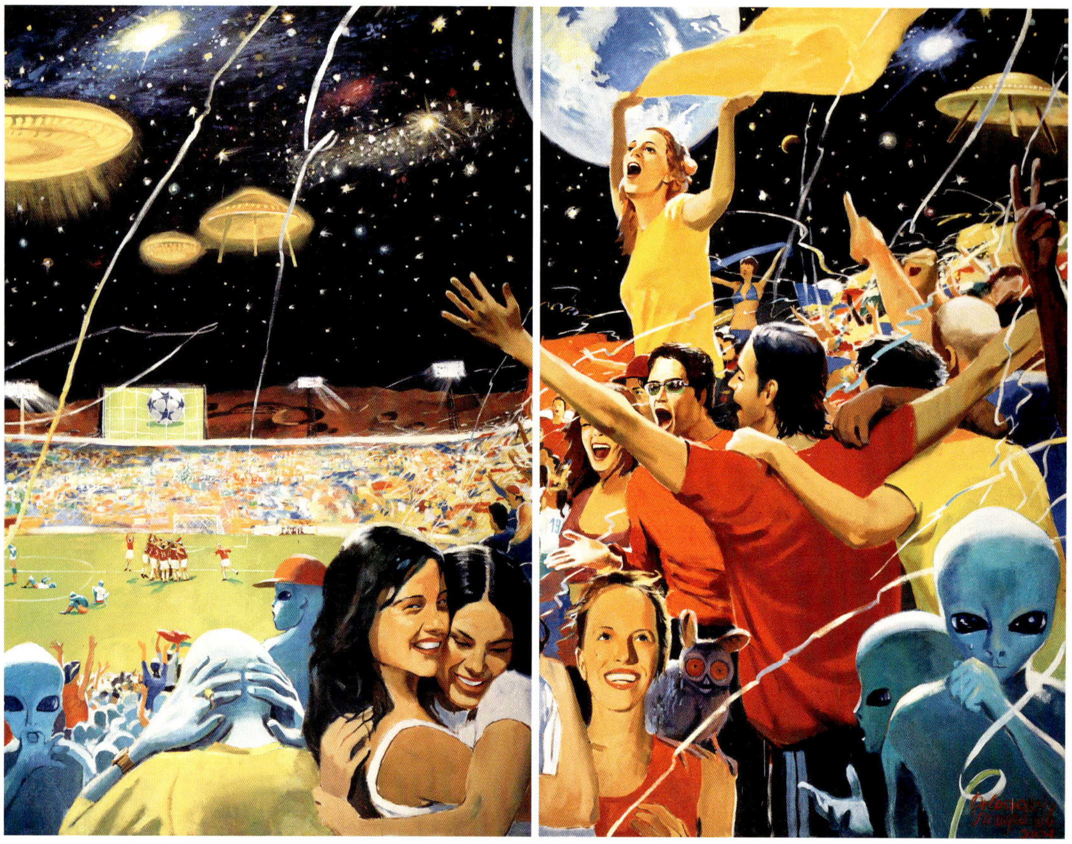

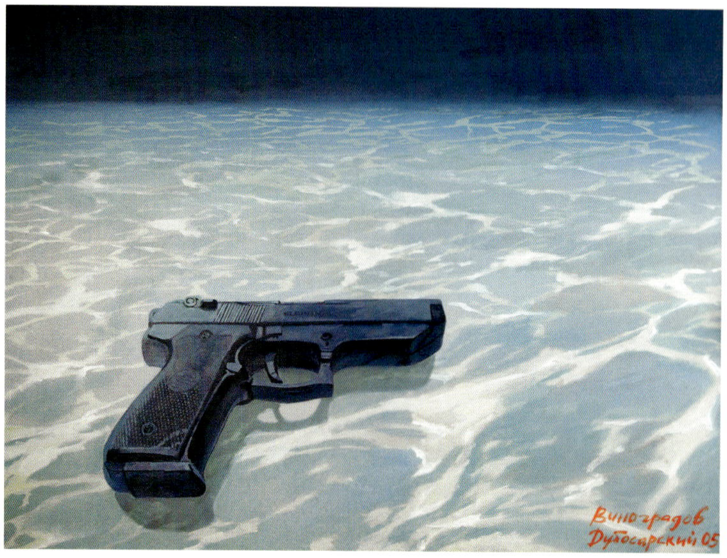

The collaborative duo Vladimir Dubossarsky and Alexander Vinogradov, based in Moscow, have been working together since 1994 to create easel paintings that depict the post-Soviet world with an air of sarcasm, humour and nonchalance. They appeared on the scene at the same time as the violent antics of Moscow Actionism were attracting wide media attention. Their longevity and success are in large part due to their winning formula, which involves introducing a plethora of icons from mass media, popular culture, art history, politics and advertising into a traditional figurative painting format. Dubossarsky and Vinogradov abstain from the political criticism and theorising of their predecessors or contemporaries. Their large-format, brightly coloured paintings offer images that are at once glamorous and kitsch; in them half-naked blondes, testosterone-pumped males, and pop-cultural, political and artistic figures inhabit bucolic landscapes. Early on in their career, the duo declared that '[t]he artist should not present to the public what he wants but what the public wants.'

The artists' early works marry Western icons of mass media and advertising, which flooded into Russia after the collapse of the USSR, with the monumentality and academicism of Socialist Realism. A project that humorously addressed the commissioning of art with works like *Russian Troika: A Painting for a Travel Agency* (1995) and *Open Air: A Painting for a School* (1995) mocked the 1990s trend for identity politics by presenting it as nothing more than a market of national brands. Despite their self-conscious, amateurish brushstrokes and gaudy, dense colours, the pair saturate their work with symbolically loaded iconography which explodes its own meaning. For example, *Total Painting: The Beatles in Moscow* (2004) depicts the Beatles in a symbolic, but impossible, situation – the group never travelled to Russia. Similarly, the series The Four Seasons of Russian Painting (2007) overlays immediately recognisable figures from the history of Russian painting in a mishmash that highlights their artificiality.

top
Earth Wins!, 2004
Oil on canvas
295 x 390 cm
Collection Ekaterina Cultural Foundation, Moscow
Courtesy of Dubossarsky and Vinogradov

above
Pistol, 2005
Oil on canvas
145 x 195 cm
© Dubossarsky and Vinogradov
Private collection, Moscow

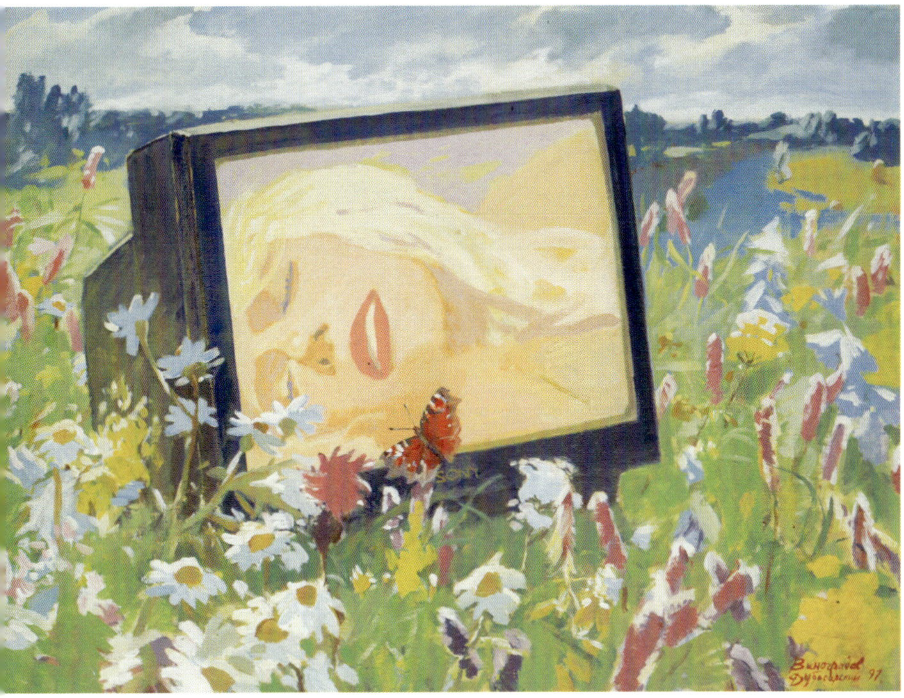

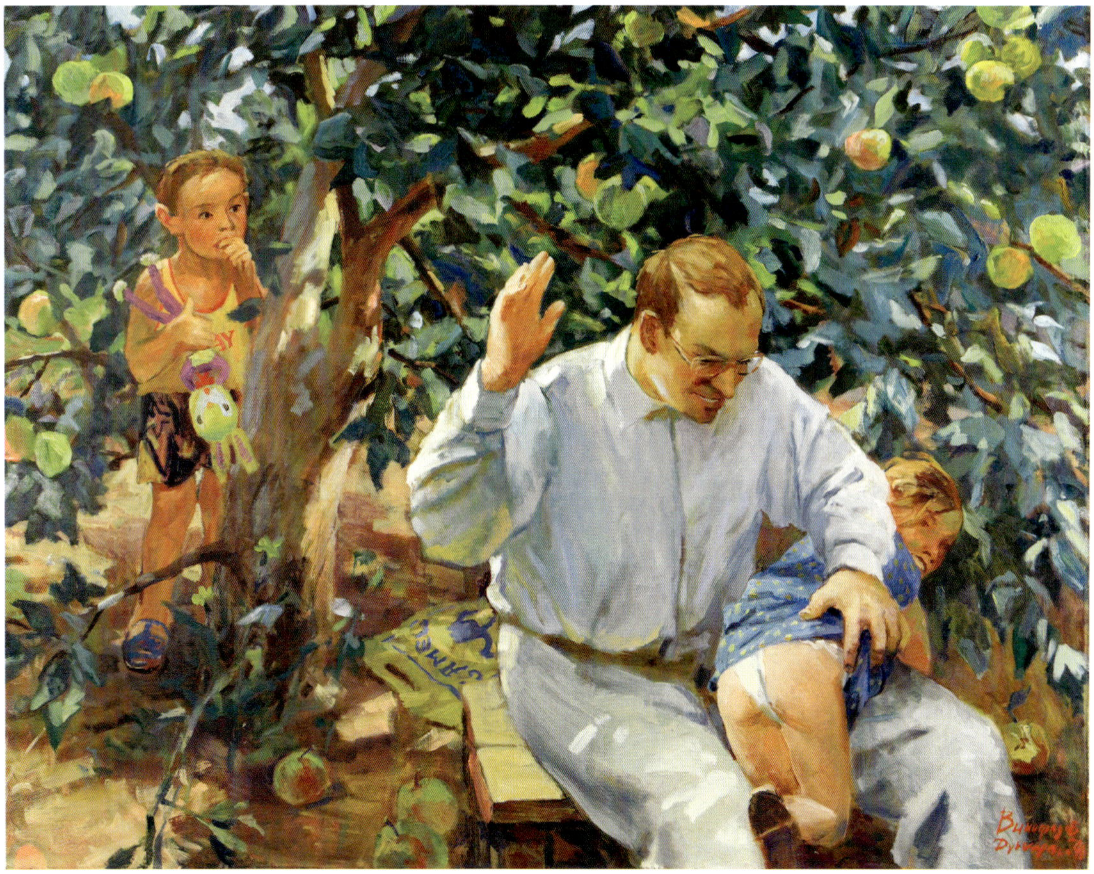

top
La Cicciolina, 1997
Acrylic on canvas
90 x 120 cm
Ekaterina Cultural Foundation
Courtesy of Dubossarsky and Vinogradov

right
Younger Brother, 1996
Oil on canvas
140 x 180.3 cm
© Dubossarsky and Vinogradov
Collection of DES

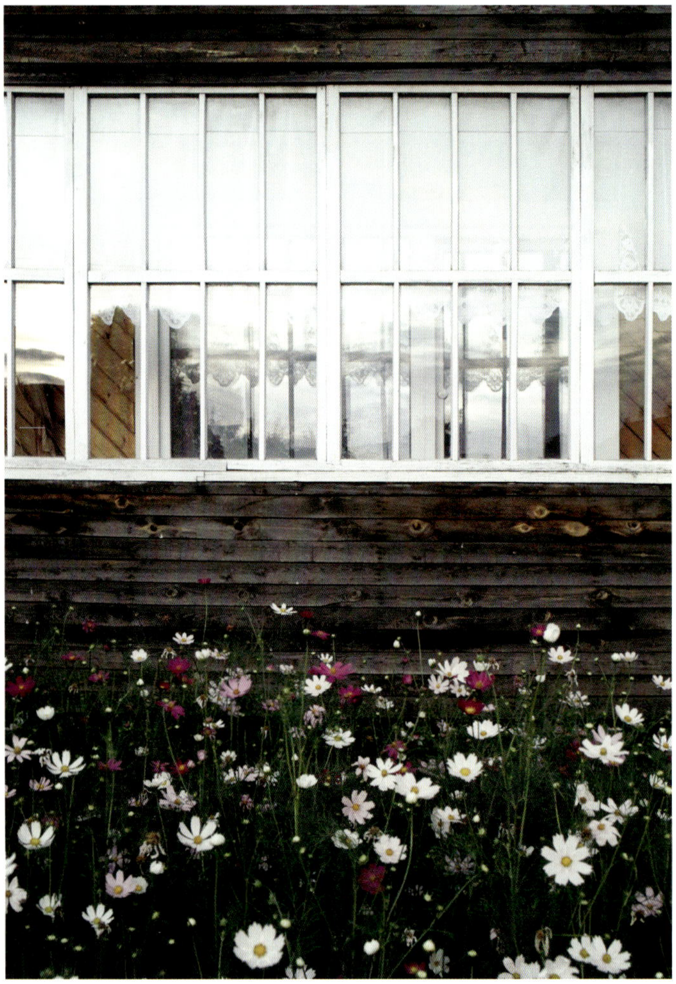

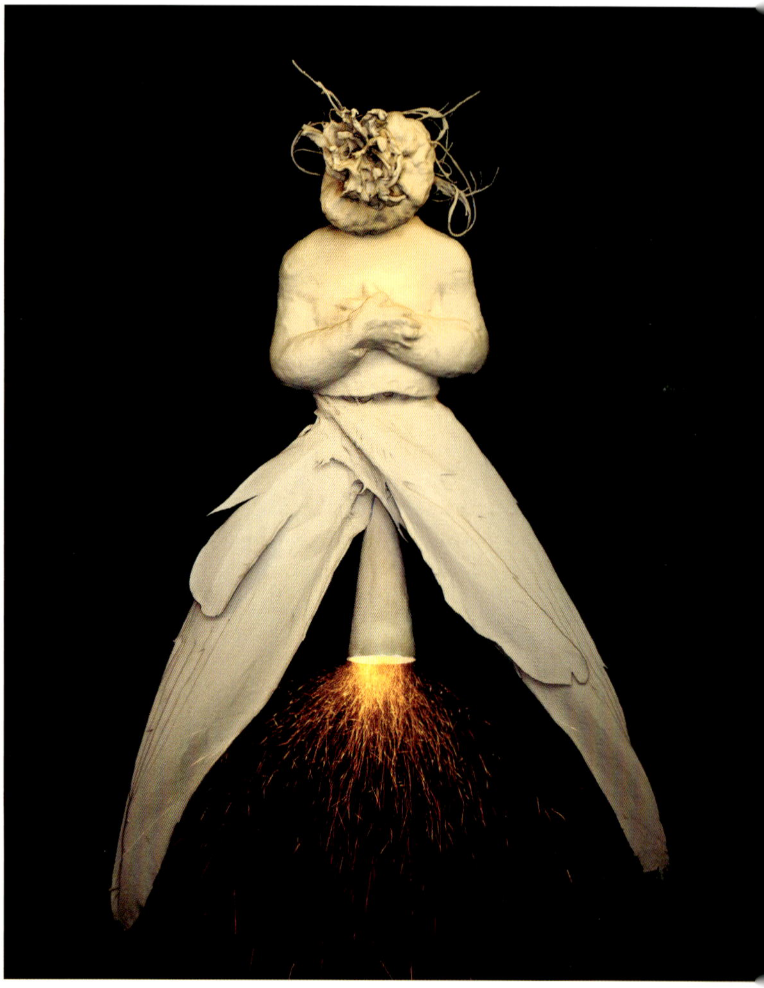

Vladislav Efimov

Vladislav Efimov was born in 1964 and lives and works in Moscow. Having graduated as a car mechanic, from the mid-1990s he started to practise art, winning a grant to study at the Academy of Fine Arts, Berlin, in 1995. Efimov works with photography, installation and interactive art, and has collaborated with Aristarkh Chernyshevsky on video projects. Collecting, classifying, documenting, mining the past and examining the present are the approaches that shape and inform Efimov's art. Using new media and high-tech equipment, he often frames objects from the past, as in his series For the Radio (2009), in which he placed and photographed old-fashioned radios in contemporary interiors. This series won him the Innovation Prize in 2009.

Efimov takes photographic portraits of everyday objects in his studio. In other works he transforms these objects into strange organisms, as in the series Burning Things (2008), where they appear to be on fire. In his 2009–10 exhibition *A Fearful Collection* at the Stella Art Foundation, Moscow, the interactive installation encouraged viewers to touch boxes in which strange objects had been placed; the objects screamed, hid or sang on being touched.

Efimov travels widely throughout Russia and Europe recording listed structures, for example early Constructivist buildings in the ongoing series New Leningrad. His landscape photography combines a spontaneous, fresh approach with a focus on design, form and pattern in the everyday environment. The photographic series ZIL (2010) saw him return to a disused Soviet factory he had worked in twenty years previously as an engineer; it documents the artist's fascination with his own memories, with change and with the decay of the familiar.

above
Burning Things, 2008
Light box
Edition of 5
20 x 25 x 15.5 cm
© Vladislav Efimov
Courtesy of Ravenscourt Galleries

left
From the series Eniseisk, 2009
C-print
© Vladislav Efimov
Courtesy of Ravenscourt Galleries

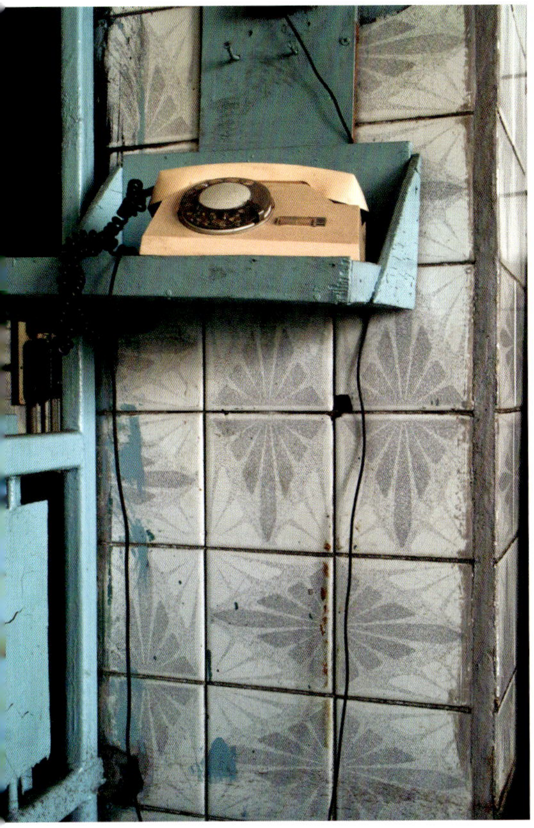

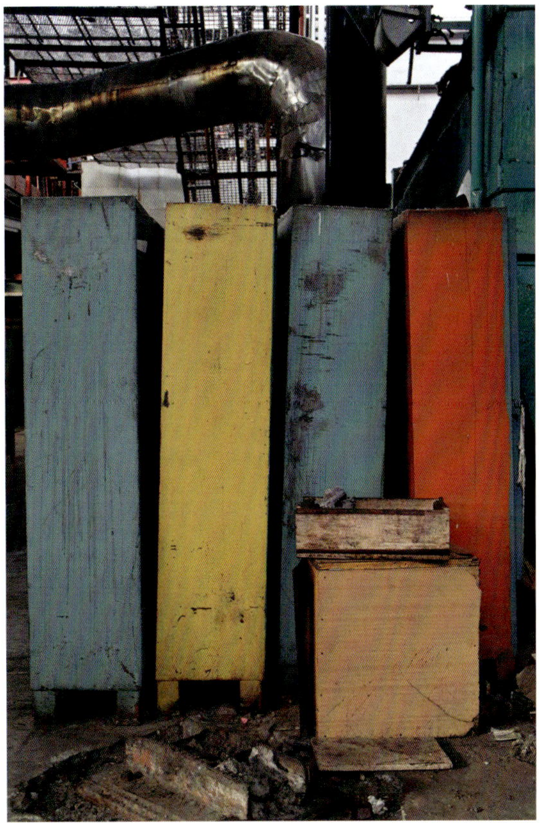

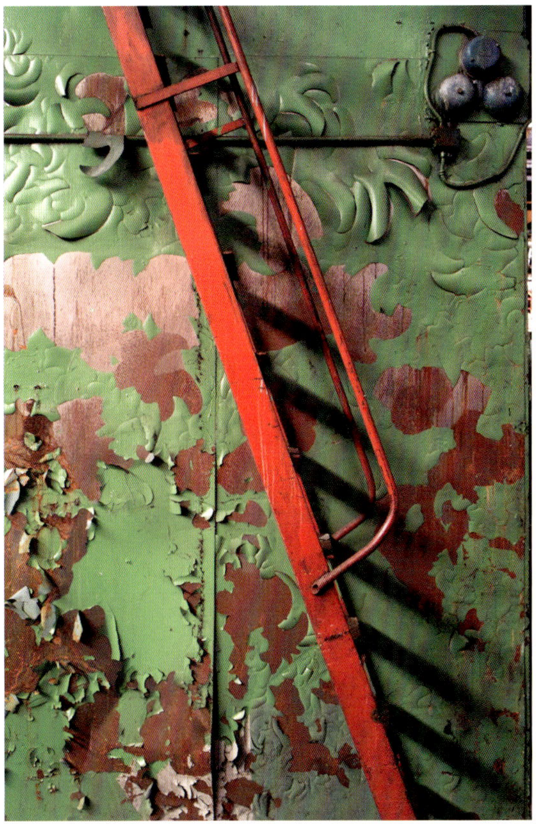

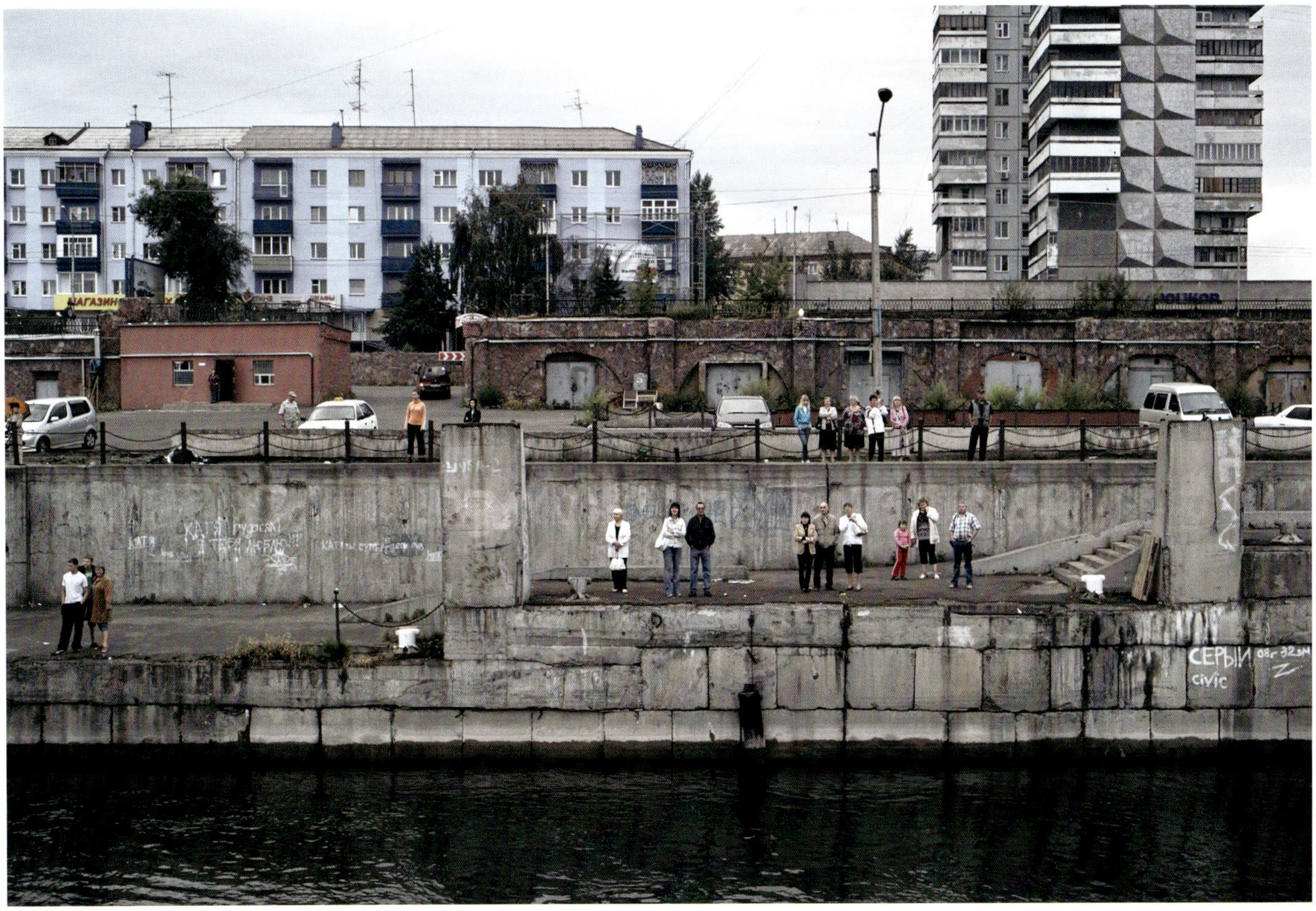

above
ZIL, 2011
Photographic paper
on foam board
Edition of 5
31 x 62 cm

Courtesy of Ravenscourt
Galleries

right
From the series Eniseisk,
2009
Colour photographs

Courtesy of Ravenscourt
Galleries

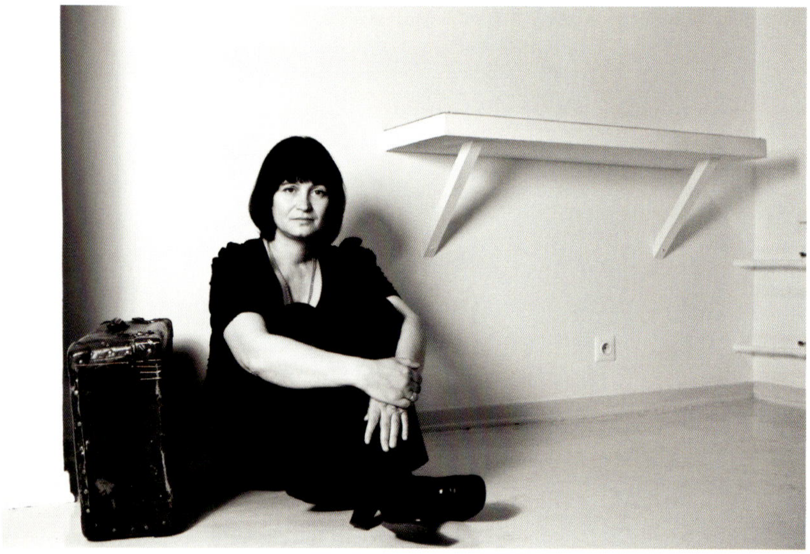

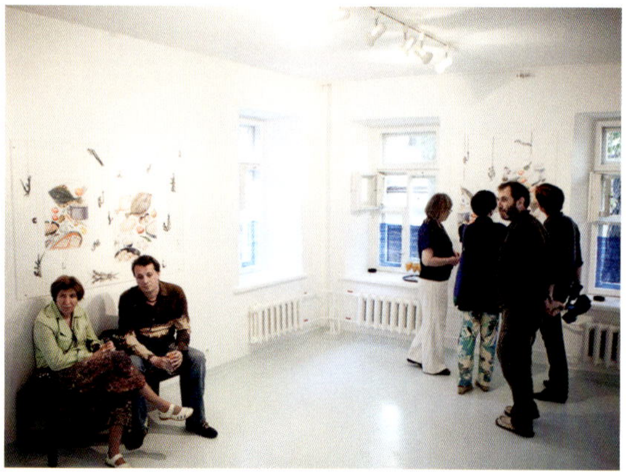

The E.K.ArtBureau is located in a nineteenth-century low-rise building close to Rozhdestvensky Boulevard, a quiet hilly neighbourhood in Moscow city centre. E.K.ArtBureau's founder, Elena Kuprina-Lyakhovich, was born in Moscow in 1965 to a family of scientists; her father was an engineer, her mother a physics teacher. After dabbling in film and journalism, she took an innovative course on curatorship at the Moscow CAC (no longer in existence) in 1993. Organised by the art historian Victor Misiano, the course was taught by Western professionals invited to Moscow at a time when independent curatorship was still in its infancy. Kuprina-Lyakhovich recalls that 'they were charismatic personalities, and [the programme] opened my eyes to the intellectual side of curating.' After setting up E.K.Art to organise arts projects, in 2002 she opened a permanent space.

With its location in a private, residential apartment block, the E.K.ArtBureau echoes the Soviet underground tradition of showing art in private homes. The atmosphere is both intimate and formal, with the small kitchen serving as a meeting space alongside a conventional, dedicated white-cube exhibition space. As an institution it defies easy definition because, despite its function as a gallery, Kuprina-Lyakovich does not like the gallery label. In her search for authenticity and liberation from the shackles of commercialism, she often shows work that is not for sale.

A passionate advocate of Moscow Conceptualism, Kuprina-Lyakovich sees it as her mission to keep the tradition alive. In 2004–5 she mounted a series of retrospective exhibitions of work by Conceptual groups, including the Toadstools (Mukhomor), Collective Actions and APTART. Artists such as Andrei Monastyrsky, Sven Gundlach and Maria Serebriakova continue to develop ideas for new shows with work that keeps pushing the boundaries of Moscow Conceptual culture. One of Kuprina-Lyakovich's strengths is her relative freedom from commercial constraint, which enables her to use her space as a laboratory for small experimental exhibitions.

Kuprina-Lyakhovich believes that, despite the plethora of important national museums and galleries in Russia, there is inadequate State funding for contemporary art due to a lack of understanding of the field. Legislative change is essential, she feels, to provide more financial support to institutions as well as tax breaks for patrons and philanthropists. Another concern is the Russian public's struggle to understand the role of the artist, which can lead to an undermining of talent. Before perestroika, artists had a clear role: to serve the State's propaganda mission. Official artists were respected and well rewarded. The fact that the status of artists has not been redefined since 1989 has left practitioners without any real professional identity or social status: 'The masses still believe artists are servants of the State; it means that now what artists do is seen as a kind of hobby; they are unemployed people with a hobby!' Meanwhile, Kuprina-Lyakhovich is critical of the impact of globalisation on Russian contemporary art, seeing it as a threat pressurising artists to create works that appeal to everyone, thereby robbing them of their true individual and national value.

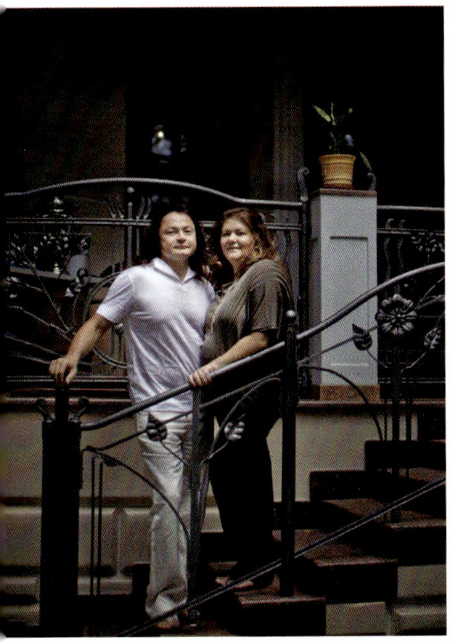

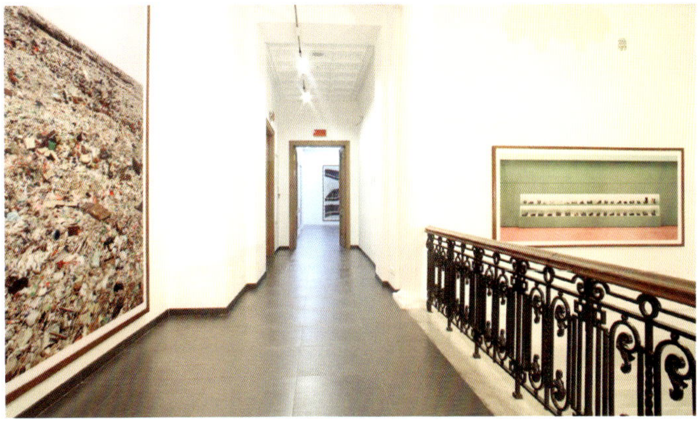

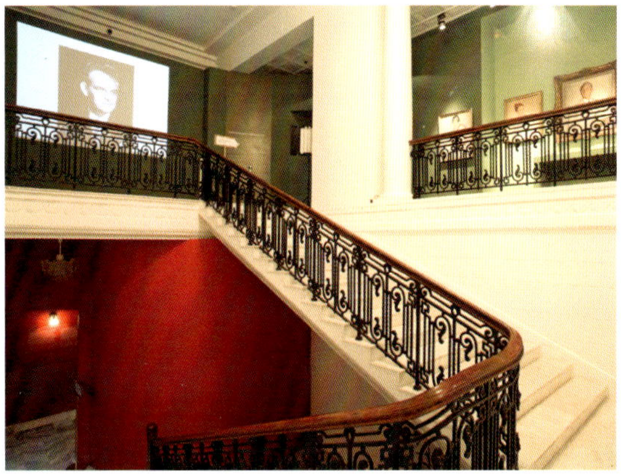

he Ekaterina Cultural Foundation was set up in 002 by Ekaterina and Vladimir Semenikhin to romote twentieth-century and contemporary ussian art. The not-for-profit foundation is ocated in a dedicated multi-storey exhibition pace on Moscow's fashionable Kuznetsky Most. supports and stages exhibitions, collaborates vith public museums, and publishes atalogues and art books. Exhibitions range om solo shows of Russian and international ontemporary artists to retrospectives and urveys of Russian post-war movements, for xample *Field of Action* (2010), which focused on Moscow Conceptualism. Collaborations with ublic museums both in Russia and abroad have ncluded *Vot*, at the Musée d'Art Moderne de a Ville de Paris (2007), and two projects at the tate Tretyakov Gallery, Moscow: *Russian Pop Art* 2005) and *SotsArt: Political Art in Russia* (2007).

Ekaterina (born 1971) and Vladimir (born 967) are both avid collectors, and their ersonal collection forms the springboard or the foundation's exhibitions programme. Native Muscovites, they met while working in eal estate; Ekaterina became an employee of Vladimir's company in 1994, and they married a year later. Today they divide their time between Moscow and Monaco.

The couple started to collect art almost immediately, and this has become a shared passion. Their first acquisitions were paintings by the Jack of Diamonds group; later they shifted their main focus to the post-war period, although their tastes remain diverse. As Ekaterina explains, 'When I like something, Vladimir almost always agrees to buy it; usually we only buy something if we both like it. Vladimir prefers monumental sculpture and I am more into painting, but we always find a common language. It is hard to say who drives the collection. I have more free time to focus on learning about new trends. Our personal collection is quite varied; we have works from the eighteenth century to today.' They both believe that Eric Bulatov is Russia's greatest talent of the past twenty-five years and own several of his important pieces.

Ekaterina observes that, despite a high level of cultural borrowing from the West, Russian contemporary art is closely connected to the country's own literary and artistic traditions. The biggest influence she sees is the Russian avant-garde. Vladimir speaks more of the practical opportunities for the exchange of ideas on a global scale that are open to Russian artists today: 'What's important is that there is development ... People are visiting exhibitions, shows and fairs, and everything happens a lot faster and more dynamically than before.' Ekaterina believes that the 1980s and '90s were strong decades for Russian artists. She advocates enthusiastically for the importance of ideas as well as strong aesthetics and skill.

Vladimir believes that the Russian art world is becoming more professional, yet he and Ekaterina share concerns about the disciplines of criticism and art history, referencing an overabundance of obscure writing which does not help to elucidate its subject matter. There is also, in their view, insufficient general and theoretical criticism being written about Russian contemporary art in the West. Ekaterina believes that artists should reflect what is happening in society in their work; Vladimir's view is that they should also attempt to predict the future. In this connection he believes that video art is a strong medium in Russia today; the couple supported the first retrospective of video artist Victor Alimpiev at the foundation in 2008.

As private patrons, despite their foundation's not-for-profit status, the Semenikhins do not receive support or tax breaks from the State; it is also the case that official bureaucracy hinders rather than helps their cause. The fact that there are different customs regulations for private and governmental organisations makes their activities even more difficult. Vladimir sees this as a problem that prevents other private patrons from supporting the arts in Russia, where State funding and legislation support public museums exclusively. Although Vladimir and Ekaterina see their role as cultural patrons as a creative activity and collecting as a source of great pleasure, responsibility for running the foundation has taken over in recent years. As Vladimir puts it, 'It's work. It was a hobby at first, but now it's a second job.'

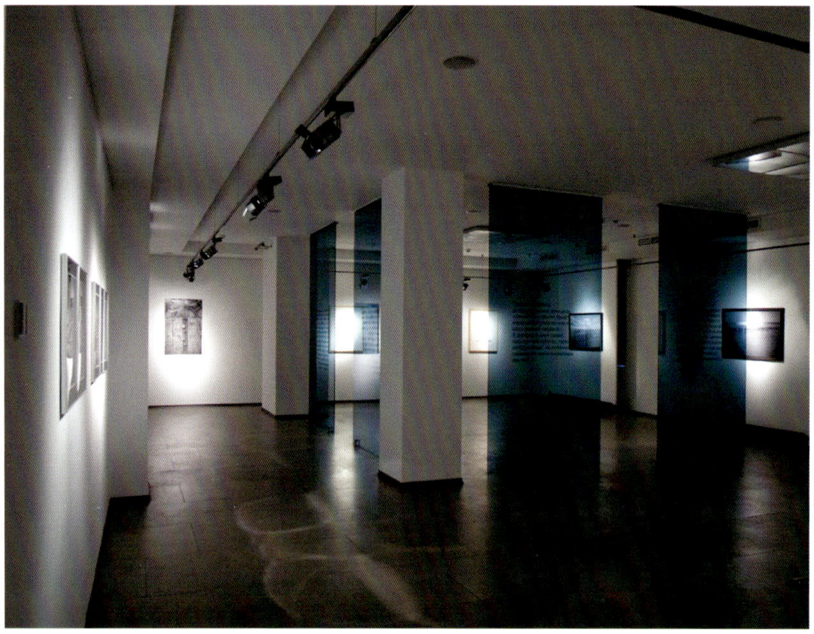

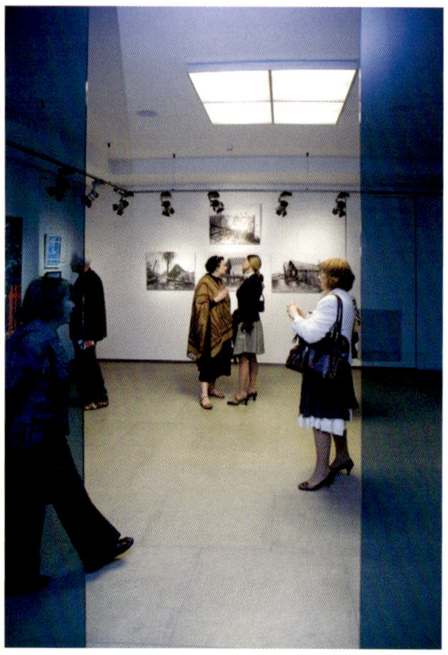

The ERA Foundation, an independent, not-for-profit organisation located in the heart of Moscow, was set up by Elena Beryozkina, its president, in 2006. It provides a central venue for exhibitions and encourages participation from other Moscow-based and international institutions within the wide-ranging scope of its activities. Its mission is to develop contemporary art in Russia and to provide a platform for artistic, research-led and educational initiatives.

The foundation's central pillar is, indisputably, the public debates and lectures it hosts. Its first organised event was the public symposium 'Formalism Forever?', which looked at the legacy of modernism within the context of contemporary art. By bringing together a panel of artists, art historians, critics, writers, musicians, theorists and museum directors such as Ekaterina Degot, Dmitry Gutov, Anatoly Osmolovsky, Andrei Erofeev and David Riff, ERA Foundation's debut demonstrated its interest in the theoretical problems and debates surrounding contemporary art, and in the necessity to make these issues accessible to the wider public. The foundation has continued to expand in this direction. In 2008, it organised and hosted the first international multimedia conference, 'A Non-canonical Classic: In Memory of Dmitry Prigov (1940–2007)', which celebrated the prolific career of the experimental artist, poet and writer Dmitry Prigov.

These public conferences and symposia have positioned the foundation as an innovative space with a desire to foster theoretical and critical thinking, and to facilitate an understanding and appreciation of contemporary art and its heritage without shying away from the latter's more intellectually demanding and less mainstream tendencies. The foundation engages directly with the most topical artistic issues in Russia today. For example, in 2011 it staged a public debate entitled 'Artist Awards in Russia: Prize or Provocation' as a means of placing problems relating to artistic prizes and competitions (such as subjective judgement and favouritism) in the forefront of public consciousness. Given that recent recipients of national awards like the Kandinsky Prize have included the ultra-nationalist Alexei Belyaev-Gintovt (2008) and the St Petersburg-based radical collective Voina (2010), the timing of the ERA Foundation's events has taken on a new prescience.

More recently, the foundation has mapped out a curatorial direction engaging with themes of childhood, motherhood and artistic legacy within the structure of the family. As part of this initiative, the organisation has developed a children's programme whose goal is to develop creative thinking and practical ability from an early age. It often schedules workshops in conjunction with current exhibitions, in which artists reveal the tricks of their trade to young children. The classes, held in the midst of the exhibition space, provide participants with the opportunity to create their own paintings, drawings and objects surrounded by existing works of art. In addition, lecture series deal with wide-ranging topics in art history and design in an informative yet entertaining fashion. Each session is divided into theoretical and practical components, so that children have a chance to create objects which address the specifics of the subjects being covered. Finally, a purpose-built theatre studio holds classes for the youngest participants, aged between three and nine, teaching the basics of stage decoration and set design.

As well as taking part in artistic fundraising events for charity, the ERA Foundation supports access to contemporary art through the publishing of exhibition catalogues which accompany its shows. Its exhibitions programme strikes a balance between the promotion of young international artists, as yet unknown in Moscow, within the framework of its Debuts series; the display of well-known fixtures on the Russian scene like Pavel Pepperstein and Nikita Alekseev; and collaborative programmes and events with the Moscow Biennale, the Multimedia Art Museum's Photobiennale and the Moscow Film Festival's Media Forum.

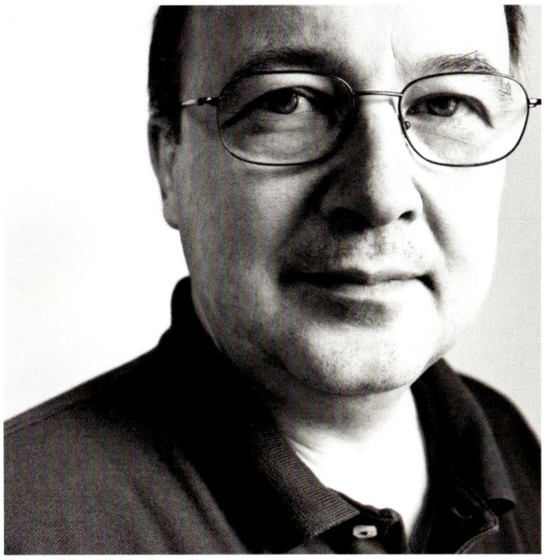

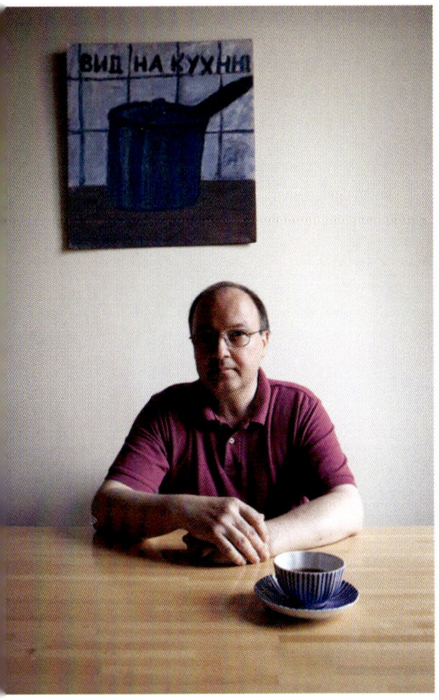

Andrei Erofeev

Moscow curator Andrei Erofeev specialises in Russian contemporary art. Born in Paris in 1956 into a family of diplomats, he studied art history at Moscow State University; today he lives in a large, bright nineteenth-century apartment in the centre of Moscow. Erofeev has a background in museum work. Between 1989 and 2002, he put together a collection of contemporary Russian art at the Tsaritsino Museum, and from 2002 to 2008 he worked at the State Tretyakov Gallery, Moscow, leading the newly formed Department of New Trends.

Erofeev's contemporary exhibitions have attracted controversy and even censorship. In 2008 he was dismissed from his position at the State Tretyakov Gallery following a high-profile scandal relating to two shows he had curated the previous year. *Forbidden Art*, at the Andrey Sakharov Museum, Moscow, brought together works which had been censored over the previous decades. *SotsArt: Political Art in Russia from 1972– the Present Day*, at La Maison Rouge, Paris, displayed a number of images that were said to discredit the Russian Orthodox Church and the armed forces. They were removed from the show and in 2010 Erofeev was charged with inciting religious hostilities.

Currently Erofeev works independently, writing articles and undertaking small exhibition projects, describing his life as 'on standby' as he waits to see whether it will be possible to return to the public arena. He is optimistic about the state of contemporary art in Russia, describing the scene as 'dynamic'. Using the metaphor of movement, he explains that contemporary art is not about 'moving things' but is reflective of life today. Erofeev believes that Russian artists already feel part of the West rather than simply 'Westernised'. During the early 2000s, practitioners such as AES+F and Dubossarsky and Vinogradov may have explored aspects of Western civilisation, but the current generation is more focused on local issues.

As far as art criticism is concerned, Erofeev notes a lack of conviction: 'Art criticism has become complimentary. It does not discriminate between good and bad art; it simply likes all artists. So there is a sense that the present, which should be selecting good from bad, is delegating its responsibilities to the future.' He believes that this situation is an inheritance from the underground culture of the past. There was solidarity, and people wanted to support one another, but this meant that they did not criticise each other's work. Interestingly, Erofeev cites similar problems in the West.

Erofeev believes that the history of Russian twentieth-century art requires reimagining: 'We need to take down Soviet art and present the Russian art of the twentieth century in the Soviet Union as "Russian art of the Soviet period".' He highlights the ideological divisions in museums that still exist today, interpreting the situation as a struggle over the meaning of art and a standoff that must be resolved. Speaking of Russian modernism, including the period before perestroika, he observes that the State museums continue to view such work as 'other art'. Erofeev challenges this view: 'There is no "other art"; there is only this art, and there should be questions cast over what exactly Soviet art is.'

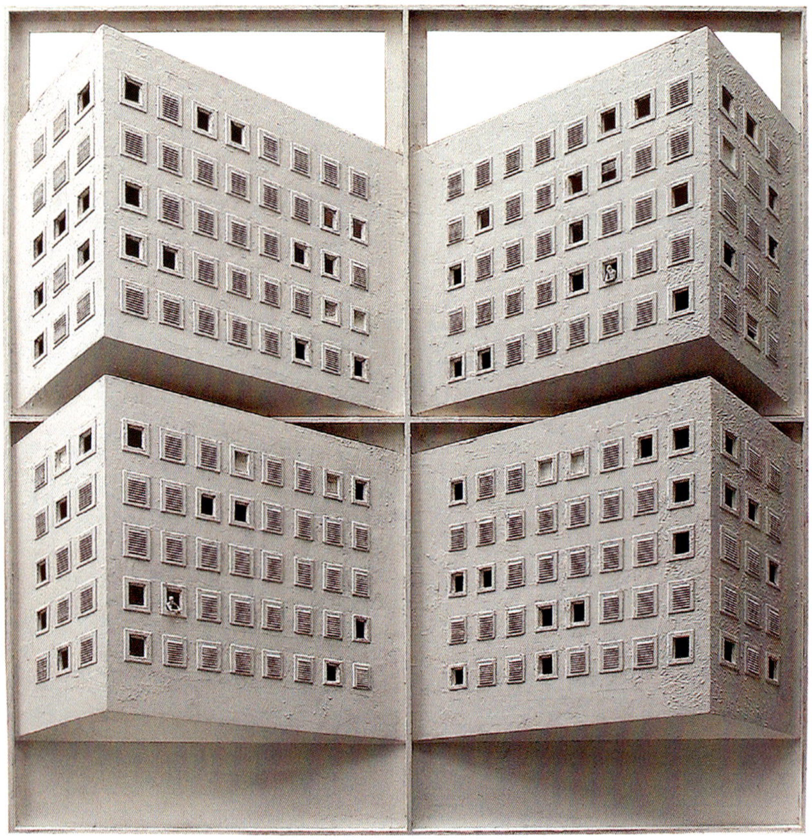

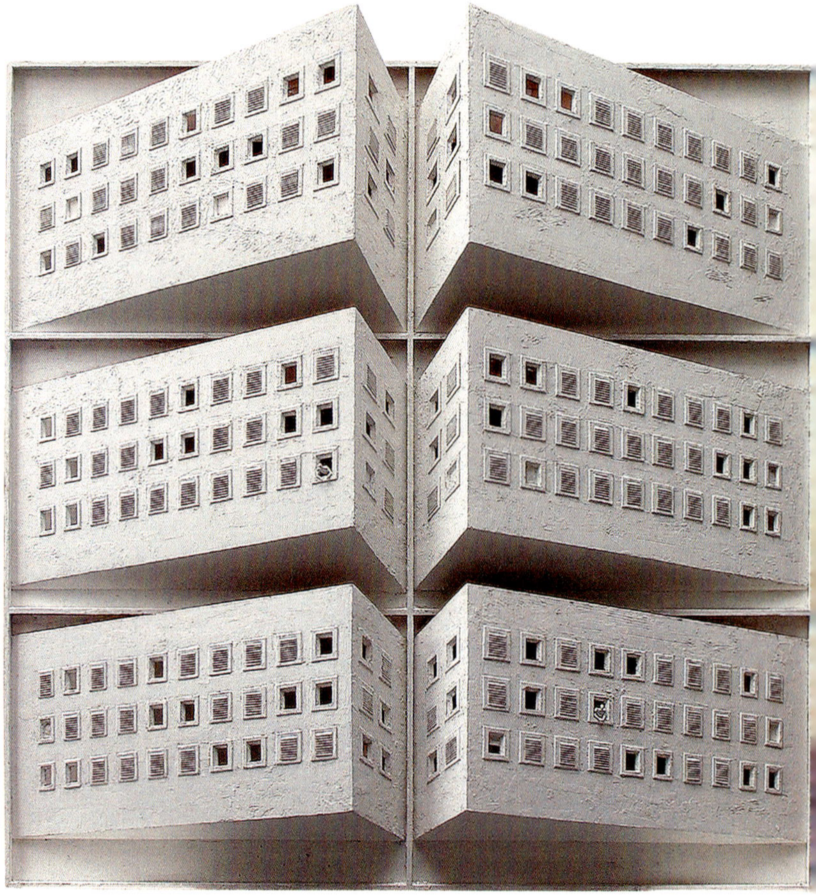

The painter, sculptor and graphic artist Sergei Essaian was born in Moscow in 1939. His father, arrested shortly before his birth, died in a gulag. Essaian's formative years were spent studying books on Western European art from his father's library. After formal art education at the Polytechnical and 1905 Memorial art institutes in Moscow, he graduated in 1960 and worked briefly as a restorer and English teacher, before taking on a job as subeditor for the magazine *Decorative Arts of the USSR*. In 1979 Essaian emigrated to Paris, where he lived and worked until his death in 2007. In 2002 the State Russian Museum, St Petersburg, organised a retrospective of his work.

Essaian's creative output can be taken as the expression of the condition and predicament of being an outsider in one's environment. Because of their exaggerated proportions, his naked, anxious figures occupying enclosed spaces or barren landscapes nearly always look small and vulnerable. His art exudes a general mood of unease, giving voice to loneliness and disengagement. A series of urban reliefs shows tiny figures in large houses reminiscent of cells. Such works were in part inspired by the stylised landscapes in Florentine Renaissance painting and in part by the memory of the house Le Corbusier designed in Moscow, which for the young artist was a seductive yet illusory symbol of Western freedom. His series of works on the theme of the runner, such as the painting *Joggers of Buttes-Chaumont* (1997), underlines the restless anxiety of contemporary life. This series, inspired by a group of runners the artist saw near his Paris studio, is a reflection on the mindlessness of jogging, which can be seen as both a healthy activity and one which distracts us from real life and the natural mind–body relationship.

above
City No. 2, 2002
Gesso on wood
152.3 x 152.3 x 10 cm
© Family of the artist
Collection of artist's family, Paris

above left
City No. 3, 2002
Gesso on wood
161 x 152.3 x 15 cm
© Family of the artist
Collection of artist's family, Paris

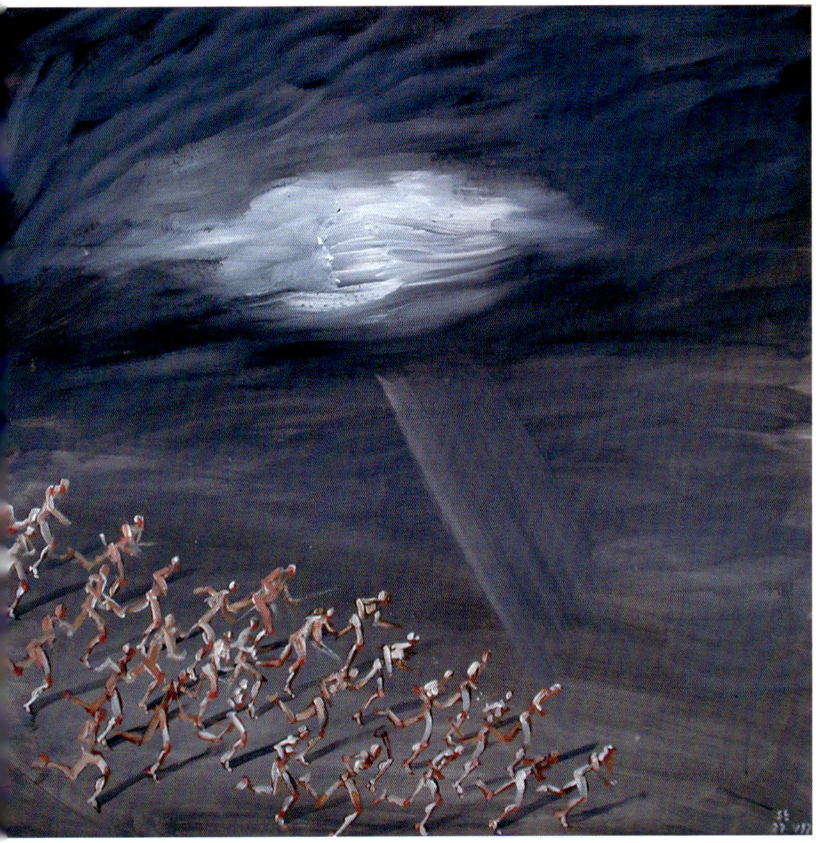

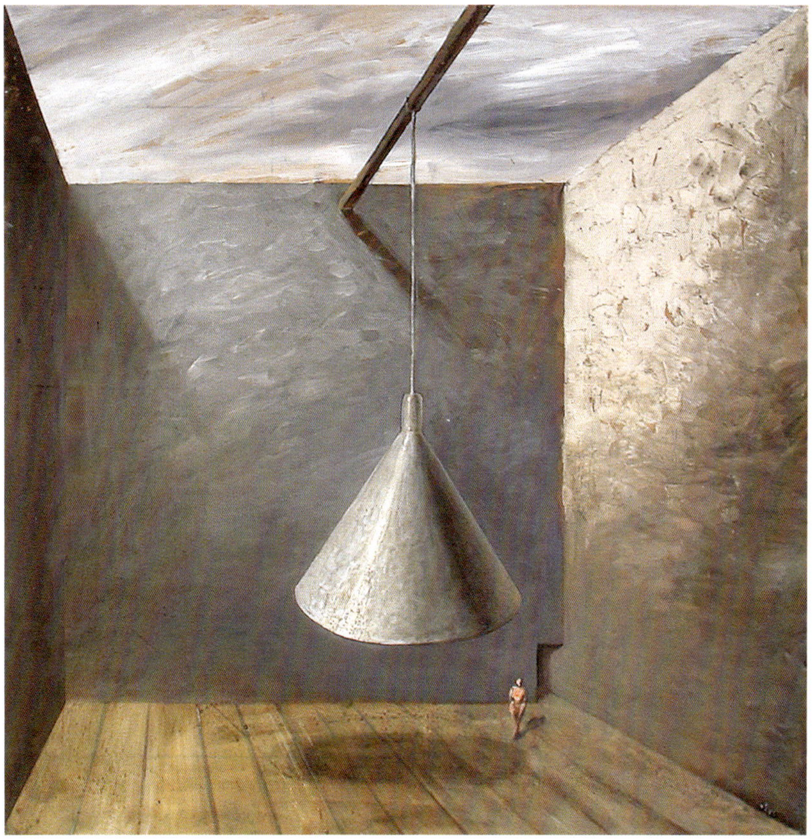

above
Joggers of Buttes-Chaumont, 1997
Acrylic on paper attached to MDF
98 x 98 cm
© Family of the artist
Collection of the artist's family, Paris

above right
Inner Courtyard No. 2, 1995
Acrylic on MDF
21.5 x 120.5 cm
© Family of the artist
Courtesy of Rostropovich-Vishnevskaya
Collection

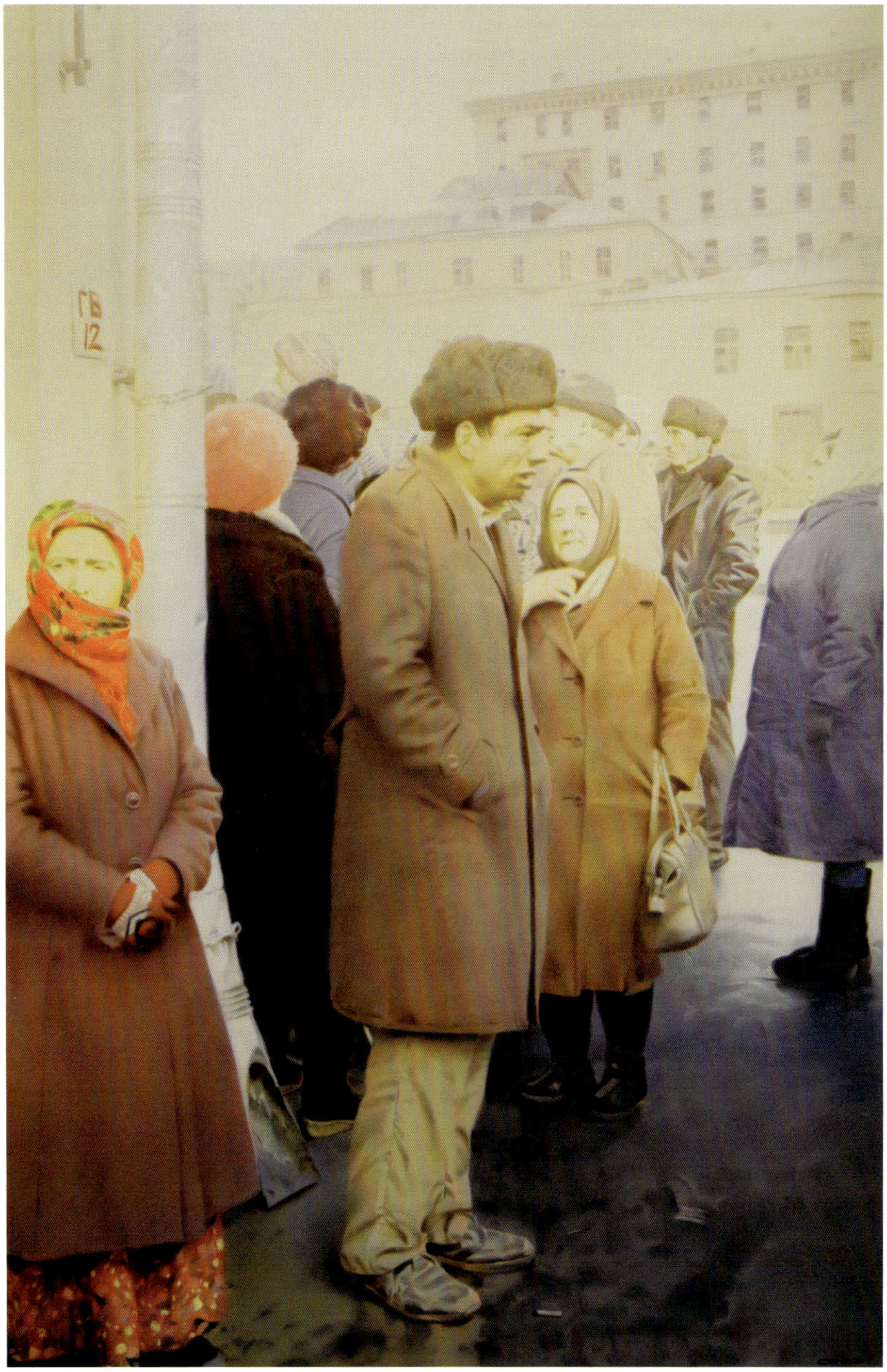

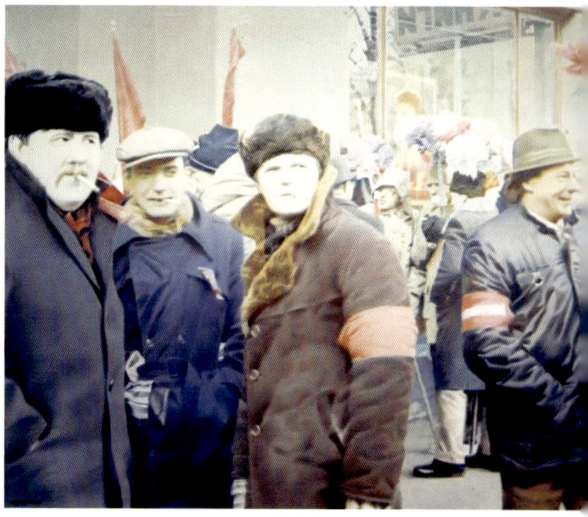

Painter and graphic artist Semyon Faibisovich was born in Moscow in 1949 and, apart from two brief stays in New York, has lived and worked all his life in his native city. His talent for drawing was discovered at an early age when he drew such an exact likeness of his brother that his parents – a military rail worker and a physicist – felt compelled to send him to art school. Having graduated from the Moscow Institute of Architecture in 1972, Faibisovich started to draw interiors at home in his spare time but quickly realised that he preferred to be out in the city combining his love of the urban landscape with an increasing interest in its inhabitants. During the 1980s he was associated with Moscow underground circles, showing his paintings in a popular alternative exhibition venue on Malaya Gruzinskaya Street. He was close to the dissident poets Lev Rubinstein, whom he painted, and Mikhail Aizenberg. Faibisovich's works have been shown in numerous important commercial and public galleries throughout Russia, Europe and the US, and he has collaborated with the Regina Gallery, Moscow, for nearly two decades. Following a period of crisis in his personal life, he abandoned painting for a decade, only returning to it in 2005. He went on to develop a new technique of recording urban views on his mobile phone, using these as a printed basis for large-scale paintings of post-Soviet Moscow.

Faibisovich's compositions most often consist of views of the Moscow suburbs and the Baumansky factory district, where he lives. One of his most celebrated series, depicting the Moscow metro, was first painted in 1984–8, with a second series, Underground Again, produced in 2011. Stylistically, his work bears some relation to American Photorealism (of which he first became aware in 1975) in its highly detailed vision of exterior reality and its focus on urban low life: people queuing in the street, piles of rubbish elevated to the status of high art. However, as the poet Aizenberg has observed, there is a fundamental difference: Faibisovich is more interested in fixing his own gaze on the canvas than employing the detached 'lens of photorealism'. Much of his art is about the experience of viewing; he often plays with reflections, introducing mirrors and similar surfaces into his work. His subdued colour palette of the 1980s has become bolder in more recent times.

During the Soviet period, Faibisovich sought to create a collective portrait of the USSR, to show Russia through the expressions and movements of its citizens. Since 2005, he has been documenting social change, especially the rise in the numbers of homeless people, street beggars and immigrants from ex-Soviet states. However, he does not have a social agenda, and, despite his scientific approach, his art is the product of a deeply personal engagement with his surroundings: 'I see myself as a post-Postmodern because I do not reject Post-modernism and what it has brought to our world view. But I come back to the conversation "What is art?" and that is still ongoing. Who knows when it started, and it will never stop because human emotions and feelings are always there.'

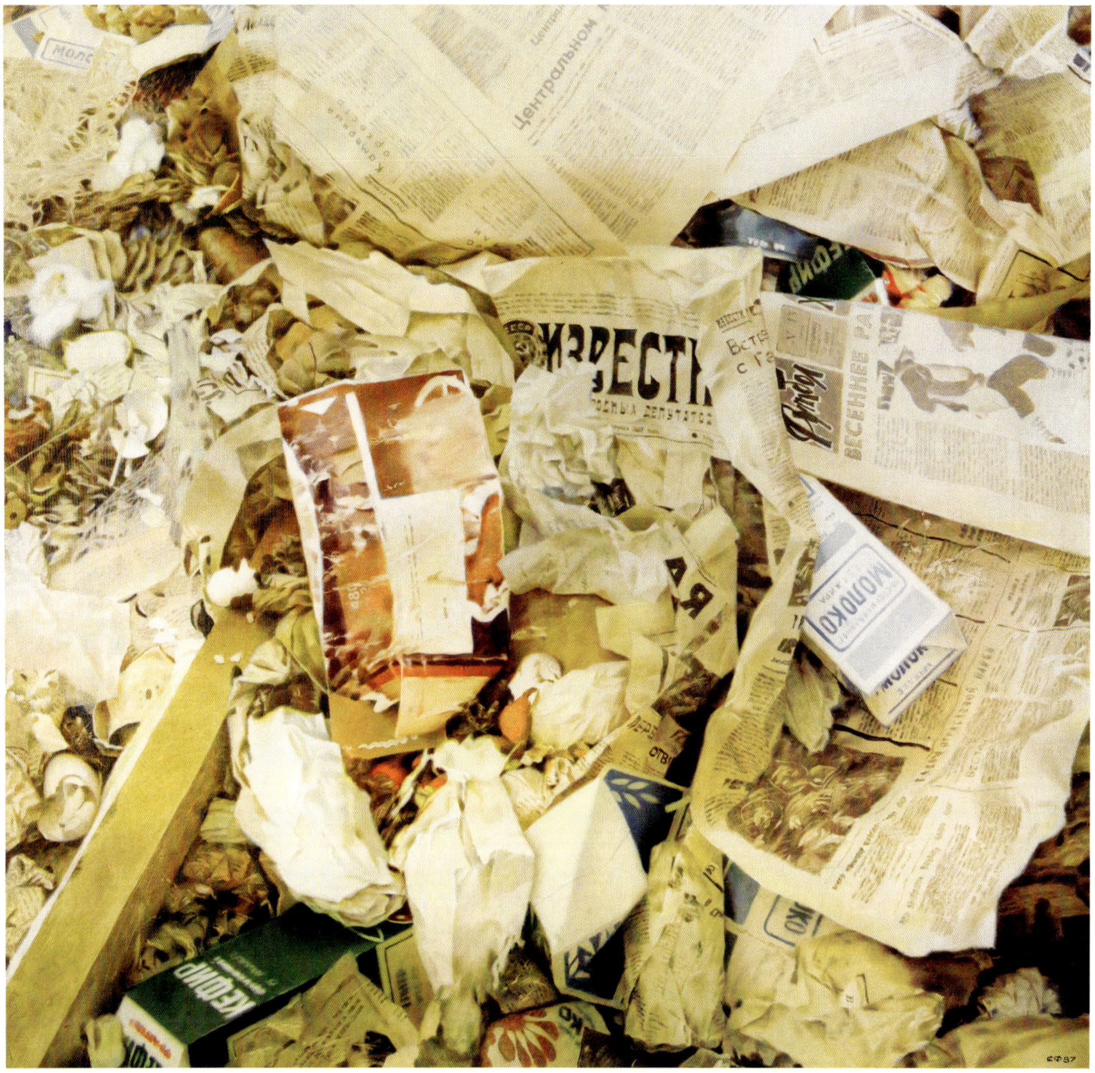

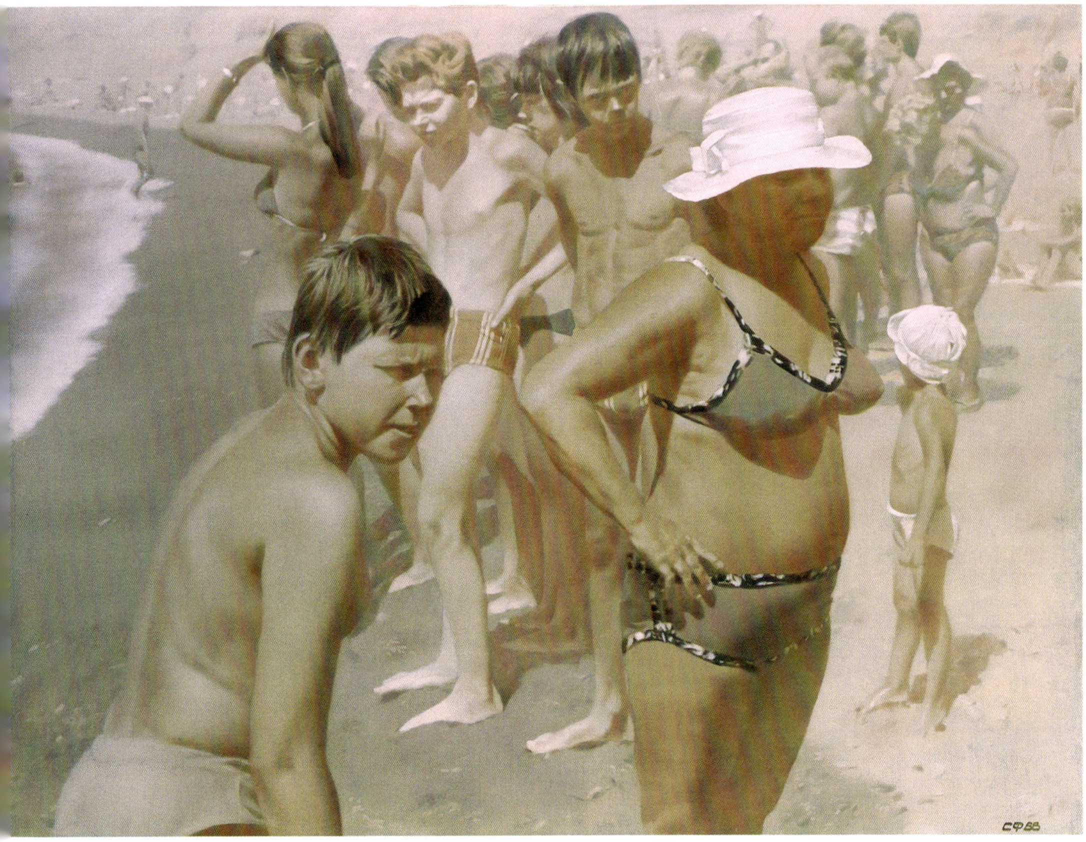

facing page top left
Sausage Line, 1989
Oil on canvas
286 x 190.5 cm
© Semyon Faibisovich
Courtesy of Sotheby's

facing page left
City Police, 1989
Oil on canvas
170 x 200 cm
© Semyon Faibisovich
Courtesy Regina Gallery, London & Moscow

above
A Spring Rubbish Pile in the Nearby Yard, 1987
Oil on canvas
189.5 x 199.4 cm
© Semyon Faibisovich
Collection of DES

left
De Luxe, 1988
Oil on canvas
160 x 270 cm
© Semyon Faibisovich
Courtesy Regina Gallery, London & Moscow

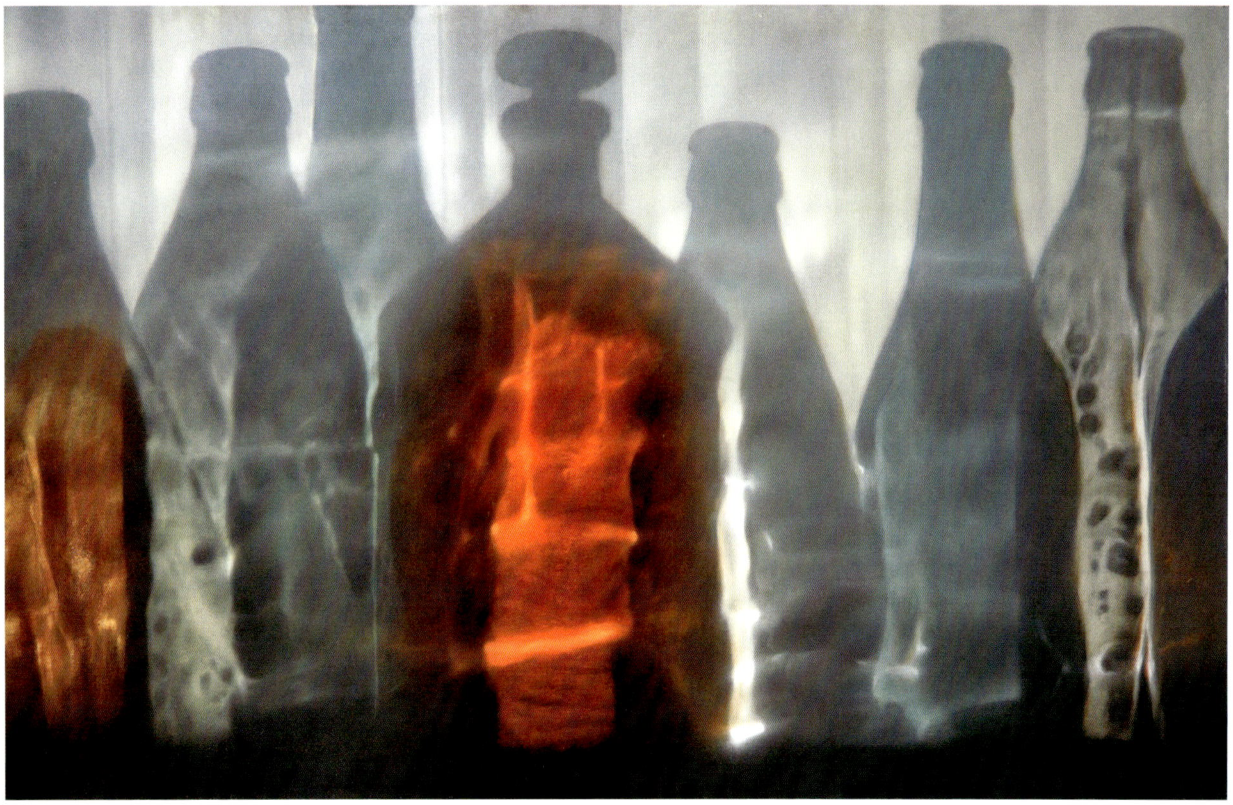

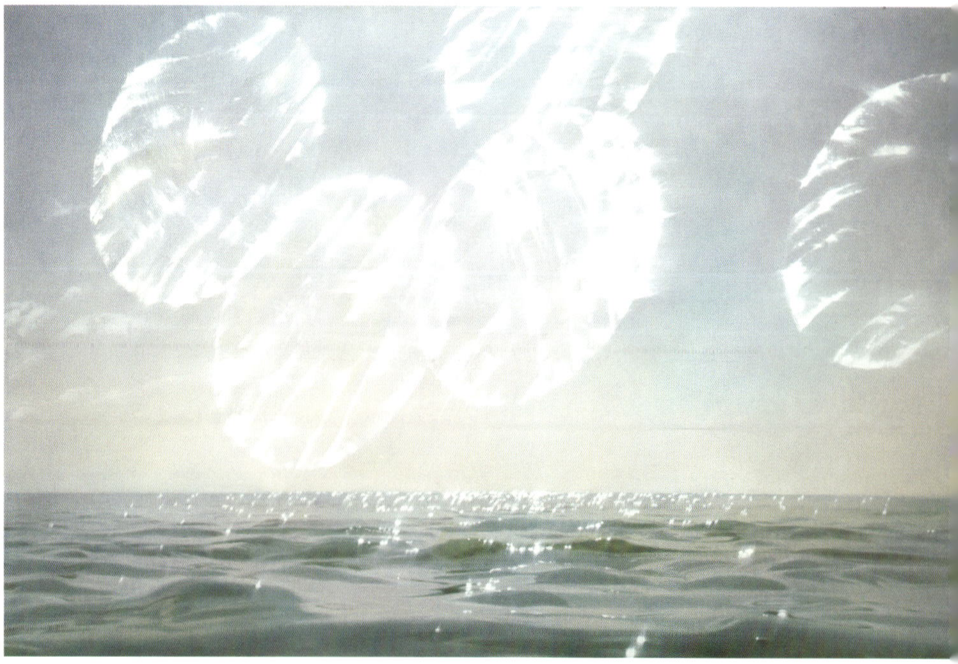

above
Memorial (from the Life of Bottles), 1984
Oil on fibreboard
100.1 x 157 cm

Courtesy of Tsukanov Art Collection

right
Drops on the Eyelashes, 1992
Oil on canvas
135 x 200 cm

Private collection

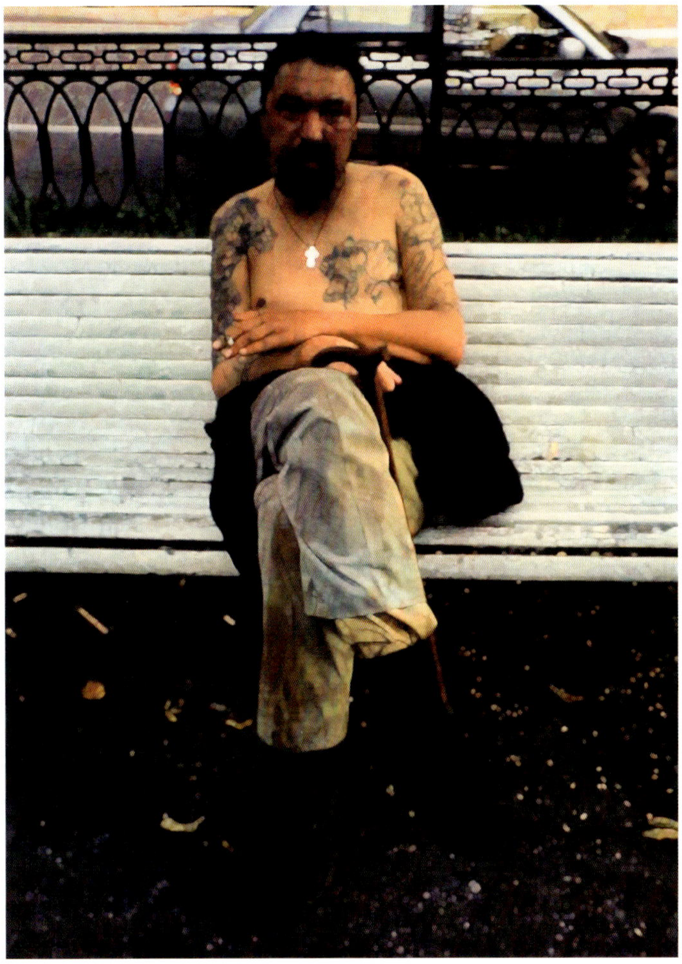

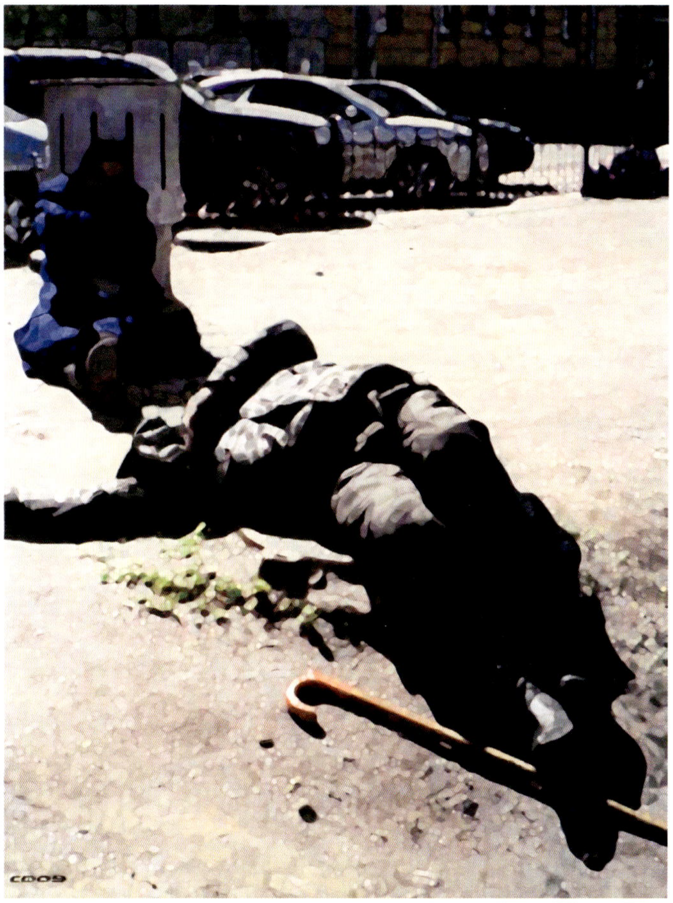

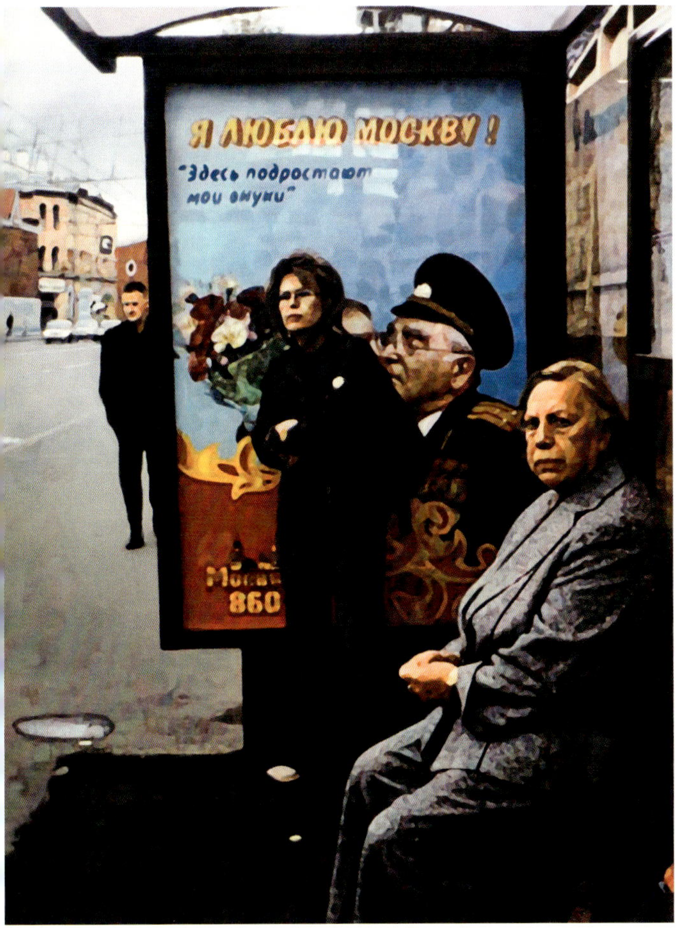

top
Christian, from the cycle RAZGULYAI, 2009
Mixed media, oil on canvas
195 x 140 cm
© Semyon Faibisovich
Courtesy Regina Gallery, London & Moscow

left
I Love Moscow, from the cycle AT THE STOP, 2008
Mixed media, oil on canvas
200 x 150 cm
© Semyon Faibisovich
Courtesy Regina Gallery, London & Moscow

above
Siesta, from the cycle RAZGULYAI, 2009
Mixed media, oil on canvas
145 x 150 cm
© Semyon Faibisovich
Courtesy Regina Gallery, London & Moscow

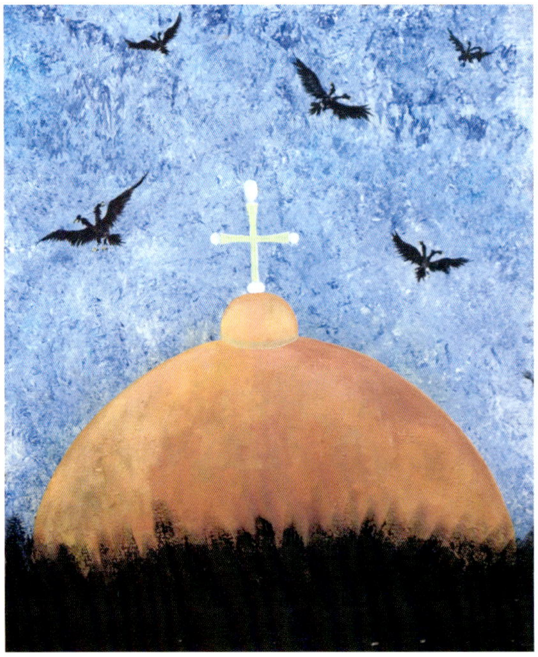

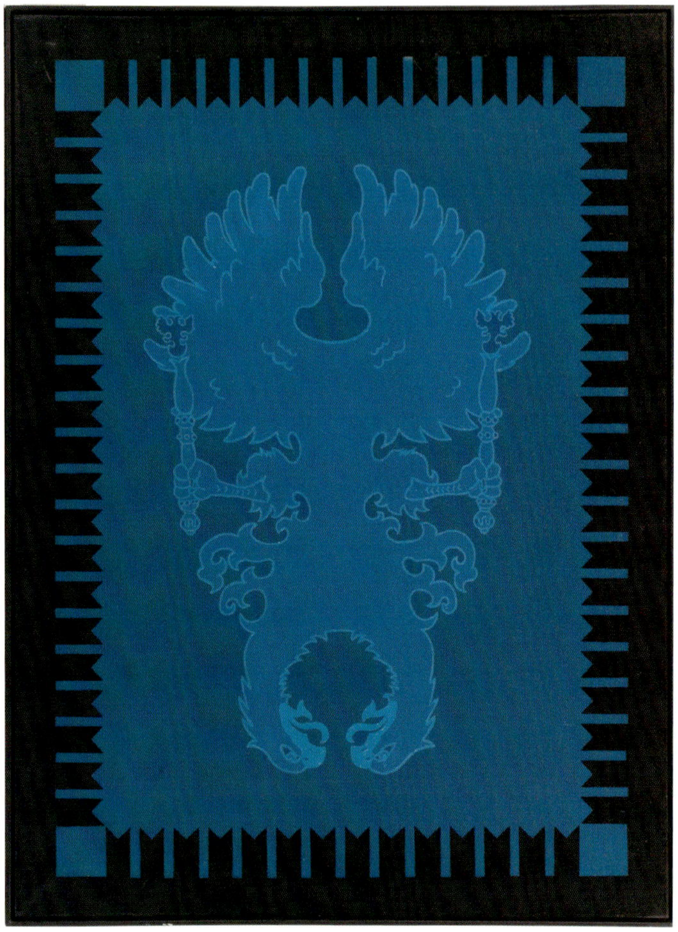

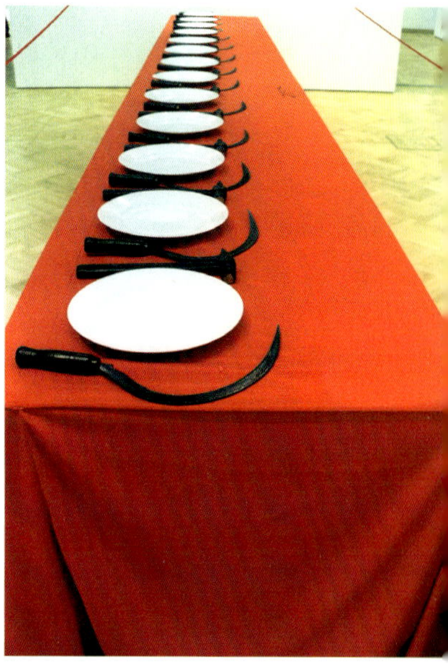

Painter, sculptor and installation artist Andrei Filippov was born in 1959 in Petropavlovsk-Kamchatsky; his father was a sea captain. After an earthquake hit the city, the family relocated to Moscow in 1960; Filippov recalls how his father saved him by throwing him out of a window. Encouraged to draw from a young age, he studied in the Department of Theatre and Set Design of the Moscow Art Theatre (MKhAT) from 1976 to 1981. During the 1980s he participated in several Moscow underground activities, most notably exhibiting with the APTART Gallery (1982–4). Filippov co-organised the cutting-edge Avantgardist Club (KLAVA), which staged exhibitions and art performances in new spaces around Moscow. His works are held in many important museums, including the State Tretyakov Gallery, Moscow; the Ekaterina Cultural Foundation, Moscow; the Jane Voorhees Zimmerli Art Museum, New Brunswick; and the Ludwig Museum, Cologne. He has participated in international group shows in Miami (2006) and London (2010), and lives and works in Moscow.

Filippov's art can be described as broadly conceptual, with a strong traditional aesthetic and references to the Russian avant-garde. He addresses Russia's historical and spiritual traditions, seeing in them not only an alternative to Soviet official culture during the 1980s but also a deeper layer of national identity. The notion of Moscow as a Third Rome can be seen in *Rim–Rimu* (Rome-to-Rome) (1983). This work plays on the Soviet propaganda slogan *Mir–Miru* (Peace on Earth), of which it is both an anagram and a pun, with each letter formed from black double-headed eagles.

The use of strong visual symbols with complex meanings serves both Filippov's aesthetics and his central message. He often uses Christian iconography in his work; the season of winter, depicted in many of his paintings, can be read as a metaphor for the Resurrection. His installation *The Last Supper* (1989) shows a red tablecloth with empty white plates, the forks and knives replaced by hammer and sickles. The double-headed eagle – a symbol of both Imperial Russia and the Russian predicament as a nation facing West and East – can be seen in many of his works beginning with *The First Swallow* (c. 1985), a sculpture in which he transformed a bound hammer and sickle into a double-headed eagle. The spiralling circle of eagles in *Balkan Baroque* (2004) is a metaphor for the crisis in the Balkans and the escalation of East-West tensions. Filippov's large installation *Saw*, first created in 1987 and reworked over several decades, also illustrates this divide, its blade imitating the Kremlin's crenellations as a potent symbol of divided power.

far left
The Cap of Monomakh, 1988
Oil on canvas
100 x 84 cm
© Andrei Filippov
Collection MANI Museum
Courtesy E.K.ArtBureaux

middle
Part I, from the series Chapters, 1990
Oil on canvas
195 x 145 cm
© Andrei Filippov
Private collection
Courtesy E.K.ArtBureau

above
Last Supper, 1989
Installation
Mixed media
80 x 80 x 675 cm
© Andrei Filippov
Courtesy E.K.ArtBureau

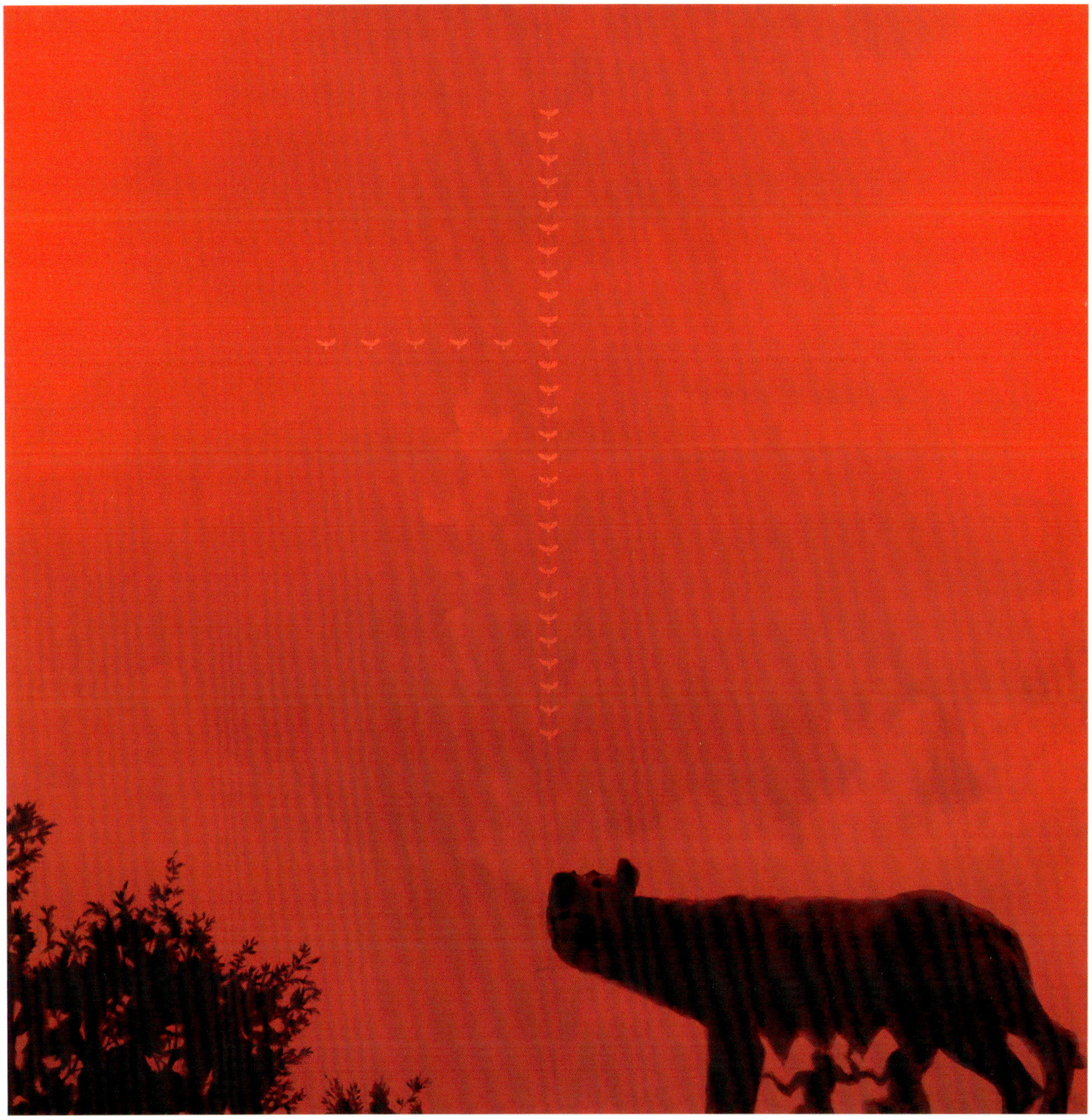

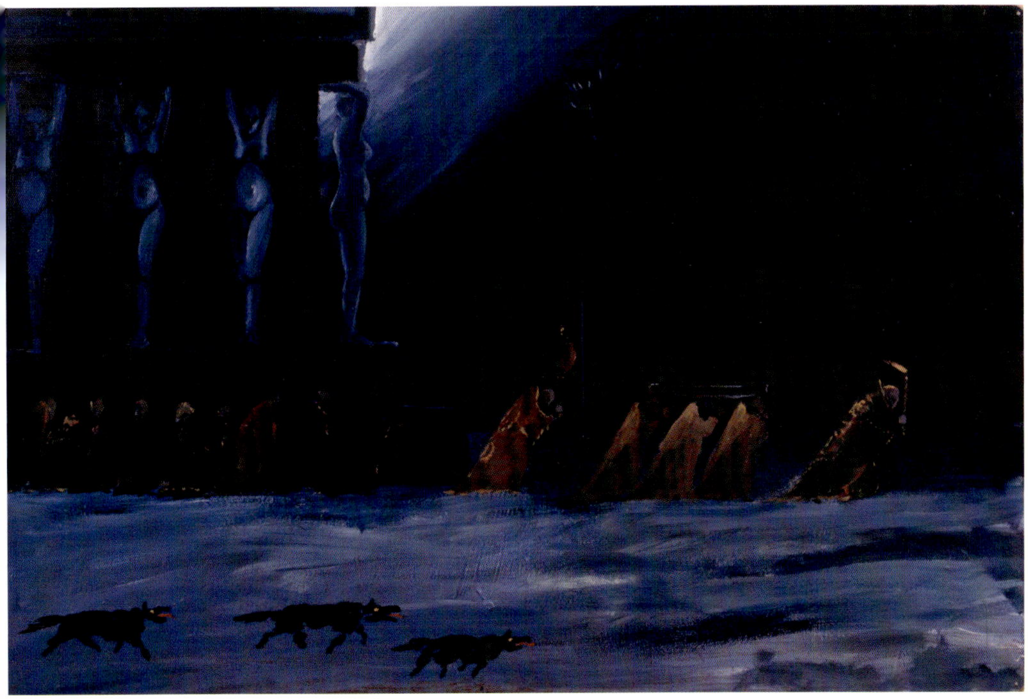

above
Untitled, from the series Line of Defence, 1991
Oil on canvas
185 x 185 cm
© Andrei Filippov
Private collection
Courtesy E.K.ArtBureau

left
Funeral, 1986
Oil on fibreboard
120 x 80 cm
© Andrei Filippov
Courtesy of E.K.ArtBureau

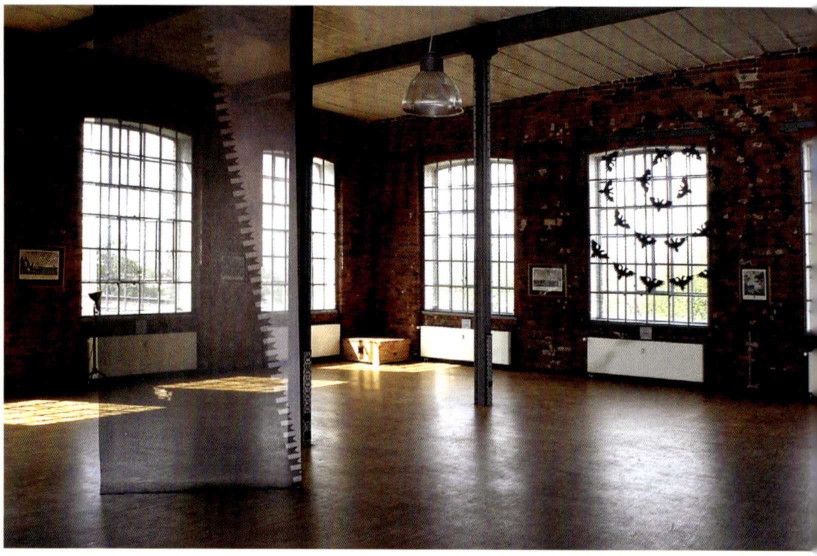

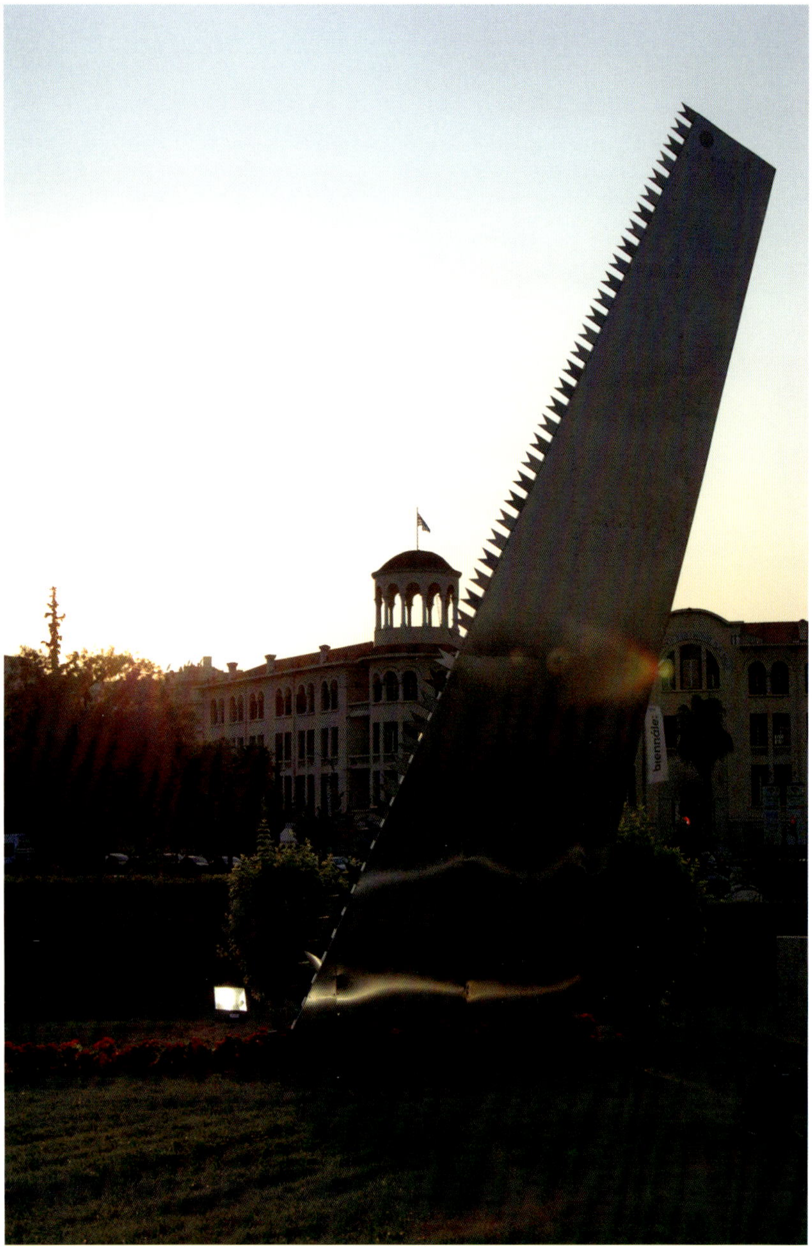

Andrei Filippov

top right
Balkan Baroque, 2004
From 'Saw It!', Loft Spinnerei, Leipzig, 2006
Photograph
© Andrei Filippov
Courtesy E.K.ArtBureau

above
Saw, 2006
1st Thessaloniki Biennale of
Contemporary Art, 2007
Metal
600 cm (h)
© Andrei Filippov
Courtesy E.K.ArtBureau

right
Book on Skates, 1989–2004
Book and pair of skates
9.7 x 15.5 x 25 cm
© Andrei Filippov
Courtesy of Ekaterina and
Vladimir Semenikhin Collection

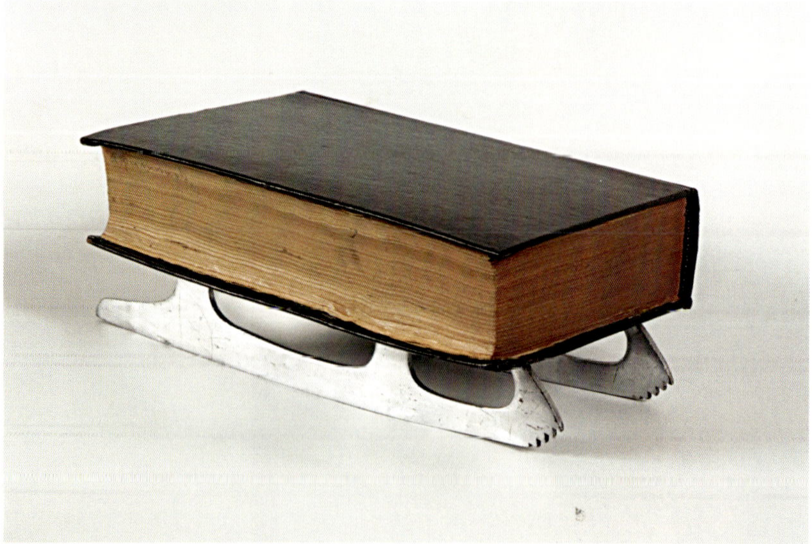

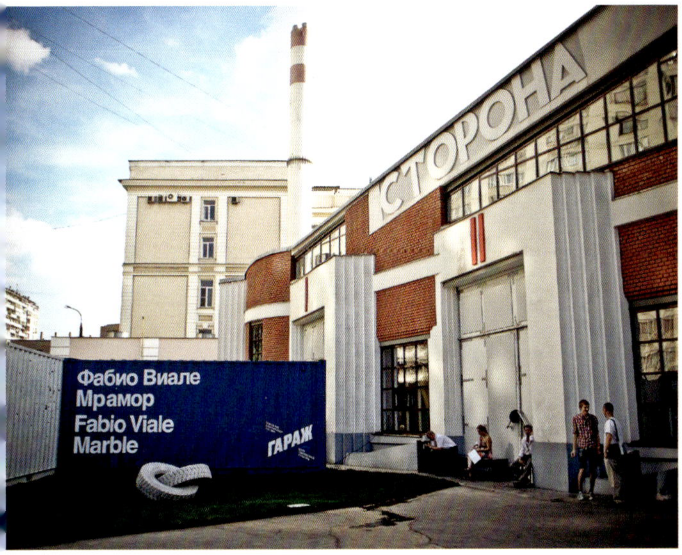

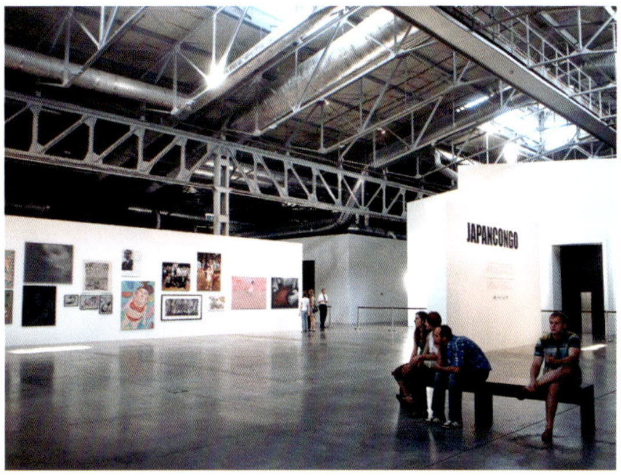

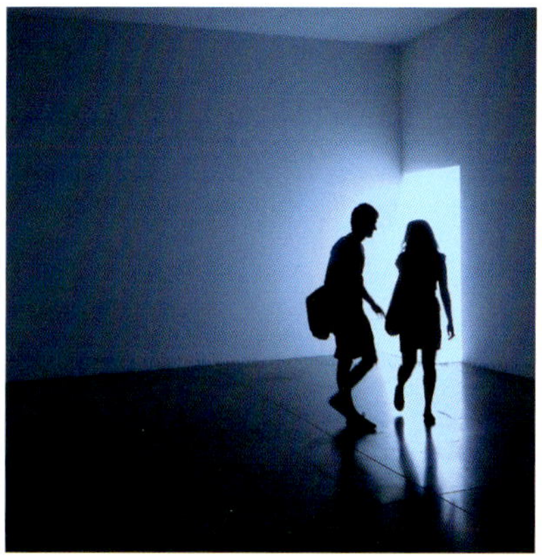

The Garage Centre for Contemporary Culture, popularly known as 'The Garage', is a not-for-profit contemporary art space established in 2008 by arts entrepreneur and patron Daria Zhukova together with her partner Roman Abramovich. Funded by private donations, it is Moscow's leading new, independent art space, dedicated to supporting, developing and promoting contemporary culture with both national and international outreach. The Garage is one of several projects supported by Zhukova's arts charity, the Iris Foundation.

The Garage takes its name from its first venue (2008–11), the former Bakhmetevsky Bus Garage, in an industrial neighbourhood to the north of Moscow's city centre. Custom-built in 1926 as a depot by the celebrated architect Konstantin Melnikov, the building is a Constructivist landmark. The award-winning architect Jamie Fobert refurbished it to create a gallery occupying 8,500 square metres of open and closed exhibition spaces, a courtyard, a purpose-built auditorium and media room, a children's zone divided into a playground and an educational area, and a café.

Since 2008, the Garage has held over thirty exhibitions of international and Russian art, including *Ilya and Emilia Kabakov: A Retrospective* (2008); *Un Certain Etat du Monde?/A Certain State of the World?: Works from the François Pinault Foundation* (2009); *Antony Gormley: Domain Field* (2009); *Mark Rothko: Into an Unknown World* (2010) and *Marina Abramovic: The Artist Is Present* (2011). Many other intellectual and cultural events are held at the Garage, including master classes, film screenings, performances and children's activities. Educational programmes are a large part of the Garage's work, both for adults and for young people; the programme for children, Garage Kids, is especially important. This series of free activities, trails and events is designed to engage children through playful experiences and hands-on exercises in order to inspire creativity and understanding.

Using its Moscow base as a springboard, the Garage creates installations, exhibitions and cultural events worldwide such as the presentation of *The History Lesson* at the Palais de Tokyo, Paris (2010), where curator Joseph Backstein brought together over twenty artists in a retrospective of Russian art since the 1980s. As part of the 54th Venice Biennale, Garage Projects and curator Neville Wakefield presented *Commercial Break*, featuring artists who explore the relationship between advertising and culture.

In the spring of 2012, the Garage will leave the Bakhmetevsky Bus Garage and move to a new location in Gorky Park in central Moscow. Inside the park, one of Europe's largest, the Garage will develop a new site occupying an 8,500-square-metre hexagonal pavilion designed in 1923 by the architects Zholtovsky, Parusnikov and Kokorin. The pavilion, consisting of six sections with a courtyard, was constructed to house the first All-Union Agricultural Exhibition, later becoming an exhibition space for Soviet artists and sculptors. The new site will include international-standard gallery spaces, open exhibition areas, children's creative spaces, education and learning facilities, a cafe and a shop. The aim is to establish a significant focus in Moscow for the presentation of new art and international culture to Russian audiences while raising the profile of Russia's own contemporary scene.

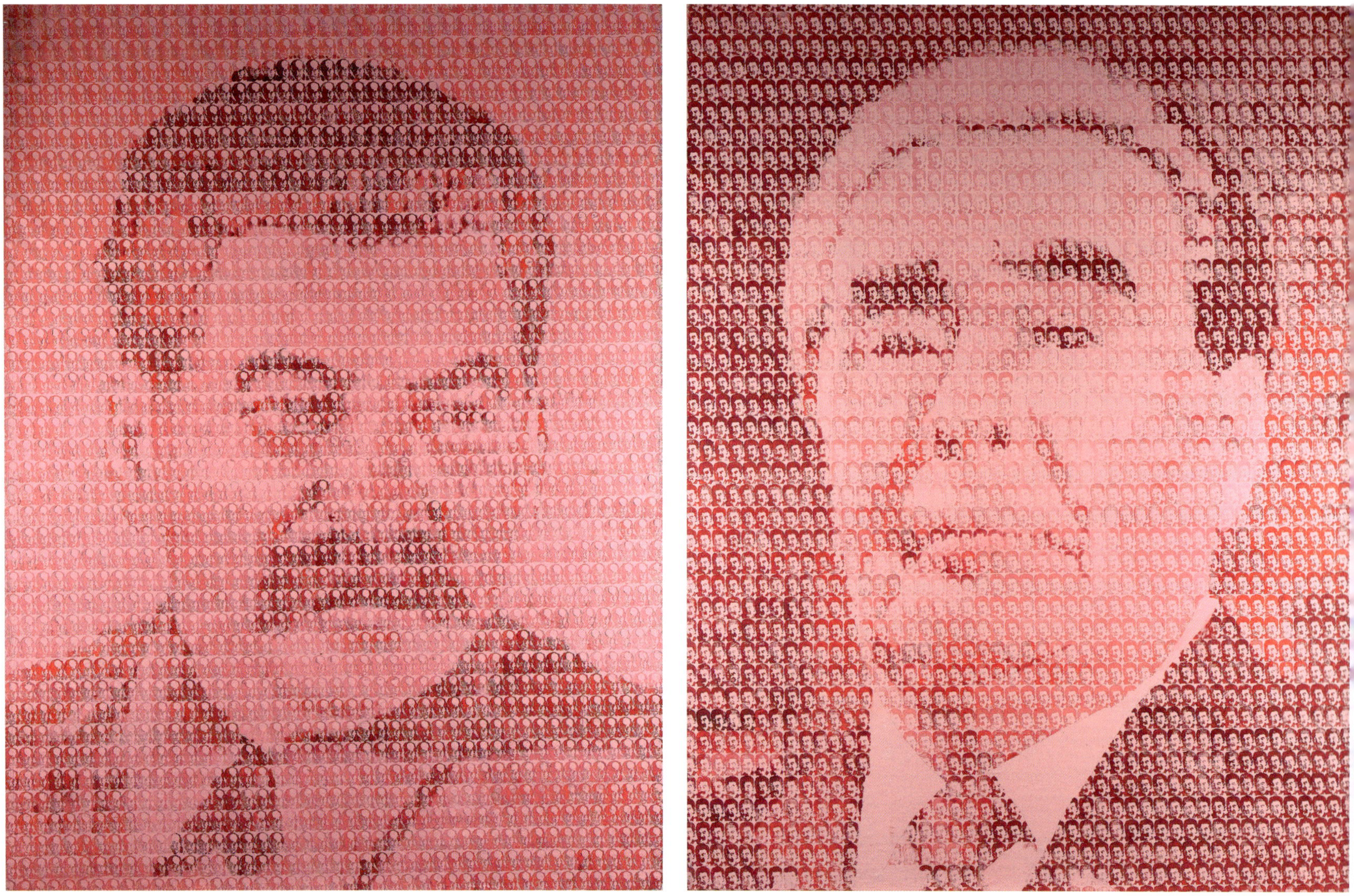

Eduard Gorokhovsky

Known for paintings which meld the realism of photographic and painterly imagery and the irony and sarcasm of American Pop art with the ideology of Socialist Realism, Eduard Gorokhovsky (1929–2004) was one of the first Soviet artists to experiment with 'photo-based art'. His compositions present a combination of visual systems. While photographs provide the main source for his prints and paintings, the picture plane is usually interrupted by an element that intrudes on the photographic space, a text, figure or superimposed image that confuses the composition's legibility. Gorokhovsky's desire to offer maximum freedom to viewers in their readings of each work paradoxically also shows the limitations of freedom. His novel approach to montage, a tradition inherited from the Russian avant-garde, reduces rather than optimises readability. At the same time, he questions the integrity and autonomy of any image, showing it to be an amalgamation of multiple dissonant narratives.

above
Festive Mosaic, 1988
Oil on canvas (diptych)
183.4 x 140 cm
© Nina Feygina
Courtesy of Sotheby's

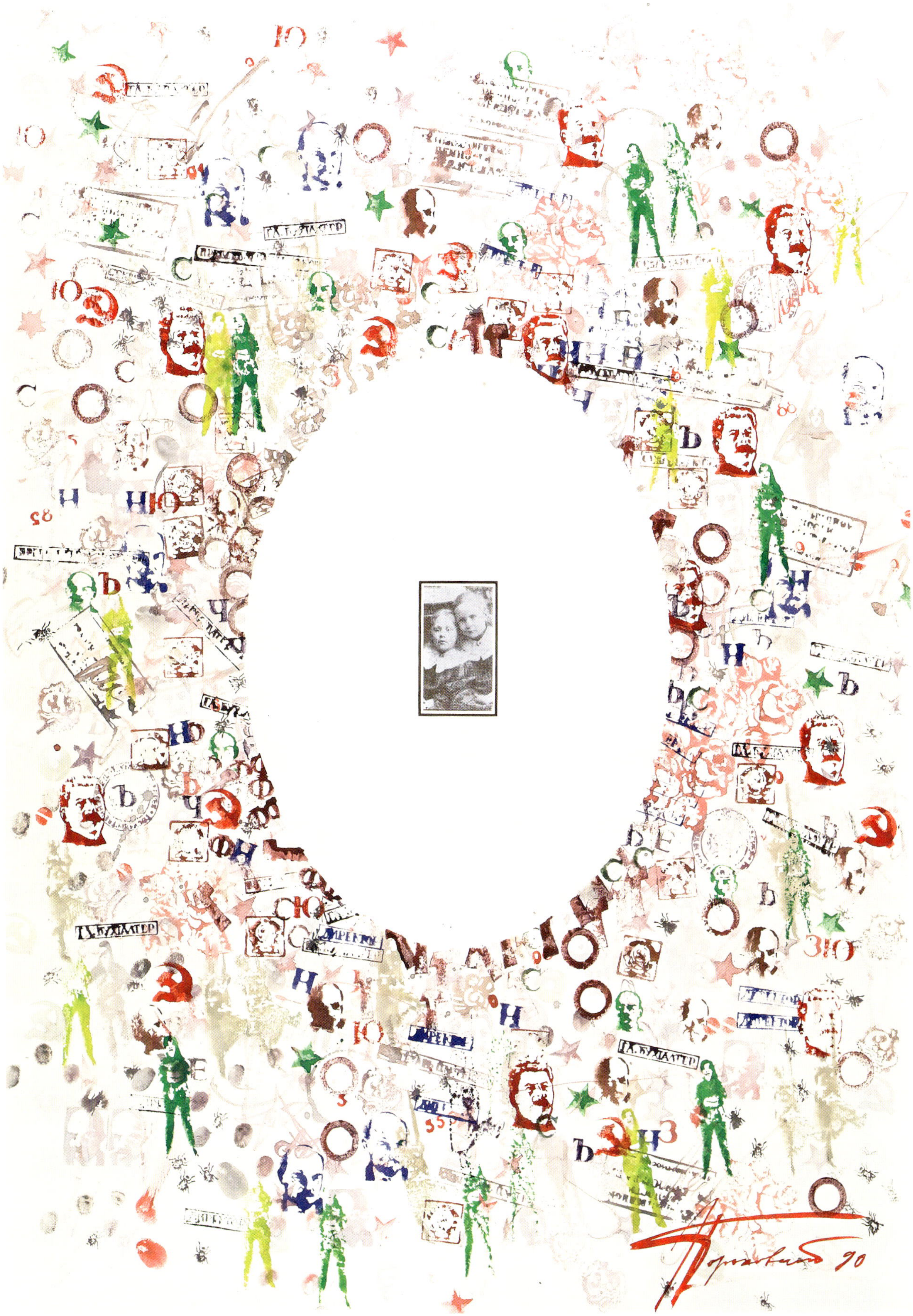

right
Oval Composition, 1990
Mixed media on paper
95.5 x 68.6 cm
© Nina Feygina
Courtesy of Sotheby's

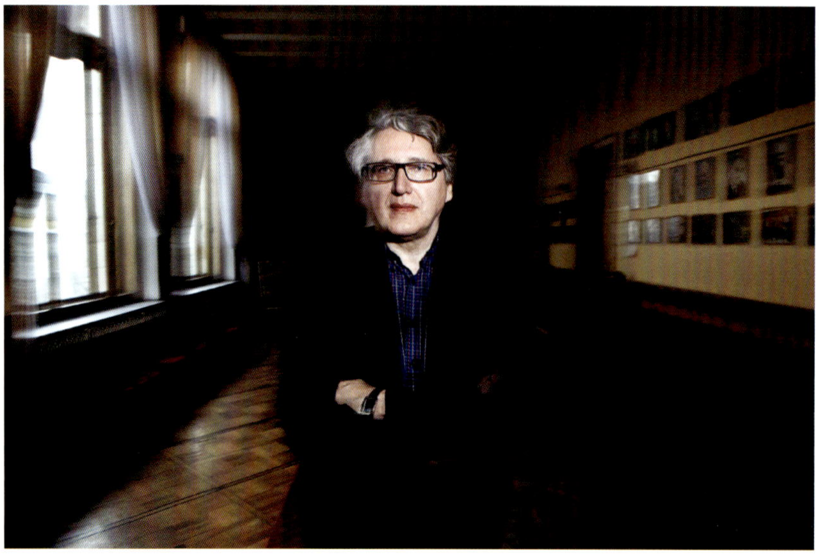

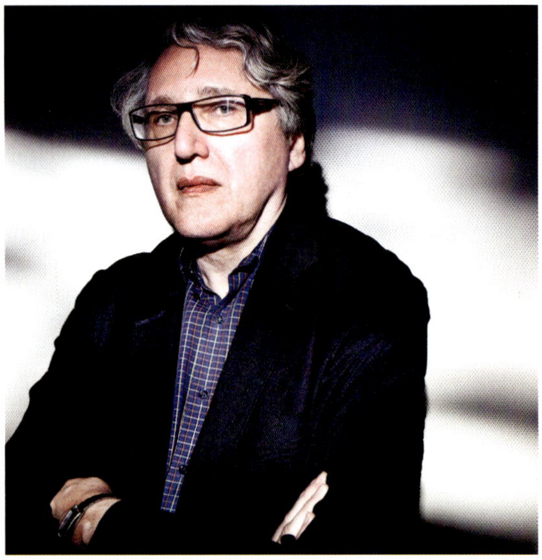

Boris Groys

Born in Berlin in 1947, the philosopher, media and culture theorist, and art critic Boris Groys first achieved international renown for his re-reading of Soviet art and culture, presenting a fresh approach that challenged decades-old Western stereotypes. Having completed his studies in Leningrad and Moscow in mathematics and linguistics, Groys developed long-lasting relationships with underground artists in both cities, regularly publishing articles about this parallel cultural scene in samizdat magazines. In particular, he forged friendships with such figures as Ilya Kabakov and Andrei Monastyrsky, becoming a first-hand witness to, and participant in, a number of their artistic experiments, often appearing in photographs documenting Collective Actions' 'Trips to the Countryside'. In 1979, Groys published his seminal essay 'Moscow Romantic Conceptualism' in the first issue of the bilingual magazine *A-Ya*, produced by Igor Shelkovsky in Paris. Although the term *Romantic* would be dropped later on, Groys effectively coined the name for a whole movement and theorised it within the Soviet context, thereby differentiating it from Western models of Conceptualist practice.

In 1981, Groys emigrated to Germany. His first published work in the West, *Gesamtkunstwerk Stalin* (1988), appeared in English as *The Total Art of Stalinism* (1992) and overturned Western interpretations and criticism of Soviet art. Groys re-evaluated socialist art production, challenging aesthetic norms by propounding a thesis based on the work of Walter Benjamin. Describing a clear trajectory through the history of twentieth-century Russian art – from the avant-garde to Socialist Realism and Sots Art – Groys argued that modernism had survived in the 'total artwork' of Stalinism. Stalin embodied the figure of the artist for Groys, who interpreted Socialist Realism as a natural inheritor of the legacy of the avant-garde.

Since then, Groys has published extensively on modern and contemporary art (both Russian and international), philosophy, politics, culture and intellectual history in such works as *The Communist Postscript* (2010), *Ilya Kabakov: The Man Who Flew into Space from His Apartment* (2006) and *Art Power* (2008). More recently, his books and articles have been concerned with the notion of production in the contemporary art market, arguing for an evolution away from consumerism; this theory is explored in *Going Public* (2010).

The subject matter of Groys's publications has been equally presented in the form of exhibitions both in Russia and abroad. *Dream Factory Communism* (2003–4), organised by the Schirn Kunsthalle, Frankfurt, explored the ideas posited in *The Total Art of Stalinism*, asking whether the transition from avant-garde practice to Socialist Realism involved a moral as well as an aesthetic break. The show demonstrated both movements' affinity with the creation of a new mass culture. Instead of rejecting the formal achievements of the avant-garde, official Stalinist propaganda used them for its own ends. Thus Groys succeeded in linking the aesthetic ambitions of the avant-garde with the political ambitions of totalitarianism. This is not to say, however, that his approach simplifies the complex histories of Russian art. Instead, he believes that the purpose of art cannot be reduced to a single instance: 'The traditional [role] is to create works that please the public. The avant-garde one is to create works that shock, surprise and criticise the public and go against accepted taste. Contemporary art inherits both of these attitudes; it lives in a paradox. It wants to be liked and to shock, to please spectators and to criticise society.'

Groys's prolific critical output maintains contemporary art's position at the forefront of public discussion: 'Contemporary art is, to use Nietzsche's words, "for everyone and no-one". Art is what potentially is open to anyone, which doesn't mean that everyone must like it ... It has to be accessible to everyone, no matter if they have money or not ... Sociologically speaking, contemporary art interested primarily the middle class. To interest the elite it has to bring in big money, and contemporary art doesn't. It's not a very profitable business.'

As well as holding a position as professor of Russian and Slavonic Studies at New York University, Groys was curator of the Russian Pavilion at the 2011 Venice Biennale and presented an exhibition exploring the ethics and aesthetics of Andrei Monastyrsky.

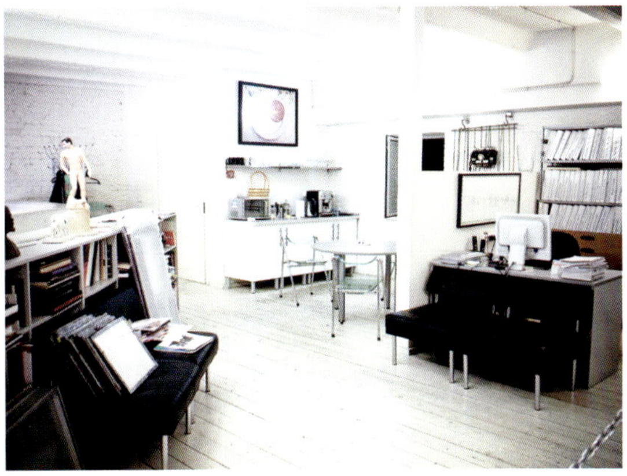

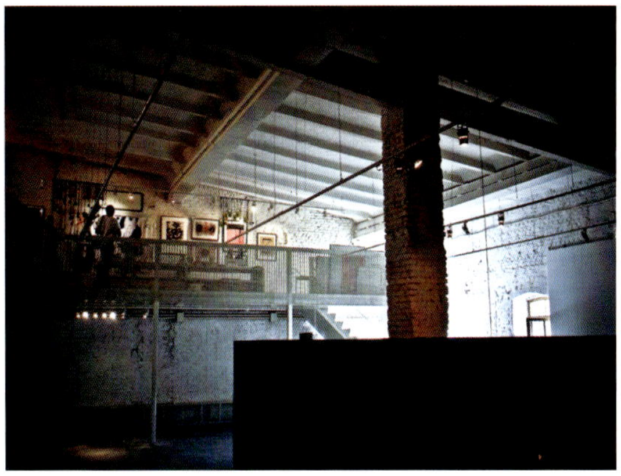

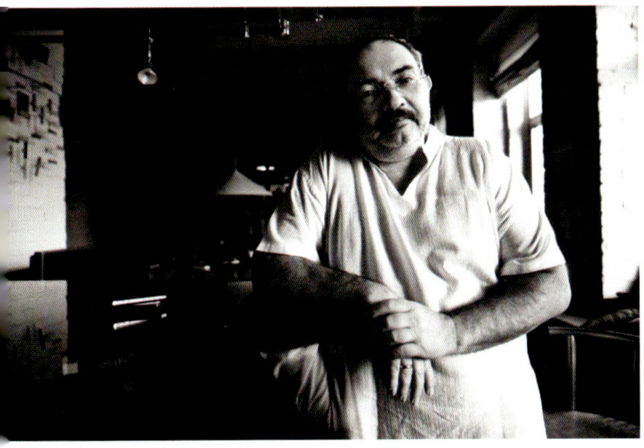

The Guelman Gallery was established in Moscow in 1990 by the Moldavian entrepreneur Marat Guelman, and his wife Yulia. One of the first galleries to showcase the work of international artists like Joseph Beuys and Andy Warhol, the gallery has achieved fame and notoriety through its promotion of artists such as Oleg Kulik, Anatoly Osmolovsky and Avdei Ter-Oganyan, and its organisation of exhibitions and festivals (such as the controversial 2005 *Russia 2* exhibition) which court socio-political criticism and confrontation.

The history of the gallery, according to Guelman, is 'a story of different chance occurrences'. He started collecting art in the 1980s while working as a research scientist in Kishenev. In 1987, he moved permanently to Moscow in order to live at the epicentre of cultural life: 'In Russia, in Moscow, after the Sotheby's sale of 1988, talented and interesting artists were very expensive and, for me at that stage, unattainable. I started travelling around the country and discovered a new, fresh scene – the southern Russian avant-garde. These were artists from Rostov, Azov, Odessa, Kishenev. This art strongly differentiated itself from what was available in Moscow. I started collecting, and, in early 1990, I organised an exhibition [*Babylon*] ... It was the first time that something significant, other than Moscow Conceptualism, appeared.' Following on the success of this first show, and with the encouragement of Leonid Bazhanov, the future artistic director of the National Centre for Contemporary Art, the Guelman Gallery opened its doors to the public.

The desire to differentiate itself from other emerging institutions and to have a long-lasting effect not only on the cultural but also on the social, economic and political situation in Russia has been the benchmark of the Guelman Gallery's strategies since its inception. Throughout the 1990s, Guelman staged a host of non-commercial projects beginning with *Conversion* (1993), whose purpose was to interact with the political events of perestroika and to modify art's role within the social context. Guelman's simultaneous involvement in the media and in political consultancy means that the gallery's activities have always followed topical issues closely. When discussing the inspiration that guides the gallery and his other projects, Marat Guelman explains that he 'was strengthened by the realisation that art is the only worthy occupation in life. When I was working in politics – one thinks that politics is more far-reaching. Compared to a little gallery or exhibition, politics concerns the whole country. But then comes the realisation that there exists a certain symbolic level at which art is more important and even more far-reaching than politics. This is what happened in Russia. Russia is a country in which contemporary art defeated politics.'

Since *Babylon*, the gallery has worked hard at promoting the totality of the Russian art scene. Its challenging of ingrained Moscow-centric attitudes has resulted in joint collaborations with national museums, including *Art against Geography* (2000), a series of exhibitions (among them *South Russian Wave*, *Poor Art* and *Dynamic Pairs*, to name just a few) that charted the gallery's ten-year history and toured the country over three years. The promotion of artists from outside of Moscow is complemented by the active decentralisation policy pursued by Guelman himself, who, since 2009, has been director of the Perm Museum of Contemporary Art.

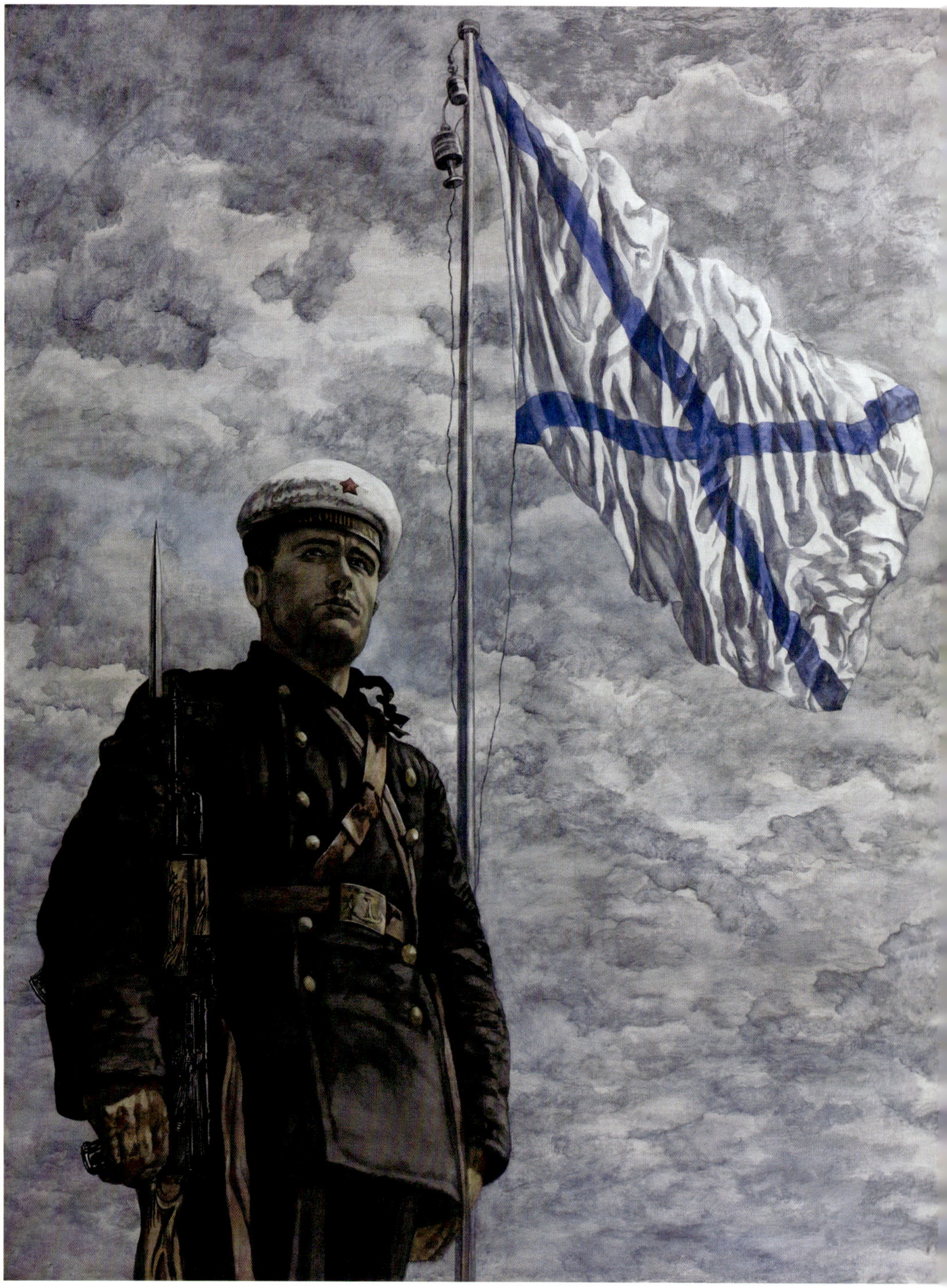

George Gurianov

Born in St Petersburg in 1961, George Gurianov was one of the key members of New Artists, founded by Timur Novikov. A well-known dandy, Gurianov was active on the underground artistic and musical scenes in St Petersburg during the 1980s. From 1984 on, he played with the avant-garde rock band New Composers, acted in various films and directed a sports programme on Piratskoye TV. Between 1984 and 1990, while continuing to paint, he was the drummer in the cult rock group Kino and a singer with the Popularnaya Mekhanika Orchestra. He also participated in the legendary Mayakovsky Club and could regularly be found at underground raves.

Despite his punk credentials, Gurianov's painting style is Neoclassical in both form and manner. A proponent of Neo-Academism, he is known for recycling Socialist Realist motifs. Compositions like *Baltic Fleet* (1998) and *Gay Games* (1998–2000) feature athletic young sailors and sportsmen against backdrops of sea and sky, their physical force unimpeded by natural barriers. The central theme of his paintings is the glorification of virility and strength, although a hint of artifice can be detected in the stylised perfection of the bodies that people his canvases and the photographs he paints over in order to smooth away reality's imperfections. In his choice of subject matter and style, Gurianov references the growing proximity between art and sport in the early twentieth century. Reminiscent of the sporting renaissance of the 1930s, his work is as much influenced by Alexander Deineka's Socialist Realist renditions of virile heroes and Alexander Rodchenko's photographs of athletes and sports parades as by the ideologically motivated art of Vera Mukhina and Leni Riefenstahl.

above
Kronstadt, 1998–2003
Acrylic on canvas
250 x 170 cm
© George Gurianov
Courtesy of the Ekaterina and Vladimir Semenikhin Collection

facing page
Aviator, 1999
Acrylic on canvas
94 x 62.5 cm
© George Gurianov
Courtesy of the Ekaterina and Vladimir Semenikhin Collection

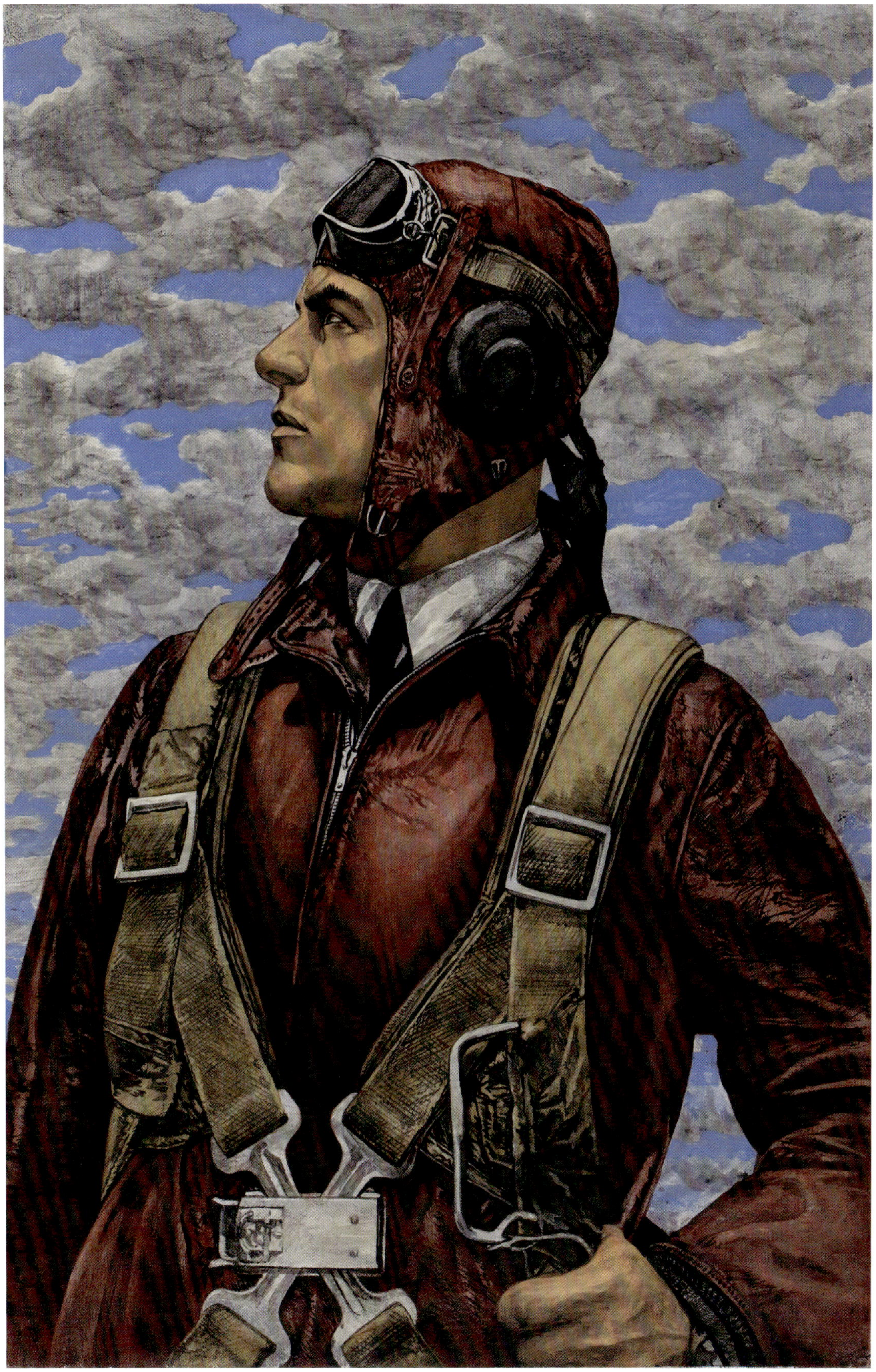

George Gurianov

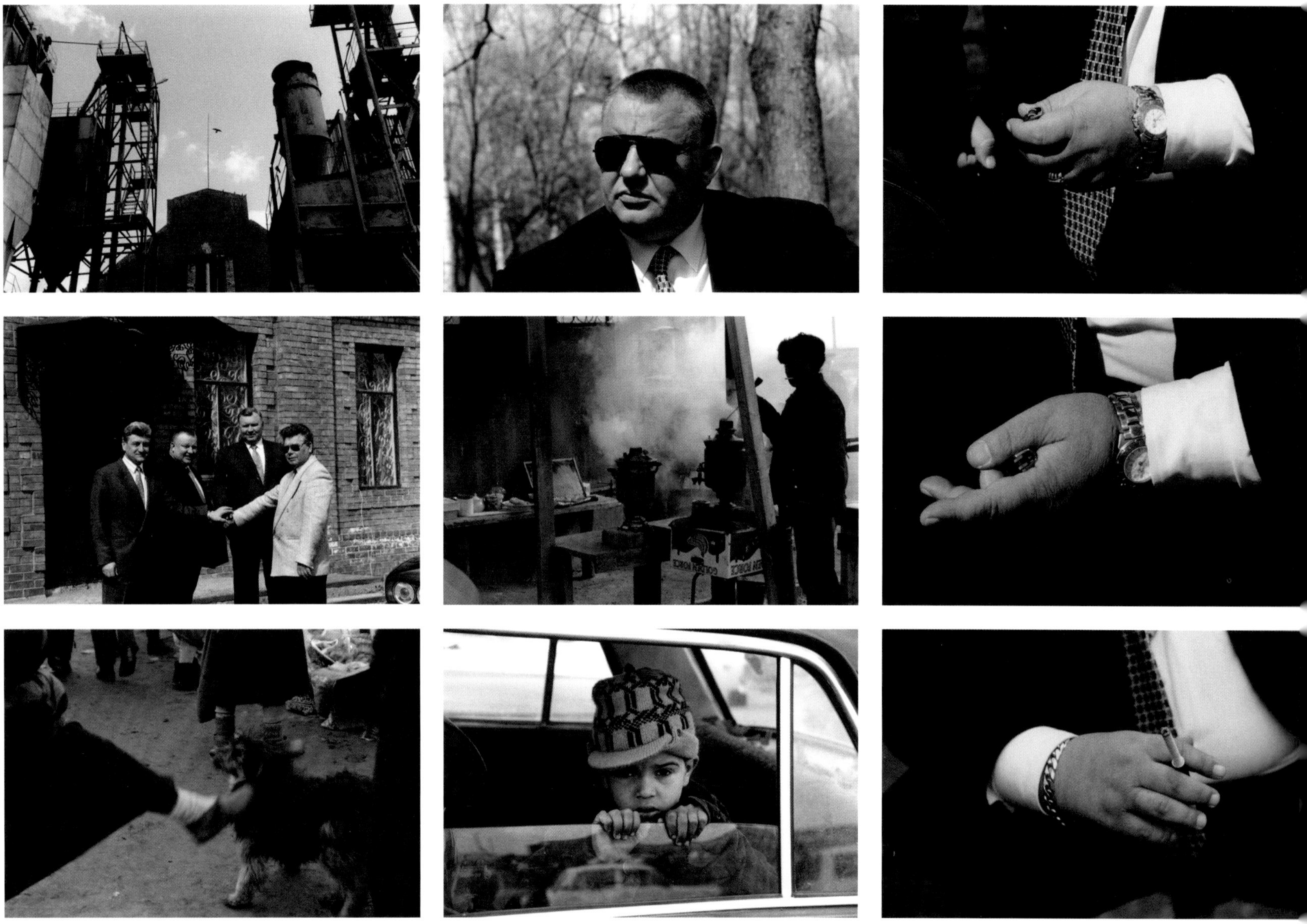

Dmitri Gutov was born in 1960 in Moscow and graduated from the Department of Theory and History of Art at the Repin Institute of Painting, Sculpture and Architecture in St Petersburg. Working in the areas of painting, photography, installation and video art, he has exhibited widely in Moscow and abroad since 1988, including at the 1995 Venice Biennale, the 1992 Istanbul Biennale, Manifesta 1 in Rotterdam (1996), the 1st Valencia Biennale (2001), the 2002 São Paulo Biennale and Documenta 12 in Kassel (2007).

In 1994, Gutov founded the Mikhail Lifshitz Institute, a laboratory group dedicated to studying the writings of the Marxist literary critic and philosopher. Inspired by his own readings in philosophy, painting, graphic design, Eastern calligraphy, Conceptual art, Soviet culture and Marxist aesthetics, Gutov has developed a unique body of work that fuses painstaking technique with a commitment to art as a vital progressive force.

Many of his compositions address the viewer directly, but, unlike some politically engaged artists, he avoids easy sloganeering. His 2011 project *Russia for Everyone* employs graphic presentation and the traditional medium of paint on canvas to attract the viewer's attention while delivering an unexpected message challenging the chauvinistic discourse of Russian nationalism. At first glance, another project, *Fence* (2007), resembles wire fences surrounding garden plots; in reality it recreates delicate calligraphy or Old Master drawings in three-dimensional constructions which shift and change with the viewer's position. The image extends beyond the frame into the onlooker's reality. Gutov explored this same connection with actual space in his 2007 project for an exhibition in Uryupinsk, where, instead of bringing contemporary art to the provincial centre, he exhibited photographs of the town he had taken in the days leading up to the show.

above
From the series Uryupinsk, 2007
Black and white photographs
Varying sizes
© Dmitry Gutov
Courtesy of Guelman Gallery

facing page top
Mary, Mother of God,
from the series Russia for All, 2011
Oil on canvas
100 x 70 cm
© Dmitry Gutov
Courtesy of Victor Bondarenko

facing page right
Dostoyevsky,
from the series Russia for All, 2011
Oil on canvas
100 x 70 cm
© Dmitry Gutov
Courtesy of Victor Bondarenko

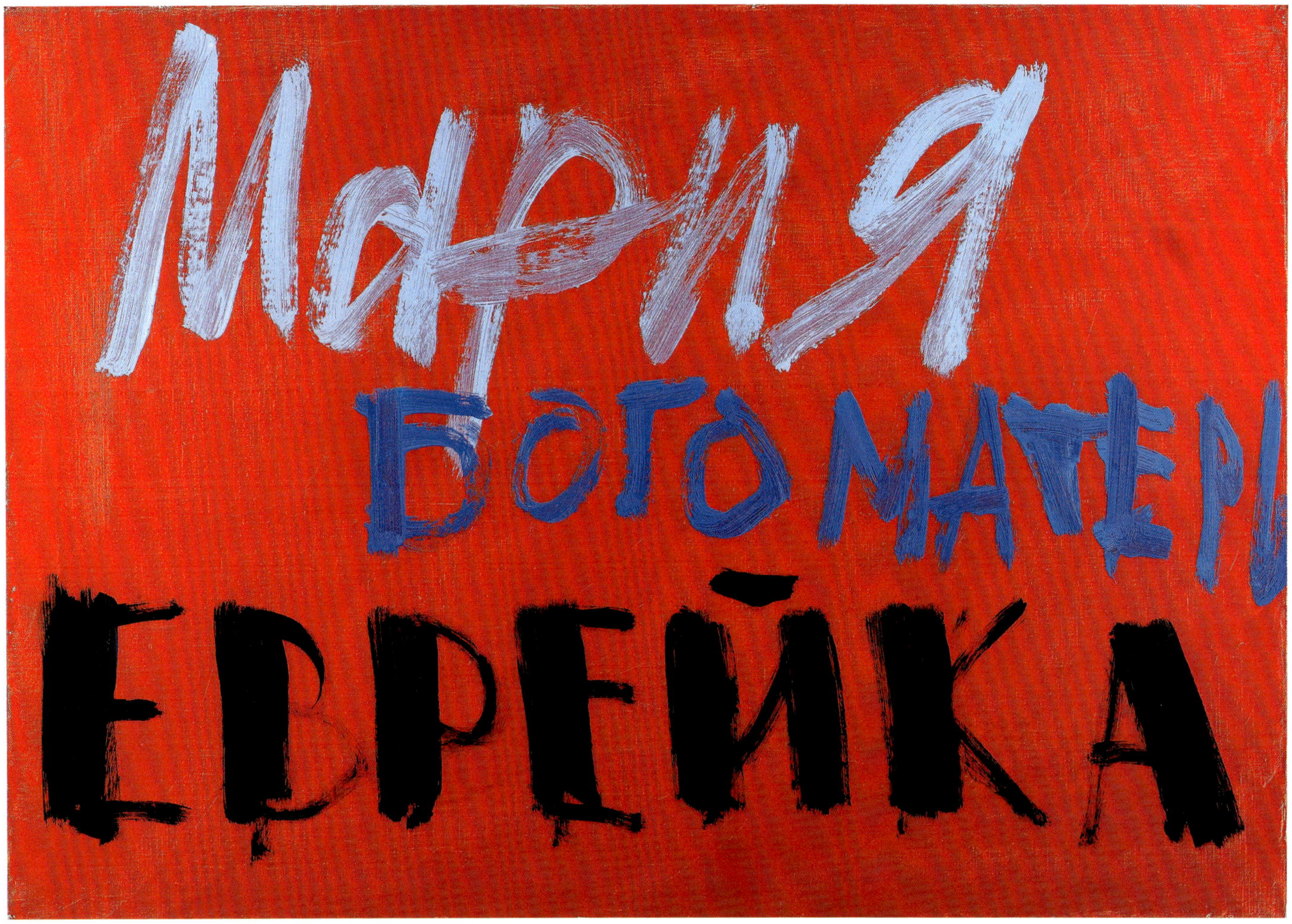
Мария
Богоматерь
ЕВРЕЙКА

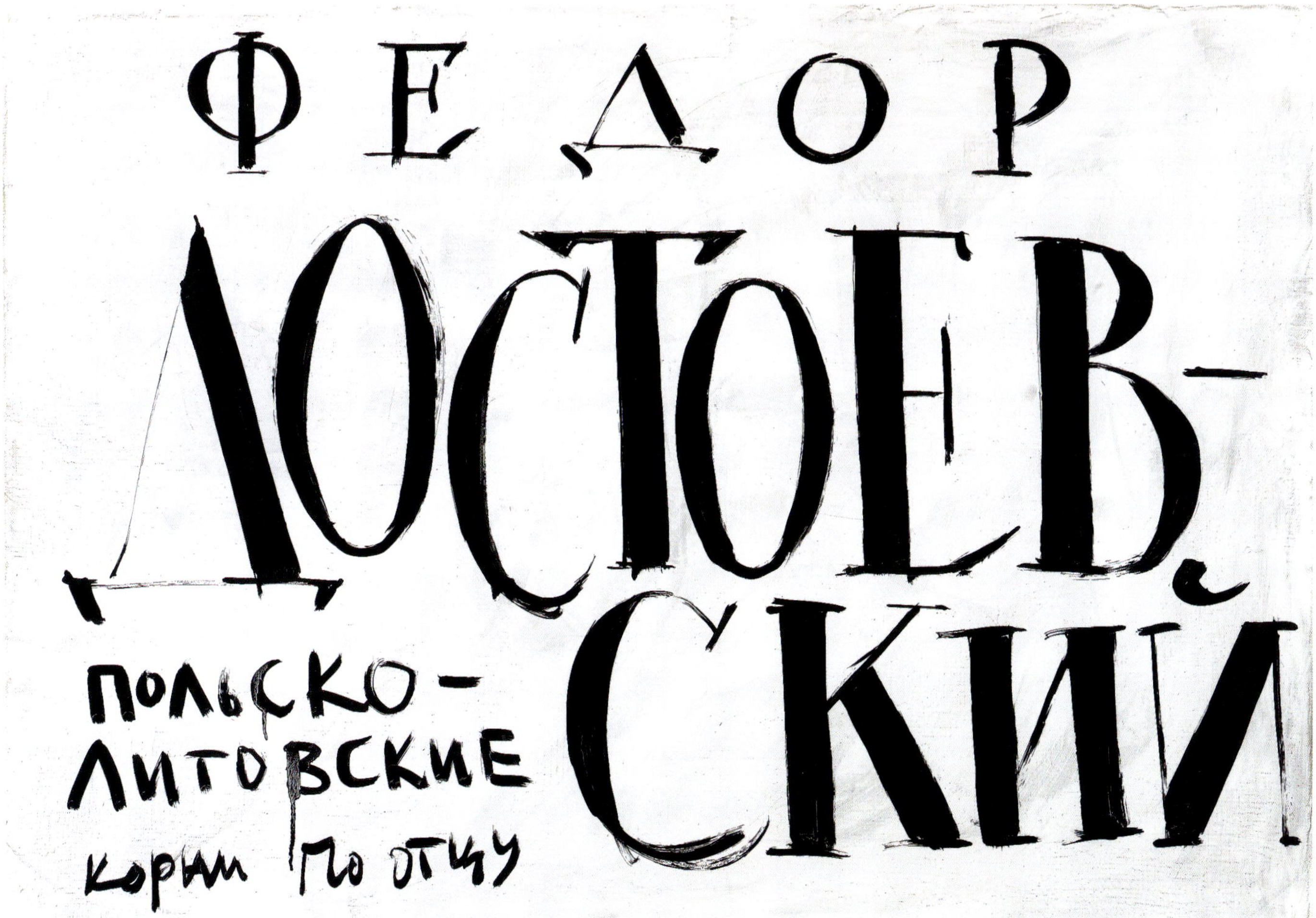
ФЕДОР
ДОСТОЕВ-
СКИЙ
ПОЛЬСКО-
ЛИТОВСКИЕ
корни по отцу

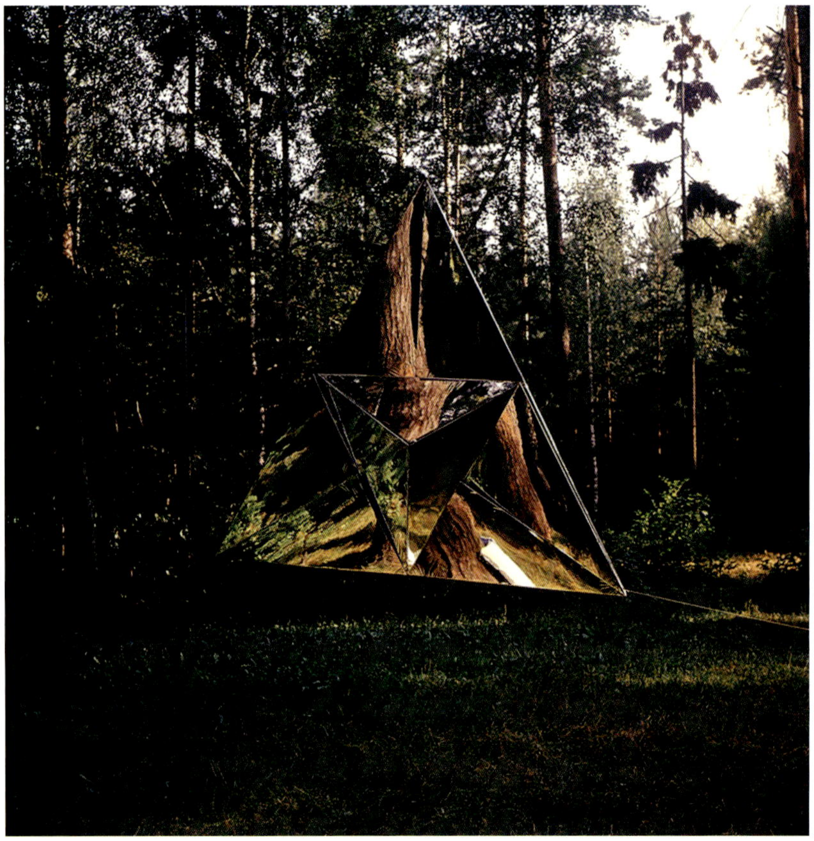

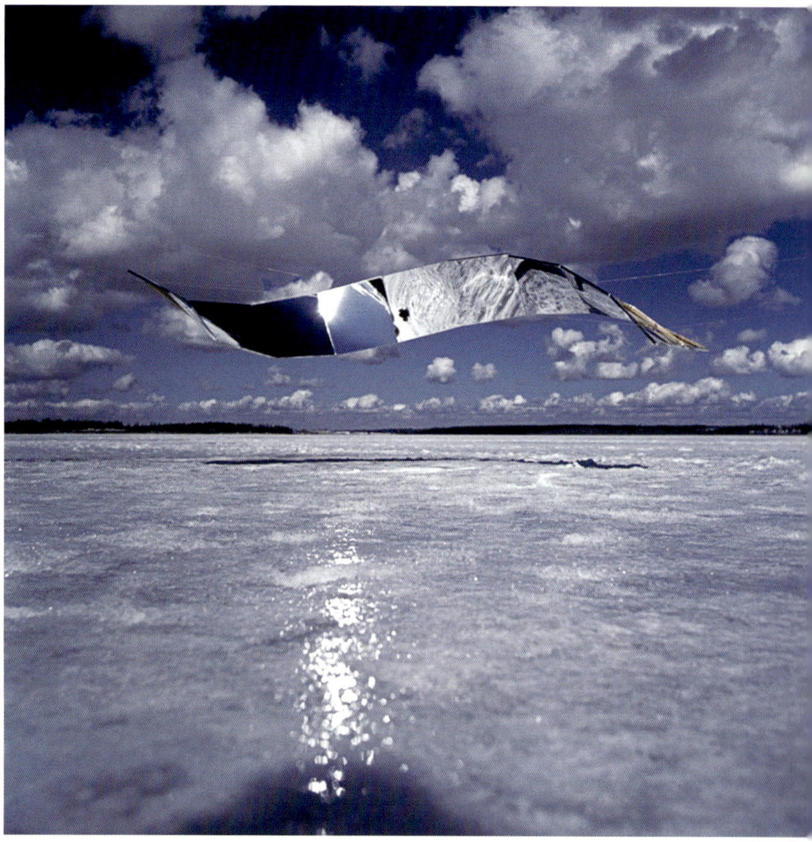

Francisco Infante

Born in Saratov Oblast in 1943 to a Spanish father and Russian mother, Francisco Infante is best known for his ongoing series Artifacts, which he began in 1968 and on which he continues to work in Russia and abroad with his wife and collaborator Nonna Goryunova. After graduating from the Stroganov Higher College of Art, Infante became a member of the Dvizheniye group of young Kineticists. Distanced from the world of Soviet politics, his career has followed a clear trajectory inspired by metaphysical notions about life, the universe, and the relationship between nature and art translated into paintings, sculptures, installations and temporary interventions in the landscape.

Early paintings such as the series The Point in Its Space (1964) demonstrate Infante's predilection for metaphysics. In these works, his aim was to visually capture infinity and eternity. His harmonious compositions, seen repeatedly in his working through and mastery of geometric forms, first on paper and canvas and then in three dimensions, have their origin in his desire to discover structure in chaos. He has explained that towards the end of his studies, he 'was struck by the feeling that the universe is infinite. It was a terrific shock to my consciousness, and I started attempting to reflect this infinity. It had absolutely nothing in common with the type of education that I had received at school. But, since I had pursued studies to become an artist, I started to make drawings – metaphors of this infinity – trying to understand and give form to this intense state of anxiety.' These works show only small facets of the structure that holds the universe in place and extends into eternity, whether in the form of spirals, grids or straight lines. 'There is a certain structure without which everything falls apart ... However, the world also contains entropy ... a push to bring everything that has structure to chaos ... Art decreases entropy,' he explains.

Infante's participation in the projects of Dvizheniye distinguished him from his contemporaries, as his work was often exhibited at, and even commissioned for, Soviet and international industrial and technological fairs. Kinetic constructions like *Sound and Light* (1970), exhibited at Chemistry-70 in Moscow in 1970, are synesthetic environments which act on the viewer through a carefully orchestrated relationship between movement, light, colour and electronic or concrete music. These are examples of the interest in modernism, science, technology and space that was dominant not only throughout the USSR but internationally throughout the 1960s.

In early 1968, while in the countryside, Infante laid out compositions of painted geometric shapes cut out of cardboard directly onto the pristine snow and then photographed them. This series, known as *Suprematist Games* (1968), was the forerunner to Artifacts. Infante compared his 'canvas' of snow with Malevich's 'white nothingness ... Snow was nothingness; it melted and there was nothing left ... What I was doing had nothing to do with Malevich; it was a conceptual gesture'. Artifacts demonstrates the interrelationship between the artificial, man-made, technological world and the natural world whose origins are symbolic and religious: 'I took the idea that a person is capable of creating his world as a second nature. At the intersection of these two worlds – the natural and artificial ones – there appears a new perspective or measure, which helps clarify the world.'

Infante and his wife are continuing to develop and expand the Artifacts series. Working with geometric shapes of increasing complexity, they

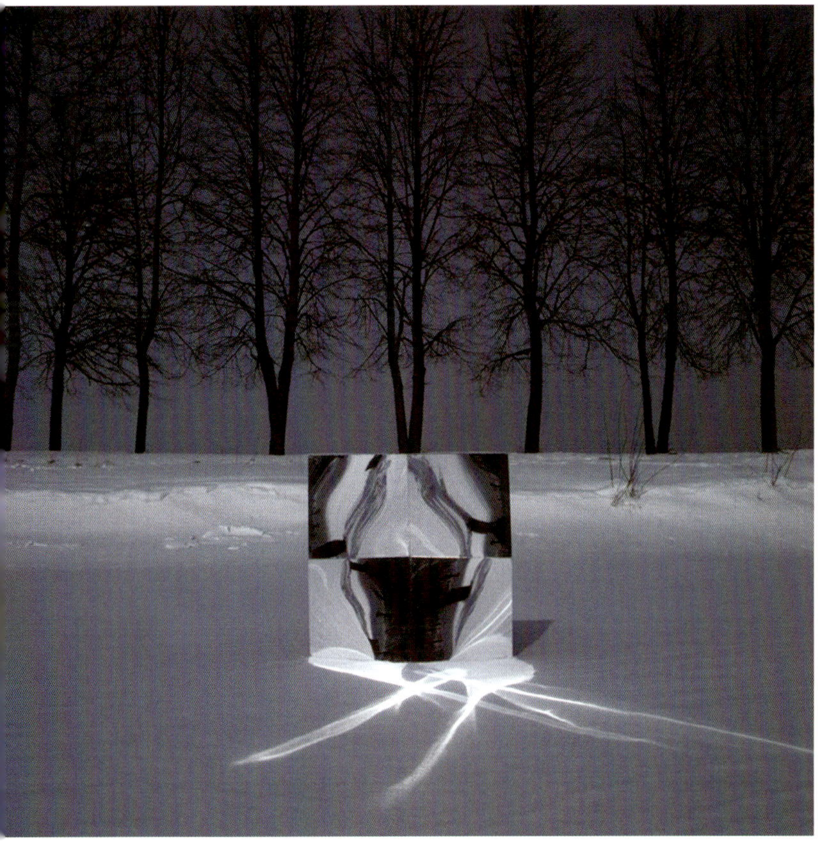

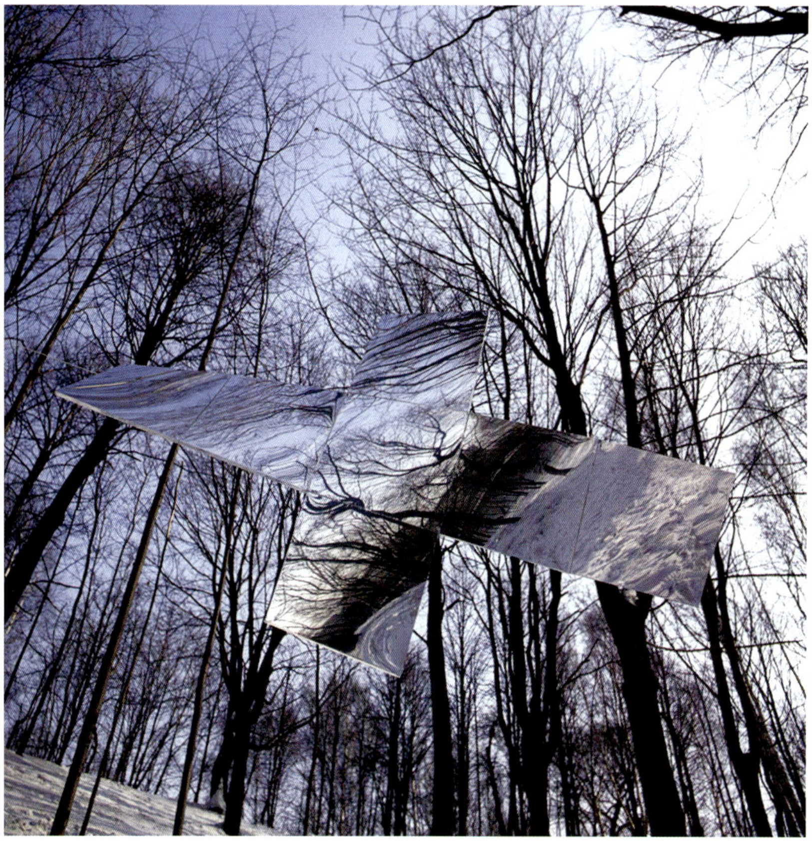

place them in nature – in water, forests, fields, during snowy winters or the summer – and photograph them. The photographs are both documentation of the momentary intersection between artifice and nature – at the centre of which is the artist-as-witness – and the final, finished work of art. Often using foil procured during the production of his State-commissioned kinetic works, Infante's strange objects float, grow up and out of, and reflect the environment in a surreal fashion. They are simultaneously a part of their surroundings and distinctly 'other'. Convinced of the artist's role as a sensitive reflector of the world, Infante explains that 'art doesn't exist without symbolism.' Things do not stand still but are constantly shifting and changing, and Artifacts – his most mature body of work – is a means of consciously seizing the world and giving it artistic form at a specific moment in time, even if unconsciously.

facing page far left
The Life of a Triangle,
from the series Artifacts, 1976
C-print
50 x 50 cm
© Francisco Infante
Courtesy of the artist

facing page left
Focuses on a Deflected Space,
from the series Artifacts, 1979
C-print
50 x 50 cm
© Francisco Infante
Courtesy of the artist

above
Focuses on a Deflected Space,
from the series Artifacts, 1979
C-print
50 x 50 cm
© Francisco Infante
Courtesy of the artist

above left
Focuses on a Deflected Space,
from the series Artifacts, 1979
C-print
50 x 50 cm
© Francisco Infante
Courtesy of the artist

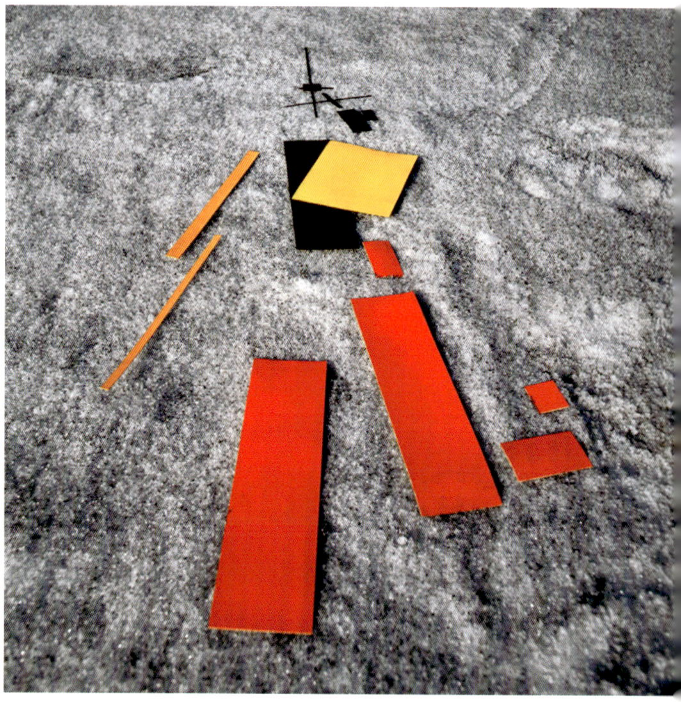

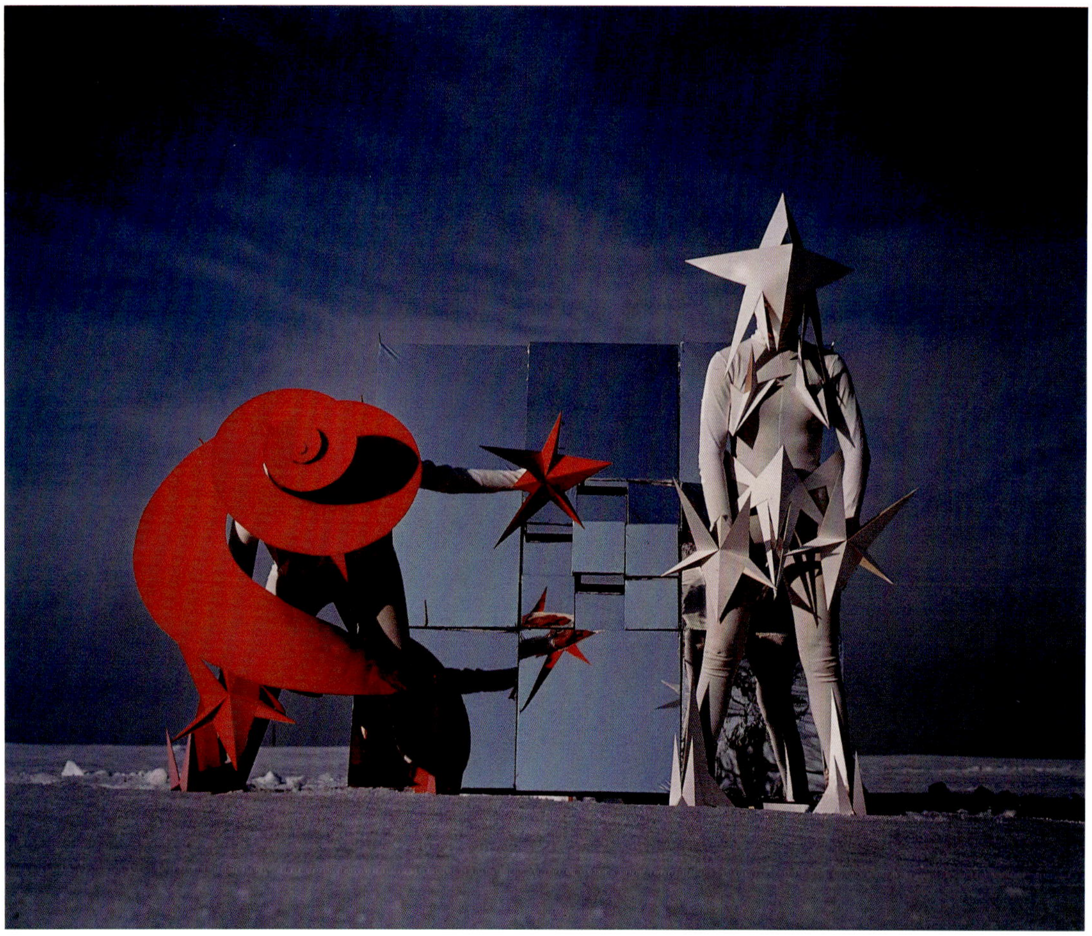

top
Signs in the Landscape,
from the series Artifacts, 1979
© Francisco Infante
Courtesy of the artist

left
Play of Gestures,
from the series Artifacts, 1977
© Francisco Infante
Courtesy of the artist

facing page
The Point in Its Space,
from the series Spiral, 1964–76
Oil on canvas
100.1 x 100.1 cm
© Francisco Infante
Courtesy of Sotheby's

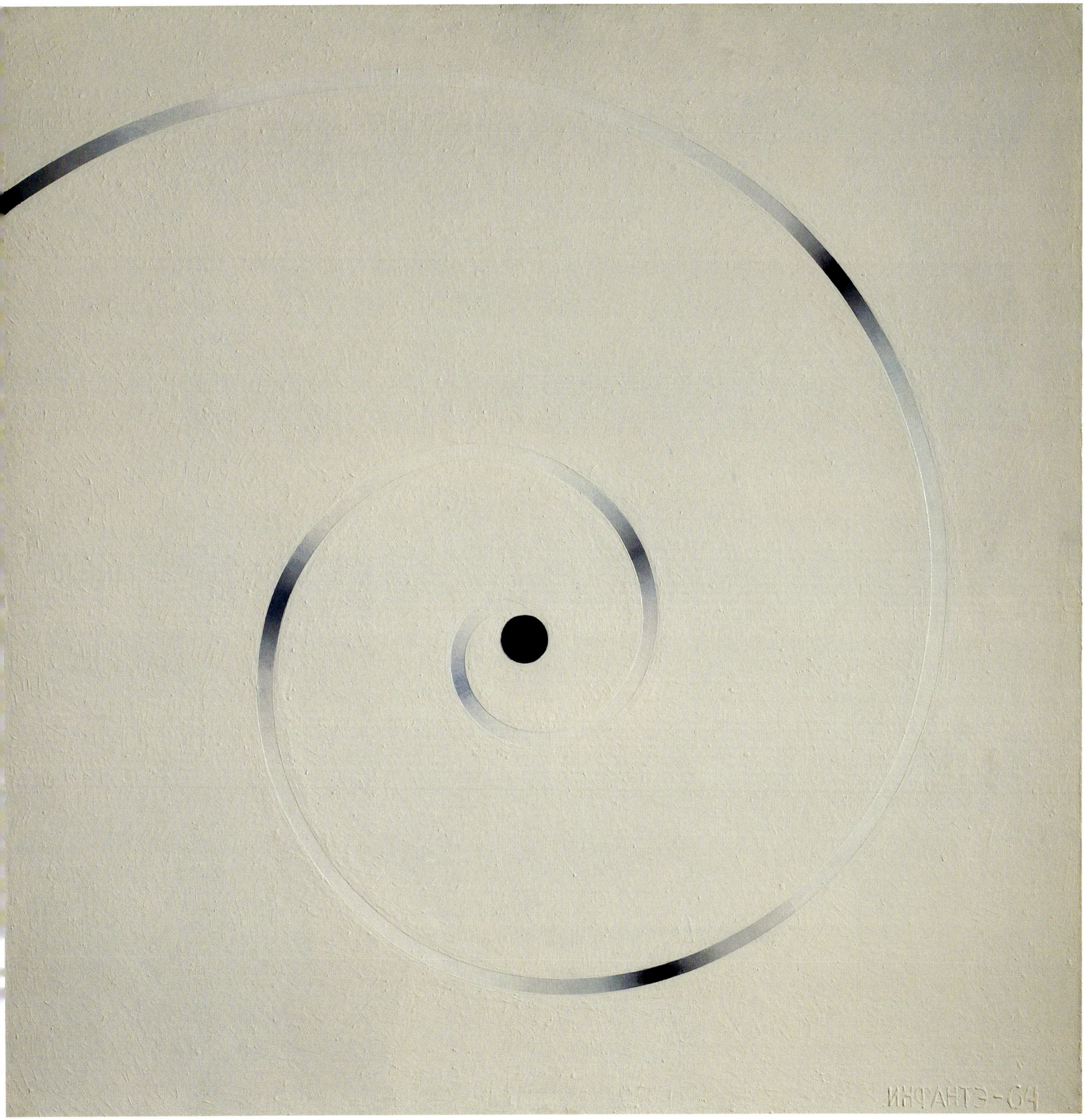
ИНФАНТЭ-64

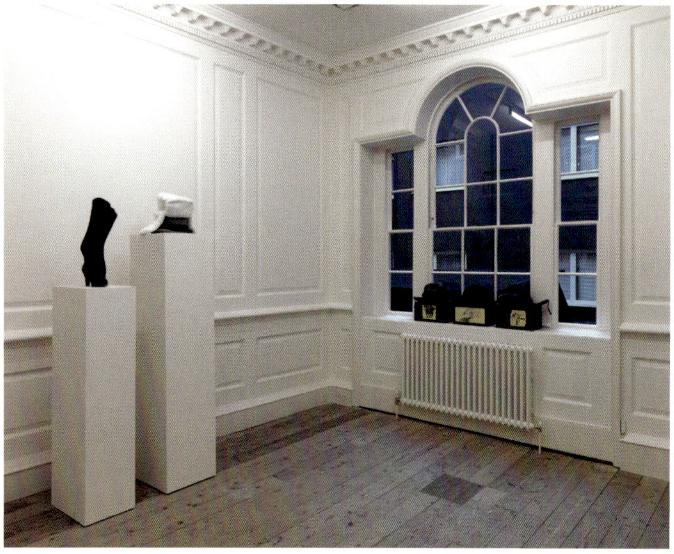

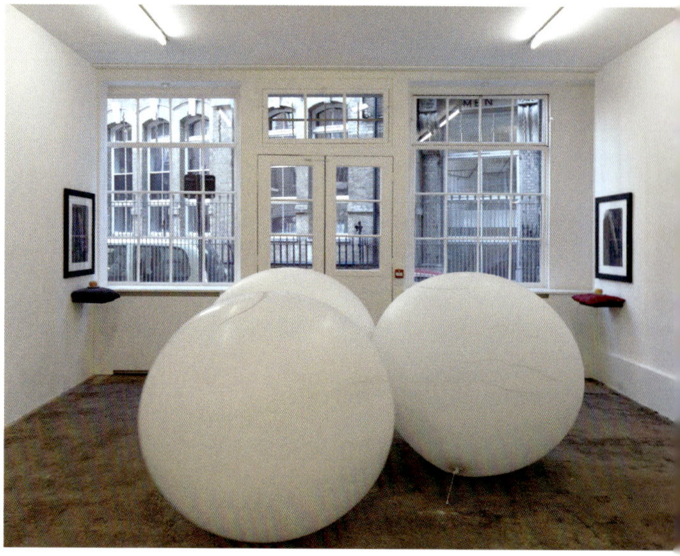

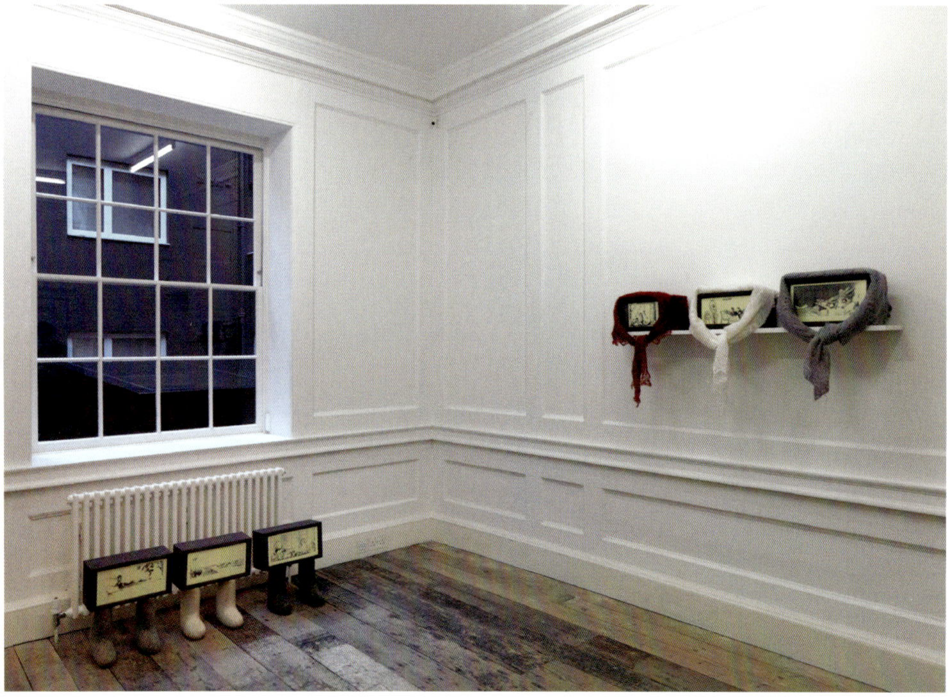

Inspection Medical Hermeneutics is an artists' collective that was established in Moscow in 1987 by Pavel Pepperstein, Sergei Anufriev and Yuri Leiderman. The group parodied Soviet-era bureaucracy both in its structure and in the form and content of its artistic output. Continuing in the tradition of the Moscow Conceptualists, the group claimed to 'inspect' symbolic content layered through everyday objects and situations. Its 'findings' were presented in the form of installations, performances, drawings, paintings and publications. These deconstructive actions drew on the visual and literary languages of Russian fairy tales, popular objects from Western visual culture, philosophy, theology, psychedelia and pseudo-scientific methodology. The group's approach found expression in its name, which suggests that Russia needs to be cured of an illness stemming from the over-signification and exhaustion of meaning following glasnost, perestroika and the collapse of the Soviet Union.

IMH's concern with studying the shifting borders between micro- and macro-social spaces is made clear in works such as *Amber Room* (1991), whose title refers to the famous long-lost Amber Room in the Hermitage, which Catherine II is said to have used as a secret hiding place. This installation mixes traditional Russian fairy tales and superstition. *Klinger's Boxes Cold Reduction* (1991), on the other hand, are eccentric, erotic etchings based on a work by the early twentieth-century German artist Max Klinger; the etchings nestle beneath a selection of Russian winter hats, gloves and scarves. Pepperstein explains that this series 'is dedicated to the theme of Russia as a memory of Europe ... Russia is a northern country with a cold climate, and this prevents things from quick degradation and decay. Therefore, traditional forms of European thought and orientation, now forgotten in Europe, have been preserved in Russia ... '

top and left
Klinger's Boxes
(second title Cold Reduction), 1991
Detail from the exhibition *A History of Irritated Material* at Raven Row Gallery, London, 2010
Mixed media
© Inspection Medical Hermeneutics
Courtesy of Nahodka Arts Ltd, London

above
Amber Room
(second title Hinterland of the Sacred), 1991
Detail from the exhibition *A History of Irritated Material* at Raven Row Gallery, London, 2010
Mixed media
© Inspection Medical Hermeneutics
Courtesy of Nahodka Arts Ltd

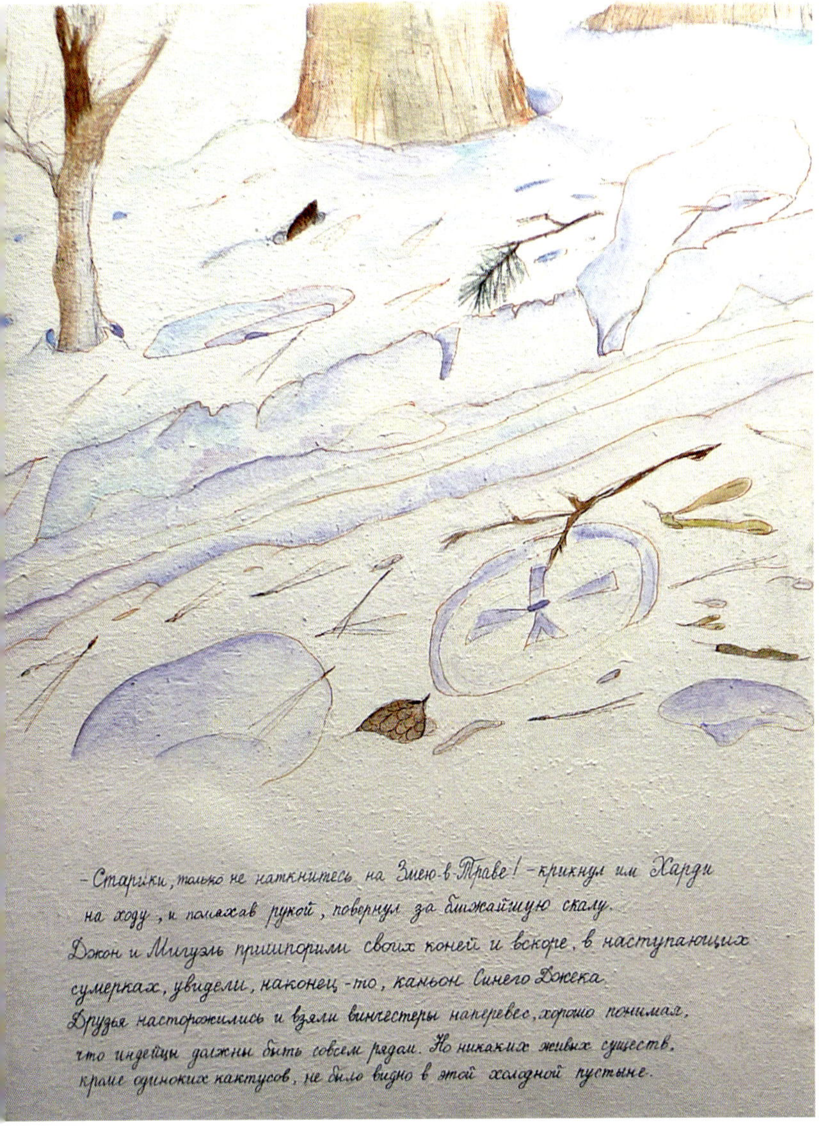

above
Paramen 1, 1994
Acrylic on canvas
50 x 65 cm

Courtesy of Nahodka Arts Ltd, London

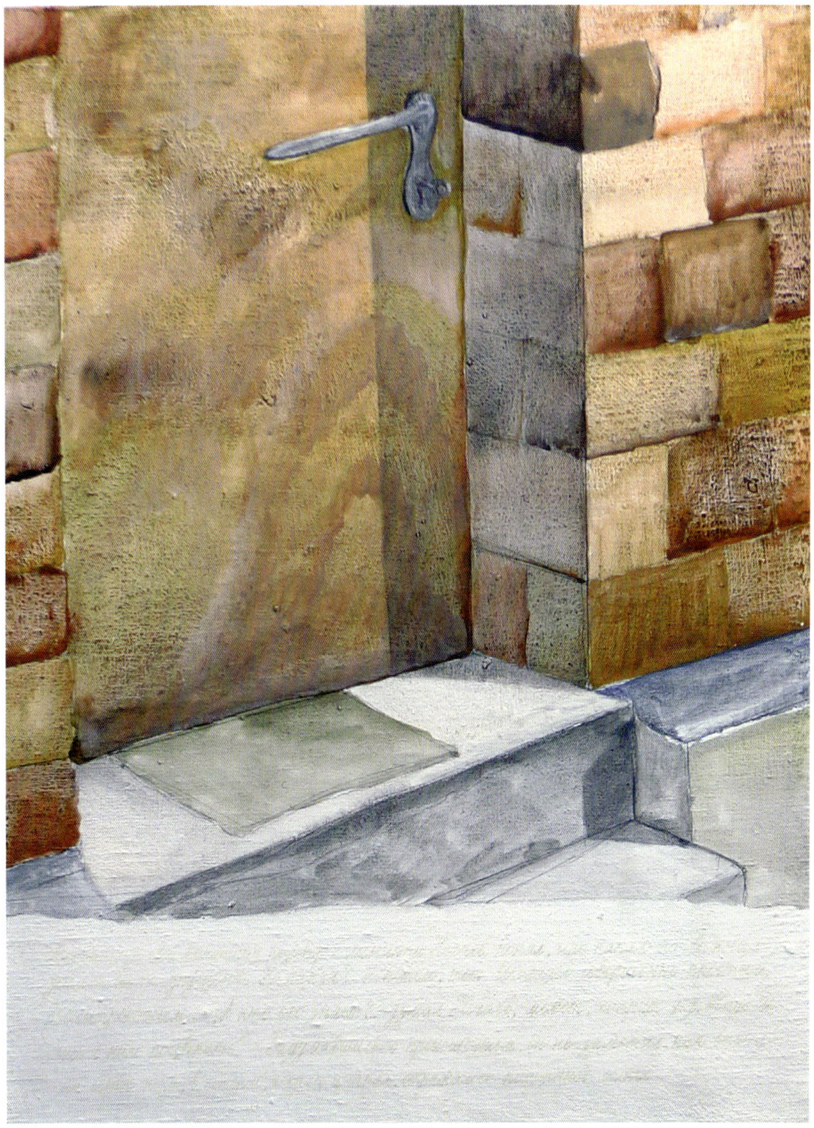

above
Paramen 10, 1994
Acrylic on canvas
50 x 65 cm

Courtesy of Nahodka Arts Ltd, London

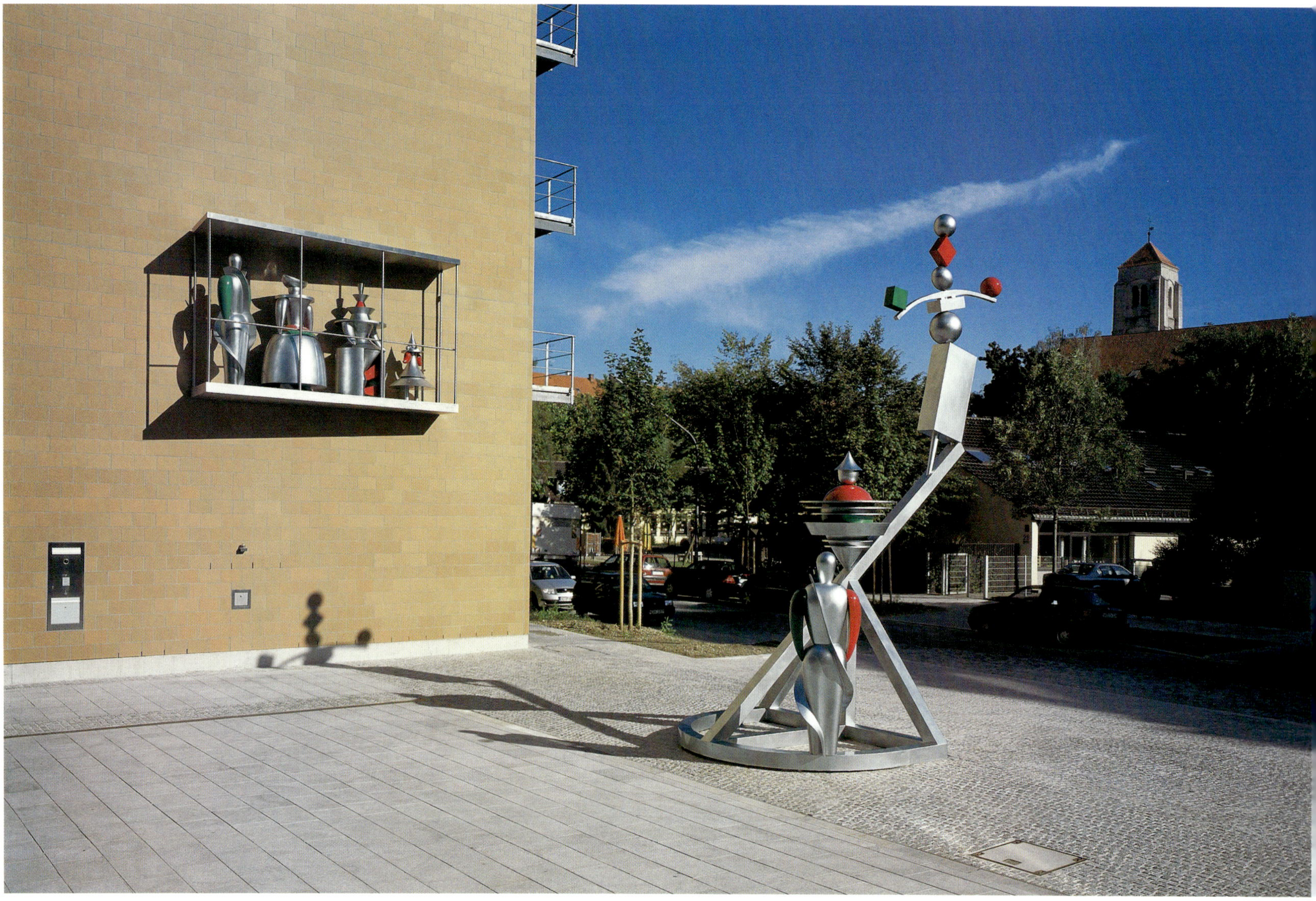

The artistic team of Ilya and Emilia Kabakov live and work together in New York. Both were born in Dnepropetrovsk, Ukraine; Emilia, Ilya's second wife, has been his collaborator since 1989. Born in 1945, she trained to be a pianist and emigrated to Israel in 1973. Ilya (born in 1933) moved to Moscow as a child and studied at an art school before entering the Surikov Institute, from which he graduated in 1957. Two years later, he joined the Soviet Union of Artists, where he worked as a children's book illustrator. It was during the 1950s that he started to produce work outside the aesthetics and ideology of Soviet official art.

Ilya Kabakov is considered to be one of the founders of Moscow underground Conceptual art. Lacking the pressure of official commissions, he developed a style in which text and image interact to create biographies of fictional characters that are typically organised into albums. From 1984 on, he developed this practice by creating installations, including the ground-breaking *Ten Characters* (1988), based on an album of the same name and first shown outside of Russia at the Ronald Feldman Gallery, New York. His art throughout the 1980s originated from the need to overcome the banalities of Soviet everyday life, with its communal apartments and petty, all-pervasive bureaucracy. Today Kabakov is seen as a pioneer in the field of installation art, with his 'total installation' projects taking over entire spaces into which viewers are typically, though not always, invited. His fictional characters all have a desire to escape into a private fantasy world. Of the Soviet Union Kabakov has said, 'Soviet life was like a kind of theatre and the play was already written by Stalin ... I was overflowing with hate and longing in relation to all the life around me; I felt I had to draw what came out of me. The awfulness, the longing, the rubbish, the Soviet bureaucracy, the falseness ... I had to free myself from it.'

Since perestroika, Ilya and Emilia Kabakov's creative collaborations have taken the form of large-scale urban installation projects which are often interactive. Ilya has described these as 'utopian projects', adding that 'Russian thought is neither pragmatic nor realistic ... but is based on a kind of craziness.' *The Palace of Projects* (1998), conceived for the Roundhouse, London, is a wood, steel and fabric structure whose form resembles Tatlin's unrealised *Monument to the Third International*. Viewers are told that they might find a personal project of their own within the palace and are reminded that life is only worth living if everyone has some kind of project. In *The Alternative History of Art* (2005), Kabakov explores a new version of the Russian avant-garde by presenting an exhibition of the work of three fictitious artists.

The Kabakovs have exhibited extensively since the early 1990s, notable shows being *Incident in the Museum and Other Installations* at the State Hermitage Museum, St Petersburg (2004), and *The House of Dreams* at the Serpentine Gallery, London (2005). They have taken part in several biennales, including Venice and Sydney, and held an important retrospective at the Garage Centre for Contemporary Culture, Moscow (2008).

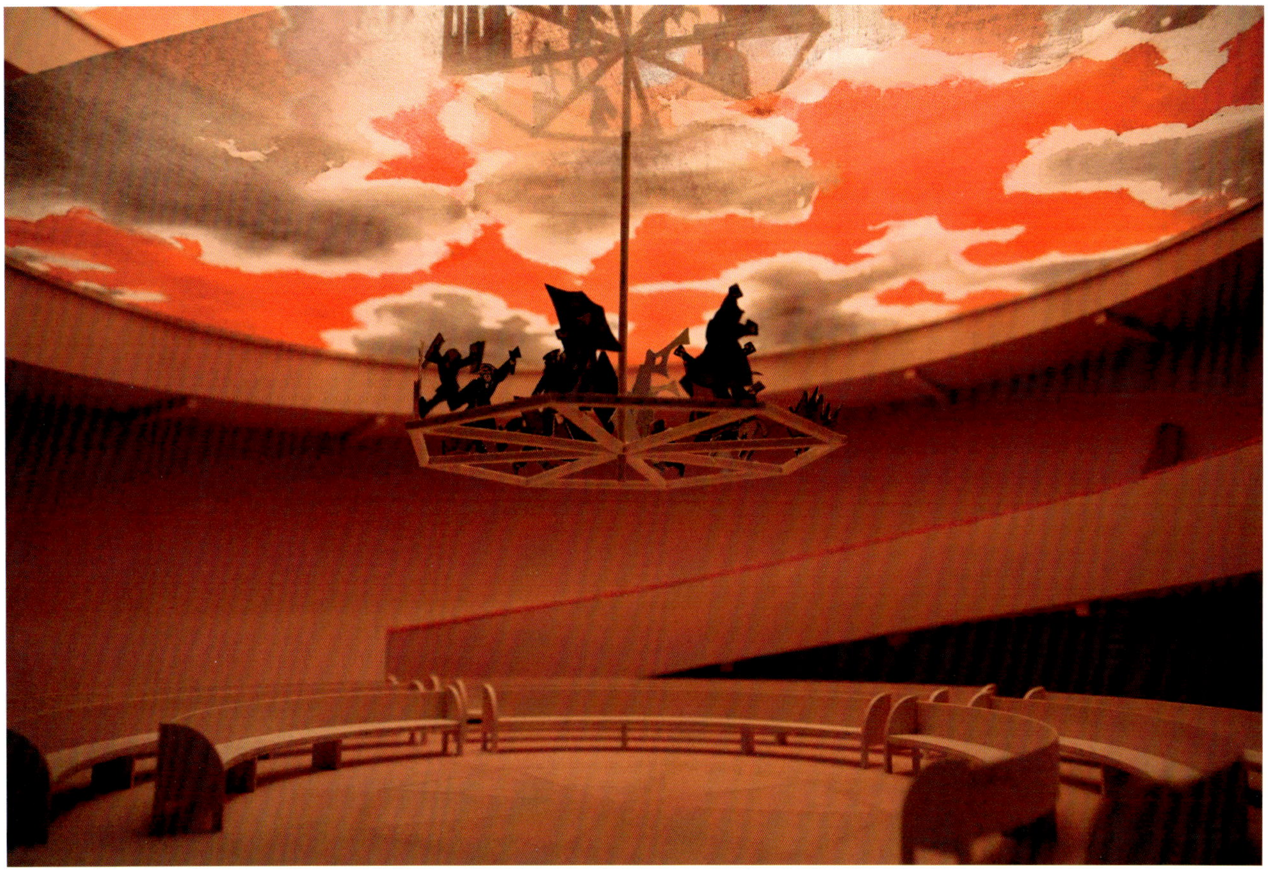

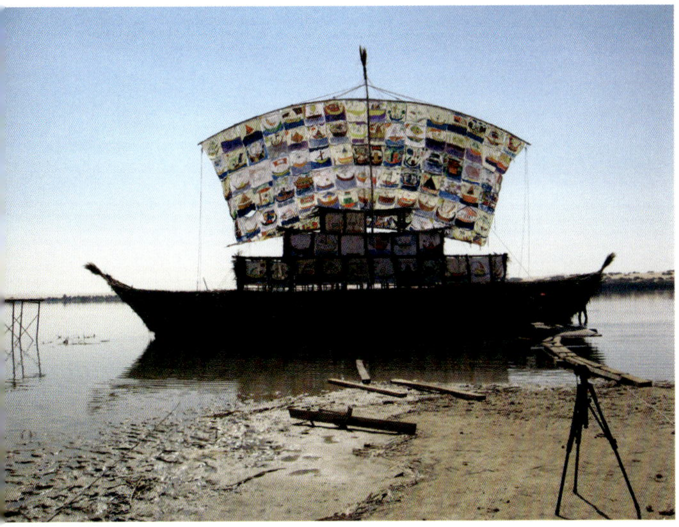

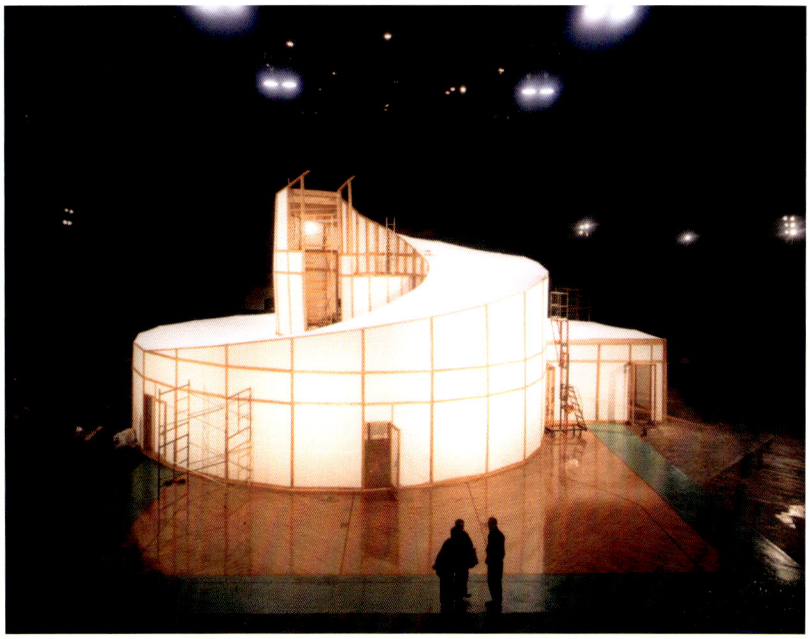

facing page
The Shining Circus and It's Spectators, 2004
Sculpture installation,
Munchen-Giesing, Germany
Aluminium, stainless steel, paint
Photo: Emilia Kabakov
© Ilya and Emilia Kabakov
Courtesy of the artists

above
The Ship of Tolerance, 2006
Siwa, Egypt
Photo: Emilia Kabakov
© Ilya and Emilia Kabakov
Courtesy of the artists

top
The Vertical Opera, 2001
Installation *Fantasmagoria* for
Guggenheim Museum, New York
Photo: Doug Dinger / Kabakov Studio
© Ilya and Emilia Kabakov
Courtesy of the artists

right
The Palace of Projects, 2000
Installation at The Armory
on 26 Street, New York
Photo: Gil Amiaga
© Ilya and Emilia Kabakov
Courtesy of the artists

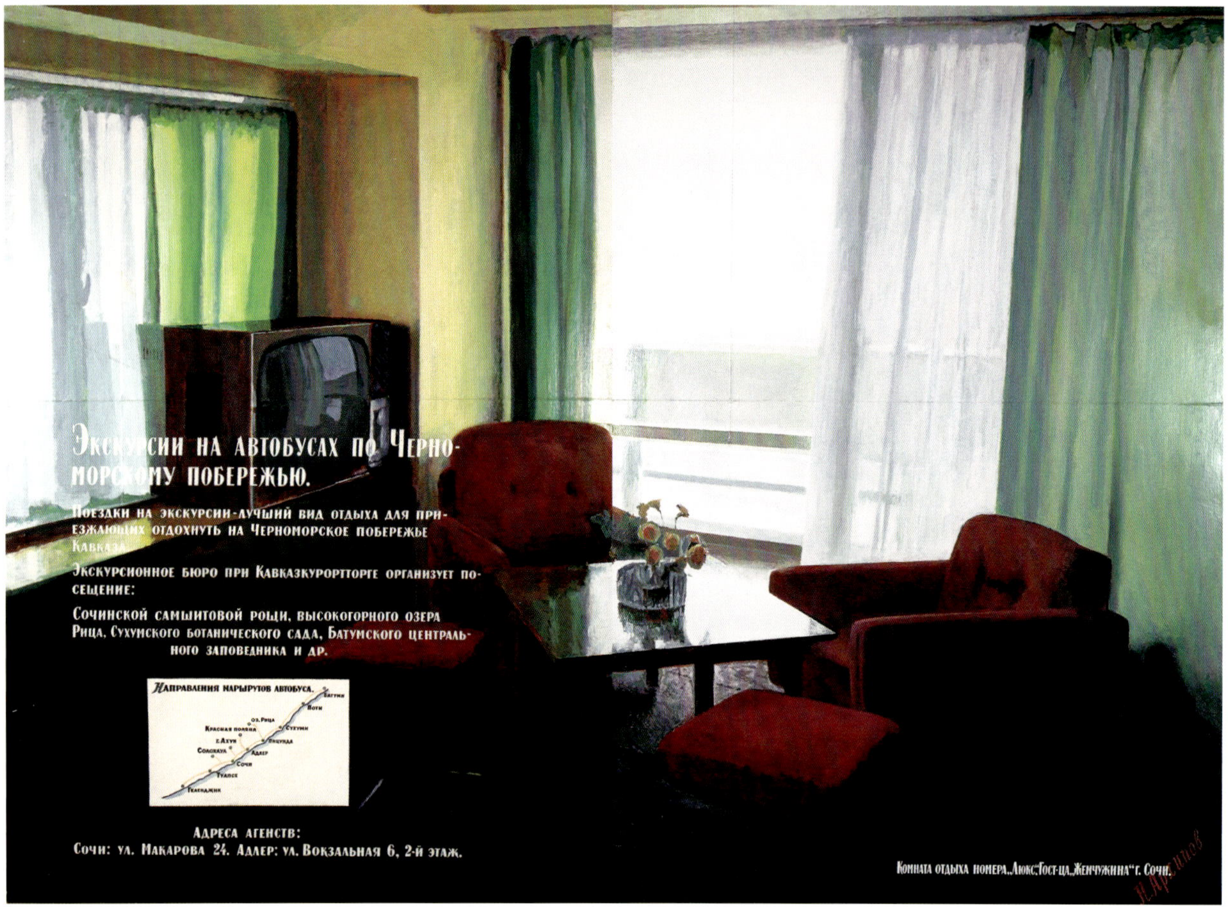

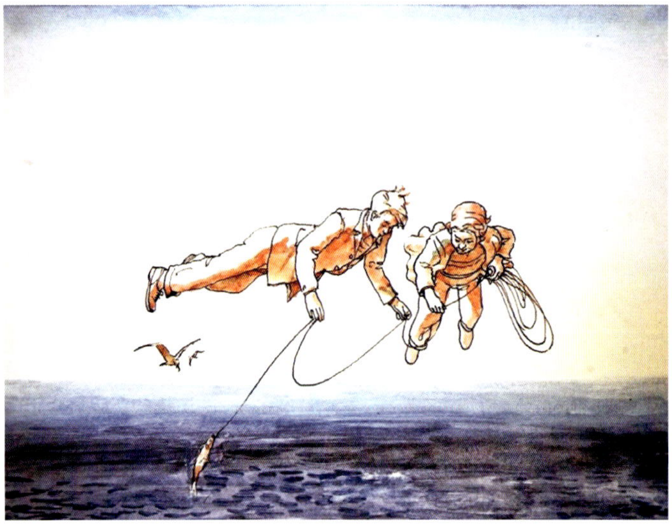

top
La Chambre de Luxe, 1981
Oil on 2 panels
214.6 x 295.9 cm
© Ilya and Emilia Kabakov
Courtesy of the Museum of Avant-Garde Mastery (MAGMA)

left
From the album The Flying Komarov, 32 sheets, sheet No. 13, Fragment, 1981
Hand coloured print
20.3 x 26.8 cm
© Ilya and Emilia Kabakov
Courtesy of the artist

above
Ch. Rosenthal: 'In The Relative's House' 1930 from The Alternative History of Art, 1997
Oil on canvas
154 x 245 cm
Photo: D. James Dee
© Ilya and Emilia Kabakov
Courtesy of the artist

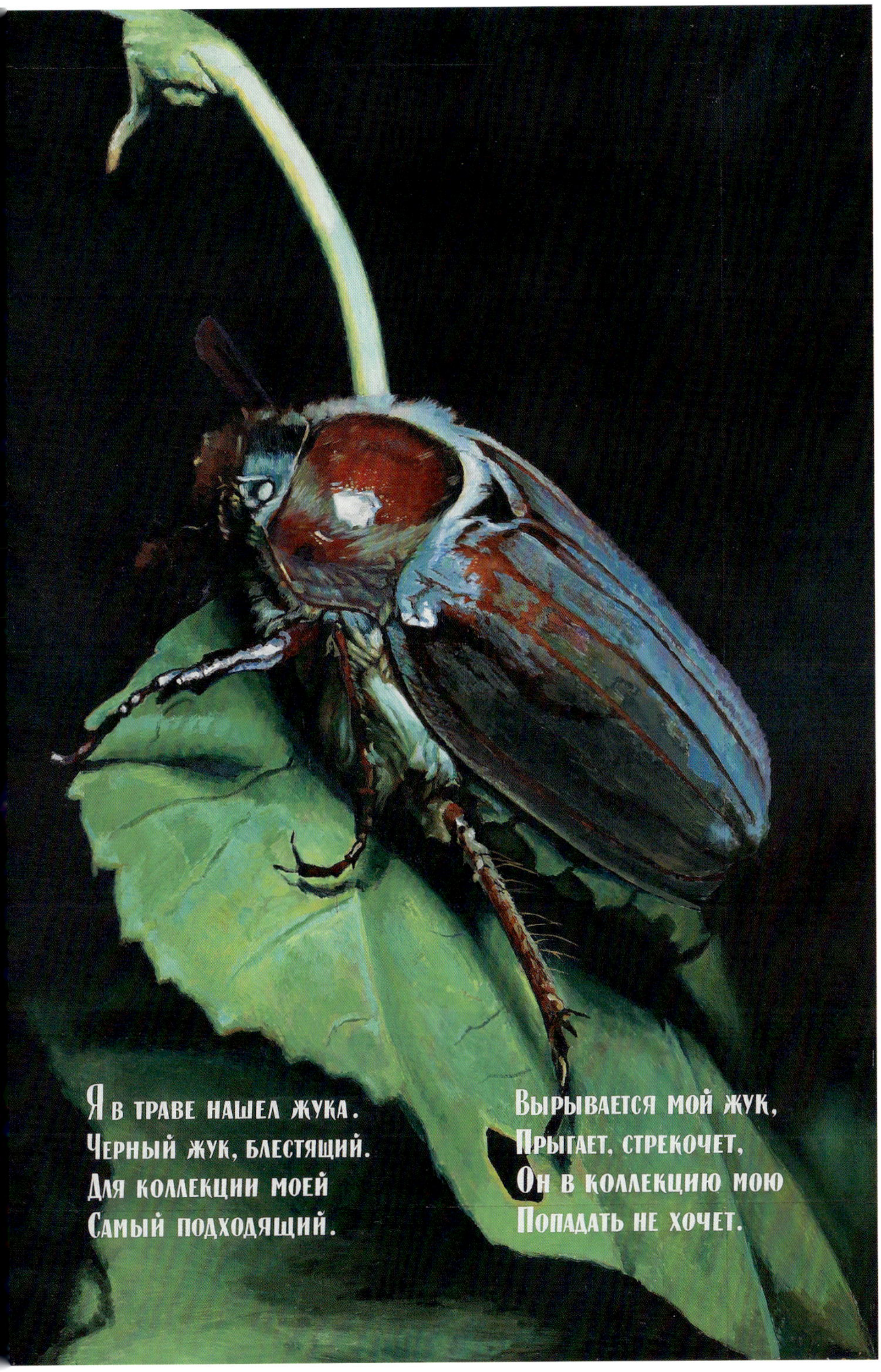

above
The Beetle, 1982
Enamel on panel
226.5 x 148.5 cm
© Ilya and Emilia Kabakov
Courtesy of the Museum
of Avant-Garde Mastery (MAGMA)

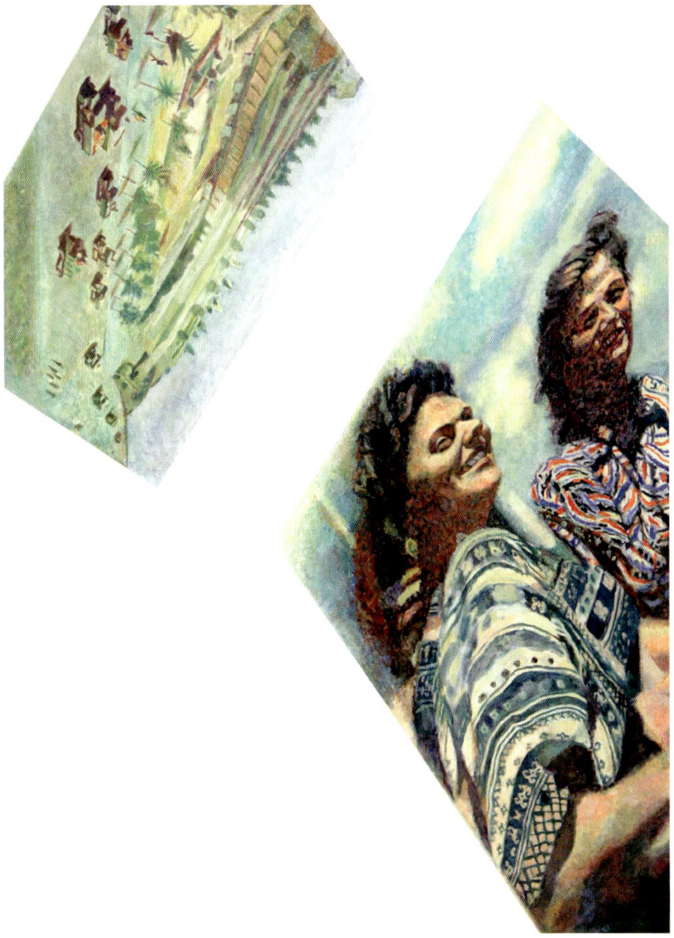

right
Flying No. 9, 2009
Oil on canvas
224 x 165 cm
Photo: Igoris Markovas / Kabakov Studio
© Ilya and Emilia Kabakov
Courtesy of the artists

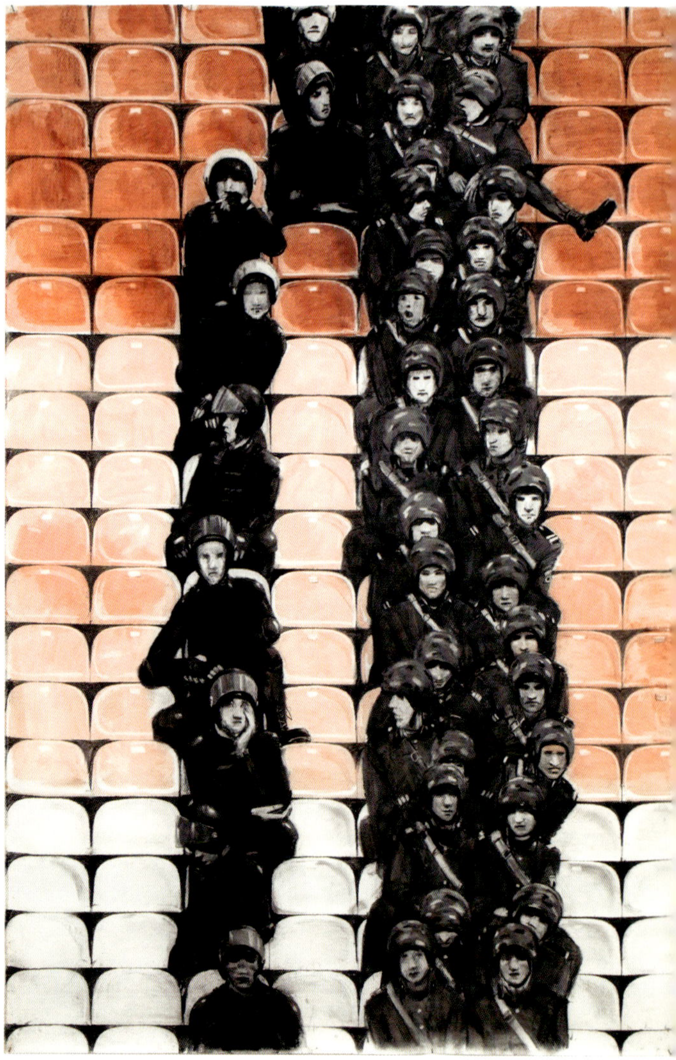

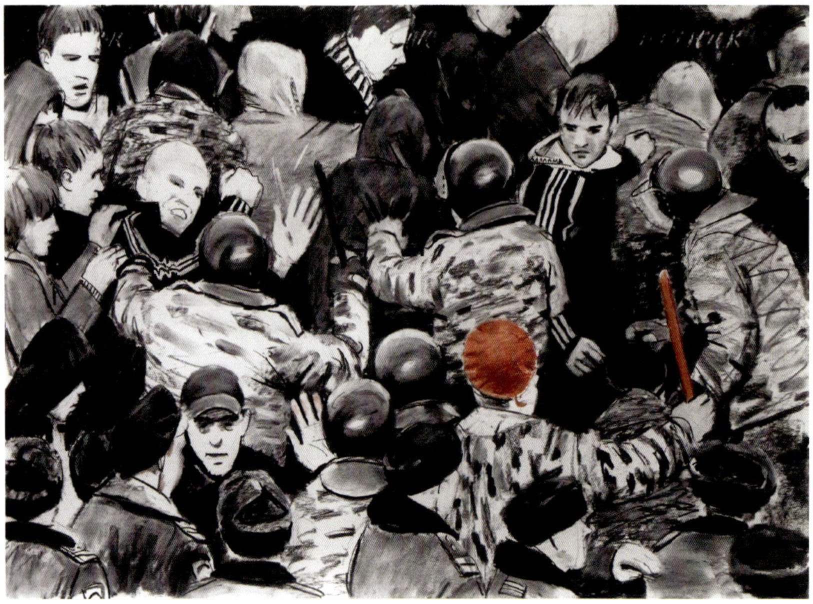

Alexei Kallima

Alexei Kallima was born in Grozny, Chechnya, in 1969 of Russian parents; his father was an engineer and his mother was a doctor. Encouraged to study art from a young age, he graduated in Painting from the Krasnodar College of Fine Arts in 1988 and, due to the conflict in Chechnya, left for Moscow in 1995. He now lives and works in Moscow. Kallima, the name of a butterfly, is the pseudonym he adopted after emigration in part due to its lack of distinct national associations.

Kallima's diverse practice can be divided into painting, graphics (the medium he increasingly prefers to work in), and performance and action art. In the late 1990s and early 2000s he often collaborated with members of RADEK, an important Actionist group. He is represented by major commercial galleries in Russia, France, Germany and New York, and has taken part in biennales in Venice, Moscow and Thessaloniki.

Kallima's upbringing and exile are central themes in his art, in which he expresses his dual identity as a Chechen living in Russia, educated and brought up in Grozny within the context of Soviet cultural heritage. Chechen rebel fighters are among his heroes; two works from his important Chechen series focus on the subject of parachuting: *Air Border* (2007) and *Chechen Women's Parachute Team* (2008–10). The open white parachutes can be seen as symbols of surrender, ecstasy and freedom. Kallima also works in fluorescent paint, which can be viewed only in the dark – a metaphor for social taboos. His best-known work in this medium, *Terek-Chelsea* (2005), for which he won Russia's Innovation Prize in 2006, is a 10-metre-long fresco showing a football game in which the Chechen team is beating the English club Chelsea 6–2 (Chelsea is owned by the Russian oligarch Roman Abramovich). Kallima's graphic works and paintings draw on aesthetics from Soviet Realism and animation art; he also cites several Western European masters as strong influences, in particular Mantegna, Goya and Velasquéz, as well as the Russian icon painter Andrei Rublev. The distinctive red colour with which he works was discovered by accident while using charcoal and sanguine. Red has personal resonances for the painter, reflecting his nostalgia for and disillusionment over the breakdown of the Soviet Union.

The early Soviet photography of Rodchenko, with its emphasis on the collective parade or large social gatherings, as well as the general theme of the heroic sportsman or -woman in Soviet Realist art, can be seen as consistent inspirations behind Kallima's art. Documenting group behaviour, one of his most celebrated series depicts football fans, capturing the surge and wave of the crowd as well as violent fans clashing after matches. When discussing his paintings, Kallima speaks of the advantage of the single image over the medium of video or film, in that a painting can tell a story in one 'still'. He further observes that although a painting shares only a small part of a story with its viewers, they can nevertheless comprehend a complex message. Kallima sees composition – the rhythm of visual form – as the most important element in any work. The arrangement of bodies and forms creates a striving dynamic, and it is the story of this striving that he sees as a painting's real narrative.

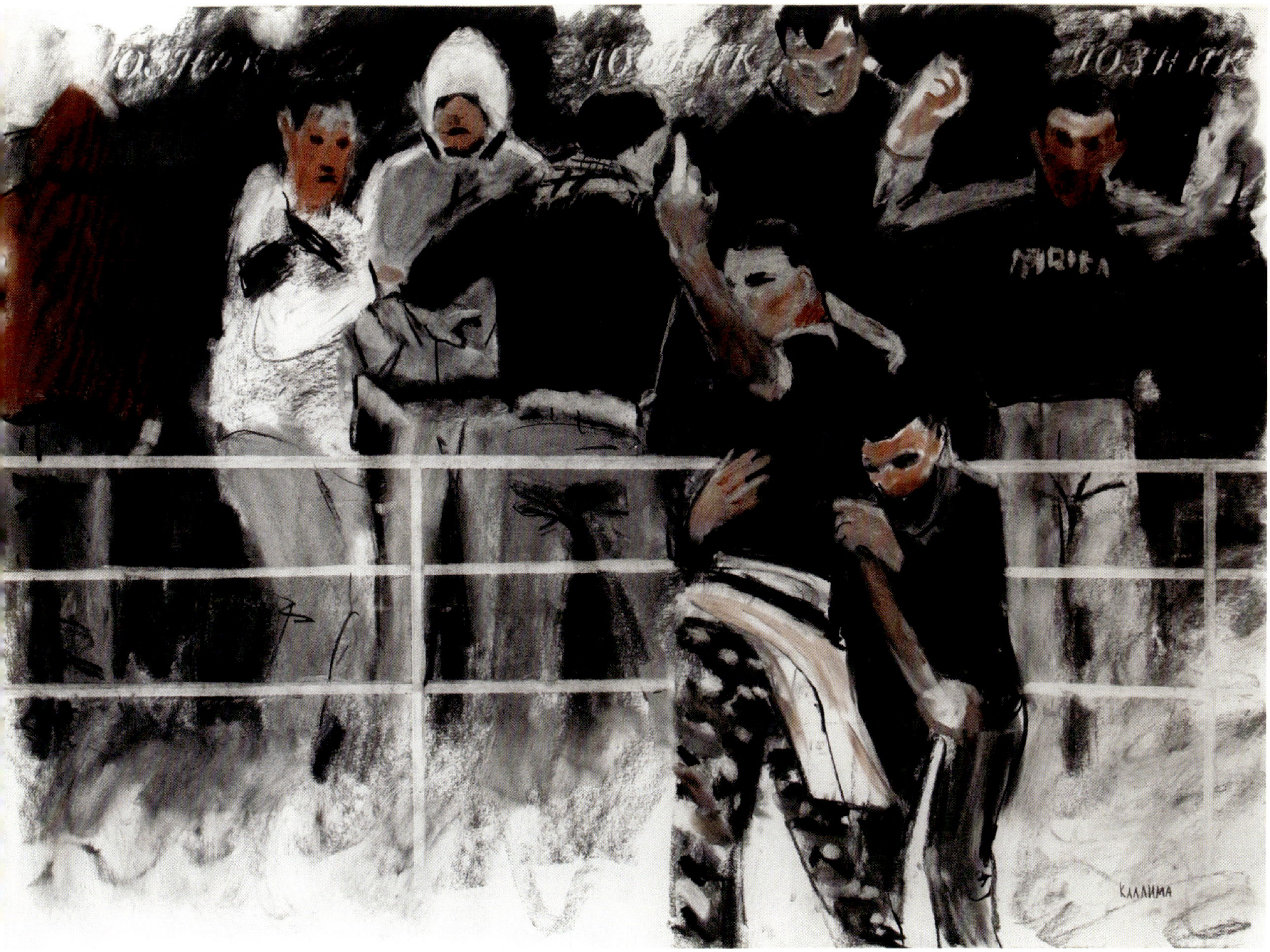

acing page far left
The Darkness Is Longer than the Night, 2010
Sanguine and charcoal on paper
72 x 97 cm (framed)
© Alexei Kallima
Courtesy of the artist and
Galerie Anne de Villepoix

acing page top
The Darkness Is Longer than the Night, 2010
Sanguine and charcoal on canvas
325 x 210 cm (unframed)
© Alexei Kallima
Courtesy of the artist and
Galerie Anne de Villepoix

above
The Darkness Is Longer than the Night, 2010
Sanguine and charcoal on paper
72 x 97 cm (framed)
© Alexei Kallima
Courtesy of the artist and
Galerie Anne de Villepoix

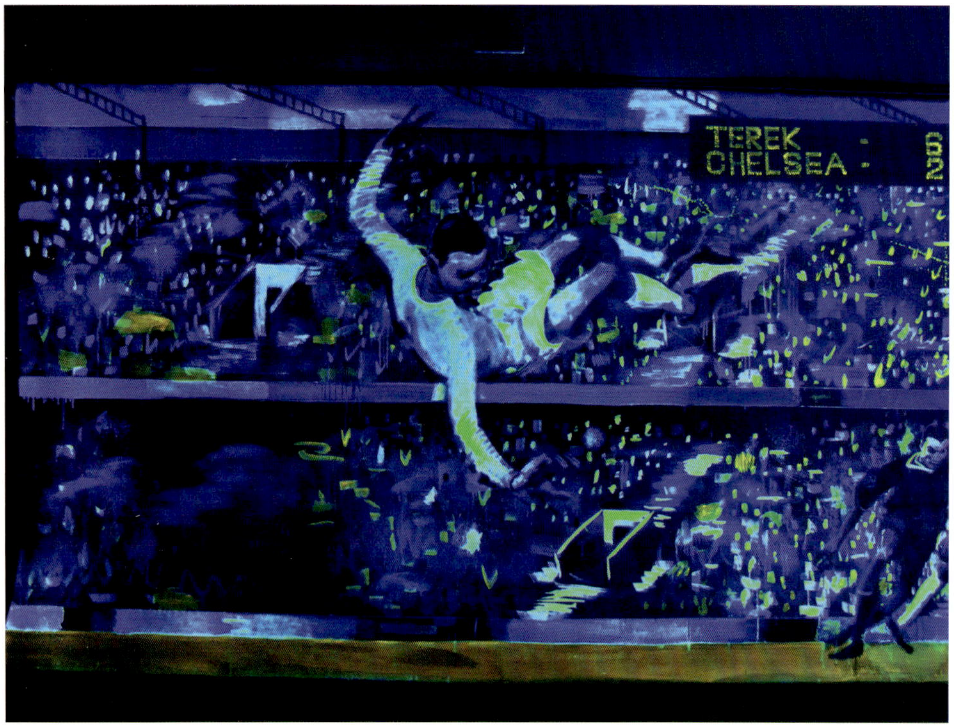

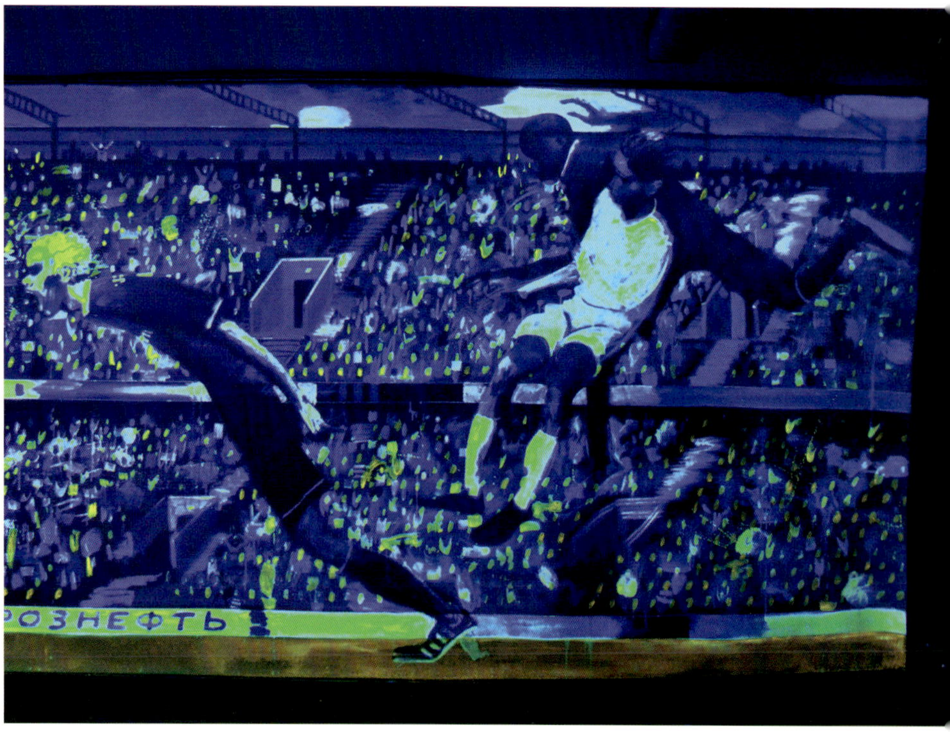

above and right
Terek – Chelsea, 2005 (detail)
Invisible ink on canvas
210 x 100 cm
© Alexei Kallima
Courtesy Guelman Gallery

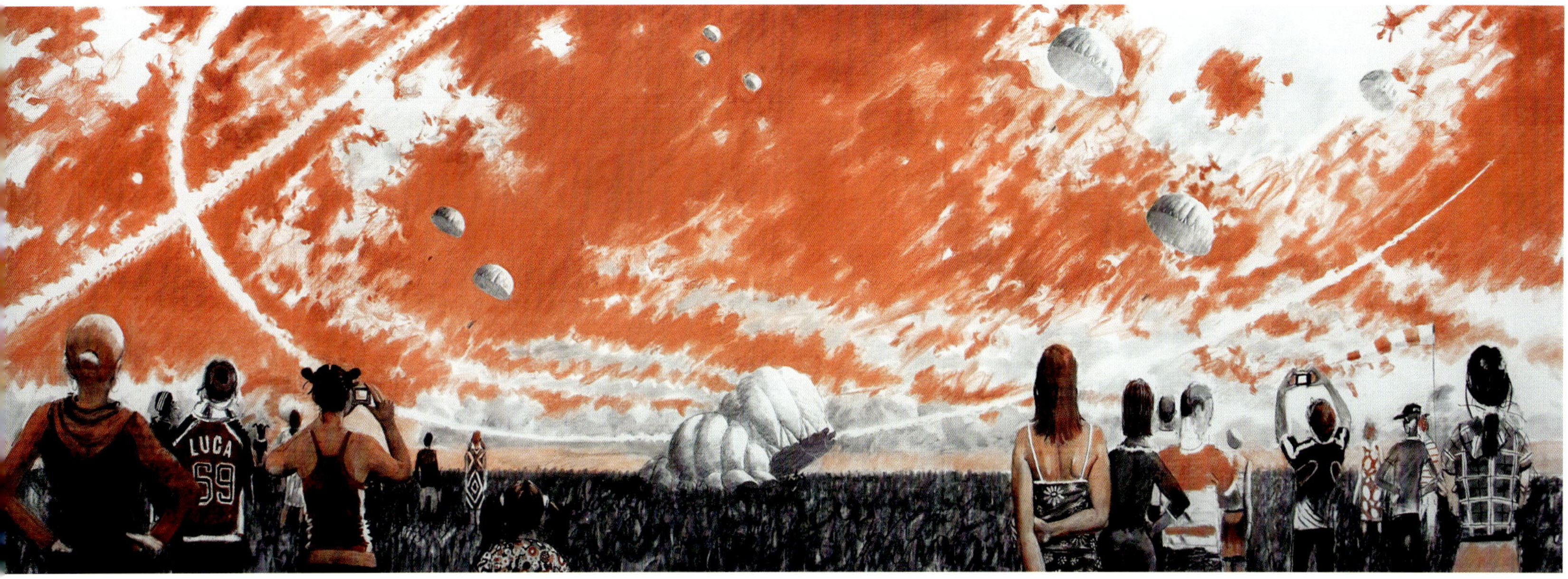

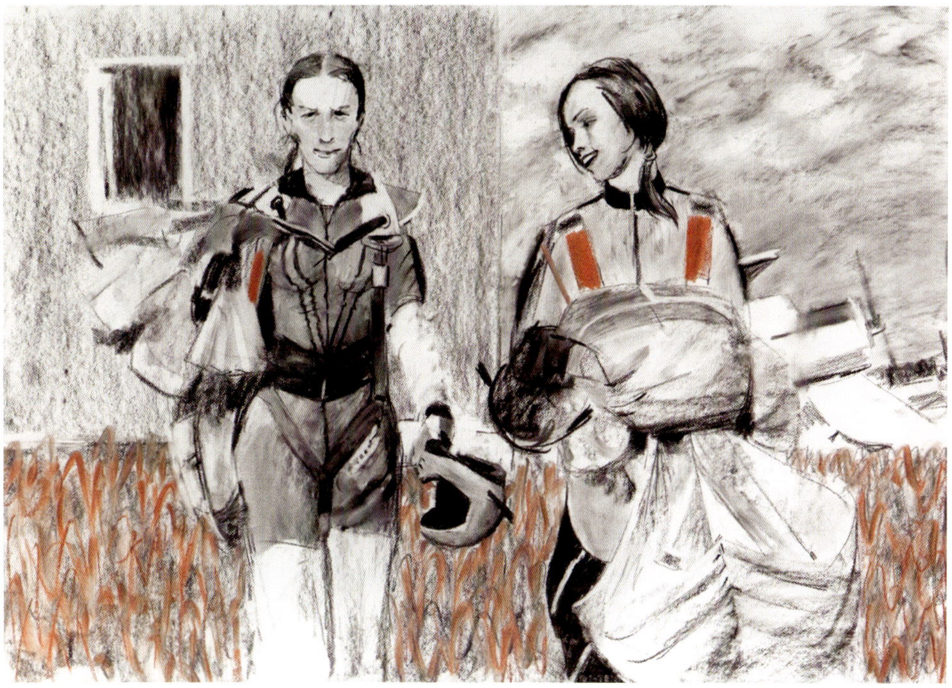

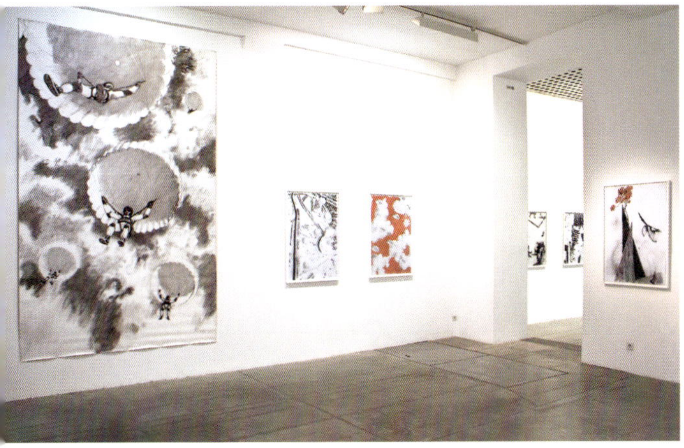

top
Chechen Women's Parachute Team, 2008–10
Sanguine, charcoal, matt lacquer on canvas
135 x 397 cm
© Alexei Kallima
Courtesy Guelman Gallery

above
Chechen Women's Parachute Team, 2008–10
Sanguine, charcoal on paper
75 x 110 cm
© Alexei Kallima
Courtesy Guelman Gallery

left
Sky Patrol, 2007
Exhibition view
© Alexei Kallima
Courtesy Guelman Gallery, Moscow,
and Galerie Anne de Villepoix, Paris

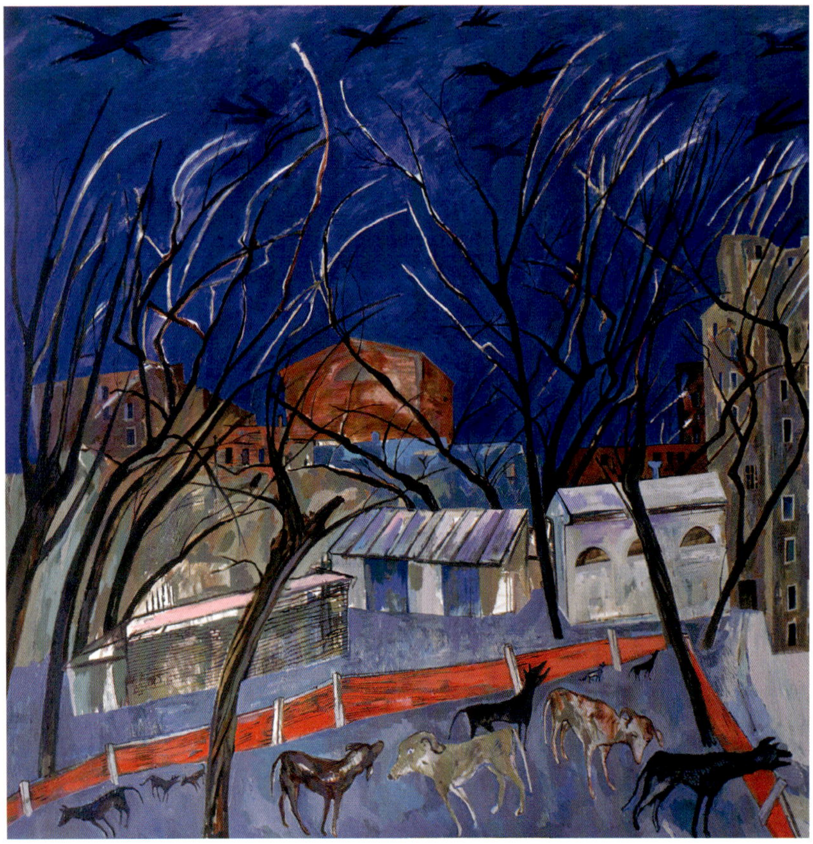

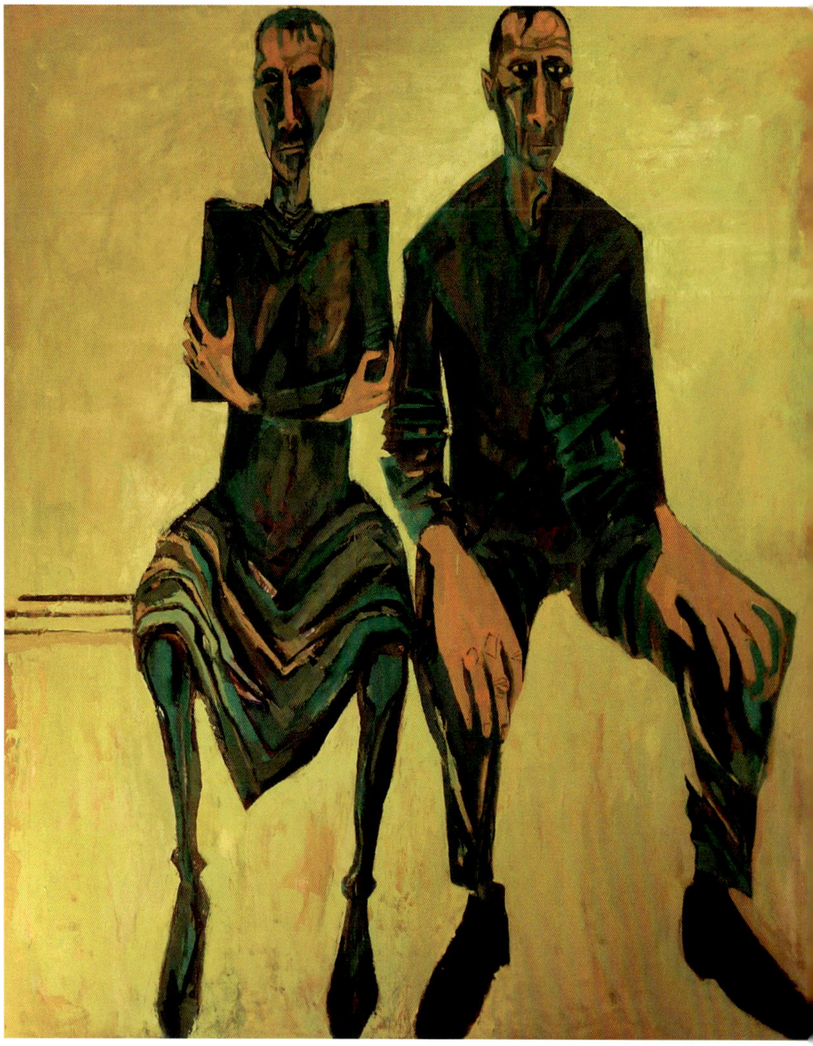

Artist and writer Maxim Kantor was born in Moscow in 1957. Having grown up among the intelligentsia – his father was a respected philosopher – Kantor studied at the Moscow Art Polygraph Institute (1975–80). During the 1980s he participated in many exhibitions of work by Moscow's underground painters; among early formative influences from this milieu he cites Vladimir Weisberg, in whose studio he spent a year, and Sergei Essaian. As Kantor's style matured through the mid-1980s, colour came to play an increasingly important role, his highly charged palette reflecting strong emotions. At the end of the 1990s, line grew more important, with drawing becoming central to his practice. Between 1999 and 2010, Kantor created a number of extensive graphic cycles which he calls 'atlases', including Wasteland, Metropolis and Vulcanus. Kantor represented Russia at the 1997 Venice Biennale, and his work is held in numerous public collections across Russia and Western Europe, including the Pushkin Museum of Fine Arts, Moscow; the British Museum, London; the Staatsgalerie, Stuttgart; and the Ludwig Museum, Cologne. In 2006 he published a two-volume part-novel, part-aesthetical treatise, *The Drawing Textbook*, in which he showed the evolution of society through the example of art history. Since then, he has published collected essays, plays and a second novel, all about contemporary Russian society and politics. Kantor divides his time between painting and writing, and lives between Moscow, Berlin, Oxford and an island off the French coast.

Key to Kantor's paintings is their openness to different levels of interpretation: the everyday, the symbolic and the metaphysical. His subject matter during the 1980s was drawn from his life under a totalitarian regime: his works showing barracks, dark canteens, stations and hospitals are portraits of Soviet stagnation. Ideology as a sickness is to be understood, endured and ultimately overcome, but in *Morning Round* (1987), the patients have little chance of being cured by evil doctors, and painting seems to be Kantor's only salvation. In working with such hopeless situations, his aim is to find a way to overcome his everyday predicament. It is this overcoming that he finds central to his art: 'A painting must be beautiful. The subject matter ... can be sad or even tragic, but the painting must be beautiful. That is the whole point of art; it fulfils its purpose to overcome misfortune.'

Portraiture occupies an important place in Kantor's work both as a traditional genre and for the role it plays in his multi-figured compositions, whether they are based on themes from Christian history or from Soviet or post-Soviet life. He finds his sitters, as in *Prodigal Son* (2001), in his circle of friends and acquaintances. Central to his practice are likenesses of his father, which offer Kantor a way of describing an archetypal image of humanity in formal terms and embody part of his own creative striving. In his works showing historical and literary figures from both Russian and global culture, the artist explores how contemporary social reality represents a complex web of past and present. Seeking to understand both, Kantor lays himself bare; his art has its roots in his autobiography. He believes that art must always be authentic rather than follow trends, observing of his own approach that 'one must try to be an artist, not an Expressionist or a Conceptualist. The painting must be returned to the world like Cézanne once tried to do.'

acing page top
Ian and Woman, 1990
)il on canvas
20 x 180 cm
© Maxim Kantor
Courtesy of Michael Neumann,
Germany

acing page left
Ten Stray Dogs, 2002
)il on canvas
40 x 240 cm
© Maxim Kantor
Private collection
Courtesy of the artist

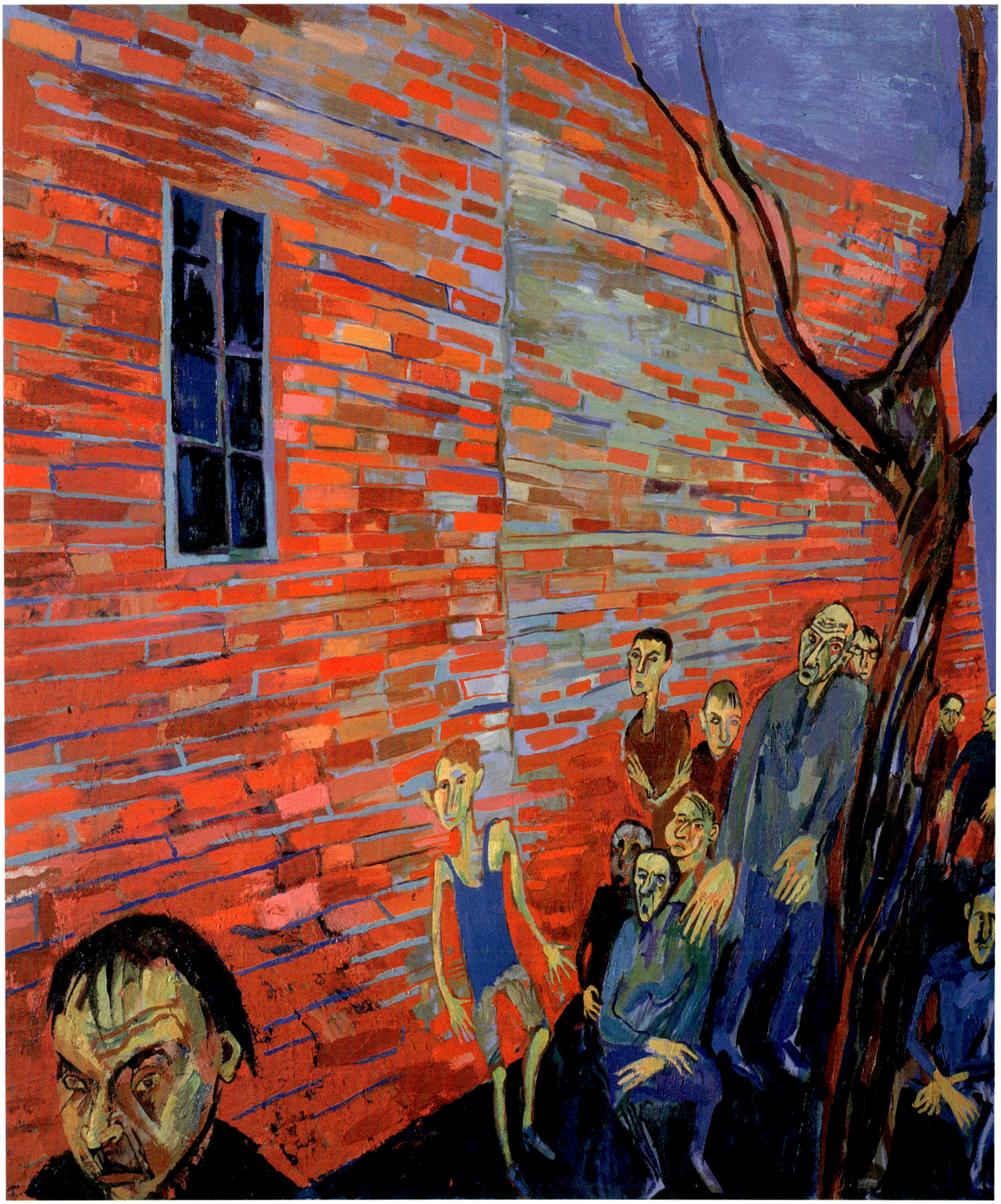

above
Prodigal Son, 2001
Oil on canvas
220 x 180 cm
© Maxim Kantor
George Ortiz Collection, Brussels
Courtesy of the artist

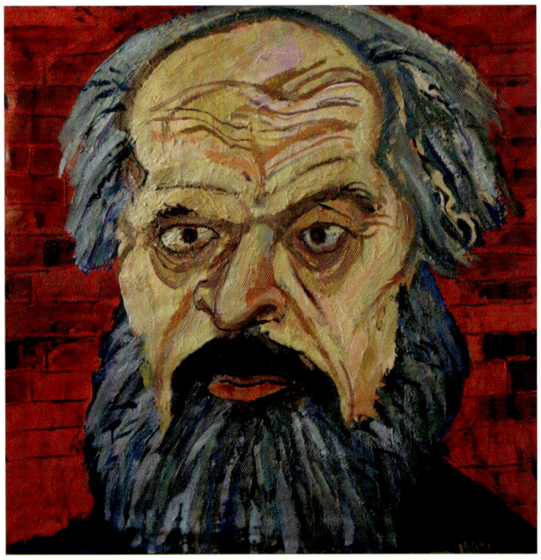

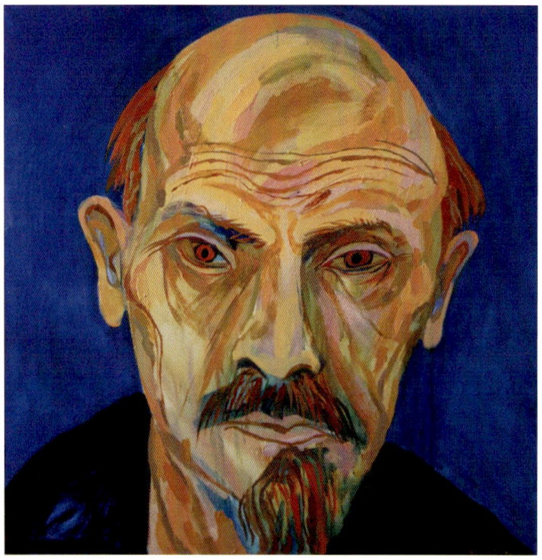

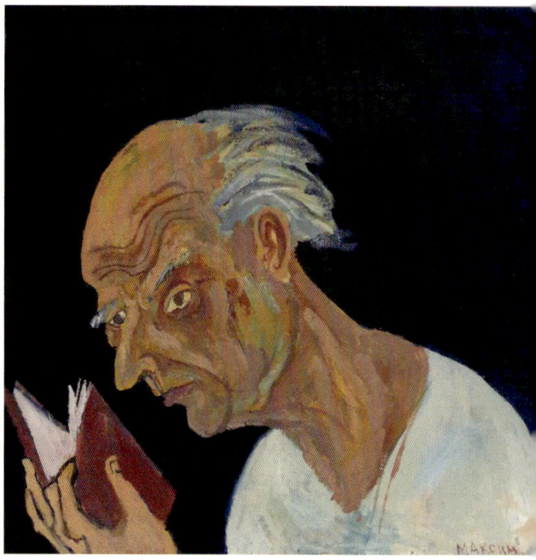

above
Karl Marx, 2010–11
Oil on canvas
110 x 110 cm
© Maxim Kantor
Galerie Nierendorf, Berlin

above
Vladimir Lenin, 2011
Oil on canvas
120 x 120 cm
© Maxim Kantor
Collection of the artist
Courtesy of the artist

above
Portrait of Father, 2010–11
Oil on canvas
100 x 100 cm
© Maxim Kantor
Collection of the artist
Courtesy of the artist

facing page
Morning Round, 1987
Oil on canvas
250 x 190 cm
© Maxim Kantor
Courtesy of Emden Kunsthalle

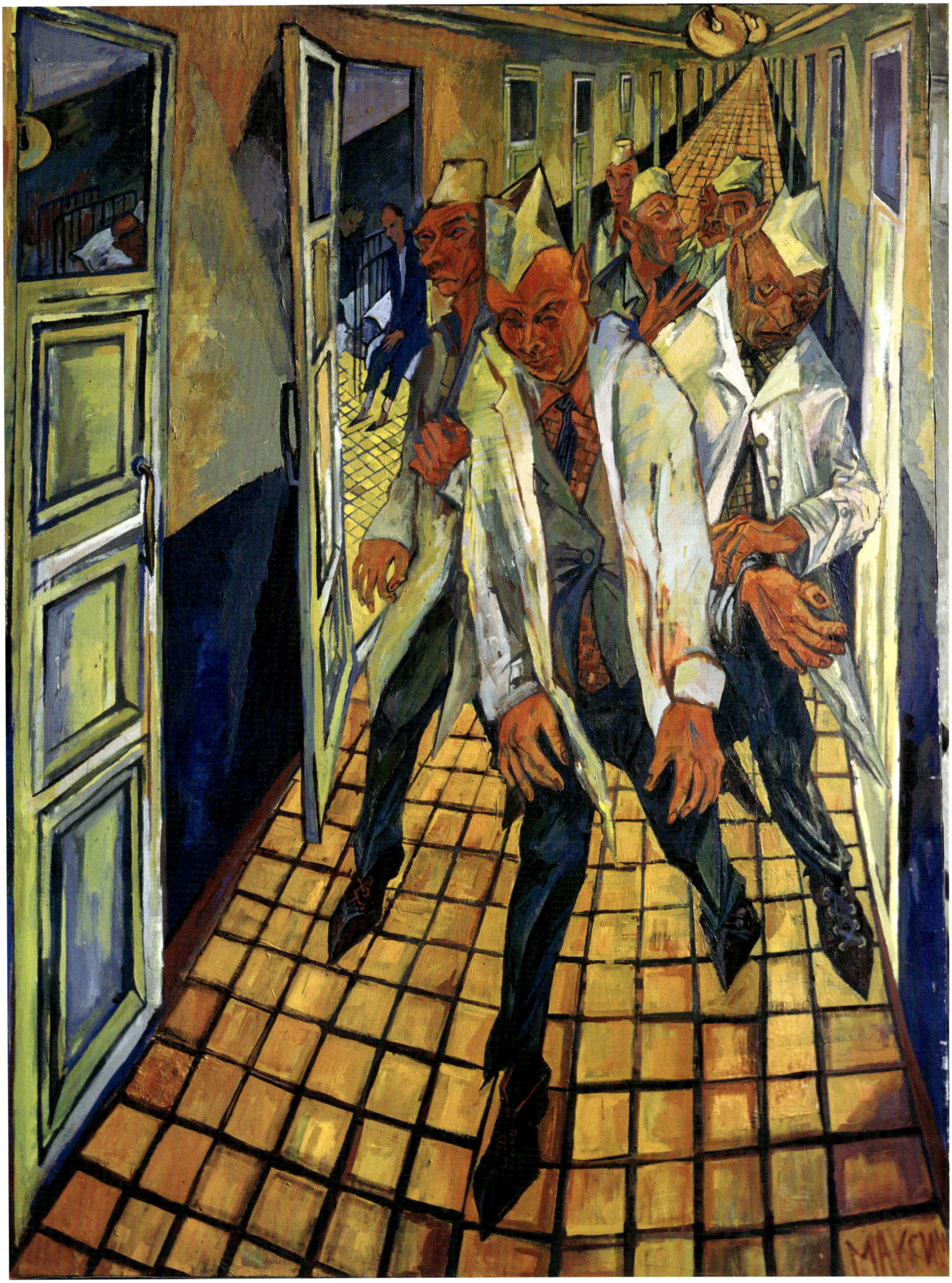

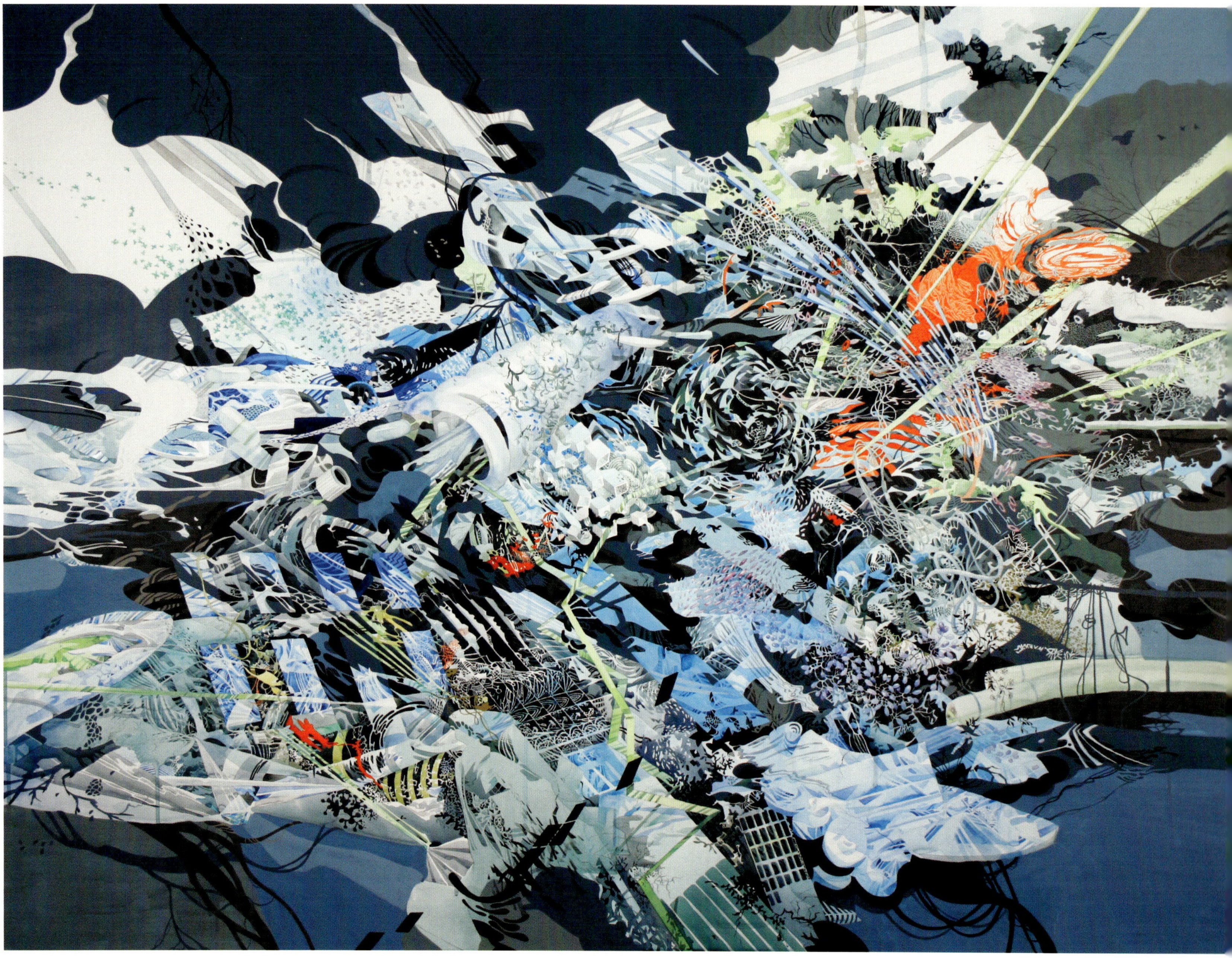

Darina Karpov

Darina Karpov's art, as if an echo of her life, is both aspiring and energetic. Born in St Petersburg, she graduated from that city's Institute of Technology before moving to the US, where she received a BFA from Maryland Institute College of Art and an MFA from Yale University. Karpov's artistic career was formed in America, where she was the beneficiary of several grants and residences, including a Pollock-Krasner Foundation grant, a Virginia Center for the Creative Arts residency and a MacDowell Colony residency.

Karpov has developed her own eclectic style. As early aesthetic influences she cites 'Renaissance paintings, miniatures from various cultures, Russian children's books ... animation from the 1970s ... contemporary architecture, experimental fiction, complexity theory and self-organisation theory'. A high degree of technical skill and a powerful command of colour are brought to bear on centralised compositions which unfold outwards to their edges. Branches and leaves can be discerned, but then abstraction takes over. There is a vague sense that further transformation will take place, as if her paintings might continue to breathe behind the grids, filigrees and templates that inform them. Perhaps this sensation is a result of Karpov's precision when it comes to rendering details, as well as her determination to create harmonious wholes. Her works are strong, airy and light, perhaps due in part to her skilful use of tiny brushstrokes. She describes her working method as 'a daily practice, a ritual, a meditation, a way of remembering. It keeps me sane'.

above
Water's Edge, 2007
Gouache and acrylic on panel
132 x 91 cm
© Darina Karpov
West Collection, Oaks

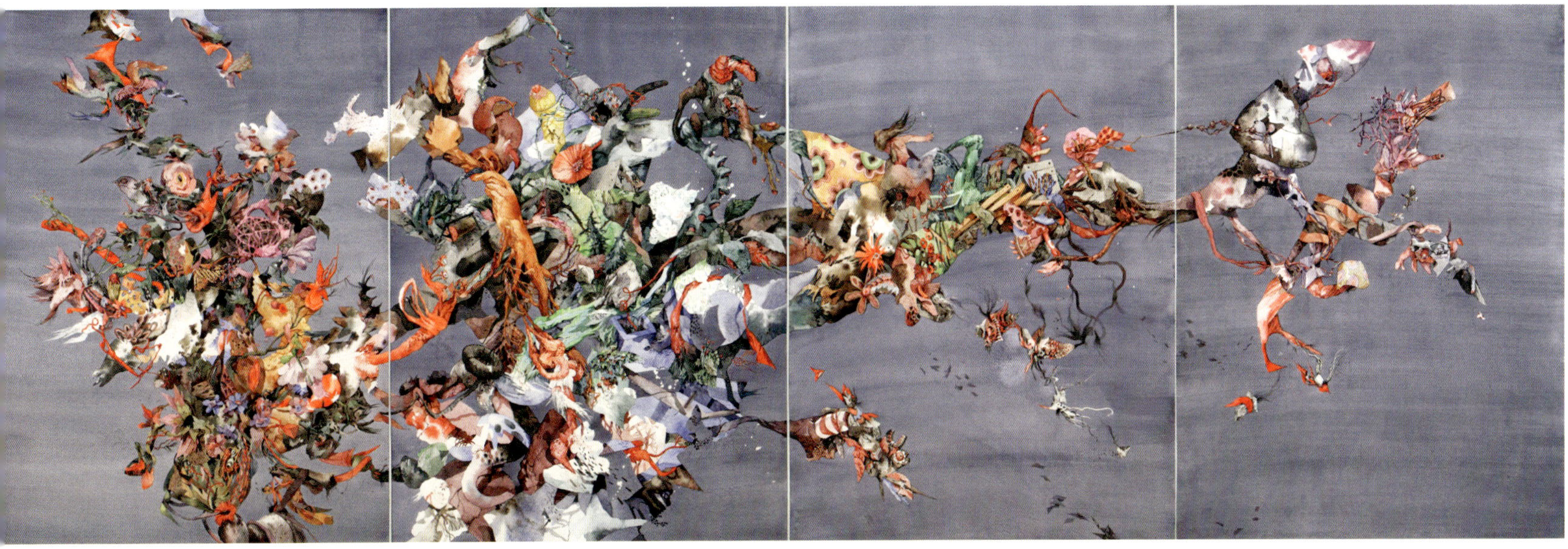

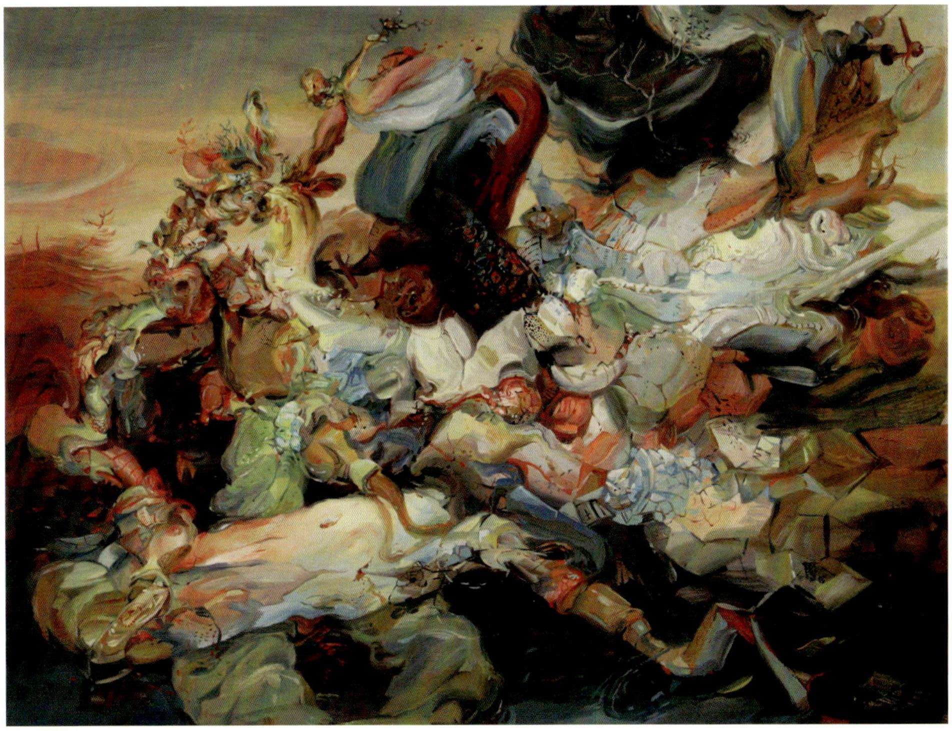

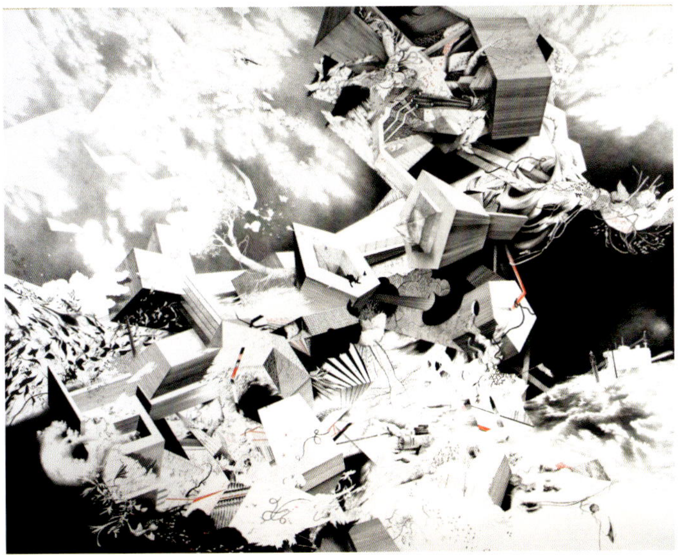

top
Wayward, 2010
Watercolor, gouache on paper
61 x 183 cm
© Darina Karpov
Collection of Patricia A. Bell

above
Dawn, 2010
Oil on canvas
22 x 25 cm
© Darina Karpov
Collection of Olok Banerjee and
Gillian Storey, London

left
Loophole, 2008
Graphite, ink on paper
131 x 104 cm
© Darina Karpov
Collection of Beth Rudin DeWoody

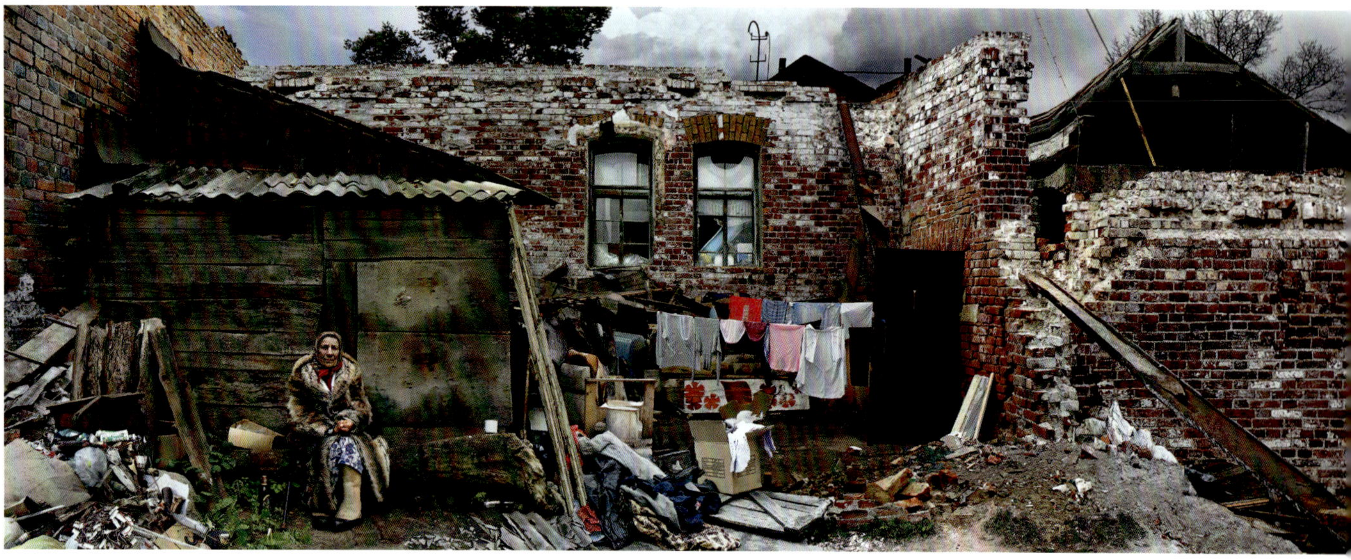

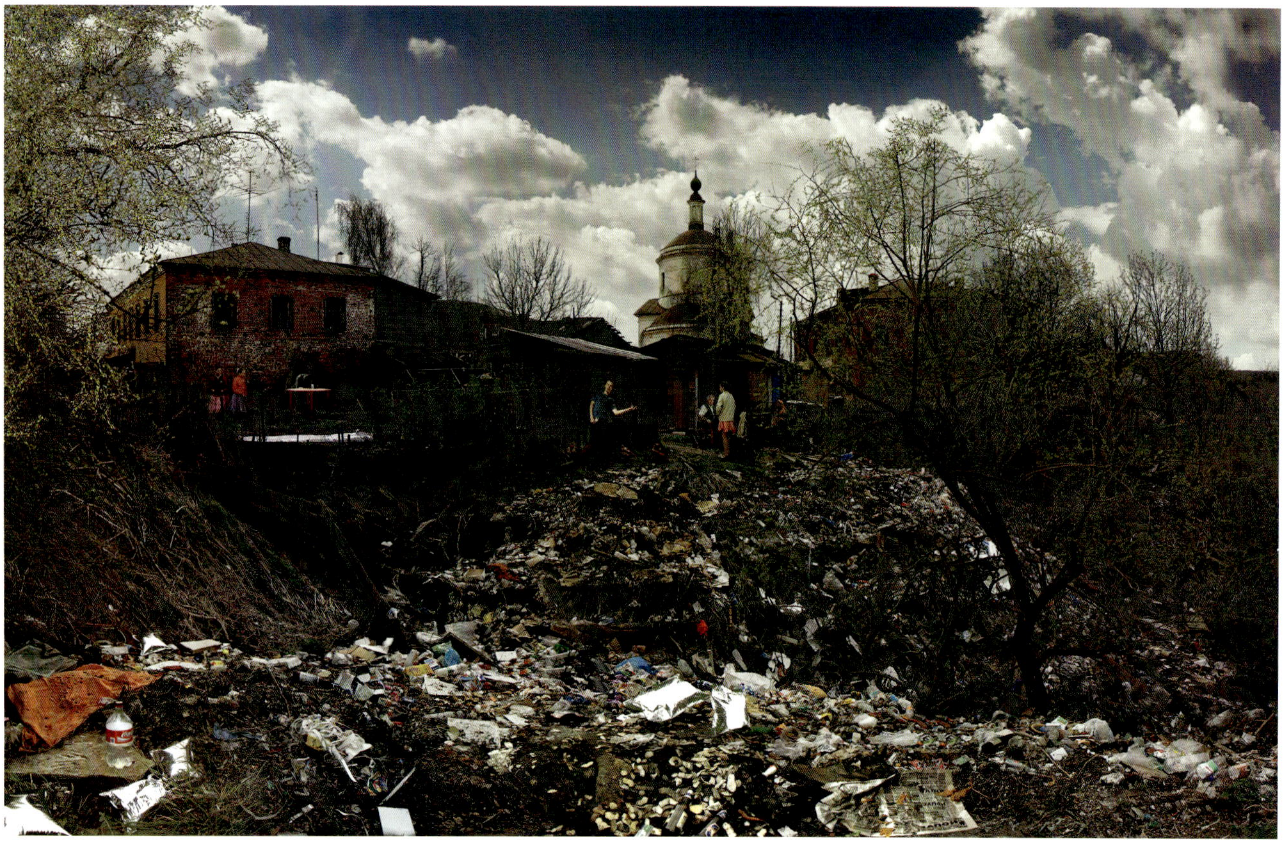

Konstantin Khudiakov

Konstantin Khudiakov was born in the village of Tsarevschina in Saratov Oblast in 1945. He studied to be an architect, graduating from the Moscow Institute of Architecture in 1971. During the 1980s he was closely associated with a group of underground artists on Moscow's Malaya Gruzinskaya Street. In 1988 Khudiakov co-founded one of Russia's first independent galleries, M'ARS, which in the years following perestroika organised group exhibitions to tour Russia and Europe.

Since the late 1990s, Khudiakov has worked increasingly with digital technology. He creates extensive series – for example, Deisis: The Coming (2001–4) and Hotel Russia (1997–) – in an attempt to reinvigorate Russia's Orthodox traditions and present sexuality as idealised, glossy and gilded. His work can be found in the State Tretyakov Gallery, Moscow; the Yaroslavl Art Museum; and many private collections across Europe, the US, Canada, Japan and Israel. He lives and works in Moscow.

top
Borovsky Courtyard. Anna, 2007–10
Ultrachrome on canvas
260 x 660 cm
© Konstantin Khudiakov
Courtesy of Victor Bondarenko

above
Borovsky Courtyard 2, 2005–10
Ultrachrome on canvas
260 x 330 cm
© Konstantin Khudiakov
Courtesy of Victor Bondarenko

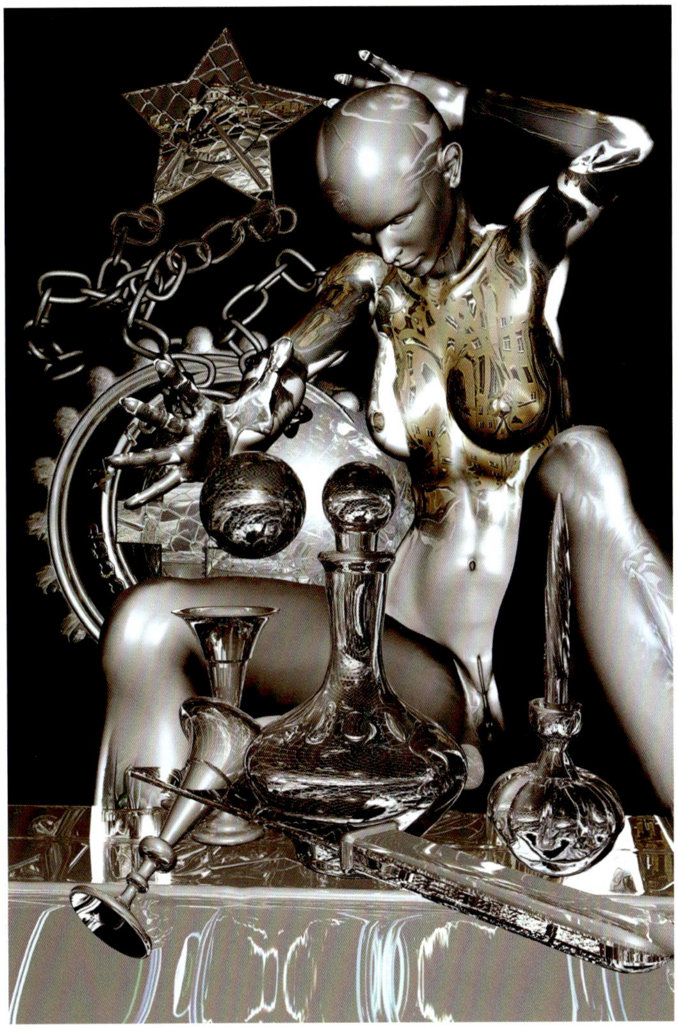

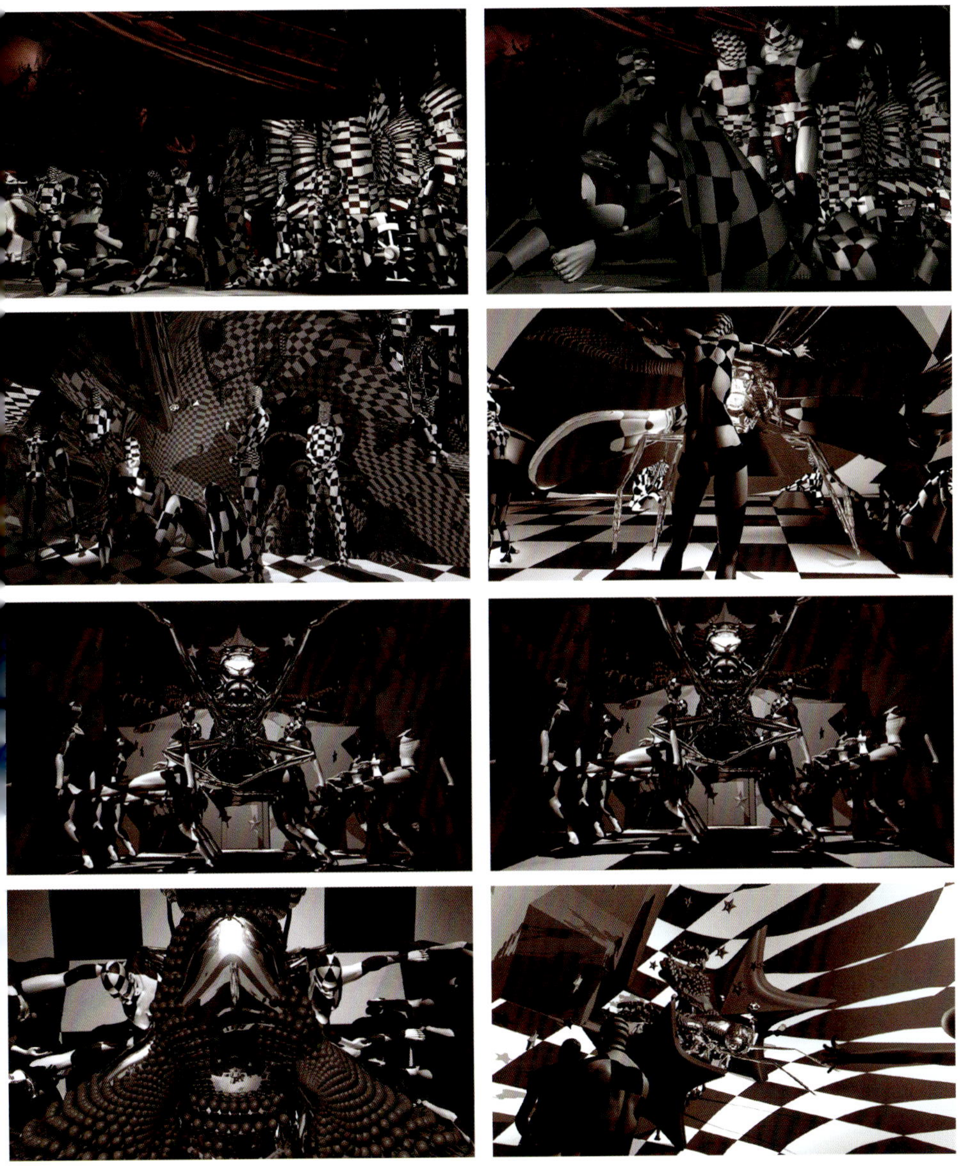

top
Magic Cream, 2006
Ultrachrome on canvas
160 x 110 cm
© Konstantin Khudiakov
Courtesy of Victor Bondarenko

left
Red Square, 2009
Multitouch-art
80 x 120 cm
© Konstantin Khudiakov
Courtesy of Victor Bondarenko

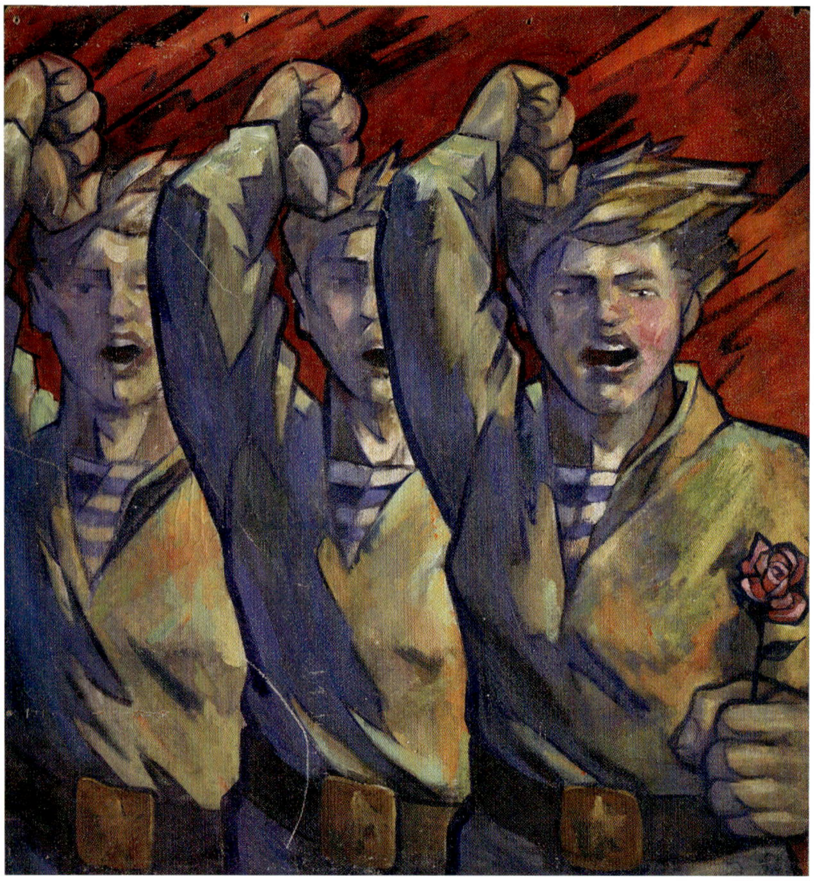

Vitaly Komar (born 1943 in Moscow) and Alexander Melamid (born 1945 in Moscow) are best known as the initiators of the Sots Art movement. Their creative collaboration, which resulted in paintings, installations and performances, endured for over thirty years, beginning in Soviet Russia and continuing after their emigration to the US in 1978. Komar and Melamid stopped working as a duo in 2002 but continue to enjoy prolific solo careers based, respectively, in New York and New Jersey.

The pair met while studying at the Stroganov Higher College of Art and started creating work together soon thereafter. They invented the term 'Sots Art' in 1972. Komar explains that 'Sots Art ... is "Sots" taken from "Socialist Realism" and "Art" taken from "Pop Art". Pop art was the result of the overproduction of consumerism and advertising. Sots Art was the result of the overproduction of ideology.' Appropriating visual and linguistic symbols of Soviet culture and politics, as well as the agitprop style of Soviet propaganda, the duo deconstructed layers of meaning as a challenge to the omnipresence of the State. Works such as *Double Self Portrait as Lenin and Stalin* (1972), destroyed during the 1974 'Bulldozer Exhibition', demonstrate the Sots Art aesthetic, an eclectic mix of Socialist Realism and American Pop in a conceptual framework with elements of the parodic, inflammatory spirit of Dadaism.

Komar and Melamid's history is closely intertwined with the New York gallerist Ronald Feldman, who organised two exhibitions of their work, smuggled out of the Soviet Union, in New York in 1976 and 1978. According to Komar, 'This is how we came to know Warhol and do a collective work – because he was [also] exhibiting at Feldman's gallery.' The *Souls* project (1978–9), a corporation for the buying and selling of human souls including Warhol's, humorously extended the concept of the American dream to its logical conclusion. If *Souls* explored the essence of American consumerism, earlier performance pieces like *Hamburgers Made out of Newspaper 'Pravda'* (1974) unmasked the false image of reality offered by the Soviet State.

The duo's best-known series since emigration was the painting project Nostalgic Socialist Realism (1981–3), which plays on the idea of 'Socialist Realism [as] a continuation of pre-Revolutionary Symbolism', and People's Choice (1994–7). The latter took the form of a survey in which the artists created the 'Most Wanted' and the 'Most Unwanted' paintings around the world; their 'polls' uncovered a surprising international consensus and predilection for landscapes and the colour blue.

top
Composition with Missiles, 1985–6
(detail from *Landscape Inspired by Rothko*)
Mixed media (1 of 3 panels)
152.4 x 366 cm

Courtesy of Sotheby's

above left
Military Parade/Demonstration, 1972
Oil on fibreboard
93 x 89 cm

Courtesy of Ekaterina and Vladimir Semenikhin Collection

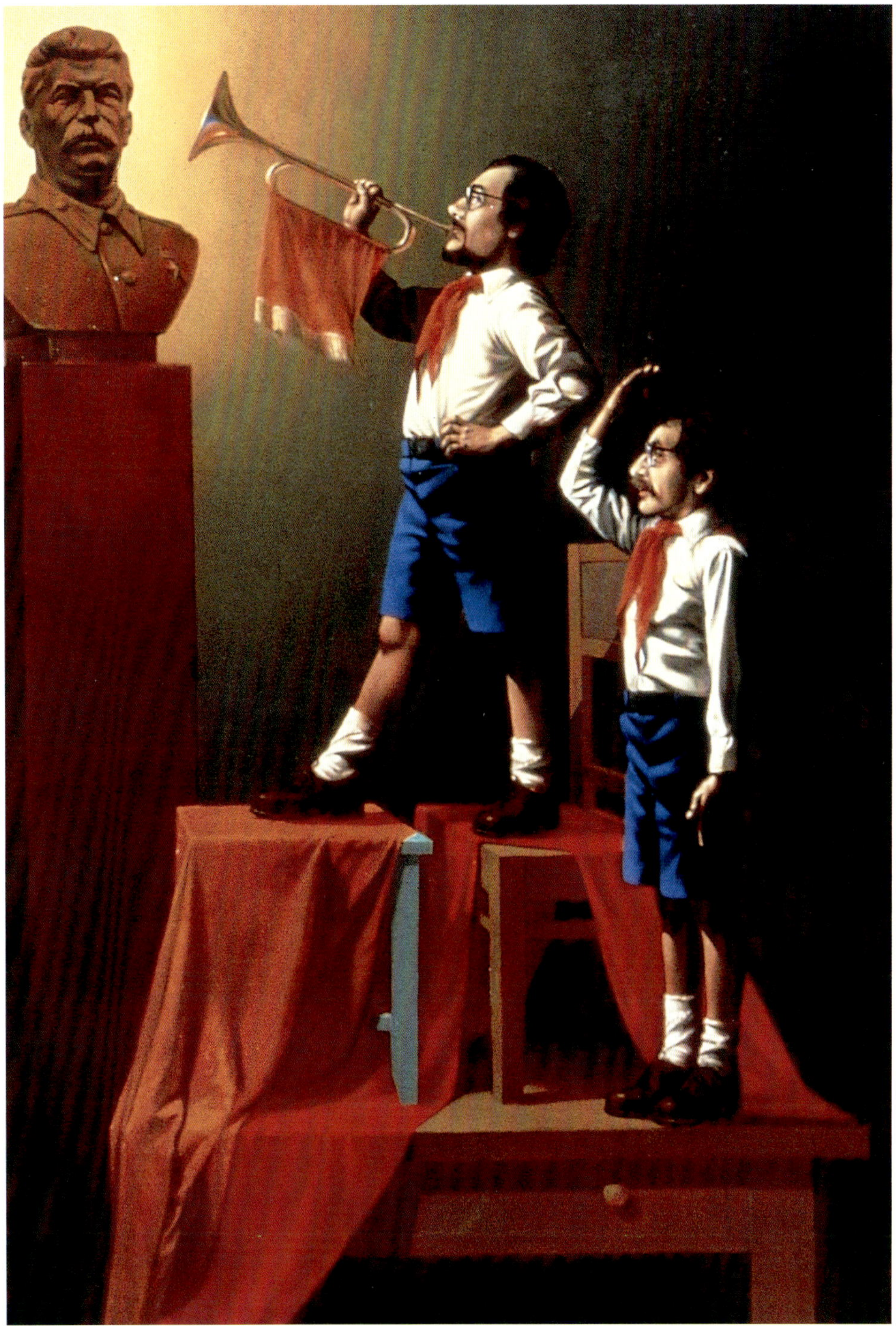

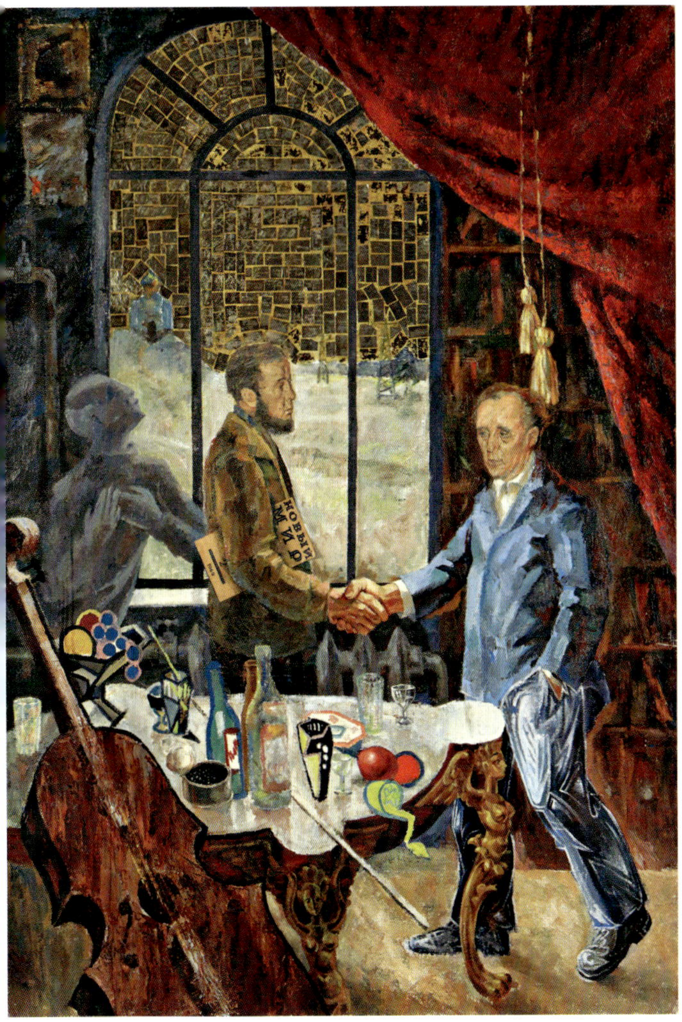

above
Double Self-Portrait as Young Pioneers, 1983
Oil on canvas
72 x 50 cm
© Komar and Melamid
Courtesy of Former Komar and Melamid
Art Studio Archive

left
The Meeting of Solzhenitsyn and Heinrich Böll
at Rostropovich's Dacha, 1972
Oil, gold foil, collage on canvas
175 x 120 cm
© Komar and Melamid
Courtesy of Shalva Breus

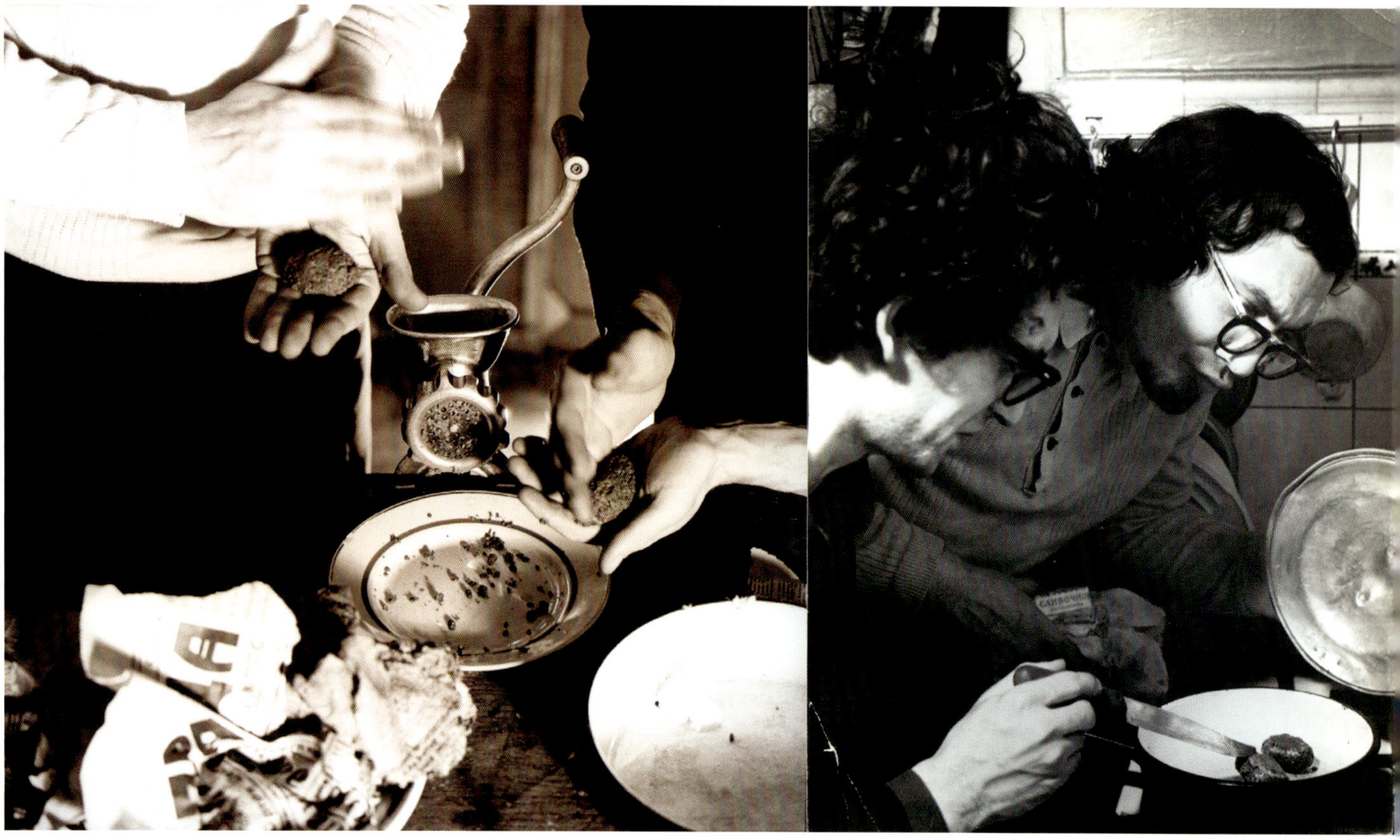

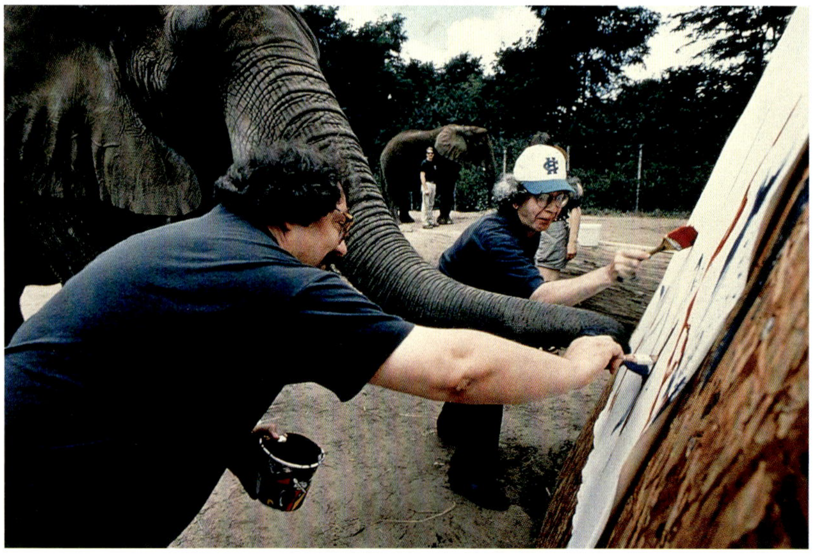

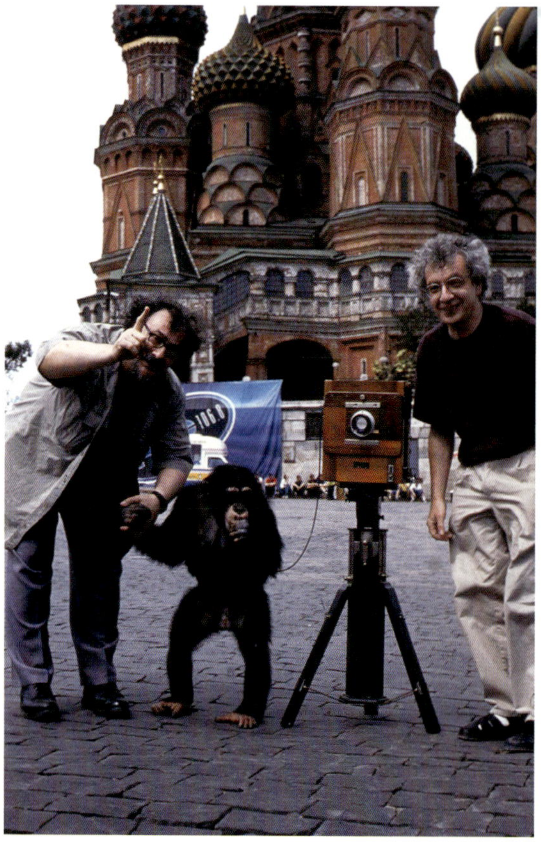

top
Hamburgers Made Out of Newspaper 'Pravda', 1974
Photo-documentation of the making of hamburgers out of *Pravda*
40 x 30 cm (diptych)
© Komar and Melamid
Photo: Valentin Serov
Courtesy of Former Komar and Melamid Art Studio Archive

above
Collaboration with Rene the Elephant, 1995
Toledo Zoo, Ohio, USA
© Komar and Melamid
Courtesy of Former Komar and Melamid Art Studio Archive

right
Collaboration with Chimp Mickey, Teaching Him Photography, 1998
Photo: Piotr Degterev
Courtesy of Former Komar and Melamid Art Studio Archive

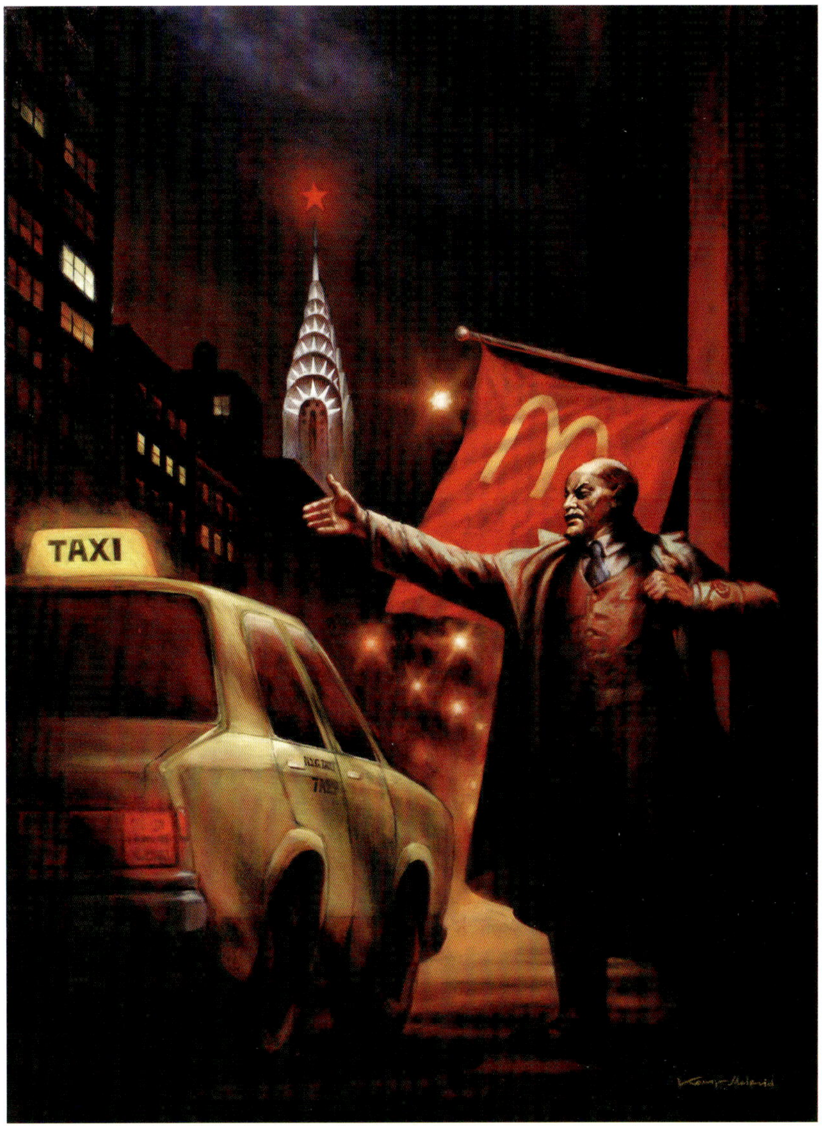

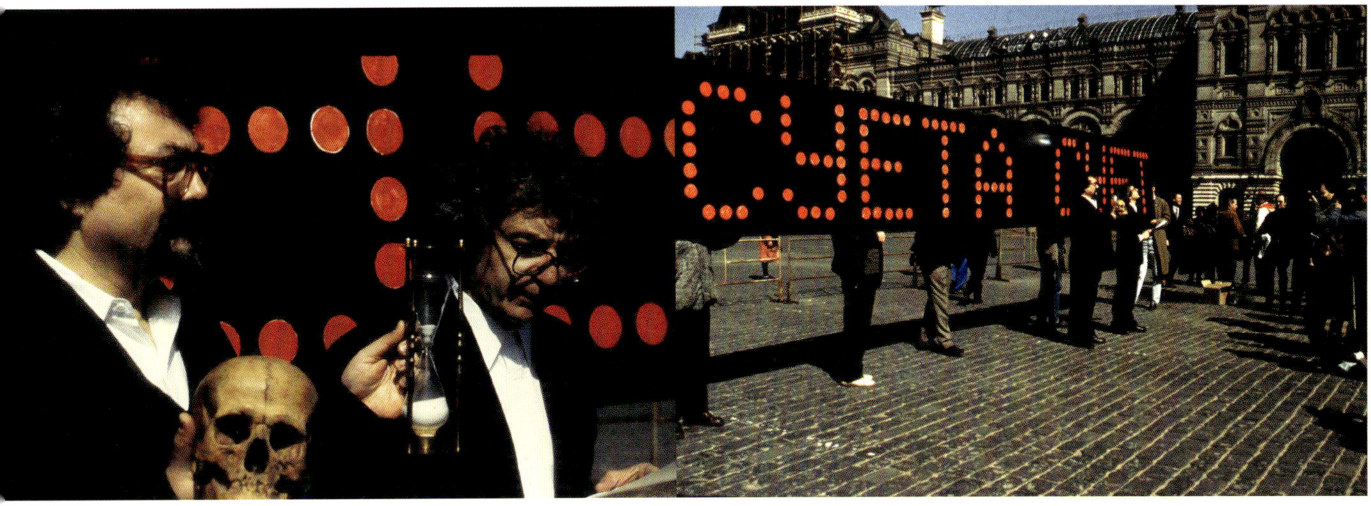

above
Lenin Hails a Cab, 1993
Oil on canvas
121.9 x 91.4 cm
© Komar and Melamid
Courtesy of Korban
Art Foundation

left
Performance in Red Square: Vanity of Vanitas from Electronic Board for Lenin's Tomb, from Monumental Propaganda Project, 1993
Photo: Piotr Degtiarev
Courtesy of Former Komar and Melamid Art Studio Archive

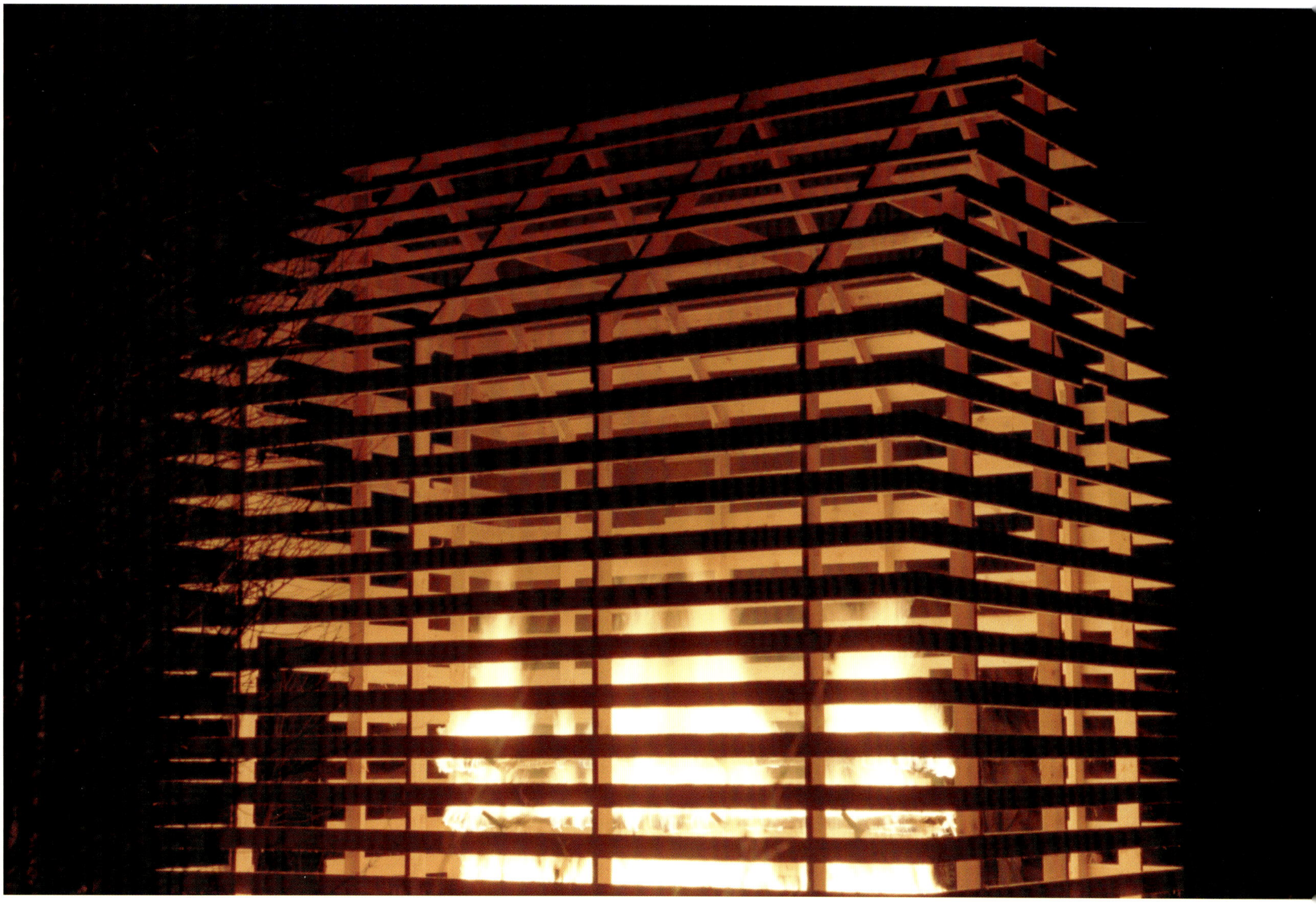

Alexander Konstantinov

Alexander Konstantinov, born in Moscow in 1953, divides his time between Moscow and New York. He creates site-specific large-scale outdoor works mainly in urban settings in Russia and Europe. Although his dream was to become an architect, in the 1970s he trained as a mathematician and became an associate professor of Mathematics at Moscow State Institute of Electronics and Mathematics. He took art classes in the evenings and continued to make art at home until perestroika, when he began to show in group exhibitions. His first solo show was at the State Tretyakov Gallery, Moscow, in 1992, and his first international exhibition, entitled *Liubov Popova 1924 – Alexander Konstantinov 1994*, took place at the Palais Liechtenstein.

Engaging with the urban environment in subtle narratives, Konstantinov's work pushes the boundaries between art and architecture. Technical draughtsmanship is central to his aesthetic. Using adhesive tape or strips of metal or wood, he clads buildings and street furniture to look as if it has been drawn. 'Being an artist,' he has said, 'I cannot build houses – no-one asks me to and no-one would let me – but I really want to do it, and so I draw them instead.' Konstantinov typically applies brightly coloured tape to cover sections of buildings or entire structures, creating the impression of cross-hatching. One source of inspiration is the dialectics of the Russian avant-garde; Constructivism underpins his choice of bold primary colours and geometric shapes. The monumental scale of his art, together with its temporary or transitory nature, strongly echoes Tatlin's famous tower project (planned but never realised). As with Constructivist art, an element of utopian longing lingers in Konstantinov's monumental constructions, which do not serve a practical purpose and are usually dismantled after a period of time.

Aluminium House (2010) and *Pediments* (2007) are site-specific commissions in a village near Moscow, where the artist covered a traditional wooden dacha in aluminium strips, thus turning an everyday rural, domestic sanctuary into a fortress. In his urban work consisting of temporary large-scale installations, such as *White District* (2005) – in which he covered part of the Pushkin Museum of Fine Arts, Moscow, in white tape – the artist playfully invites passers-by to become spectators. His aim is to 'remind an individual to think and feel' rather than passively absorb the subliminal messages of advertising that dominate contemporary urban space.

above
Izba, Basilica, Archstoyanie Festival, Kaluga Area, 2008
Wood
600 x 400 x 600 cm
© Alexander Konstantinov
Courtesy of Ravenscourt Galleries

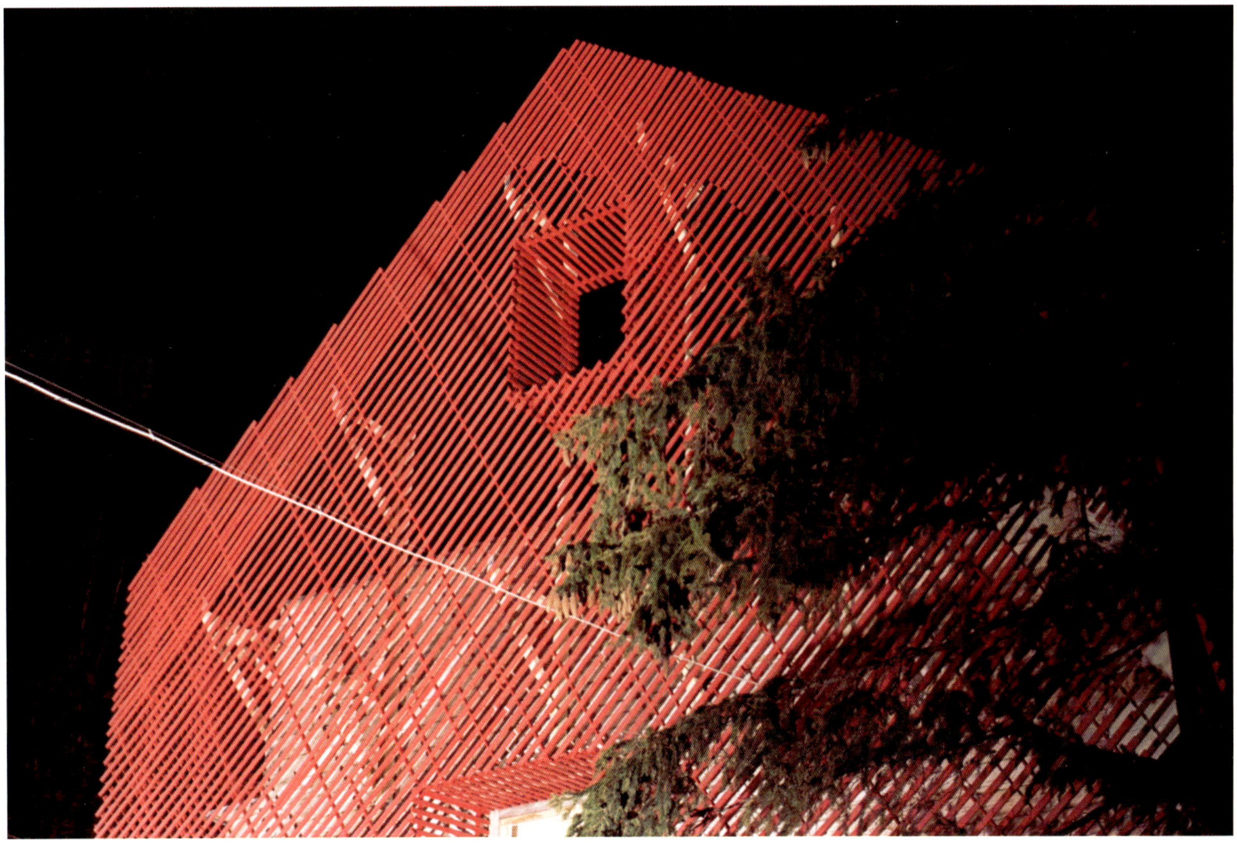

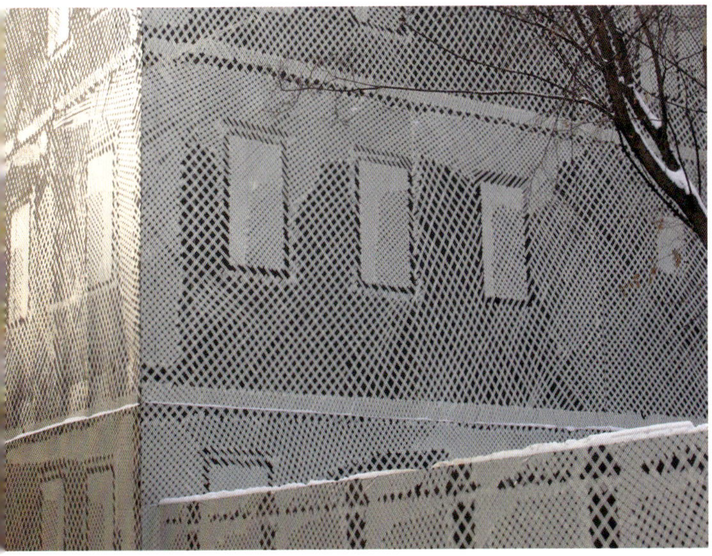

above
White District, 2005
White tape over black plastic
1,200 x 10,000 cm
© Alexander Konstantinov
Courtesy of Ravenscourt Galleries

top
Red House, Pediments, Moscow Area, Russia, 2007
Painted wood
450 x 145 x 900 cm
© Alexander Konstantinov
Collection of Maxim Bokser
Courtesy of Ravenscourt Galleries

right
Aluminum House, Moscow Area, Russia, 2010
Aluminium strips
1,100 x 1,200 x 850 cm
© Alexander Konstantinov
Collection of Maxim Bokser
Courtesy of Ravenscourt Galleries

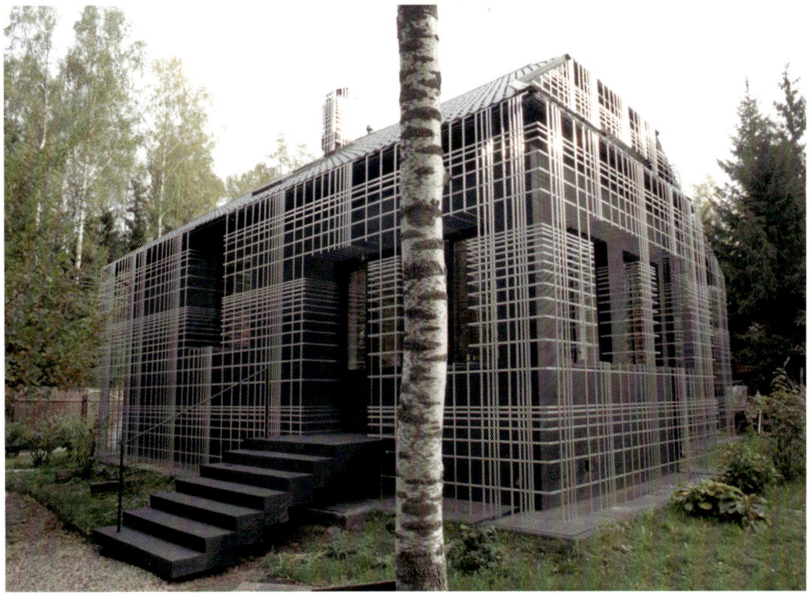

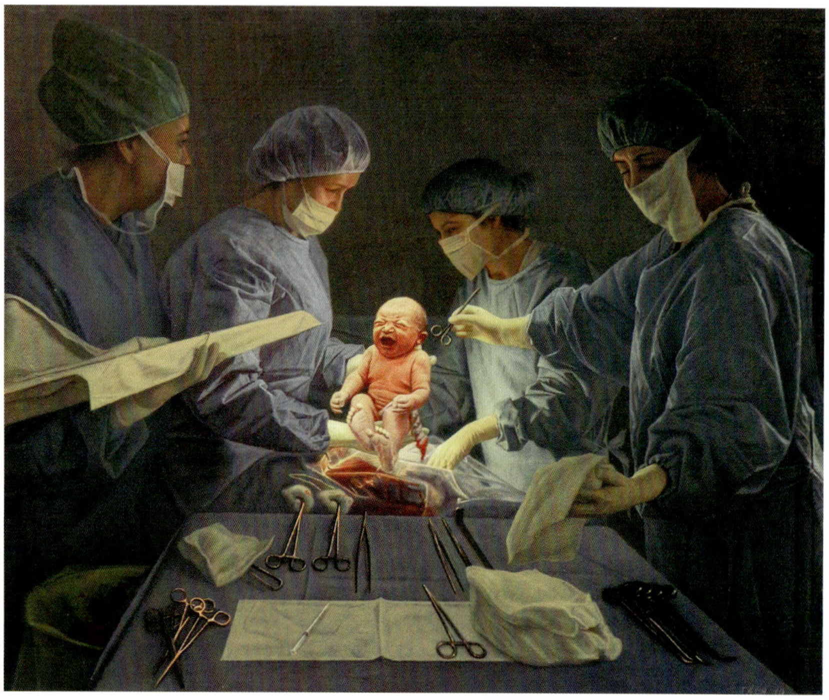

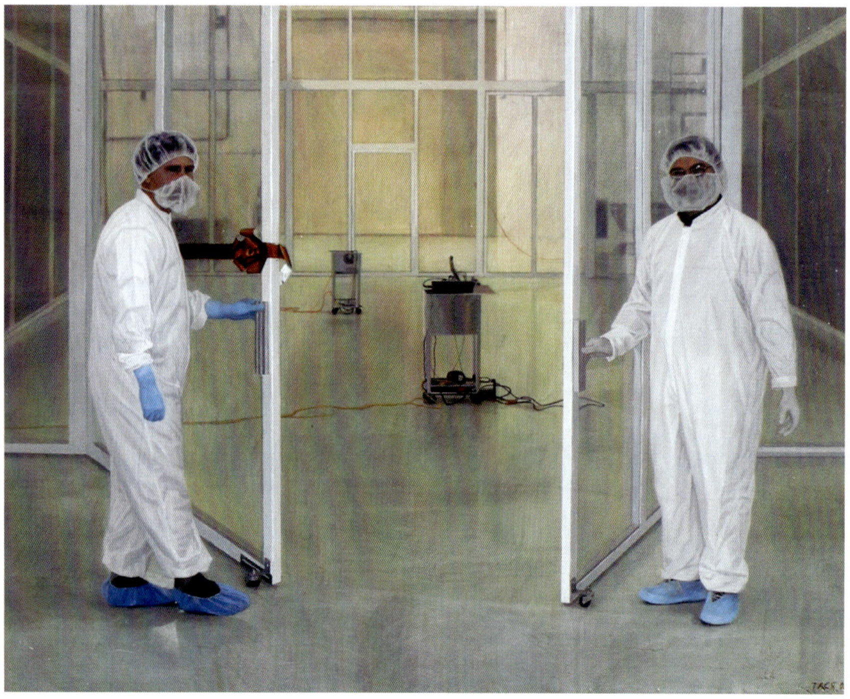

Taisia Korotkova

Born in 1980 into a family of artists, Taisia Korotkova lives and works in Moscow. After graduating from the Moscow Secondary Art School, she continued her studies at the Institute of Contemporary Art and the Surikov Institute. Korotkova was one of the joint recipients of the Young Artist. Project of the Year award, part of the Kandinsky Prize 2010, for her series Reproduction.

Working in a hyper-realist style influenced by Socialist Realism, Korotkova uses the medium of egg tempera, which she mastered through icon painting, to create compositions that mix scientific and technological content, thus producing images reminiscent of science fiction and dystopian novels. However, she is adamant that her visions have little to do with fantasy. In her series, whether she is casting her interrogative eye over spaceships – in Technology (2008) – or childbirth in a technologically advanced world – in Reproduction – Korotkova is inspired by 'vivid, real-life impressions'. Works like Reproduction, which depict IVF and neonatal intensive-care units, are, in her words, 'technological, I would even go so far as to say realistic, because there is very little in them that comes from the imagination'. However, her concerns are broadly humanist rather than feminist.

Blending meticulous research skills and preparatory work into her creative process, Korotkova lends a non-judgemental, distanced gaze to her productions. The motivation behind her art lies in investigating the interconnection between 'the role of humanity ... and the role of advanced technology'.

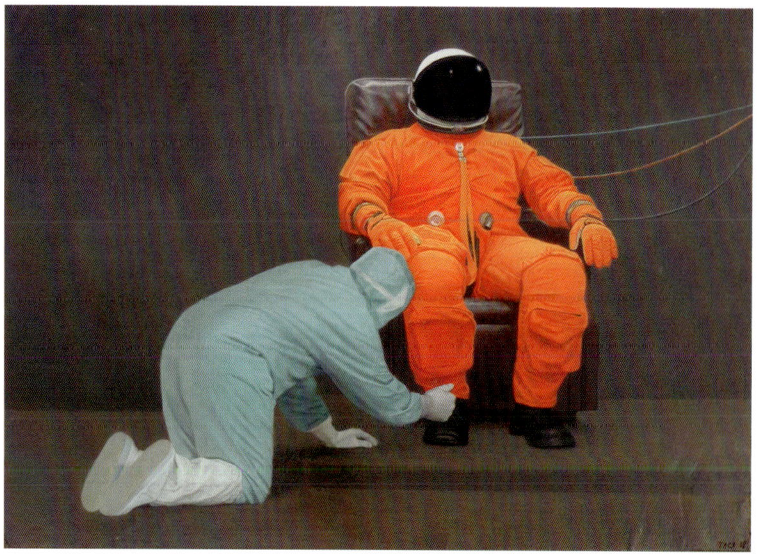

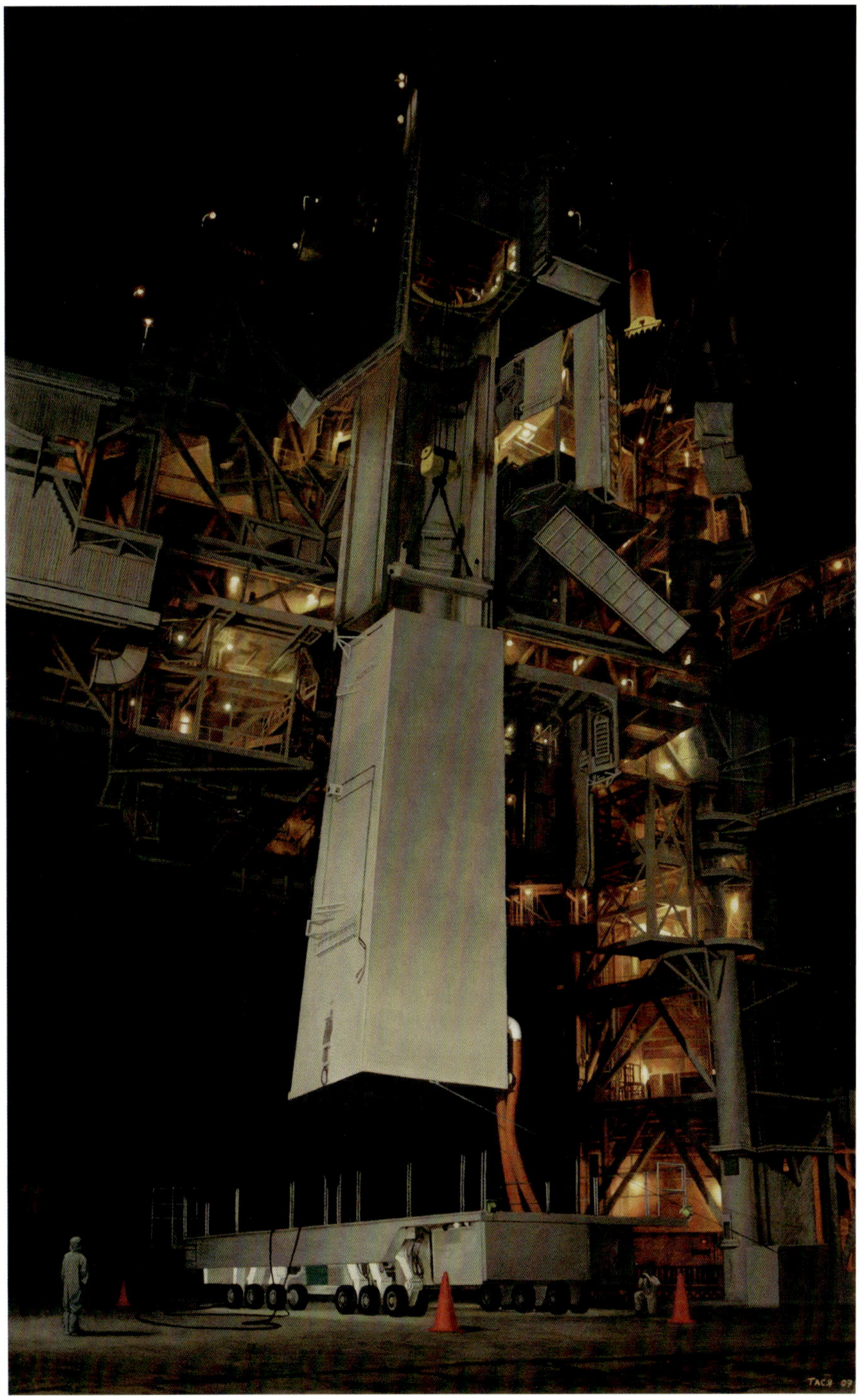

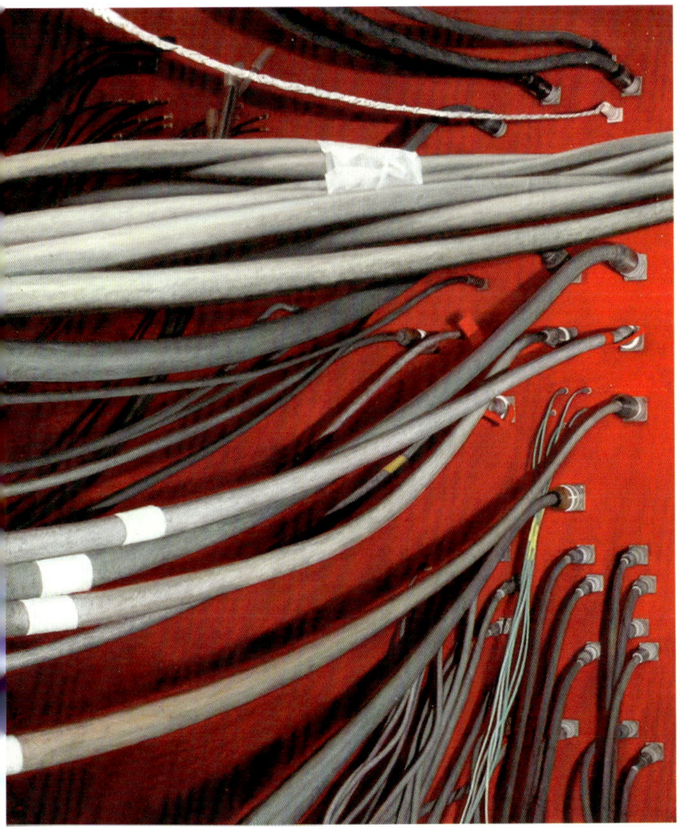

facing page top
Caesarean Section, from the series Reproduction, 2010
Tempera on panel
50 x 60 cm
© Taisia Korotkova
Courtesy of the artist

facing page middle
From the series Technology, 2008
Tempera on panel
50 x 69 cm
© Taisia Korotkova
Courtesy of Regina Gallery

facing page bottom
From the series Technology, 2008
Tempera on panel
50 x 72 cm
© Taisia Korotkova
Courtesy of Regina Gallery

above
From the series Technology, 2007
Tempera on wood
80 x 51 cm
© Taisia Korotkova
Courtesy of the artist

left
From the series Technology, 2008
Tempera on panel
50 x 42 cm
© Taisia Korotkova
Courtesy of Regina Gallery

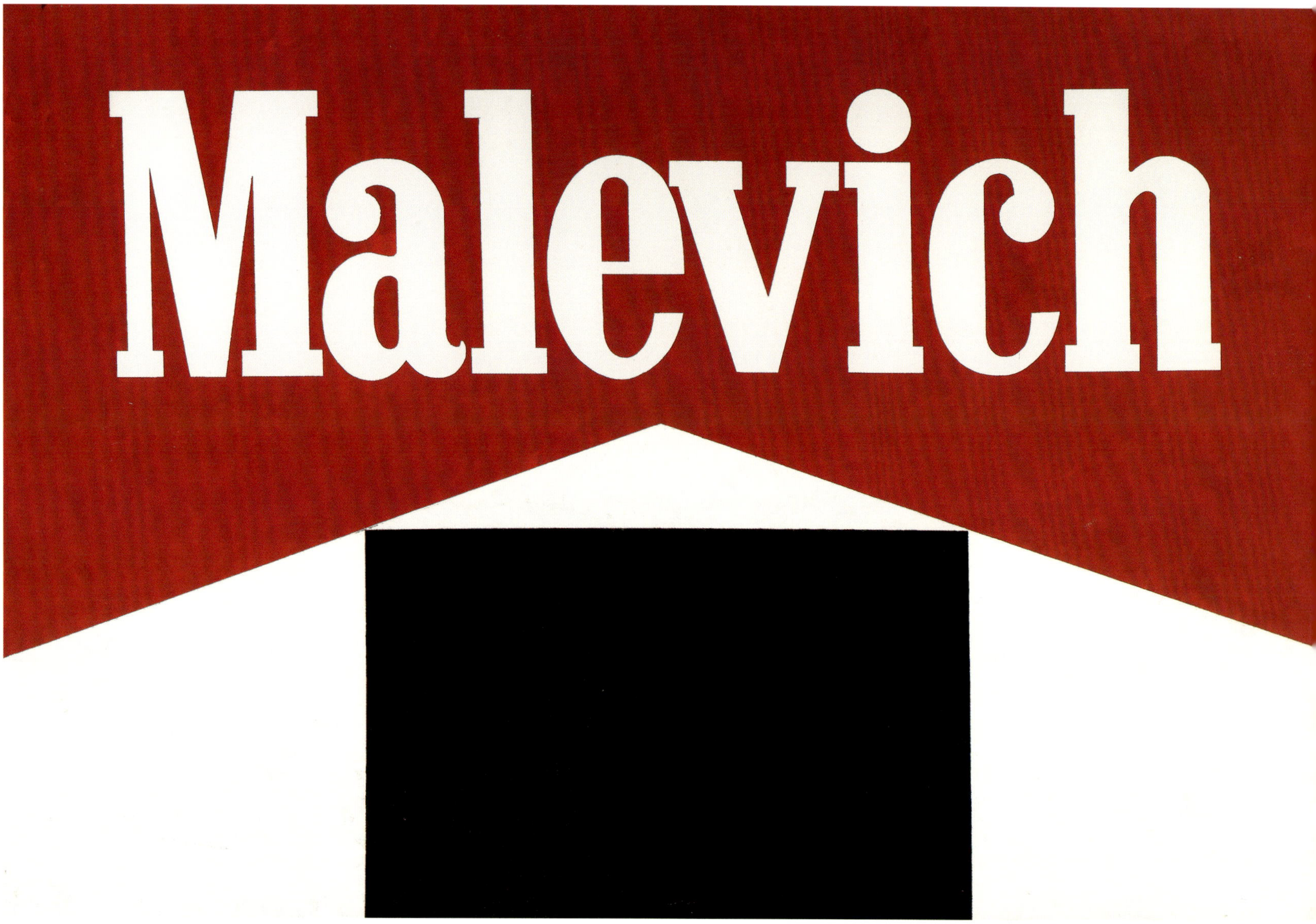

Alexander Kosolapov

Painter and sculptor Alexander Kosolapov was born in Moscow in 1943. After a long period of residence in the US, beginning in 1975, he now divides his time between New York and Moscow. Having studied at the Surikov Institute, Moscow, Kosolapov graduated from the Stroganov Higher College of Art, Moscow, in 1968. He has exhibited widely in group exhibitions throughout America and Europe and in Moscow, including *Berlin–Moscow/Moscow–Berlin 1950–2000* (2004–5); *Sots Art* (La Maison Rouge, Paris, 2007); and *Glasnost* (Haunch of Venison, London, and Galerie Volker Diehl, Berlin, 2010). His works are held in numerous public collections, including the Museum of Modern Art, New York, and the State Tretyakov Gallery, Moscow.

At the beginning of the 1970s, while still in Russia, Kosolapov worked as an official sculptor as a member of the Soviet Union of Artists but then became associated with Komar and Melamid's Sots Art movement. After moving to the US, he began to explore witty, stark juxtapositions of images from Soviet officialdom, Western consumerism and American Pop art. His first image of this kind, which he reworked several times, was of Lenin and the Coca-Cola logo on a red background and was shown at the Kazimir Passion Group's performances at the Kitchen in New York. Kosolapov has exploited numerous variations, both painted and in print, of Soviet caviar pots as a play on Warhol's Campbell's soup cans, as well as combinations of the McDonald's logo with Soviet imagery and sculptures of Mickey Mouse and Lenin. Icons of Russian avant-garde art are often combined in clever visual puns with everyday objects, as in the ironic painted series Marlboro-Malevich, where the word *Malevich* is applied to the Suprematist-inspired 1950s design of a Marlboro cigarette packet as though the former were an advertising brand.

above
Malevich – Black Square, 1987
Oil on canvas
119.5 x 173 cm
© Alexander Kosolapov
Courtesy of Tsukanov Art Collection

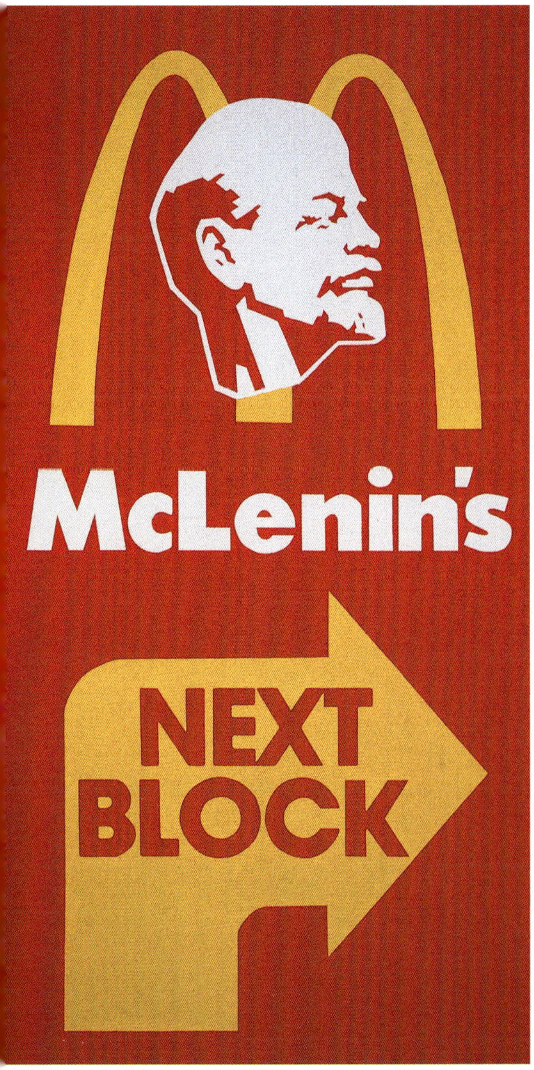

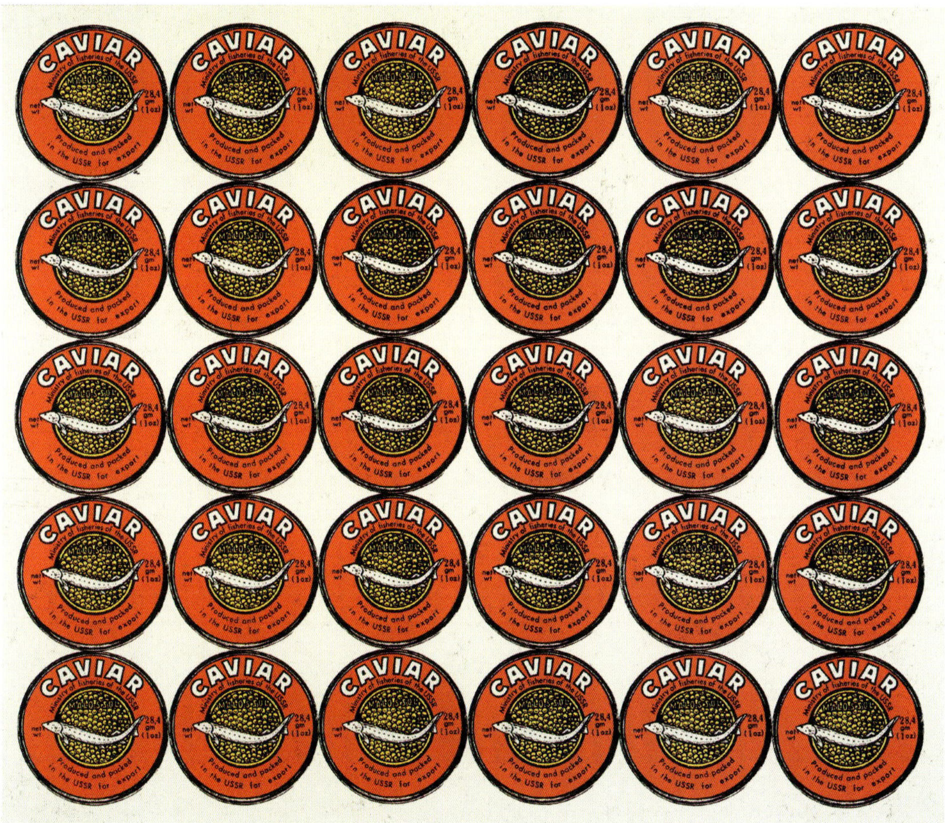

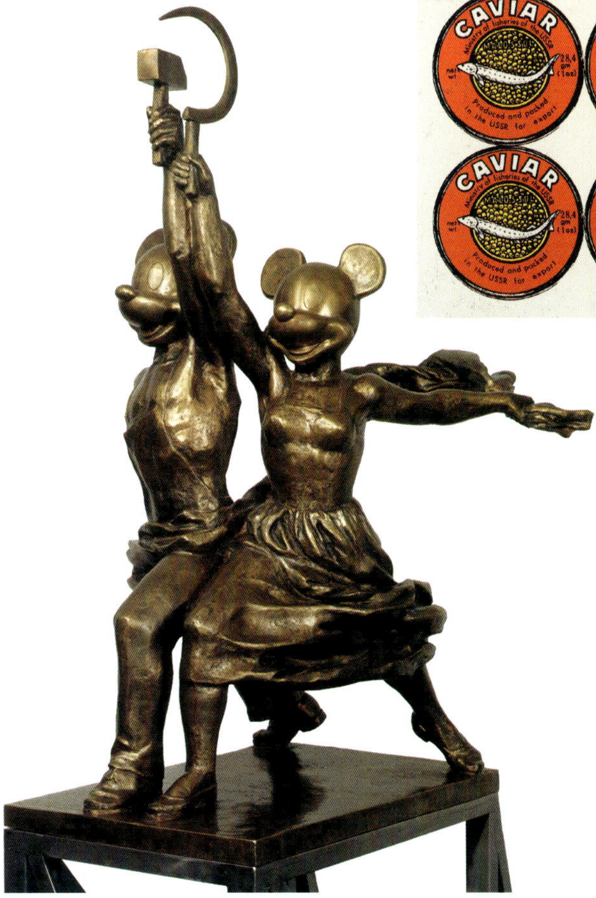

top
McLenin's, 1990
Acrylic on canvas
178 x 91 cm
© Alexander Kosolapov
Private collection

right
Mickey and Minnie, 2006
Bronze
58.6 x 56.4 x 50.8 cm
© Alexander Kosolapov
Courtesy of the artist
Private collection

above
Red Caviar, 1990
Acrylic and silkscreen on canvas
132 x 157 cm
© Alexander Kosolapov
Private collection

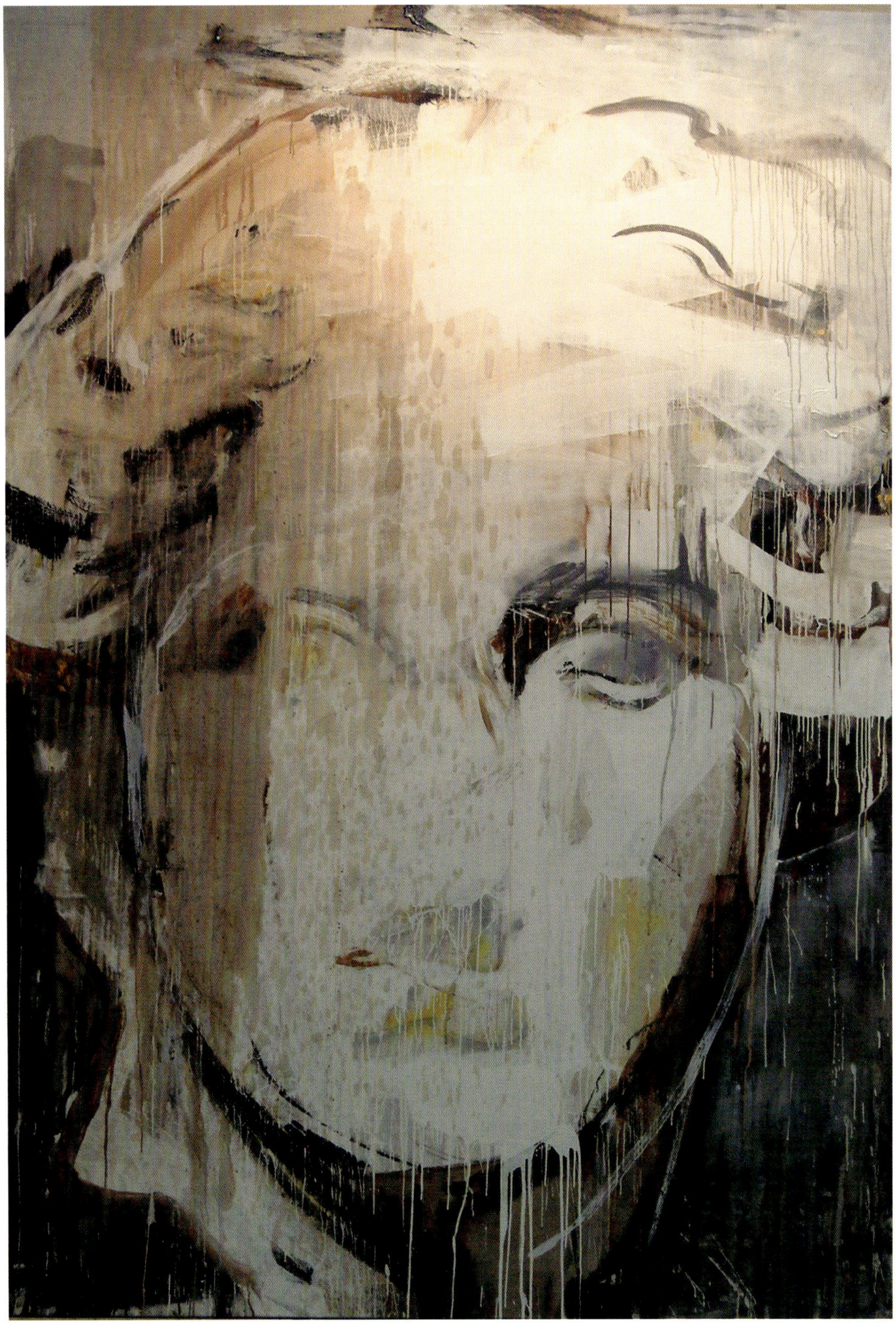

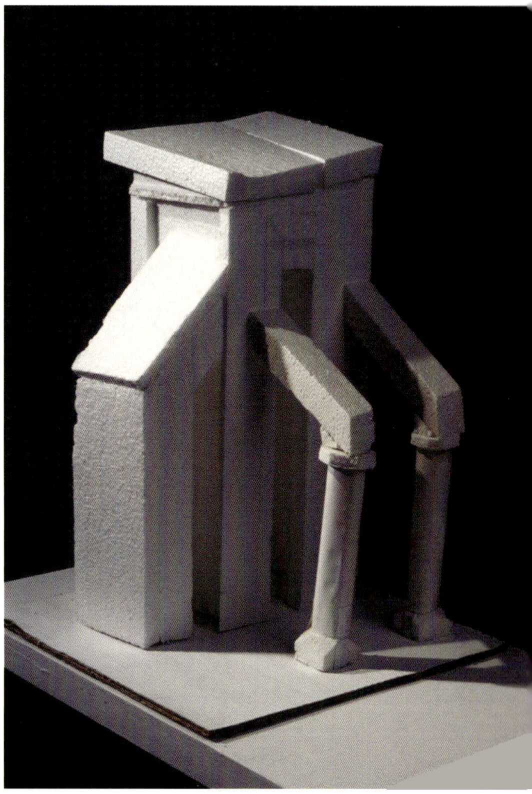

Currently splitting his time between Paris and Moscow, Valery Koshlyakov was born in 1962 in Salsk in the Rostov-on-Don region of southern Russia. Having graduated from the Grekov School of Art in 1985, he was employed for a time as a theatre decorator, an occupation that left an indelible mark on his style, as can be seen in his grandiose, sweeping brushstrokes. In 1987 he became a member of Art or Death. Koshlyakov belongs to the group dubbed the 'south Russian wave' by the influential collector and curator Marat Guelman. Swamping Moscow in the late 1980s and early '90s, these artists ignored the capital's traditions and taste, challenging the mainstream with their distinctive version of ideal beauty.

Gluing together pieces of corrugated cardboard, Koshlyakov then paints ancient Greek and Roman temples and theatres, Renaissance palaces and churches, and monumental Soviet architecture on them in an energetic monochromatic style. Architectural icons treated in this way include *Coliseum* (1995) and *Brunelleschi's Dome* (1997). An idiosyncratic juxtaposition of classical order and symmetry with the cheapness, anonymity and ephemeral nature of recycled materials, these works explain the artist's association with another movement formulated by Guelman, Russian Povera.

In the last decade, Koshlyakov has also created monumental architectural installations and sculptural objects from recycled materials such as cardboard, packing tape, polystyrene and plastic bags. And he has started to 'paint' on walls and on cardboard with Scotch tape, recreating iconic buildings and artworks such as Ingres' *Odalisque* (2003) and the *Mona Lisa* (2003). Of his predilection for packing tape, Koshlyakov says, 'The speed of its adhesion, its brilliance, the poverty and purity of its colour make it an extremely lively and contemporary material.' Of his work as a whole, he has stated, 'I am not searching for innovation. I break with the cult of authorship. I dislike signing my works. I have not invented them ... I am not dealing with Contemporary Art as a cult of self-expression. I am searching for the clash, for the meeting with culture, with tradition.' His works unpack the baggage of collective and individual memory locked away in cultural icons dotted throughout history; he unlocks and releases these icons back into the social consciousness with a powerful new energy.

above left
Aphrodite, from Empire of Culture project, 200[illegible]
Bitumen and acrylic on canvas
350 x 200 cm
© Valery Koshlyakov
Collection of the artist

above
Iconus, 1999
Polystyrene
40 x 25 x 25 cm
© Valery Koshlyakov
Collection State Tretyakov Gallery, Moscow
Courtesy of the artist

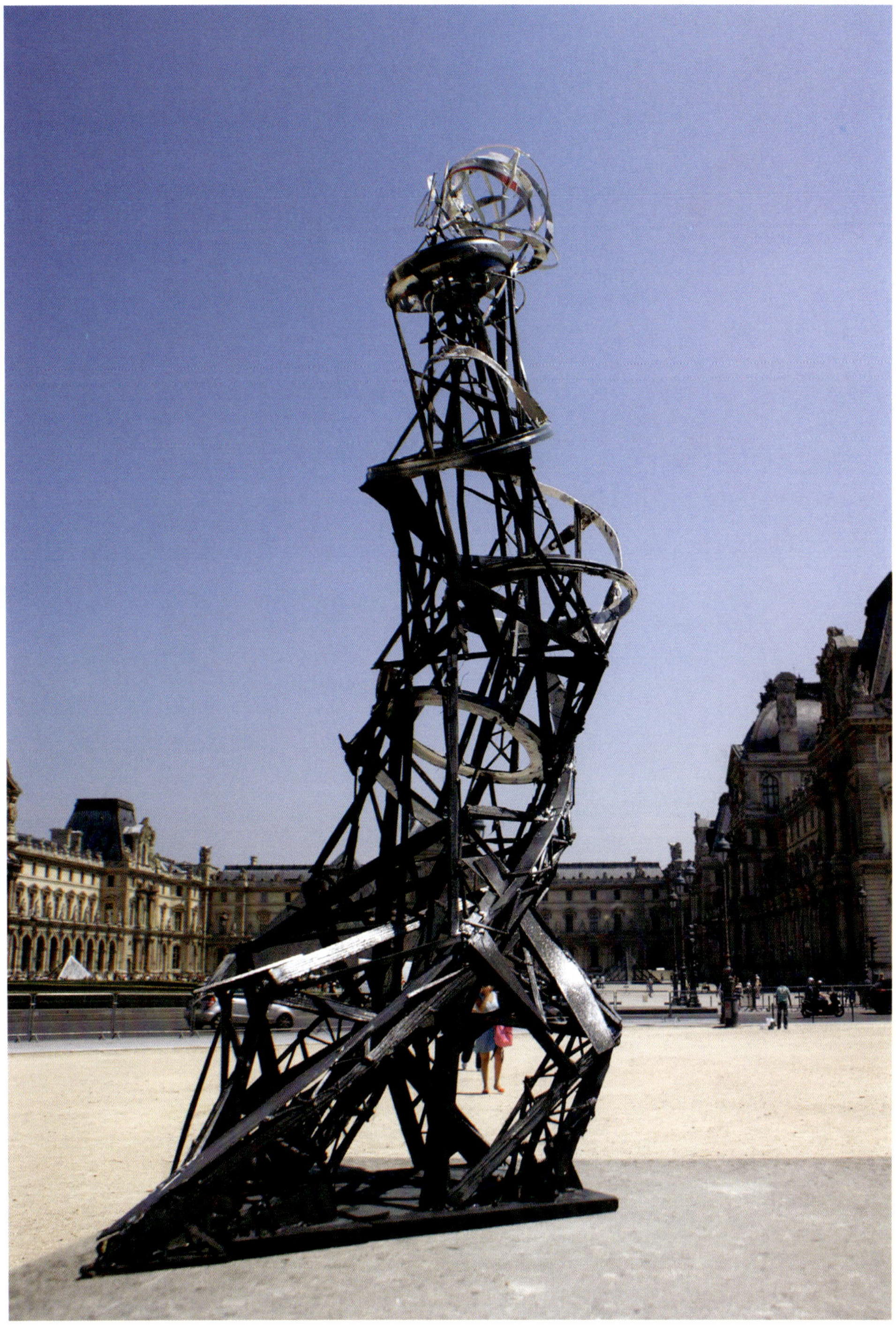

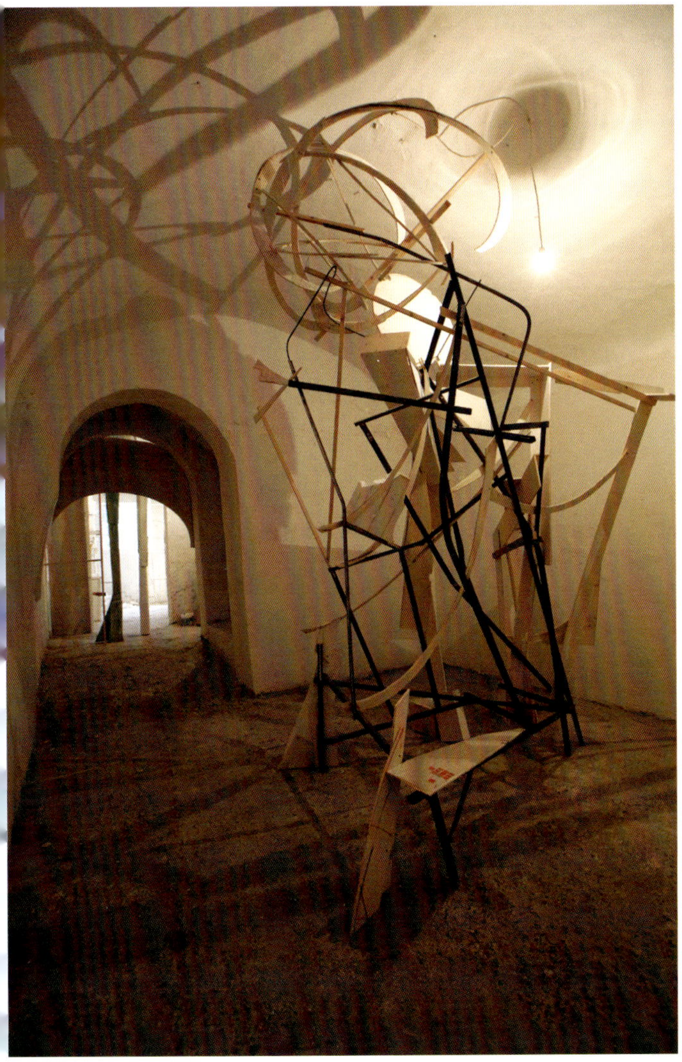

above
Construction Monument, 2010
Project for the Louvre, Paris
© Valery Koshlyakov
Courtesy of the artist

left
Tower, 2009
Installation view, Fondazione Volume, Rome
© Valery Koshlyakov
Courtesy of the artist

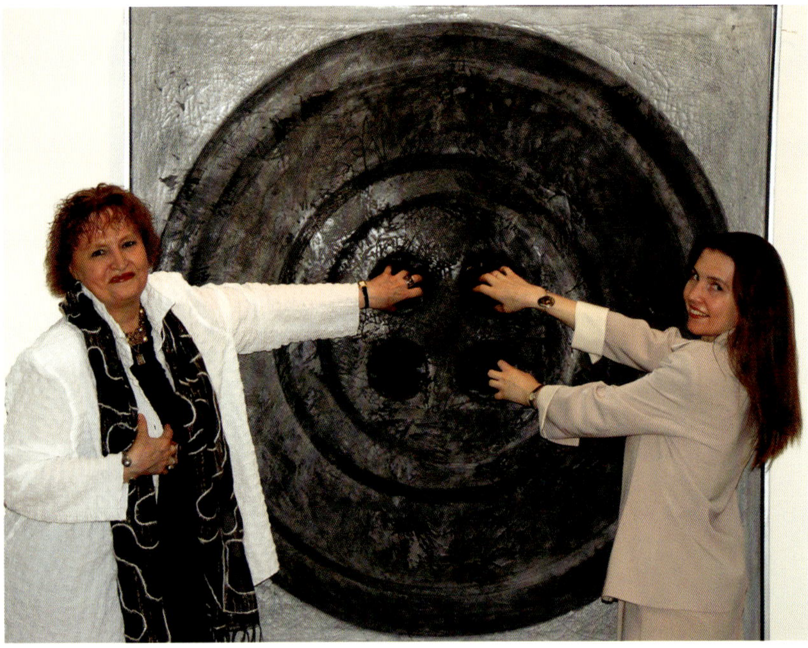

Tatiana Kolodzei started amassing her art collection in the 1960s, at the height of the Cold War and therefore at one of the most arduous moments for Soviet nonconformist art. Thanks to a close friendship with George Costakis, who quickly became her mentor, Kolodzei had the opportunity to see his unique collection, which included works by Liubov Popova and Ivan Kliun, and to formulate her own artistic taste. Kolodzei's daughter Natalia relates that her mother 'was only seventeen [when] she met George Costakis ... saw his collection and "caught the collecting bug" for life.' Having nourished a love of art in her daughter from a young age – 'On my first birthday, the artist Petr Belenok gave me my first work of art, which became the seed of my own collection' – the mother-and-daughter team have continued to introduce new works into their collection ever since.

The Kolodzei Collection now boasts 7,000 works representing over 300 artists and is one of the world's largest collections of Soviet unofficial and Russian contemporary art. With representative works by such artists as Eric Bulatov, Ilya Kabakov, Komar and Melamid, and Oleg Vassiliev, among many others, the collection reads like a forty-year history of underground activity, whose survival is wholly connected to the energy and entrepreneurism of collectors like the Kolodzeis. It is Natalia's view that '[d]ogma and politics certainly influence art; under Stalin, for instance, there was no potential to produce anything other than official Socialist Realism, under the severest of penalties. However from the late 1950's in Russia "unofficial" art was somewhat tolerated. Not allowed, but tolerated. This meant that those who didn't want to produce works glorifying the Soviet State would not be persecuted, but they would have difficulty gaining access to materials ... and to venues to publicise their works.' Nevertheless, Tatiana Kolodzei worked hard at organising exhibitions in the Soviet Union throughout the 1970s and during the cultural clampdown and censorship of the arts under Brezhnev. In 1991, with the help of American friends, she founded the Kolodzei Art Foundation, a not-for-profit public foundation based in New Jersey. The foundation's purpose, says Natalia, is 'to promote the art of Russia and the former Soviet Union to the public through art exhibitions in museums, universities and cultural centres throughout the United States, Russia and Europe, and publish books on Russian art'.

Today, mother and daughter organise exhibitions within the framework of the foundation, one example being *From Non-Conformism to Feminism: Russian Women Artists from the Kolodzei Art Foundation* at the Chelsea Art Museum, New York (2008). They also lend actively to exhibitions of Russian art around the world. Their support of unofficial art is based on a desire not only to educate the Western public but to reacquaint Russian audiences with their neglected national heritage. 'In Russia,' they observe, 'there was no open art collecting and there was little to no scholarship ... Once the Russians were again able to join the world art market after perestroika, they started to collect art in a "checklist" fashion, feeling the need to fill their walls mostly with traditional Russian art. Now, the Russian collectors are re-discovering, or even discovering, their own great artists, and likewise American collectors are also discovering the greatness of Russian art.'

Spanning over forty years of Soviet art, the Kolodzei Collection is richly democratic in its representation of localities and styles. As such, it creates an ongoing, open-ended history of Russia. Speaking about the purpose of art, Natalia explains that 'on a macro, societal level, the artist creates art at a historical moment; the art not only reflects that historical moment, it is a reflection of that reality. Through the presentation and then perception by others within the community, the artist is able to reflect and project into the society an awareness of the moment ... For instance, one can learn much about *kommunalka*, living in a communal apartment, by looking at some of the works of Ilya Kabakov. The language he employs is what people would say in a communal apartment, where living together and sharing facilities was imposed, while still maintaining distance.' Like art, the Kolodzei Collection is a living entity that continues to grow, develop and reflect the ongoing changes in society and contemporary art alike.

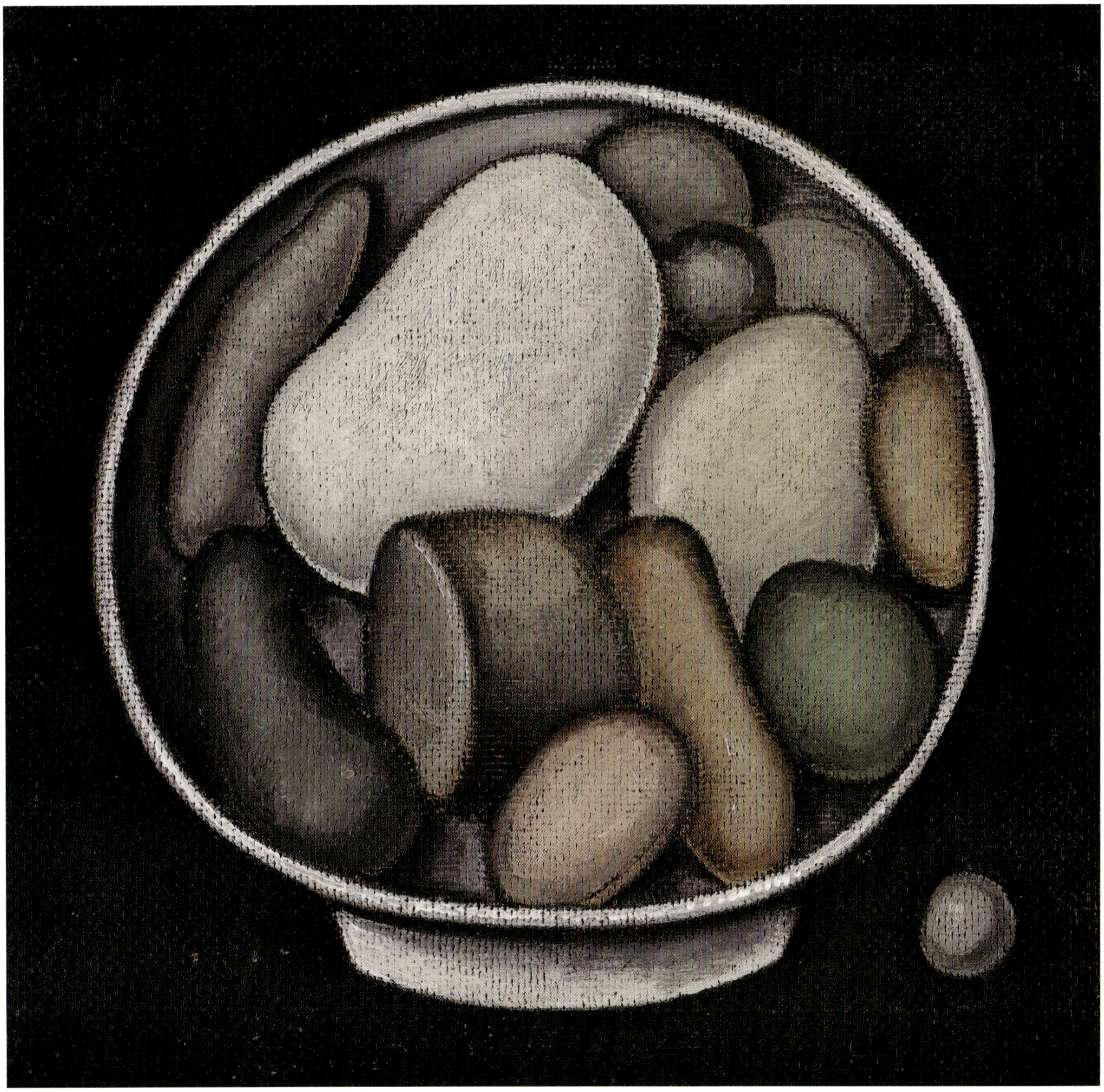

above
Still Life with Bowl and Pebbles, 1968
Oil on board
23.9 x 24.4 cm
Courtesy of Sotheby's

Born in Moscow, Dmitry Krasnopevtsev (1925–1995) is known for his still-life paintings in which he consistently worked through the theme of time, thus creating a separate universe of art. Although modest in scale and using a subdued palette of grey, brown, beige and black, Krasnopevtsev's paintings invariably convey a sense of monumentality. He used the same objects in multiple configurations: broken bottles, rolled-up scrolls, shells, stones, twigs, ceramics. Shown against neutral backgrounds, these compositions are both a-temporal and ahistorical. As Krasnopevtsev put it, 'The objects with which I compose my still lifes have shed all geographical or temporal characteristics. I don't paint from nature, but sometimes I turn to nature for information.' He also observed that 'a painting is an island – an independent country – that lives according to its own laws and under its own flag.'

Krasnopevtsev graduated from the Surikov Art Institute in 1955 and supported himself financially as a graphic artist, painting cinema advertisements. However, his work was already being collected by George Costakis in the late 1950s. Thanks to this connection, Krasnopevtsev was one of the first Russian modernists to find recognition abroad. In 1967 the Museum of Modern Art, New York, acquired some of his paintings. Permeated with silence, they make a clear distinction between life and art. *Still Life with Bottles and Twigs* (1968) and *Still Life with Bottles* (1984) are characteristic of his approach. Through the stability, order and harmony of the compositions and tonalities, they demonstrate the timelessness of art and the immortalisation of the past. About still life, Krasnopevtsev observed, 'It's the genre that allows the artist the greatest freedom if he aspires to express something spiritual.'

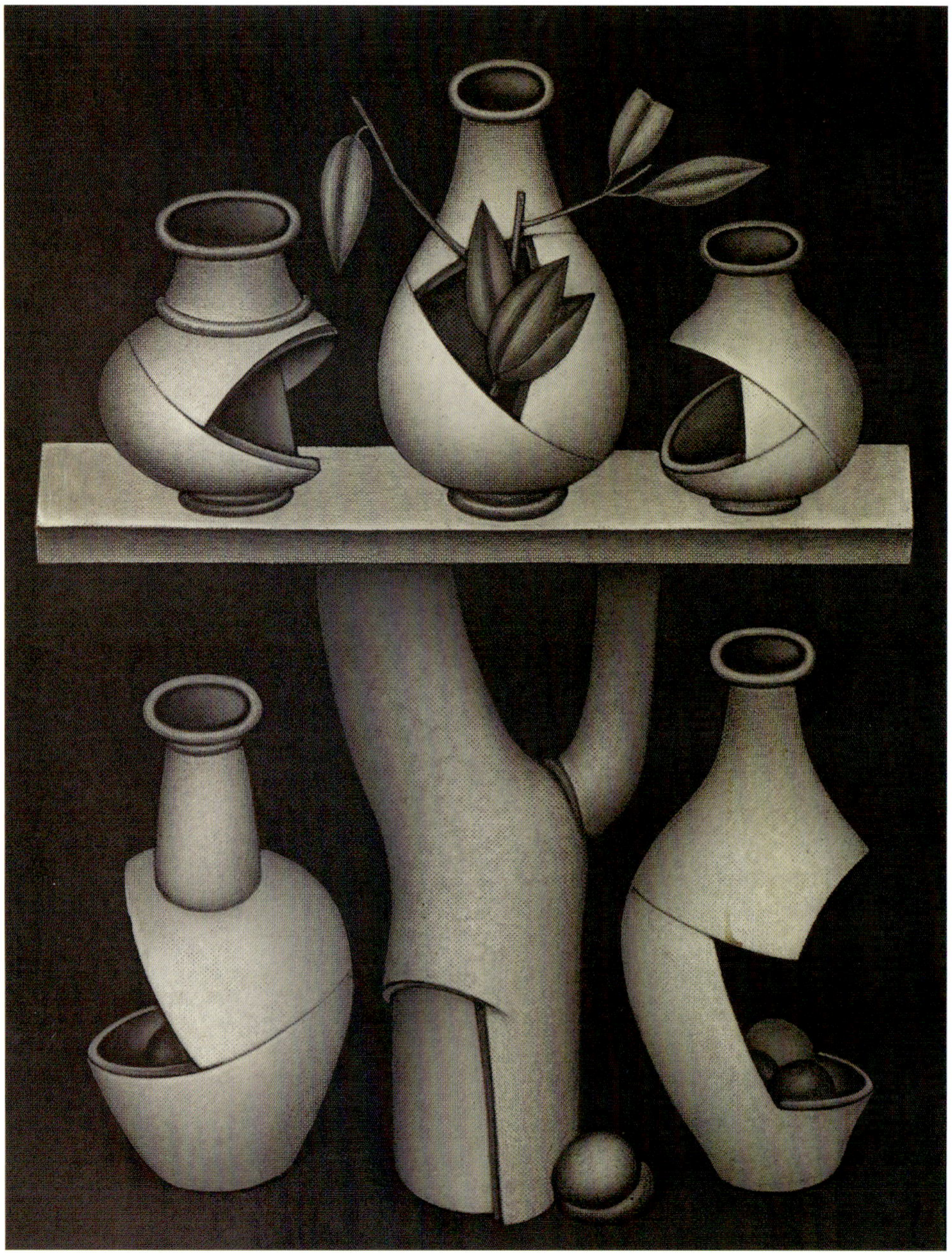

above
Five Broken Jugs, 1972
Oil on fibreglass
75 x 60 cm
Courtesy of The State Pushkin Museum
of Fine Arts, Moscow

right
Two Pink Pitchers, 1970
Oil on fibreglass
58.8 x 47.3 cm
Courtesy of The State Pushkin Museum
of Fine Arts, Moscow

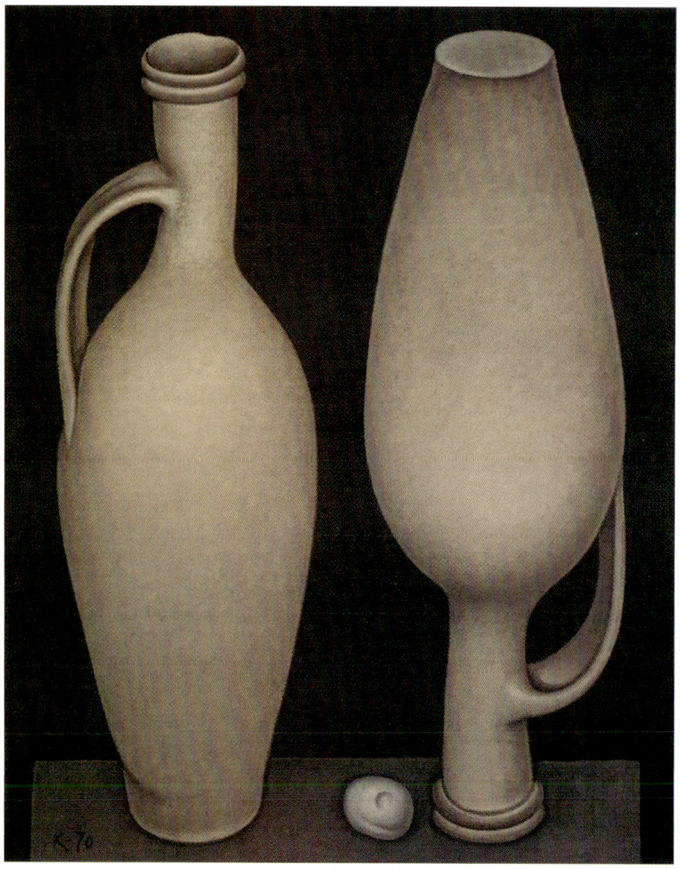

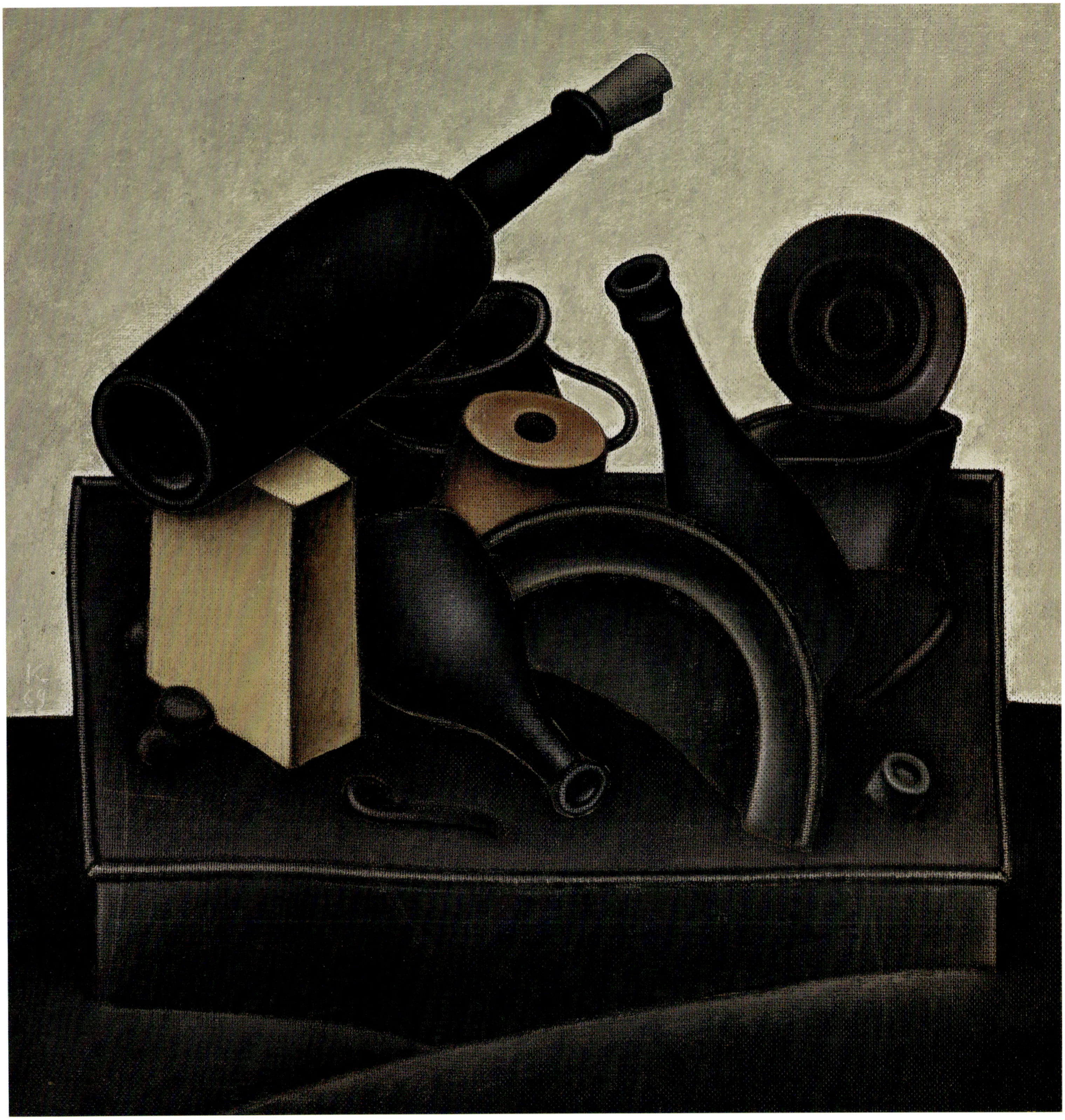

above
Still Life with Bottles, 1969
Oil on board
58.7 x 57.4 cm
Courtesy of Sotheby's

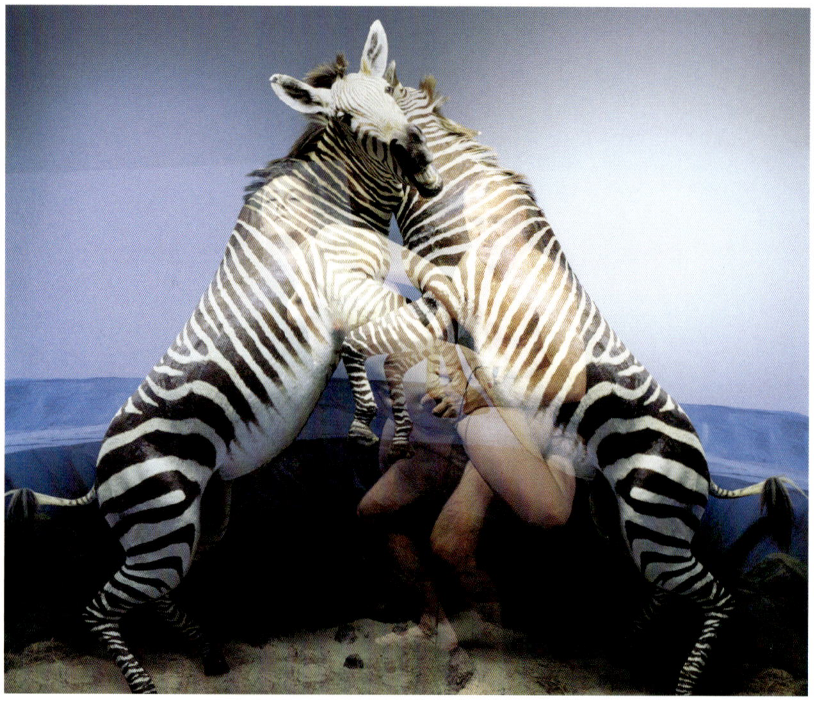

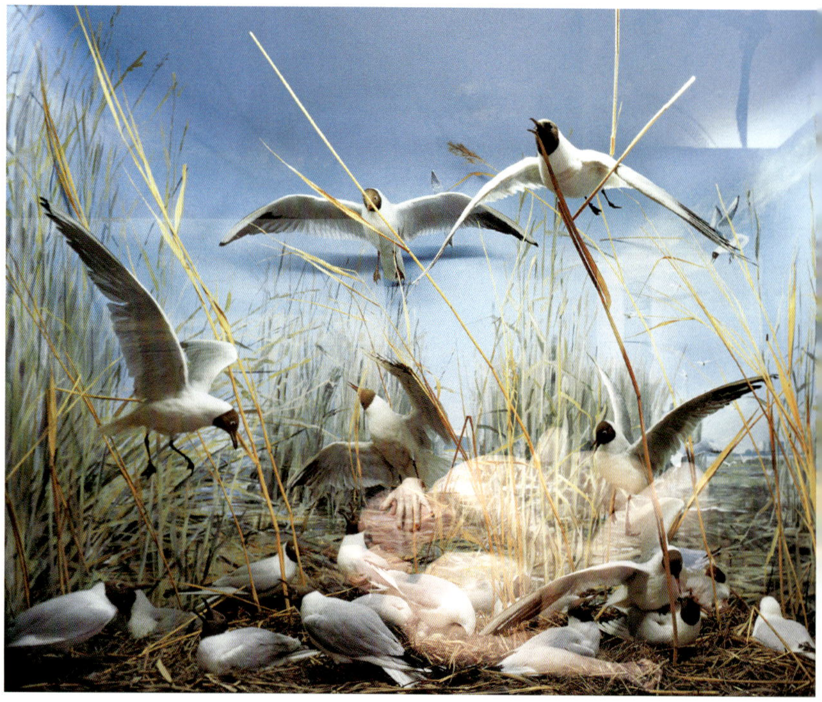

Born in Kiev, Ukraine, in 1961, artist and curator Oleg Kulik relocated to Moscow in 1987. Deciding not to pursue his formal education, he became a protégé of artist Boris Orlov, famous for his sculptures that parody Soviet power via a Sots Art aesthetic. While working as a curator with the then newly established Regina Gallery, Kulik exploded onto the Russian and international art scenes in the 1990s with his provocative, confrontational and sometimes violent street actions. He has exhibited in Moscow, Paris, New York, Stockholm and London, and participated in biennales in Moscow and Venice. His latest projects have been synesthetic opera productions staged at the Théâtre du Châtelet, Paris. In 2008 Kulik was the recipient of the award for Curator's Project at the 3rd Innovation Prize for his group exhibition *I Believe*. He was made an *Officier dans l'Ordre des Arts et des Lettres* in 2009.

One of the key figures of 1990s Moscow Actionism, this artist-provocateur performed spontaneous actions in the city's public spaces – at gallery openings, food markets, the zoo – often having recourse to animal alter egos, the most infamous of which became his artist-dog persona. In these actions Kulik questioned the essence of humanity, demonstrating the possibility that people might easily revert to a state of wildness. At the same time, they were a bitter recognition of Russia's belated arrival on the contemporary stage of art and politics; Kulik's brutish antics created a stereotypical portrait of 1990s Russia, fulfilling the international public's expectations concerning the country's innate character. These gestures were indelibly linked to the monumental changes that Russia was experiencing at the time: 'On the eve of perestroika, I was working a lot with the theme of transparency ... But perestroika started, and with it life changed vastly. A wild, animal spirit erupted into the open. Everything became aggressive, brutal. And life was changing at such a fast pace that it was impossible to react, to provide a context, to guess what would follow. The only reaction was spontaneous, animalistic, from which came the idea of fusing the form of a human being with a canine one, to create a two-sided creature – on the one hand, loyal, tame, and on the other hand, aggressive.' Kulik staged performances around the world over a period of several years, achieving infamy at the *Interpol* exhibition in Stockholm in 1997, when he was arrested for biting a member of the public.

Interested in the fine lines between art and life, ethics and aesthetics, sculptural installations like *Tennis Player* (2002) and *Cosmonaut* (2003) from the Museum series blur those boundaries. Life-size realistic sculptures of well-known figures such as Anna Kournikova and Yuri Gagarin denote their own artificiality through the 'taxidermy' stitches that run across their bodies. As Kulik explains, 'Art is what helps make sense of life, but it is governed by its own laws.' Convinced of a growing renaissance of spiritualism, he has refocused his artistic output on producing multi-sensory operas. His recent staging of works by Monteverdi (2009) and Handel (2011) 'combined all my previous investigations – animalistic, ethical, spatial, formal ... The theatre is an exhibition space which contains massive, purely expositional potential'. Kulik sees the future of art as a multidisciplinary endeavour: 'The theatre is the temple's inheritor – people go there and watch a ceremony ... The audience will come not just to look at a work of art on a white wall ... but to make some form of contribution.'

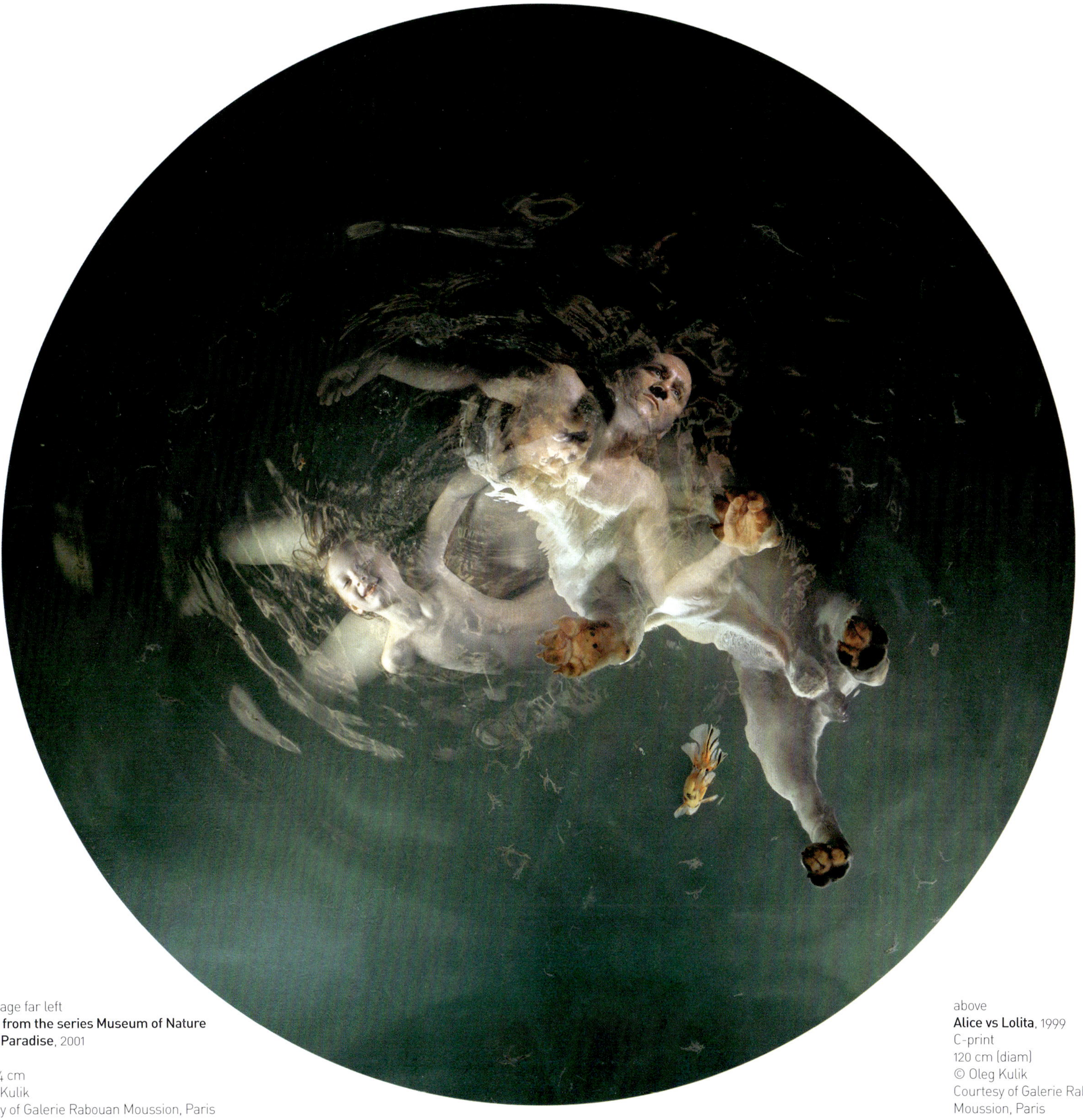

facing page far left
Zebras, from the series Museum of Nature or New Paradise, 2001
C-print
120 x 144 cm
© Oleg Kulik
Courtesy of Galerie Rabouan Moussion, Paris

facing page left
Seagulls, from the series Museum of Nature or New Paradise, 2001
C-print
120 x 148 cm
© Oleg Kulik
Courtesy of Galerie Rabouan Moussion, Paris

above
Alice vs Lolita, 1999
C-print
120 cm (diam)
© Oleg Kulik
Courtesy of Galerie Rabouan Moussion, Paris

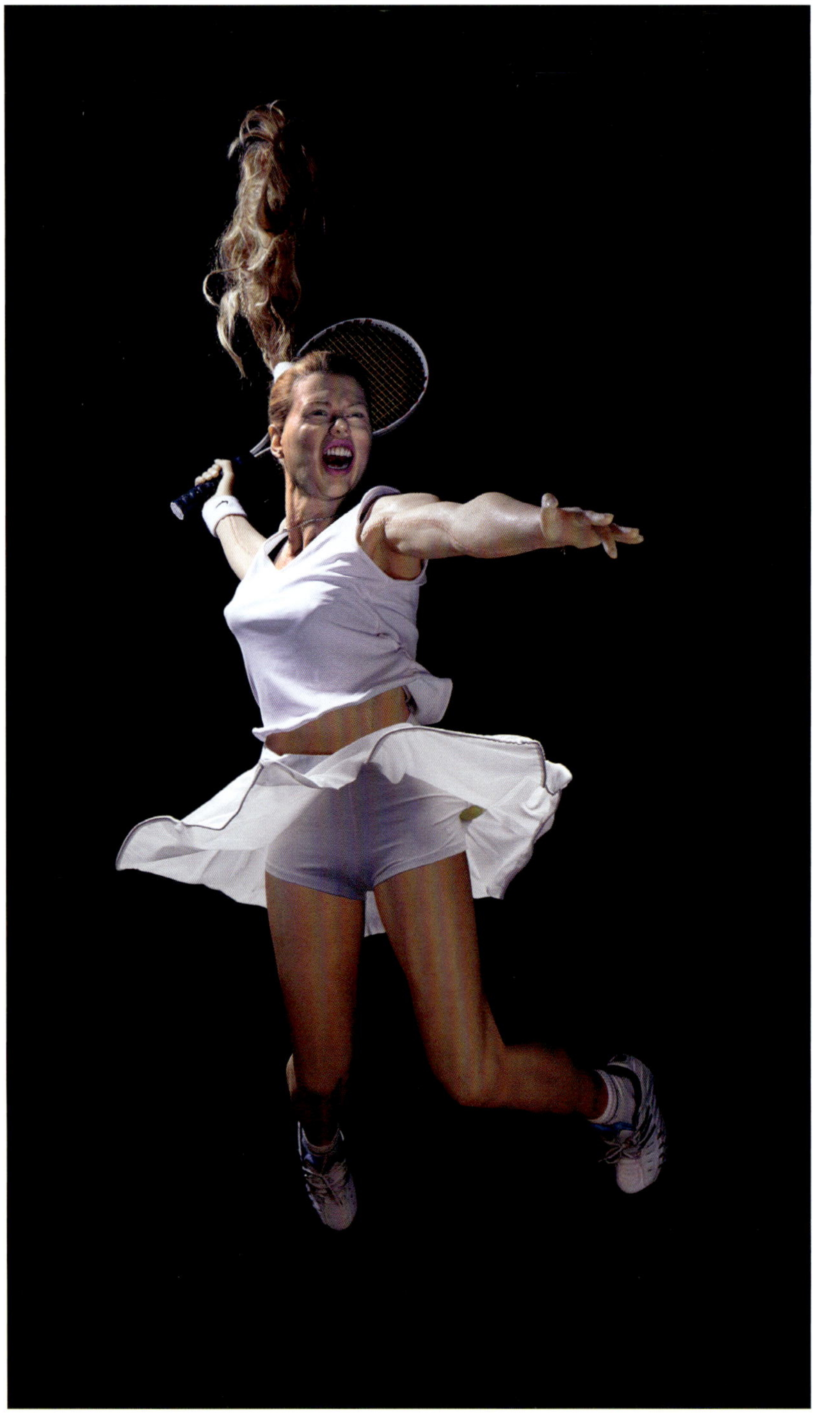

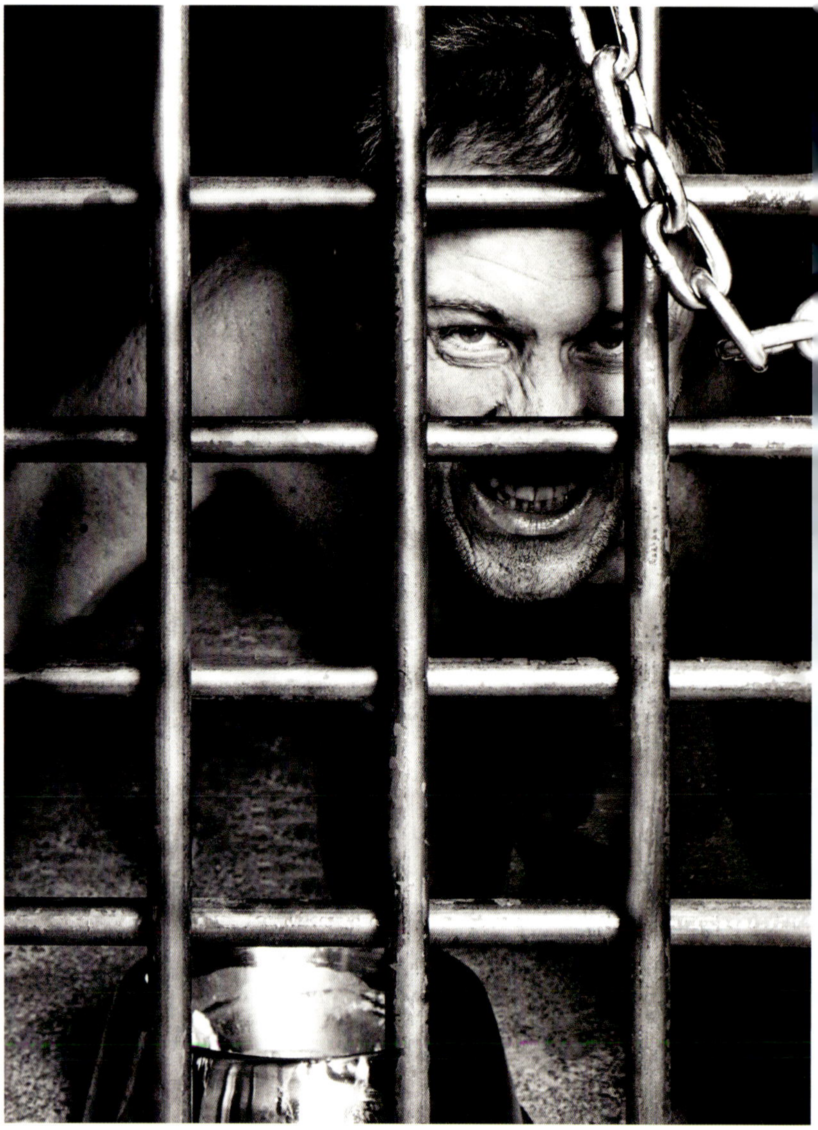

above
Tennis Player, from Museum project, 2002
Wax, taxidermist's stitching, hair, suit,
shoes, glass showcase
250 x 200 x 200 (showcase)
© Oleg Kulik
Courtesy of Galerie Rabouan Moussion, Paris

right
I Bite America and America Bites Me (with Mila Bredikhina), Deitch Projects, New York, 12–26 April 1997
Documentation of performance
Black and white photograph
160 x 120 cm
© Oleg Kulik
Courtesy of Galerie Rabouan Moussion, Paris

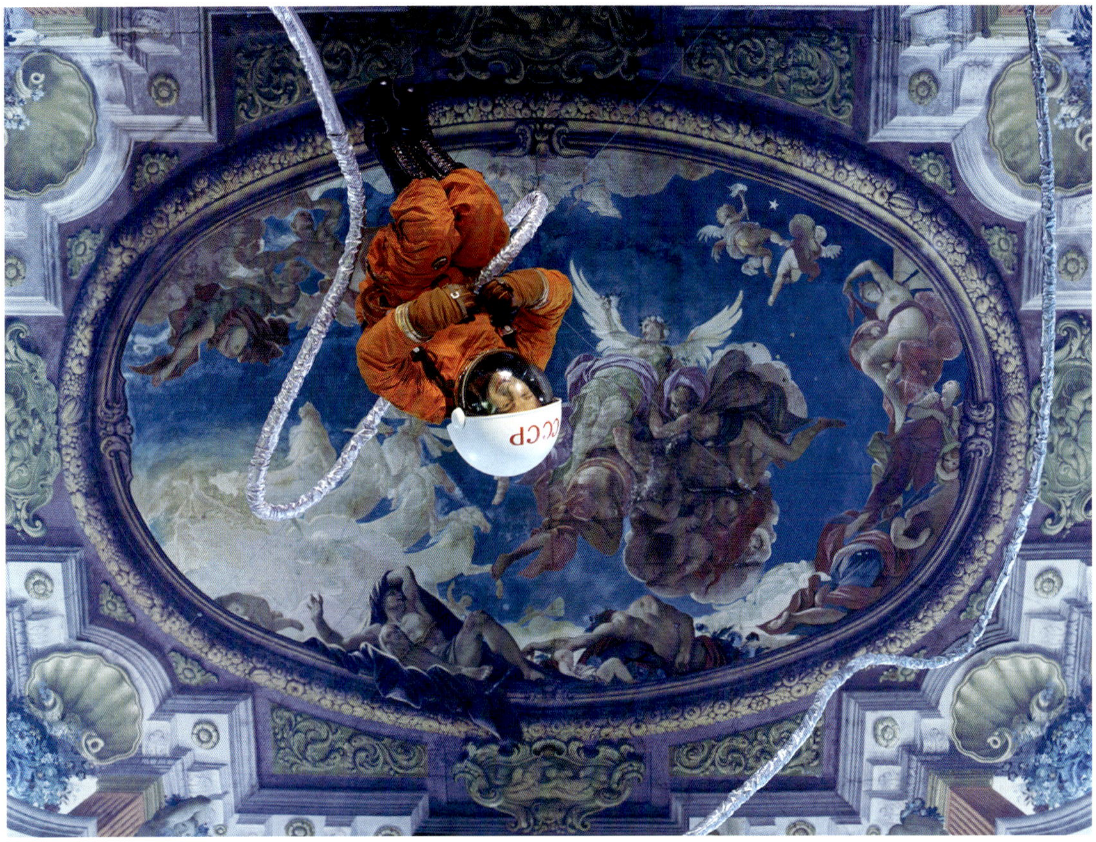

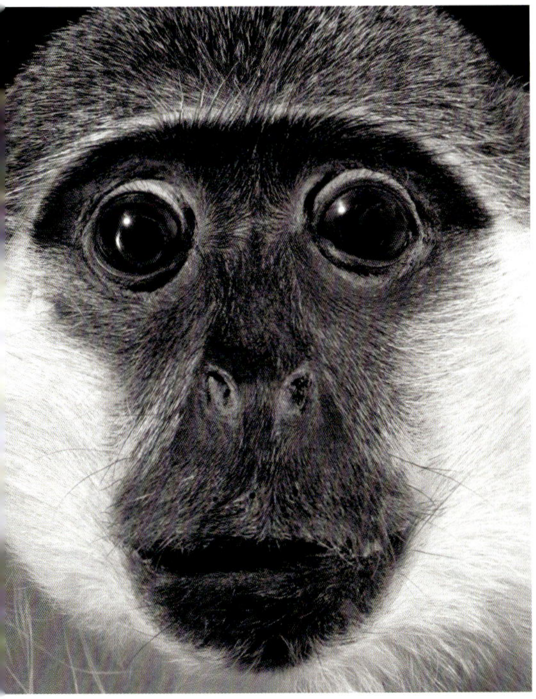

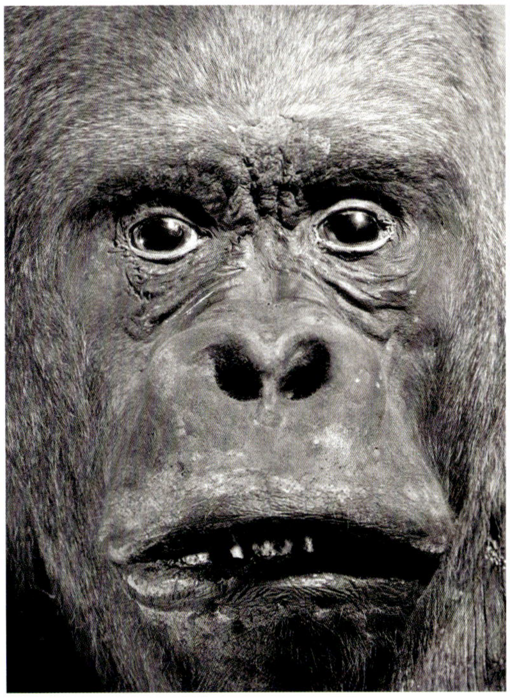

top
Cosmonaut, from Museum project, 2002
Wax, taxidermist's stitching, space suit, cord
140 x 70 x 75 cm (figure)
© Oleg Kulik
Courtesy of Galerie Rabouan Moussion, Paris

left
Dead Monkeys, or Memento Mori, 1998
Series of 12 black and white photographs
100 x 75 cm (each)
© Oleg Kulik
Courtesy of Galerie Rabouan Moussion, Paris

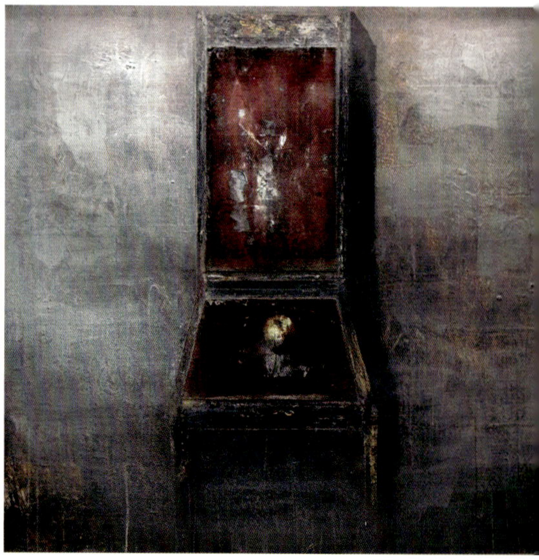

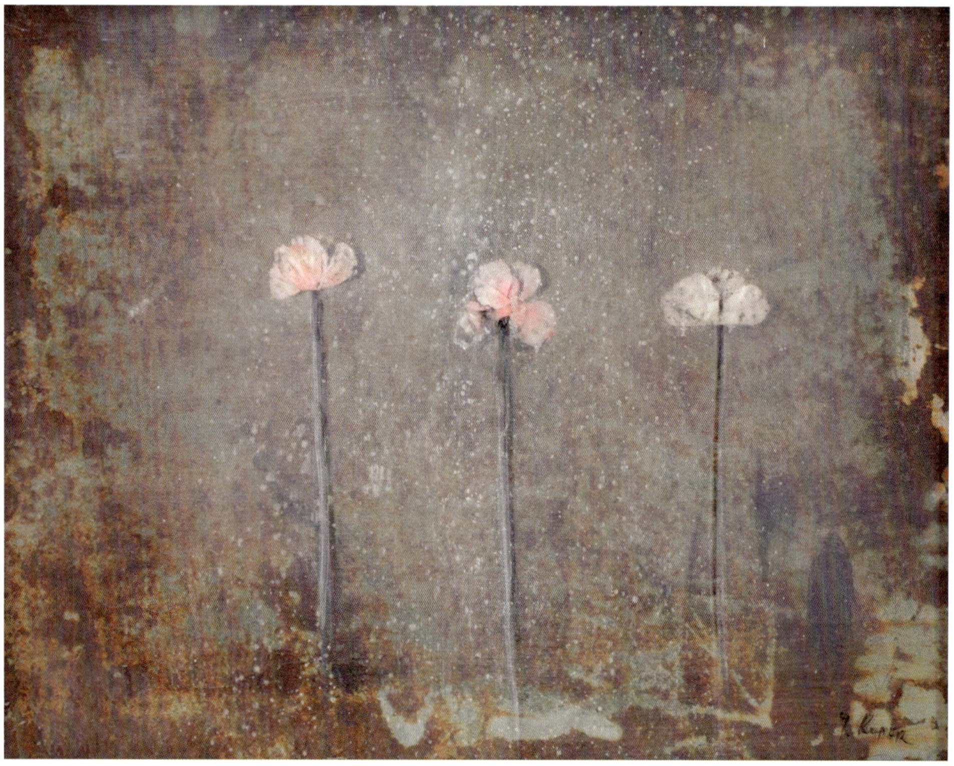

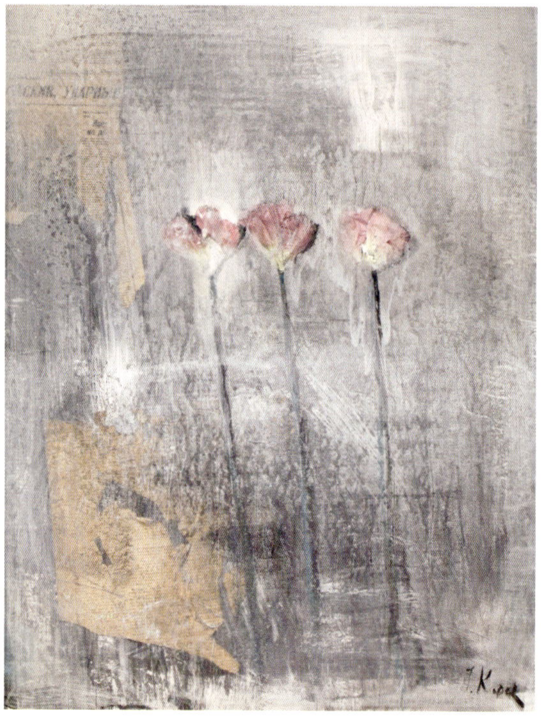

Painter, sculptor, graphic artist and theatre designer Yuri Kuper was born in Moscow in 1940, and today divides his time between New York and Paris. He studied at the Moscow State Pedagogical University, in the Department of Art and Graphics, graduating in 1963. From 1967 on, he was a member of the Soviet Union of Artists until he emigrated to Israel in 1972. Kuper's works have been shown in many leading commercial and public galleries across Europe and the US, as well as at the Pushkin Museum of Fine Arts, Moscow. He works in diverse media, creating assemblages or sculptural reliefs using a selection of found objects, in particular tools of the artist's trade. He favours objects worn by the passage of time and which possess the patina of decay, including pieces of corrugated cardboard, old drawers, bits of rusty tin, glass shards, old locks and bricks.

Since 1965, Kuper has worked for both theatre and film as a designer and creative advisor in Russia and internationally. Notable achievements have included designing the costumes and decor for Zorin's *Copper Grandmother* (Moscow Art Theatre) and for Chekhov's *The Seagull* (Théâtre de L'Ouest Parisien de Boulogne-Billancourt), and stage and set designs for Nikita Mikhalkov's production of Chekhov's *Unfinished Play for a Piano Player* (Teatro Argentina, Rome). Kuper has also collaborated with film maker Alexander Sokurov, producing set designs for Mussorgsky's opera *Boris Godunov*, and was artistic director for Sokorov's film *The Sun* (2004). Of this body of work, Kuper says, 'Being a theatre set designer has as much influenced my career as an artist, as being an artist has influenced my career as a set designer. I paint what I like and the way I like, but both of these activities are part of me.'

top
Red Chair, 2008
Oil and collage on canvas
150 x 150 cm
© Yuri Kuper
Courtesy of Kournikova Gallery

above
Ice Flowers No. 3, 2010
Oil and collage on canvas, painted glass
90 x 70 cm
© Yuri Kuper
Courtesy of Kournikova Gallery

above left
Ice Flowers No. 8, 2010
Oil and collage on metal, painted glass
88.5 x 112 cm
© Yuri Kuper
Courtesy of Kournikova Gallery

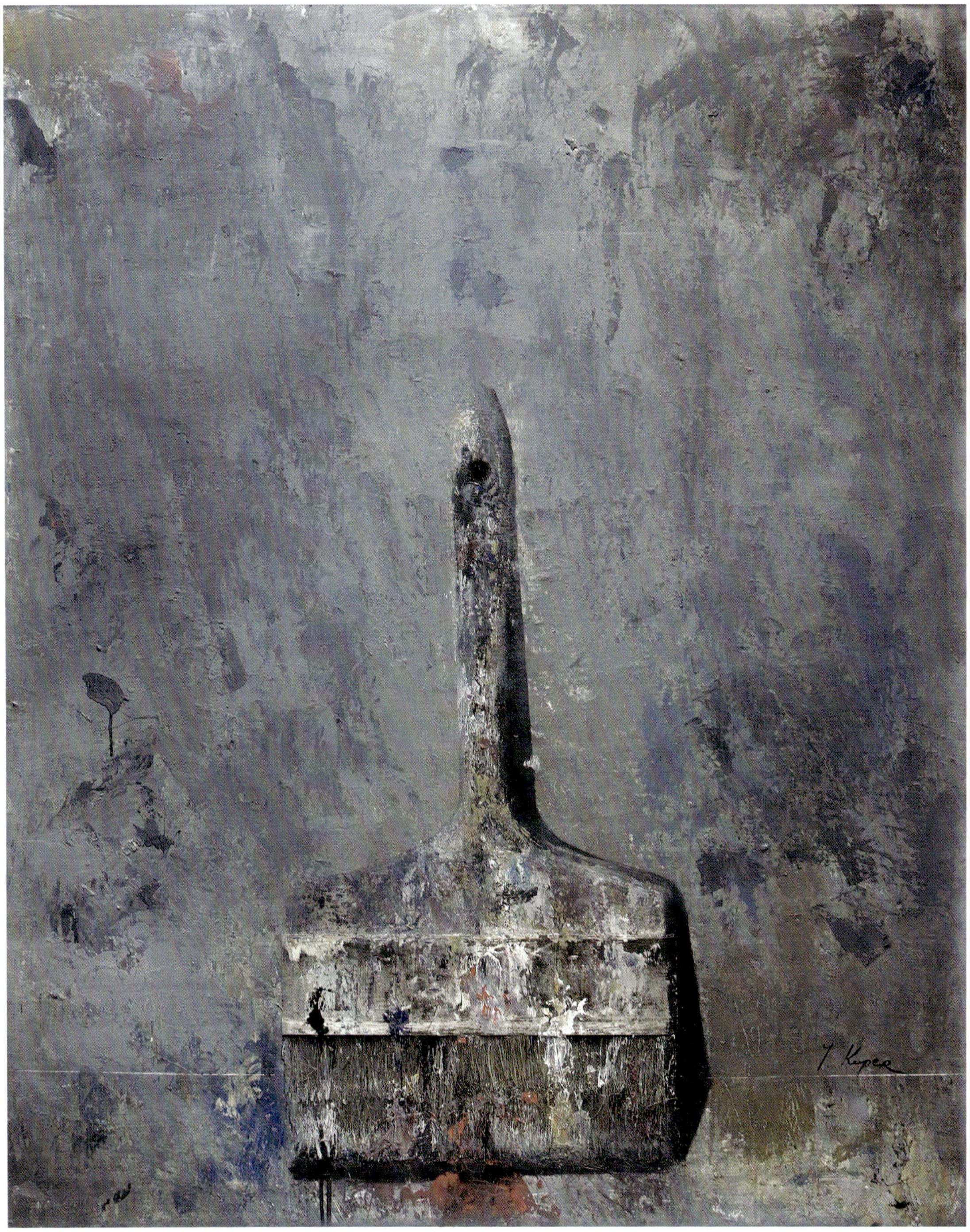

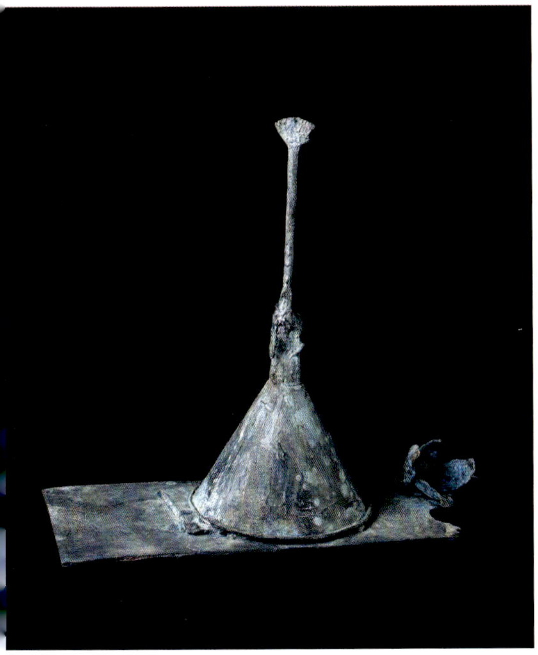

above
Brush, 2008
Oil and collage on canvas
162 x 130 cm
© Yuri Kuper
Courtesy of Kournikova Gallery

left
Funnel, 2006
Bronze
37 x 18 x 44 cm
© Yuri Kuper
Courtesy of Kournikova Gallery

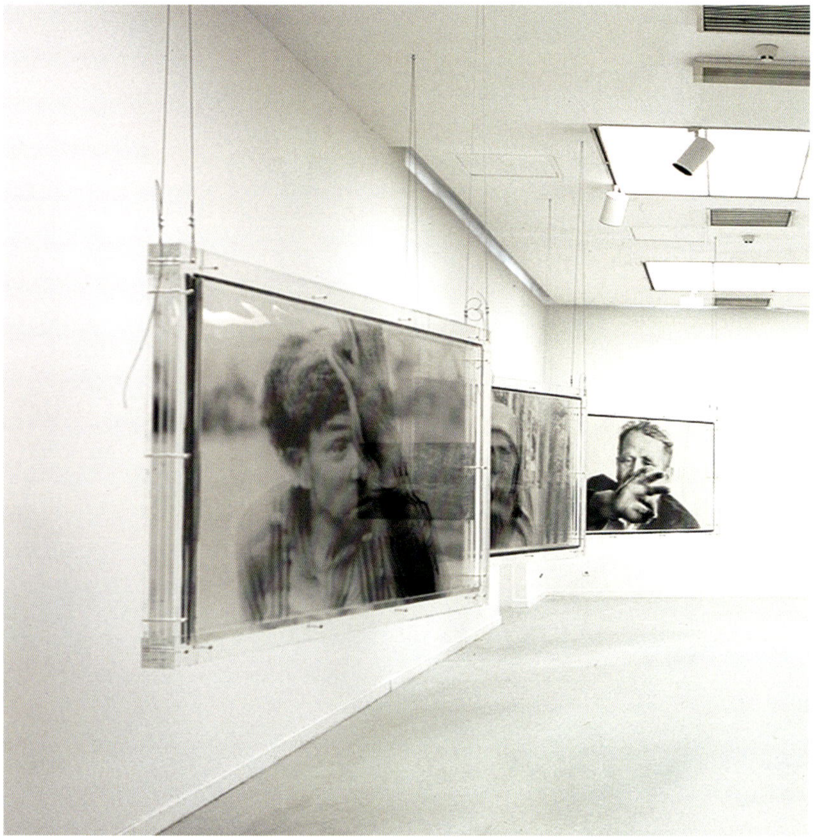

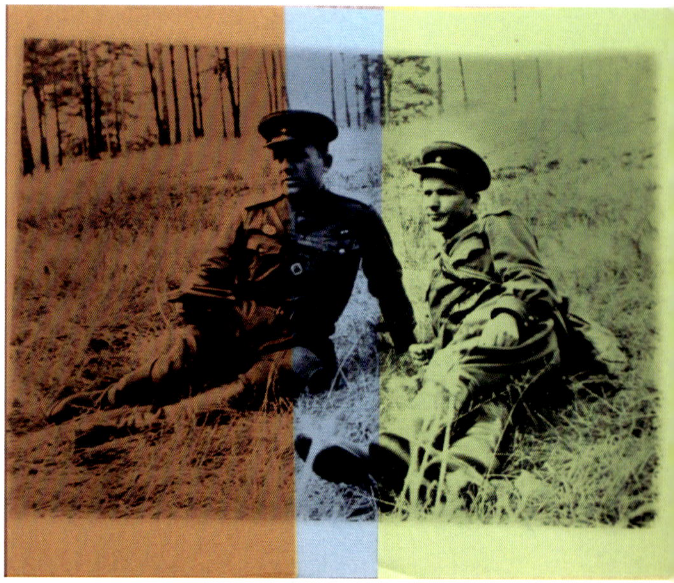

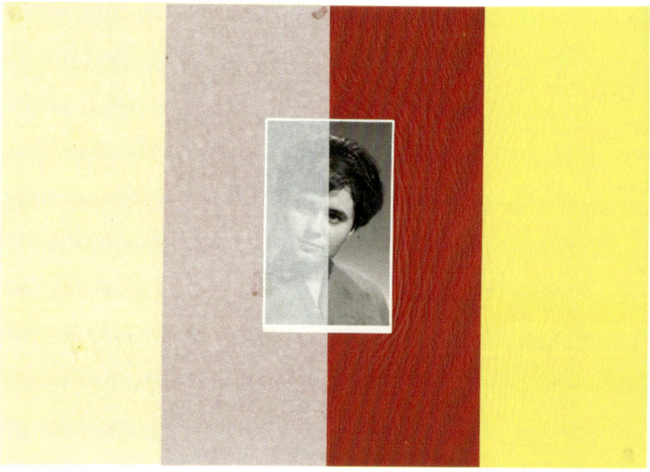

Vladimir Kuprianov was born in Moscow in 1954. Having trained to be a theatre director at the Institute of Culture, he graduated in 1976 and then spent a year in the Soviet Army. During his time as a student, Kuprianov began to work with both painted and sculptural objects, becoming close to some of the Moscow Conceptualists, including Dmitry Prigov, Boris Orlov and Rostislav Lebedev. During the 1970s he explored abstraction, only later coming to photography, the medium that has become central to his practice.

In 1983 Kuprianov created the photo-illustrations for Alexander Tvardovsky's book *Lyrika*. He has exhibited widely in Russia and throughout Western Europe. In 1989 he took part in the first Foto-Triennale in Esslingen, Germany, and his work has been shown at the Centre Pompidou, Paris. Since 2007 he has been associate professor of Art Photography at the Alexander Rodchenko Photography and New Media School, Moscow, where he also lives.

Kuprianov often incorporates recycled vintage photographs into his work, for example in his series *Photographic Investigations* (1980), in which he photographed images from old books, calendars and postcards. Exploiting one of photography's most common uses as a medium for documentation – be it of family portraits or of world events – he creates incisive and reflective works addressing the passage of time. Kuprianov's mining of the past is not just an act of nostalgia, however; he seeks catharsis by working with the Soviet propaganda imagery of his youth, as well as reconciliation with his memories of childhood and his family heritage. The collective experience is a fundamental aspect of his work as well.

top left
From the series
Sergievsk Village, 2003
Black and white print on photographic film, plastic
125 x 176 cm
© Vladimir Kuprianov
Courtesy of the artist

top right
From the series
Family Photo Album, 2009
Black and white print on photographic film, coloured paper
30 x 40 cm
© Vladimir Kuprianov
Courtesy of the artist

above
From the series
Nadusha, 1992
Black and white print on paper, coloured paper
30.5 x 42.5 cm
© Vladimir Kuprianov
Courtesy of the artist

facing page
From the series
The 1950s, 2008
Colour print on film
65 x 48 cm
© Vladimir Kuprianov
Courtesy of the artist

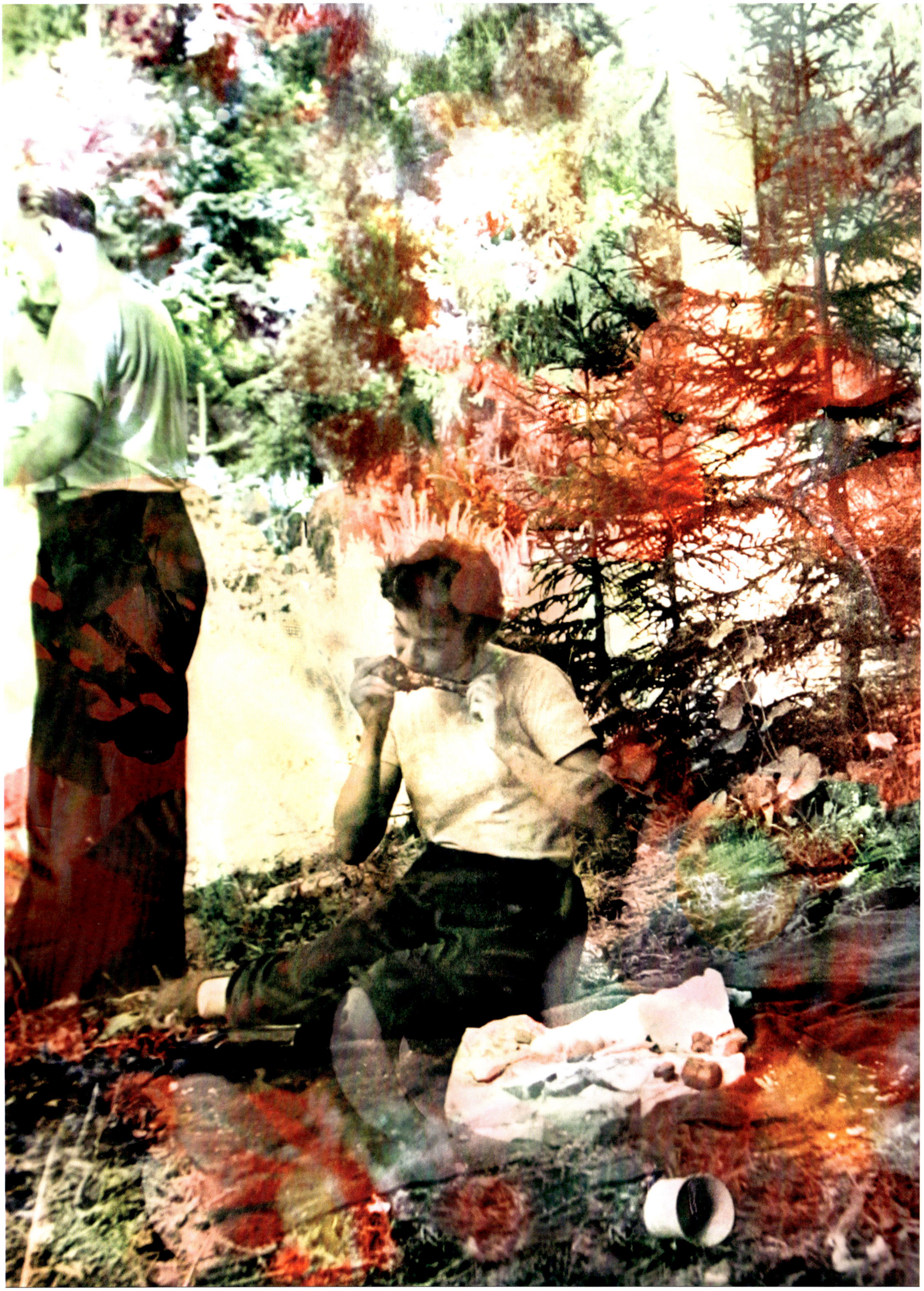

Vladimir Kuprianov

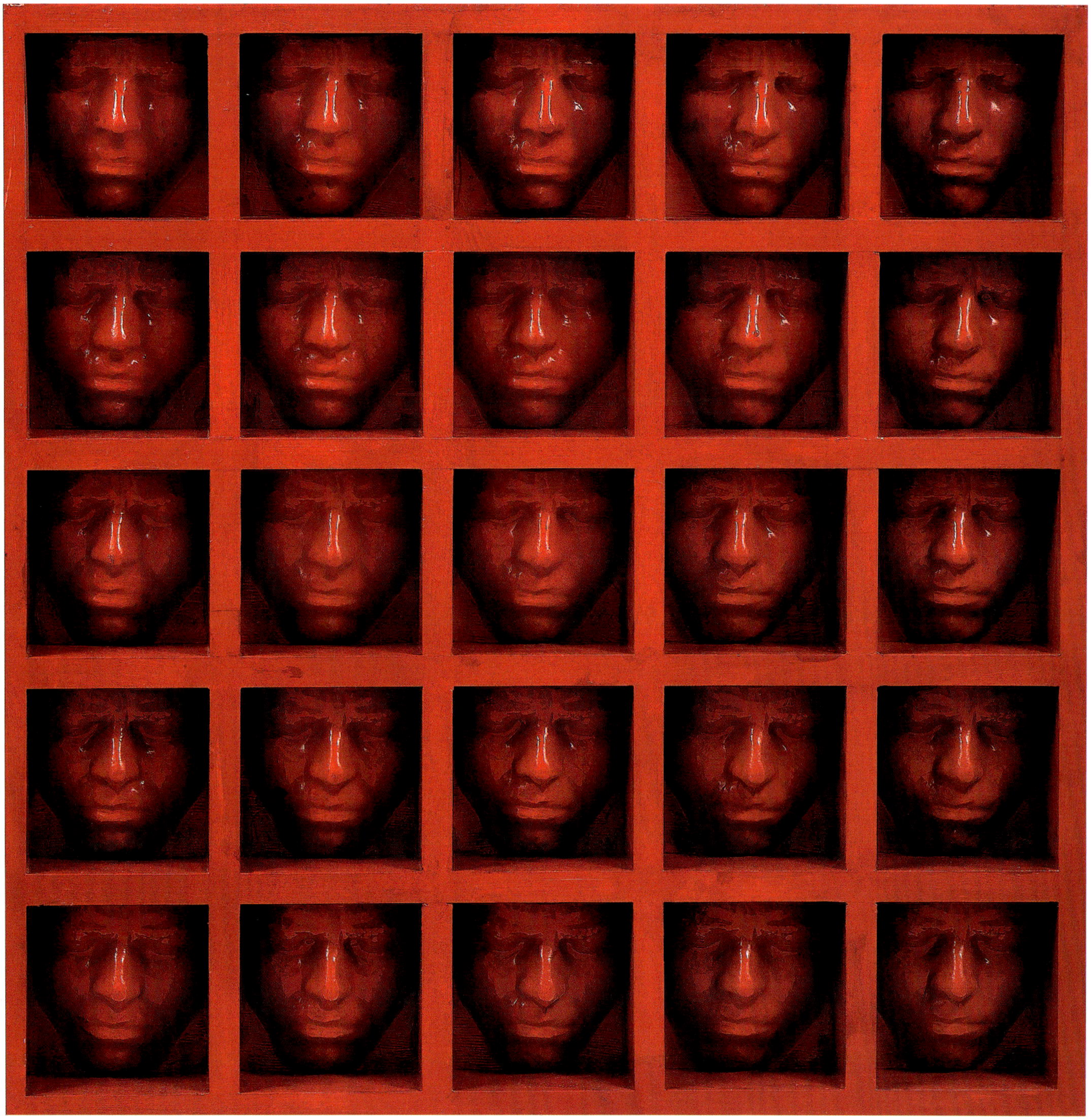

Igor Makarevich & Elena Elagina

Makarevich (born 1943) & Elagina (born 1949) are partners in both art and life. Both joined the Collective Actions group in 1979, participating in numerous performances and documentary projects with fellow members including Ilya Kabakov and Andrei Monastyrsky. Concurrently, they worked on individual projects until 1990, after which they collaborated exclusively with each other. A conceptual archaeology, their joint projects reread historical and archival material, re-evaluating symbols from Soviet mass culture and its avant-garde antecedents. While their practice sometimes distorts historical facts, the artists have also chosen to reflect on some of the more speculative aspects of Soviet 'science', by appropriating the discredited agricultural theories of Lysenko, for instance. Whether true or false, the 'factographic' rhetorical dimension of their artworks charts the interaction between collective myth and private fantasy in Russian history. This concern with the indefinite boundaries of social and linguistic institutions, and their relation to personal fantasy, situates Makarevich & Elagina's practice firmly at the centre of Moscow Conceptualism.

above
Composition with Red Faces, 2002
Wood, plastic, enamel
82 x 82 x 10 cm

Courtesy of Victor Bondarenko

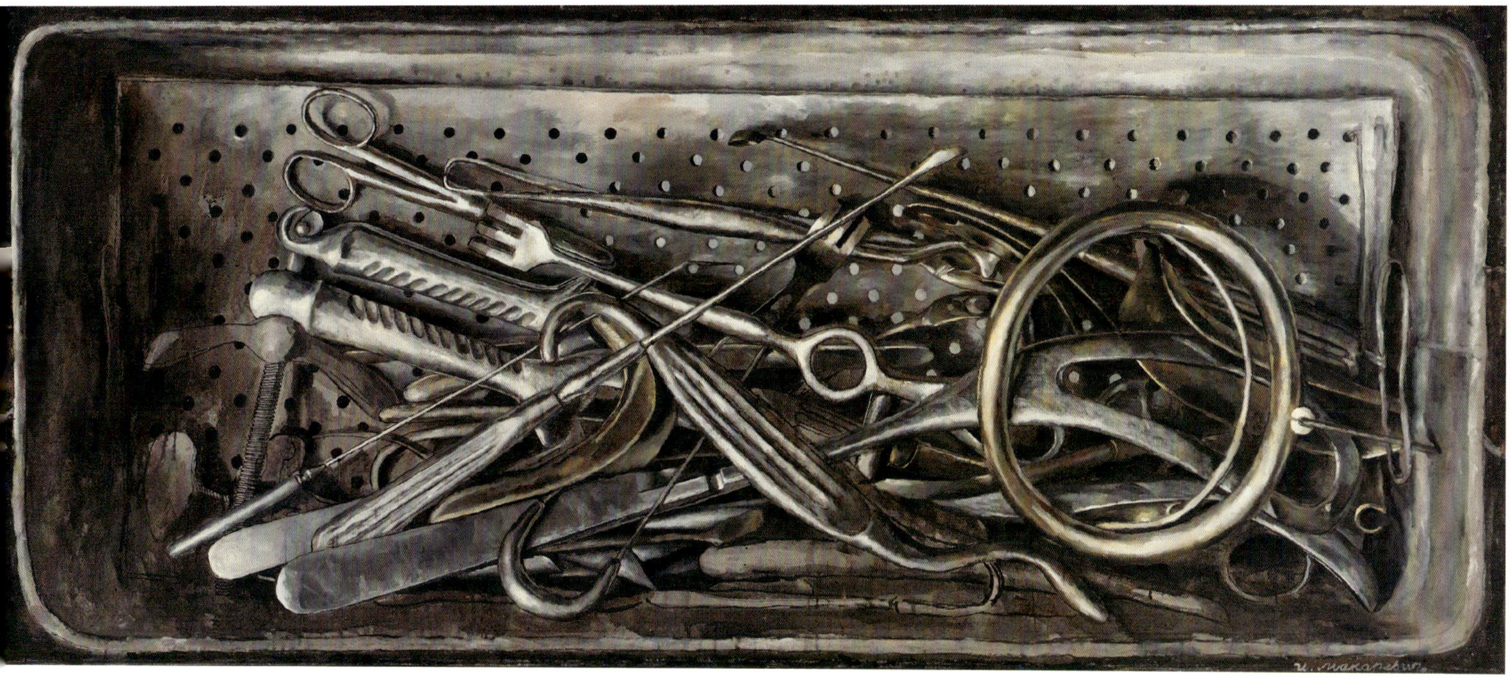

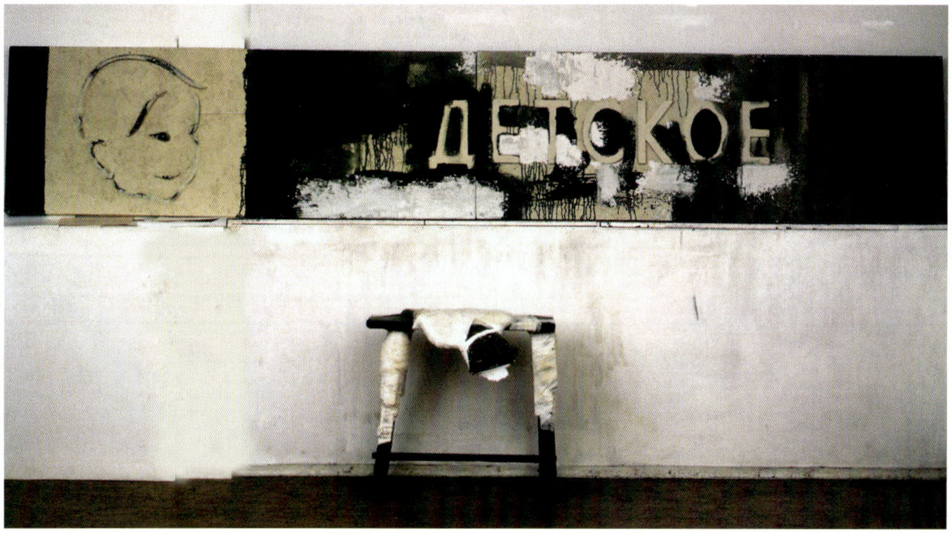

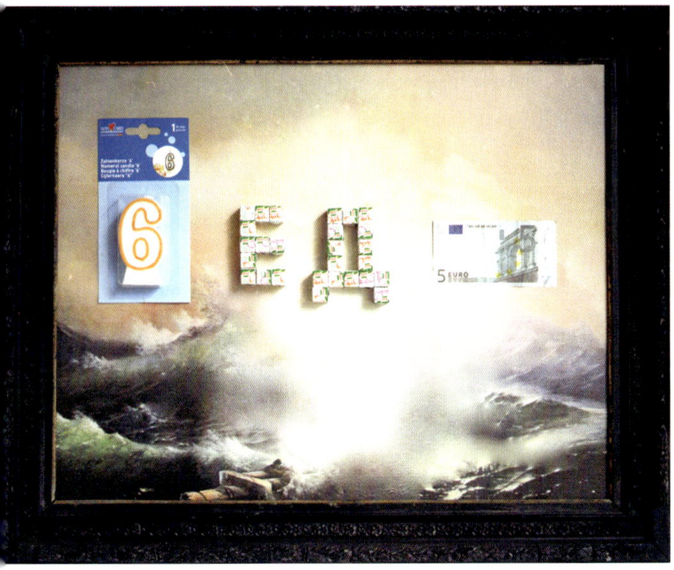

top
Surgical Instruments, 1978
Tempera on canvas
88 x 204.5 cm
© Igor Makarevich
Courtesy of the artist

left
Untitled, 2011
Mixed media
54 x 65 cm
© Elena Elagina
Courtesy of the artist

above
Children's, 1987
Mixed media
70 x 200 cm (2-part table, each part);
70 x 72 x 50 cm (bench)
© Elena Elagina
Courtesy of Stella Art Foundation, Moscow

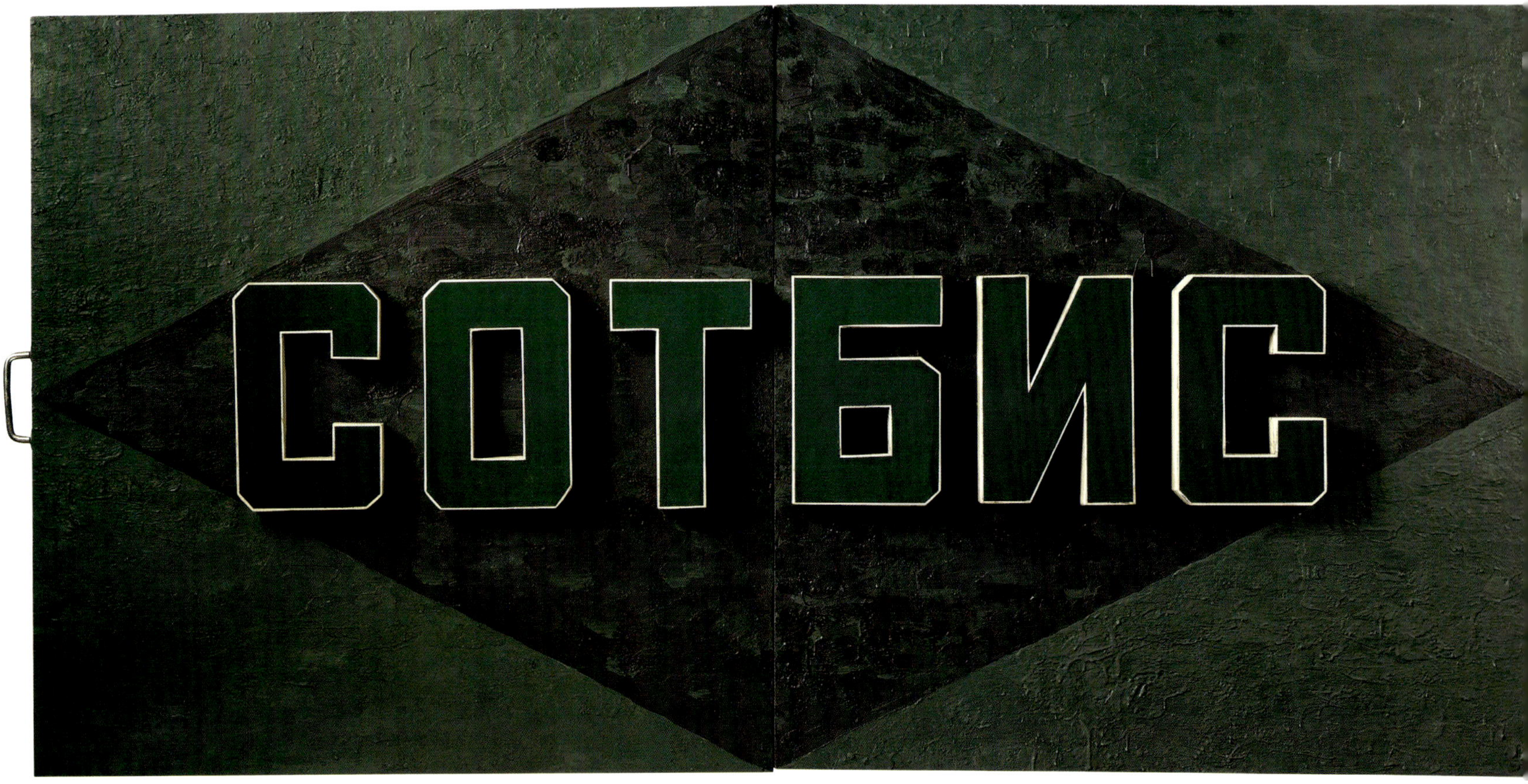

above
Sotheby's, 1998
Plywood, enamel, mixed media
100 x 210 x 6 cm
© Igor Makarevich
Courtesy of Sotheby's

right
I LOVE USSR, 1989
Mixed media on board
89.5 x 69.5cm
© Igor Makarevich
Courtesy of Sotheby's and
Private Collection, US

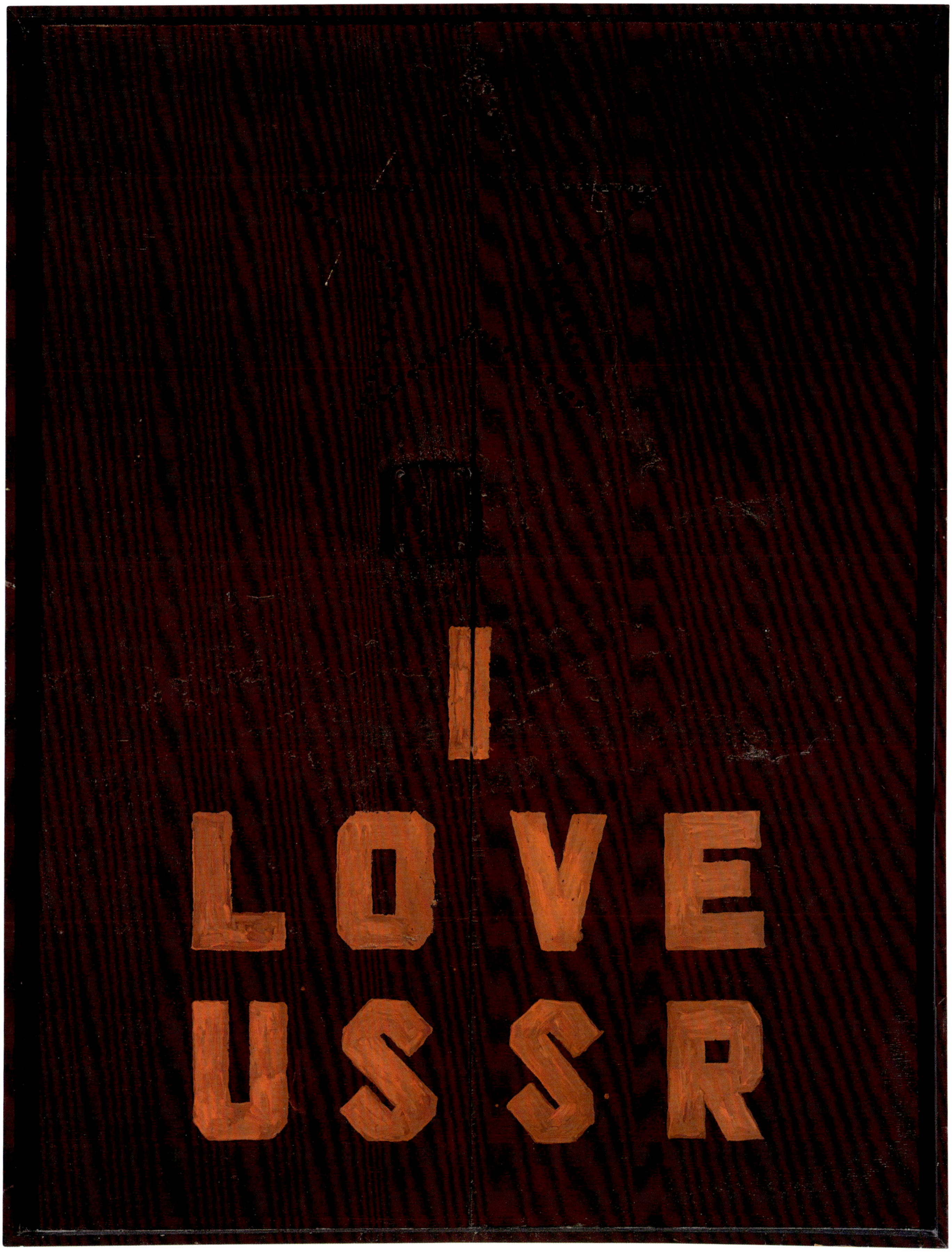
I
LOVE
USSR

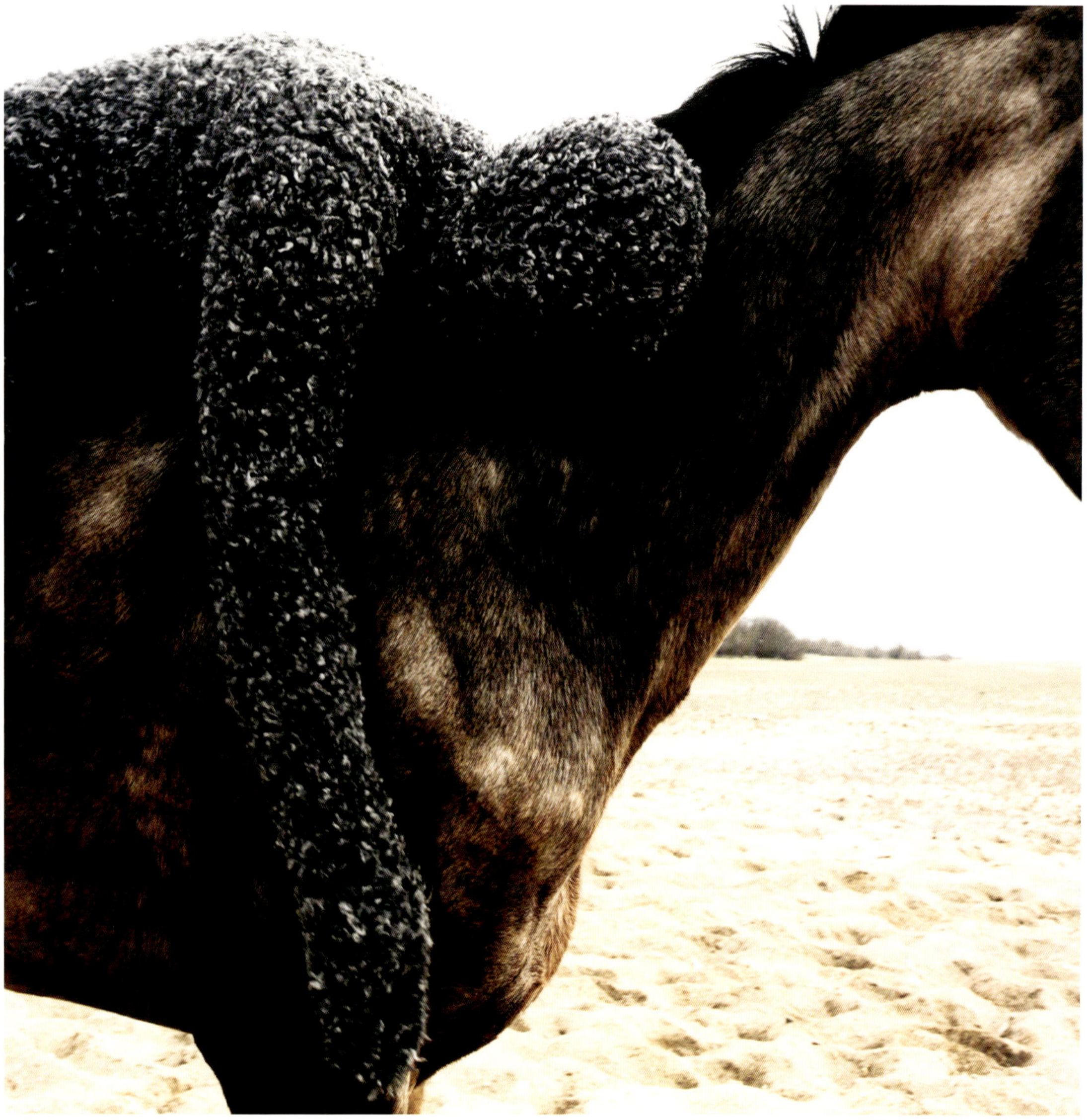

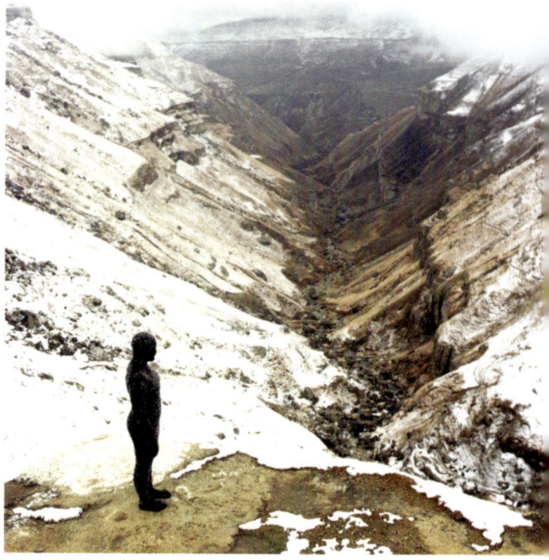

Taus Makhacheva

Born in 1983, Taus Makhacheva divides her time between her native Makhachkala in Dagestan and Moscow. As a member of an ethnic minority, her work is informed by investigations into the construction of social and cultural identities, the meaning of community, and the politics at play behind these socio-cultural structures. She describes a deep familiarity with habitual reactions to members of other cultures; the essence of her work, which largely takes the form of video, photography and performances, resides in the difficulty of overcoming differences.

Works like *Karakul* (2007) and *Rekhen* (2009) demonstrate a subtle use of irony and sarcasm in figuring the 'other'. Both pieces explore the concept of boundaries and the interaction between social hierarchies through recourse to anthropomorphism. In *Rekhen*, a young man wears the sheepskin coat traditionally worn by shepherds. His attempts to scramble as close as possible to the surrounding flock consistently end in failure, yet he perseveres. In *Karakul*, a human figure wrapped in karakul is stripped of all human characteristics, instead interacting with and mimicking a horse – the embodiment of domesticity. Makhacheva deconstructs social relations in order to test the limits of the human desire for integration and acceptance, and to discover to what extent human interaction is built upon social codes rather than organic, mutual understanding. These investigations are expanded into public space in *A Space of Celebration* (2009), in which spherical anthropomorphic forms move effortlessly and silently through the gaudy interiors of a Dagestani marriage hall.

Makhacheva graduated from Goldsmiths College, London, in 2007 before completing her studies at the Institute of Contemporary Art, Moscow. She has participated in numerous exhibitions in Russia and abroad, including the Third Moscow Biennale.

above left
Karakul No. 5, 2007
C-print
90 x 90 cm
© Taus Makhacheva
Courtesy of the artist and Impronte Contemporary Art, Milan

above
Karakul No. 2, 2007
C-print
90 x 90 cm
© Taus Makhacheva
Courtesy of the artist and Impronte Contemporary Art, Milan

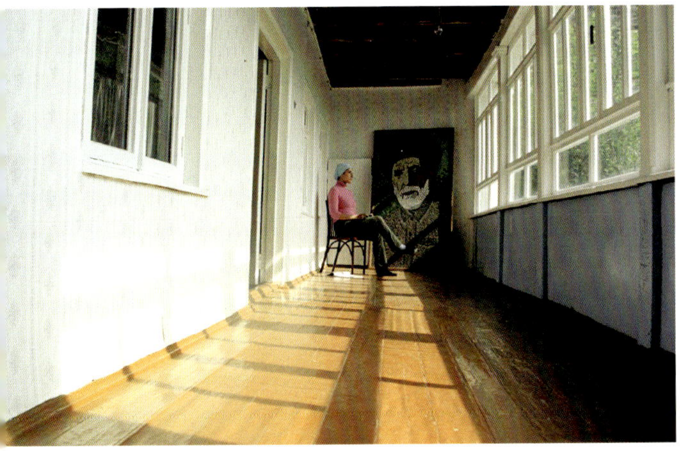

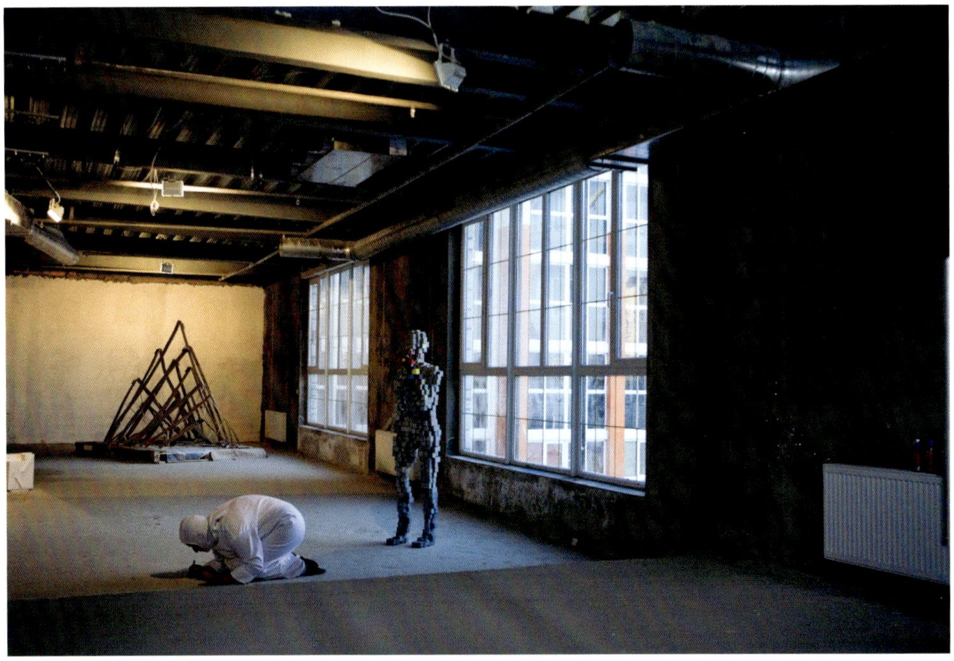

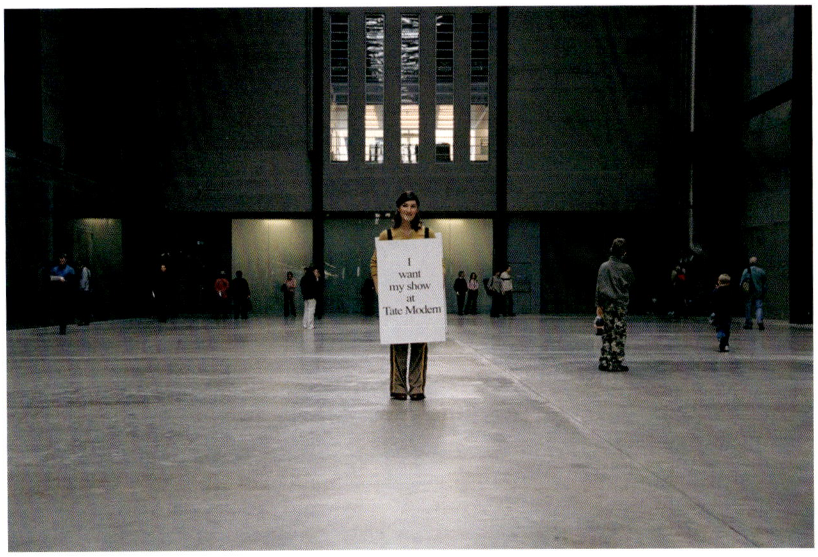

top
Formation No. 2, 2006
C-print
40 x 60 cm
© Taus Makhacheva
Courtesy of the artist and Impronte
Contemporary Art, Milan

above
Me and My Friend OCD
(Obsessive-Compulsive Disorder), 2009
Photo-documentation of performance
C-print
30 x 45 cm
© Taus Makhacheva
Photo: Nikolai Alekseev
Courtesy of the artist and Impronte
Contemporary Art, Milan

left
Maturity II, 2004
Photo-documentation of performance
C-print
40 x 60 cm
© Taus Makhacheva
Photo: Olga Hoffman, Tate Modern, London
Courtesy of the artist and Impronte
Contemporary Art, Milan

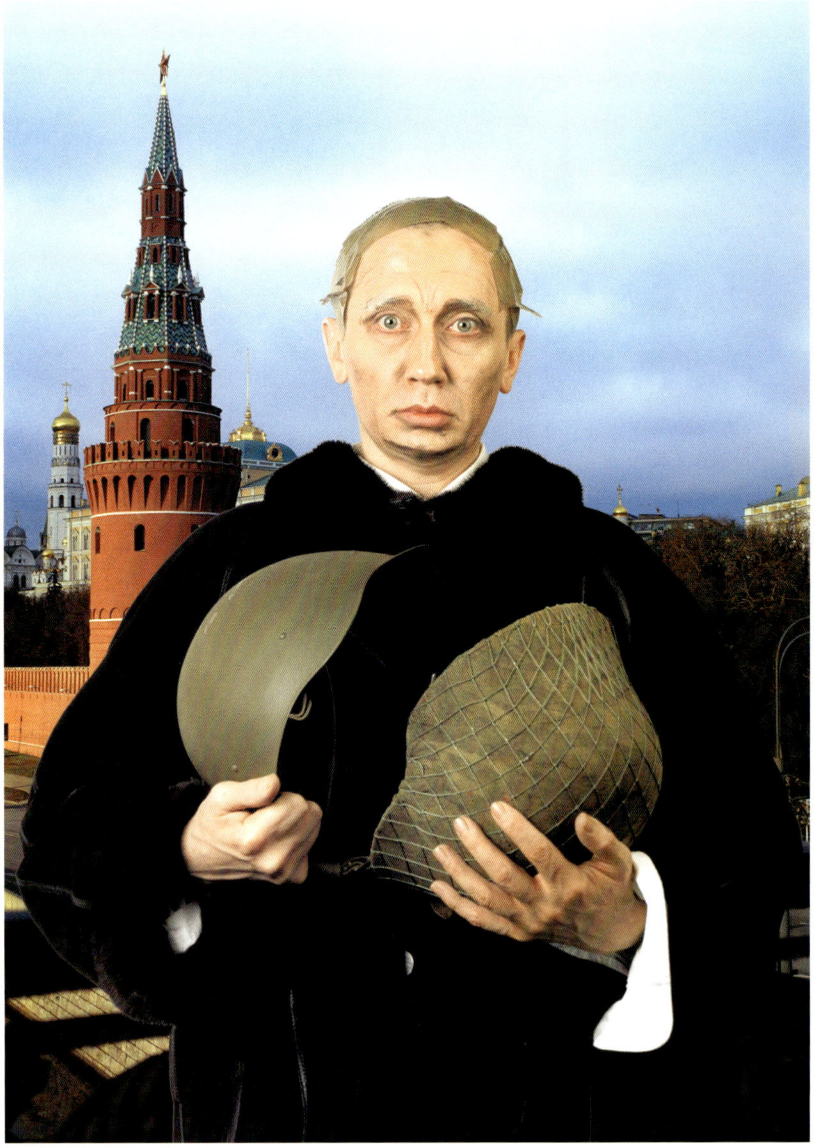

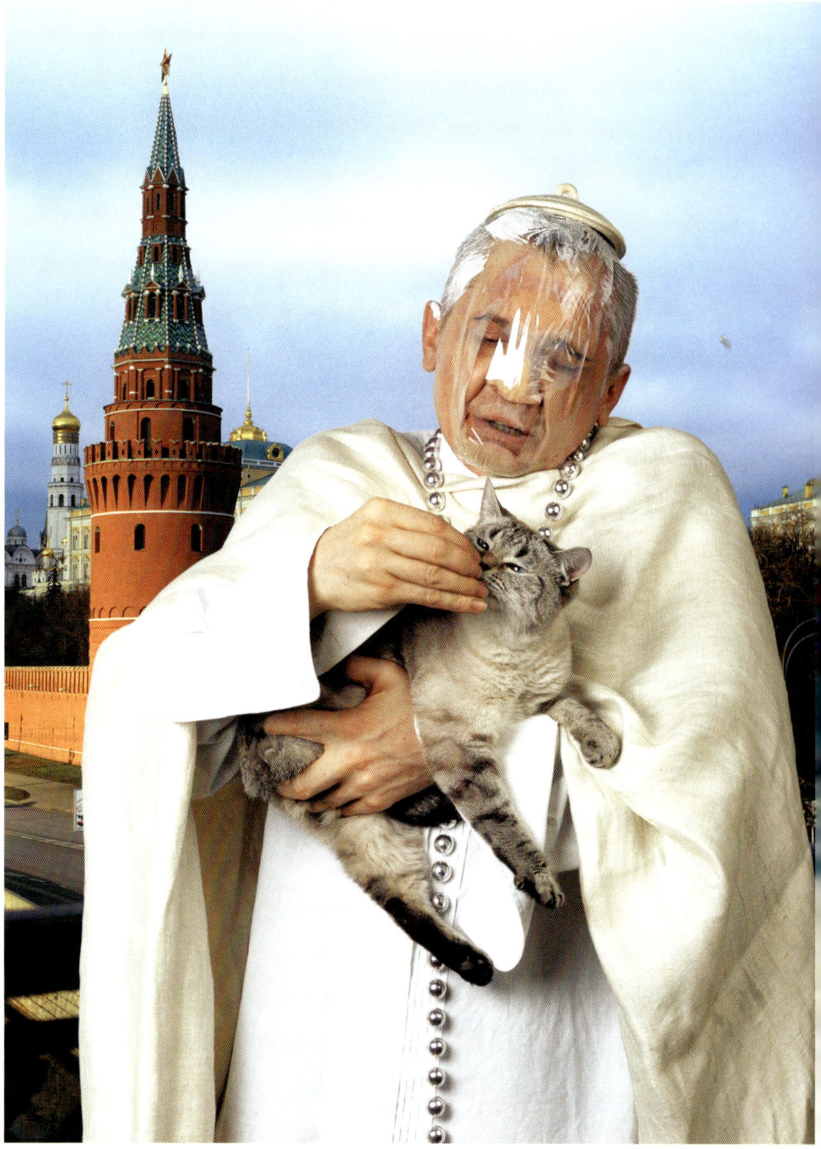

Performance artist and artist-photographer Vladislav Mamyshev-Monroe is his own subject in works in which dressing up and transvestitism play the main roles. Born in Leningrad in 1969, he studied literature, at the age of seventeen meeting artist Timur Novikov, whom he cites as a major influence. Mamyshev-Monroe joined Leningrad exhibitions of work by the New Artists group and participated in Sergei Kuryokhin's alternative orchestra Popular Mechanics. While serving in the army in 1987–9, he started to photograph himself dressed as Marilyn Monroe, eventually taking her name in order to create an alter ego. Together with Novikov, Mamyshev-Monroe founded Piratskoye TV.

One of Mamyshev-Monroe's most ambitious shows, *The Life of Great People* (1996) at the Yukut Gallery, Moscow, comprised an epic display of large photographic images of himself dressed as some of the world's most famous historical figures, including Jesus Christ, Catherine the Great, Hitler and Lenin. Other impersonations are taken from myth and legend. Mamyshev-Monroe's frequent shows in Russian commercial and public galleries have included *My Name Is Trinity*, at XL Gallery, Moscow (1997); *Russian Questions*, at the State Russian Museum, St Petersburg (1997); and *Liubov Orlova*, at the Guelman Gallery, Moscow (1999). Since going abroad for the first time in 2002, he has actively participated in the international art scene.

In 2006 Mamyshev-Monroe collaborated with directors Pavel Labazov and Andrei Silversterov to remake the Soviet classic film *Volga-Volga*. Mamyshev-Monroe's head was superimposed on that of the heroine, and the film was dubbed and partly rewritten with the artist doing the lead voice-over. Having premiered at the Rotterdam Festival in 2006, in 2007 it was awarded the Kandinsky Prize as Media Project of the Year.

above left
Veteran, from the series Stars, 2005
Colour photograph
90 x 65 cm
© Vladimir Mamyshev-Monroe
Courtesy of XL Gallery, Moscow

above
Pope, from the series Stars, 2005
Colour photograph
90 x 65 cm
© Vladimir Mamyshev-Monroe
Courtesy of XL Gallery, Moscow

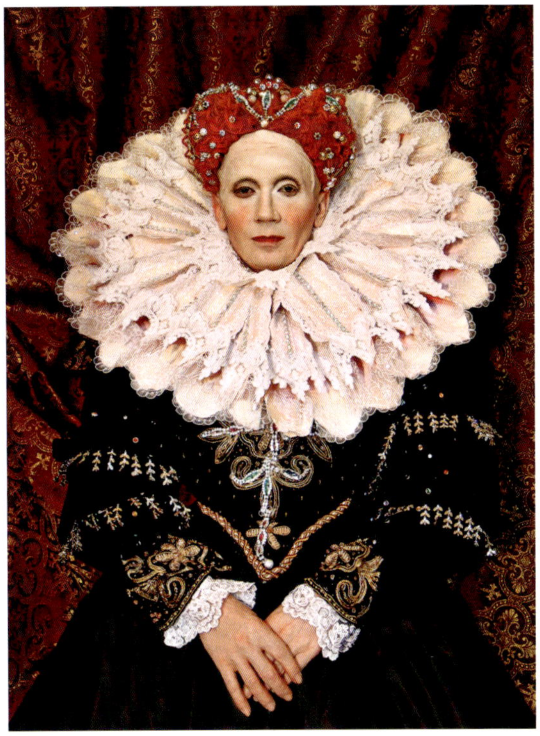

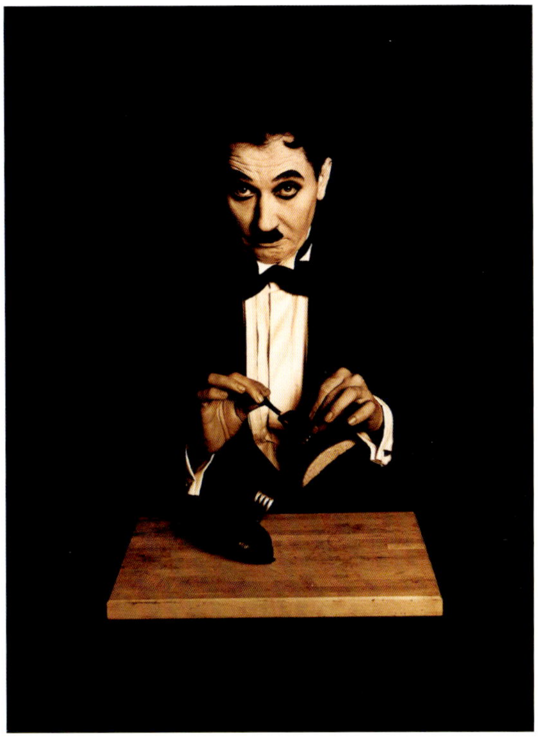

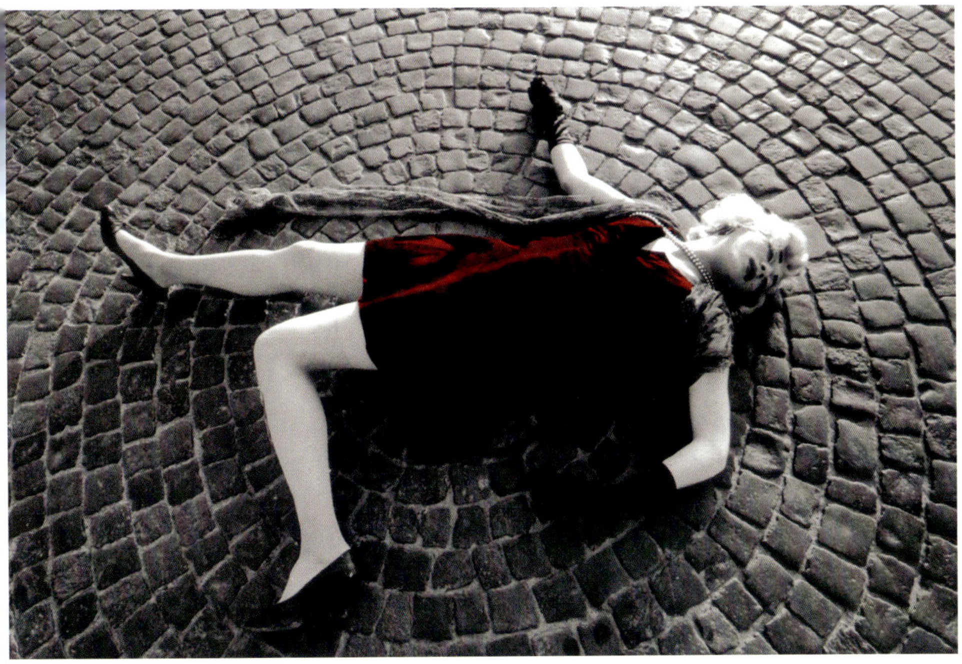

above
Elizabeth, 2006
Colour photograph
130 x 100 cm
© Vladimir Mamyshev-Monroe
Courtesy of XL Gallery, Moscow

left
Marilyn, from the series Her Story, 1991 (printed 2010)
Hand-coloured
black and white photograph
49 x 75 cm
© Vladimir Mamyshev-Monroe
Courtesy of XL Gallery, Moscow

above
Chaplin, from the series Silent Film, 2005
Gelatin silver print
150 x 108 cm
© Vladimir Mamyshev-Monroe
Courtesy of XL Gallery, Moscow

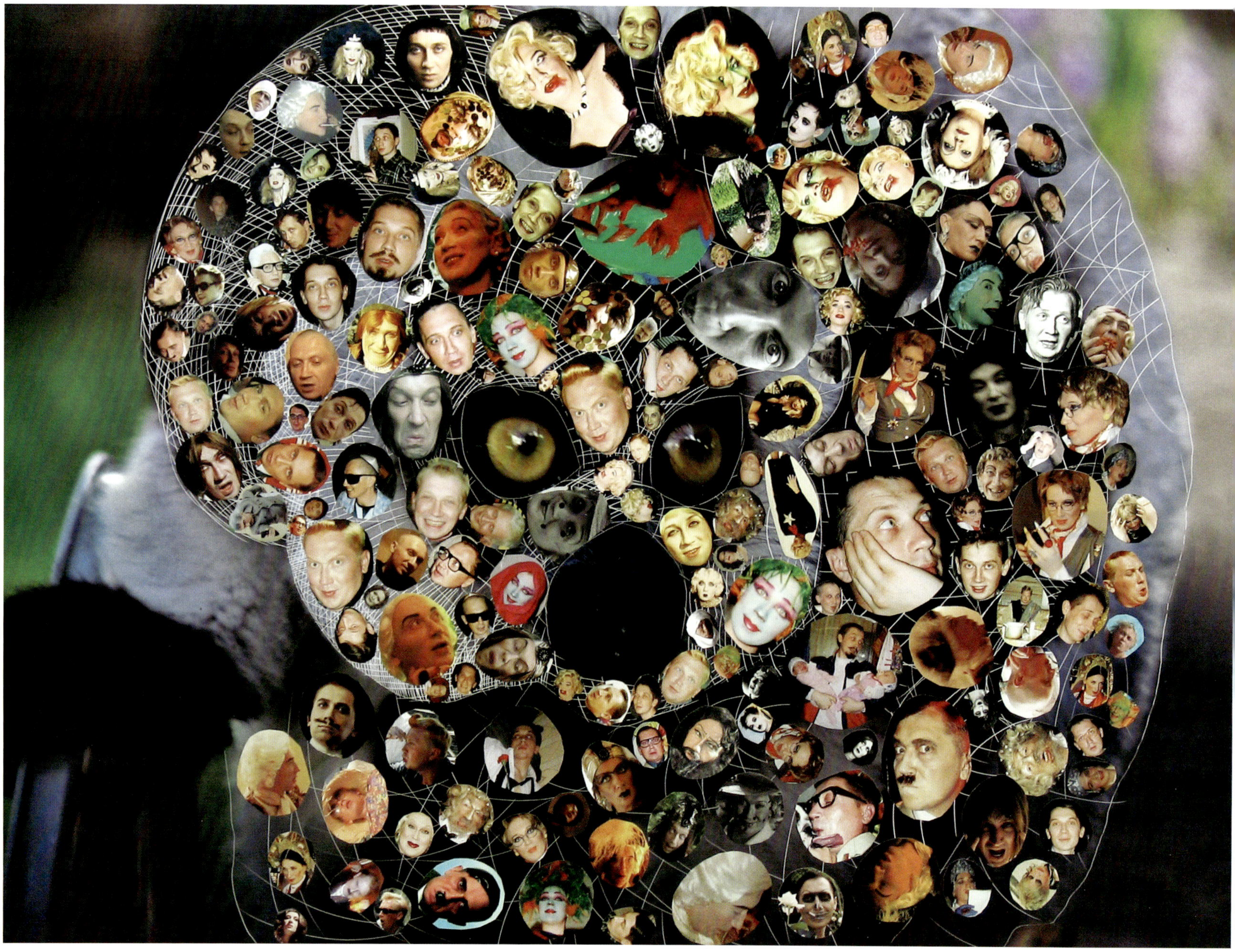

above
Every beast has a bit of Monroe, 2006
Digital photograph, collage
60 x 80 cm
© Vladimir Mamyshev-Monroe
Courtesy of XL Gallery, Moscow

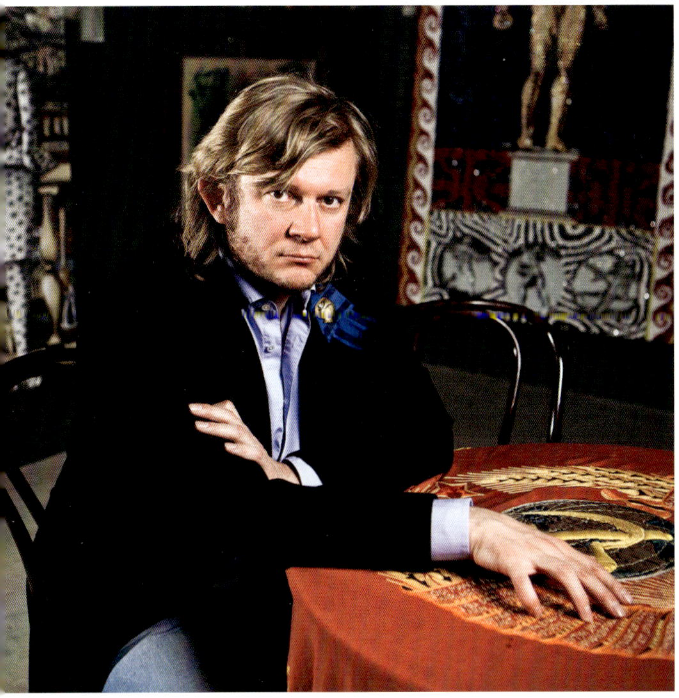

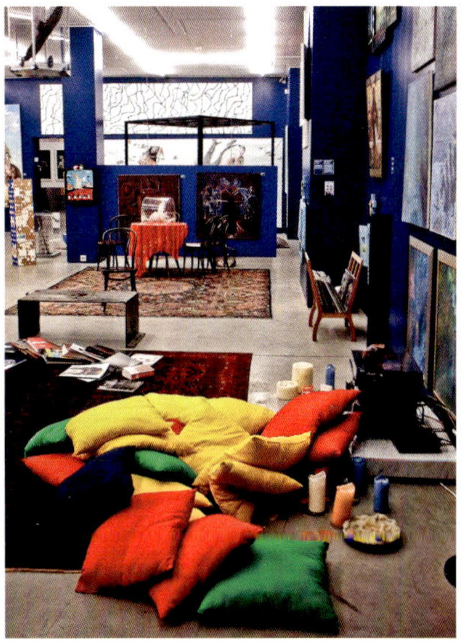

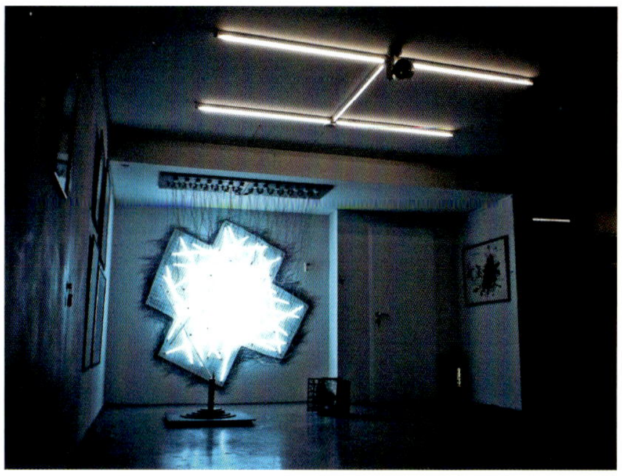

Igor Markin was born in Moscow in 1967. Following the collapse of the Soviet Union, he went into the construction business, subsequently becoming a plastics magnate.

Collecting is Markin's passion. As a child he bought old cameras and coins; later on he purchased works by the nonconformists Anatoly Zverev and Vladimir Yakovlev. Around 2002, Markin started to buy art in earnest, quickly amassing one of the largest collections of Russian contemporary art in Moscow. Totalling over a thousand works, it took five years to assemble; Markin bought directly from artists and from Moscow galleries, international auctions and private collectors, at one point acquiring four new works per week. As he began collecting at a time when few others were interested in the field, he was able to buy important works.

Markin's collection covers the late 1940s up to the present day and includes paintings, graphics, photography, objects and installation art. Highlights include notable works by Eric Bulatov from the early 1990s and several by Semyon Faibisovich, including his 1997 portrait of Lev Rubinstein, the only likeness of one of his contemporaries made by the painter. Markin also has a representative collection of work by painters of the '60s generation, most notably Vladimir Weisberg, Dmitry Krasnopevtsev, and the post-Soviet duo Dubossarsky and Vinogradov, with their ironic take on Soviet Realism represented by the great *Andy Warhol in Moscow* (2000).

In 2007 Markin set up Art4.ru, the first completely privately funded, independent art gallery in Moscow, to show post-war unofficial and contemporary Russian art. His 600-square-metre museum houses roughly a third of his collection and is a strong reflection of its founder's personality and drive. Over time the space has evolved into something far more personal than a conventional gallery; initially accessible to the public, it is now open by appointment only. The exhibition space, crammed with artworks from floor to ceiling, serves as an extension of Markin's home and office, with sofas, armchairs, large floor pillows and music playing in the background.

Markin's mission with Art4.ru has been to bring contemporary art into the public arena, with the goal of making contemporary Russian art fashionable and popular. He likes to compare his achievements to those of Russia's two most famous twentieth-century collectors, Shchukin and Morozov – whose French Post-Impressionist pictures are today in the State Hermitage Collection, St Petersburg – or to the great nineteenth-century patron Pavel Tretyakov, whose collection forms the core of the State Treyakov Gallery, Moscow. As Markin puts it, 'I really love art and I love collecting paintings. Now I have more than 700 paintings; Tretyakov had less even at the time of his death.'

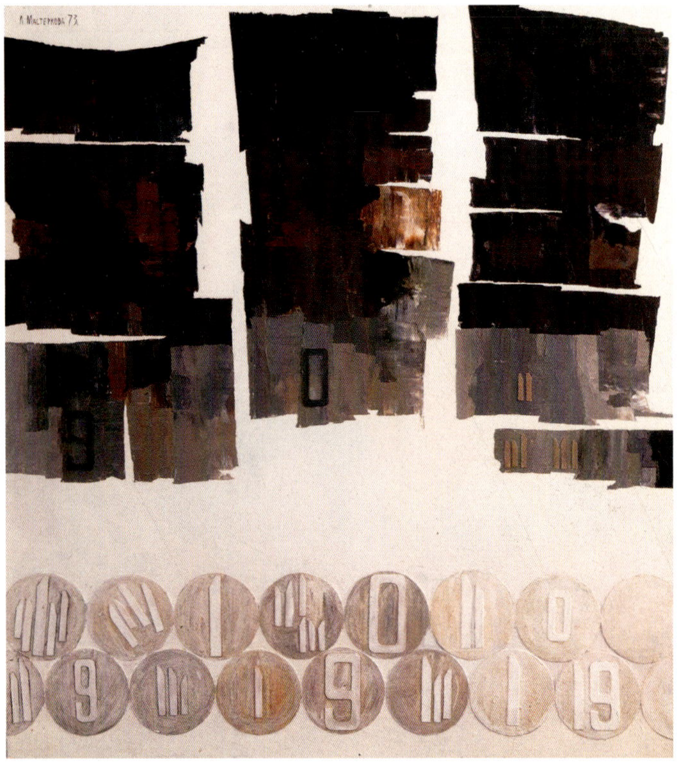

Abstract painter and graphic artist Lydia Masterkova was born in Moscow in 1927. She studied at the Surikov Institute, Moscow, graduating in 1950. Together with her husband, the painter Vladimir Nemukhin, she was a member of the Moscow underground. Along with Oscar Rabin, Evgeny and Valentina Kropivnitsky, and others, Masterkova and Nemukhin organised themselves into a community of artists and poets living and working in a small village near Moscow; they were known as the Lianozovo Group. Masterkova took part in the 'Bulldozer Exhibition', during which the authorities demolished and confiscated her paintings. A year later she moved to France, initially residing in Paris and finally moving to the village of Saint-Laurent, where she lived as a semi-recluse, continuing to paint until her death in 2008. She visited Moscow regularly in the post-Soviet period, and in 2006 the State Tretyakov Gallery, Moscow, held an important retrospective of her work.

Abstract art was outlawed in Russia from 1932, when the Union of Artists was founded and the Soviet Realist school was introduced, so until the late 1980s it remained an aspect of dissident practice. That it was often combined with religious imagery is evident in Masterkova's application of fragments of liturgicial robes to her paintings. Having worked in her early career with bright colours and fluid forms, her mature paintings combine Russian avant-garde geometry with American post-war abstraction, examples of which she first saw exhibited in Moscow in 1959. Shying away from a totally expressive approach, Masterkova's abstract art is more controlled. Graphics make up a strong part of her oeuvre, typically taking the form of circular black-and-white collages with Indian ink on paper.

top
Composition, 1973
Oil on canvas, collage
102 x 77 cm
Courtesy Margarita and Victor Tupitsyn Archive

above
Abstract Composition, 1970
Oil and sand on canvas with impressions
125 x 100.1 cm
Courtesy of Sotheby's

facing page
Composition, 1985–6
Chinese ink, collage
72.9 x 57.9 cm
Collection of Ravenscourt Galleries
Courtesy of Sotheby's

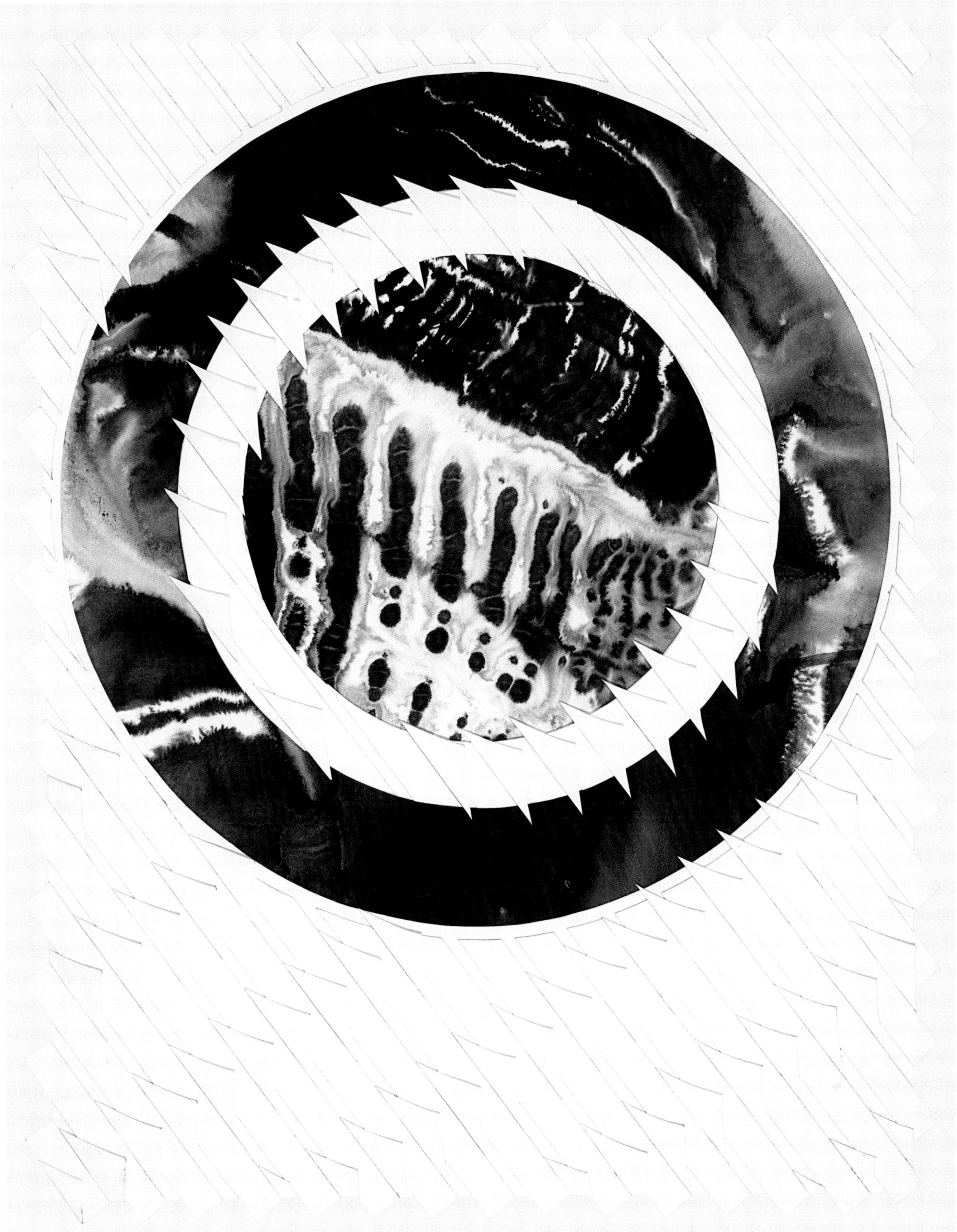

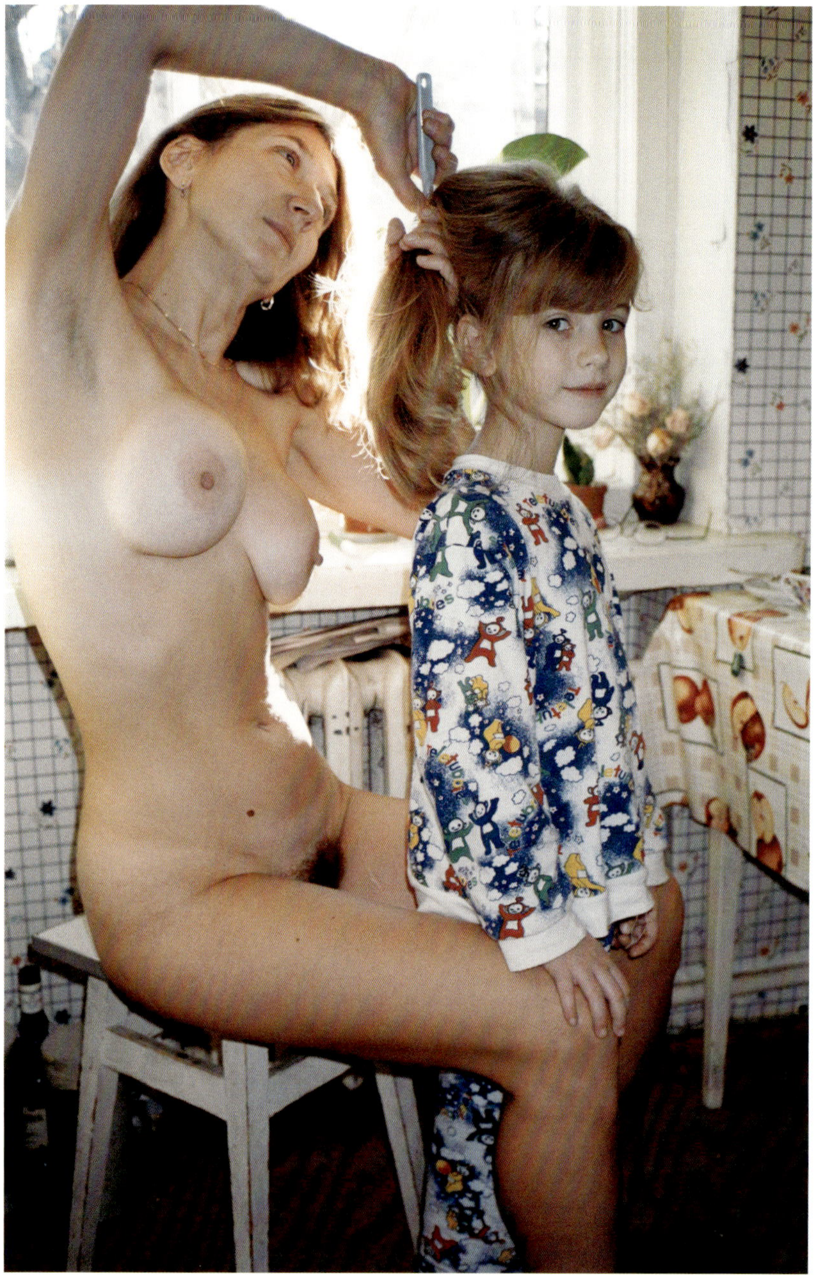

Photographer Boris Mikhailov, who was born in Kharkov, Ukraine, in 1938, lives and works in Berlin. Self-taught, he initially trained as an engineer but was dismissed by the KGB from his job in a camera factory when naked photographs of his wife were discovered at work. He then supported himself as an underground entrepreneur and showed his photographs in small galleries and private apartments. Beginning in the mid-1990s, he exhibited openly in both Ukraine and Western Europe, winning numerous awards, including the Hasselblad Award (2000) and the Citibank Private Bank Photography Prize (2001). His photographs are held in major museum collections worldwide, including the Museum of Modern Art, New York, and the Saatchi Gallery, London.

Mikhailov's work is typically arranged in large thematic series, with his subjects ranging from intimate, tender, often erotically charged family portraits to raw, frequently disturbing documentaries of urban life. He employs a variety of techniques and styles, including hand-coloured black-and-white photographs, superimposition, amateur snapshots, blue and brown colouration, and panoramas. During the 1970s, Mikhailov explored the visual language of Soviet official imagery and culture in series such as Red (1968–75) – exploring the use of the colour red in everyday life – and Luriki (1971–85) – a conceptual work in which he hand-coloured found photos. In Sots Art (1975–8), influenced by the Moscow underground movement of the same name, Mikhailov's photos faithfully reflect official ideology but are heightened by bold multi-coloured retouching. In *I Am Not I* (1992) the artist turned the lens on his own naked body in a startling series of grotesque postures.

During the 1990s, Mikhailov created several important series which document the social breakdown of the Soviet Union, including On the Ground (1991) and At Dusk (1993), both of which depict gritty urban panoramas. In 1996 he won a DAAD Fellowship. Immediately after his return to Kharkov from Berlin, he started working on his most celebrated series, Case History (1997–8), consisting of over 500 life-size colour photographs showing homeless people on the margins of post-Soviet society. Despite epitomising the tradition of social-documentary photography, this series makes use of age-old Christian iconography such as the *Pietà* to stage the artist's anonymous homeless heroes like actors. The series' power is due to its raw insights into social disintegration. Mikhailov often shoots his subjects naked, thus revealing scars and sores, and introducing an element of the erotic.

above
Naked, 2003
C-print
151 x 99 cm
© Boris Mikhailov
Courtesy of Matthew Bown Gallery

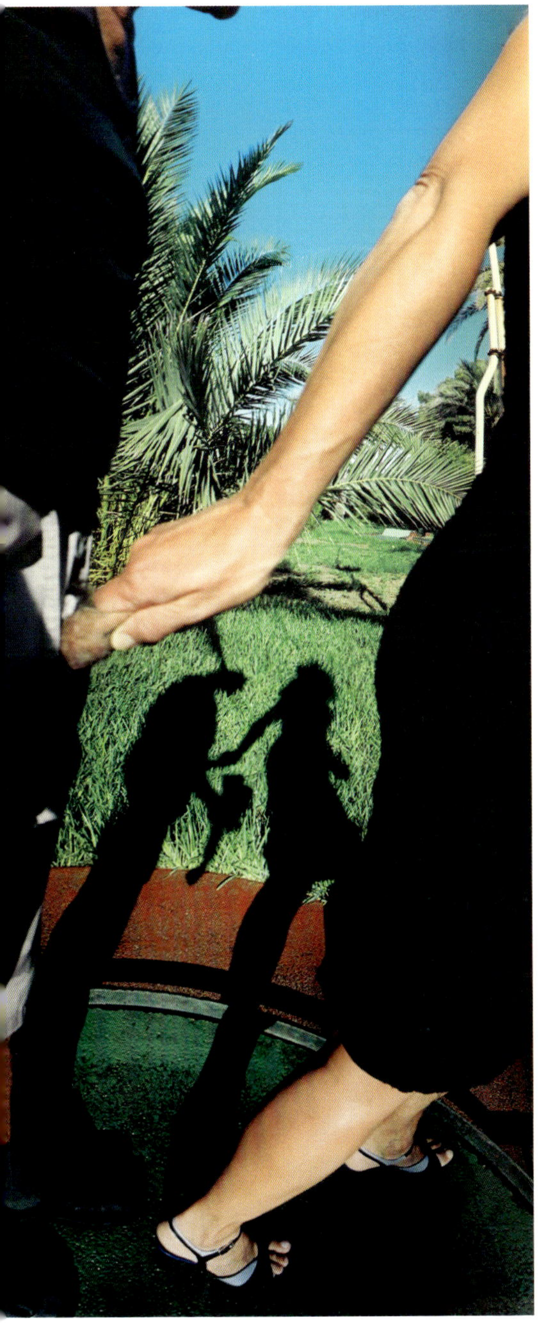

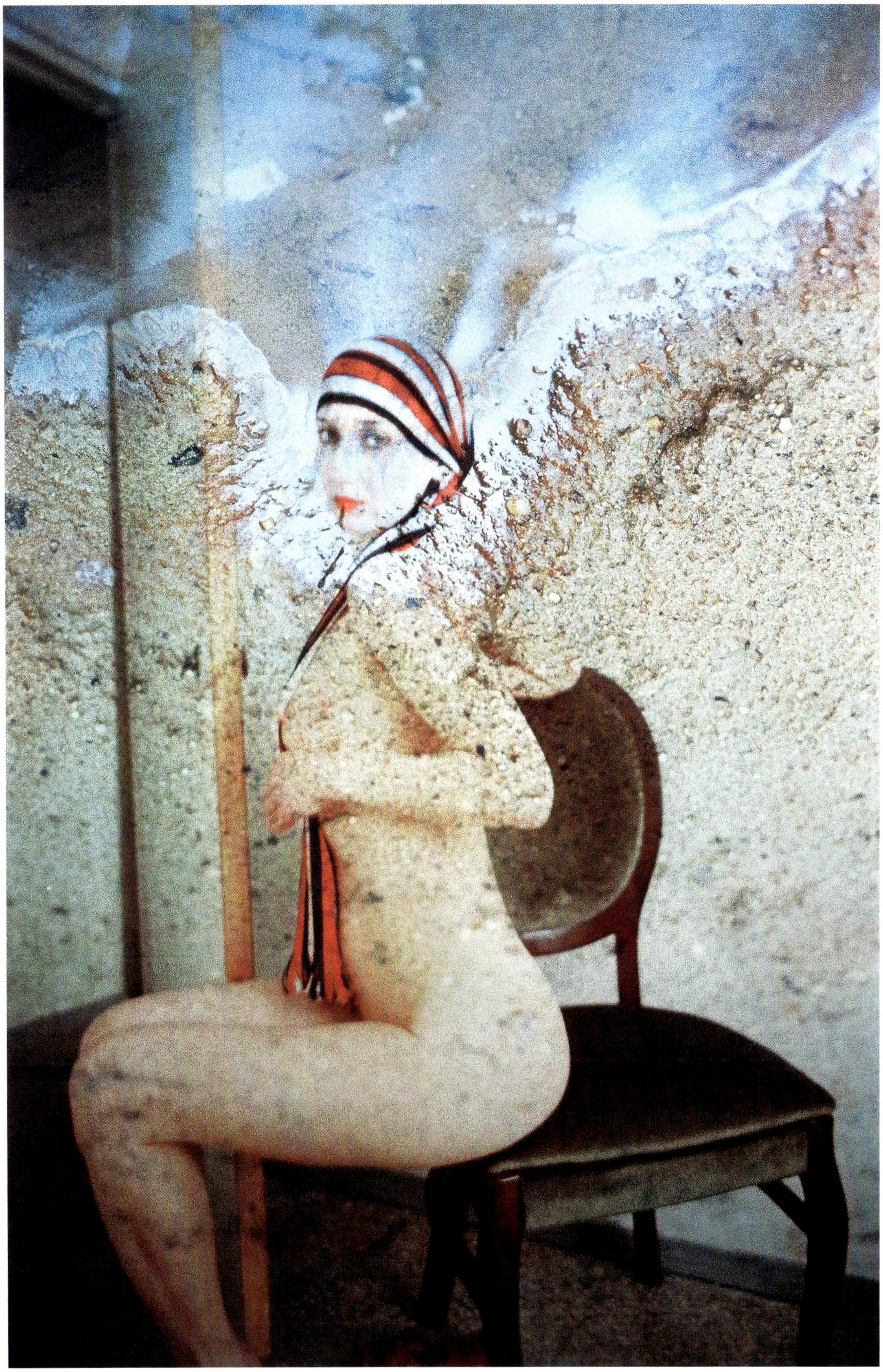

left
Untitled, 2001
C-print
198 x 83 cm
© Boris Mikhailov
Courtesy of Matthew Bown Gallery

above
From the series Superimpositions,
Late 1960s–70s
C-print, 1/5
147 x 107 cm
© Boris Mikhailov
Courtesy of Victor Bondarenko

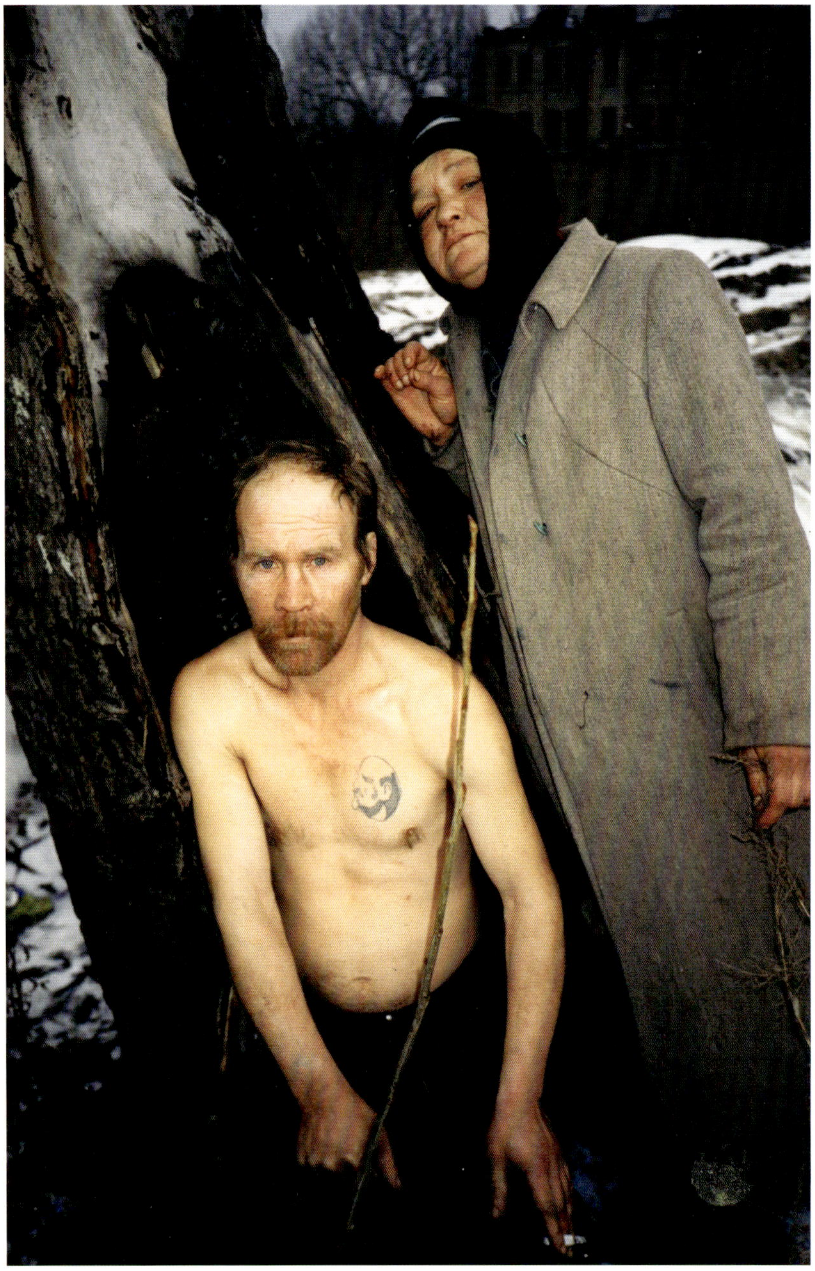

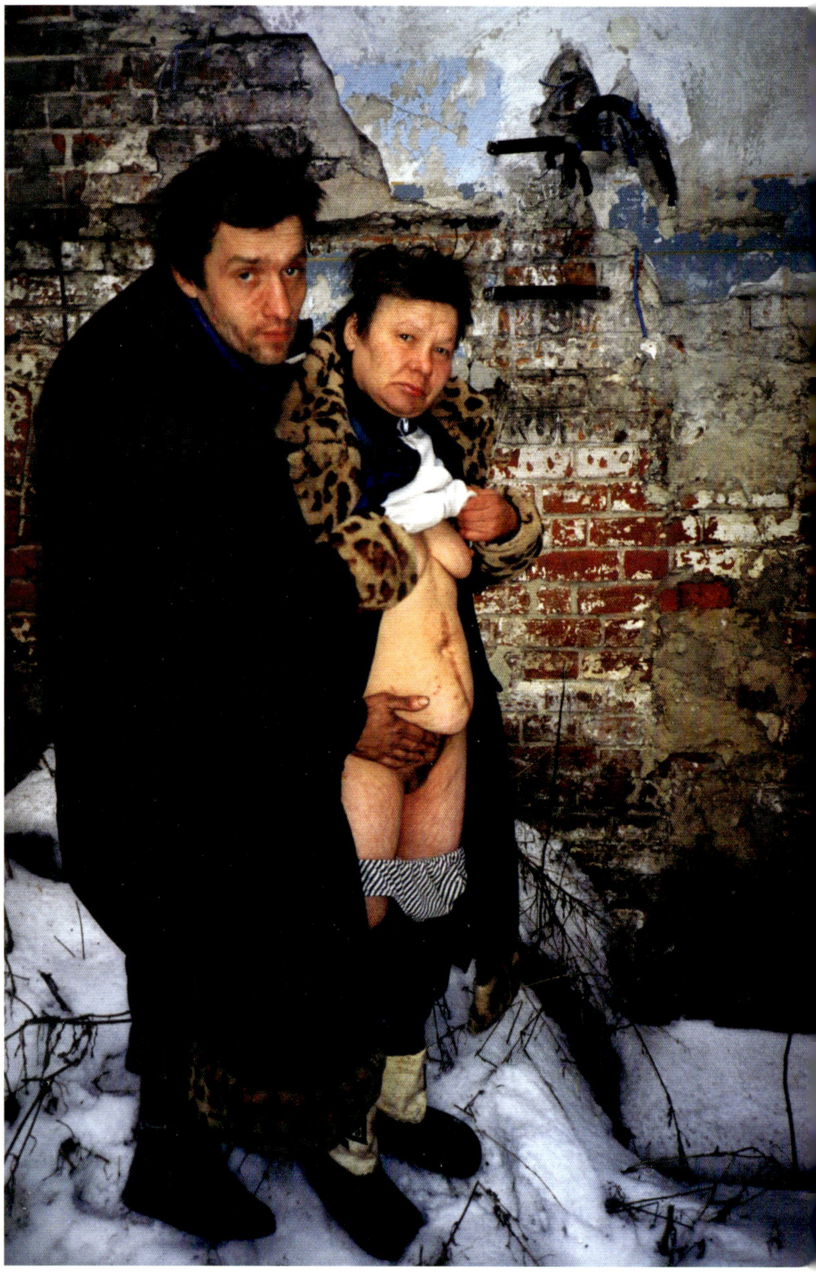

both images
Case History,1997–8
C-print from negative
190 x 127 cm

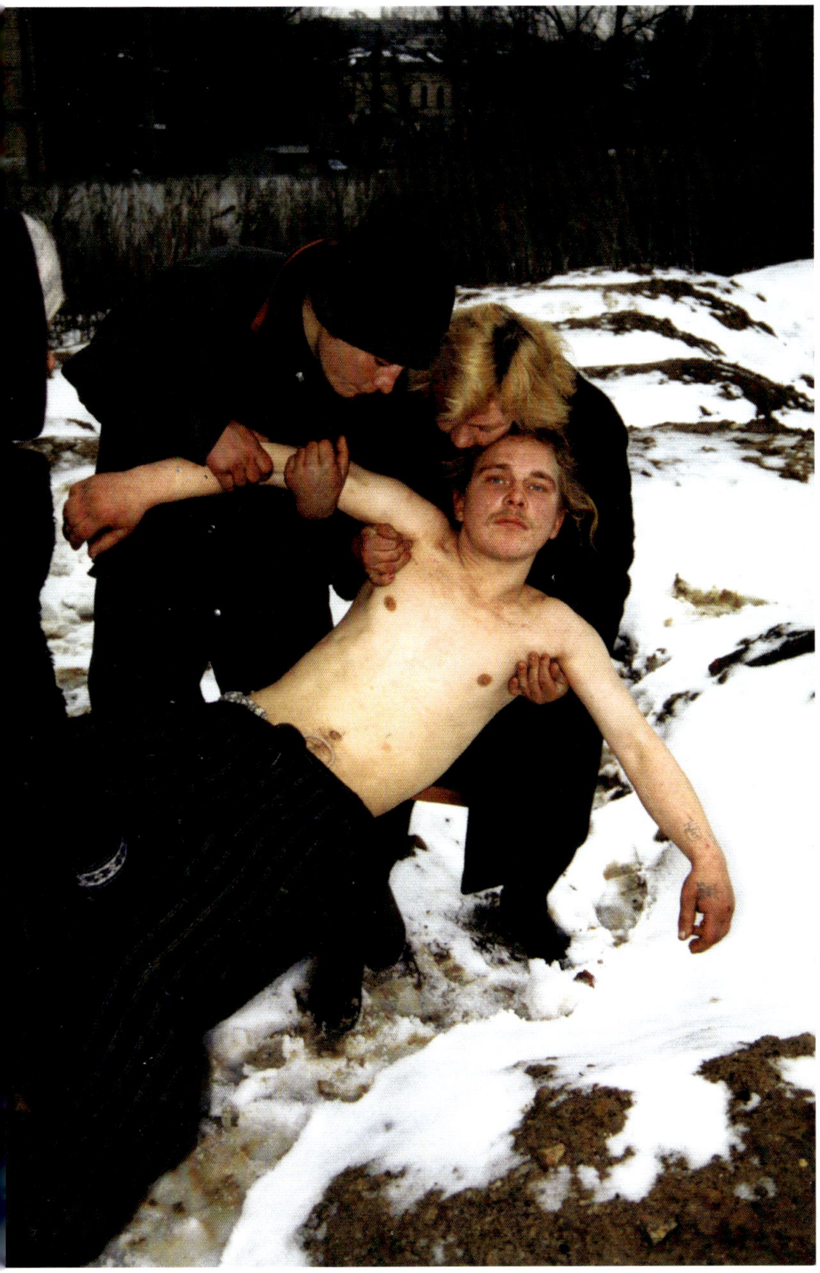

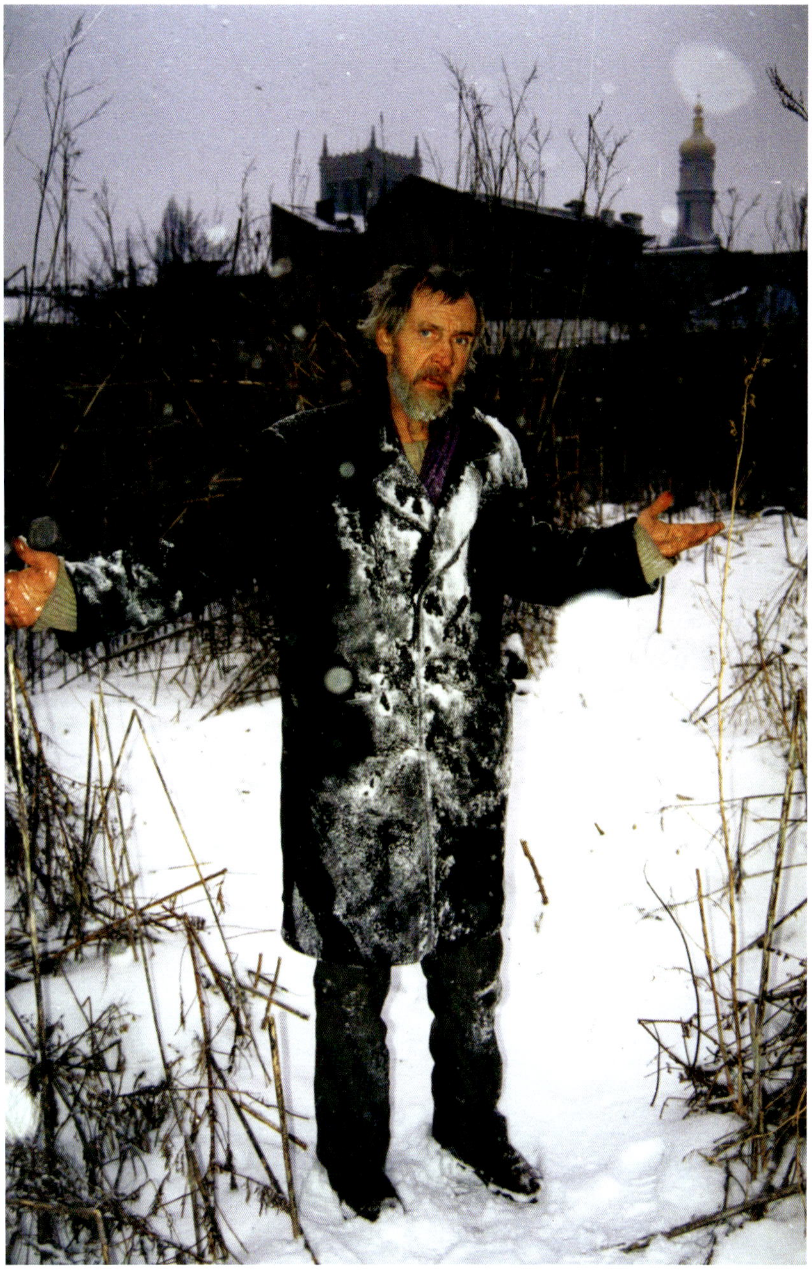

both images
Case History,1997–8
C-print from negative
190 x 127 cm

Courtesy of Boris and Vita Mikhailov

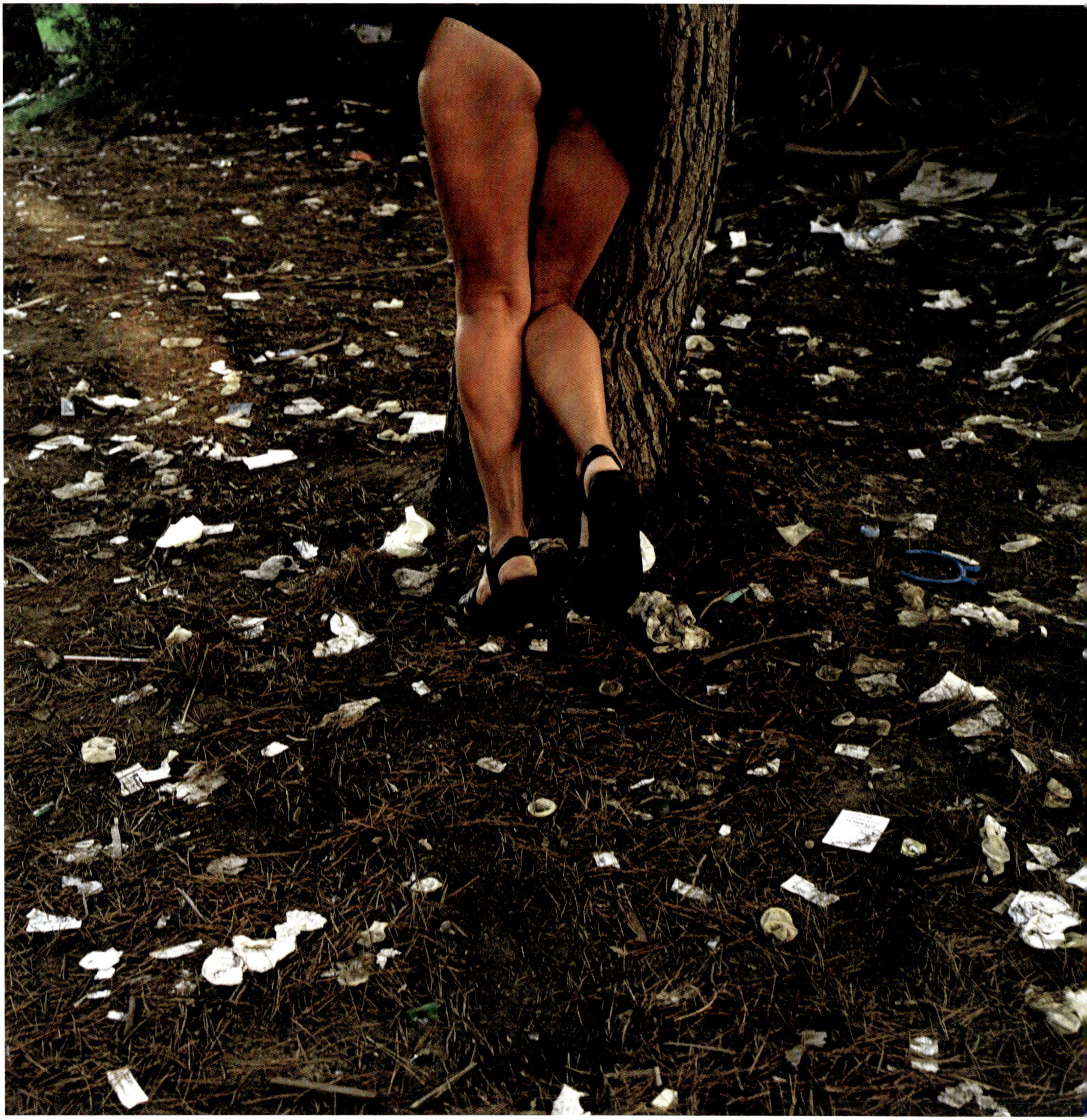

above
Untitled (Park in Marbella), 2007
C-print
100 x 100 cm

Courtesy of Matthew Bown Gallery

Boris Mikhailov

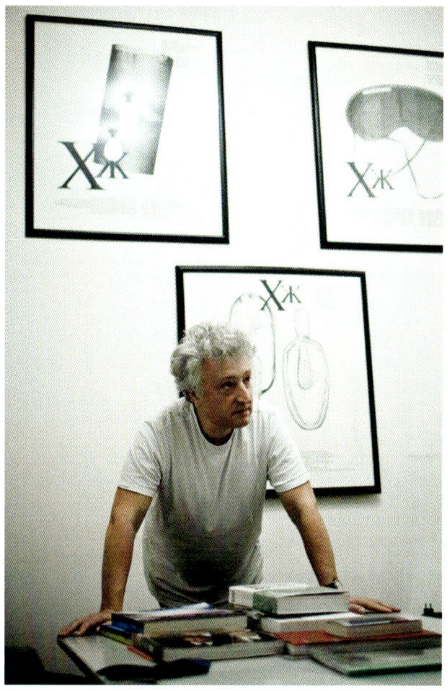

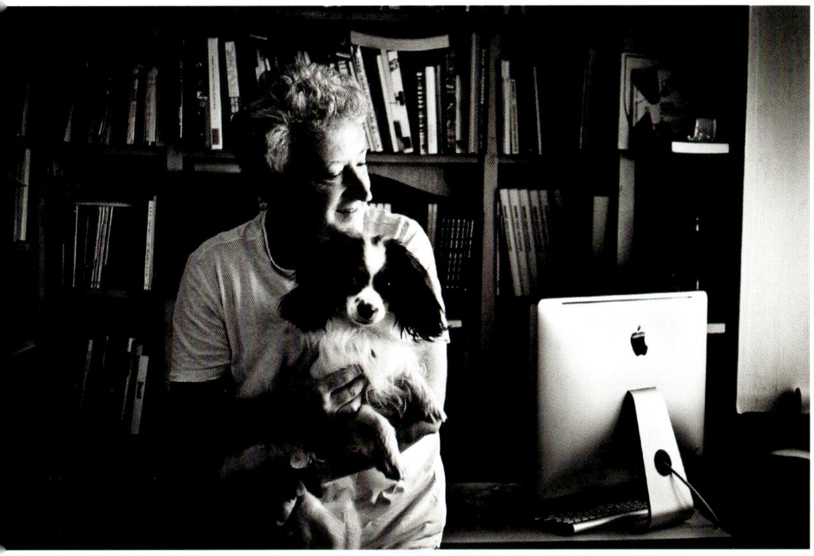

'ictor Misiano (born in 1957) is a curator and art :ritic based in Moscow. From 1980 to 1990 he vas curator of contemporary art at the Pushkin Auseum of Fine Arts, Moscow, and from 1992 to 997 he was director of the (now closed) Centre or Contemporary Art, also in the captial. In 996 he co-curated Manifesta-1 at the European 3iennale of Contemporary Art in Rotterdam nd Amsterdam. He has also curated many iennales on his own, including Venice, Istanbul, São Paulo and Valencia. Misiano was co-founder of the *Moscow Art Journal*, of which he is :urrently editor-in-chief. In 2005 he organised he first-ever Central Asian exhibition at the 'enice Biennale, and two years later he realised *Progressive Nostalgia: Art from the Former JSSR*, which toured Europe. Misiano, who vas awarded an honorary doctorate from the Jniversity for Art and Design Helsinki, divides is time between Moscow and Italy.

Surveying the past quarter of a century, Misiano acknowledges that the 1990s were a time of transition in both social and artistic terms that forced people to live for the moment. All of that changed in the 2000s, when artists began to reflect on the transformations of the preceding decade and question their cultural heritage. It was during the 2000s that 'the establishment of connections with the Soviet past became crucially important, a process that was both conscious and subconscious.' Misiano observes that 'it has become fashionable in Russia today to think of this experience in post-colonial and post-Soviet terms. I think it is absolutely justified; of course they are not identical, but still there is a lot in common.'

Today Misiano sees artists looking for answers: 'I would say that now the crucial topic has become the future: what kind of vision should we have?' This complex challenge is one that the Russian art scene, given its current resources, will struggle to negotiate. The rate of change is creating problems for the whole of post-Soviet society: 'This is a country without clear understanding of what its aim is and what its position is in the world, except for that of its gas and oil production.' Interestingly, Misiano sees Soviet cultural heritage as a hidden strength. The Soviet art world, though academic, 'was up-to-date with its age in terms of methodology and it understood its position in society'. He senses a complete rejection of intellectual values, observing that culture essentially has become part of the entertainment industry. Although this might be said for the rest of the world as well, for Misiano the Russian situation is more acute because of an unquestioning rush to accept Western values. He feels that there is a need to set boundaries between productive and regressive culture: 'I think the major problem nowadays is a certain moral majority which really is willing to be uncritical, which is refusing any form of criticism, which is blindly and uncritically accepting that the position of art in contemporary society is to be close to money and power.' Misiano's aim is to help to re-establish some level of critical distance.

Born in the late 1950s, Misiano belongs to the generation who knew the countries of Central Asia, in which he is especially interested, as part of the Soviet Union. He believes that there is a certain common experience which could be a basis for communication beyond national cultures: 'I want to go beyond multiculturalism to find some common ground.' His stance regarding the cultural interests of the West and Russia is similarly open: 'The borders between West and East are a fiction. It is a time when we should insist on the opposite; we should think about what we have in common and not on what separates us.'

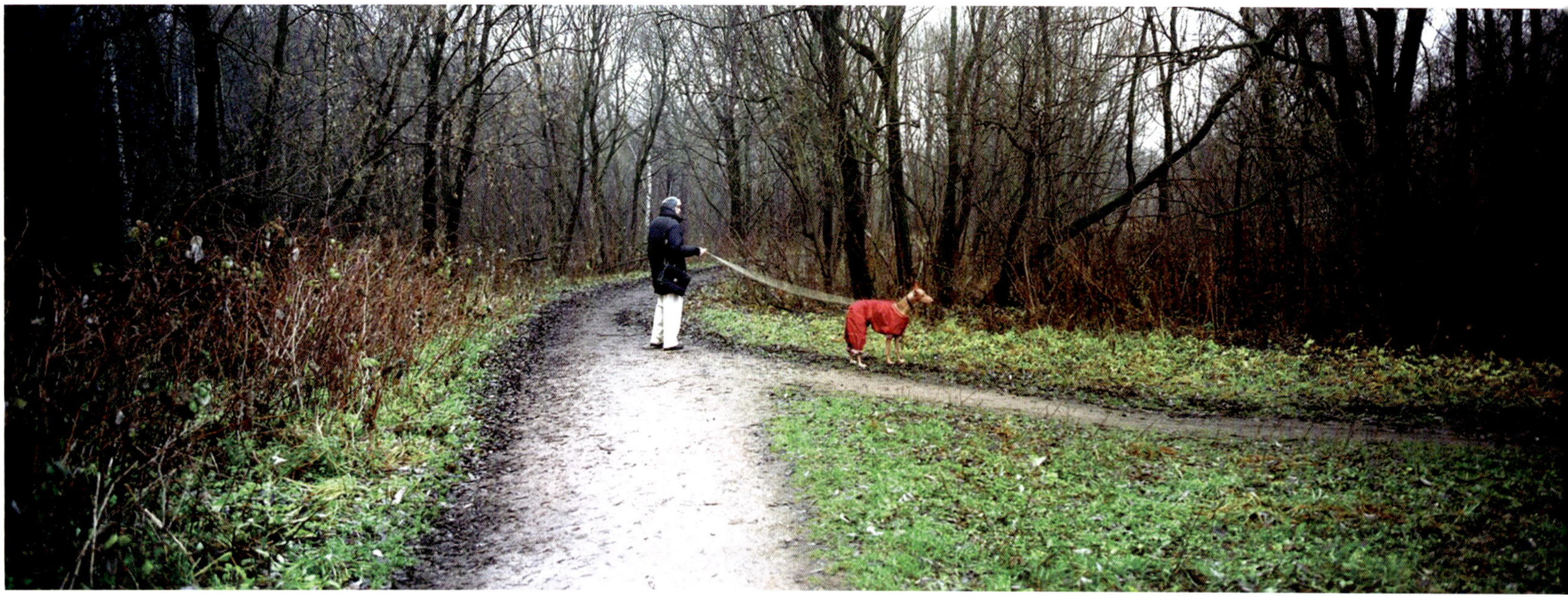

above
Walk in Losiny Ostrov, 2009
Digital photograph
Dimensions unknown
© D. Novgorodova
Private collection
Courtesy of the artist

Andrei Monastyrsky

Conceptual artist and poet Andrei Sumnin was born in Petsamo in the north of Russia in 1949. He adopted the pseudonym 'Monastyrsky' as a pen name when he began writing poetry while still a child. Monastyrsky moved to Moscow in the 1970s and studied Modern Languages at Moscow State University, graduating in 1980. He is a leading exponent and theoretician of Moscow Conceptualism, and in 1976 co-founded the influential Collective Actions group, of which he is still a member. During the 1980s he exhibited in several important underground shows in Moscow, including *APTART* (1982) and the Avantgardist Club's *KLAVA*. In 2011 he represented Russia at the Venice Biennale. His works can be found in several Russian public and private collections, including the State Tretyakov Gallery, the Moscow Museum of Modern Art and the Stella Art Foundation. He lives and works in the capital.

Monastyrsky explores language and the meaning of art in a diverse practice embracing performance art, installation and 'action objects'. The latter are a type of concrete interactive poetry that originated in the 'visual poetry' of the Russian Futurists. Both Monastyrsky's action objects and his performance works typically require the viewer's participation. His most famous action object is *Finger: Or Pointing at Oneself like an Object Outside of Oneself* (1978). It consists of a simple black box with a small hole through which the viewer can insert his hand to point at him- or herself. Thus the observer becomes part of the artwork. These works play on the interaction of text, image, space and time. Monastyrsky has described his work as 'an existential experience. It is a process so it does not play a role.' Despite the intellectual nature of his art, he speaks of his process as having its origin in moments of pure inspiration.

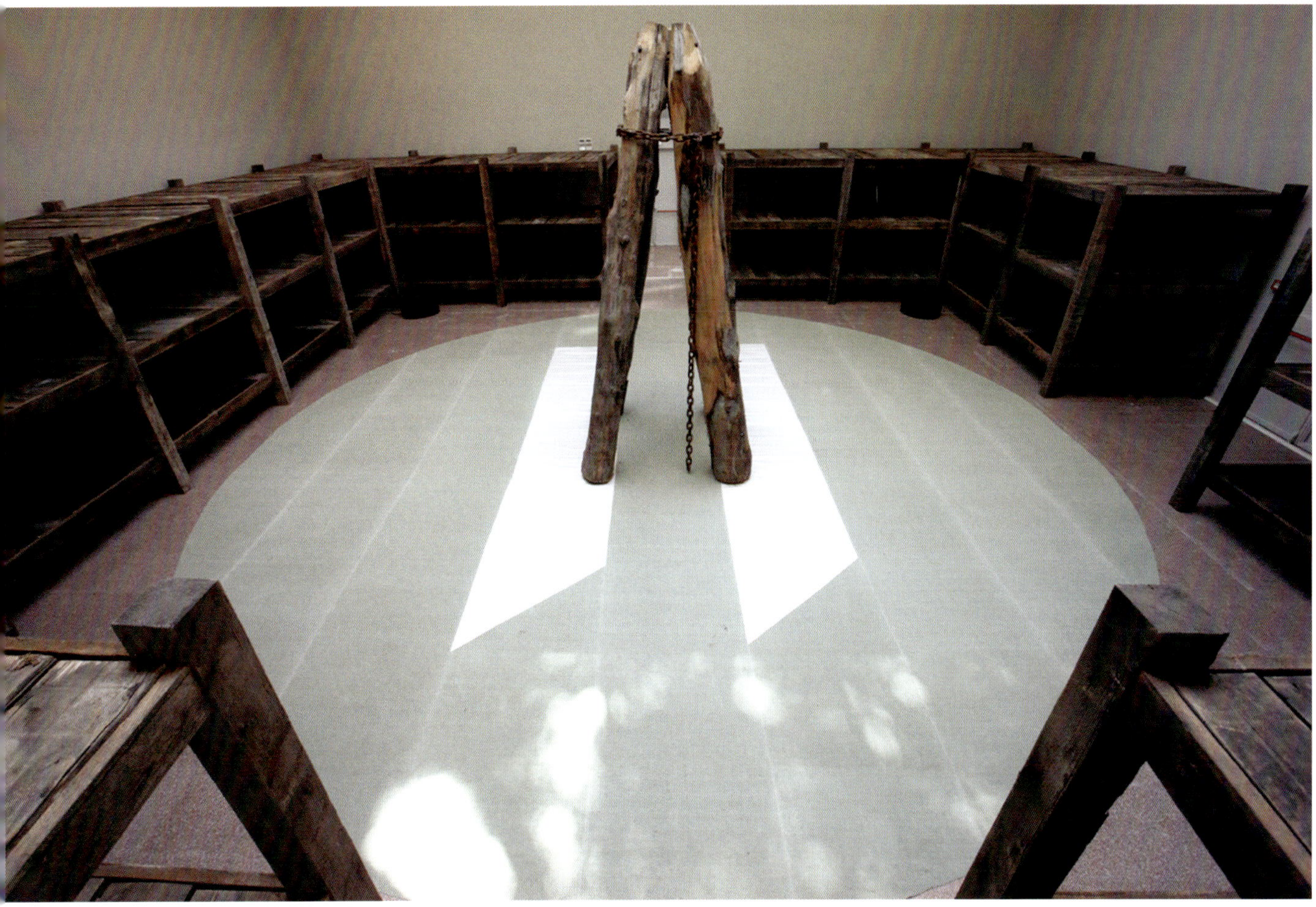

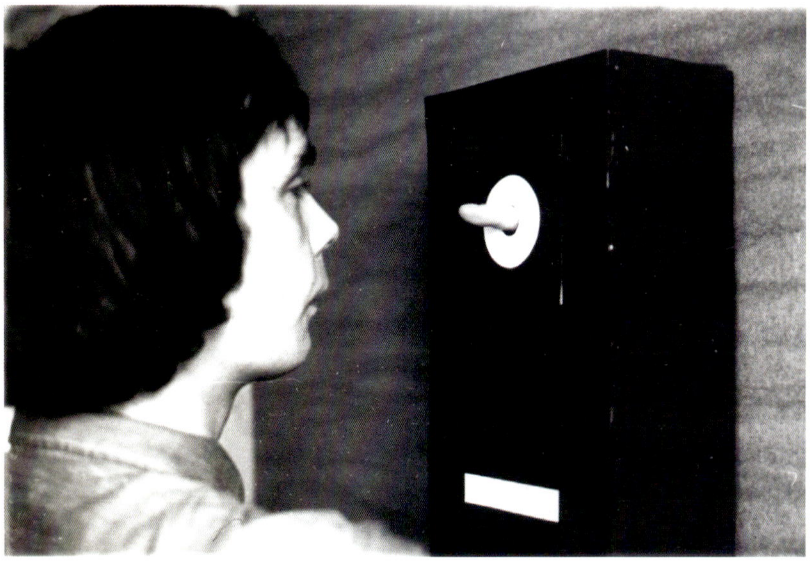

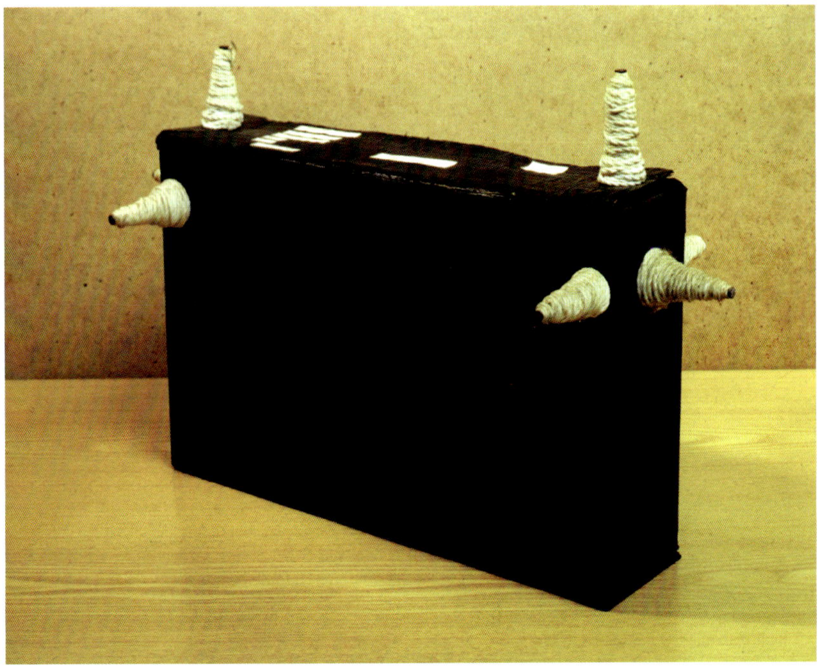

top
11, 2011
Installation with wood, iron
1200 x 1200 cm
© Andrei Monastyrsky
Private collection
Courtesy of the artist

left
The Music of Consent, 1986
Action object with cardboard, string, nails, text
55 x 35 x 22 cm
© Andrei Monastyrsky
Private collection
Courtesy of the artist

above
Finger, 1978
Action object with plywood, text
40 x 17 x 10 cm
© Andrei Monastyrsky
Private collection
Courtesy of the artist

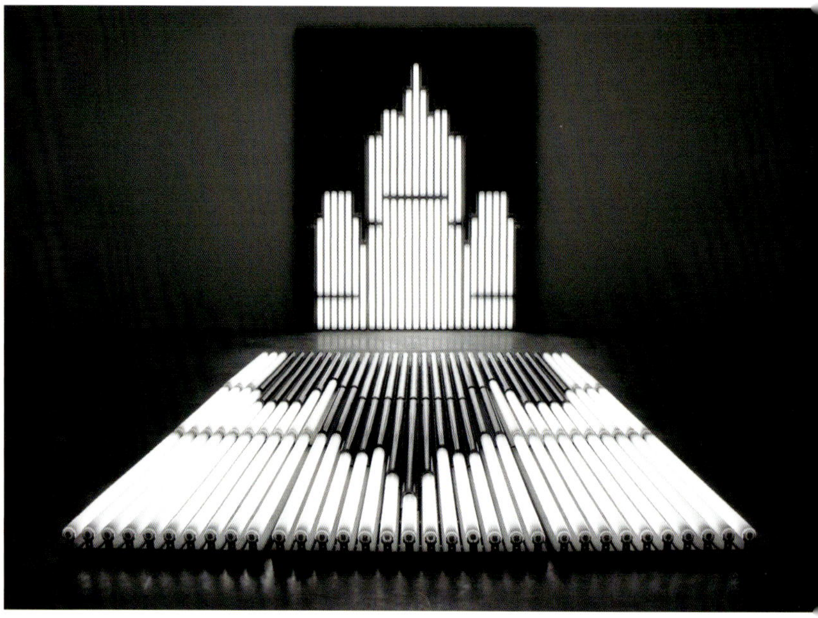

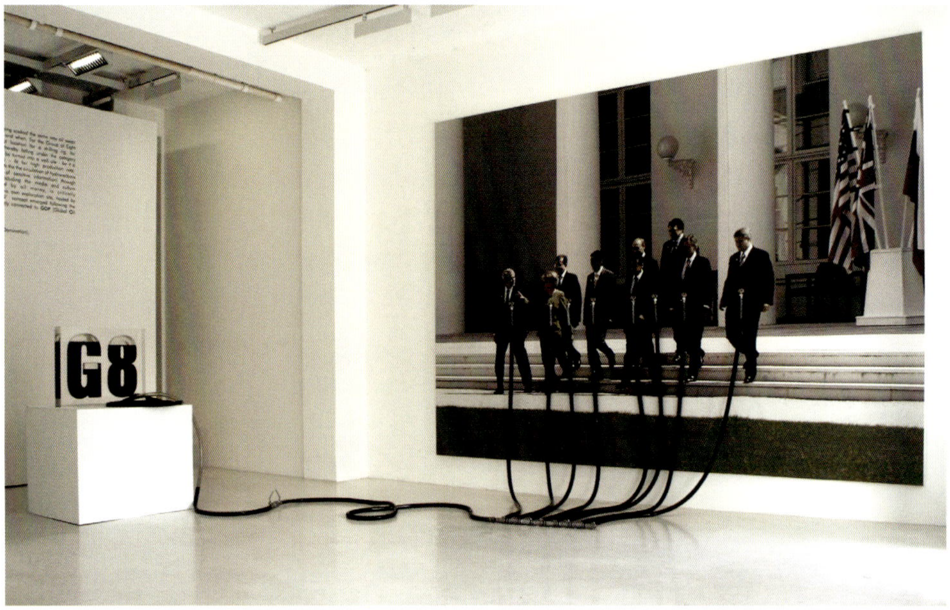

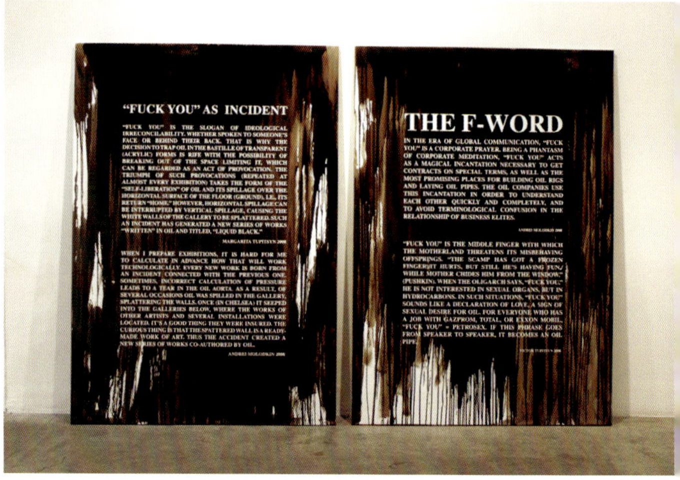

Andrei Molodkin

Andrei Molodkin was born in Boui in 1966 and currently divides his time between Paris and Moscow. After completing obligatory military service in 1985–7, he graduated from the Department of Architecture and Interior Design of the Stroganov Higher College of Art, Moscow. His work has been widely exhibited in solo and group exhibitions in Moscow, St Petersburg, New York, Miami, Paris and Zurich. In 2009, he represented Russia at the Venice Biennale.

Ranging from monochromatic large-format drawings to technically complex petrol-filled sculptures, Molodkin's work has acquired notoriety due to its politically charged language and the materials he uses. His army experience, with its '[cycle of] death and rebirth', left a lasting impression on the artist. Works such as *Democracy* (2005) and *Untitled* (2006) demonstrate his critical attitude 'towards the use of resources as a means of self-enrichment, towards the exploitation of resources, both human and natural ...' Molodkin manipulates linguistic and visual clichés and stereotypes to deconstruct the vocabulary of contemporary culture and unmask the void of meaning behind them.

Despite the critique inherent in his oeuvre, Molodkin proposes a notion of freedom and protest through his choice of media. His engagement with geopolitics is most evident in his sculptures in which acrylic blocks, which take the shape of currency signs or religious symbols and figures such as Christ and the Virgin Mary, are hollowed out and the resulting negative space filled with crude oil. The source of the crude – often Iraq, Iran or Chechnya – is as polemical as the political and popular symbols that it 'occupies'. Undeniably aesthetic and influenced by modernism and Russian avant-garde practice, Molodkin's works achieve a state he likes to describe as 'political formalism', offering a timely statement on human waste exploitation, corporate and political greed, and the misappropriation of democratic values.

top
Installation view of New Architecton, Garage Centre for Contemporary Culture, Moscow, 2010
Steel rails, transparent acrylic tubes filled with crude oil, neon tubes
375 x 375 x 15 cm (each)
© Andrei Molodkin
Rosenblum Collection

above left
Installation view of G8, Kashya Hildebrand Gallery, Zurich, 2007
Acrylic block and transparent tubes filled with crude oil, C print on canvas
© Andrei Molodkin
Rosenblum Collection

above
The F-Word, 2008
Installation view of *Guts à la Russe*, Orel Art Gallery, Paris
Crude oil and text on canvas
230 x 170 cm (each)
© Andrei Molodkin
Collection of the artist

facing page
Installation view of Liquid Modernity, Orel Art UK Gallery, London, 2009
Acrylic transparent tubes filled with crude oil, pumps, compressors
© Andrei Molodkin
Collection of the artist

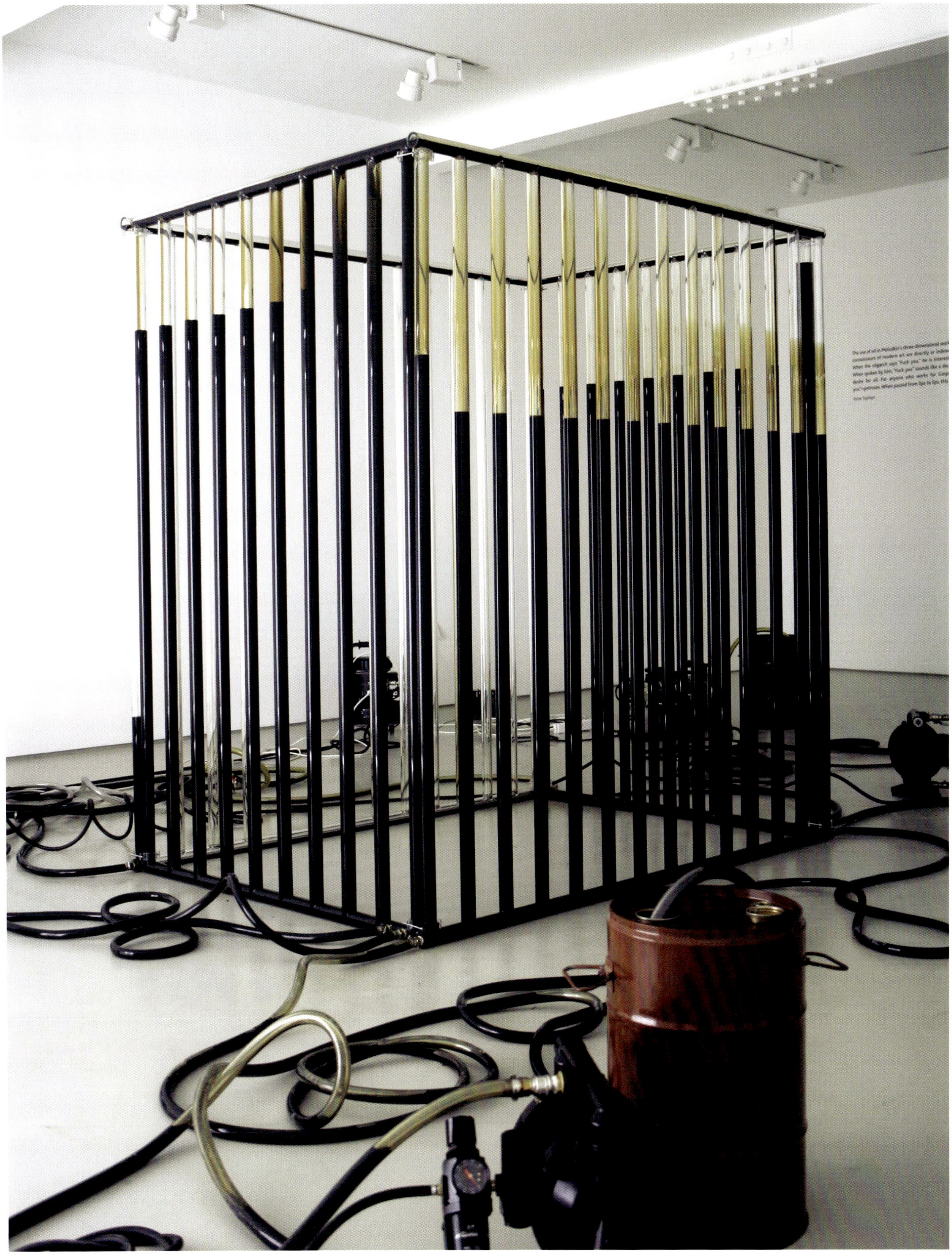

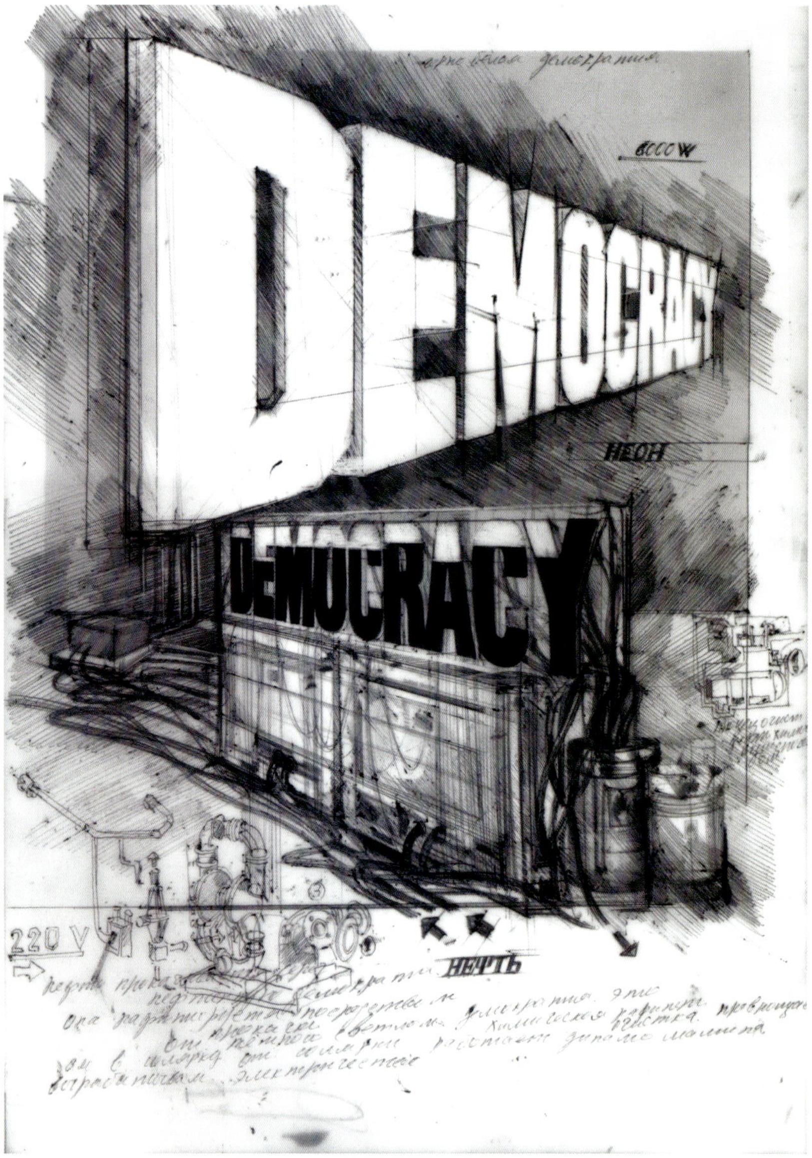

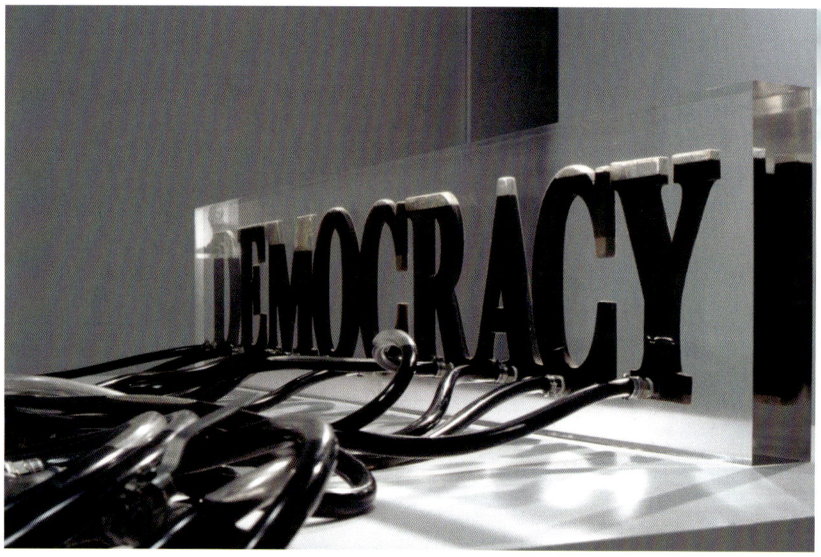

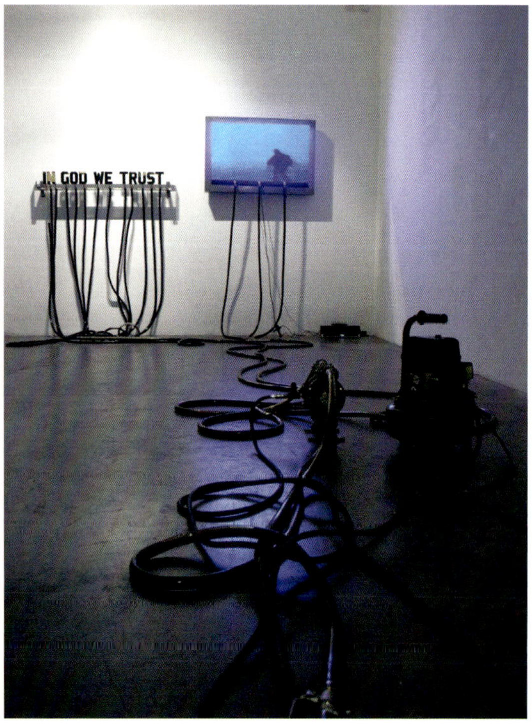

top left
Drawing for the installation Democracy, 2008
Biro on tracing paper
45 x 35 cm
© Andrei Molodkin
Courtesy of the artist
Collection of the artist

left
In God We Trust, 2008
Installation view of *Liquid Black*,
Galleria Pack, Milan
Acrylic block and transparent tubes filled
with crude oil, pump, compressor, video
© Andrei Molodkin
Private collection

above
Democracy, 2005
Acrylic block and transparent tubes
filled with crude oil
40 x 180 x 15 cm; tubes 300 cm
© Andrei Molodkin
Courtesy of the artist
Private collection

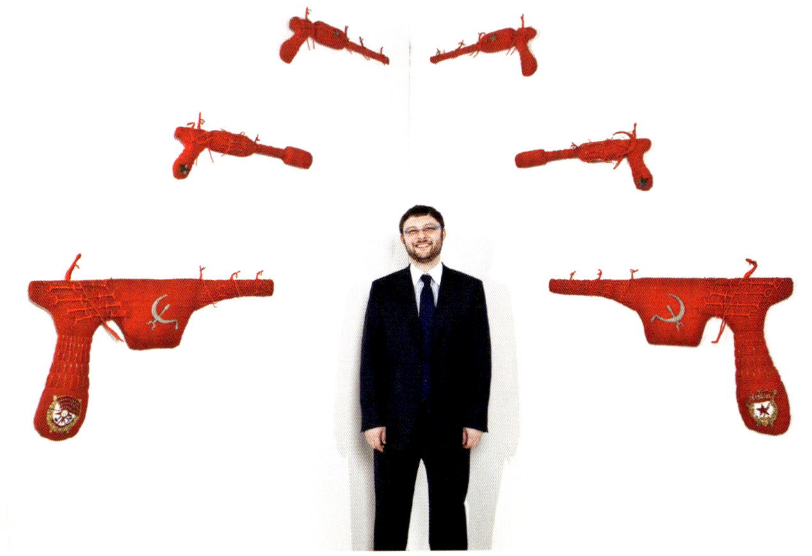

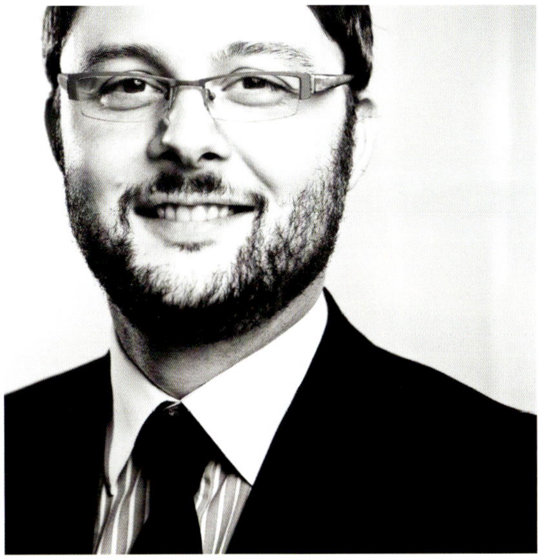

The Moscow Museum of Modern Art, founded in 1999 by Zurab Tseretelli, is run today by his grandson Vasily Tseretelli. MMOMA was the first museum to open in Russia after the break-up of the Soviet Union, its aim being to bring modernism and contemporary art together. It exhibits both international and Russian art and is funded by the Moscow municipal government.

Zurab Tseretelli, born in Tbilisi, Georgia, in 1932 and himself an accomplished sculptor and painter, is president of the Russian Academy of Arts. Vasily Tseretelli is an energetic, talented arts manager with a creative vision and many plans for MMOMA's development as a leading arts institution. Born in Tbilisi in 1978, he went to the US to study at the School of Visual Arts, New York, from 1999 to 2002. He returned to Moscow after graduation at the invitation of his grandfather to take up the post of director of MMOMA. Both Tseretellis live in Moscow, whose cultural life has been strongly affected by this small Georgian dynasty.

Under Vasily's directorship, MMOMA has become one of the most successful large-scale museum projects in post-Soviet Moscow. Having expanded quickly over the past decade, it occupies five buildings in the city centre. The main building is an eighteenth-century Neoclassical mansion on Petrovka Street which once belonged to the Moscow merchant Gubkin. There is also a building on Ermolaevsky Lane and a gallery on Tverskoi Boulevard, and parts of the museum are located in the Russian Academy of Arts and the Zurab Tseretelli Studio Museum. MMOMA welcomes around half a million visitors annually, attracting tourists and Muscovites alike.

MMOMA's initial holdings were built around Zurab's private collection, which numbered around 1,500 works at the time. Currently the museum is expanding its holdings of Russian contemporary art through an exhibitions programme funded by the Moscow municipality. Zurab's collaborations with former mayor Yuri Luzhkov and his links to local government have resulted in a wealth of other creative projects which have transformed the city. He has himself designed and executed several large-scale urban sculptures, including the controversial monument to Peter the Great on the Moskva River, and he redesigned the steps of the Okhotny Ryad complex in the heart of the city.

When speaking about his grandfather, Vasily Tseretelli emphasises their complex and close collaboration: 'Whatever he envisioned, I am trying to implement that. I have managed the museum for a decade now; I have a certain vision that I am going towards. He agrees in general with my exhibition plans, but how the overall strategy evolves is my own vision.' The two men share a passion for collecting: 'My grandfather has a great collection of icons, rifles, antique medals and antiquities; I have always collected stamps and pens. I also started to collect art in the 1990s, when we first planned to set up the museum.'

One of the strengths of MMOMA's post-war collection lies in its focus on art from countries of the former Soviet Union such as Ukraine, Azerbaijan, Armenia and Georgia. Vasily maintains that, despite the enormous cultural diversity of these countries, during the Soviet period they shared the same arts education based on Academic Realism, although there were also dissidents working outside of the system and evidencing greater aesthetic diversity. In fact MMOMA has an important collection of Soviet nonconformist art by Ilya Kabakov, Vladimir Nemukhin, Komar and Melamid, and others. And there is a Georgian emphasis: important works by the modernist Niko Pirosmani and by Vasily Shukhaev, a major Russian painter who emigrated to Georgia after the Revolution and taught at the Tbilisi Academy of Fine Art, are included.

Looking towards the next phase in MMOMA's development, Vasily Tseretelli sees a need for consolidation, fewer shows and greater ambition in the curatorial sphere, perhaps in a new dedicated space: 'We need a cinema, a conference centre; we need to build further our institutional presence with a research centre and more home-grown curators.' He reveals the extent of his and his grandfather's ambition with a sense of comfortably worn determination: 'The challenge is to make an institution that will survive one, two, even three hundred years from now.'

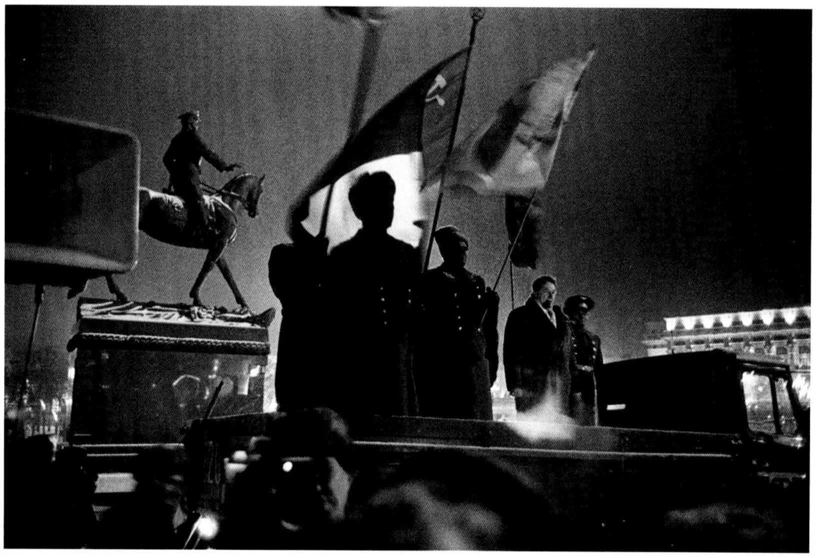

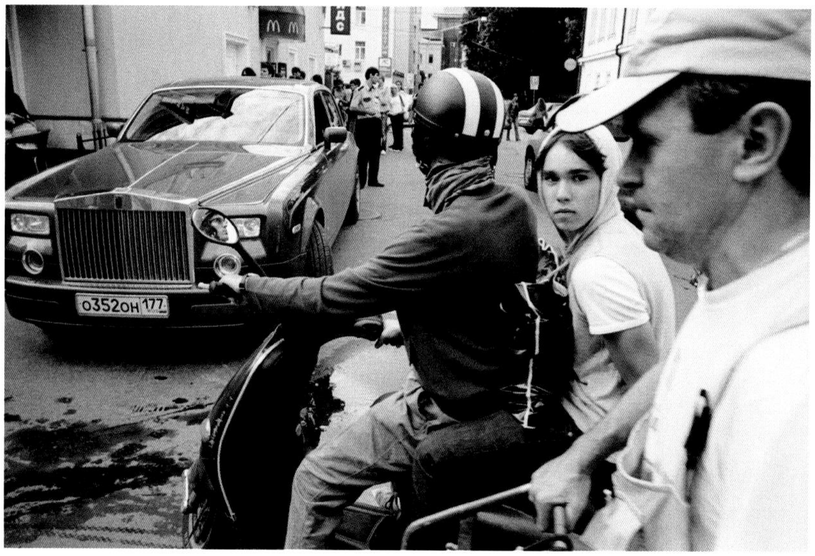

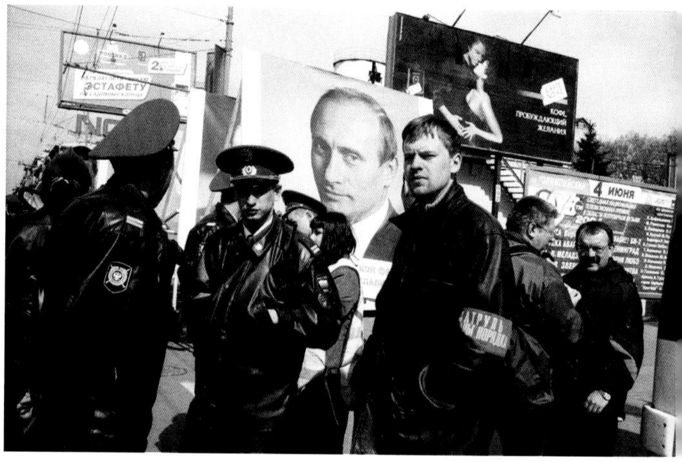

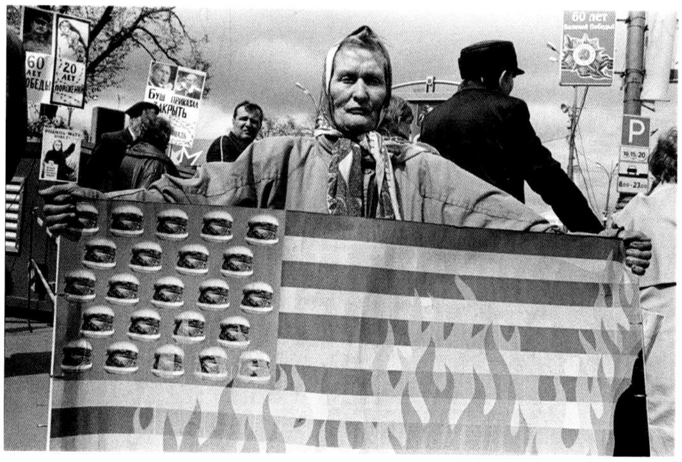

Photographer Igor Moukhin was born in Moscow in 1961. Although he did not pursue a formal art education, in 1986 he spent a year attending classes at the studio of Alexander Lapin. Moukhin prefers traditional methods and shoots with a Leica. During the late 1980s he spent time with Moscow's leading underground rock musicians, including Victor Tsoi and Boris Grebenschikov, whom he photographed. He also joined the unofficial Immediate Photography group founded in 1987 by Alexei Shulgin, another of whose members was the Ukrainian Boris Mikhailov. Moukhin began working on the street, where he developed a penchant for photographing the youth of the new Russia against the backdrop of the Soviet past. His work has been published in *TimeOut*, *Elle*, *Vogue*, *Harper's Bazaar* and *Le Monde*, and is held in the collections of the Museum of Modern Art, New York; the Multimedia Art Museum, Moscow; and the National Centre for Contemporary Art, Moscow. He lives and works in the Russian capital.

top left
From the series Moscow, 23 February 2000
Gelatin silver print
30 x 40 cm
© Igor Moukhin
Courtesy of XL Gallery, Moscow

above left
From the series Moscow, 2008
Gelatin silver print
30 x 40 cm
© Igor Moukhin
Courtesy of the artist

top
From the series Moscow, 2005
Gelatin silver print
30 x 40 cm
© Igor Moukhin
Courtesy of XL Gallery, Moscow

above
From the series Moscow, 2005
Gelatin silver print
30 x 40 cm
© Igor Moukhin
Courtesy of XL Gallery, Moscow

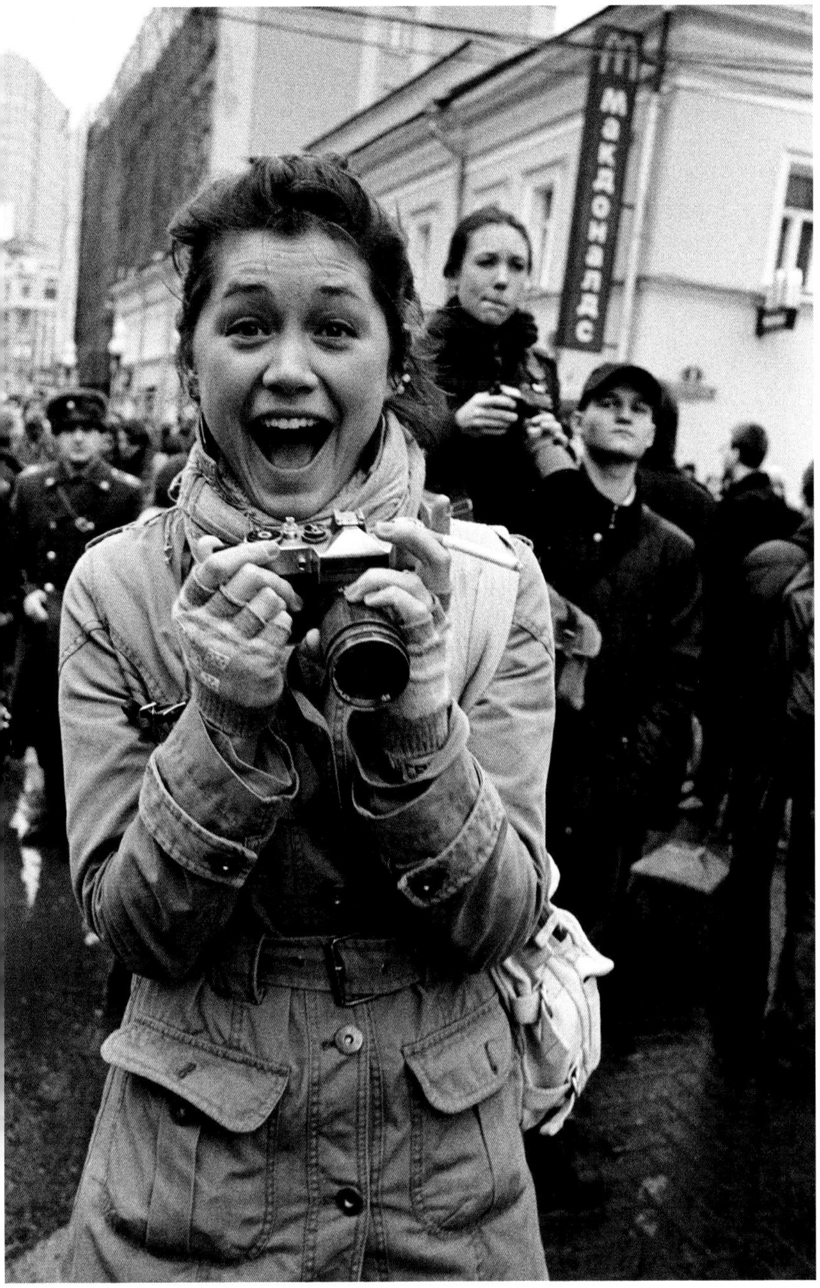

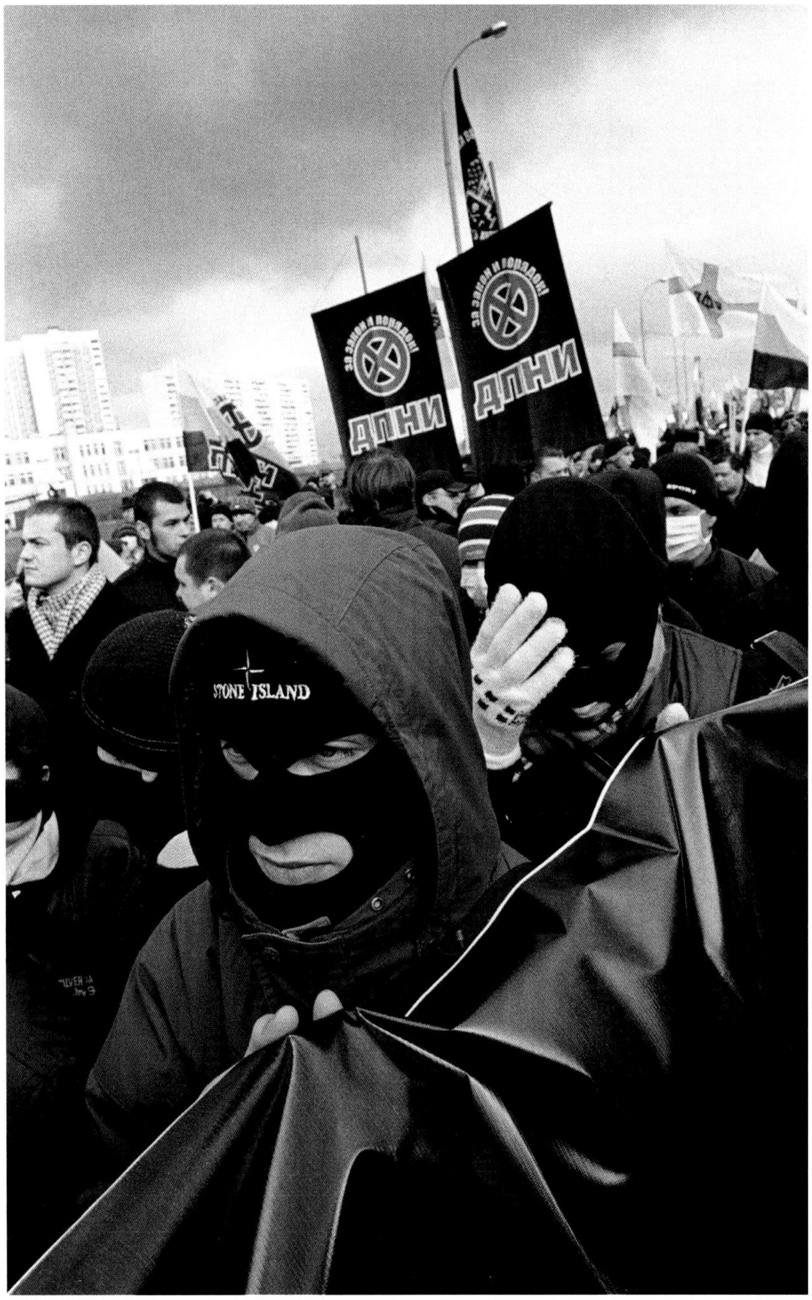

above
From the series Moscow, 2009
Gelatin silver print
30 x 40 cm
© Igor Moukhin
Courtesy of Galleria Impronte
Contemporary Art, Milan

right
From the series Moscow, 2009
Gelatin silver print
30 x 40 cm
© Igor Moukhin
Courtesy of XL Gallery, Moscow

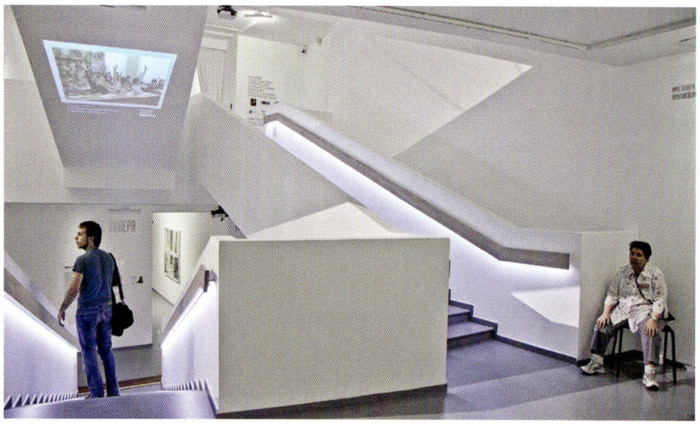

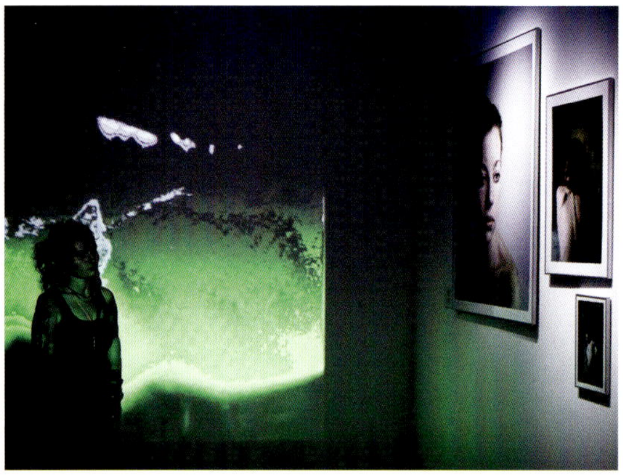

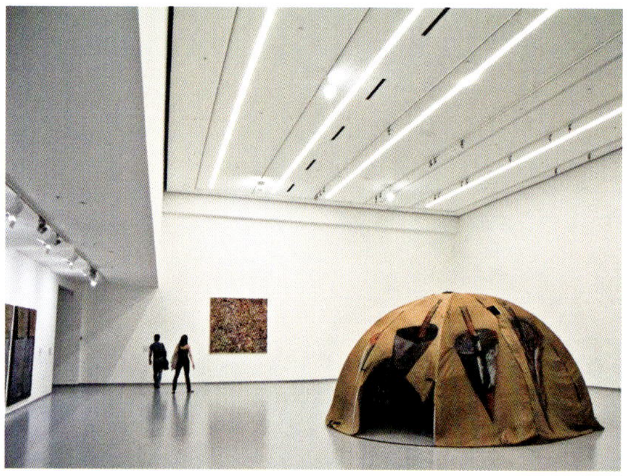

The Multimedia Art Museum was established in Moscow in 2001 as an extension of the Moscow House of Photography (founded in 1996). The museum specialises in all types of multimedia art, from photography to video art, Internet art, video and tape recordings of performances, and Action art. In 2010 the museum opened in a multi-storey custom-built, state-of-the-art exhibition space on the Ostozhenka in the centre of Moscow, its interior architecture reminiscent of Constructivist design.

The Multimedia Art Museum's evolution from the Moscow House of Photography has shaped its history and remains a part of its institutional ethos. Photography continues to be a strong force as a crucible for the exploration and representation of new types of creative media. The institution's founder is Moscow-born curator, critic and art historian Olga Sviblova, known as the 'saviour of Russian photography' for setting out single-handedly during the early post-Soviet era to establish a national archive of photography. At the time, photography was underappreciated as an artistic genre; certainly the significance of the country's own avant-garde photographers was not fully recognised.

The Multimedia Art Museum's photographic archives are extensive, numbering over 80,000 works. There are many rare historical and iconic images by early Russian photographers, as well as a growing archive of contemporary digital ones. The highlights of the collection include works by Alexander Rodchenko, the pioneer of Russian photography in the 1920s and '30s. There are also significant holdings of work by El Lissitsky, Boris Ignatovich, Alexander Grinberg and Nikolai Andreev. The museum has a growing collection of work by contemporary photographers, including Sergei Borisov, Vladimir Kuprianov and AES+F.

In the decade since its foundation in the late 1990s, over 500 exhibitions have been curated and organised by the Multimedia Art Museum and its parent, the Moscow House of Photography. The exhibitions programme includes shows arranged to travel to the Russian regions and to Europe. Notable exhibitions have been *Russia: The 20th Century in Photography* (Moscow, 2000) and *Contemporary Russian Photography* (Nizhny Novgorod, 2001). Among recent shows in the new premises have been *Tazio Secchiaroli: The First Paparazzi* (2011) and *Arte Povera in Moscow* (2011).

In 1996 the Moscow House of Photography pioneered a new international photo biennale. The first show comprised nearly a hundred separate exhibitions co-hosted by major Moscow museums, including the Pushkin Museum of Fine Arts and the State Tretyakov Gallery. Another international arts festival launched in 1999 by the Moscow House of Photography, Fashion and Style in Photography, continues to be supported today and illustrates how the museum's scope reaches into the world of fashion.

Alongside its exhibition programme, the Multimedia Art Museum is a resource for research. Russia's first photographic library, which contains publications on the history and theory of photography, rare exhibition catalogues, and monographs on photographers, both Russian and international, was opened there. The museum has brought about a change in public perception regarding the importance of new media, in particular the appreciation of the country's role in the history of twentieth-century photography. Among its aims is a reintegration of Russian photographic achievements into the international history of art.

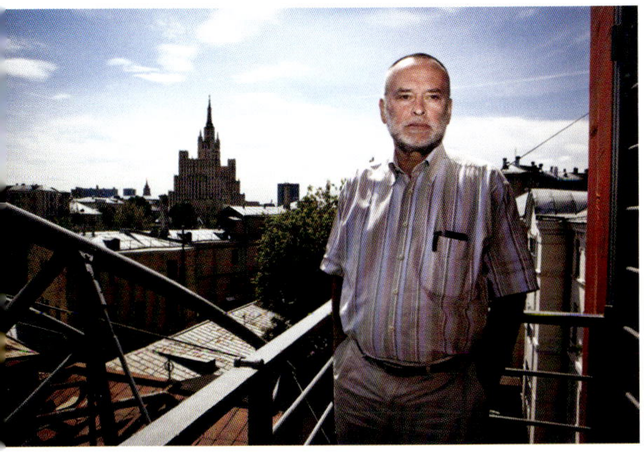

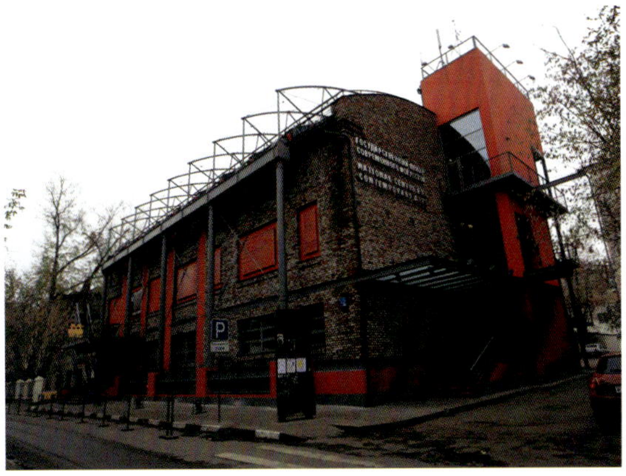

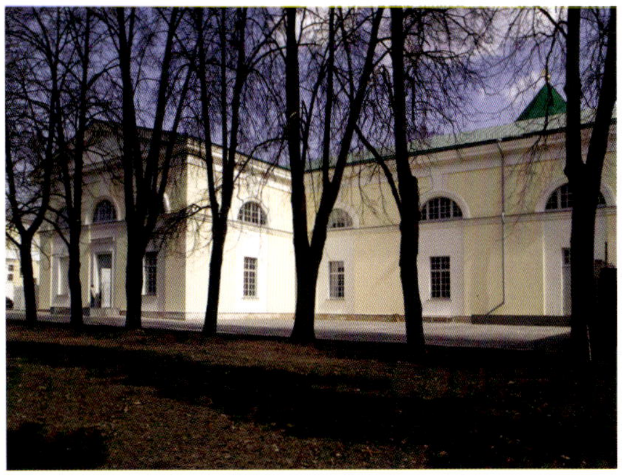

Founded in 1992 and occupying the site of a former factory in central Moscow since 2000, the National Centre for Contemporary Arts is a State-sponsored museum, exhibition and research organisation whose goal is to develop and promote Russian contemporary art both within the country and abroad. According to Leonid Bazhanov, one of the founders of the NCCA and its current artistic director in Moscow, the idea to create 'a Russian Centre Pompidou' originated in 1986, during perestroika, under the auspices of Hermitage, an independent association whose members included some of the country's most prominent artists and art historians. Nowadays, the 'main lines of work are curating, research, education and a permanent collection. The format that these take includes exhibitions, talks, concerts, performances, conferences, festivals and biennials.'

The NCCA, which currently boasts affiliate centres around the country, is progressively leading the decentralisation of Russia's artistic infrastructure. As Bazhanov explains, 'We created a network of affiliates ... in St Petersbrug, Nizhny Novgorod, Kaliningrad, Ekaterinburg, this year in Vladikavkaz. We are planning to open a branch in Siberia [and] in the Far East.' The goal, however, is not to export and mimic the Moscow original in the regions: 'Its role is important, although one shouldn't exaggerate it. It is perhaps one of the most stable structures that was created a long time ago now, and which will continue to exist and develop. But it is not unique, and shouldn't be. It should interact with other institutions that come into being and that already exist, and which will be created in the future.' The five existing branches all have individual programmes and agendas. For example, the Nizhny Novgorod NCCA focuses attention on the development of contemporary architecture, photography and video art, while in Kaliningrad the focus is directed towards new media and the dissemination and popularisation of new artistic trends.

As one of the longest-running art centres in Russia, the NCCA is unique in having acquired government funding and support early on in its history. Bazhanov enabled its establishment through the Ministry of Culture after having been invited to work there in 1992. It was with the ministry's continuing support that the NCCA finally found a permanent site in 2000. Its position as a State-funded body should not be underestimated in a country where a large amount of support for the promotion and development of contemporary art still comes from the private sector. Bazhanov explains that there is further room for development, however: '[The State] offers support, although I don't think it does so judiciously ... it offers aid to material structures in which contemporary art has to station itself, rather than to creative projects.' Nevertheless, the outlook is promising, since 'the Ministry of Culture actively supports Russia's participation in the Venice Biennale, the Moscow International Art Biennale and the Moscow International Biennale of Young Artists. It [also] organised the Industrial Biennale in Ekaterinburg.' A joint effort by the Ministry of Culture and the NCCA was the creation in 2005 of 'Innovation' – The All-Russian Contemporary Art Competition, whose role is to provide support and recognition for emerging and established artists, curators, critics and art historians, as well as for active supporters of the country's contemporary art scene.

If, says Bazhanov, Russia did not capitalise on the opportunity for integration with the West that was offered by the infamous Sotheby's sale in Moscow in 1988, it can still rely on its own rich history to propel it into the international community. Russian art has a strong background in the form of its modernist avant-garde, the memory of which continues to '[exist] in the artistic consciousness', as well as a rich history of private patronage. The hope is that current buyers and collectors will not invest in artworks purely to follow fashion or as a source of entertainment, but will remember the role played by individuals like Schukin, Morozov, Ryabushinsky and Ostroukhov in forming and determining Russia's cultural heritage. As Bazhanov puts it, 'There is a base from which to restore, to reanimate, and to learn – meaning even from Russia's own experience, let alone the West's.' While lending their names to newly created galleries, foundations and organisations, Russia's art investors should not forget the most effective means of offering their support: through patronage and sponsorship of existing professional institutions.

One of the main concerns expressed by the NCCA, and shared by a variety of individuals and institutions across Russia, is the lack of public education regarding post-war and contemporary art. Because of art's stunted evolution during the Soviet period, the country lacks contemporary art 'in a developed condition with a consistent, normal evolutionary history'. The sporadic bursts in which artistic creation has characteristically manifested itself means that cultural politics are also inadequately developed to bridge the gap between culture and the market. One of the main activities of the NCCA, therefore, involves growing an easily accessible educational network. Its centres provide education and research outlets like the Mediatheque in Moscow, which houses a growing collection of Russian and foreign-language publications, including exhibition catalogues, articles, reviews, monographs and *catalogues raisonnés*. The NCCA's outreach network is developing through a programme of lectures, talks and workshops, as well as the dissemination of free information via the Internet. It is continuing to evolve, always conscious of the fact that there is 'more work in the future that lies ahead than what has already been achieved'.

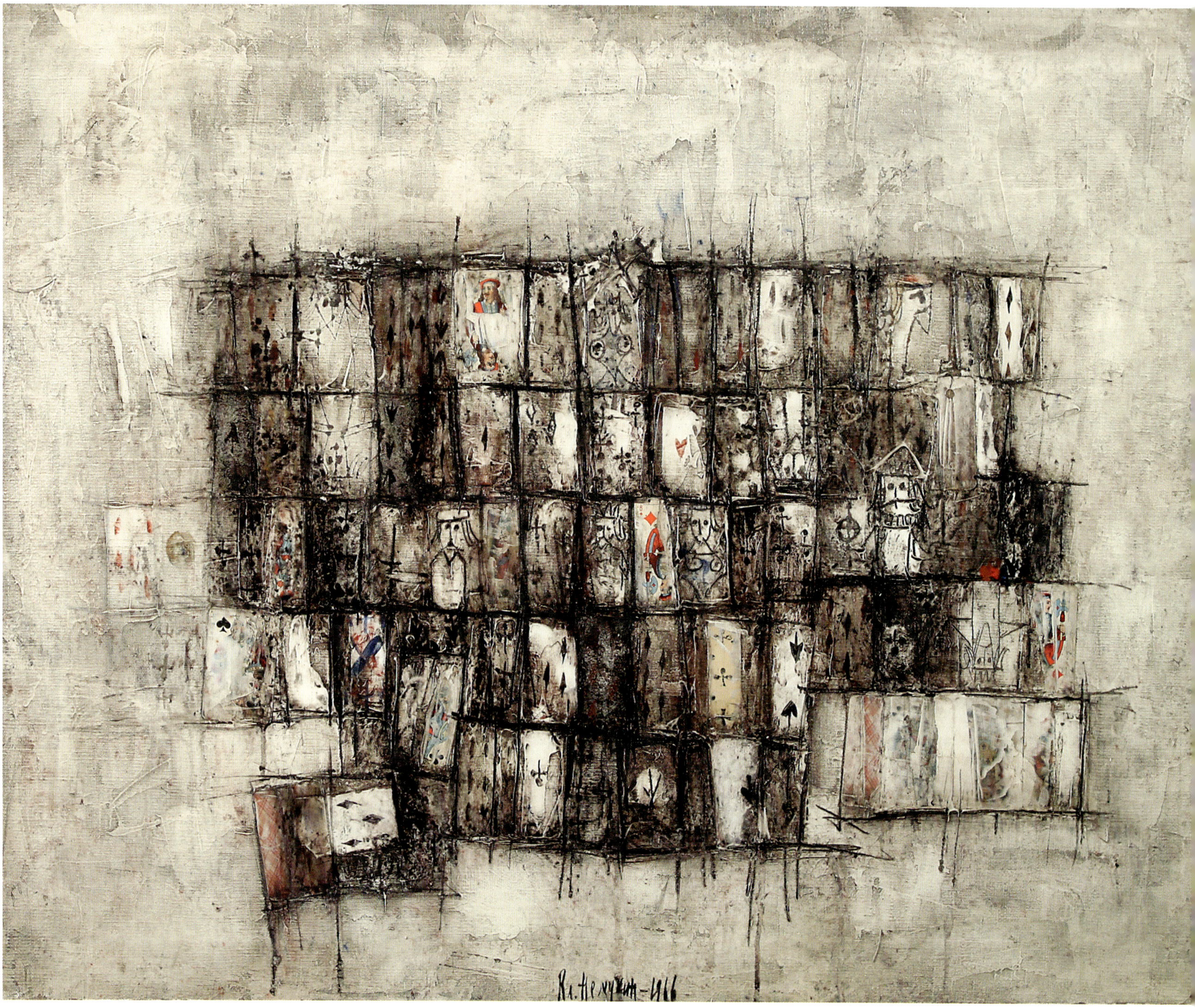

Vladimir Nemukhin was born in Moscow in 1925. Predominantly a painter and graphic artist, he also makes sculptures. At the age of nine he drew a white bear on ice which won him a prize in a local talent contest. During the early war years, while working in a military factory, he decided to become an artist, making paintbrushes by tying his hair to a pencil and trading bread for paints. Between 1943 and 1946 he attended the Moscow Art Studio (AUCCTU); his most important formative influence was artist Petr Sokolov, a pupil of Malevich, who introduced Nemukhin to Cubism by way of reproductions of work by Western masters. During the Stalin years, Nemukhin reverted to the style of the nineteenth-century Realist Isaac Levitan as a means of survival from persecution until the Thaw in the mid-1950s. The American National Exhibition in 1959 exposed him to the work of the American Abstract Expressionists Jasper Johns and Robert Rauschenberg, who influenced his own approach. Throughout the 1960s he worked with artist Lydia Masterkova, his first wife, and exhibited with the members of the Lianozovo Group. He also took part in the two key unofficial outdoor exhibitions in 1974, the 'Bulldozer' at Belyaevo, and at Ismailovo Park later in the same year.

Nemukhin's paintings contain both abstract and figurative elements. Influenced by the non-objective art of the Russian avant-garde, his compositions unite modernism's formalist aesthetics with the emotional freedom of Abstract Expressionism. Commenting on the place of abstraction in both the Soviet past, when Realism was the only official style, and today, he has said, 'For [the Soviets] abstract art was the most terrible villain, whereas today formalism does not play any role at all.' In 1963–4 Nemukhin started to paint playing cards and apply them to his work, making them a hallmark of his art. This practice grew out of formalist explorations into the aesthetic and geometric qualities of such cards, especially the 7 of Diamonds with its configuration of red triangles on white. The Jack of Diamonds is a recurring motif, for its reference to the Russian modernist group of the same name. The red colour of the Diamonds suite is also significant: the word red – *krasni* in Russian – shares the same root as the word for 'beauty', *krasota*. Through the figure of the Jack, Nemukhin's abstract art arrived at the human figure: 'I could not paint a person's face like Picasso, because I could not deform a human being, but with the Jack of Diamonds I was able to do this.'

Nemukhin's work is held in numerous major public and private collections worldwide, including the State Tretyakov Gallery, Moscow; the Museum of Modern Art, New York; the Metropolitan Museum of Art, New York; the Ludwig Museum, Cologne; and the Jane Voorhees Zimmerli Art Museum, New Brunswick. Having emigrated to Düsseldorf after the break-up of the Soviet Union, the artist now lives and works in Moscow. The period of dissidence in the 1960s, when many artists worked in closed groups or in isolation, is often contextualised in official and unofficial terms, overshadowing aesthetic concerns. But Nemukhin questions this critical approach: 'We have to talk about art and not politics. We are all different from one another ... we all had our own style and voice.' He acknowledges, however, that 'if it had not been for Stalin or the Thaw, art would have changed; it would have been different.' Nemukhin was made an honorary member of the Russian Academy of Arts in 2008.

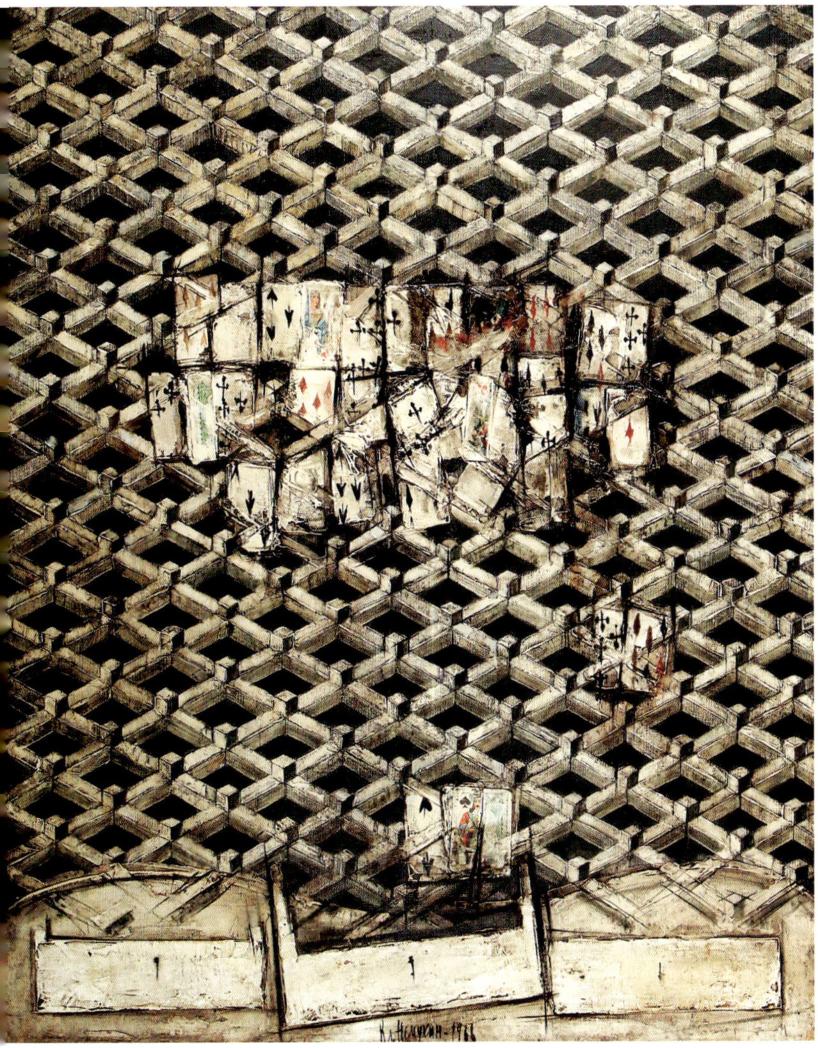

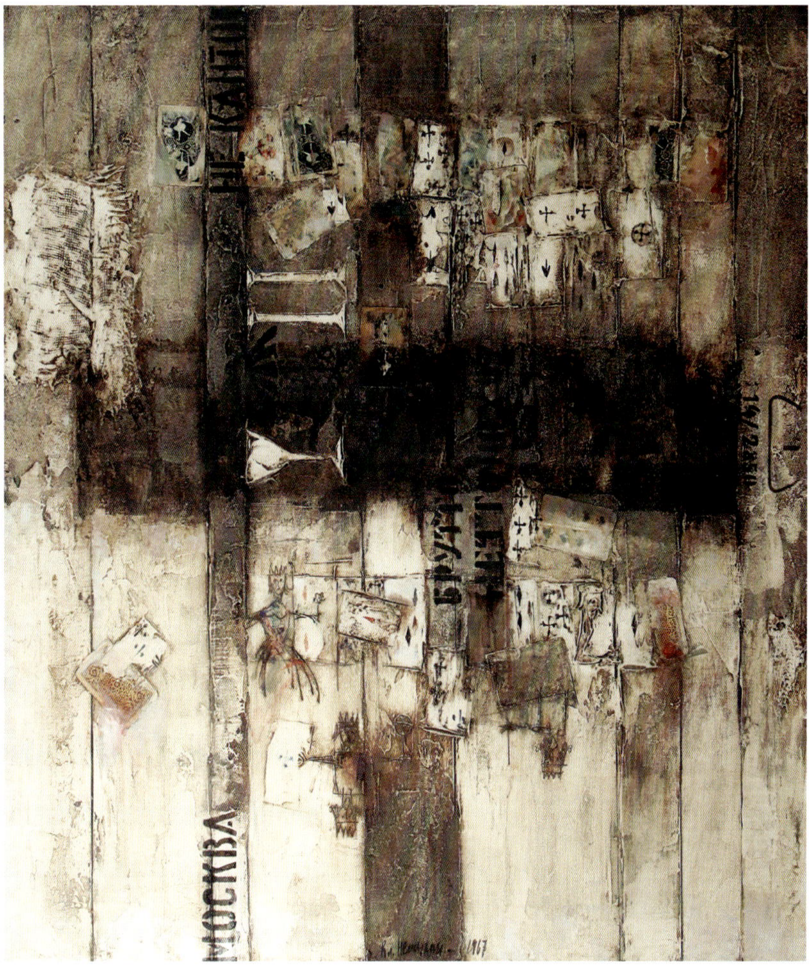

left
Marquetry, 1966
Oil and mixed media on canvas
90 x 100 cm
© Vladimir Nemukhin
Collection of Carole Rector Bankhead and Todd Bankhead, US

facing page
Discarded Solitaire, 1966
Oil and mixed media on canvas
100 x 80 cm
© Vladimir Nemukhin
Collection of Neil Rector, US

above
Game of Fool on a Box, 1967
Oil and mixed media on canvas
96.5 x 109 cm
© Vladimir Nemukhin
Collection of Neil Rector, US

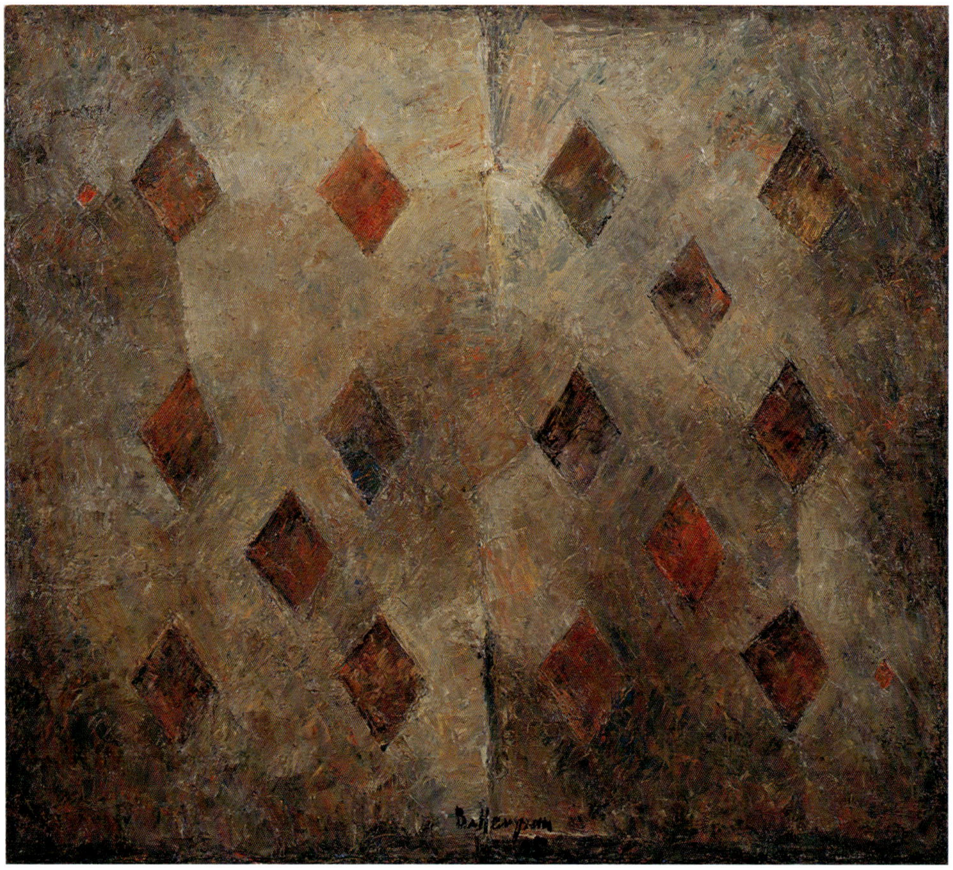

above
Two Cards, 1965
Oil on canvas
65 x 75 cm

Iveta and Tamaz Manasherov Collection, Moscow
Courtesy of the artist

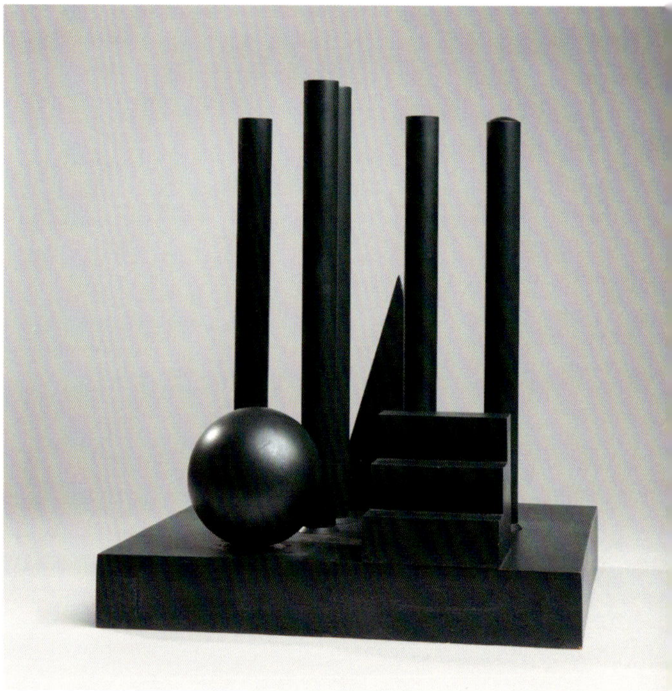

top
Dedicated to Pyotr Efimovich Sokolov, 1983
Bronze
32 x 28 x 28 cm

Collection of the artist
Courtesy of the artist

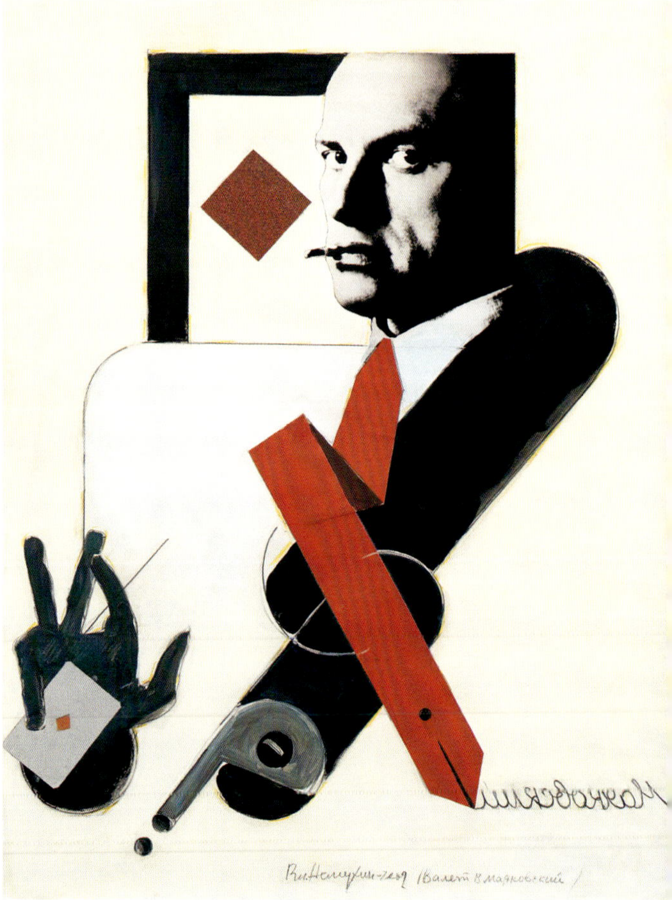

right
Jack 'Vladimir Mayakovsky', 2001
Paper, tempera, collage
80 x 60 cm

Collection of the artist
Courtesy of the artist

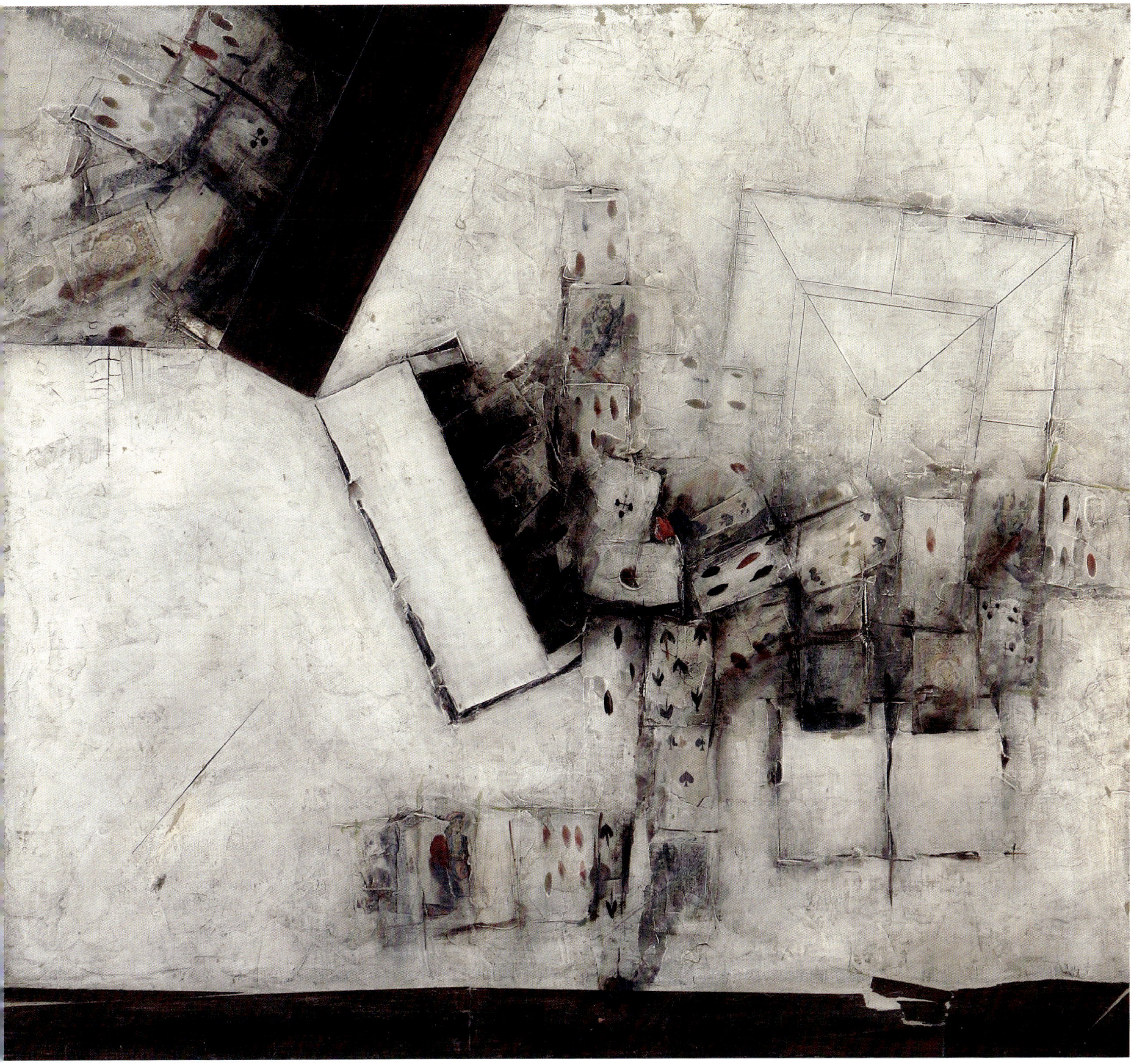

above
Soiree, 1974
Oil on canvas
100 x 100 cm
© Vladimir Nemukhin
Courtesy of Tsukanov Art Collection

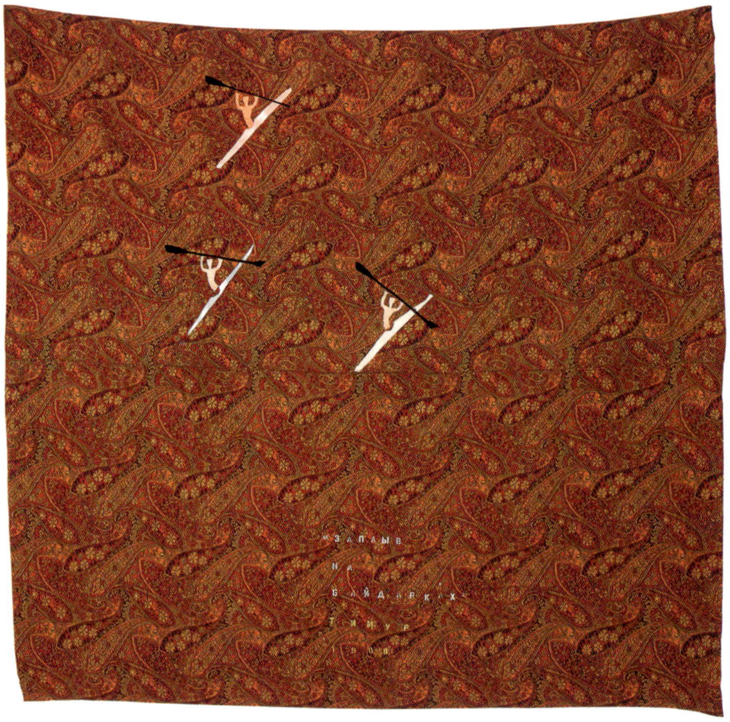

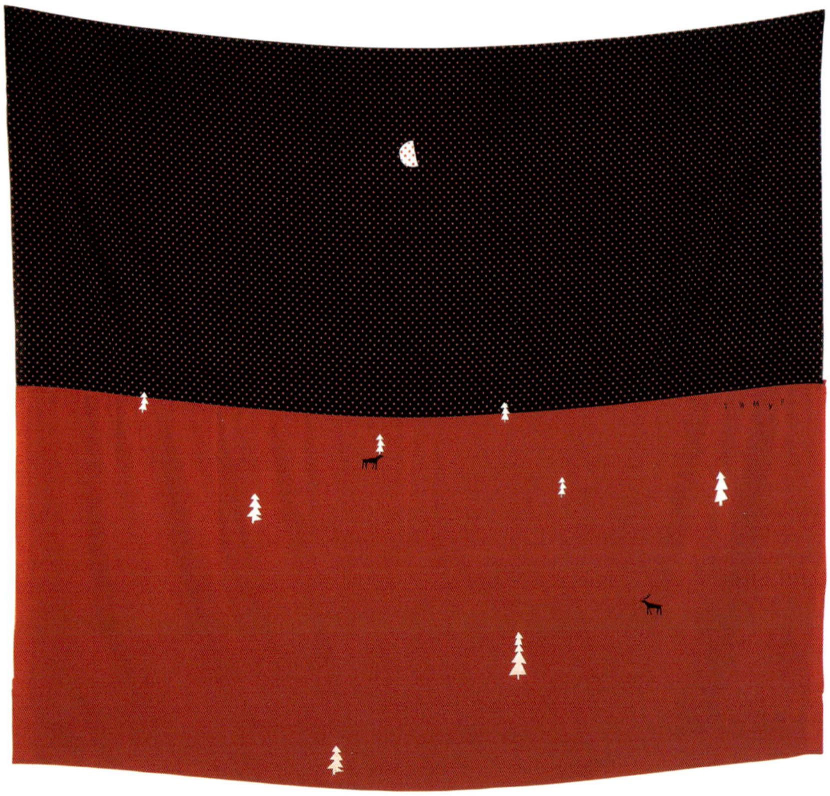

Timur Novikov

Timur Novikov was born in Leningrad in 1958. As a child he lived for several years in Novaya Zelandia in the far north of Russia; the stark Arctic horizon had a strong influence on his mature work. Novikov took art classes as a child but was not formally trained. During the 1980s, he became a cult figure in Leningrad's unofficial subculture, where art, rock music and theatrical performances cross-fertilised, thus fostering a strong creative community. In 1982 he founded a group called the 'New Artists' who exhibited at the ASSA Gallery (initially Novikov's own apartment), which became a cultural hub. By 1988, he was reacting against the cultural anarchism of his early years, going on to found the New Academy and introduce Neoclassicism into his work.

Travel, space exploration, homosexuality and the Russian landscape are among the diverse subjects addressed by Novikov's art. Using a minimal, decorative aesthetic, he reduces the main figurative elements in his compositions to small signs dominated by the horizon line. About merging abstract Suprematism with figurative art, he wrote, 'If you place a sign on Malevich's black square you construe it in a humanistic way. By placing a circle on a black background you create an image of the moon.' In the 1920s the avant-gardists reinvigorated Russia's tradition of textile art, which had originated in the folk art of the country's early nomadic tribes; these sources inspired Novikov as well.

Novikov, who died in 2002, was given a major retrospective at the State Russian Museum, St Petersburg, in 1998. His works can be found in several public collections, including the State Russian Museum; the State Tretyakov Gallery, Moscow; the Stedelijk Museum, Amsterdam; the Jane Vorhees Zimmerli Art Museum, New Brunswick; and the Victoria and Albert Museum, London.

above
White Nights in Siberia, 1988
Acrylic, stencil on textile
160 x 155 cm
© Xenia Novikova
Collection of Michel Roux

above left
Travel on Kayaks, 1988
Acrylic on textile
59 x 59 cm
© Xenia Novikova
Collection of Jeffrey Schaire, New York

facing page
Andy Warhol's Sadness, 1989
Acrylic on textile
205 x 194 cm
© Xenia Novikova
Collection of The State Russian Museum, St. Petersburg
Courtesy of Xenia Novikova

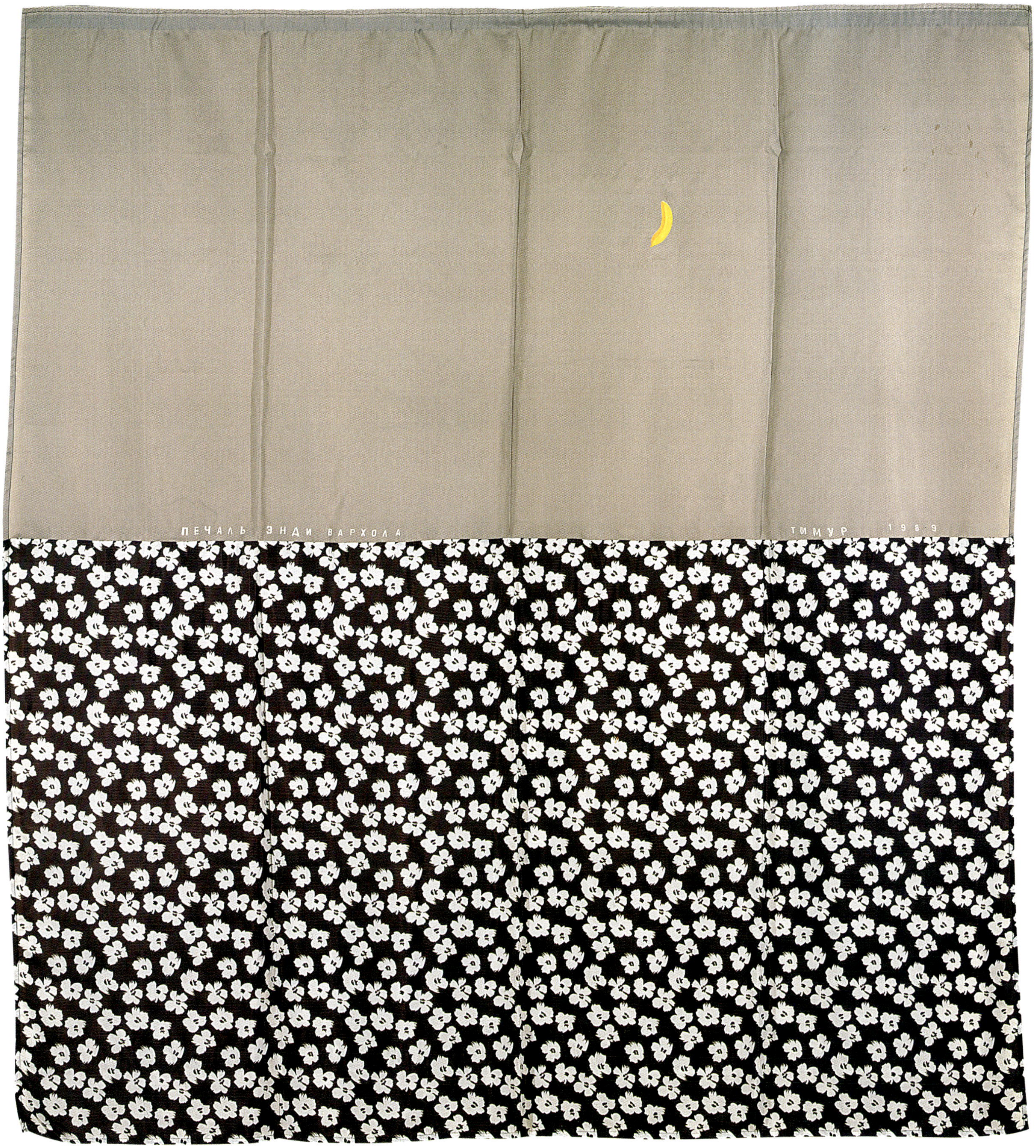

Timur Novikov

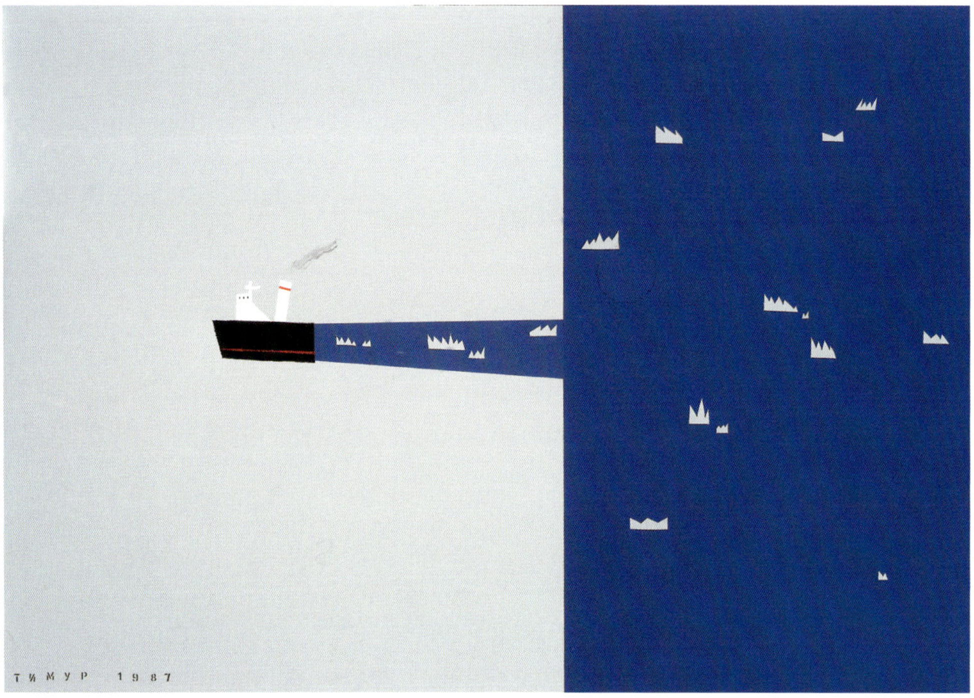

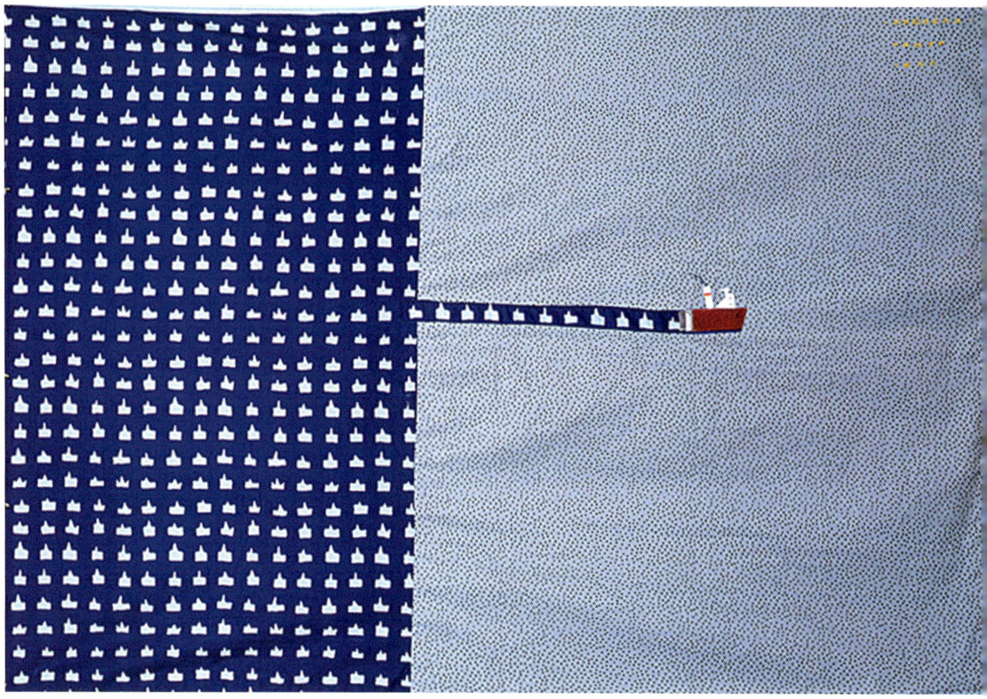

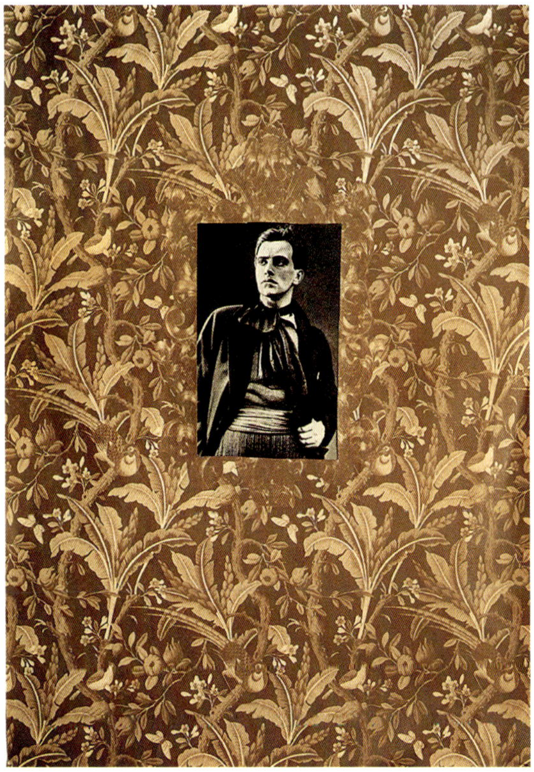

top
Icebreaker, 1987
Acrylic and paper on cardboard
60 x 80 cm
© Xenia Novikova
Collection of artist's family, St Petersburg

above
An Icebreaker, 1989
Acrylic on textile
100 x 169 cm
© Xenia Novikova
Courtesy of V. Dubrovolsky

left
V. V. Mayakovsky, from the series
In the Land of Literary Heroes, 1994
Mixed media on paper
38.5 x 27.5 cm
© Xenia Novikova
Sergey Bugayev–Africa Collection, St Petersburg

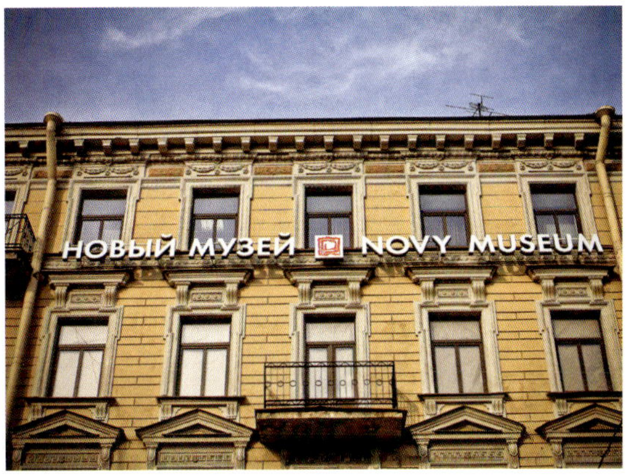

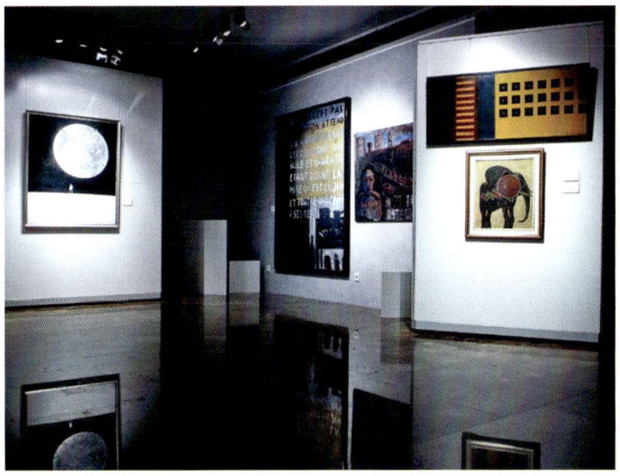

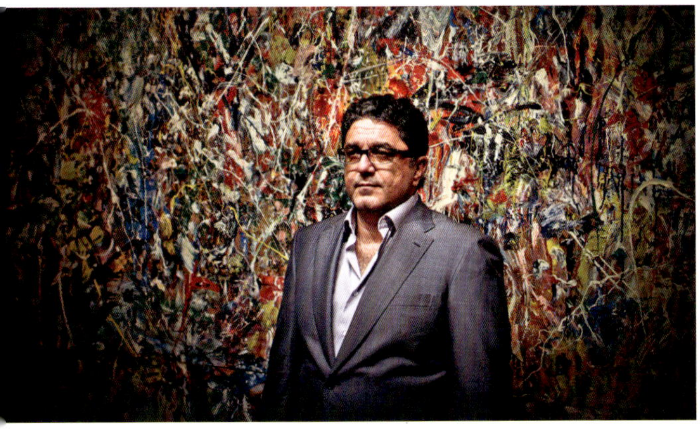

The Novy Museum was founded in St Petersburg in 2010 by Russian energy entrepreneur Aslan Chekhoev and his wife Irina. It is located over three floors in a refurbished nineteenth-century building on historic Vasilievsky Island, close to the Russian Academy of Arts. The Novy, or New, Museum is the first private art museum in St Petersburg and that city's only permanent collection dedicated to Russian contemporary art. The founder has emphasised that the museum's name relates to his mission, which is to show both new art and a new approach to exhibiting work as part of a private collection. Chekhoev, who began collecting around 2000, has amassed around 300 works to date, many of which are shown in the museum. His activities as a collector and promoter of the arts are related in that he prefers not to make a distinction between what he shows at the museum and what he displays at home.

Chekhoev was born in Tskhinvali into an educated South Ossetian family and moved to Leningrad in 1983 at the age of seventeen to study medicine. He practised as a doctor until 1993, when he left the profession in the difficult years following the break-up of the Soviet Union. In order to provide for his family, he went into business, starting out in trading and then getting into coal mining. Today electrical energy is his main business concern. Having learnt about art history at home, he started going to museums and galleries, finally realising that his passion lay with contemporary Russian art. Chekhoev is particularly interested in the Soviet underground artists from as early as the late 1940s, when Stalin was still alive, up to perestroika. What intrigues him as much as the art itself are its historical context and development.

Chekhoev is aware that the Russian public's suspicion of contemporary art is based on a lack of education and information, a situation he seeks to address with his museum. He sees the legacy of Communism, with its official art system, as an important factor in this lack of understanding: 'We lost seventy years; there was no contemporary art like the avant-garde of the 1920s. It completely disappeared from our everyday lives ... In the West there were gradual and organic changes in the twentieth century. New movements came and went, but we did not have that in Russia.' Chekhoev understands that the Russian public needs time to engage with new forms of art, and that people are not accustomed to the process of enquiry essential to an appreciation of new things. He also has observed that Western visitors can be more receptive: 'Many Westerners come to the museum and seem to understand it better than the Russians; they are more tolerant and less critical.'

When speaking about the problems of centralisation, Chekhoev expresses his concern that the departure of strong artists from the regions for Moscow is leaving a cultural void in the provinces. Despite this, he is optimistic about the numerous cultural initiatives in the regions today. He admits that even in St Petersburg there is a lack of public spaces where contemporary art can be viewed: 'There is not one centre or museum of contemporary art, no big state museum; everything is based on small private initiatives.' Chekhoev believes that the State should not help private investors in this field, but that it should give more general support to contemporary art by helping to fund biennales, opening new exhibition spaces and encouraging the public to engage with contemporary art in an active and positive way.

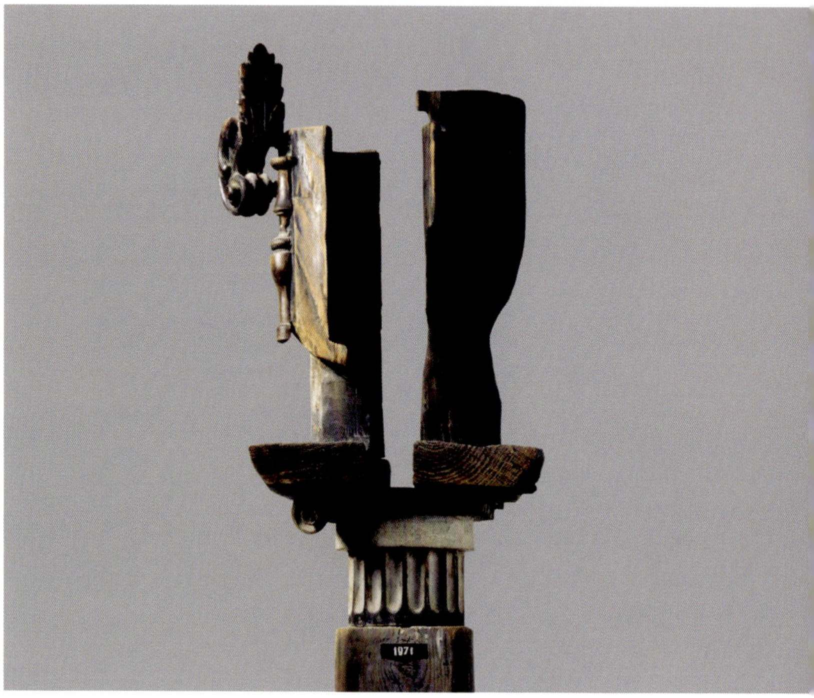

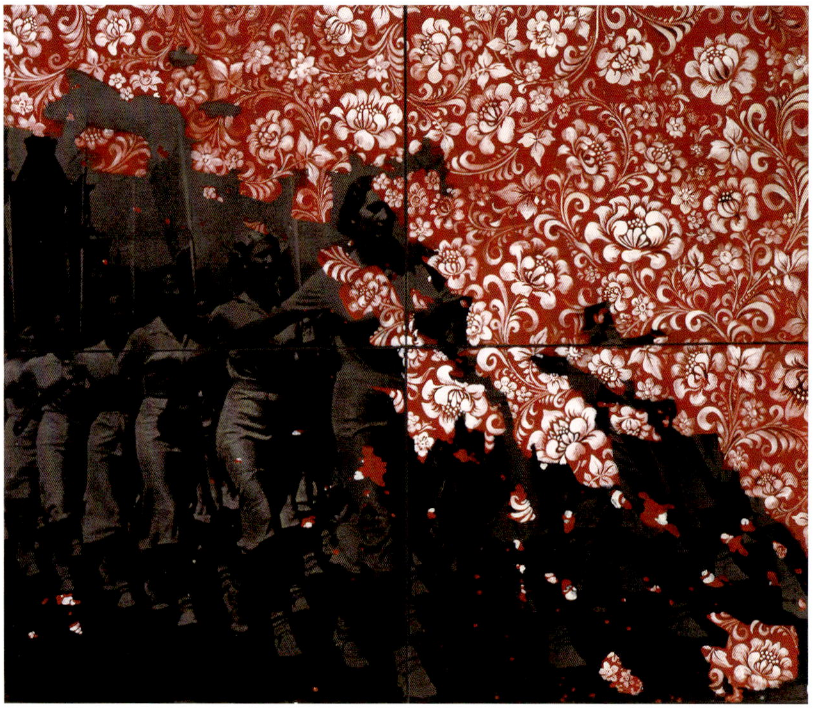

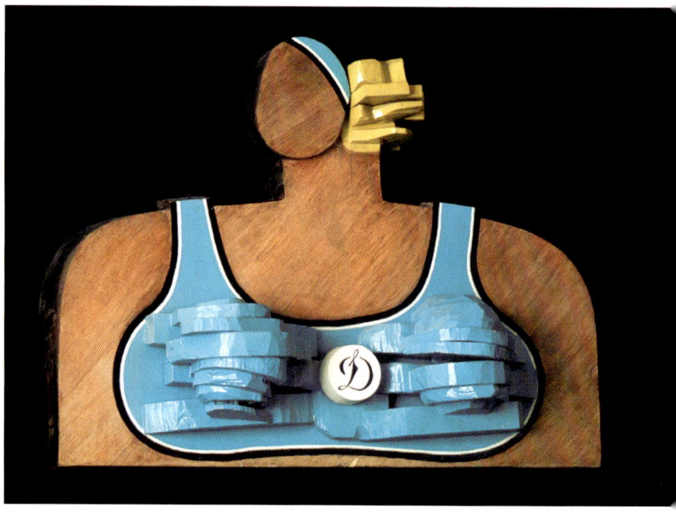

Boris Orlov

Born in Khimki, near Moscow, in 1941, sculptor Boris Orlov worked as a welder before giving up manual labour for academic studies. From 1960 until 1966 he was enrolled in the Sculpture Department of the Stroganov Higher College of Art in Moscow. After graduating, he shared a studio with fellow future Sots artists Leonid Sokov, Alexander Kosolapov and Rostislav Lebedev.

Since the beginning of his career as a sculptor, Orlov has demonstrated an interest in philosophy and metaphysics, interpreting Soviet power via ancient Greek and Roman art, history and mythology. Early sculptures include terracotta or plaster casts of mythological symbols and heroes such as *Icarus* (1970) or *Phoenix* (1971), metaphors for a Soviet utopia.

Orlov developed the aesthetic for which he is famous in the early 1980s: Russian naval heroes made out of porcelain, wood or bronze, and covered in enamel medals, military honours, ribbons and weapons. Their rudimentary, exaggerated forms satirise the State's delusions of grandeur. Orlov's stylised, idiosyncratic manner is evident in earlier works as well, for example *Imperial Bust (Sailor)* (1975), which appropriates a classical portrait bust of Julius Caesar but gives it the exaggerated attributes of a Soviet naval figure. Caesar's classical features are juxtaposed with the artisanal quality of the torso – a nod to the traditional arts and crafts beloved by early twentieth-century artists. Balanced precariously on a 'classical' pedestal, this sculpture is at once a devaluation of images of imperial power and a mocking acknowledgement of Soviet pomp.

Inspired by totems and symbols of historical empires, Orlov's eclectic intermixing of codes and symbols demonstrates his belief that history does not consist of individual moments in time and space but is cyclical and repetitive. In his sculptures and installations, all historical attempts at flight, at moving beyond the horizon, are ultimately fated to fall back down to earth.

top
The Emperor's Head, 1971
Wood
210 x 35 x 30 cm
© Boris Orlov
Collection of Novy Foundation, Moscow

above
Dinamovka, 1978
Enamel on wood
76 x 100 x 33 cm
© Boris Orlov
Collection of Regina Gallery, London and Moscow

above left
From the series Contours of Time, 1999
Enamel on photograph
100 x 120 cm
© Boris Orlov
Private collection, Moscow
Courtesy of the artist

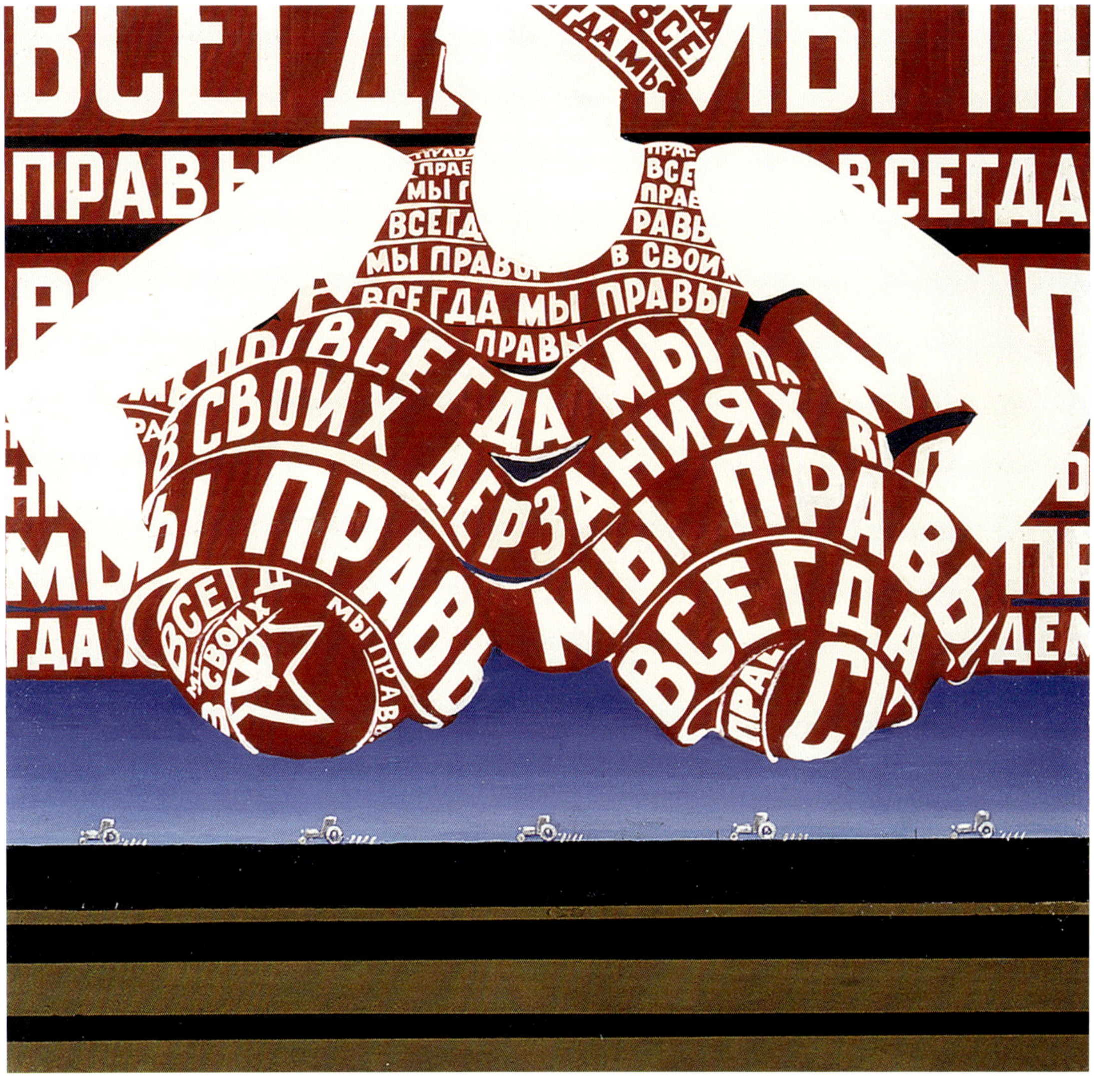

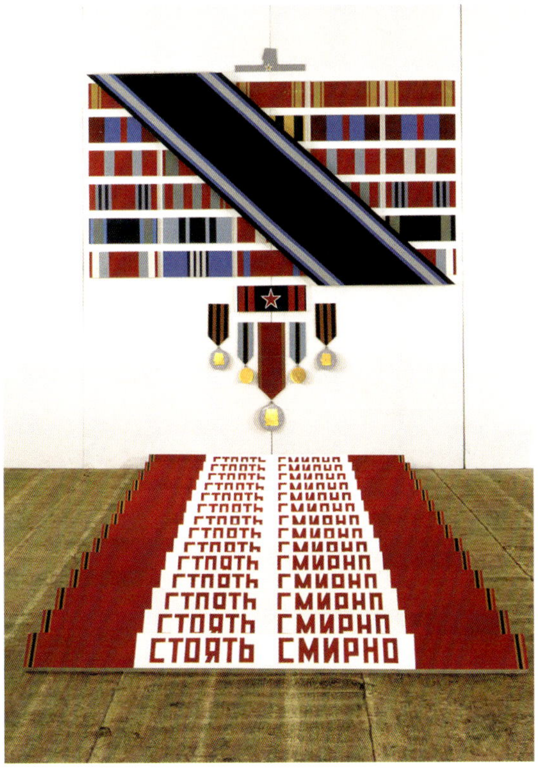

above
Red Cloud, 1989
Oil on plywood
75 x 78 cm

Courtesy of Shalva Breus

left
Pantocrator, 1990
Enamel on wood
300 x 300 x 500 cm

Collection of the State Tretyakov Gallery, Moscow

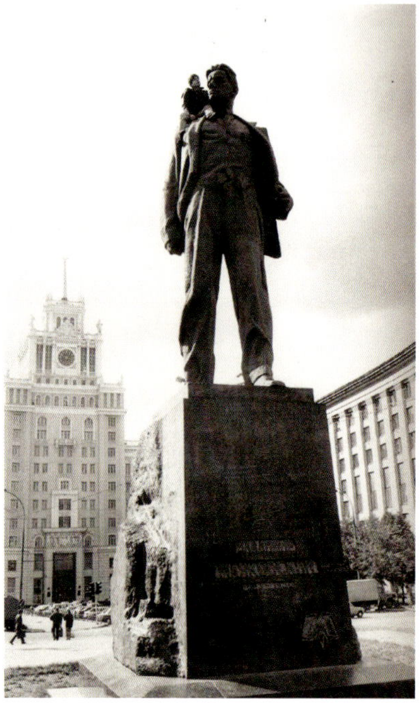

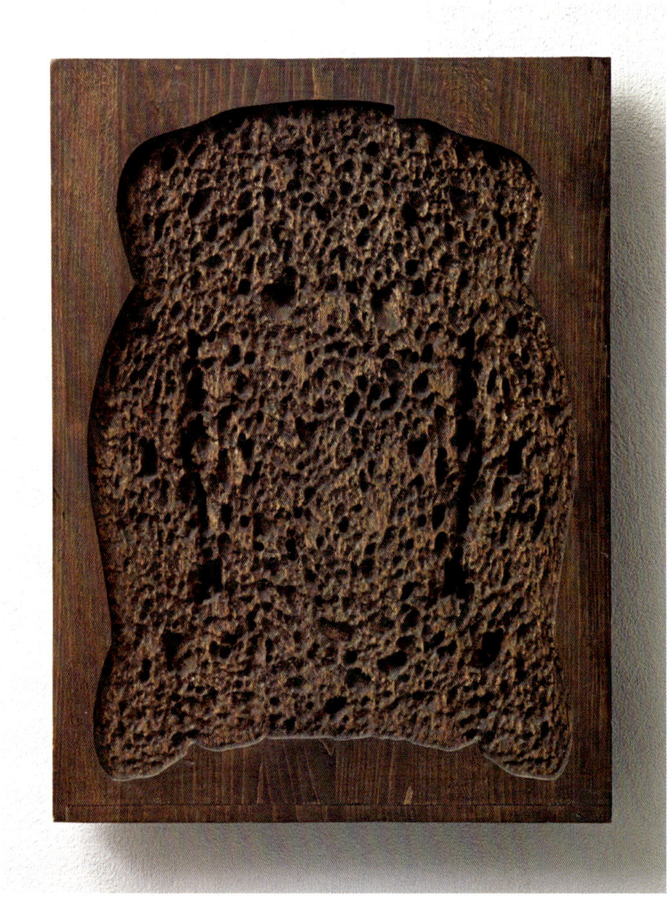

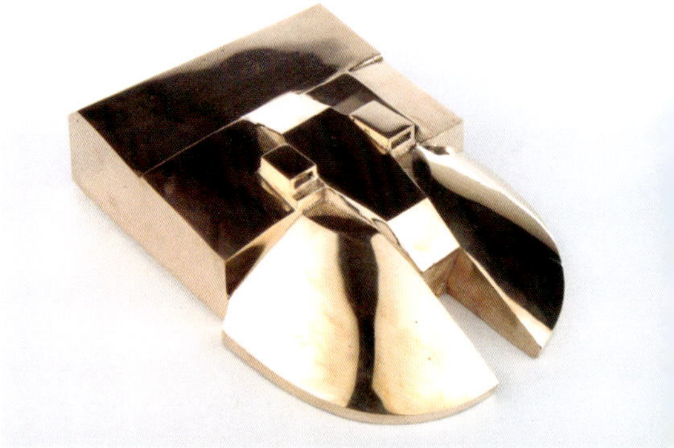

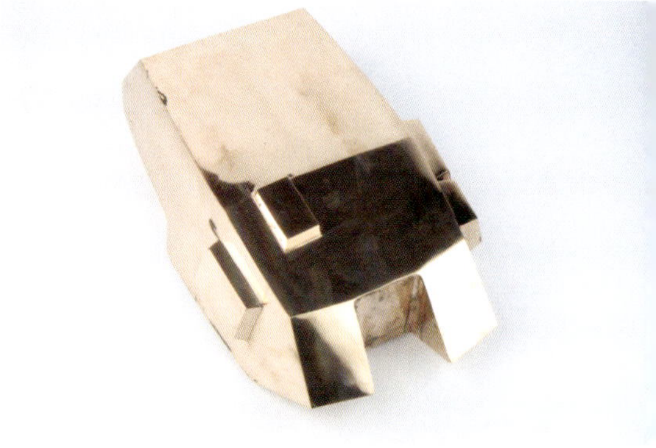

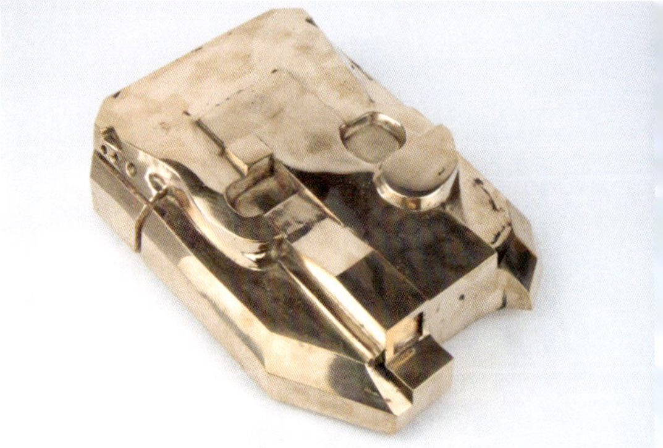

Artist, activist, writer and theoretician Anatoly Osmolovsky was born in 1969 in Moscow, where he continues to live and work. Osmolovsky first came to prominence during the 1990s, the heyday of Moscow Actionism. Advocating the taking of politically engaged Leftist art to the streets, he organised and participated in anarchic solitary and group actions, performances and happenings. Since 2000, influenced by the philosophy of Theodor Adorno, he has challenged the usefulness and impact of artistic activism, developing in its place a strategy for 'non-spectacular art' that directly addresses the contemporary art market.

A spirit of anarchy is present in many of Osmolovsky's early gestures, such as *A Trip to the Land of Brobdingnag (Mayakovsky/ Osmolovsky)* (1993). This period was also marked by collaborative efforts instigated by his organisation of the ETI (Art Territory Expropriation) movement (1989–92) and Vote Against Everyone! Now (1997–2000), among others. It was the latter group that staged *Barricade (Dedicated to the Events of Prague, 1968)* (1998) in protest against the breakdown of parliamentary democracy. In 1995 Osmolovsky founded *Radek* magazine, whose aim was to create a space for the exploration of radical philosophy and politics in the wake of the unstable political climate at that time.

Many of Osmolovsky's 'non-spectacular' objects play with the idea of the ready-made. In *Hardware* (2006), he produced highly finished casts of polished bronze miniature tanks, which, divested of their military purpose, became art objects. The artist explains his approach this way: 'The awareness of the social limits of art inevitably turned into the search for its *aesthetic* limits ... The political dimension of art appears when art is understood in a concrete way ... I believe that the most consistent and natural thing for these speculations is to state the new potential of objectless visuality. Silence is the only possible response of art to the present situation.'

top
Travel to the Brobdingnag Land, Mayakovsky Square, Moscow, 1993
Photograph of performance
© Anatoly Osmolovsky
Courtesy of the artist

above left
From the series Bread N1, 2007
Wood, mixed media
40 x 30 cm
© Anatoly Osmolovsky
Courtesy of the artist

above
From the series Hardware, 2007
Bronze, mixed media
45 x 20 cm (each)
© Anatoly Osmolovsky
Courtesy of the artist

facing page
Bread series N2, 2007
Wood, mixed media
15 parts, largest 170 x 65 cm
© Anatoly Osmolovsky
Perm Museum of Contemporary Art
Courtesy of Perm Museum of Contemporary Art and the artist

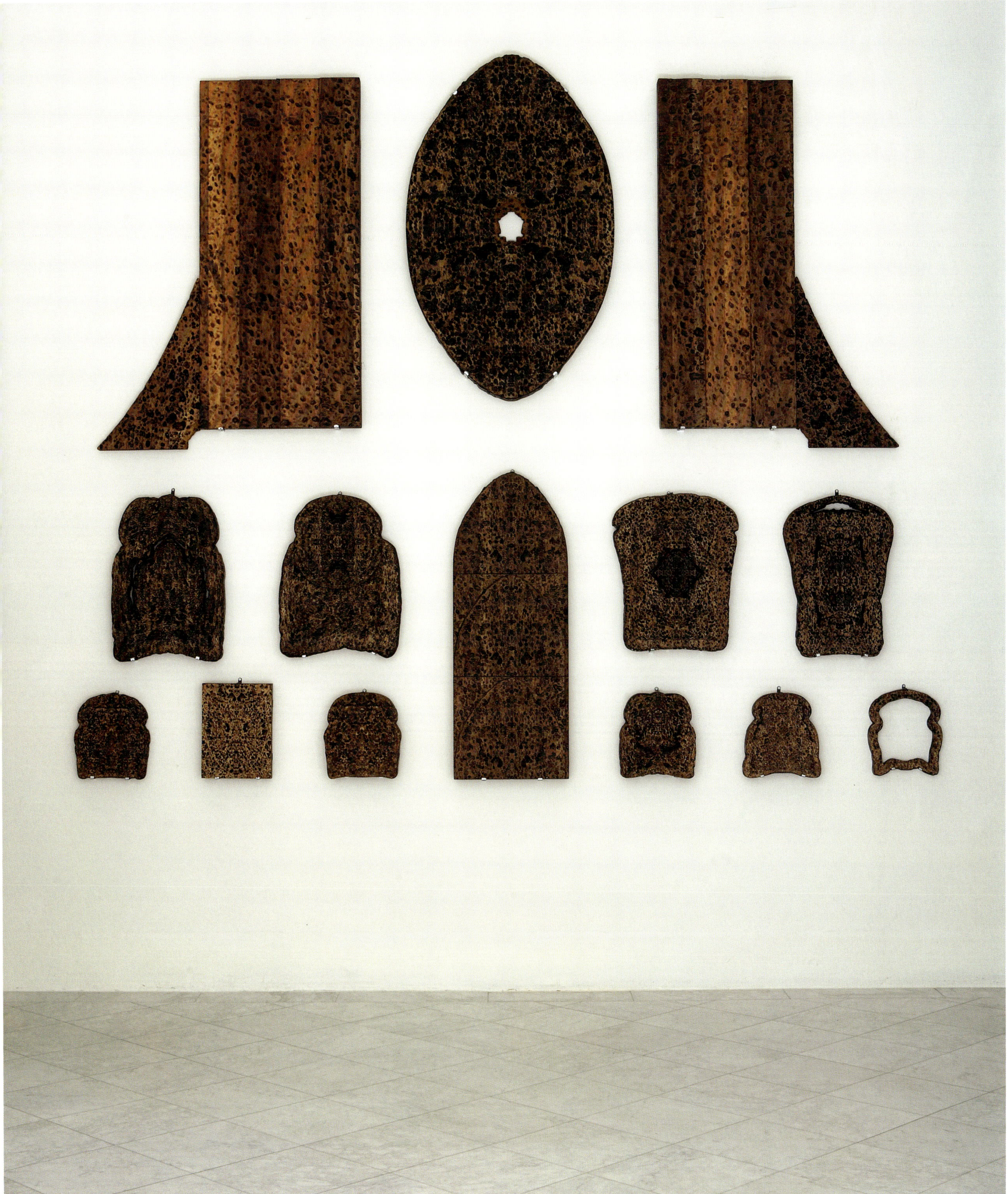

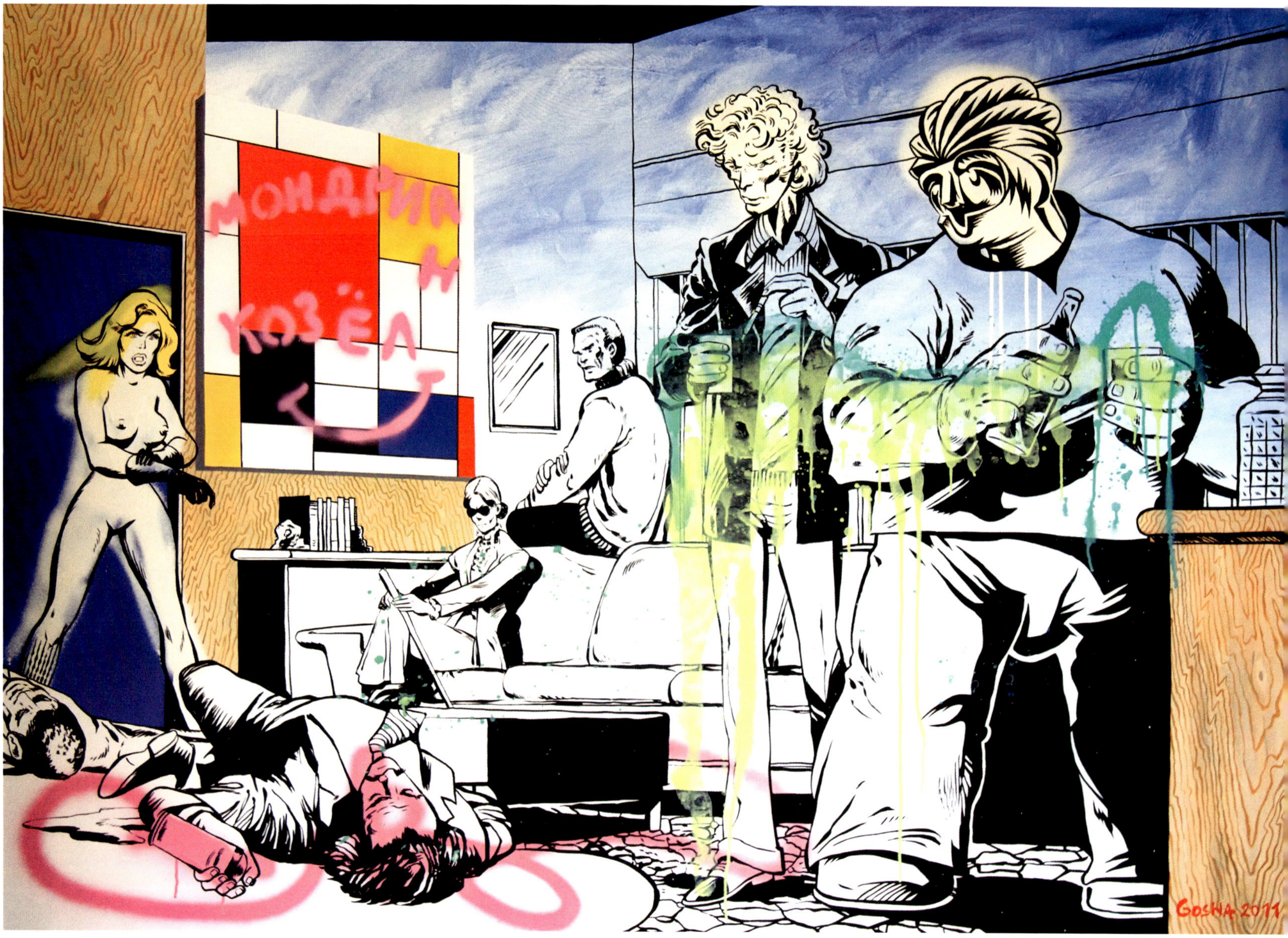

Gosha Ostretsov was born in Moscow in 1967. At the age of seventeen he graduated from the Theatre Art School at the Bolshoi Theatre, Moscow; a year later, he began to show work in underground exhibitions in the capital, with, among others, Andrei Roiter's Kindergarten group. During the perestroika era, Ostretsov went to Paris, where he lived for a decade, rediscovering Russian Orthodox theology and iconography. After working for a time in the fashion industry, he abandoned it in favour of his true calling as a politically engaged artist. Ostretsov's practice is diverse, encompassing installations, performances and painting; his paintings employ cartoons and slogans to interrogate such universal themes as war, propaganda and crime. Works by Ostretsov are held in many public collections, including the State Tretyakov Gallery, Moscow; the State Russian Museum, St Petersburg; the National Centre for Contemporary Art, Moscow; and the Moscow Museum of Modern Art.

above
Mondrian Is a Jerk, 2011
Acrylic on canvas
120 x 170 cm

Courtesy of the artist

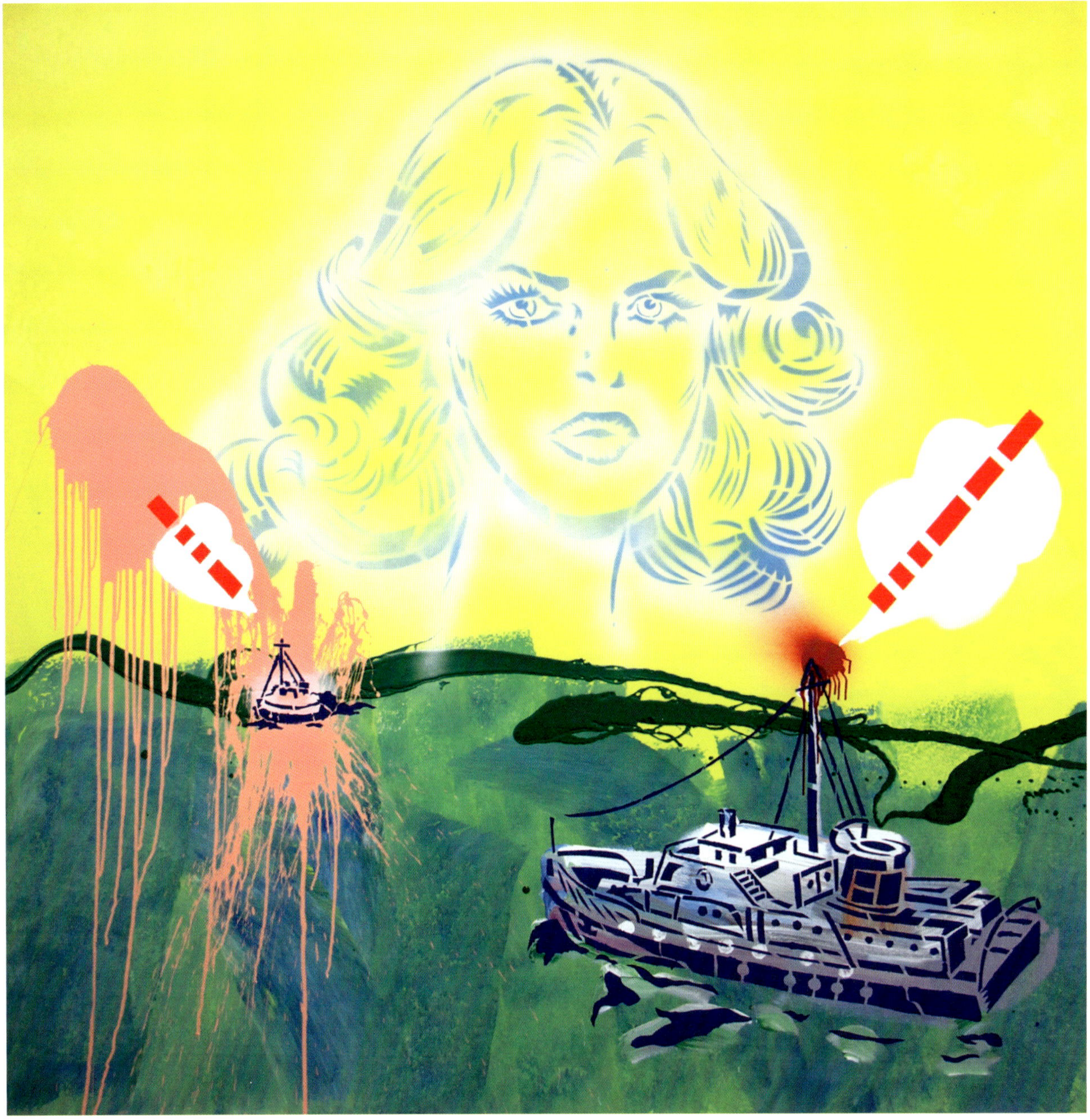

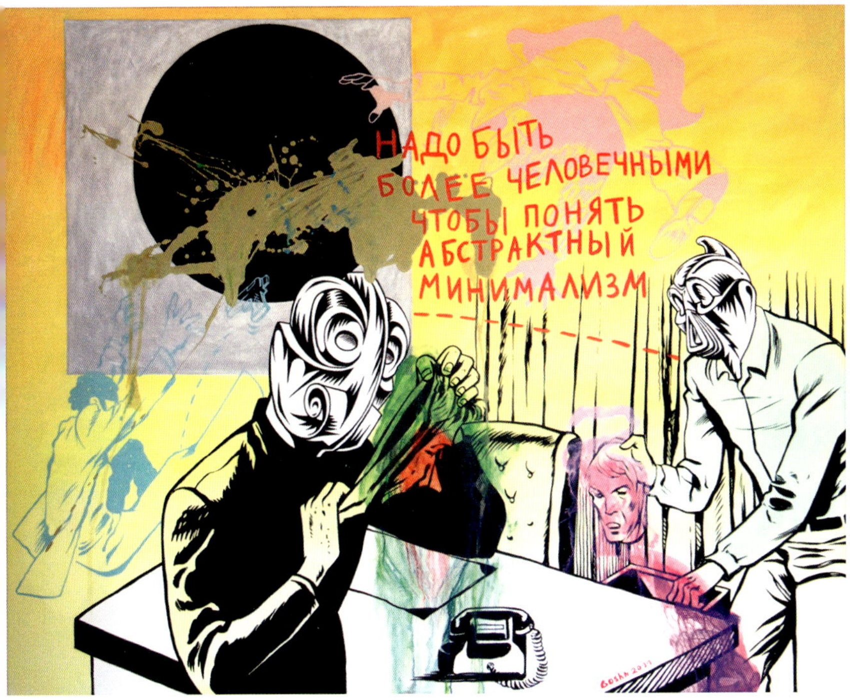

above
Two Ships, 2010
Acrylic and enamel on canvas
200 x 200 cm
© Gosha Ostretsov
Private collection

left
Black Circle, 2011
Acrylic on canvas
120 x 160 cm
© Gosha Ostretsov
Courtesy of the artist

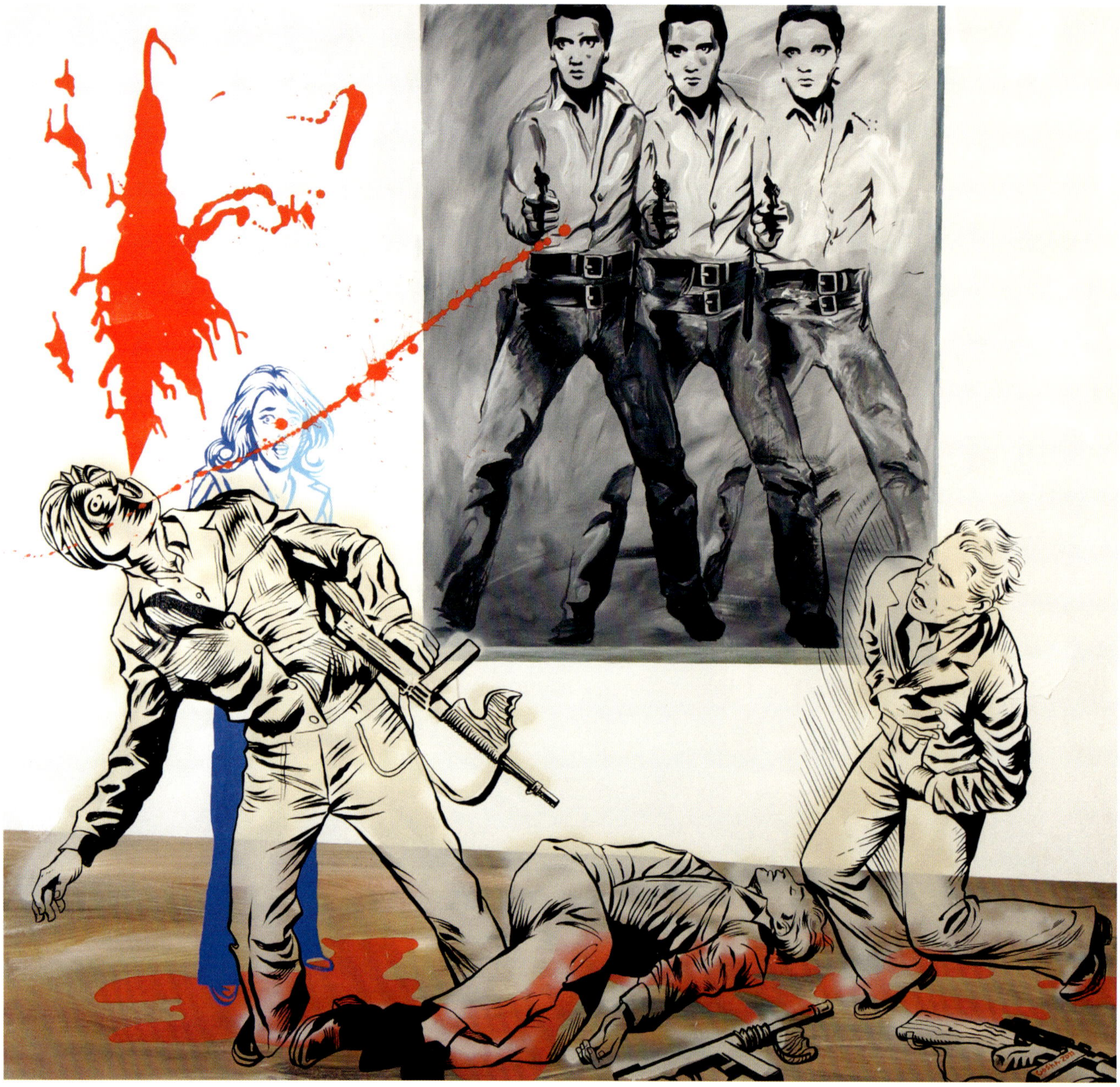

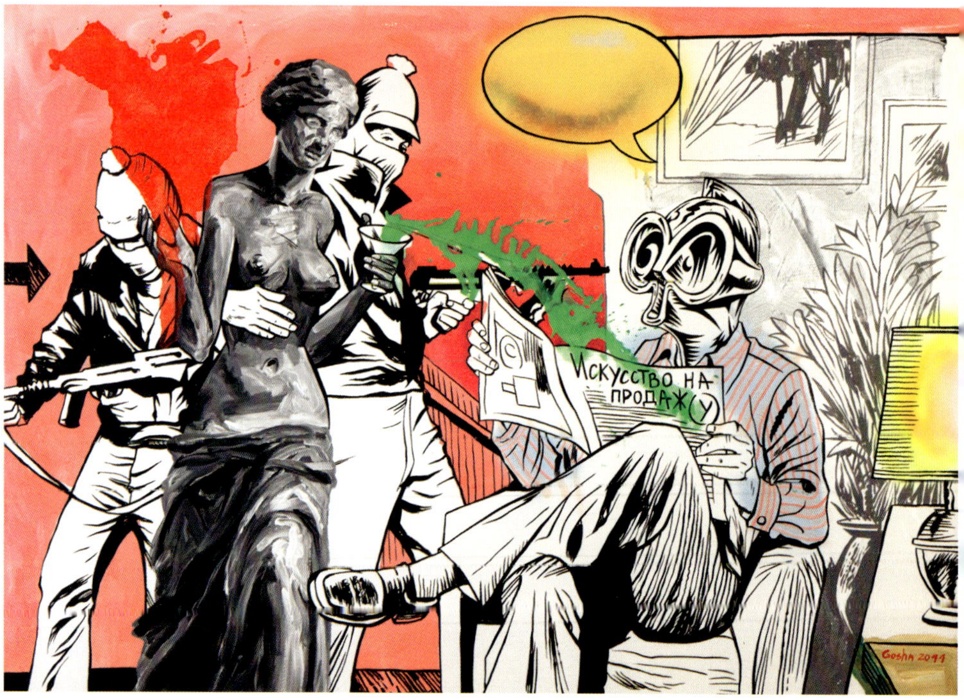

above
The Elvises, 2011
Acrylic on canvas
150 x 160 cm
© Gosha Ostretsov
Courtesy of the artist

right
Venus, 2011
Acrylic on canvas
120 x 170 cm
© Gosha Ostretsov
Courtesy of the artist

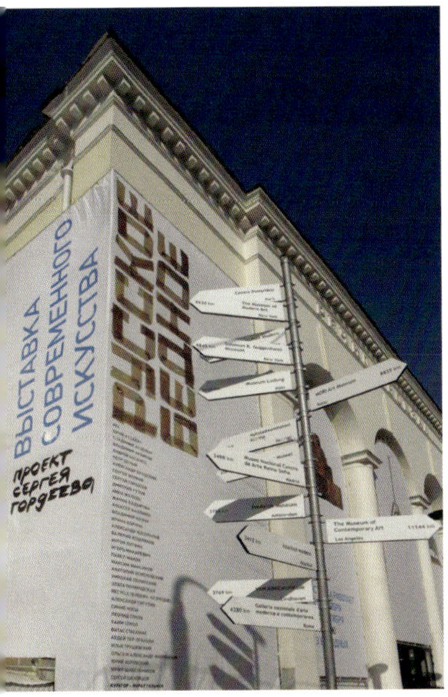

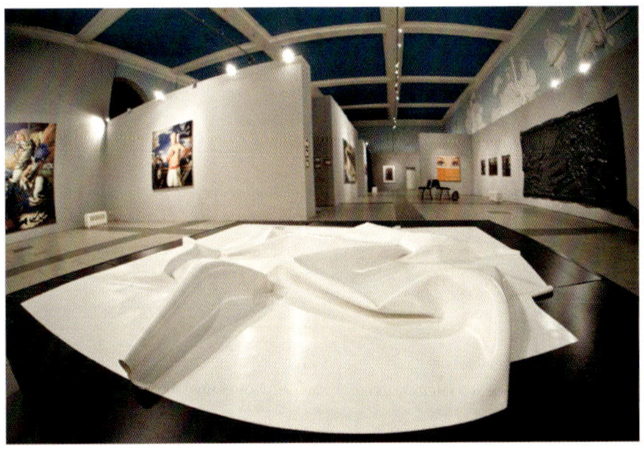

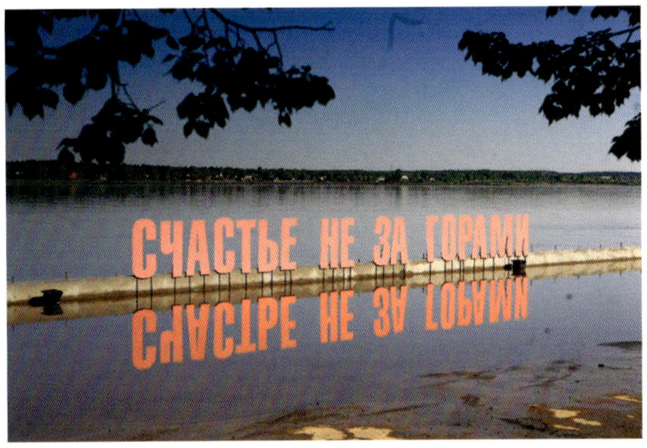

PERMM (Perm Museum of Modern Art) opened in 2008 in the city of Perm at the edge of the Ural Mountains. One of the most important contemporary art museums outside of Moscow, it has regenerated the city, which is fast turning into a new cultural hub.

PERMM was conceived, and has mainly been funded, by the property entrepreneur Sergei Gordeev, former senator of Perm Oblast and an art enthusiast. Through his Russian Avant-Garde Foundation, Gordeev has subsidised a number of creative projects, from architectural exhibitions at Moscow's Museum of Architecture to reconstruction work on the Russian Pavilion for the 2007 Venice Biennale. Gordeev realised that a contemporary art museum would serve as a regenerating impulse for Perm and a catalyst for facilitating cultural integration of the city into the international art scene, thus encouraging economic growth and tourism. The idea of creating such a museum was supported by Oleg Chirkunov, Perm's governor. Chirkunov was willing to help to transform a disused site into a contemporary space by making available part of the regional budget for urban and cultural development projects. An inspired gesture for the development of PERMM was the hiring of Marat Guelman, the Moscow-based commercial gallery owner, art critic and collector, as director and curator.

PERMM held its inaugural exhibition, *Russian Povera*, in 2008. The show, which attracted critical acclaim, brought thirty thousand visitors to PERMM over a two-month period and later travelled to St Petersburg, Moscow, Milan and New York. In Perm the exhibition was presented in the former River Station Hall, which had been renovated for the occasion by Gordeev's foundation. The building was subsequently kept as the premises for PERMM as it met all the requirements for an exhibition space, a quality of railway stations exploited to huge advantage in Europe in previous years; witness the successes of the Musée d'Orsay in Paris and the Hamburger Bahnhof in Berlin.

Since *Russian Povera* there have been other big shows, including *New Testament Project* (2009), which featured contemporary reportage together with quotations from the Bible. And *IF* (2010), curated by Ekaterina Degot, featured contemporary Ukrainian art reflecting upon life since the Orange Revolution.

Alongside major temporary exhibitions, there is a plan to establish a permanent collection. Guelman is proud of what has been achieved so far: 'Having seen how many sheets of paper there were for every part of the programme, I understood that Perm is living. The main task is to show Perm that it is living.' Gordeev has observed that 'the role of a contemporary art museum in our country is to change people's thinking or reasoning; to introduce tolerance in action ...' PERMM's support through the regional budget is important, as State support for contemporary art is perceived as an important step in its acceptance by the public. It also increases the region's status and acts as a catalyst to build visitor numbers and inspire press interest.

It is also controversial, however, because some at the local level believe that there are more immediate priorities for public spending. Another difficulty is the unwillingness of local patrons to accept contemporary art alongside the traditional work to which they are accustomed. Despite these obstacles, Guelman believes that 'a phenomenon is being created in Perm that will pull all of Russian art up to international level.' As if in support of this statement, the city has been compared favourably in the international press with another industrial city-turned-cultural centre, Bilbao.

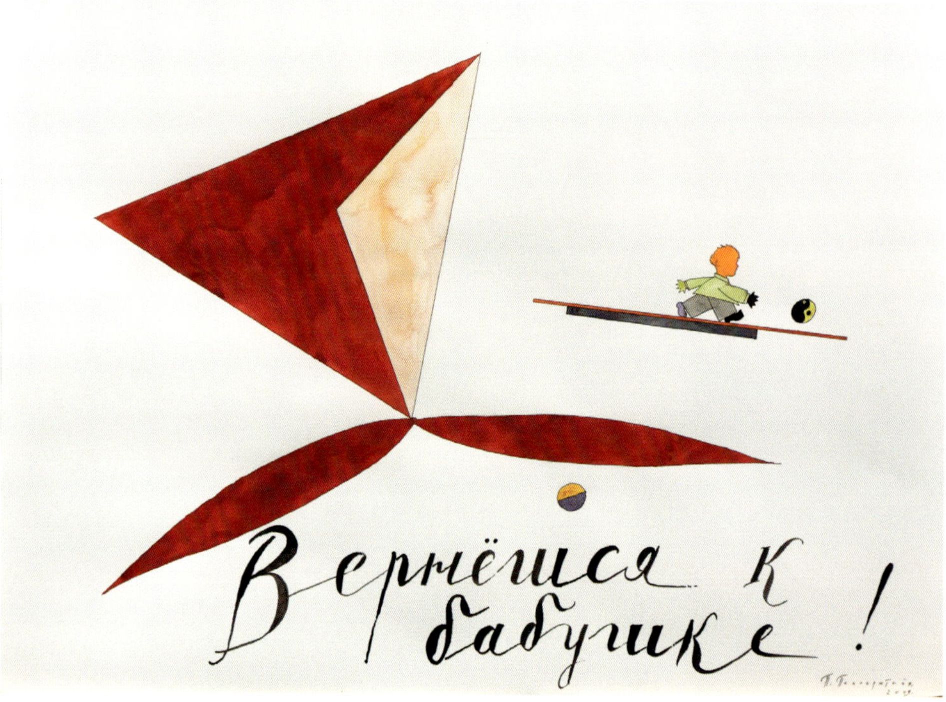

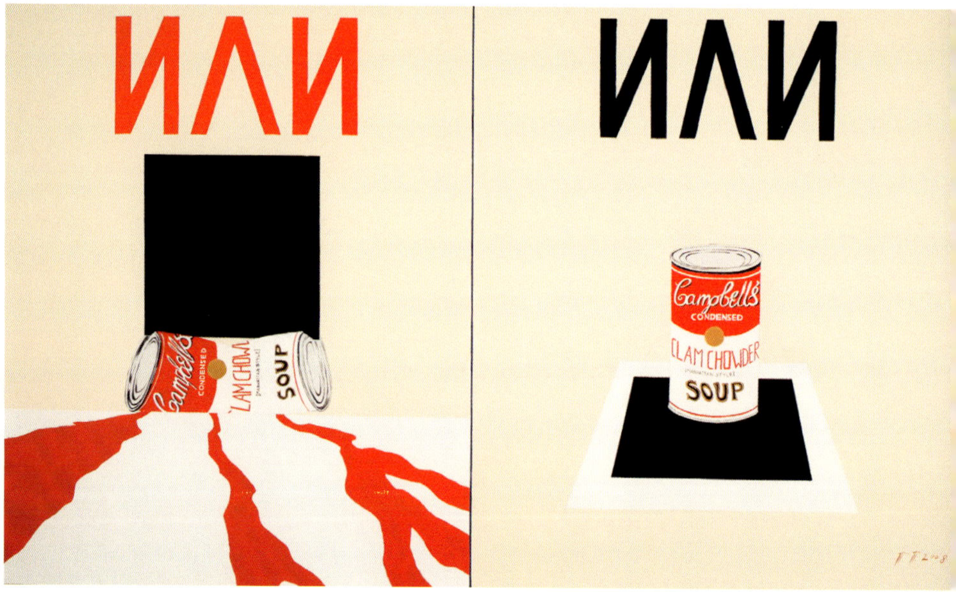

It comes as no surprise that Pavel Pepperstein has been busy for the last two and a half decades producing installations, paintings, drawings, criticism, novels and rap music. Born in Moscow in 1966, Pepperstein – an alias – is the son of Moscow Conceptualist Victor Pivovarov and the children's book illustrator Irina Pivovarova. 'I was born into the family of an artist', he explains. 'My father was a great artist and he created a powerful aura around himself, and I was pulled into it. My mother worked with literature and created a charged aura as well, so I simply started working with these two, following in their footsteps.' Growing up in this artistic circle, Pepperstein forged close relationships, most notably with Ilya Kabakov, with whom he has collaborated. On his return to Moscow in 1987 after completing his studies at the Prague Academy of Fine Arts, Pepperstein co-founded Inspection Medical Hermeneutics. His independent work, on which he has been focusing since the late 1990s, has extended the deconstructive ethos of IMH. Pepperstein's name is largely associated with series of fanciful pictures and drawings combining cultural symbols and codes, word games, children's fables and fairy tales to form, as he puts it, a kind of 'psychedelic realism'.

That Pepperstein's work inspires a game of free associations and subconsciously generated thought might well be due to his wide-ranging interest in topics including, but not stopping with, Freudian psychoanalysis, Soviet and Western cultural ideologies, Zen Buddhism, the schizo-analysis of Deleuze and Guattari, literature and psychedelia. By intertwining these disparate sources, he aims to deactivate culturally loaded myths and symbols and make them fit again for public consumption. In the diptych *Black Square and Campbell* (2000), for example, he playfully reactivated Cold War antagonisms on an artistic battlefield inhabited by Malevich's *Black Square* and Warhol's *Campbell's Soup Cans*.

Pepperstein draws heavily on the utopian aesthetics of the historical avant-garde, notably Suprematism, and of the space-age optimism of the 1960s. One example is *Landscapes of the Future* (2006–7), which was exhibited in the Russian Pavilion at the 2007 Venice Biennale. Half-playful, half-serious, *City of Russia* (2007) develops this highly topical investigation into social utopias, architecture and urbanism. The paintings and the associated letter addressed to Vladimir Putin and the mayors of Moscow and St Petersburg came into being due to the fact that 'Moscow was ruthlessly destroyed, then St Petersburg and other cities, too. This caused these feelings of despair, and I wanted to oppose it with something, so this utopia was created, mostly from the desire to save old cities. To channel the activity of the bourgeoisie who build their ... skyscrapers and to place them in a neutral space where they won't ruin our beautiful cities.' Thus Pepperstein proposed the establishment of a new capital, City of Russia, and charted its evolution. Despite his quirky sense of humour and wild imagination, these works sound a note of desolation and express an awareness of the failed utopias of the 1920s and 1960s and, therefore, of the fantastical nature of his own creations.

Pepperstein has exhibited widely across Europe and Russia. Alongside his visual works, in 1999 he co-authored the hugely popular *The Mythogenic Love of Casts* with Sergei Anufriev and then, in 2005, *The Interpretation of Dreams* with Viktor Mazin. He leads a nomadic lifestyle, on occasion reappearing in Moscow.

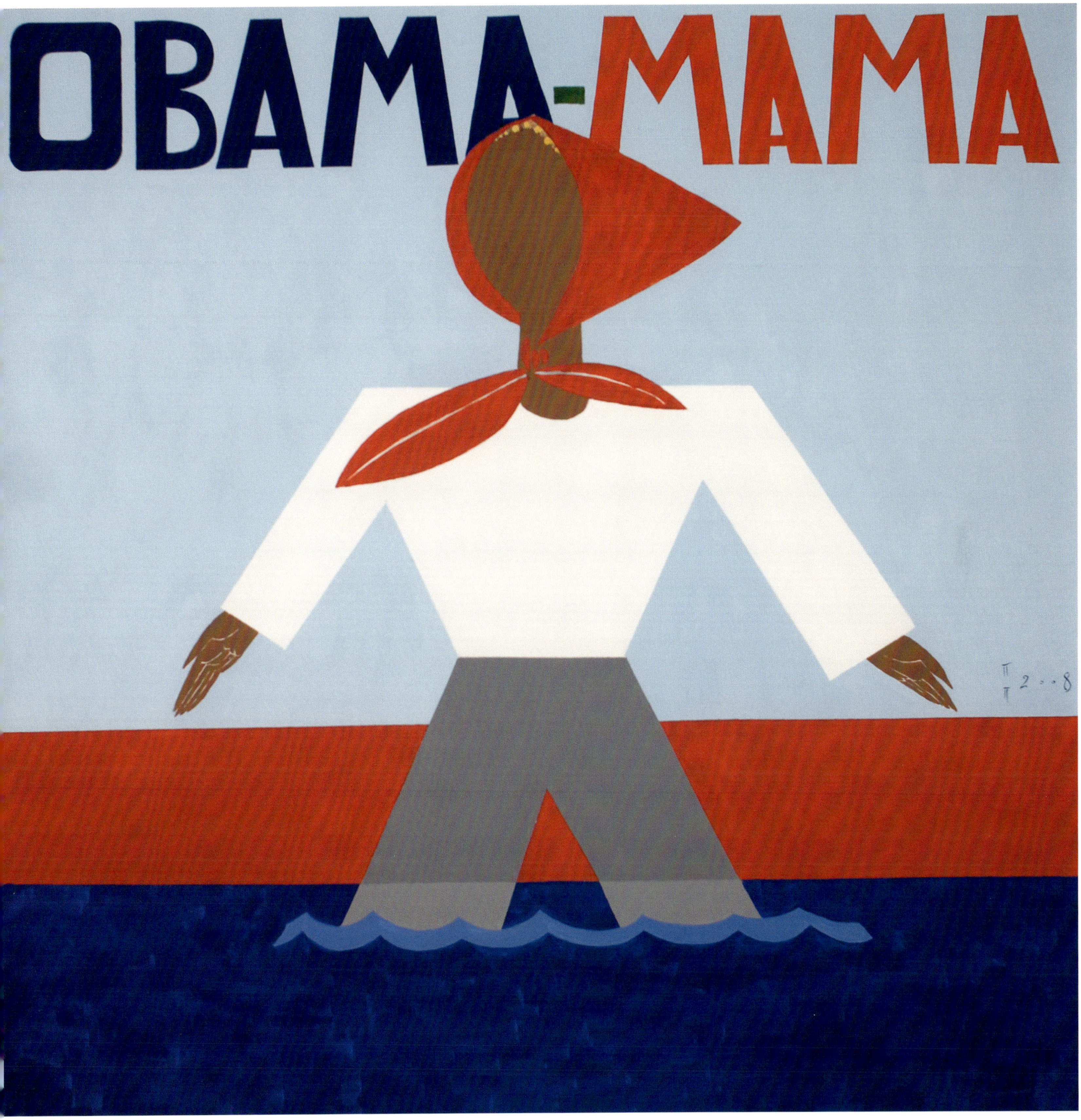

facing page far left
Let's Go Back to Granny!', 2009
Watercolour on paper
49.5 x 69.5 cm
© Pavel Pepperstein
Courtesy of Regina Gallery, London & Moscow

facing page left
Black Square and Campbell, 2008
Acrylic on canvas
250 x 150 cm
© Pavel Pepperstein
Private collection

above
OBAMA-MAMA, 2008
Acrylic on canvas
150 x 150 cm
© Pavel Pepperstein
Private collection

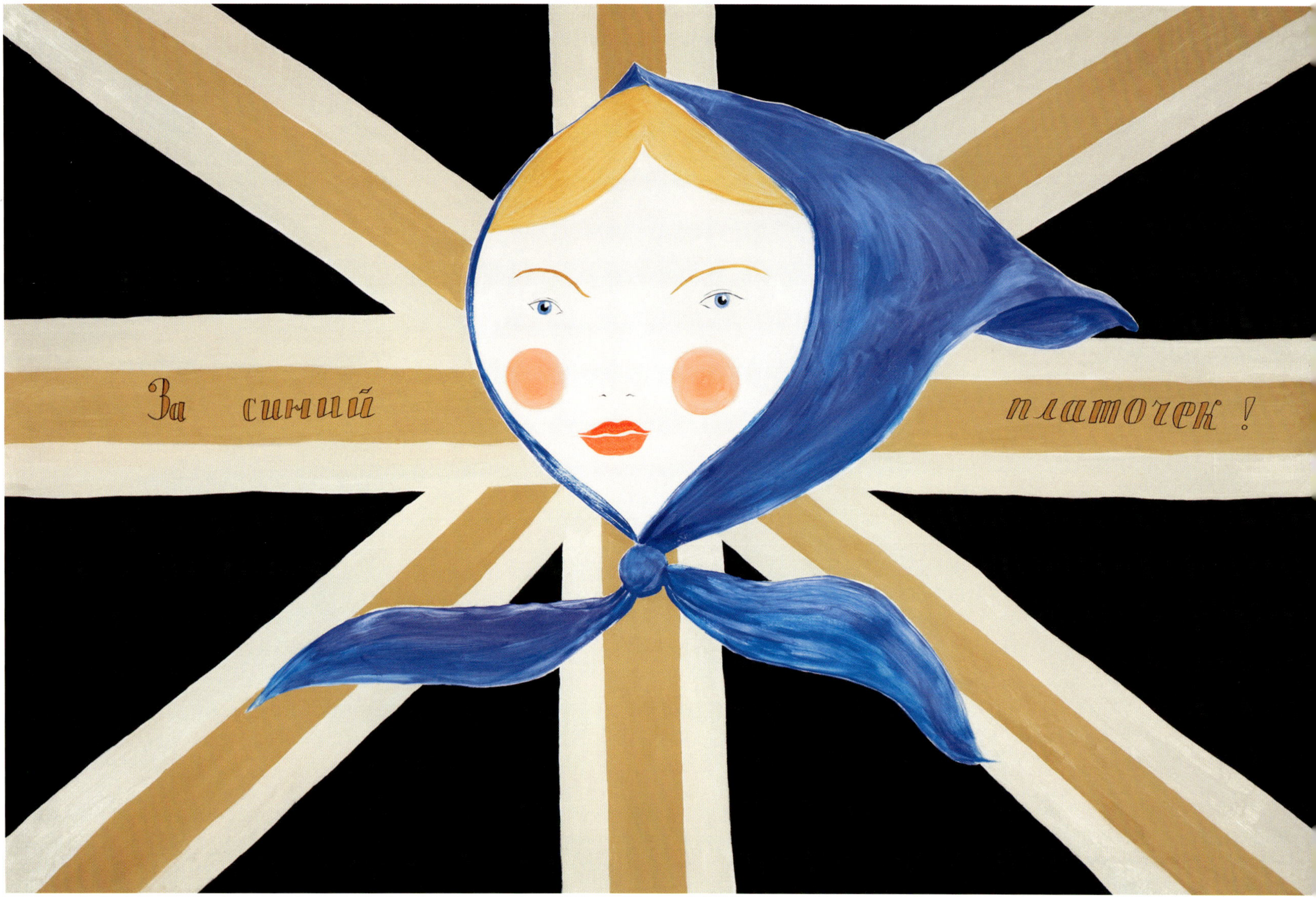

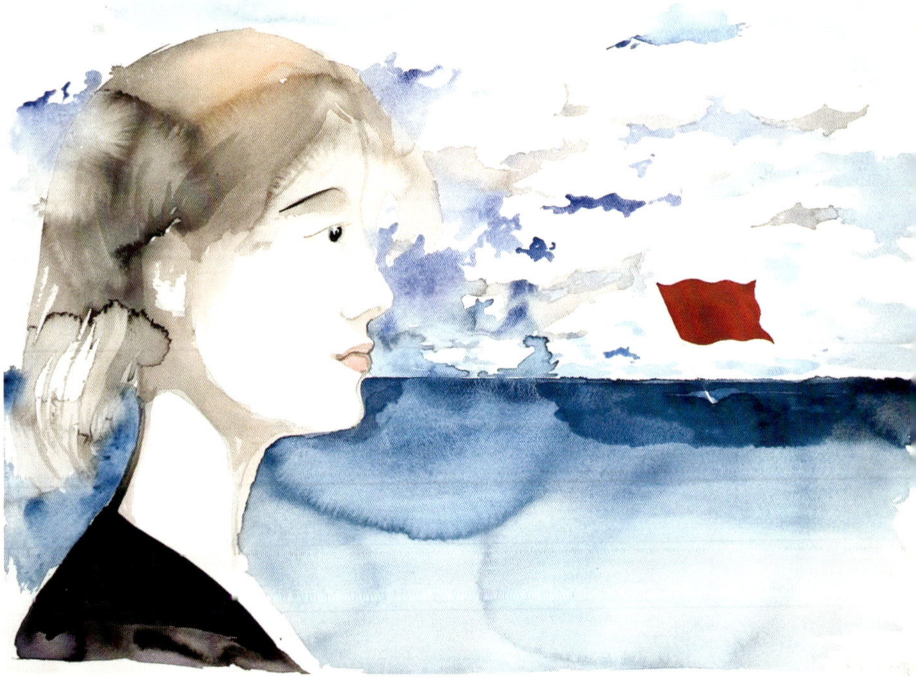

above
For Blue Kerchief, 2010
Oil on canvas
200 x 300 cm
© Pavel Pepperstein
Courtesy of Regina Gallery, London & Moscow

right
No. 2, from the series Hypnosis, 2004
Watercolour on paper
56 x 76 cm
© Pavel Pepperstein
Private collection

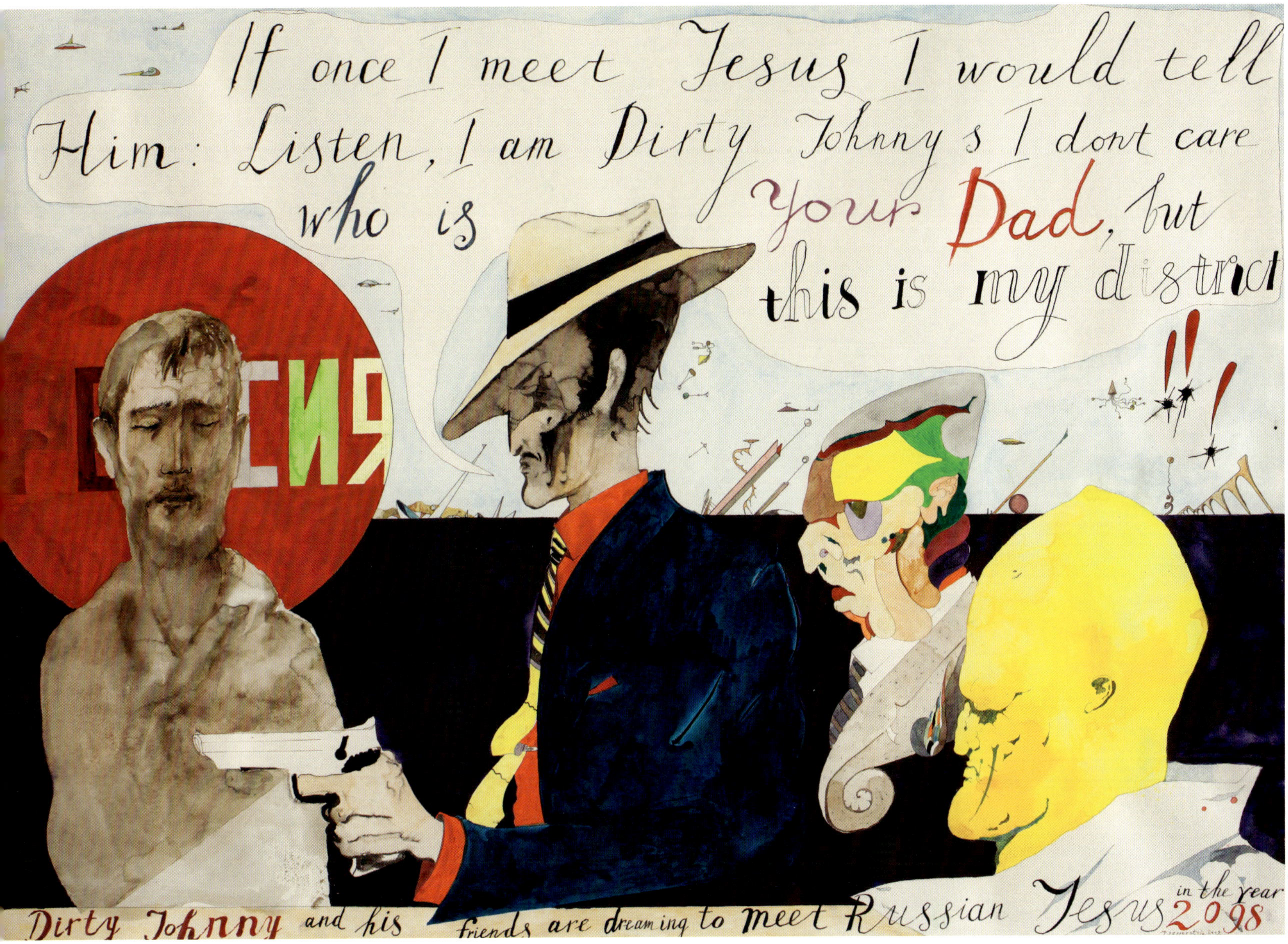

above
Dirty Johnny, 2009
Watercolour on paper
62 x 85 cm
© Pavel Pepperstein
Courtesy of Nahodka Arts Ltd, London

Pavel Pepperstein

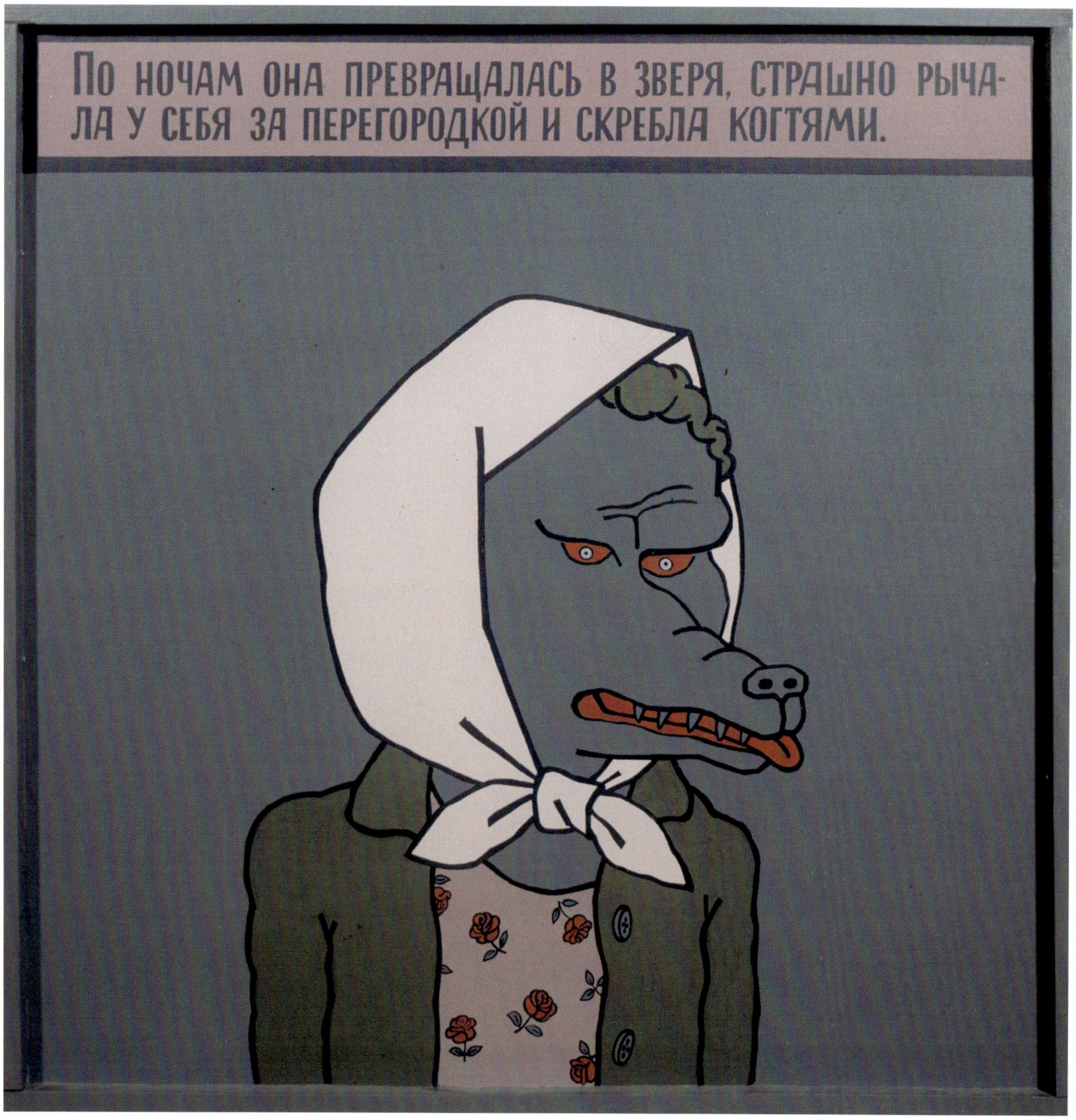

One of the key figures associated with Moscow Conceptualism, Victor Pivovarov was born in Moscow in 1937 and received his formal education in the department of Book Illustration at the Moscow Polygraphic Institute. With his friend the artist Ilya Kabakov, Pivovarov created a new artistic genre, the album, a format in which he continues to work to this day. He explains his predilection this way: 'The album as genre unites text and image, and gives a greater opportunity for the fullness of expression ... Works in series provide greater opportunity not only for the artist but for the viewer too, because they lead and help him along.' Famed for these Surrealist-influenced albums projects as well as for his paintings, Pivovarov has also enjoyed an illustrious career as a book illustrator. Since 1982 he has lived and worked in Prague.

Pivovarov sets out to depict a neutral, romantic, introspective existence distanced from the virulent, sarcastic social critique of his Moscow Conceptualist contemporaries. His works are often linked by an investigation into the themes of childhood and solitude. Life's bittersweet nature is explored in the aptly named *Lemon Eaters* (2006), which takes as its point of departure Van Gogh's painting *The Potato Eaters* (1885) but which presents consumption within the context of Soviet history. Works like this one feature individuals alienated from the rest of society and existing in dreamlike conditions. Pivovarov understands loneliness not as 'a state of suffering, because of course it can very often be arduous, but as a moment of contact with the world, with being, and with nature'.

above
At Night She Turned into..., 1992–95
Nitro-enamel on canvas
101 x 101 cm
© Victor Pivovarov
Ekaterina and Vladimir Semenikhin Collection

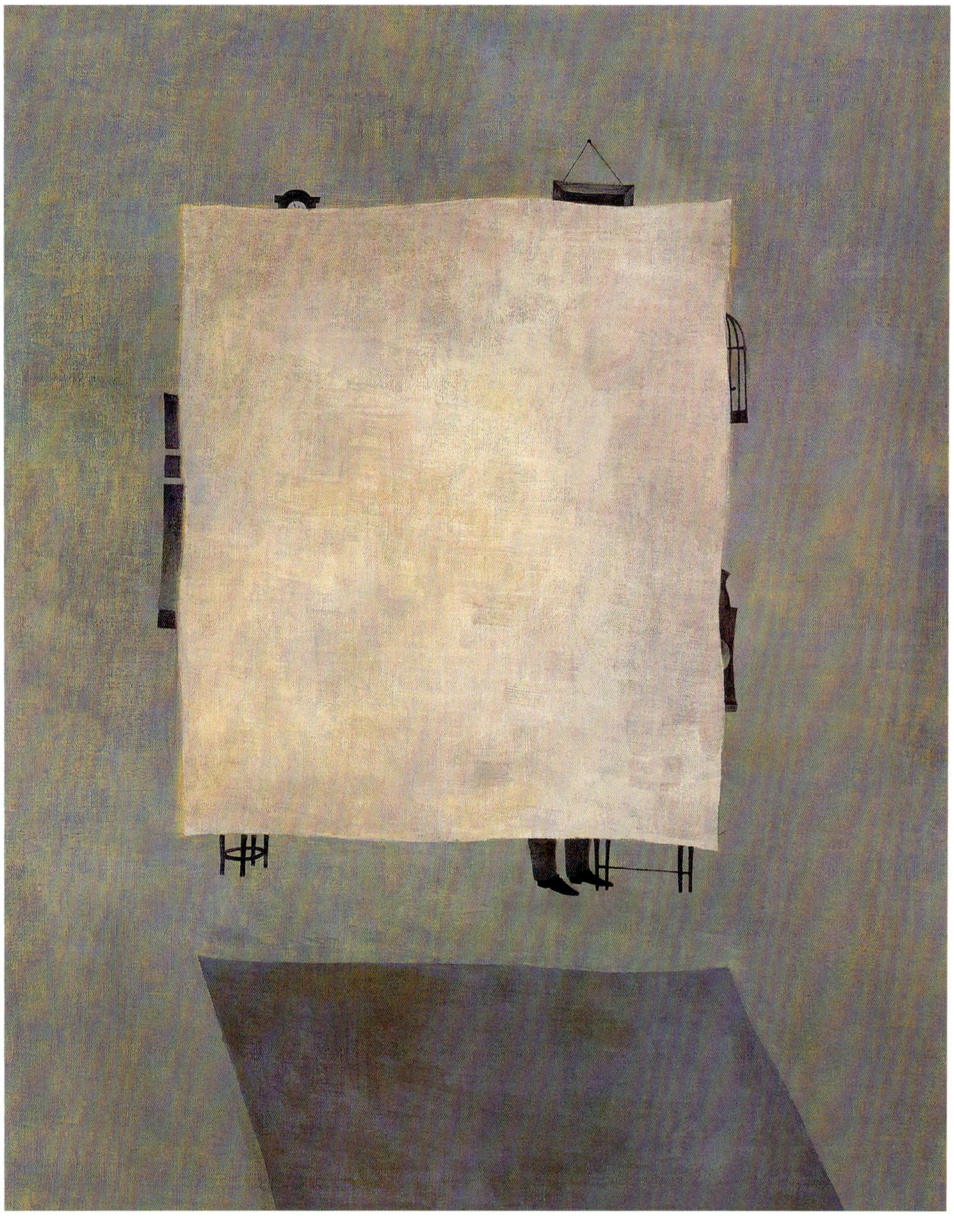

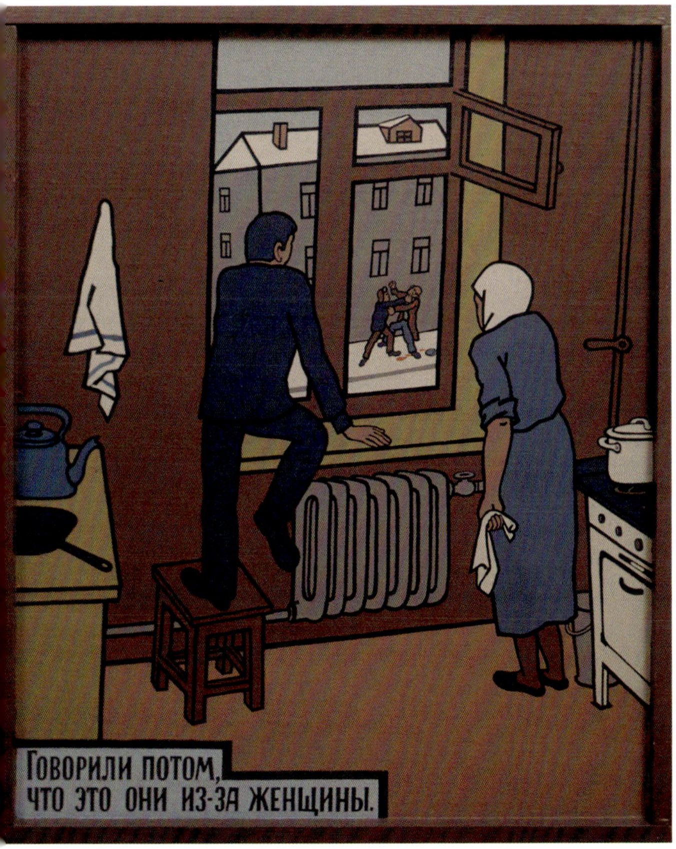

left
From the cycle Apartment 22, 1992
Oil on plywood, wood and enamel
100.5 x 83 x 5.5 cm
© Victor Pivovarov
Ekaterina and Vladimir Semenikhin Collection

above
House of the Wind, 1974
Oil on canvas
86 x 107 cm
© Victor Pivovarov
Courtesy of Yuri Traisman Art Foundation

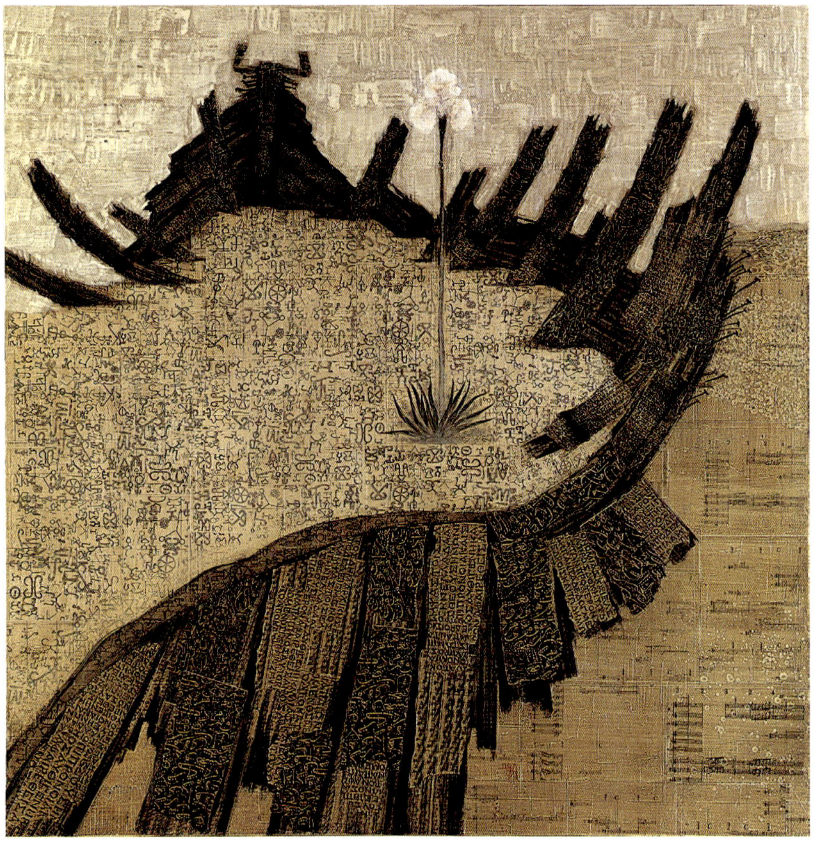

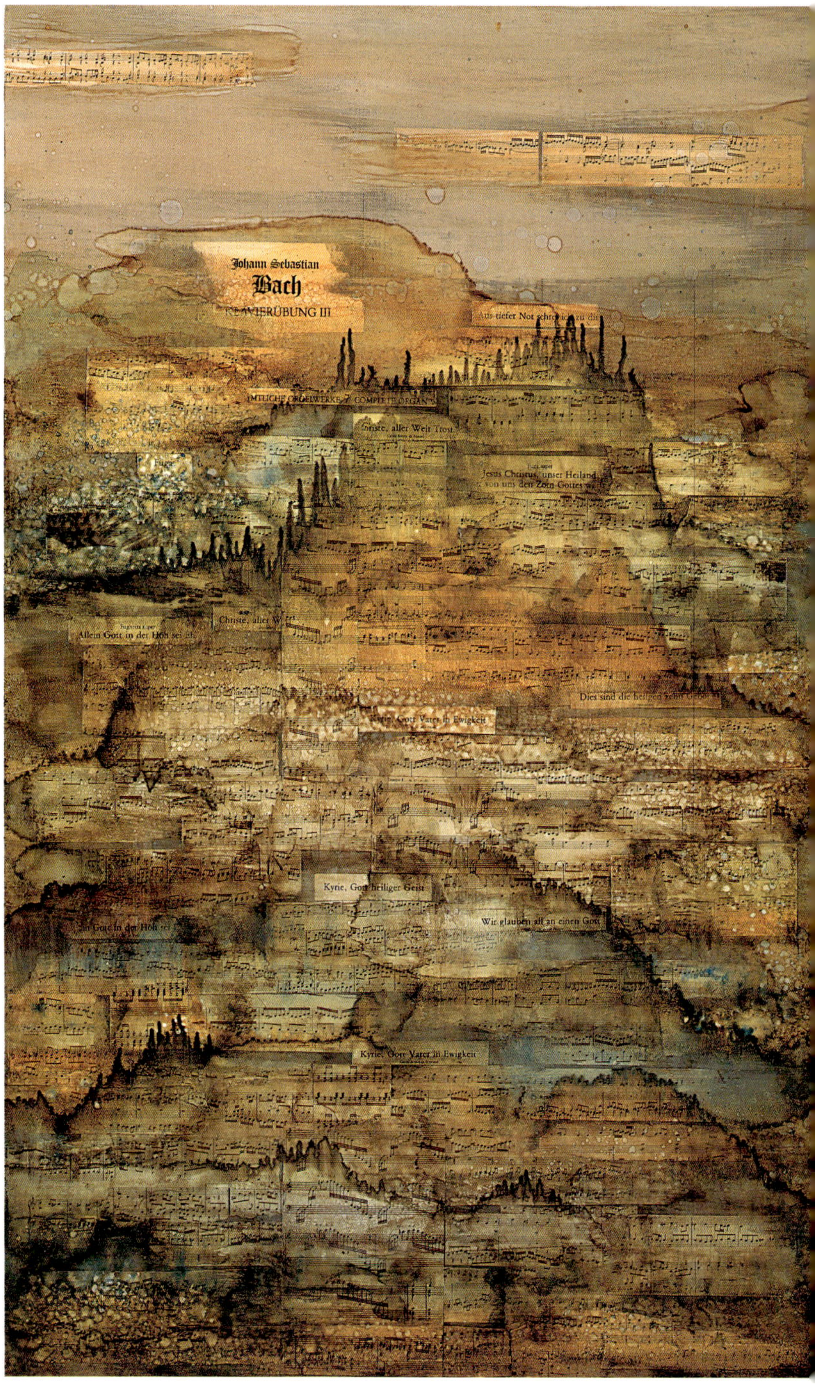

Dmitry Plavinsky

Painter and graphic artist Dmitry Plavinsky was born in 1937 and grew up in Moscow's Arbat district. Having started to draw at the age of ten, he studied theatre design in Moscow's Art School in Memory of 1905, graduating in 1956. The International Festival of Youth a year later was a turning point for Plavinsky, as he was able to see modern art from Europe and America for the first time. In 1960 he met the collector George Costakis, who became a patron. At the time, Plavinsky was developing a style of painting using a pared-down colour palette and exploring both abstract and figurative approaches. His paintings are held in numerous public collections, including the Museum of Modern Art, New York; the Metropolitan Museum of Art, New York; the Ludwig Museum, Cologne; the State Tretyakov Gallery, Moscow; and the State Russian Museum, St Petersburg. He lives and works in Moscow.

The forms and colours of the natural world as seen in Plavinsky's series of paintings of turtles and studies of plant life form the foundation for a practice that explores formal continuities as well as harmonies and spiritual traditions from past civilisations and contemporary urban life. Focusing on signs and symbols, he documents things that have endured over time. During the 1960s he made several trips to the north of Russia to explore medieval towns and record church buildings that were falling into disrepair. He has also travelled widely in Central Asia, incorporating Islamic motifs into his art. Plavinsky emigrated to New York in 1991; one of his celebrated works painted while there depicts Manhattan Island as a fossilised prehistoric fish. As well as visual culture, his art explores the diverse realms of music, poetry, mathematics, geology and astronomy.

top left
Boat of Remembrances, 1997
Oil, acrylic, collage on canvas
153 x 153 cm
© Dmitry Plavinsky
Private collection

above
Bach's Fugue, 1987
Oil, polyvinylacetate tempera, collage on canvas
140 x 90 cm
© Dmitry Plavinsky
Private collection

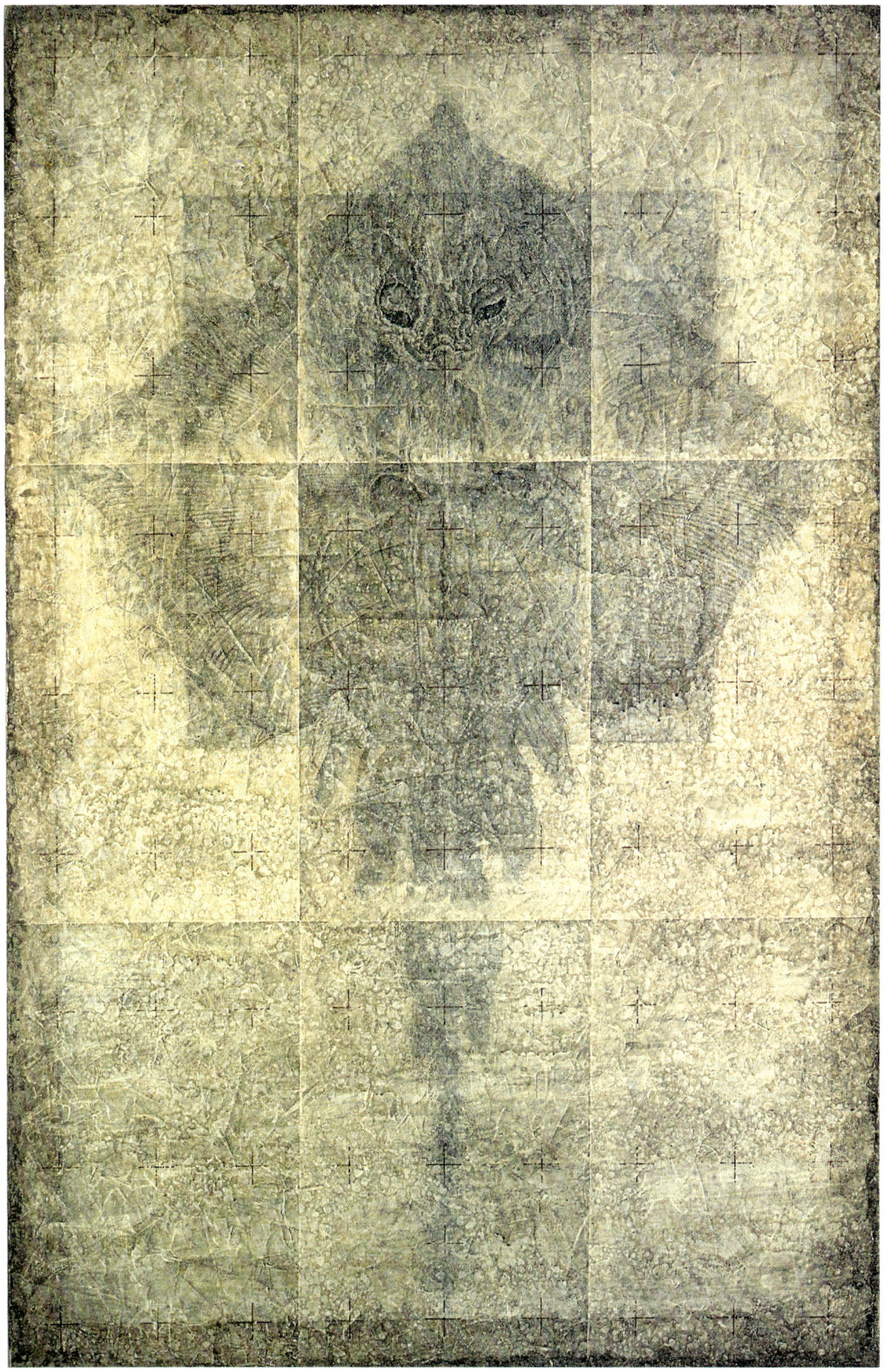

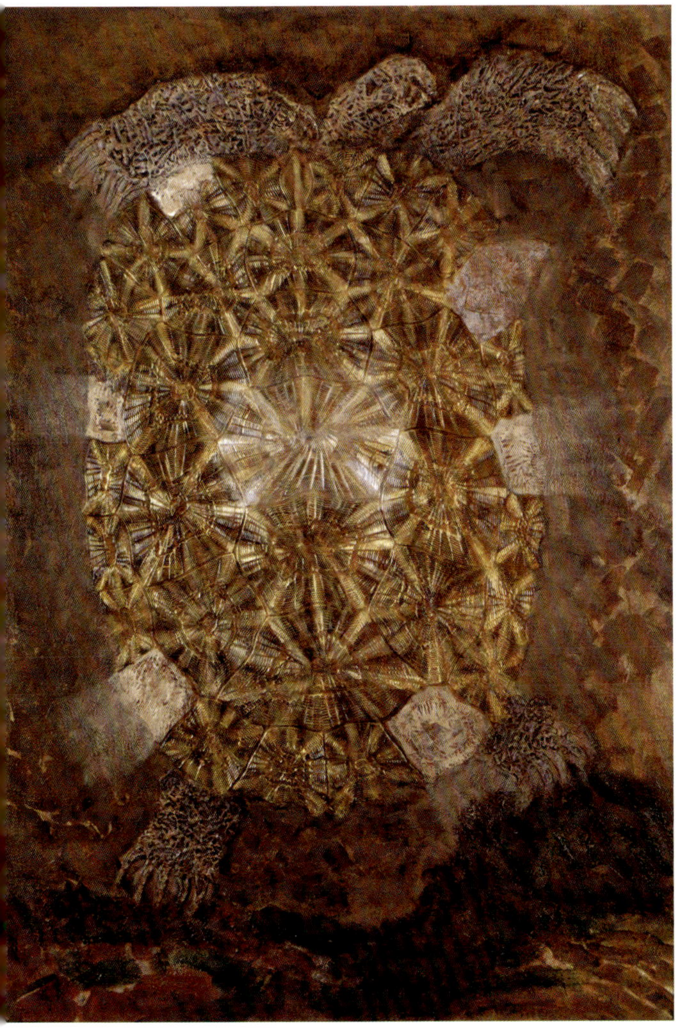

above
Skate, 1981
Oil, polyvinylacetate tempera on canvas
150 x 100 cm
© Dmitry Plavinsky
Collection of the artist

left
Radiated Tortoise, 2009–10
Oil, acrylic, collage on canvas
160 x 110 cm
© Dmitry Plavinsky
Private collection

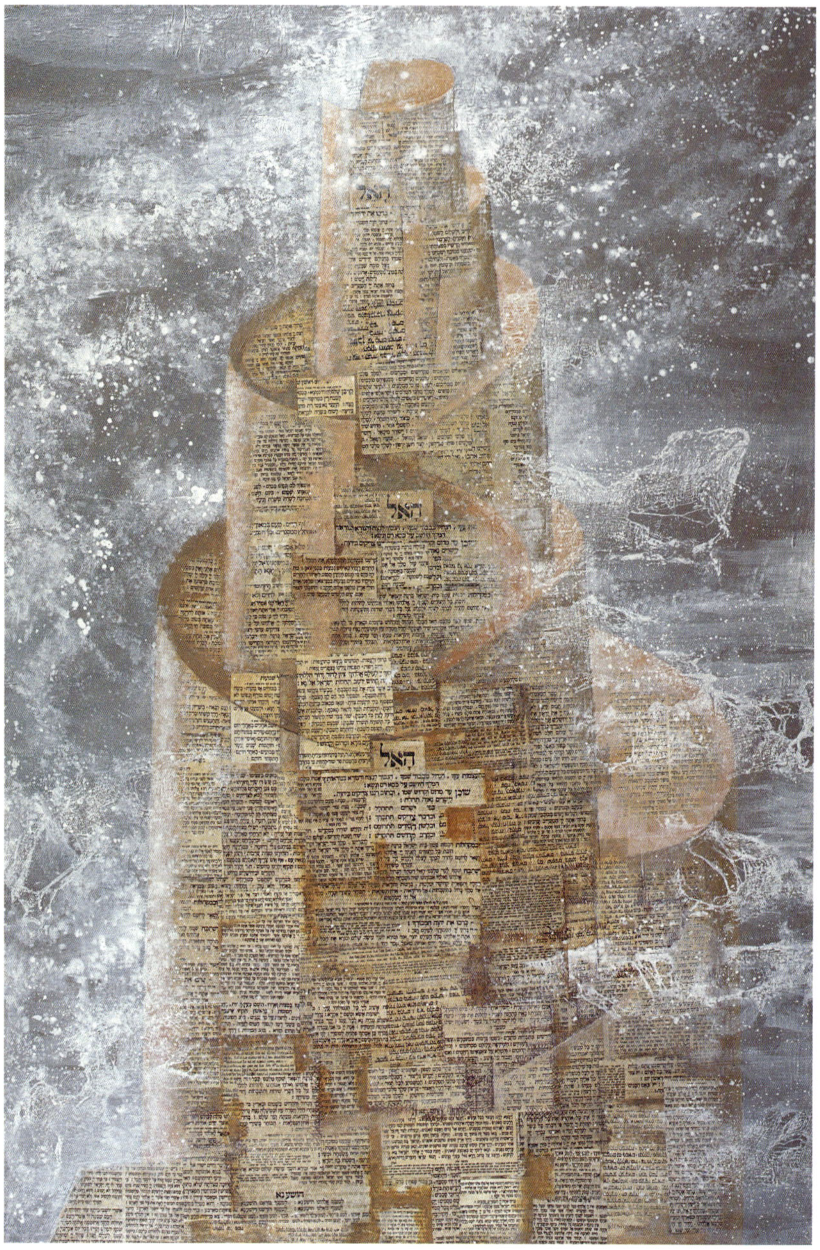

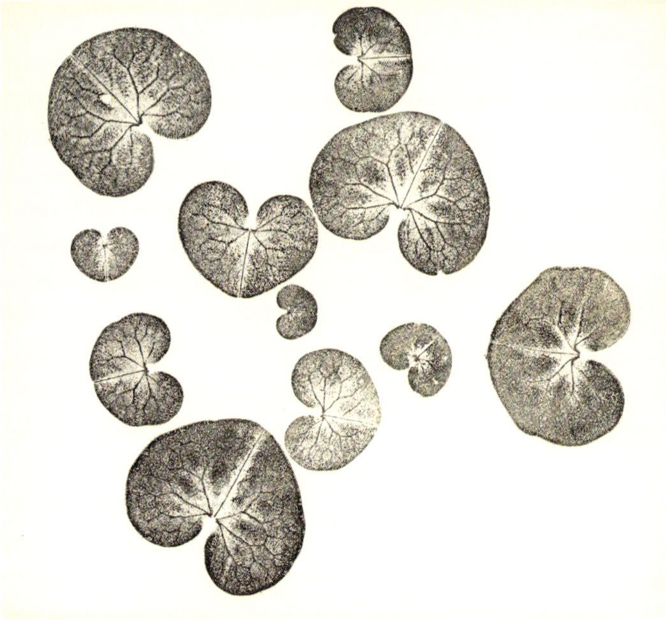

above
Sheet from Book of Grass, 1963
Pen and ink on paper
27 x 30 cm
© Dmitry Plavinsky
Collection of the artist

top
Wanderer's Vision, 1989
Oil, polyvinylacetate tempera, collage on canvas
143 x 98.5 cm
© Dmitry Plavinsky
Collection of the artist

right
Moonlight Leaf from Book of Grass (2 parts), 1963
Nature print
27 x 60 cm
© Dmitry Plavinsky
Collection of the artist

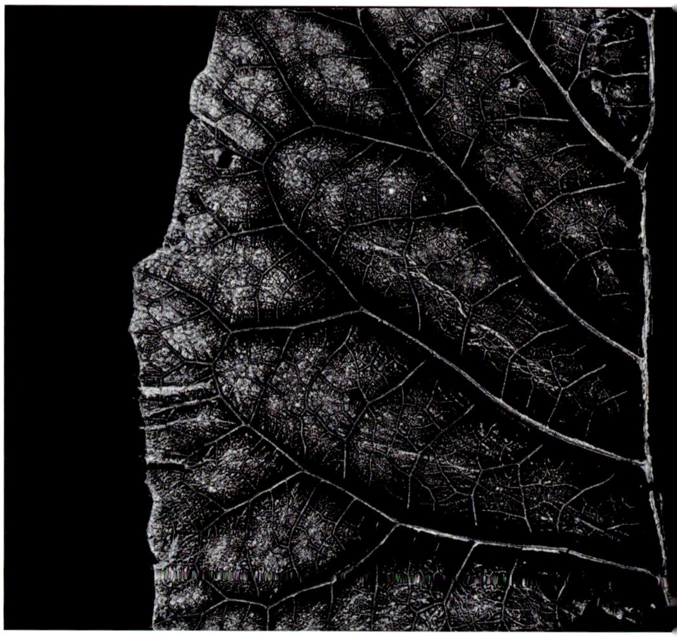

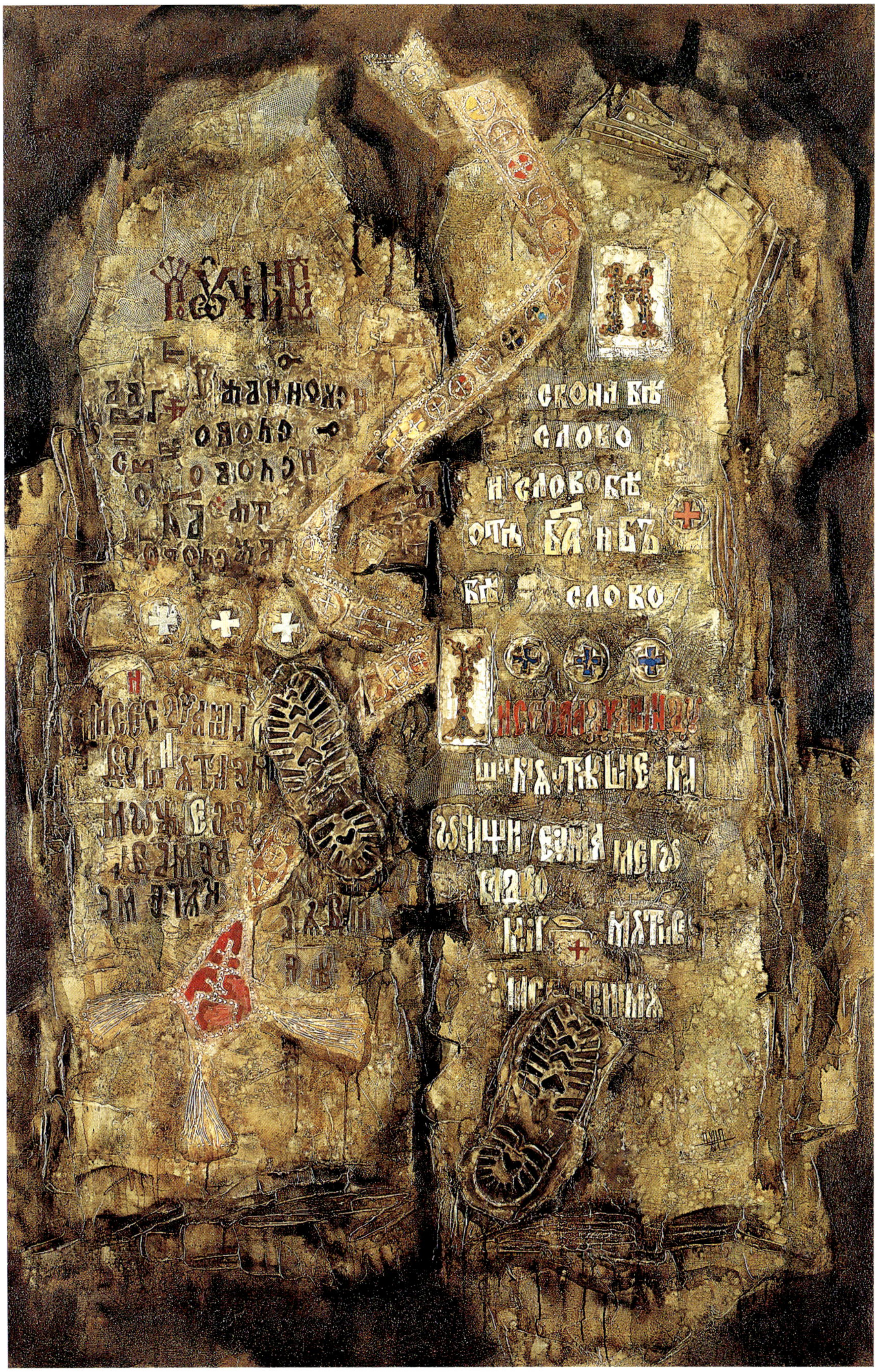

right
St John's Gospel, 1967
Oil, polyvinylacetate tempera, plaster, collage on canvas
180 x 120 cm
© Dmitry Plavinsky
The Tabakman Collection, US

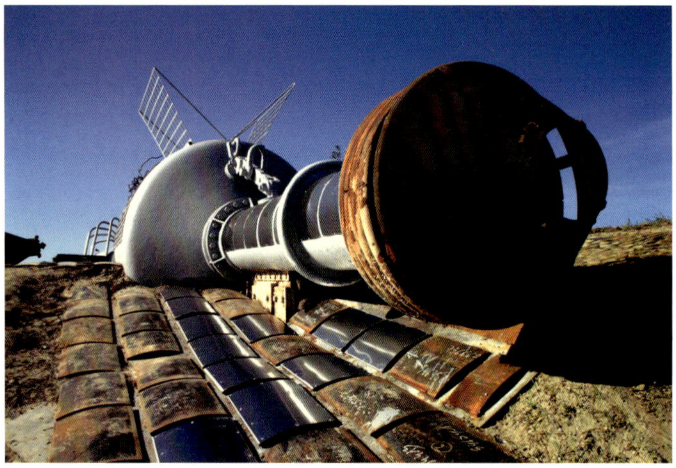

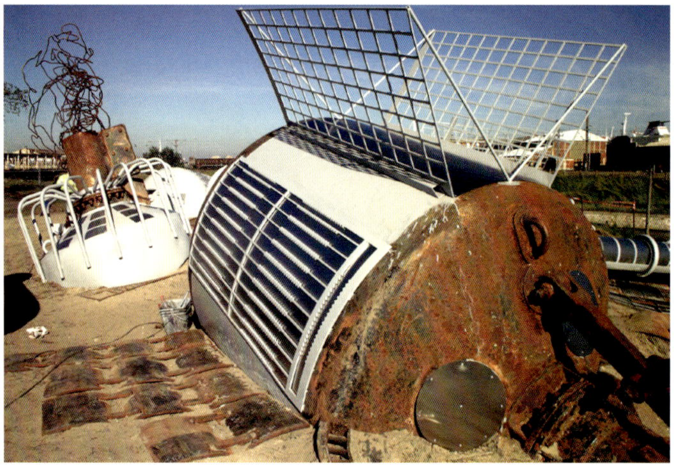

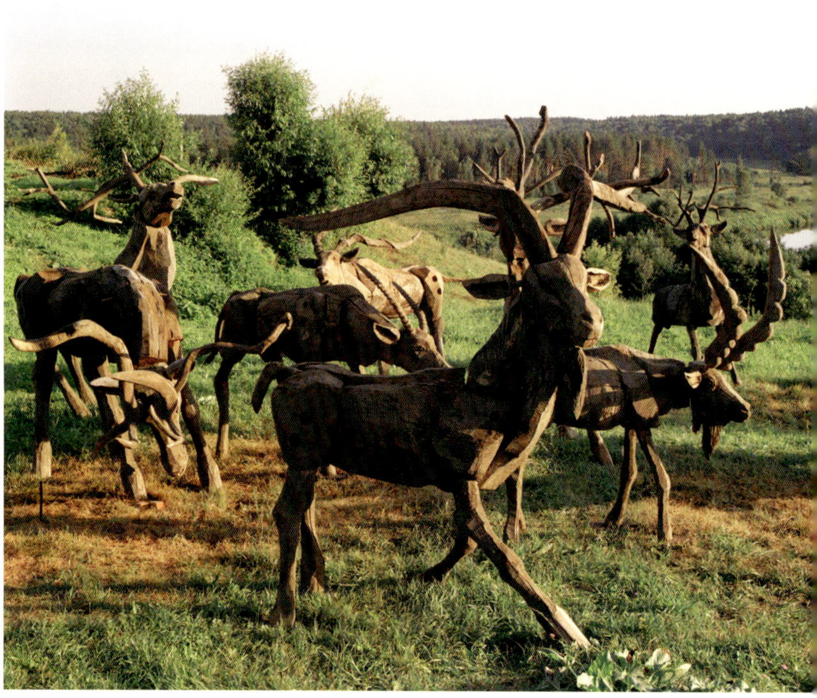

Nikolai Polissky

Nikolai Polissky was born in Moscow in 1957. He studied at the Leningrad Higher Industrial Art Institute, specialising in ceramics, and graduated in 1982. From the mid-1980s on, he became associated with Mitki, a group with a strong literary focus as well as a collaborative, multidisciplinary approach emphasising irony and the absurd. Since 2000 Polissky has become known for his large site-specific installations or sculptures in the tradition of Land art.

Polissky divides his time between Moscow and the small village of Nikola-Lenivets, 200 kilometres west of the capital. Together with a group of locals, he creates large-scale temporary installations, drawing inspiration from the ancient pagan rites of pre-Christian Russia and using cheap local materials. *Snowmen* (2000) was a collaborative project with fellow Mitki members Konstantin Batinkov and Sergei Lobanov and local inhabitants, who together made an army of 220 snowmen-warriors with carrot noses and buckets for helmets. Polissky's works all have connections with national mythology, peasant rites and ancient customs, which he reinvigorates. Many of his installations are set alight and the performances recorded in photographs and on film. Since 2006 he has created an annual Land art festival, Arch-Stoyanie, at Nikola-Lenivets.

top left
Sputnik, 2010
Metal, ready-mades
Varying dimensions
© Nikolai Polissky
Courtesy of City of Dunkerque

above left
Sputnik, 2010
Metal, ready-mades
Varying dimensions
© Nikolai Polissky
Courtesy of City of Dunkerque

above
Hunting Trophies, 2010
Wood carved with chainsaw
Varying dimensions
© Nikolai Polissky
Courtesy of Le Royal Monceau

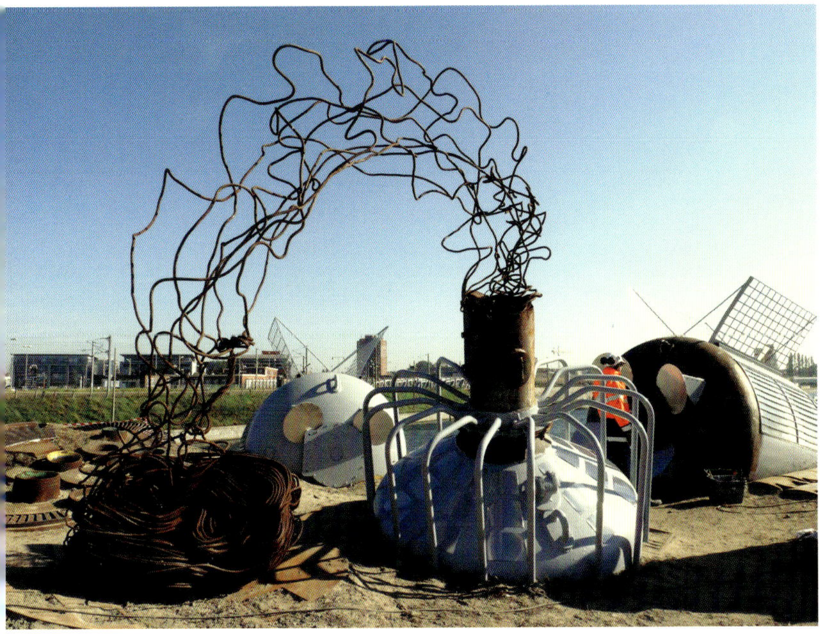

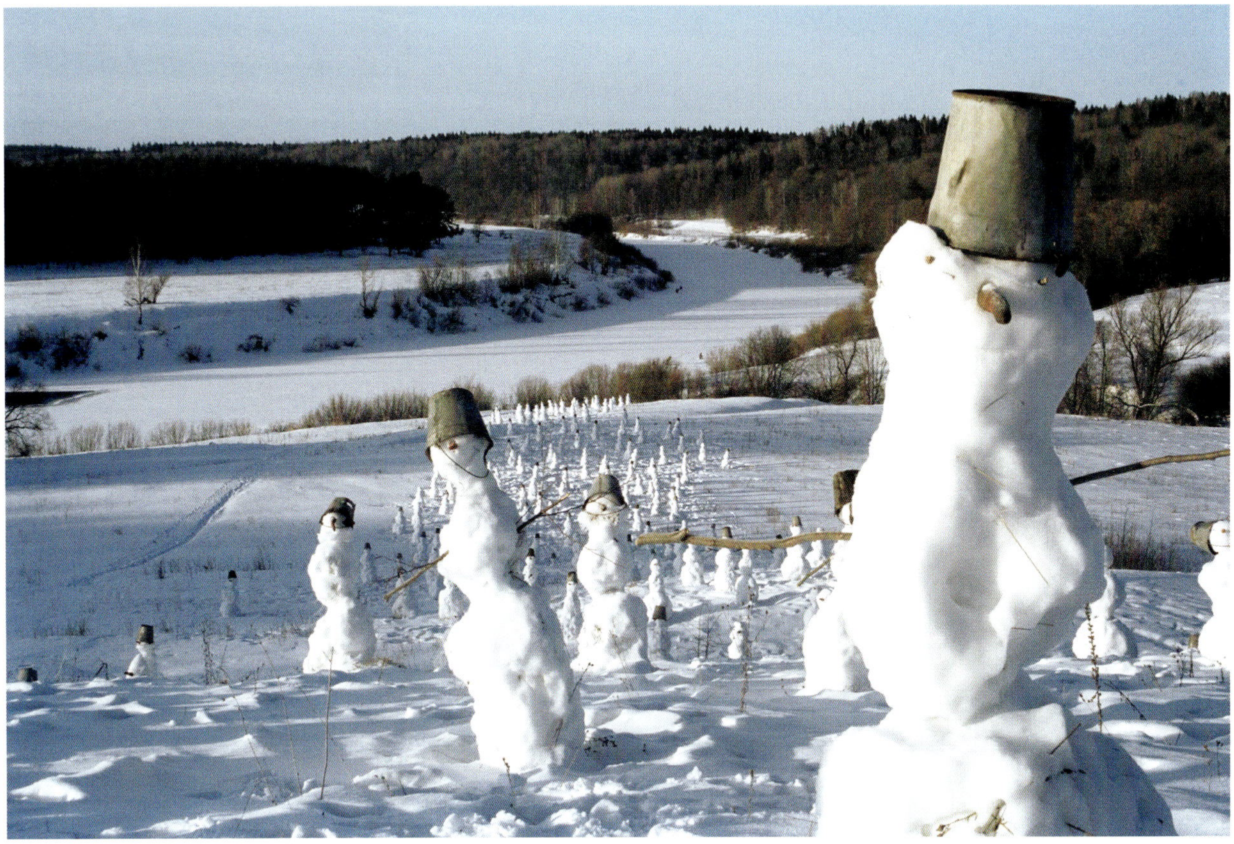

top
Sputnik, 2010
Metal, ready-mades
Varying dimensions
© Nikolai Polissky
Courtesy of City of Dunkerque

right
Snowmen, 2000
Snow, rusted buckets, carrots
Varying dimensions
© Nikolai Polissky
Courtesy of the artist

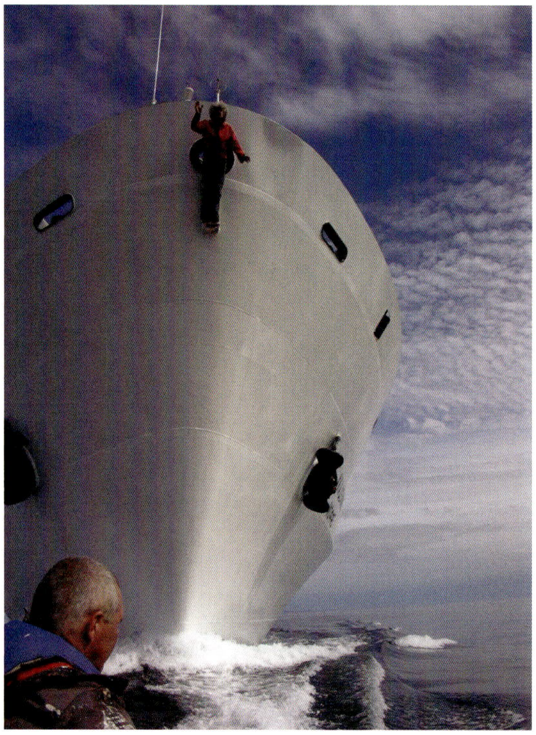

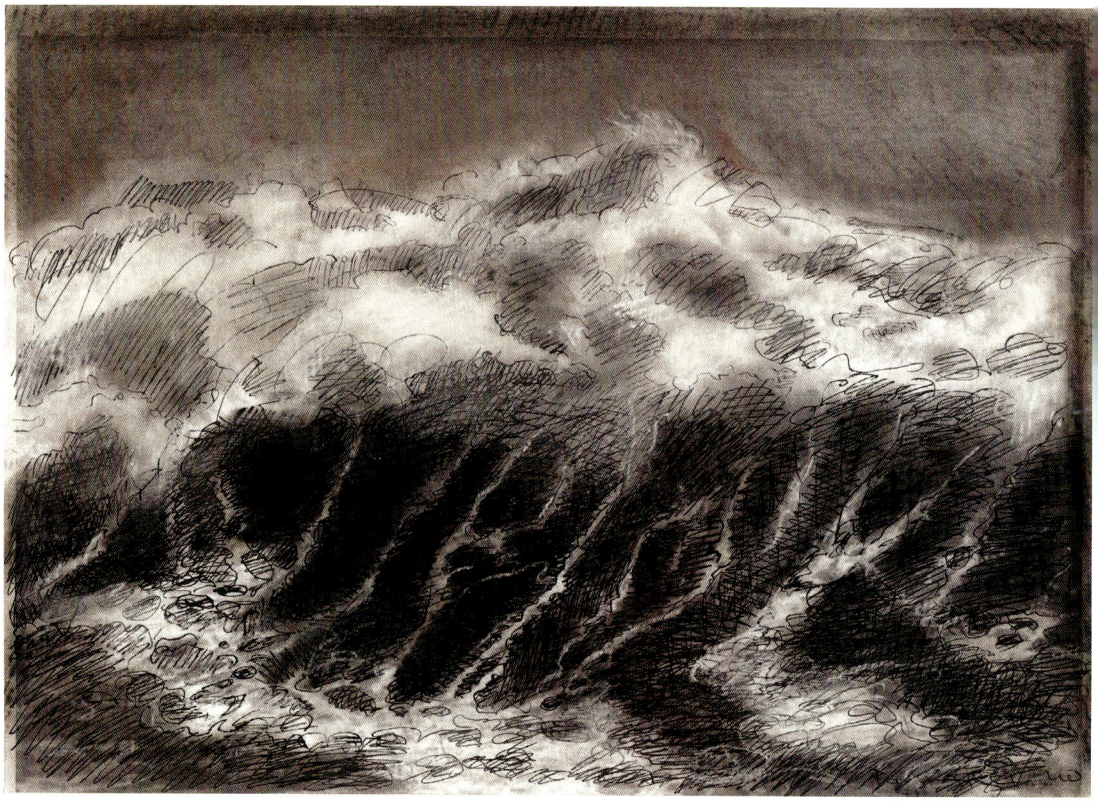

Alexander Ponomarev's formal education began at the Orel Art School and finished at the USSR Nautical Engineering College in Odessa. On graduating from the latter in 1979, he spent two years as a torpedo officer onboard a diesel submarine before joining the merchant navy. 'In Soviet times it was the only way to see the world,' he has said. Ponomarev's career as a seaman would leave an indelible mark on his subsequent artistic practice, which is dominated by epic aquatic installations and performative engagement with remote seas and arctic terrain. Throughout his work, he marshals industrial, military and scientific structures to poetic and revealing effect. While refashioning the role of explorer for the twenty-first century, his art also invites meditation on the relationship between illusion/fiction and 'reality', the utility of creativity, and the shifting tides of personal and social history. Throughout, he forges powerful and surprising conjunctions between aspects of cultural and natural life that are often considered separate – between naval officers and esoteric philosophy, the Italian Renaissance and Russian Constructivism, Romantic landscape and geopolitical conflict over natural resources. His art is at once metaphysical and intensely material.

Monumental gestures are characteristic features of Ponomarev's practice. That the man can – in a figure of speech not far removed from the truth – move mountains is demonstrated by *Maya: A Lost Island* (2005), in which the artist, collaborating with the 5th Fleet of the Russian Navy, made a land mass in the Barents Sea disappear. In 1996, he gained access to a secret naval base and painted an operational nuclear submarine in 'anti-camouflage designs'. When the vessel was properly decorated, it left the harbour and sewed his signature into the ocean. Further works have included a fleet of handmade submarines, one of which surfaced outside Turner's studio on Venice's Grand Canal during the 53rd Biennale; the erection of a 12-metre periscope beneath the dome of the Chapelle Saint-Louis de la Salpêtrière in Paris; and the construction of his own aeroplane in *Feedbacks* (2009). Such pieces are united through their embrace of significant technical challenges and what the artist calls his 'strategy of adventure'.

Ponomarev has been awarded the title of *Officier des Arts et des Lettres* by France's Minister of Culture and is a member of the Russian Academy of Art. He represented Russia at the 52nd Venice Biennale and features in public collections worldwide, including the Centre Pompidou, Paris. When not crossing oceans he is most at home in Moscow.

top left
Baffin Figure, 2006
Performance, Baffin Sea
Mixed media
© Alexander Ponomarev
Courtesy of the artist

above
Waves, 2000
Ink and pencil on paper
20 x 28.5 cm
© Alexander Ponomarev
Courtesy of the artist

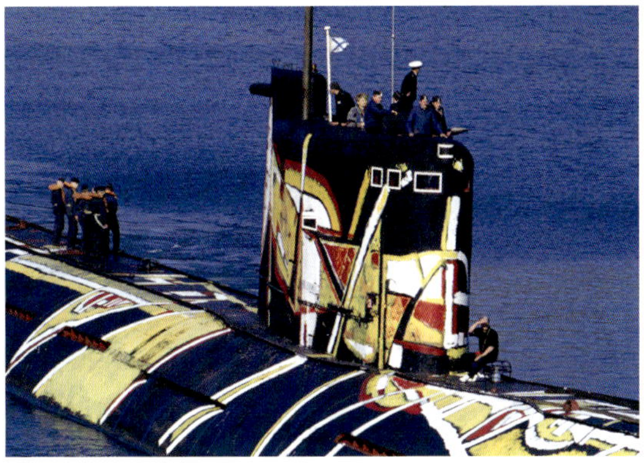

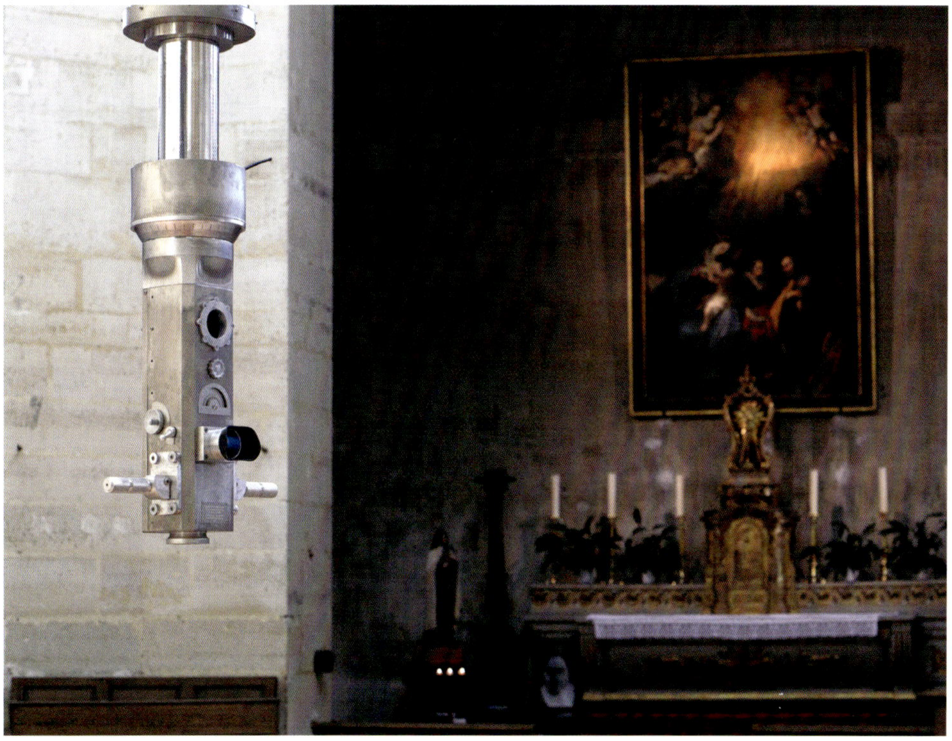

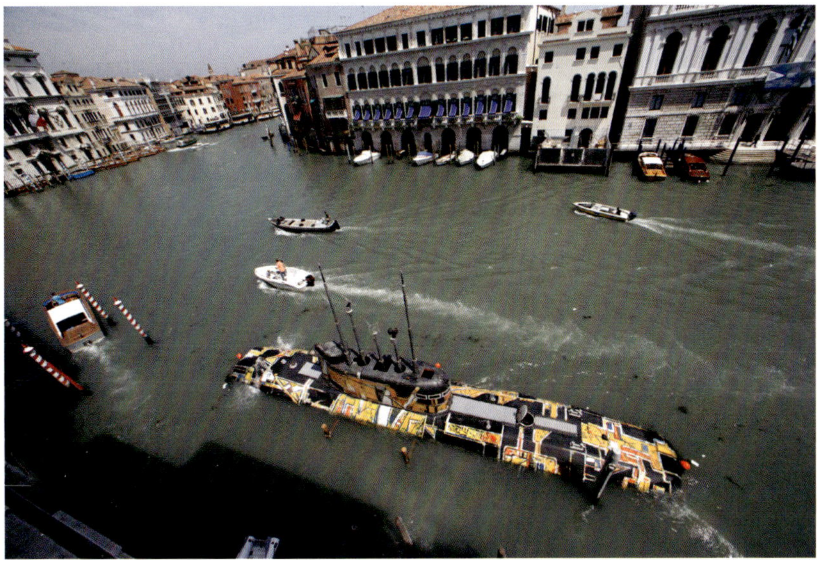

above left
The Northern Trace of Leonardo, 1996
Happening/object, Barents Sea
© Alexander Ponomarev
Courtesy of the artist

above
Verticale Parallele, 2007
Chapelle St-Louis-de-la-Salpêtrière,
Festival d'Automne, Paris
© Alexander Ponomarev
Courtesy of the artist

left
SubTiziano, 2009
Università Ca' Foscari di Venezia,
Grand Canal, Venice
Official collateral project
for the 53rd Venice Biennale
© Alexander Ponomarev
Courtesy of the artist

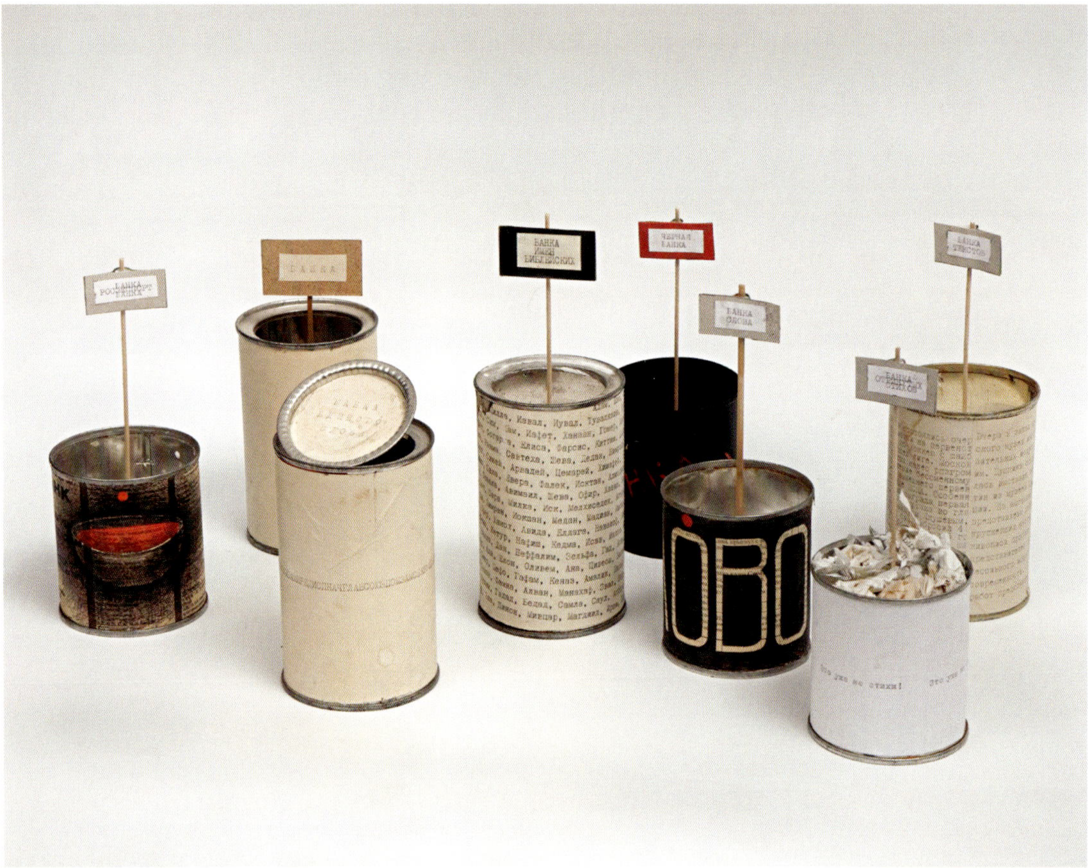

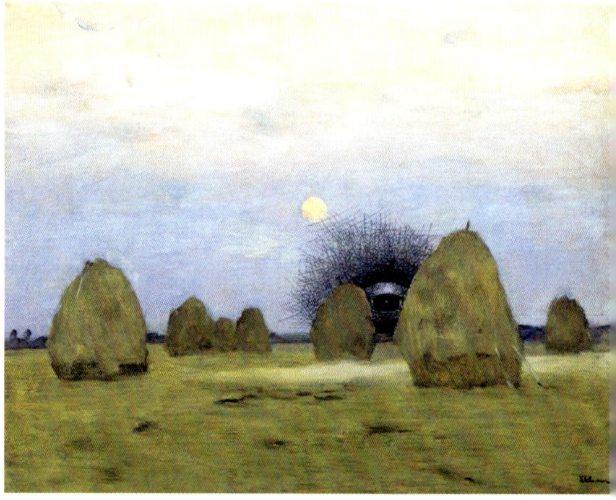

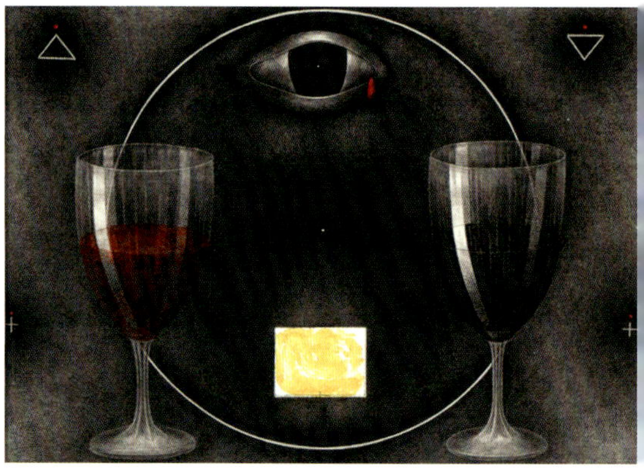

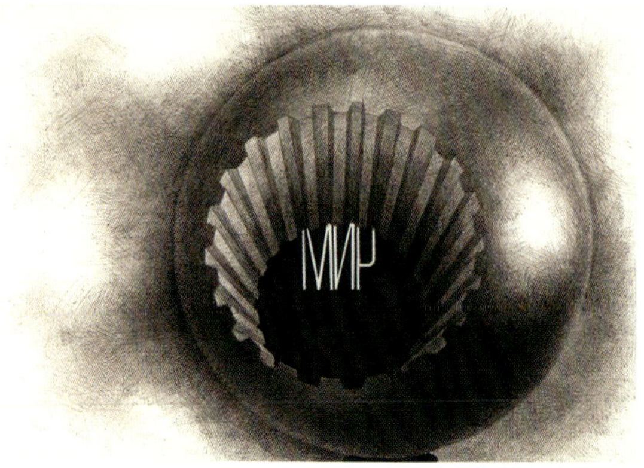

Dmitry Prigov (1940–2007), artist, poet and sculptor, lived and worked in Moscow. The interplay of text and image lies at the centre of his art. Prigov was closely associated with the circle of underground Moscow Conceptualists, particularly Ilya Kabakov and Andrei Monastyrsky. Having trained initially as a sculptor at the Stroganov Higher College of Art, in 1956 he started writing poetry, which he began to publish after the breakdown of the Soviet Union. In 1986 Prigov spent time in a mental institution for his unorthodox art performances. He died of a heart attack while preparing to take part in a performance by the young activist group Voina in which he was due to be carried up a Moscow high-rise sitting inside a wardrobe – an homage to Kabakov's famous fictional Soviet anti-hero Primakov.

Prigov's graphic works are typically drawn in biro on newspaper, an incongruous meeting of the individual imagination and mass media. They often combine text, whether typeset or handwritten, with mythological figures, such as the series Bestiary, which presents his circle of friends and acquaintances along with poets and painters of the past in the form of mythological beasts. As a Conceptual sculptor, Prigov created works inspired by Pop art. In his most famous series, Cans (1970s–2000s), he designed labels for empty tins purporting to contain different elements of written language. Prigov also created installations, took part in performances and was a talented musician. In 1993 he was awarded the Pushkin Prize by the Alfred Toepfer Stiftung, and in 2002 he won the Boris Pasternak Prize for his literary work. The State Hermitage Museum, St Petersburg, organised an important retrospective at the Venice Biennale in 2011.

top
Eight objects from the series, Cans, 1970s–2000s
8 objects
Collection of the artist's family
Courtesy Ekaterina Cultural Foundation

above
Untitled, c. 1990s
Ballpoint pen and gouache on paper
21 x 30 cm
© Family of the artist
Courtesy of the artist's family

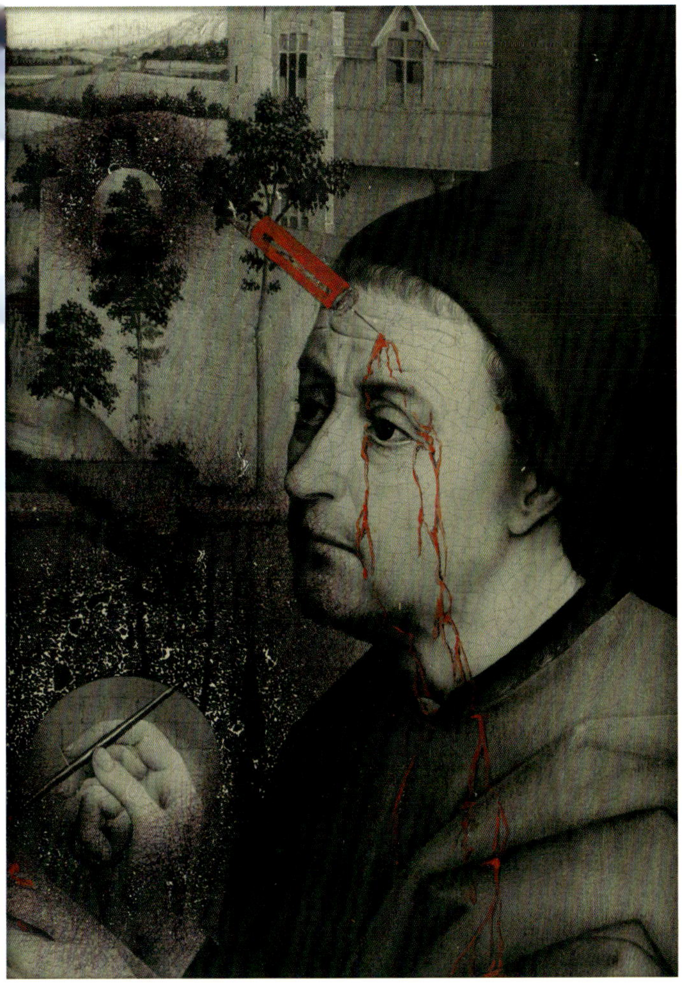

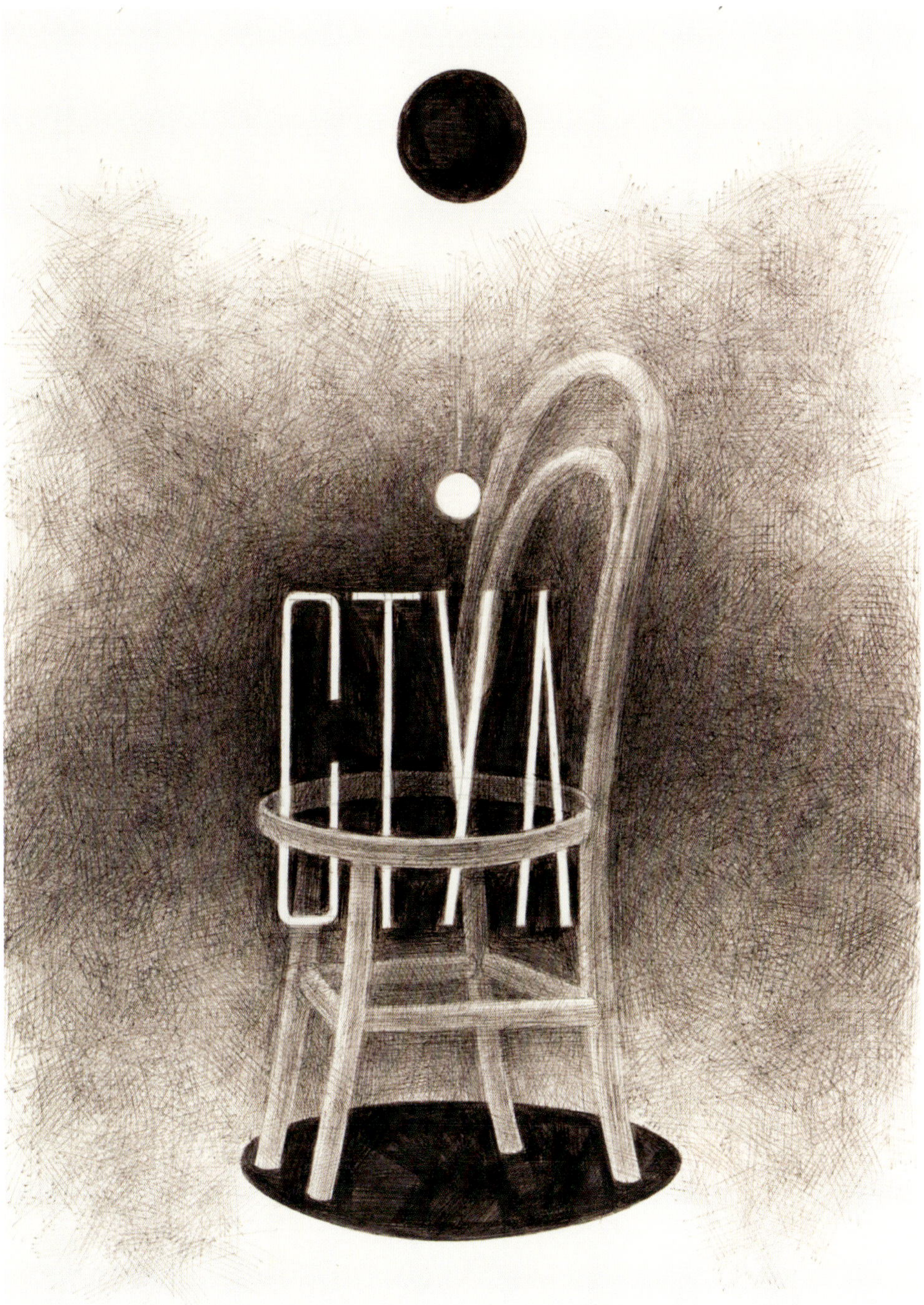

top
Untitled, c. 1990s
Drawing on a reproduction
Ballpoint pen and gouache on paper
42 x 30 cm
© Family of the artist
Courtesy of the artist's family

right
Untitled (Chairs)
(composition of 25 sheets), 1996
Ballpoint pen on paper
29.6 x 20.9 cm
Photo: The State Hermitage Museum /
Yuri Molodkovets
© Family of the artist
Courtesy of The State Hermitage Museum,
St Petersburg

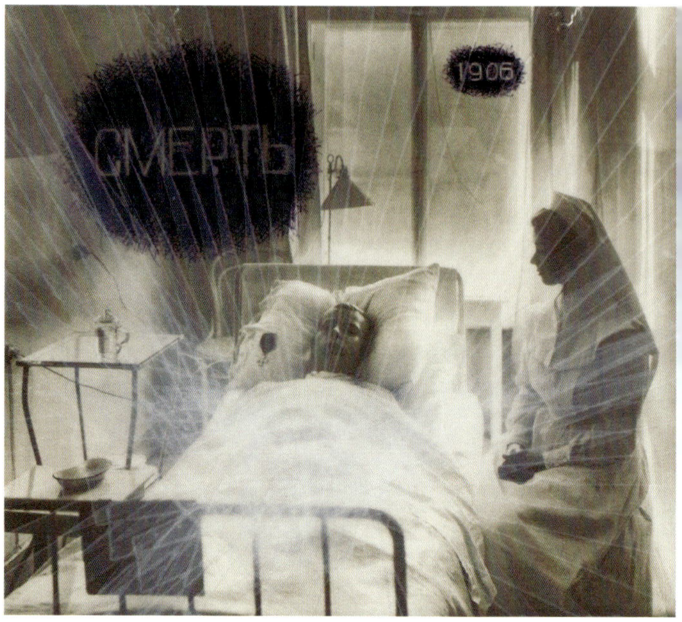

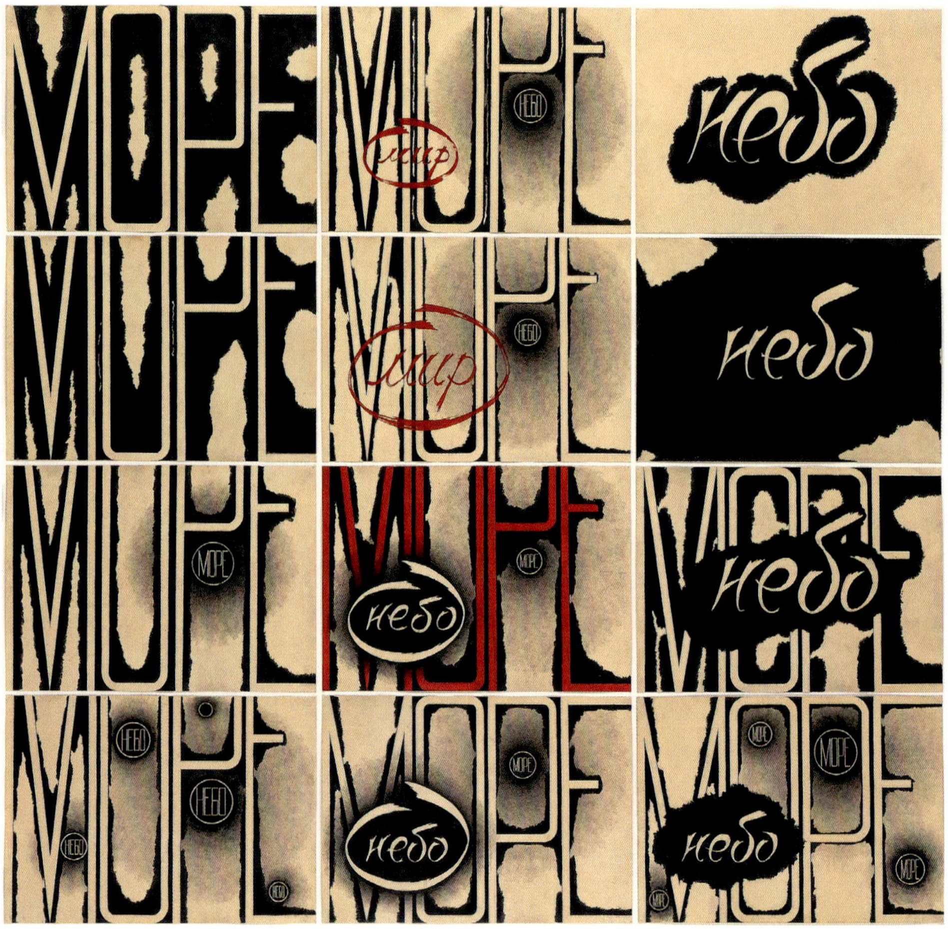

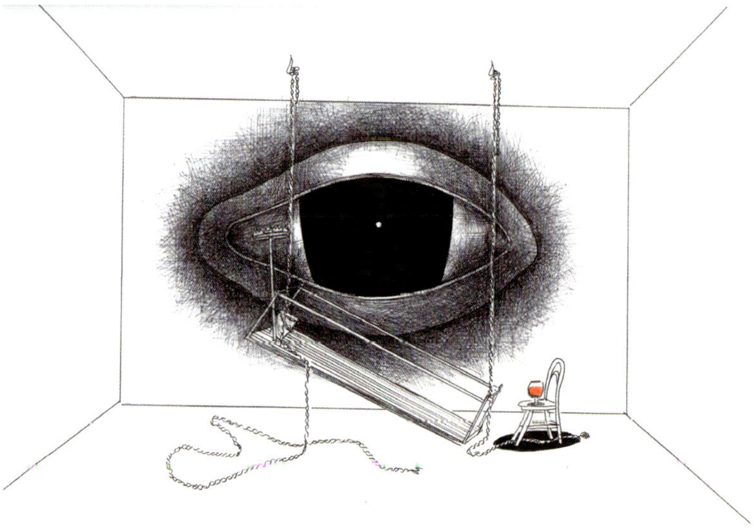

above
Sky, Seas, Peace, 1982
Ink on paper
119 x 127 cm
© Family of the artist
Courtesy of Yuri Traisman Art Foundation

top right
Death 1906, 2001
Reproduction, Scotch tape, ballpoint pen
23 x 26 cm
Photo: The State Hermitage Museum / Yuri Molodkovets
© Family of the artist
Courtesy of The State Hermitage Museum, St Petersburg

right
Untitled, c. 1990s
Ballpoint pen and gouache on paper
21 x 30 cm
© Family of the artist
Courtesy of the artist's family

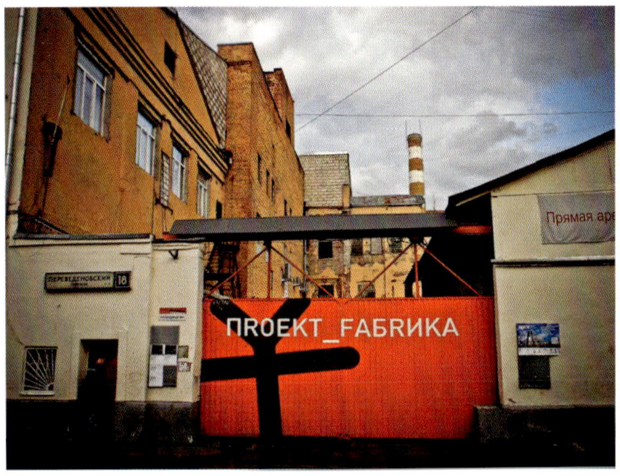

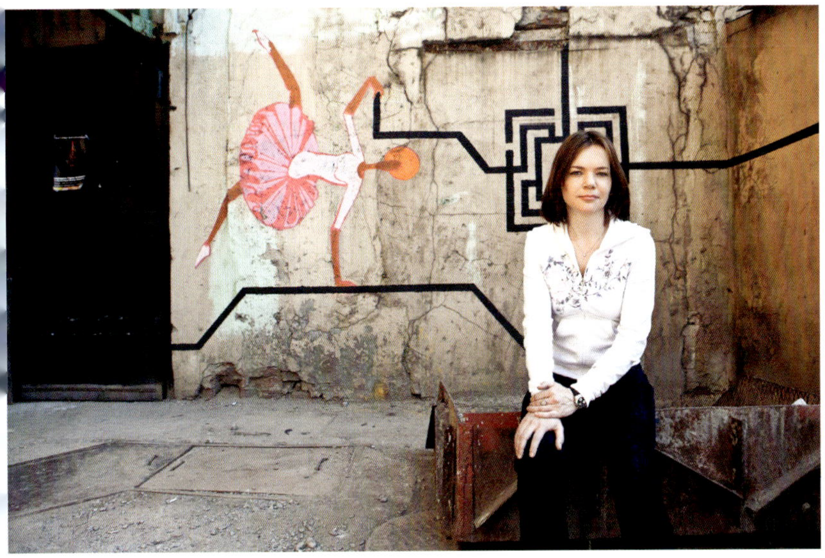

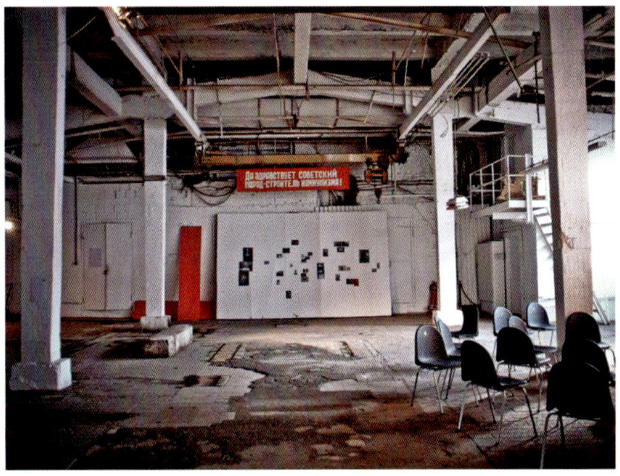

Founded in 2004, PROEKT_FABRIKA is one of the first independent, not-for-profit contemporary arts organisation in Moscow. Its unique identity is characterised by its location in a nineteenth-century paper plant where one third of the space is still a functioning production site for technical paper. Asya Filippova, director of the October factory and the founder and director of PROEKT_FABRIKA, holds a degree in Economic Cybernetics. She first became aware of the factory in 1995 while working for the investment fund that later held shares in it. After completing an MBA in Production Management, she was offered the job of factory director in 2003. The situation, as she remembers it, was dire: 'There was no work to give to the employees and nothing to pay them with. Demonstrations and strikes greeted me.' Dealing with the after-effects of industrial decline, Filippova decided that the only answer was to requisition space no longer used for industrial purposes: 'Free space was created as we stopped using some of the equipment. Since working in just the industrial sphere in this post-industrial world was sad, I was leaning towards contemporary art and culture, and the idea was born eventually to use this space for exhibitions and projects, and to make it available for cultural events. In 2005, when the first Moscow Biennale was held, we opened our first exhibition hall. At the time, it was almost uniquely large in Moscow – over 700 square metres.'

With a total of seventeen buildings, most of which have been handed over to PROEKT_FABRIKA, the organisation offers unparalleled amounts of exhibition space. Another thousand square metres of venue space is aimed at dance, theatre and music events. In addition to a café, the factory is also home to a theatre and to film and photography studios, and – as part of its mission to foster an interdisciplinary community with an experimental ethos – it leases converted studio space. The initial success of the exhibition space led to 'people ... coming in asking about more free space, studios, exhibition halls. So the Assembly Hall was formed for staging plays, showing documentary films, hosting indie music, contemporary performances and so on. Space was created that people could rent and work in, and there were people from all kinds of industries coming here – theatre, film, design, graphic art, publishing'. The premises are shared with the publishing house Ad Marginem, the production company Cinemateka and the contemporary dance agency TsEKh, among others.

The resulting creative energy illustrates PROEKT_FABRIKA's mission, which is to challenge familiar ideas and provide a forum for projects that do not follow the mainstream. As Filippova says, 'I long for a new, fresh, energetic direction in Russian art. Moscow Conceptualism has had its era. It's time for something new.' The factory collaborates with established artists like Viktor Skersis,Yuri Leiderman and Yuri Albert, and focuses on a new generation of Russian and international artists, including Arseny Zhilyaev and Taisia Korotkova, all of whom are invited to exhibit and curate in the vast spaces. An openness to creativity fuels PROEKT_FABRIKA's activities. 'I do not support the Leftist view that an artist has to reaffirm equality and criticise inequality,' says Filippova.'In general, this politicised view of art exists everywhere, and it should exist. But I do not think this is the main mission. An artist has to offer society a breath of fresh air. And what is the role of fresh air? To remind us that there is something fresh, eternal and essential. It is the same with artists ... giving people the possibility to follow the artist beyond the existing horizon.' This strong sense of individuality is evident in the physical appearance of the spaces, many of them left raw and unfinished, their industrial origins shining through. This treatment is unique both in Moscow and abroad, where the white-cube aesthetic is still de rigueur.

PROEKT_FABRIKA has forged relationships with other Moscow-based spaces such as the Moscow House of Photography, the National Centre for Contemporary Arts and E.K.ArtBureau. These collaborations have resulted in exhibitions like *GESAMT(KUNST) WERK*, shown as part of the 2005 International Biennale for Young Art, and *Interpreting the Object in the Moscow Conceptual School: From the MANI Collection (The Moscow Archive)*, curated by Alexandra Danilova and Elena Kuprina-Lyakhovich. One of the most important aspects of PROEKT_FABRIKA is the guest-residency programme launched in 2008. Offering apartments and studios to participants in factory events as well as to individuals taking part in cultural-exchange programmes, it is the first initiative of its kind in Moscow.

The factory's current success and future are linked, of course, to its director. Filippova explains that 'it is a very special situation, since I am the director [of the paper plant] and also interested in contemporary art. I can't imagine bringing two people here and dividing those functions. And finding someone else as weird as me – who would spend half the day discussing the reconstruction of the boiler room, and the other half talking about contemporary art?' Meanwhile the space is thriving; future projects include the further development of the residency programme and a stronger involvement with the dramatic arts.

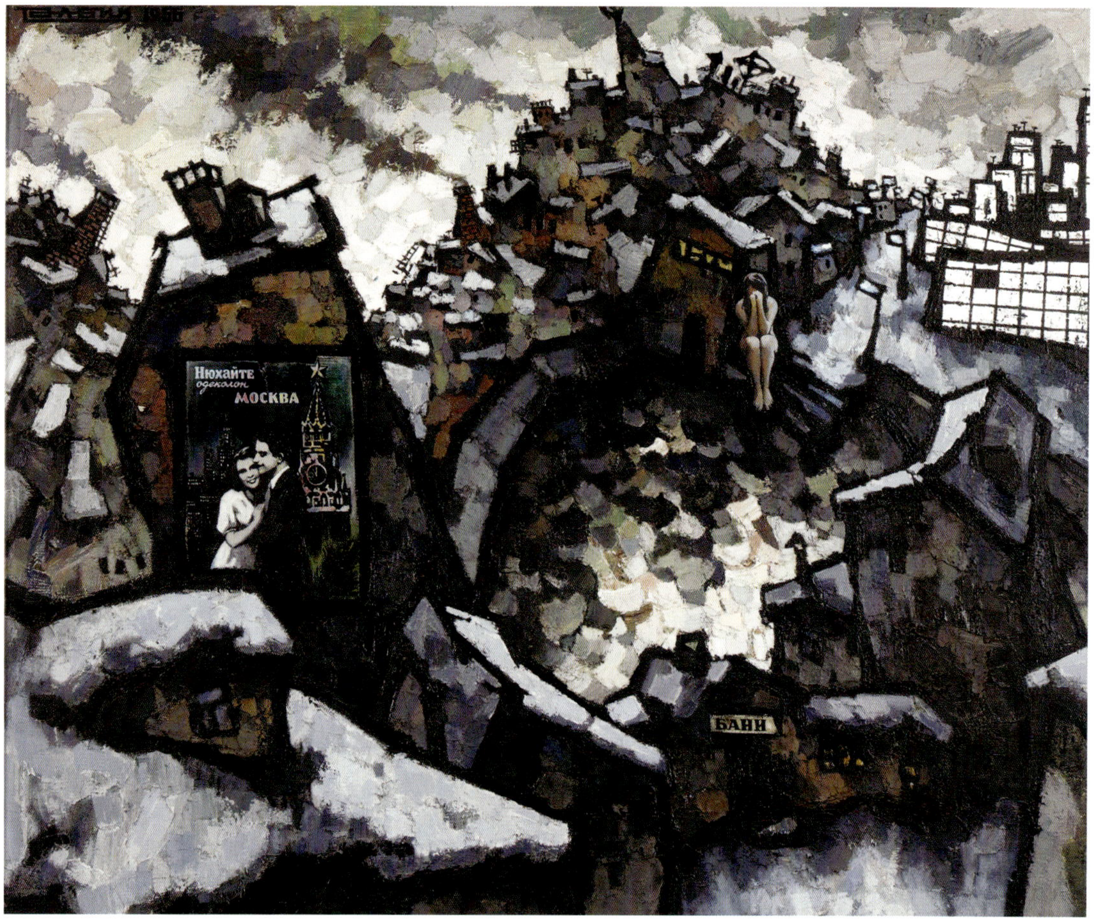

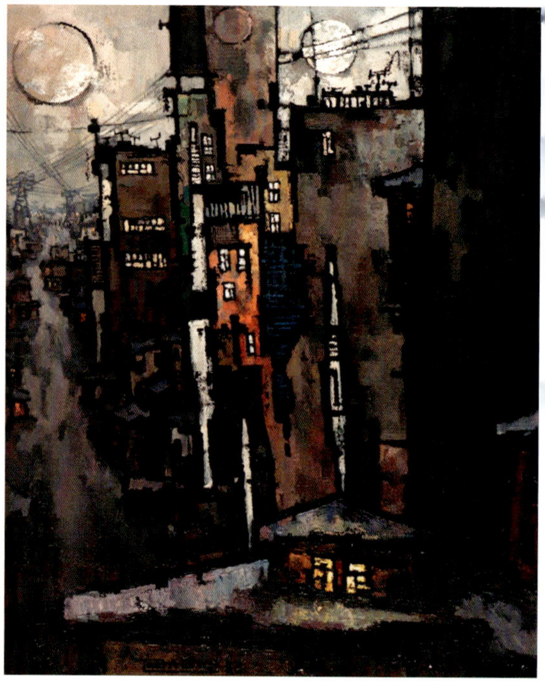

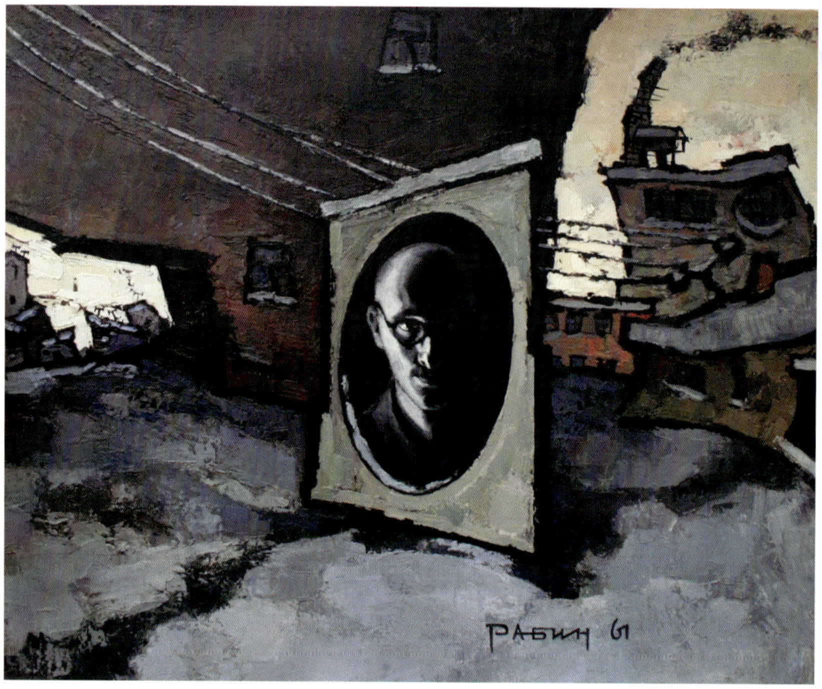

Born in Moscow in 1928, Oscar Rabin has been at the forefront of seminal events in Russian post-war art. Throughout his long career, he has continued to produce oil paintings in a lyrical, expressionistic manner; their iconography of litter, herrings, vodka bottles, religious icons, passports and barracks set against desolate urban and rural landscapes function as metaphors for lived experience.

'All my life, the subject of my paintings, the emotions that are portrayed, are based on my life and what I observe around me,' Rabin has explained. 'I can name about ten to twenty objects that I repeat and use regularly that mean something to me – the barracks in which I lived in Russia, documents – there is so much behind the Soviet passport –, money – behind which is human passion –, alcohol and wine.' *Still Life with Vodka* (1960) and *'Pompes Funèbres' with Rothschild Champagne* (2003) demonstrate the way in which this iconography criss-crosses geography, history, politics and time to acquire universal values.

A member of the Lianozovo Group, which met regularly for philosophical and artistic discussions, Rabin was a central figure in the artistic life of Moscow, often hosting open houses for artists and visitors from abroad. George Costakis acquired his works as early as 1961, and he had his first solo exhibition in 1965 in London. Active in the fight for artistic freedom, Rabin was arrested following his co-organisation of and participation in the infamous 'Bulldozer Exhibition' (1974), 'a collective action, although the government pointed its finger at me afterwards'. Following another arrest in 1977, he suffered forced emigration when he was officially and permanently stripped of his Soviet citizenship while on a trip to Paris, where he lives and works today.

top left
Baths (Sniff Eau de Cologne Moscow), 1966
Oil on canvas
89.4 x 109.5 cm
© Oscar Rabin
Private collection

top right
Russian Cityscape with Two Moons, 1962
Oil on canvas
100.3 x 80 cm
© Oscar Rabin
Courtesy of Korban Art Foundation

above
Self Portrait , 1961
Oil on canvas
64 x 79 cm
© Oscar Rabin
Private collection

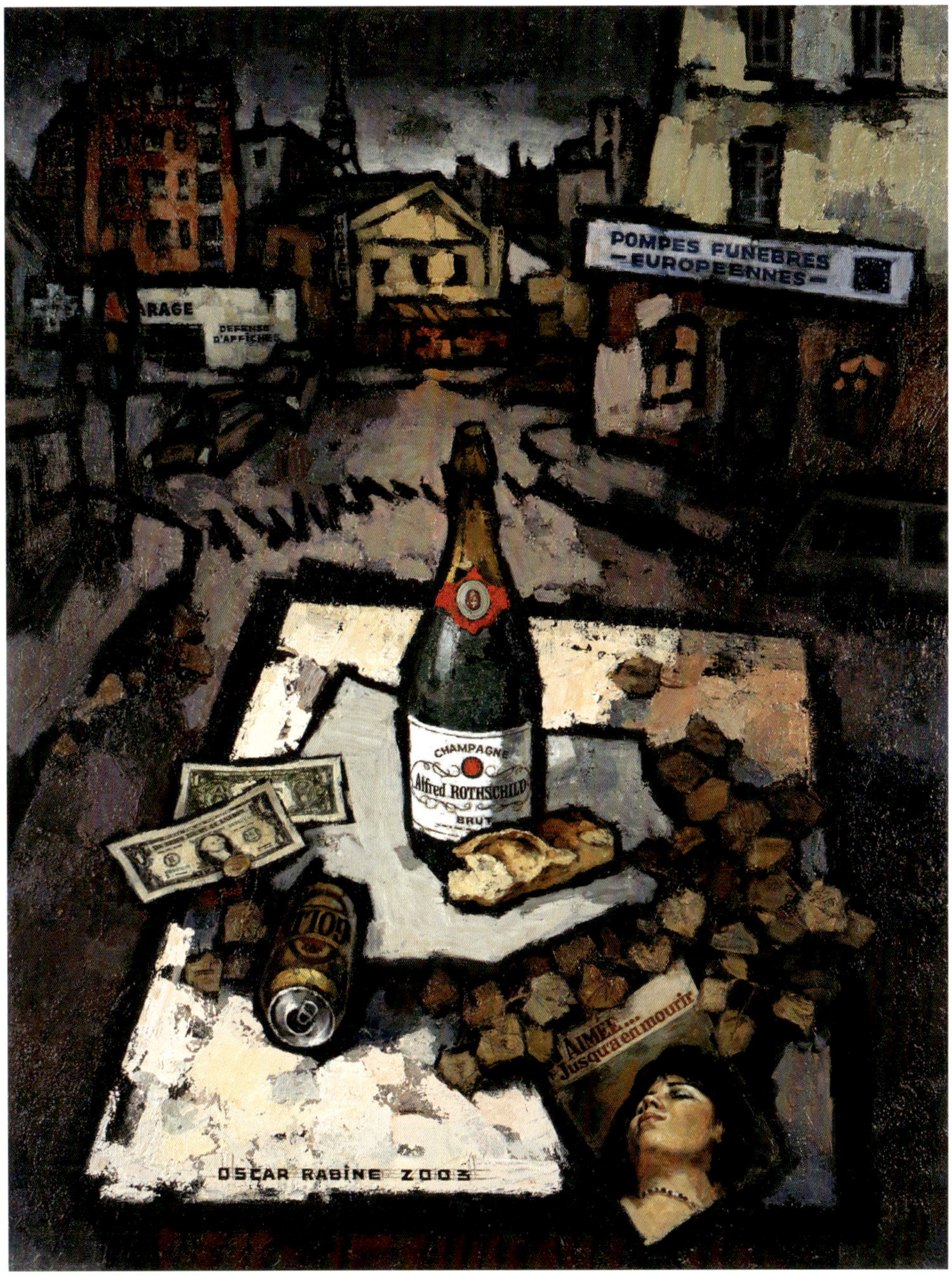

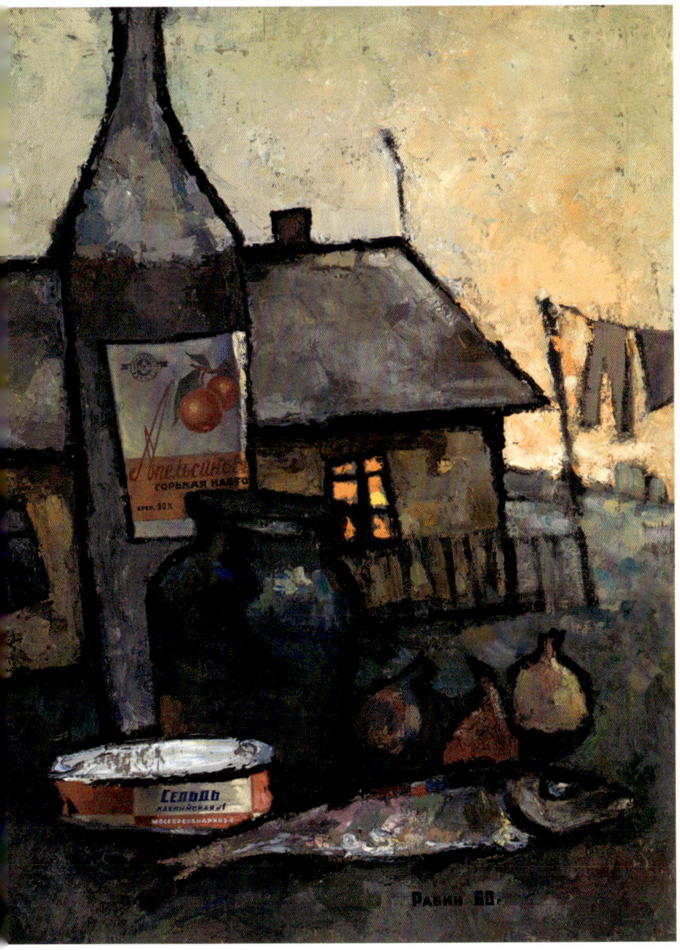

above
Pompes Funèbres with Rothschild Champagne, 2003
Oil and mixed media on canvas
116 x 90 cm
© Oscar Rabin
Private collection

left
Still life with Vodka, 1960
Oil on canvas
71.5 x 54 cm
© Oscar Rabin
Courtesy of MacDougall's Fine Art

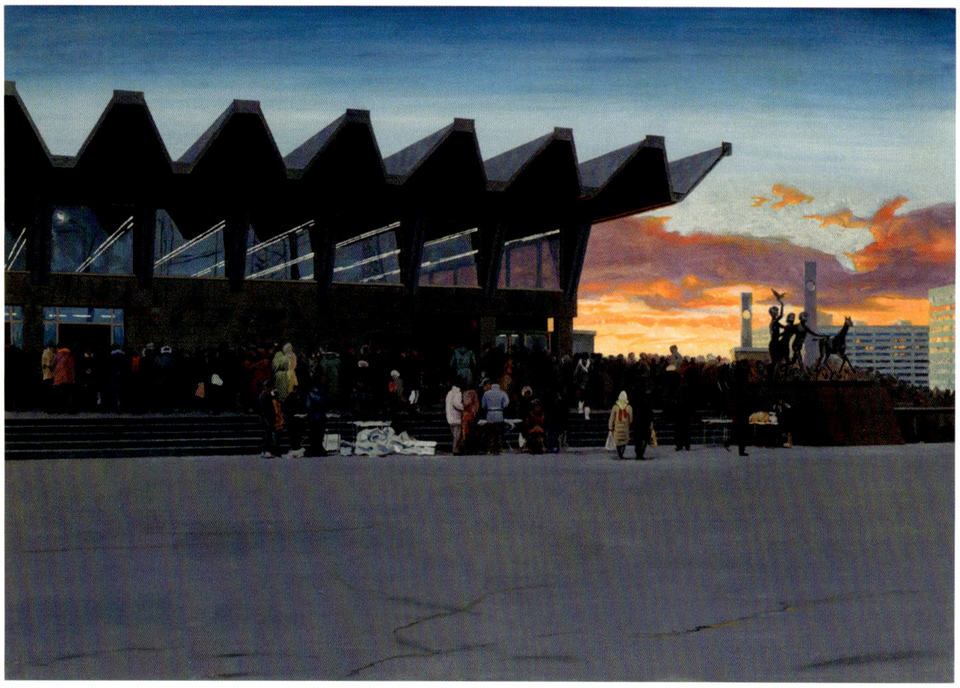

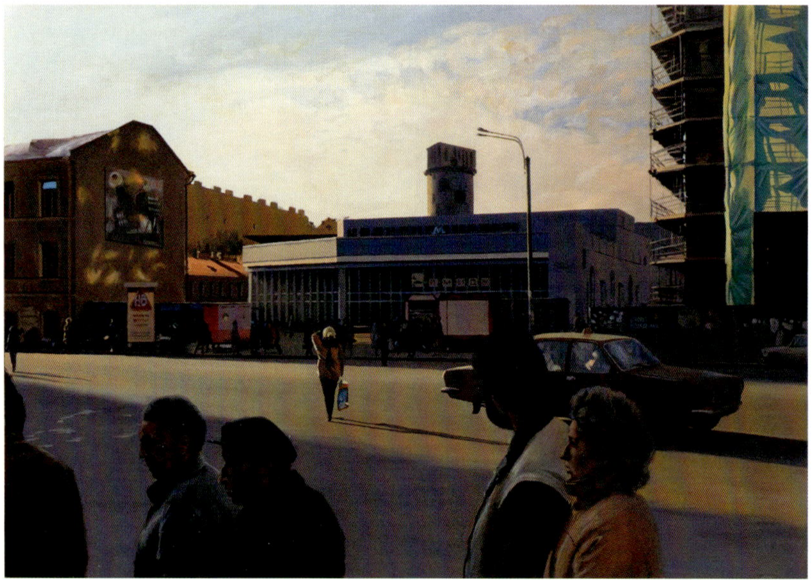

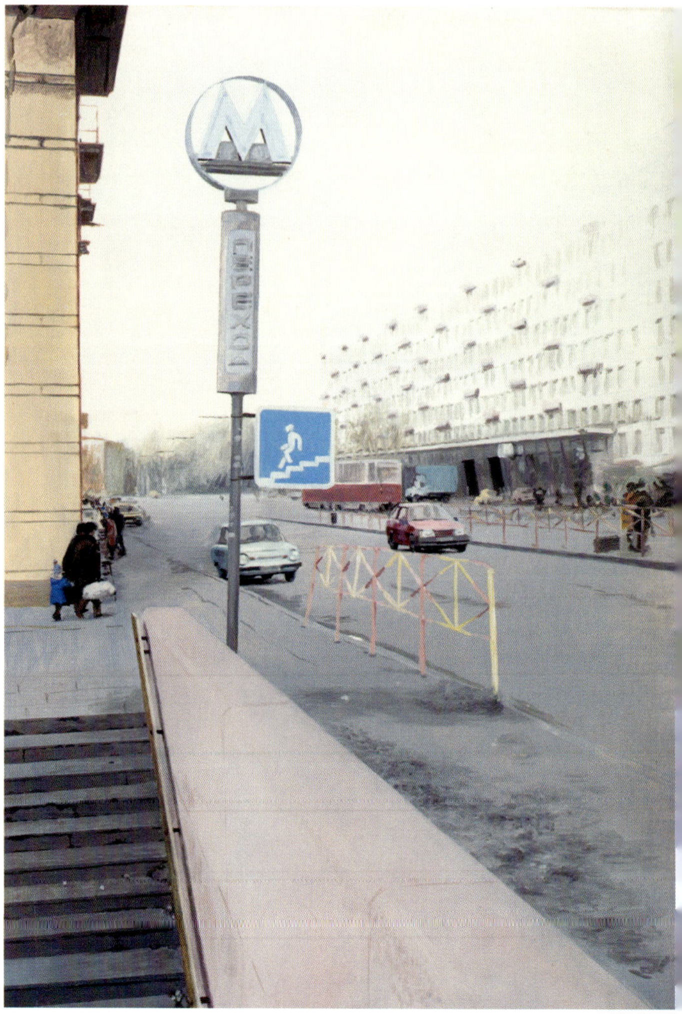

Kerim Ragimov's long-term painting projects, executed in an expressive photorealist style, employ images from the mass media as their source material. Born in St Petersburg in 1970, Ragimov graduated from the Nicholas Roerich School of Fine Arts, St Petersburg, in 1989. He has exhibited widely in Russia, as well as in Milan, Tel Aviv, Berlin, Warsaw and London.

Best known for his series Metro Project (1993–) and Human Project (1994–), Ragimov melds images from daily life, commercials, magazines and films by means of a painstaking, time-consuming artisanal process. In Metro Project, he has set himself the task of painting the pavilions of all fifty-four metro stations in St Petersburg, resulting in a work he has described as 'both historical and biographical'. Working in styles that range from St Petersburg Neo-Academicism to computer-generated post-digitalism, his oil paintings are not static renditions of banal reality. Rather, they exude a diversity of psychological and emotional states which individualise otherwise repetitive, homogenous scenes. Referencing Russian spiritualism and the tradition of icon painting, works like *Metro Project – Baltiskaya* (1997) seem to glow with an inner light.

In Human Project, Ragimov copies stickers as well as images found in newspapers and magazines and on posters to create group portraits. The anonymity of the 'sitters' is enhanced by his focus on the formal execution of perfect copies. Explaining his process, he has said, 'I make the pictures in this series anonymous, removing all attendant information and explanations to be found in the originals. This information blackout seems to me to be the ideal silent soundtrack for this work.' Repudiating his own identity as author by replicating even the shortcomings of his sources, Ragimov has made the subject of Human Project humanity itself.

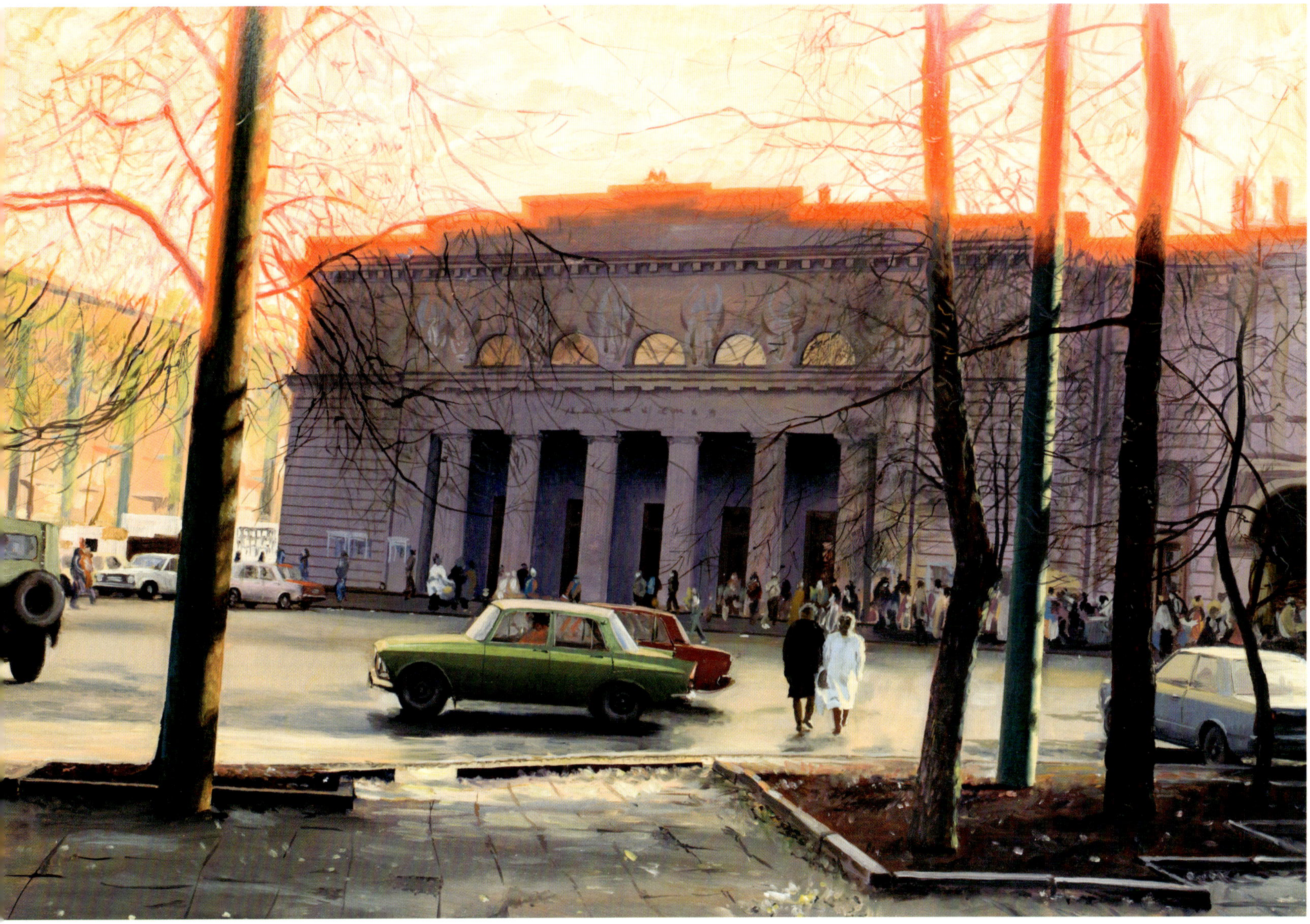

facing page top
Metro Project – Pionerskaya, 1997
Oil on paper
56 x 81 cm
© Kerim Ragimov
Courtesy of the artist

facing page far left
Metro Project – Dostoevskaya, 1998
Oil on paper
56 x 81 cm
© Kerim Ragimov
Courtesy of the artist

facing page left
Metro Project – Novocherkasskaya, 1998
Oil on paper
56 x 81 cm
© Kerim Ragimov
Courtesy of the artist

above
Metro Project – Baltiskaya, 1997
Oil on paper
56 x 81 cm
© Kerim Ragimov
Courtesy of the artist

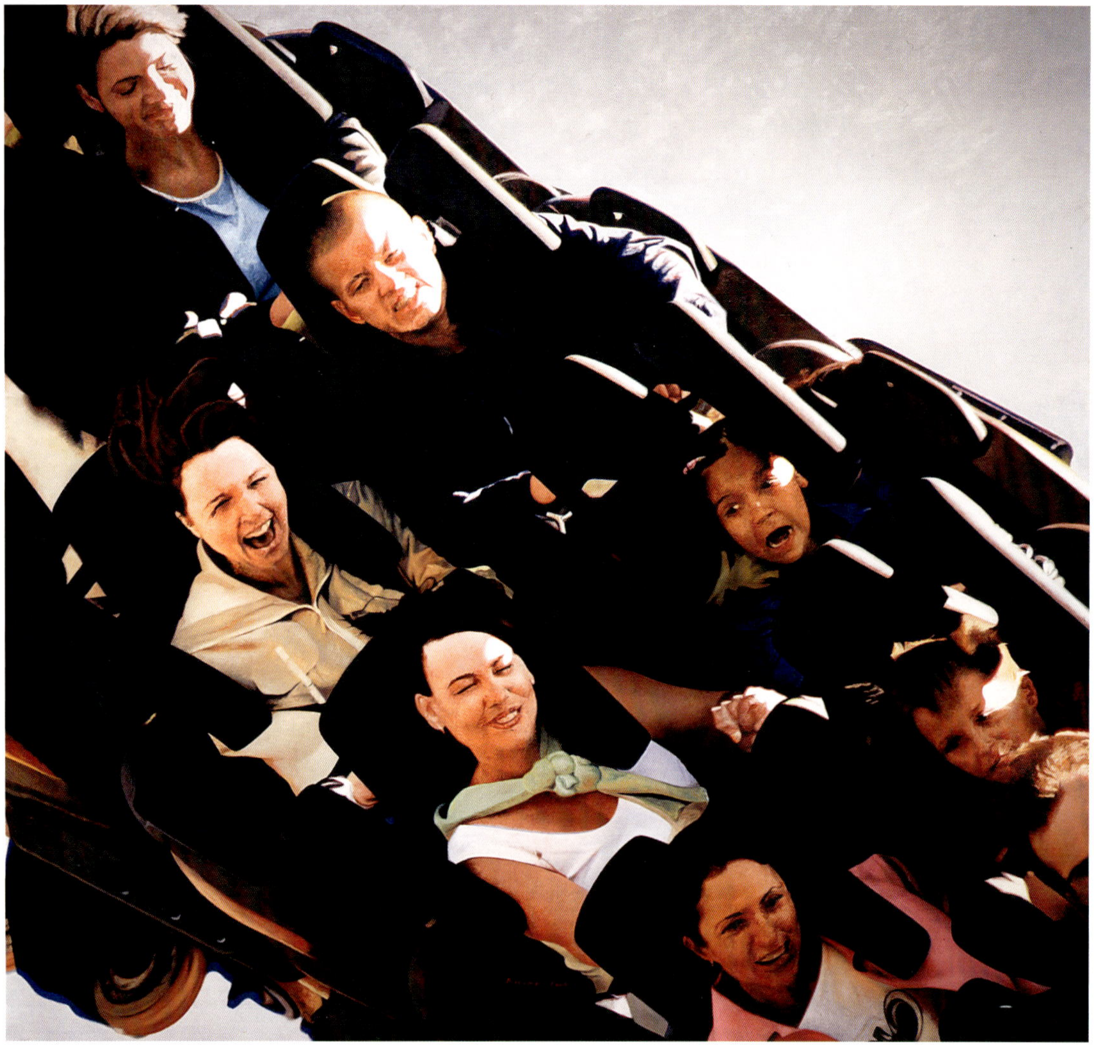

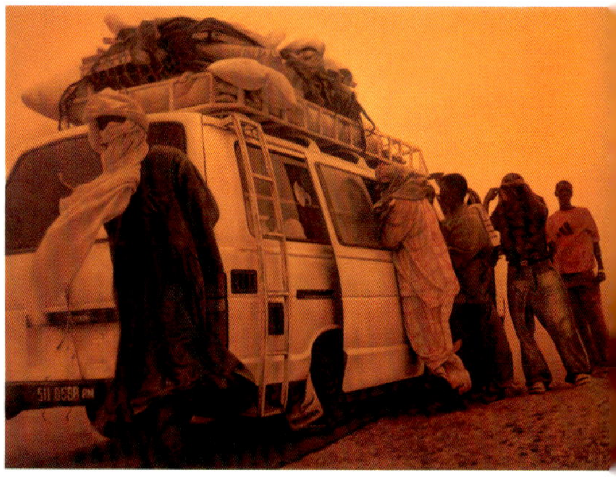

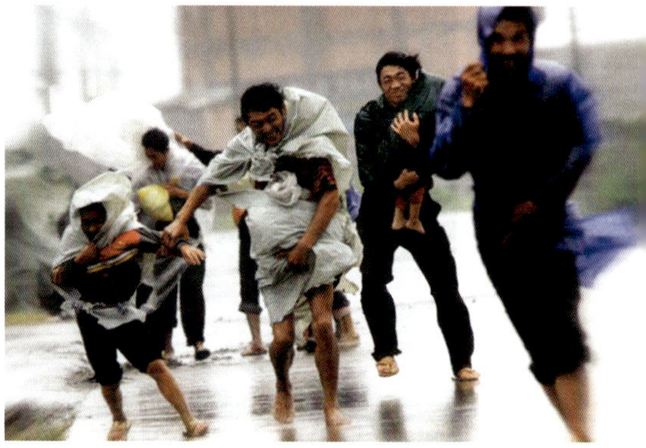

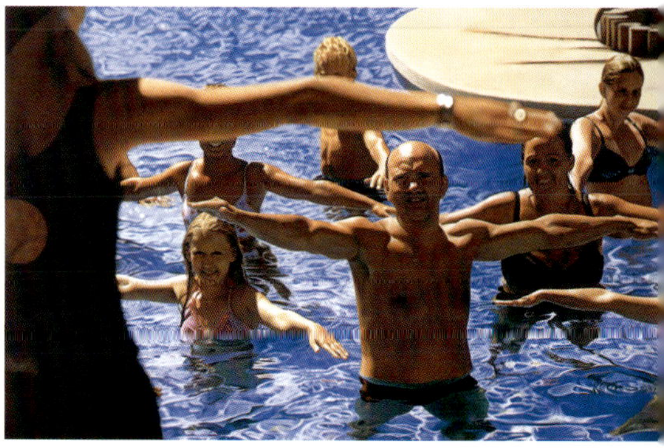

above
Human Project. Portrait No. 23, 2004
Oil on canvas
196 x 207 cm

Collection of Ekaterina Cultural Foundation, Moscow
Courtesy of the artist

above right
Human Project. Episode No. 33, 2007
Oil on canvas
189 x 252 cm

Courtesy of Marina Gisich Gallery and the artist

middle right
Human Project. Episode No. 28, 2006
Oil on canvas
180 x 248 cm

Courtesy of Marina Gisich Gallery and the artist

bottom right
Human Project. Episode No. 31, 2007
Oil on canvas
189 x 292 cm

Courtesy of Marina Gisich Gallery and the artist

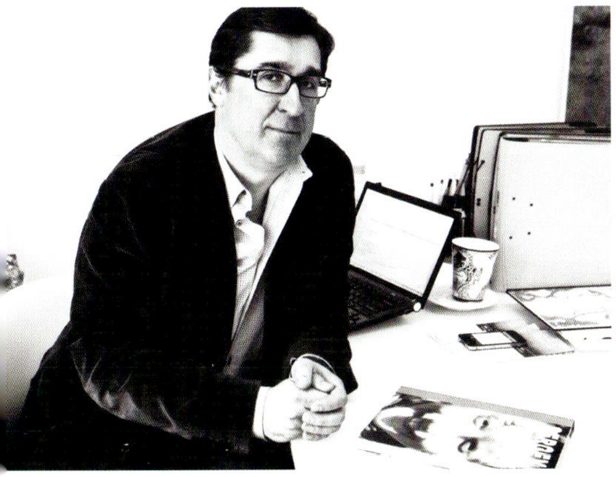

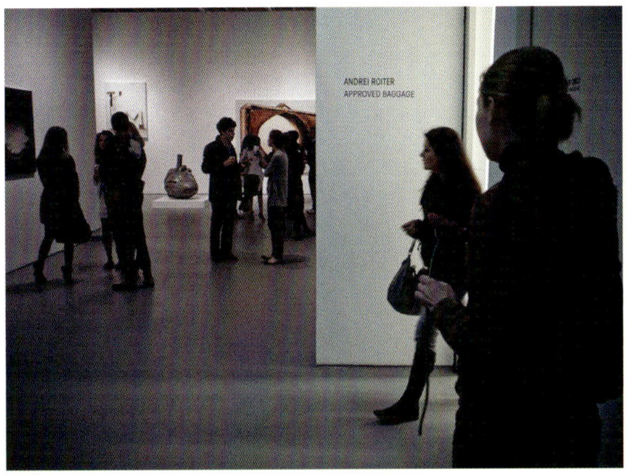

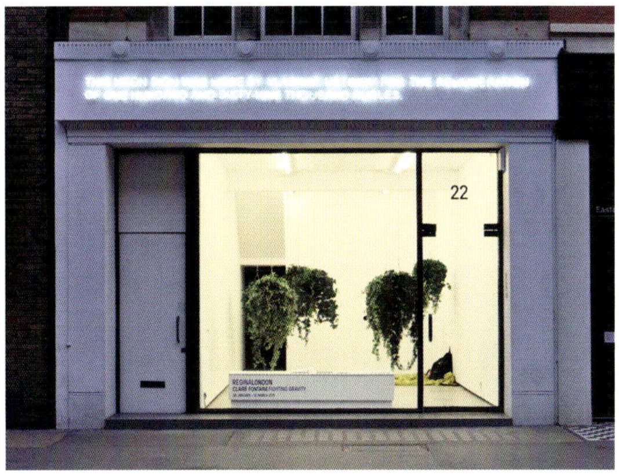

The Regina Gallery was founded by Vladimir and Regina Ovcharenko in Moscow in 1990. In 2007 it moved to its current premises in Vinzavod, Moscow's vibrant arts complex in an industrial neighbourhood of Moscow. Three years later Ovcharenko opened a second space, in London's Eastcastle Street, an up-and-coming enclave just north of Mayfair and Soho. The London gallery is a two-storeyed space in a nineteenth-century warehouse.

Vladimir Ovcharenko, who grew up in Moscow, divides his time between that city and London. His Moscow gallery is the only major commercial contemporary-art outlet with a subsidiary located outside of Russia, the aim being to bring Russian contemporary art to a wider audience. Ovcharenko's ambition is to see his country's artists rediscover their place on the cultural map of Europe, a position they have not occupied since the early years of the twentieth century. At the same time he does not wish the gallery to become a Russian ghetto in London, so he also exhibits and represents international artists, including such young British practitioners as Ryan Mosley and Graham Dolphin, who are also shown in his Moscow space. Ovcharenko has an international vision and has plans to expand into Europe.

In its early years the Regina Gallery was a place in which to make interesting, not necessarily commercial, projects for which there was no market. As the Russian economy developed, the gallery expanded. The artists Ovcharenko represents today include Semyon Faibisovich, Pavel Pepperstein, Andrei Roiter, Victor Alimpiev and Ivan Chuikov. The gallerist also has worked closely with artist-photographer Sergei Bratkov, whom he discovered in Ukraine in the mid-1990s and brought to Moscow; he considers this to have been one of his major professional successes. In the gallery's early years, the Moscow Actionist Oleg Kulik was its artistic director; Ovcharenko still represents Kulik today.

Ovcharenko believes that there is a lot to do both in Russia and abroad to raise the profile of the country's contemporary artists and provide them with adequate support. On a positive note, he agrees that change is happening, though he finds the pace frustratingly slow. The political impulse to repatriate Russian art is a double-edged sword, he feels. Although it is important to return art to Russia, building the country's cultural presence internationally will, he feels, ultimately bring about a greater understanding and appreciation of its cultural and historical values throughout the world. For Ovcharenko this is a political imperative.

Ovcharenko has an enormous passion for art and thrives on the social aspect of his life as a gallerist. Working directly with artists gives him strength and inspiration: 'Art gives you another life which you can switch into at any time. It seizes you as though you are watching a film for two hours and become engrossed; in the same way you can plug into art and find something interesting to do.' Most importantly, he believes that art is like a mirror showing us reflections of things we cannot see clearly in everyday life.

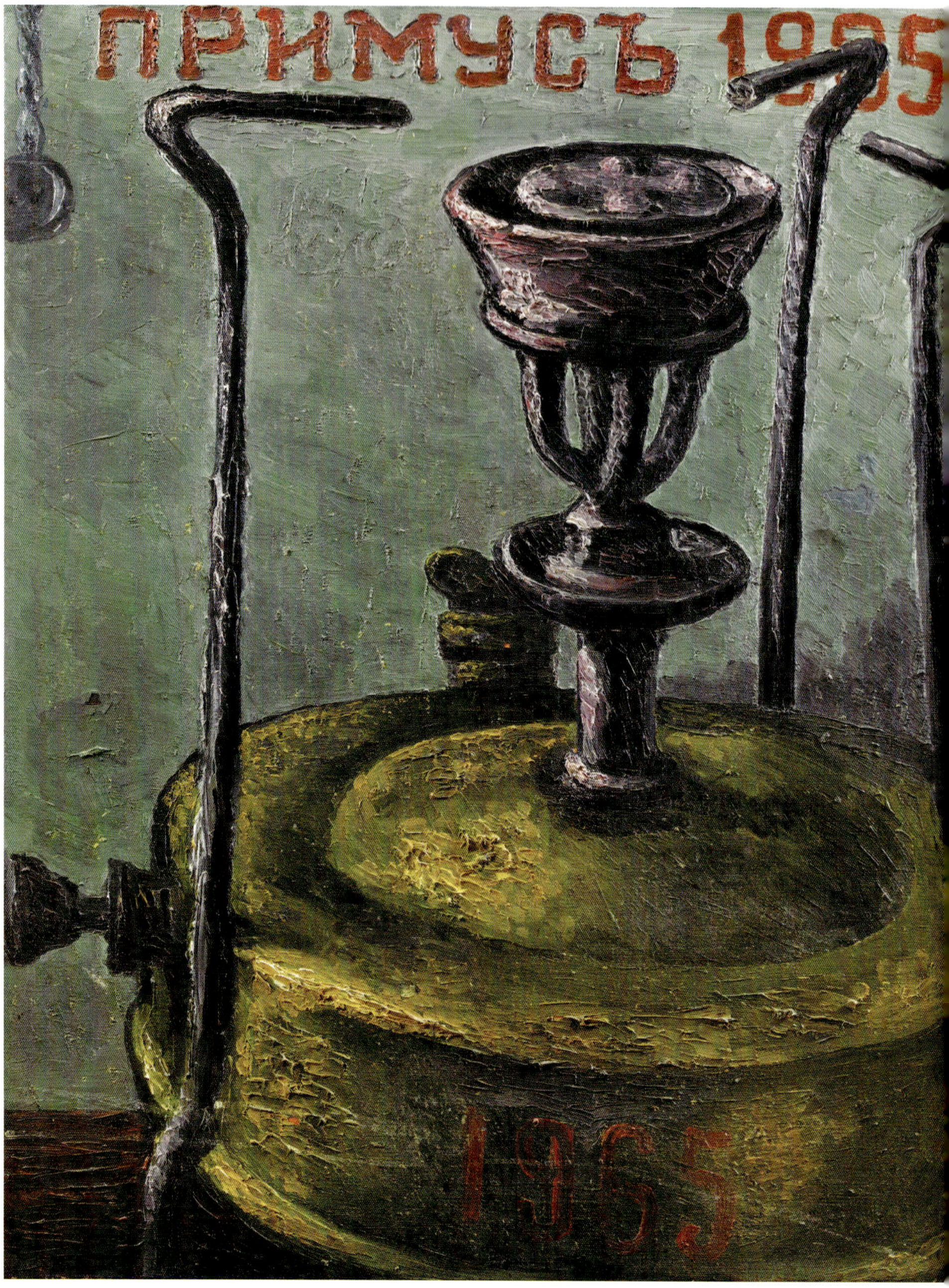

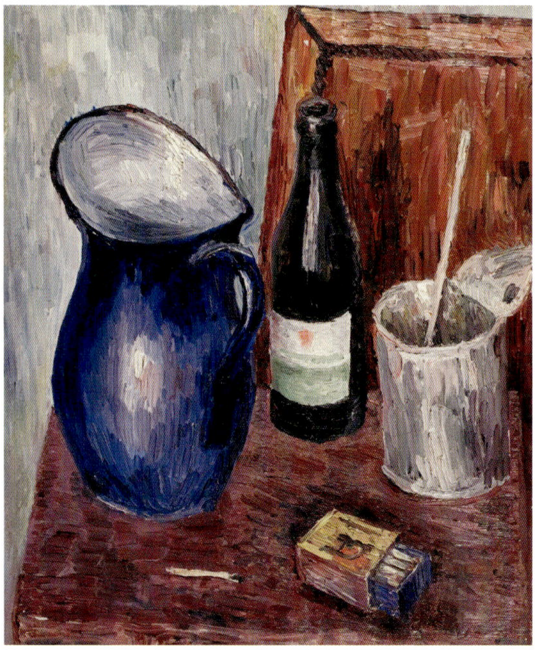

Mikhail Roginsky was born in 1931 in Moscow; in 1978 he emigrated to Paris, where he died in 2004. Having graduated in 1951 from the Scenography Department of the Moscow Art School in Memory of 1905, he worked in provincial theatres before returning to the capital in 1960. During the '60s he developed a style of genre painting presenting everyday household objects tinged with an existential mood. The kitchen was his most typical setting for still lifes of unassuming domestic utensils such as primus stoves, kettles and matchboxes. Such works were often executed in tempera on cardboard.

By the late 1960s Roginsky had started to conceive of the painting itself as a simple utilitarian object, thus opening his practice out into a form of Pop art. *Door* (1965) is a piece of plywood painted bright red to which a real door handle was attached. Roginsky shared with the Pop artists a belief that objects can symbolise the banality of everyday life, yet, unlike Pop art, his objects are everyday things rather than items from the world of consumerism. They have metaphysical properties, their ugliness and simplicity acquiring a certain beauty in his compositions. In the 1970s, the artist returned to more traditional methods of painting, using a muted palette and concentrating on still lifes, interiors and urban views.

Roginsky's work has been widely exhibited throughout Russia and in Europe, and can be found in numerous private collections, including the State Tretyakov Gallery, Moscow; the National Centre for Contemporary Art, Moscow; and the Jane Voorhees Zimmerli Art Museum, New Brunswick.

above
Primus Stove, 1965
Mixed media on canvas
© Family of the artist
Courtesy of DES

above left
Still life with pitcher, 1966
Oil on canvas
69 x 59 cm
© Family of the artist
Courtesy of Ekaterina and Vladimir Semenikhin Collection

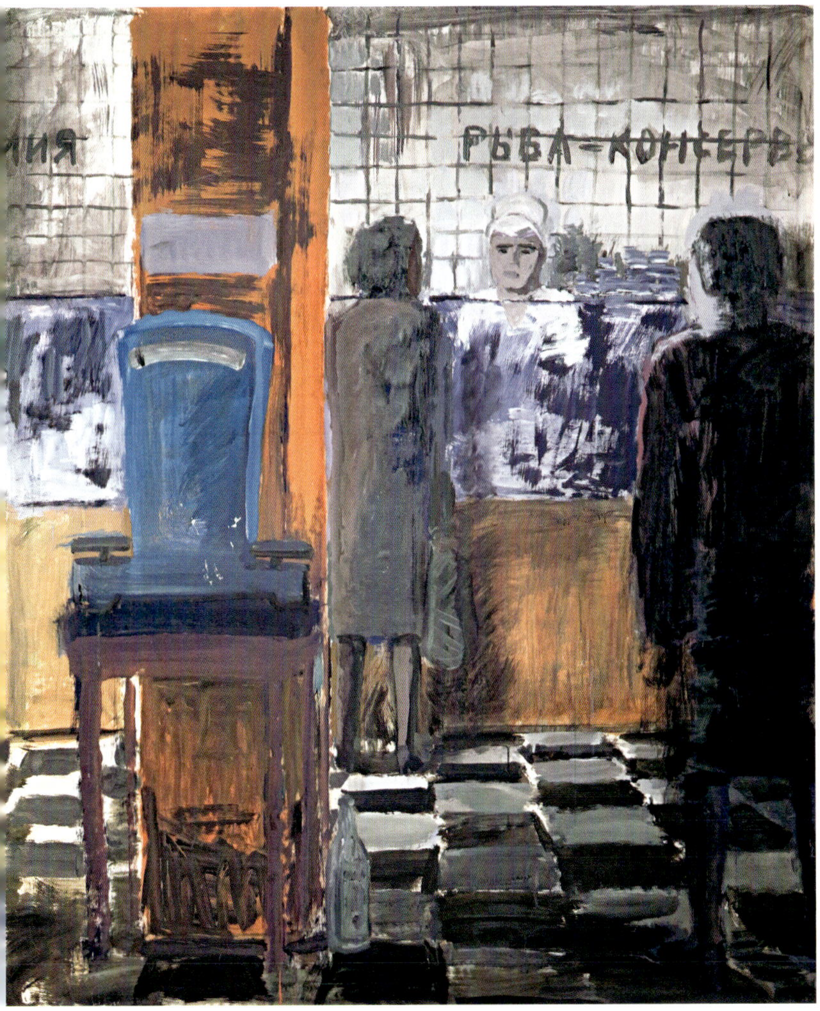

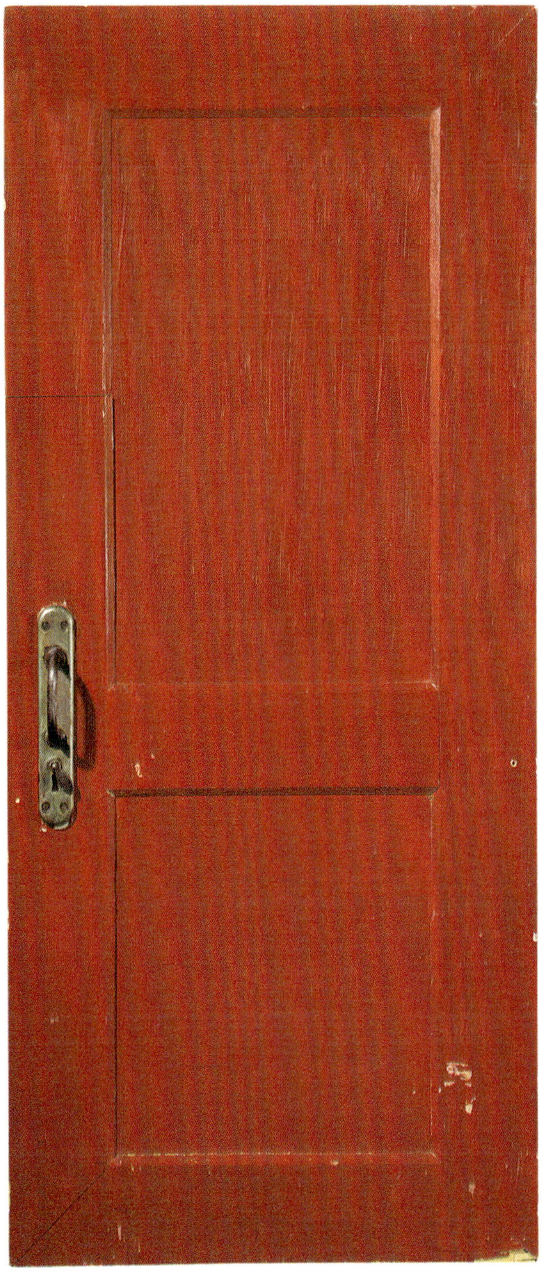

above
Red Door, 1965
Painted wood, door handle
© Family of the artist
Courtesy of Victor Bondarenko

left
Store No. 3, 1981–2
Acrylic on paper
190 x 150 cm
© Family of the artist
Courtesy of Victor Bondarenko

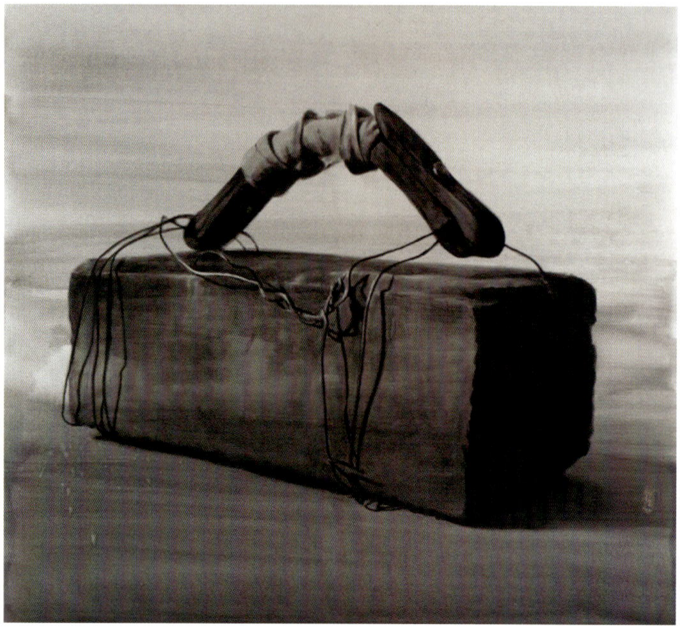

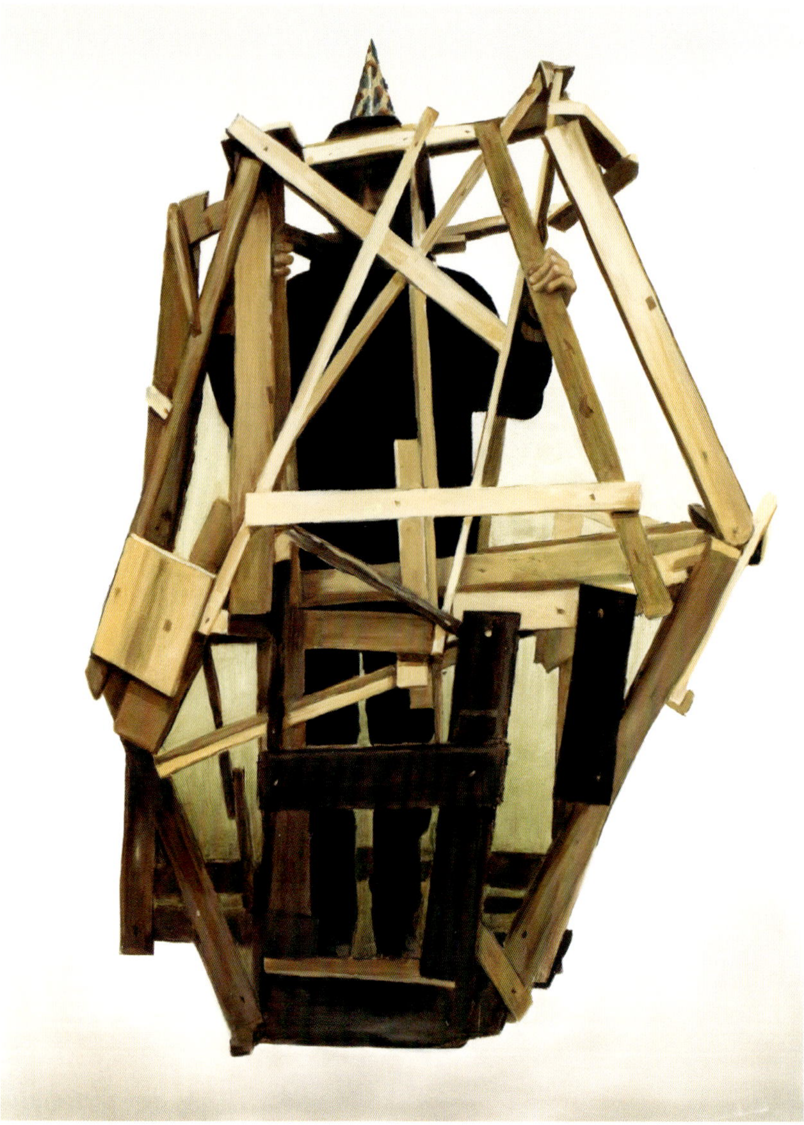

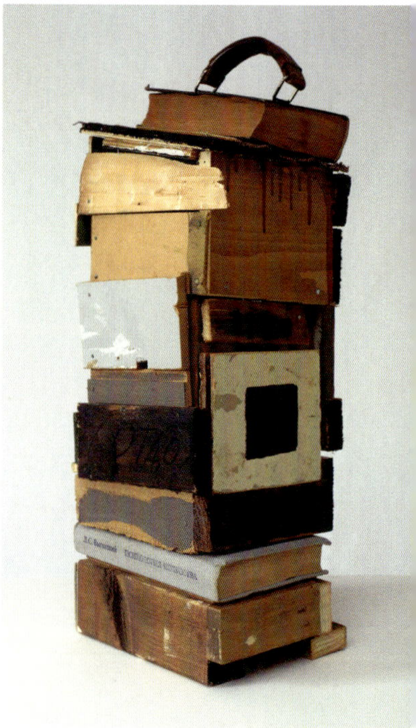

Andrei Roiter was born in Moscow in 1960. His parents, both engineers, encouraged him to become an architect, and he studied at the Moscow Institute of Architecture between 1978 and 1980. With no formal art education, he has described his true university as a combination of personal therapy and socialising. During the 1980s Roiter worked as a nightwatchman at an abandoned kindergarten in Moscow, which quickly developed into a popular underground exhibition venue. Arte Povera was a formative influence on his mature style, with recycled, found or discarded objects appearing in his sculptures. From 1985 he was a member of the Union of Artists as an illustrator of children's books, and in 1986 he was invited to take part in an officially sanctioned exhibition at Kuznetsky Most in Moscow. In 1988 Roiter travelled abroad and exhibited in Europe and the US; today he divides his time between Amsterdam and New York. He has exhibited widely in Europe and Japan, and his works are held in several public collections, including the State Tretyakov Gallery, Moscow; the Deutsche Bank Collection; Duke University Museum of Art, Durham; and the Jane Voorhees Zimmerli Art Museum, New Brunswick.

The fact that Roiter's work addresses the predicament of the outsider has to do with his experiences in the Soviet Union as an 'internal immigrant'. Intellectual dissidents divide their time between providing themselves with social and legal status and channelling their real selves into independent creative work. Having lived abroad since the 1990s, Roiter has said that this experience prepared him for the integrated yet unique sense of identity he feels existing in two multicultural cities, he thinks of himself as neither fully Russian nor Dutch nor American.

His working process is based on travelling and daydreaming, recording impressions and gathering material as visual notes with a camera or putting objects into his pockets. He reworks these things in the studio, selecting and editing them to form public installations. Roiter sees his practice as a way of preserving the past, a combination of his own history and roots with visual analysis that crystallises into organised statements. He often refers to his sculptural works as 'props', and to his art as a performance: 'The most pleasant way of seeing reality for me is thinking about endless tragic-comic performance in the theatre and seeing the artist as a travelling comedian.' Recently he has begun to refer to his props as 'relics', thus giving them a personal religious or spiritual value, as well as an aura of being preserved, even cherished.

top
Hand Luggage, 2010
Acrylic on canvas
180 x 200 cm
© Andrei Roiter
Private collection, Waalre, Netherlands
Courtesy of Galerie Akinci, Amsterdam

above left
Artist at Work, 2010
Oil on canvas
200 x 150 cm
© Andrei Roiter
Private collection, New York
Courtesy of Impronte Contemporary Art, Milan

above
My Luggage, 2007
Mixed media
54 x 20 x 20 cm
© Andrei Roiter
Collection of the artist
Courtesy of the artist

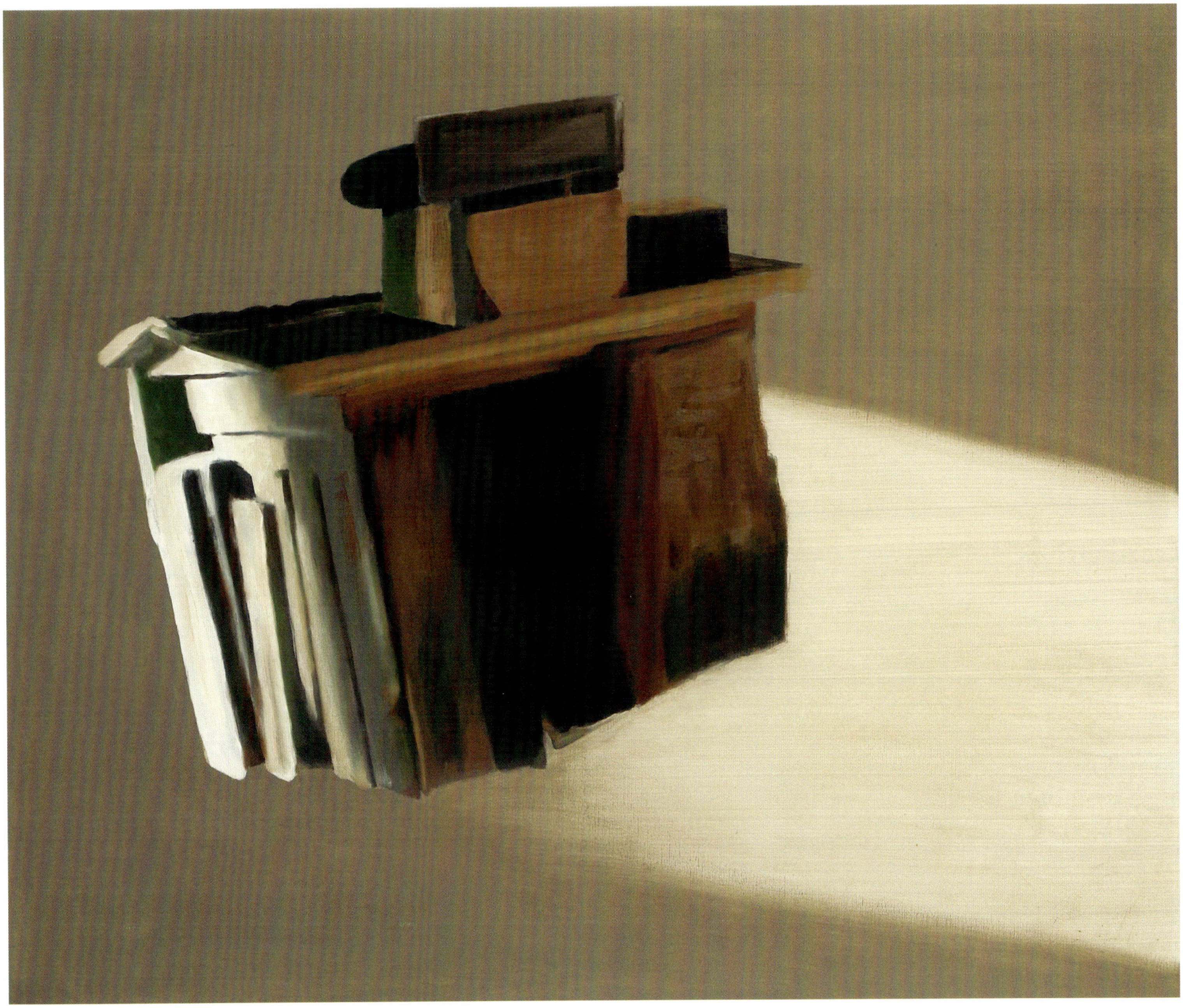

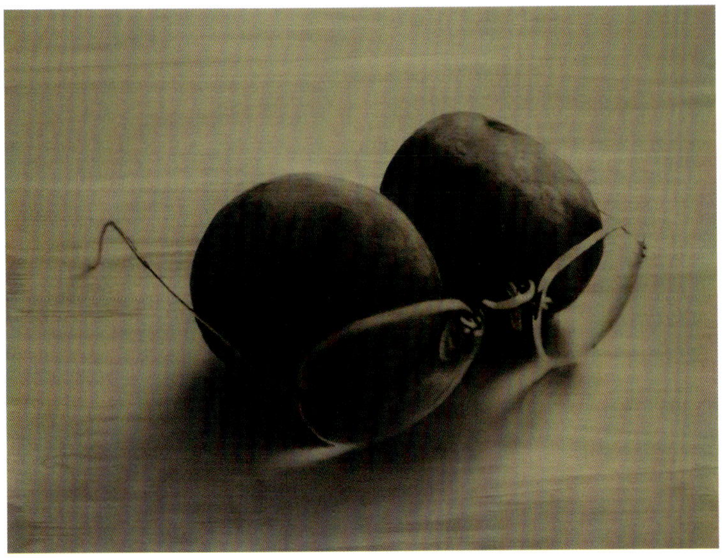

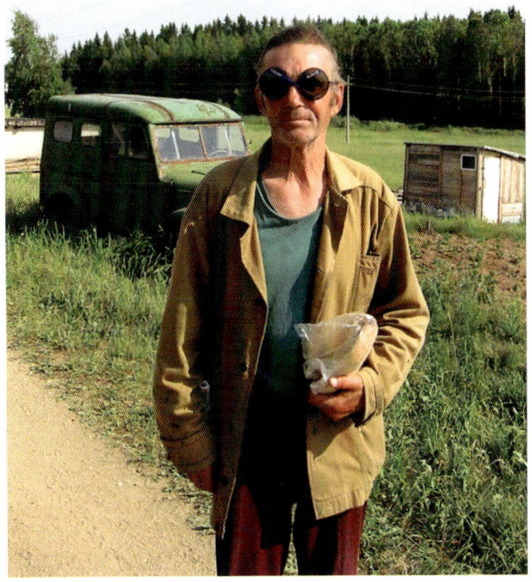

above
Sputnik, 2008
Oil on canvas
100 x 120 cm
© Andrei Roiter
Collection of the artist
Courtesy of the artist

far left
My Russian Eyes, 2010
Acrylic on canvas
150 x 200 cm
© Andrei Roiter
Collection of the artist
Courtesy of the artist

left
Moscow, 1998
Digital photo
© Andrei Roiter
Courtesy of the artist

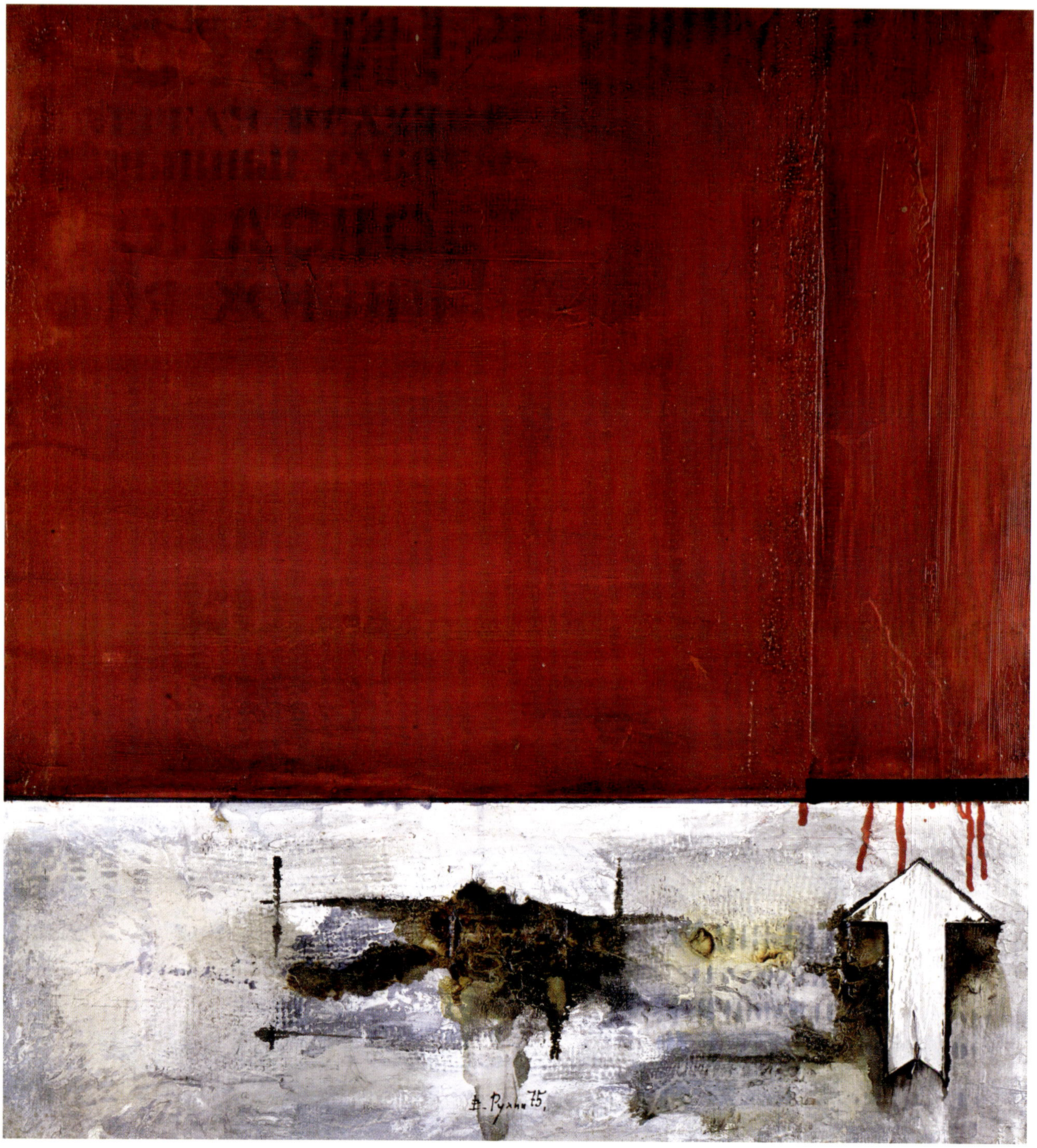

Born in Saratov, painter Evgeny Rukhin (1943–1976) lived and worked in Leningrad. Coming from a family of scientists, he studied geology at university; as an artist he was entirely self-taught. In the mid-1960s he was associated with important older artists of the Moscow underground, notably Vladimir Nemukhin, Oscar Rabin and Dmitry Plavinsky, all of whom had a formative influence on his art. A prolific painter, Rukhin produced, over the dozen years of his career, more than 500 works. His many important foreign and Russian patrons included George Costakis, Norton Dodge, Leonid Talochkin and Alexander Glezer. Rukhin died in suspicious circumstances in a fire in his studio; some have suggested this was at the behest of the KGB. As with many of his underground contemporaries, his association with international collectors and unofficial practice brought him constantly to the attention of the Soviet authorities. In 1974 he showed his paintings in the 'Bulldozer Exhibition'; he was arrested and his paintings seized. Today his work can be found in the State Russian Museum, St Petersburg; the State Tretyakov Gallery, Moscow; and the Jane Voorhees Zimmerli Art Museum, New Brunswick.

Rukhin's art represents a nostalgic longing for the past, in particular Russian Orthodox Christianity and the avant-garde of the 1920s. His use of a square format and his typical palettes of either monochrome or red and black on a white background derive from Suprematism and Constructivism; his addition of stencilled text was inspired by avant-garde book design. Rukhin emphasised the three-dimensional potential of his paintings' surfaces by using a mixture of synthetic tempera and plastic to serves as a cradle for found objects, thus often transforming paintings into assemblages. The found objects can be discarded bits of urban detritus or parts of broken furniture. The parallel between collapsed chairs and the imprints of metal icon covers points up the way in which useful things can become broken and no longer needed: Christianity discarded in favour of Soviet ideology. Yet political metaphor often comes second to Rukhin's simple lyricism, as the critic Svetlana Darsalia has observed: 'Rukhin poeticises the object. It is the poetic perception found in the works of Kandinsky.' The highly decorative quality of Rukhin's art often gives way to a darker mode of expression with impassioned brushstrokes, burned and cracked paint surfaces, forms and objects which press against one another, and the application of chains and locks.

above
Untitled (Composition with Red Field and Arrow), from the series Danger for Life, 1975
Oil, mixed media, relief on canvas
81.3 x 76.2 cm

Private collection

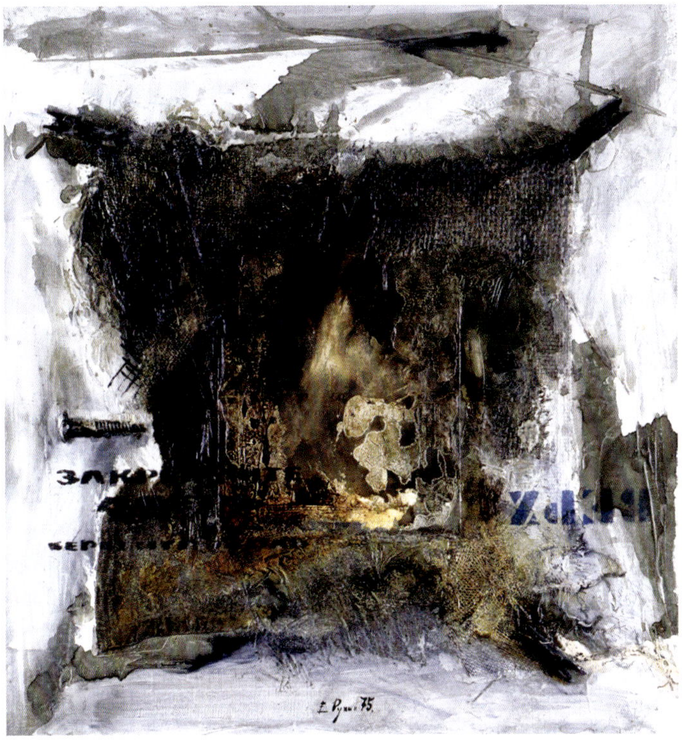

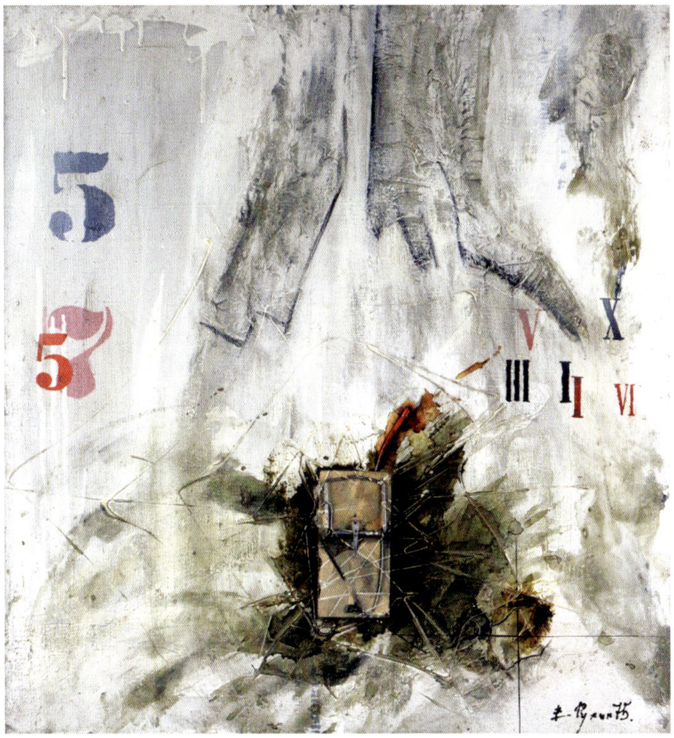

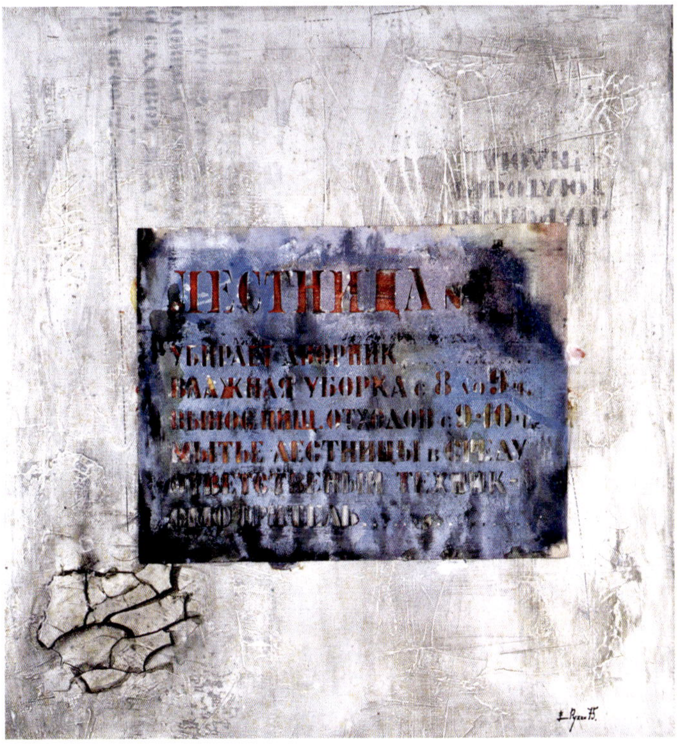

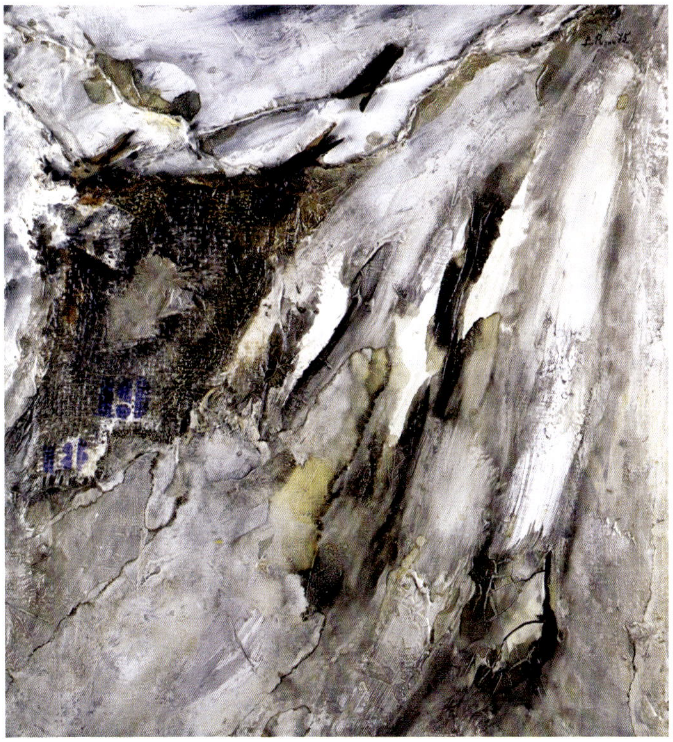

top
Untitled (Composition with Four Clothespins),
1975 (damaged in studio fire)
Oil, mixed media, collage on canvas
69.9 x 66 cm
© Evgeny Rukhin Foundation
Private collection

above
Untitled (Composition with Stencils), 1975
Oil, mixed media, collage on canvas
69.2 x 64.1 cm
© Evgeny Rukhin Foundation
Private collection

top
Untitled (Composition with Mousetrap), 1975
Oil, mixed media, collage on canvas
69.9 x 66 cm
© Evgeny Rukhin Foundation
Private collection

above
Untitled (Composition with Burlap and Blue-ink Numbers), 1975
Oil, mixed media, collage on canvas
69.9 x 66 cm
© Evgeny Rukhin Foundation
Private collection

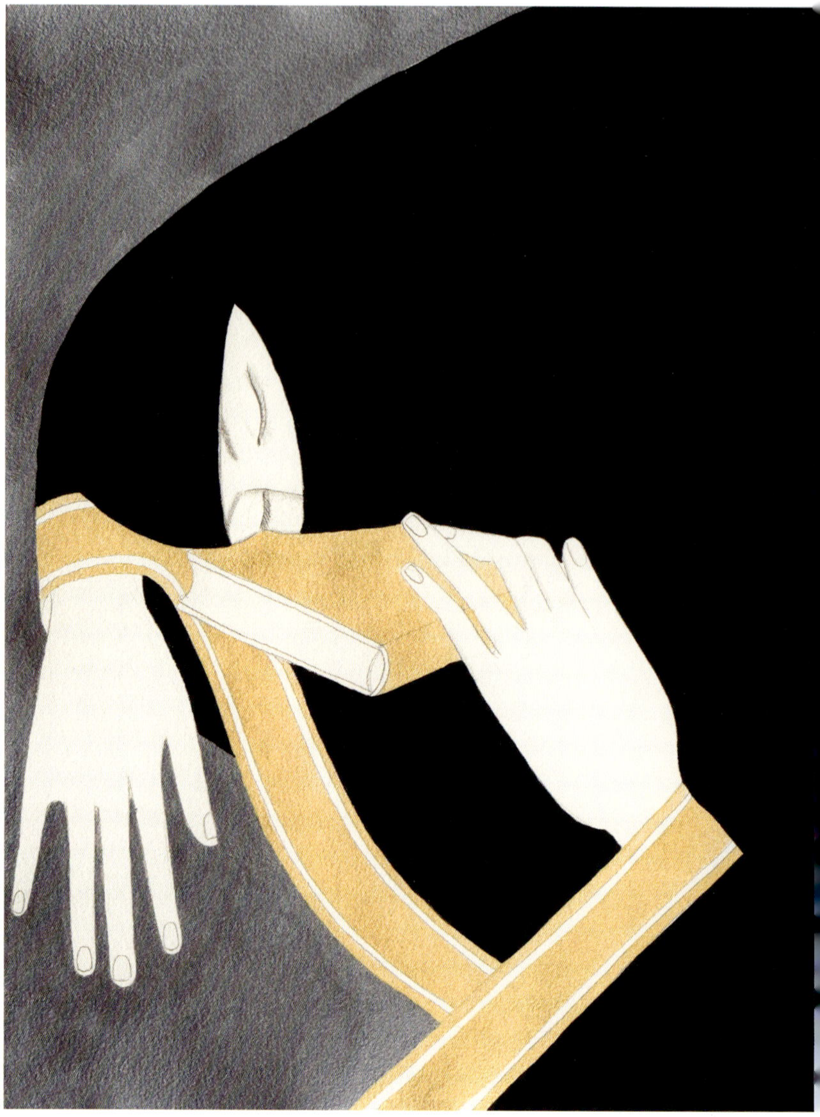

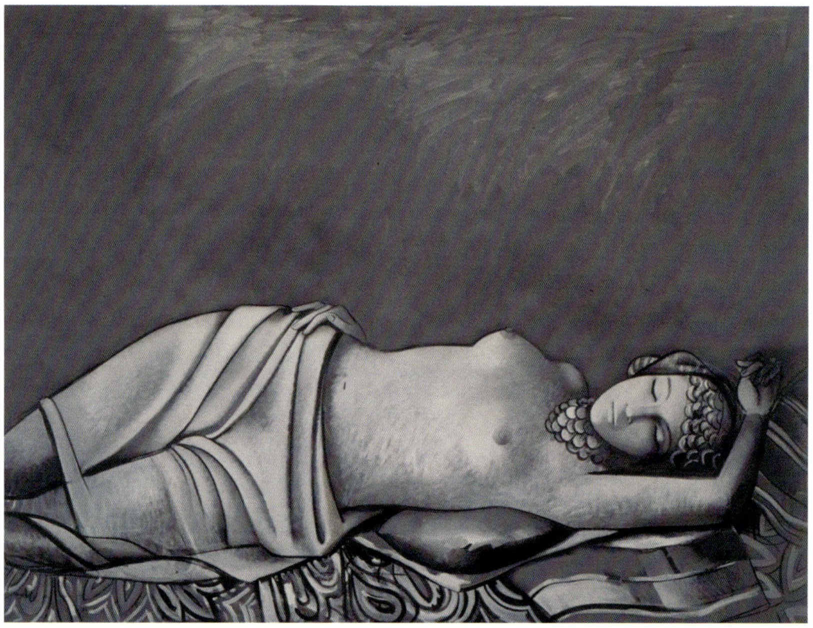

Salakhova, born in 1964, divides her time between Moscow and Baku. The daughter of Azeri artist Tair Salakhov, she started painting at an early age, graduating from the Surikov Institute, where she is now a professor, in 1987. Salakhova – who is known by her first name, Aidan – founded the first commercial art gallery in Russia in 1992. In 2007 she became an Academician of the Russian Academy of Arts. Aidan exhibited in the Soviet Pavilion at the 1990 Venice Biennale, and in 2011 works from her sculpture series Destination (2010) were shown at the Pavilion of Azerbaijan in Venice. MMOMA hosted a major solo retrospective in Moscow in 2006.

Aidan works in a variety of media, notably painting, graphics, video, installation and sculpture. Using traditional methods of representation, her art explores female sexuality and identity through her own dual nationality as Russian and Azeri, referencing her cultural and spiritual roots in Soviet Russia and Islam. By reinventing the odalisque of nineteenth-century European Orientalism, she empowers the feminine, creative spirit in works which can be seen both as an expression of herself as a woman artist and as an unfettered celebration of female sensuality and fertility. According to Maria Kravtsova, Aidan 'has returned sensuality to the realm of contemporary art'. Sometimes this sensuality gives way to eroticism, as in the series I Love Myself (2005). The monumental marble sculptures of Destination (2010–11) are powerful reinterpretations of classical Greek sculpture which employ an aesthetic of traditional beauty, Aidan's models being veiled Muslim women and symbols of Islamic culture.

above
Untitled, from the series Persian Miniatures
Watercolour, pencil, gouache on paper
64 x 48.2 cm
© Aidan Salakhova
Ekaterina and Vladimir Semenikhin Collection

left
Sleeping Beauty, 1999
Acrylic on canvas
150 x 200 cm
© Aidan Salakhova
Courtesy of the artist

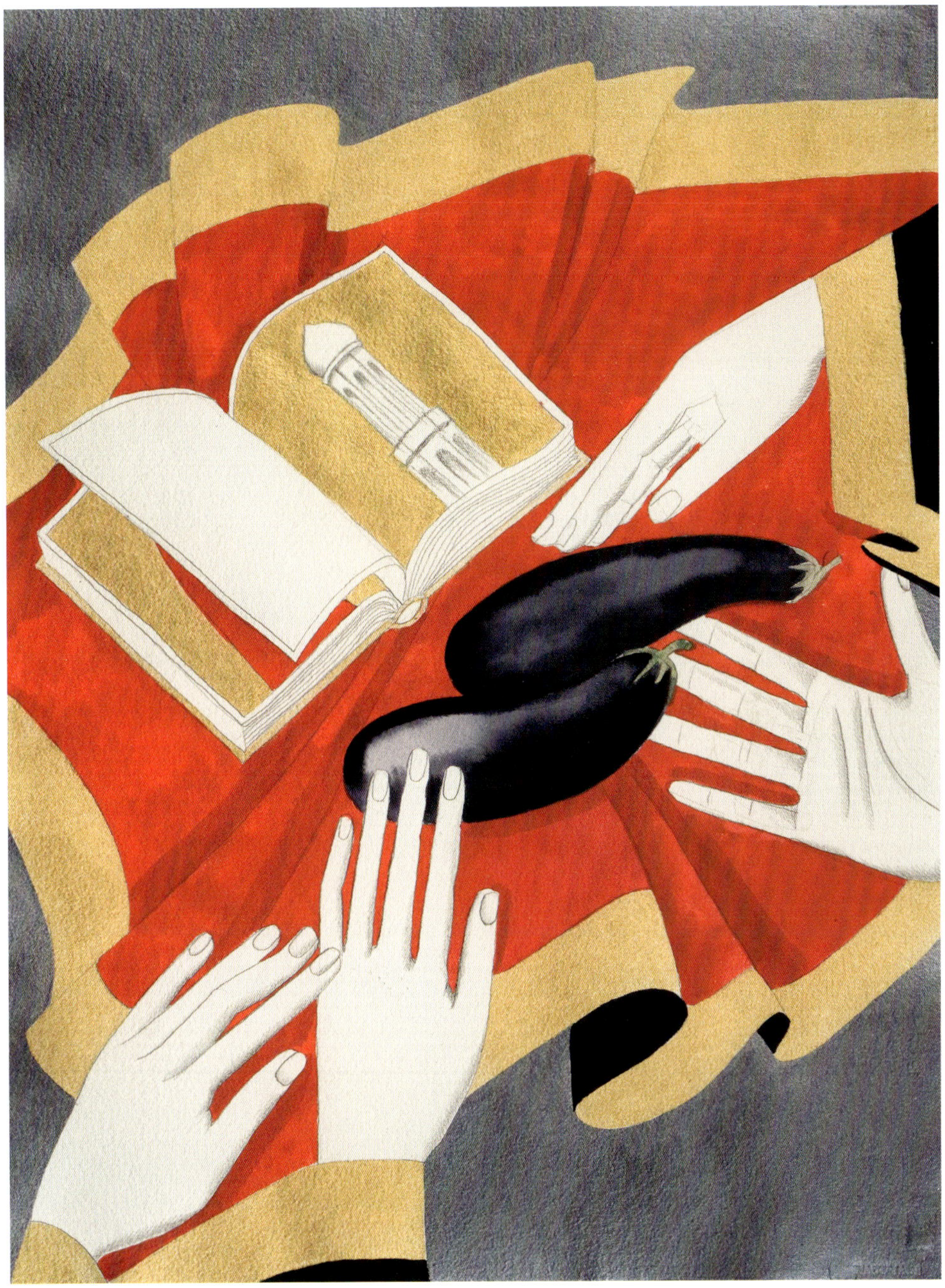

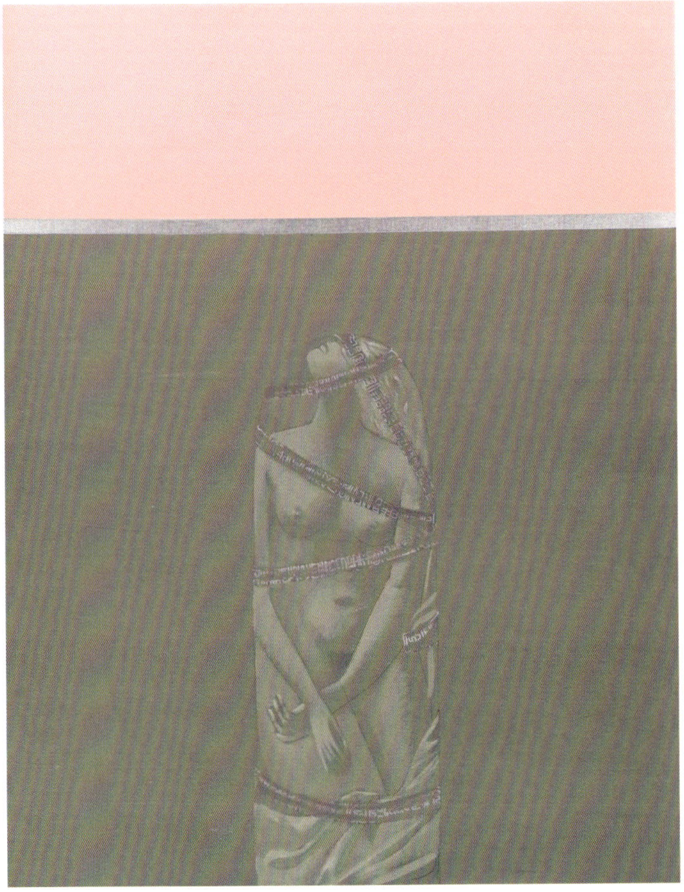

above
Untitled, from the series
Persian Miniatures
Watercolour, pencil, gouache on paper
64 x 48.2 cm
© Aidan Salakhova
Ekaterina and Vladimir Semenikhin Collection

left
Green Abstract, 1998
Oil on canvas
173 x 136.9 cm
© Aidan Salakhova
Courtesy of the artist

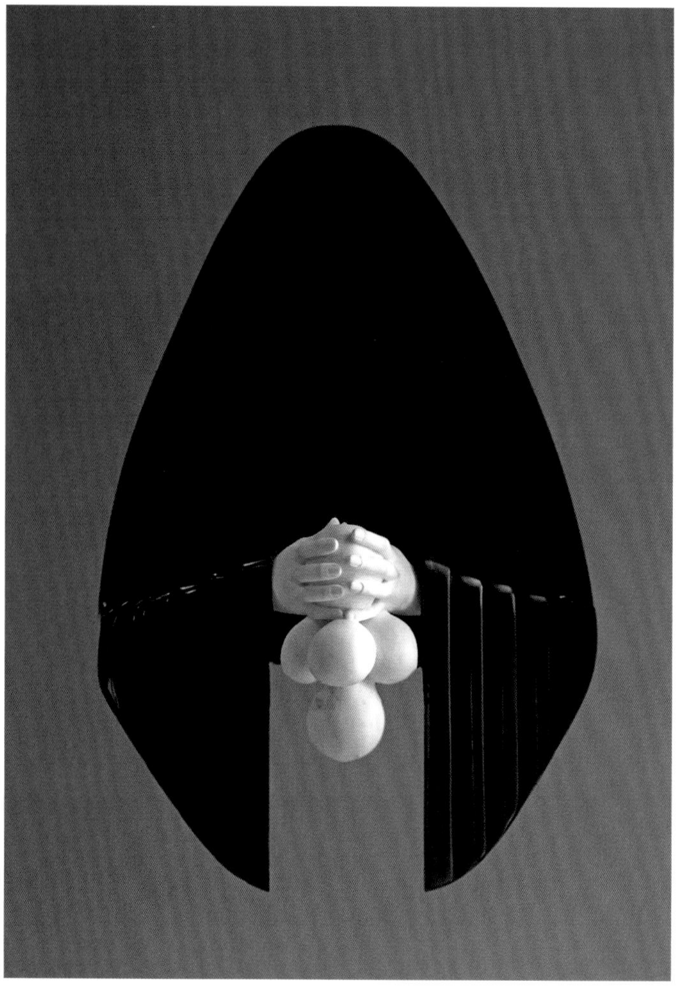

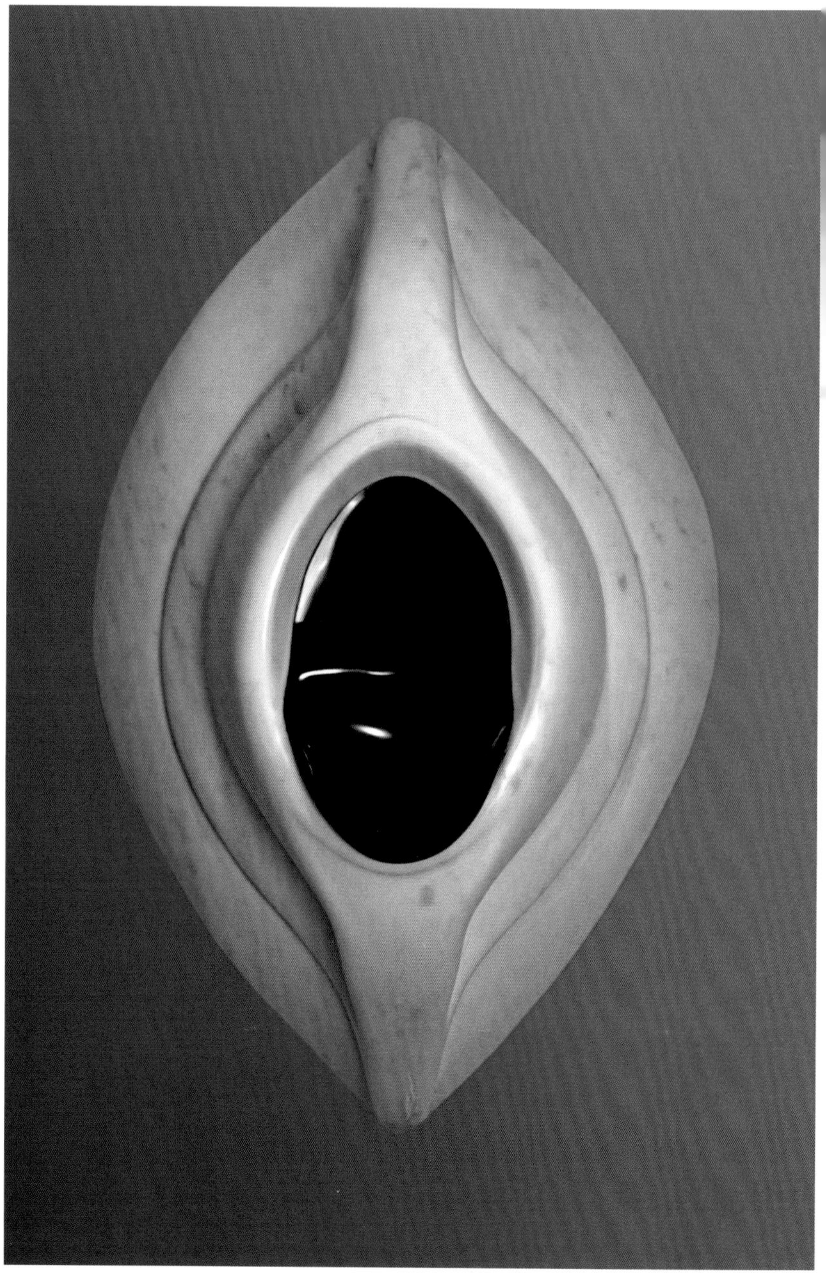

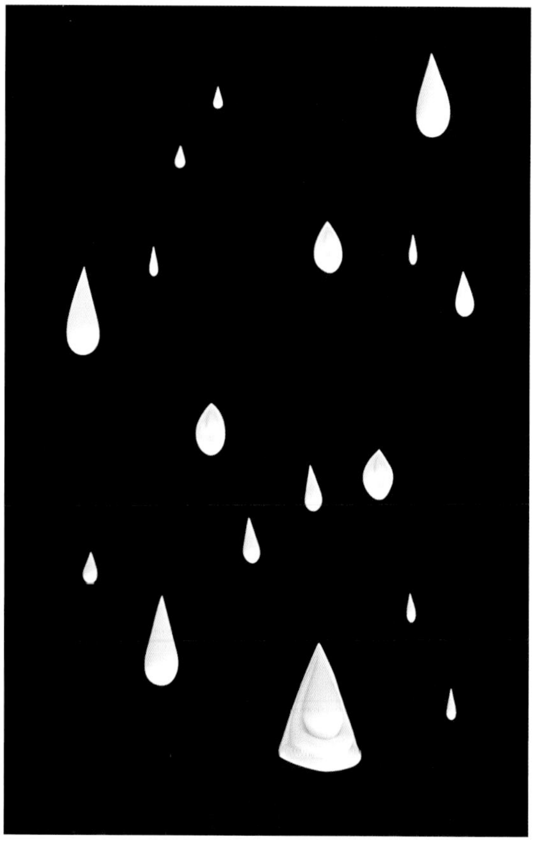

top
White, from the series Destination, 2010–11
Marble
90 x 70 x 40 cm
© Aidan Salakhova
Courtesy of the artist

right
Tears, from the series Destination, 2010–11
Marble
Varying dimensions
© Aidan Salakhova
Courtesy of the artist

above
Black Stone, from the series Destination, 2010–11
Marble
125 x 75 x 40 cm
© Aidan Salakhova
Courtesy of the artist

facing page
Prestanding, from the series Destination, 2010–11
Black granite, white marble
80 x 68 x 170 cm
© Aidan Salakhova
Courtesy of the artist

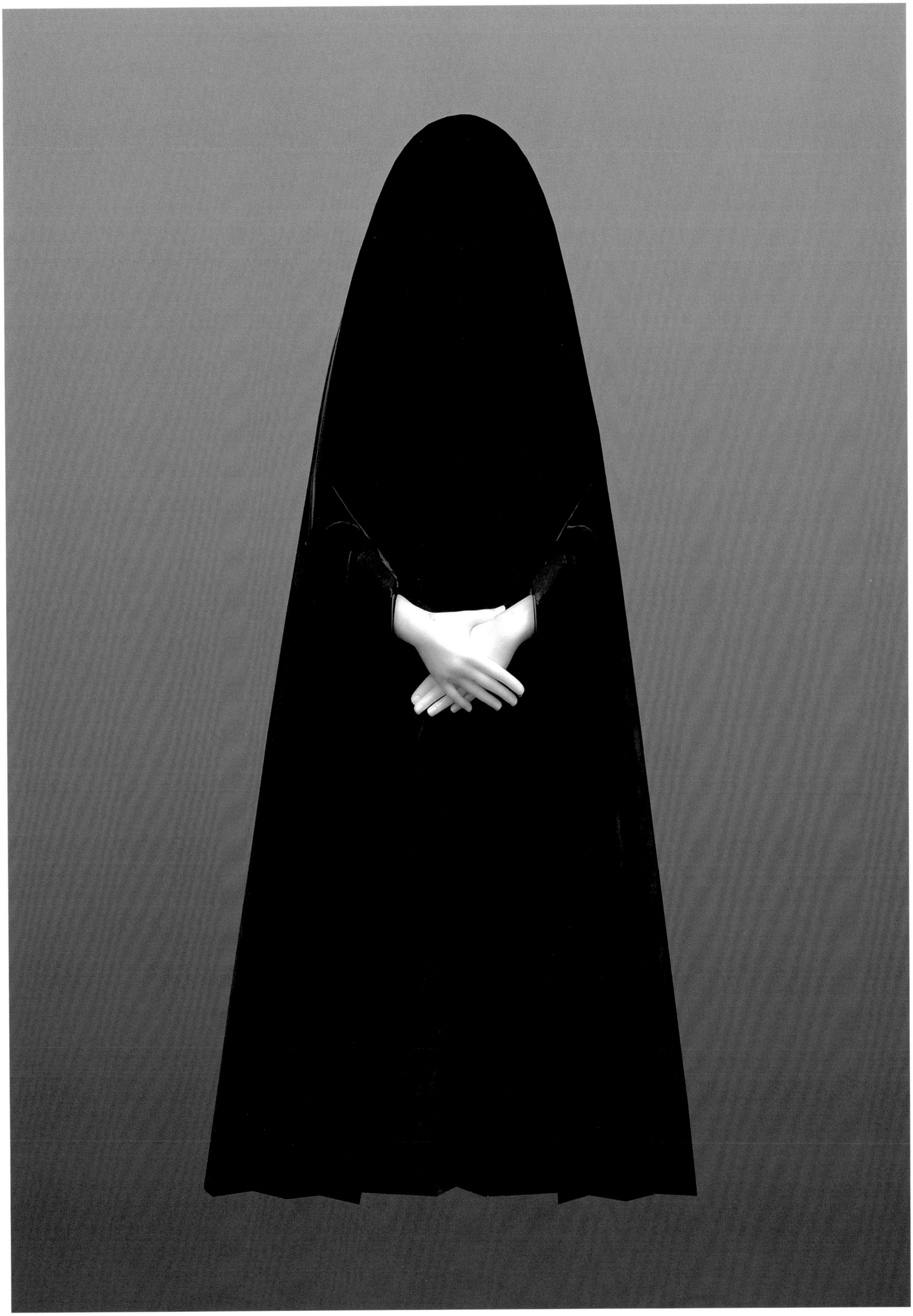

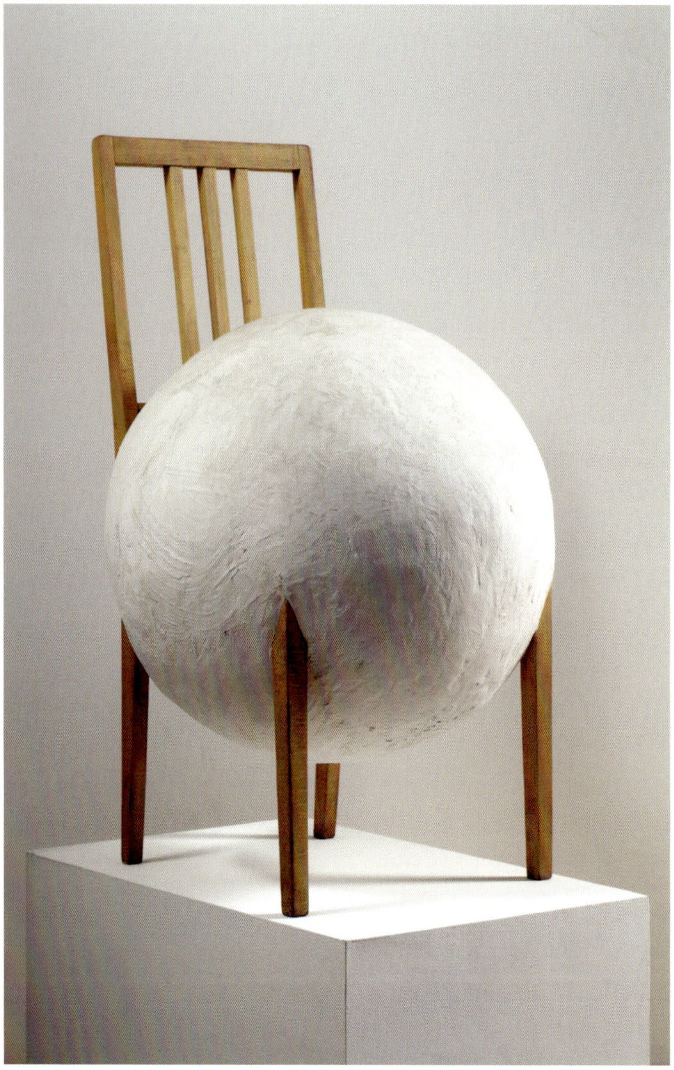

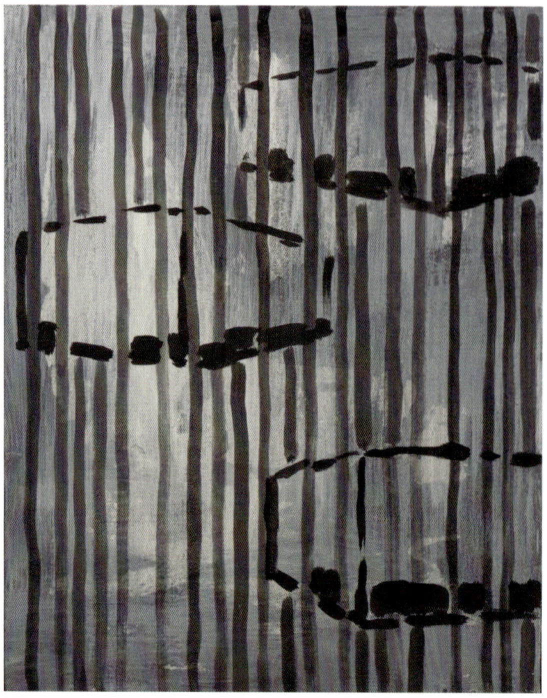

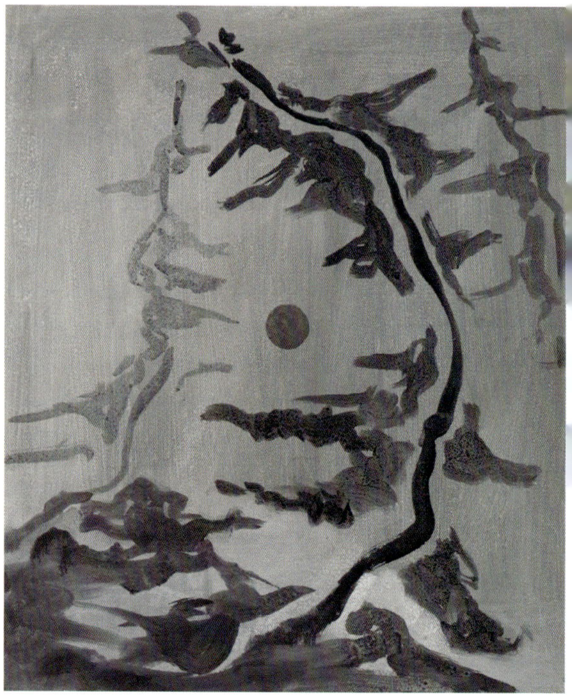

Born in Moscow in 1965, Maria Serebriakova works predominantly as a painter and across various media including installation, graphics and photographs. Throughout her oeuvre, natural imagery, such as plants, landscapes, and man-made architectural details are put forward as personal metaphors for emptiness, loneliness, tragedy and the search for identity. These motifs are rendered with an economy of expression and subtle rhythm, offering the viewer catalysts for meditation. The artist's work is included in the collections of the Museum of Modern Art, New York; SMAK, Ghent; the State Russian Museum, St Petersburg; and the UCLA Hammer Museum, Los Angeles. Her work has been included in a number of international exhibitions, including Documenta IX and the first and second Moscow biennales.

top
Feather No. 2, 2007
Oil on cardboard
30 x 42 cm
© Maria Serebriakova
Courtesy Regina Gallery,
London & Moscow

above
Untitled, 2008
Acrylic on wooden panel
60 x 50 cm
© Maria Serebriakova
Private collection

above left
Untitled, 1993
Chair, plaster
95 x 60 x 65 cm
© Maria Serebriakova
Courtesy Regina Gallery,
London & Moscow

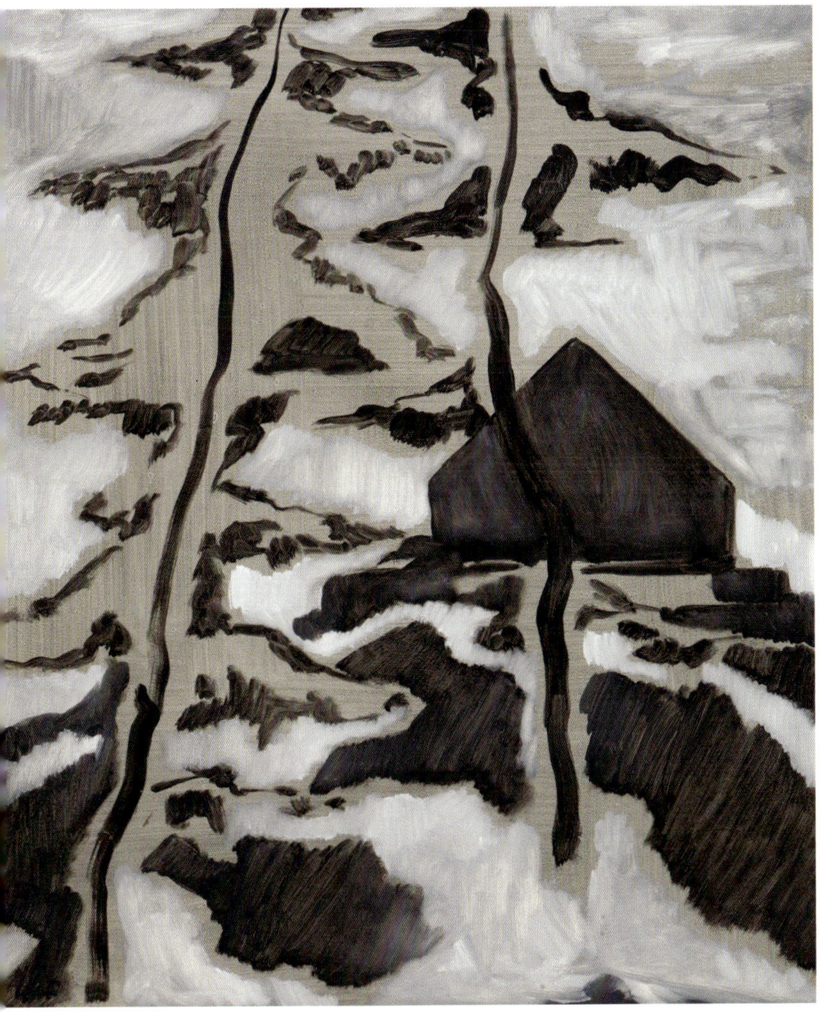

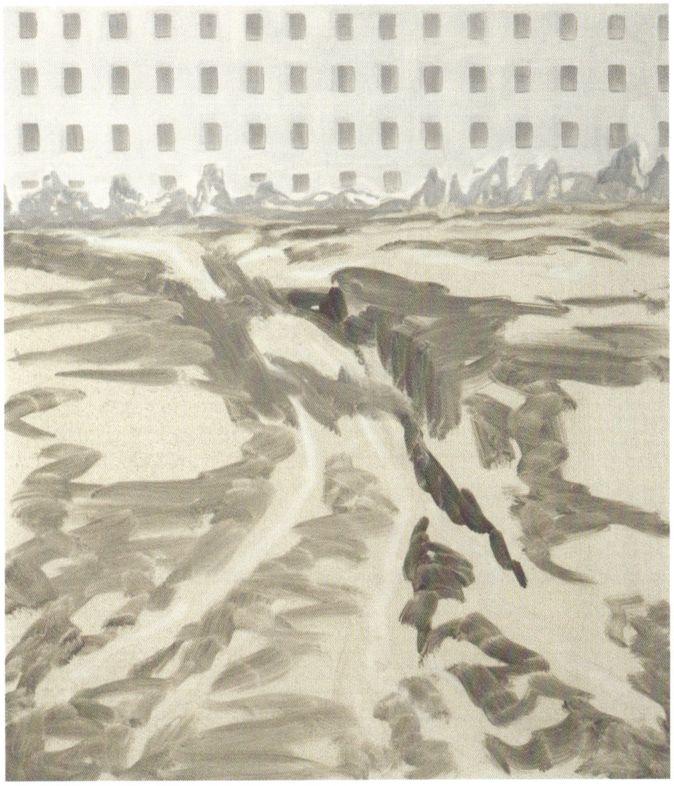

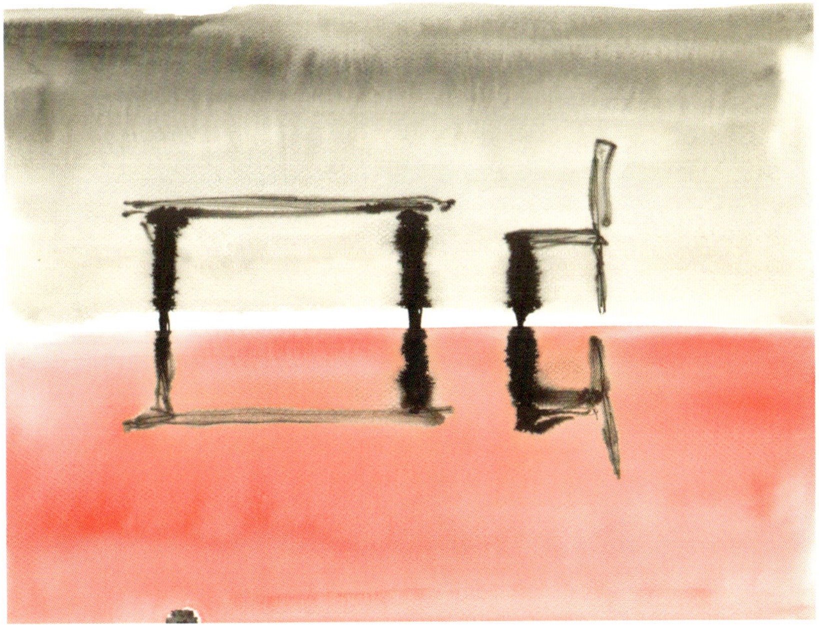

top left
Untitled, 2007
Oil on wooden panel
60 x 50 cm
© Maria Serebriakova
Courtesy Regina Gallery,
London & Moscow

left
Untitled, 2010
Watercolour on paper
32 x 24 cm
© Maria Serebriakova
Courtesy Regina Gallery,
London & Moscow

above
Wasteland, 2007
Oil on wooden panel
57 x 50 cm
© Maria Serebriakova
Courtesy Regina Gallery,
London & Moscow

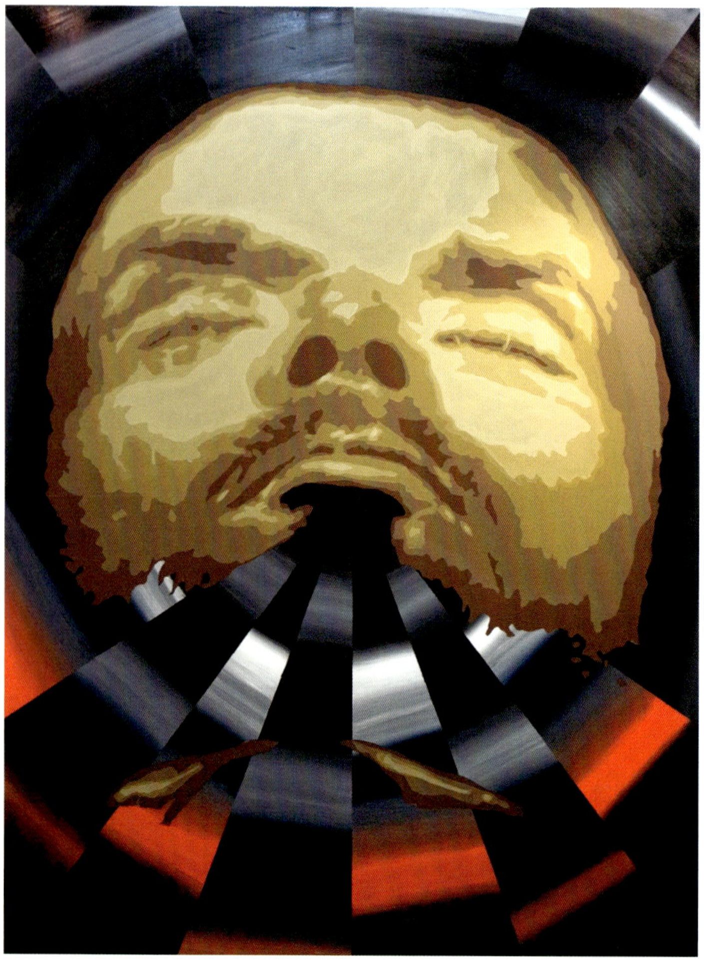

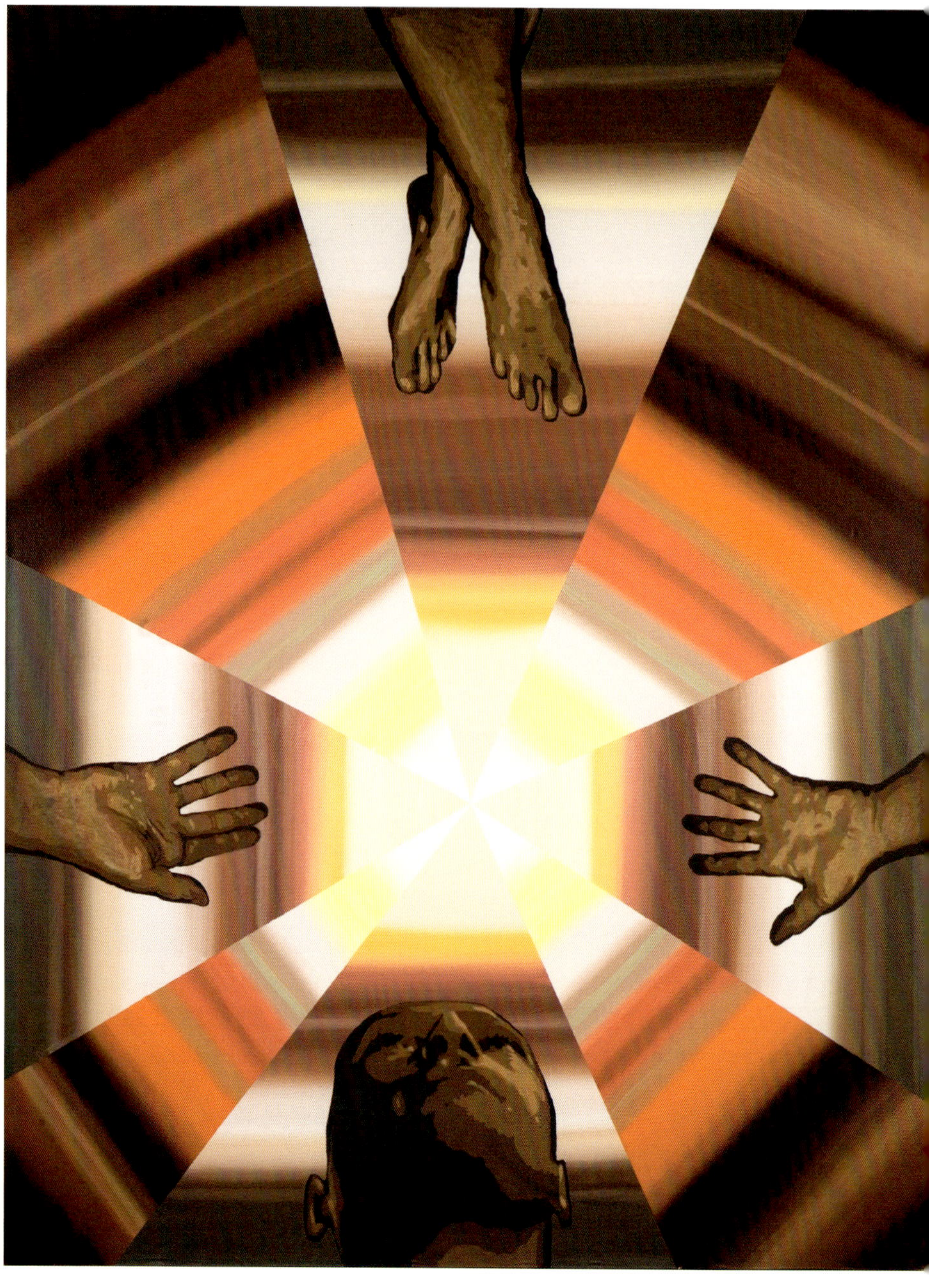

Born in 1955 in Potsdam, Germany, Sergei Shutov is active across a wide range of media despite the fact that he has had no formal art education. He has been a musician, curator and theoretician, lectured at the Moscow Planetarium, and worked in the Pushkin Museum of Fine Arts and the Moscow Zoo. He became famous as the production designer of the cult film *ASSA* (1987), in which he also acted. During the 1990s Shutov became Russia's first VJ; in the early days of Moscow club life he did real-time video mixing at the legendary Ptyuch club. He has never been a member of an art group.

Shutov's early work consists of bold new-wave paintings. Following on from these, he founded the Institute of Art Technologies in 1993 as a return to traditional media, imparting an intentionally rugged, hand-crafted look to his work. His art is an emotional reflection of his multiple interests, which embrace everything from ethnography and allusions to cult imagery to the unknown and unexplored. All things cosmic – from metaphysics to cartoonish aliens to psychedelic experiences to the advances of science and world religions – engage his attention.

In 2001 Shutov represented Russia at the 49th Venice Biennale with the installation *Abacus*. Having participated in numerous important exhibitions, he was nominated for the State Prize of the Russian Federation in 2002. He has had many solo exhibitions and been included in group shows in Russia and elsewhere. Shutov lives and works in Moscow.

above
From the series Elevation I, 2007
Mixed media on canvas
200 x 150 cm
© Sergei Shutov
Courtesy of the artist

top left
From the series The First Kilometer, 2009
Mixed media on canvas
200 x 150 cm
© Sergei Shutov
Courtesy of the artist

Sergei Shutov

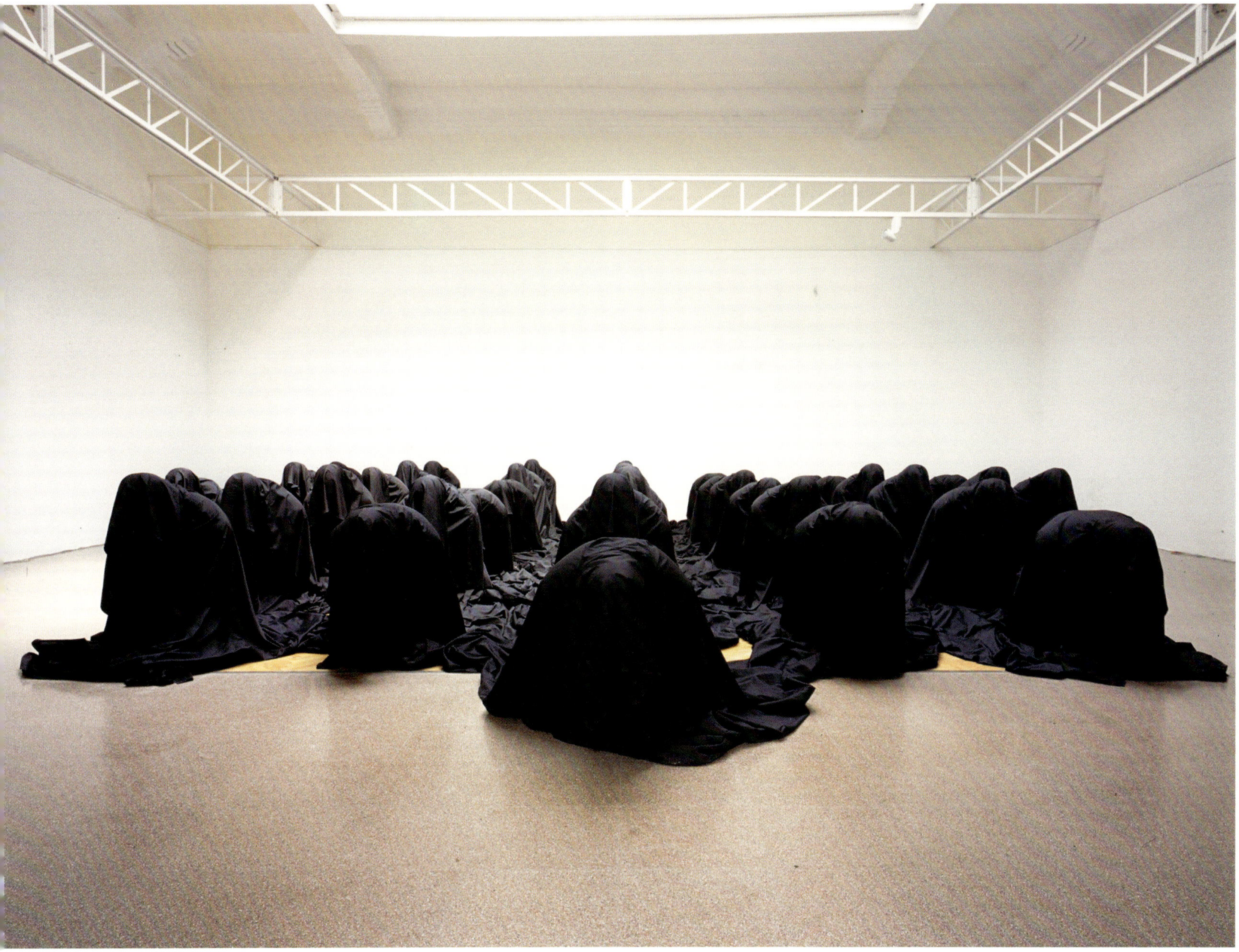

above
Abacus, 2001
Mechanisms, lay figures, fabric (40 figures)

Courtesy of the artist

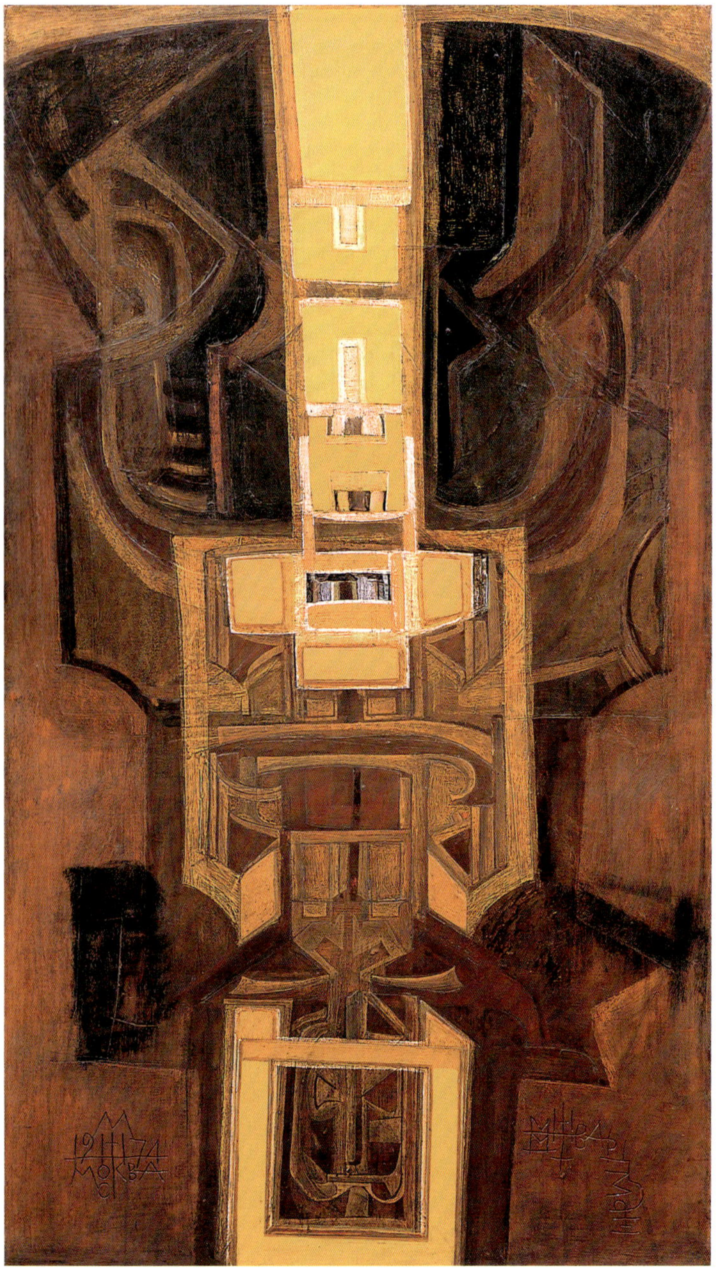

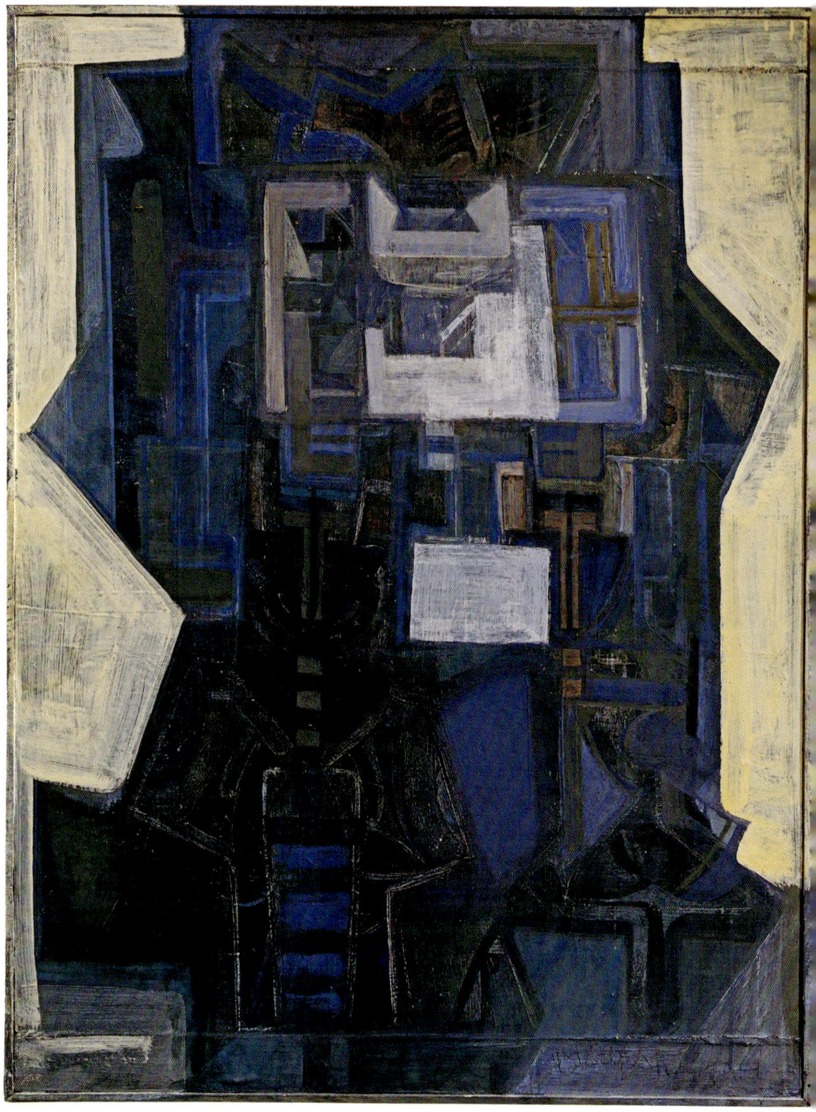

Painter Mikhail Shvartsman (1927–2007) lived and worked in Moscow. When he was ten years old, his father was arrested, later dying in a labour camp in Nizhny Tagil. Shvartsman served in the Soviet Army for five years before entering the Moscow Institute of Industrial Art. After graduation, and with a young family to support, he worked as a designer specialising in industrial design, graphic art and posters. Painting in his free time, he developed his own abstract style. In 1966 Shvartsman was given the post of head designer of the graphic arts section of the newly formed Special Office of Art and Construction. Under the auspices of the design workshop, and in spite of the government's insistence on Soviet Realism in the fine arts, Shvartsman and his students studied the work of the Russian avant-garde, including Malevich, Tatlin and Rodchenko. Throughout this time, he had his own studio and sold paintings to collectors such as Norton Dodge and George Costakis. Shvartsman mounted his first-ever solo show after perestroika at the State Tretyakov Gallery, Moscow (1994), and in 2001 there was a retrospective of his work at the State Russian Museum, St Petersburg.

Shvartsman's abstract art has a spiritual basis, drawing inspiration from both icon painting and the non-objective art of Malevich, whom Shvartsman had met as a child. Often painting at twilight when the light most suited his vision, he worked slowly, using meditation and spiritual contemplation (a practice common to icon painters when depicting saints and religious festivals). As in the icon-painting tradition with its set forms, he devised an underlying system, thus giving his practice a structure within which to create spiritual works.

Shvartsman's oeuvre can be divided into two main themes: semi-abstract 'countenances' and fully abstract works, which he called 'hieraturae'. The countenances are the faces of saints, *liki* in Russian; as Shvartsman wrote, 'They are images and not real heads, but the face as the entrance into a spiritual world.' These countenances bear a superficial resemblance to African masks but must not be confused with such objects: 'They are not masks; that would be demonic.' Shvartsman's fully abstract compositions can be compared closely to the avant-garde architectonics of Popova and Exter: abstract art which creates a structural form sufficient in itself to convey aesthetic power. Shvartsman's hieraturae are spiritual rather than artistic; he likened them to sacred handicrafts. They are painted on panel, with the colours teased out until, in the words of George Costakis, 'they shine'. The term *hieraturae* comes from the Greek word *hieros*, meaning 'sacred'. These works can be seen as expressions of the language of the sacred spirit; Shvartsman believed that the role of the artist's imagination is to bring out the spirit in form.

above left
Snow on Selmona, 1974
Levkas and tempera on board and canvas
130 x 75 cm

Courtesy of Shvartsman Heritage Art Foundation

above
The Chain, 1975
Levkas and tempera on board and canvas
100 x 75 cm

Courtesy of Shvartsman Heritage Art Foundation

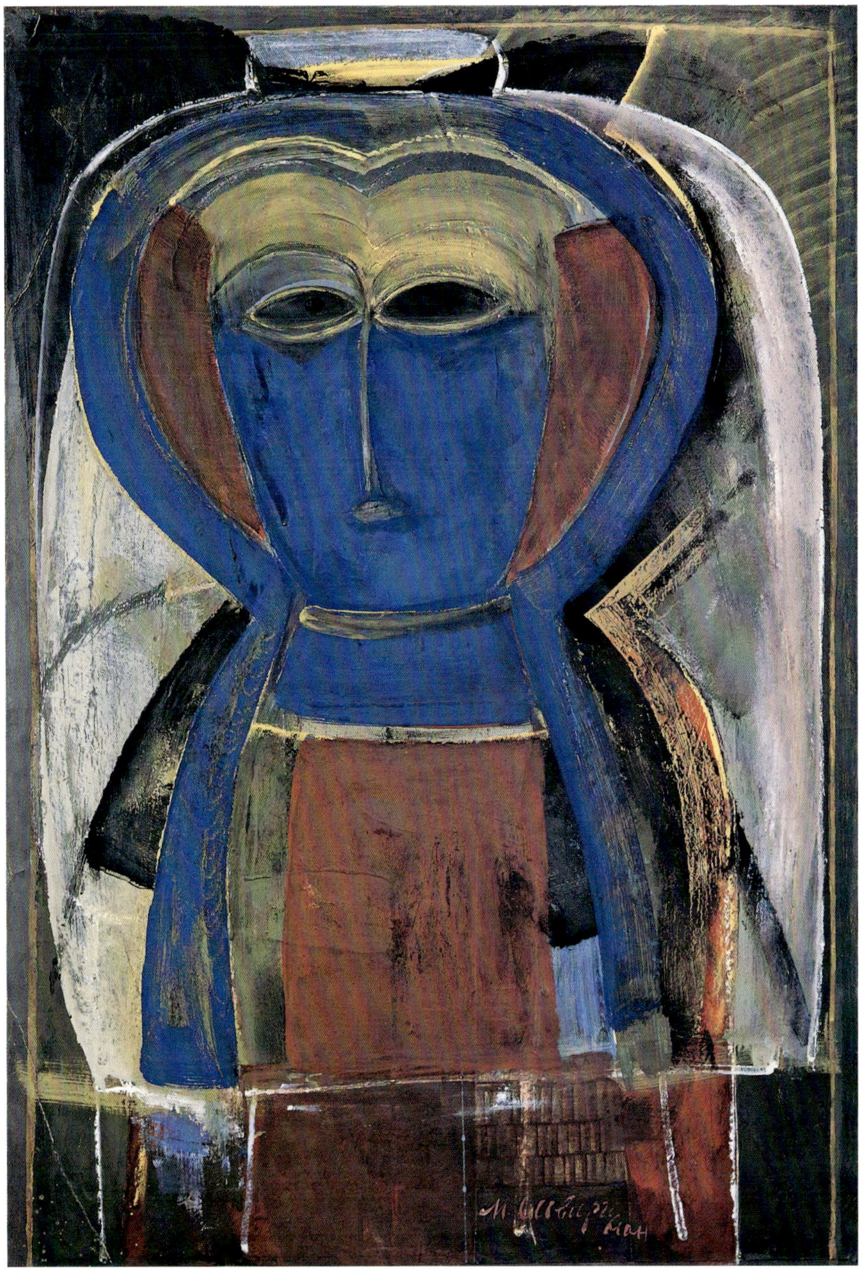

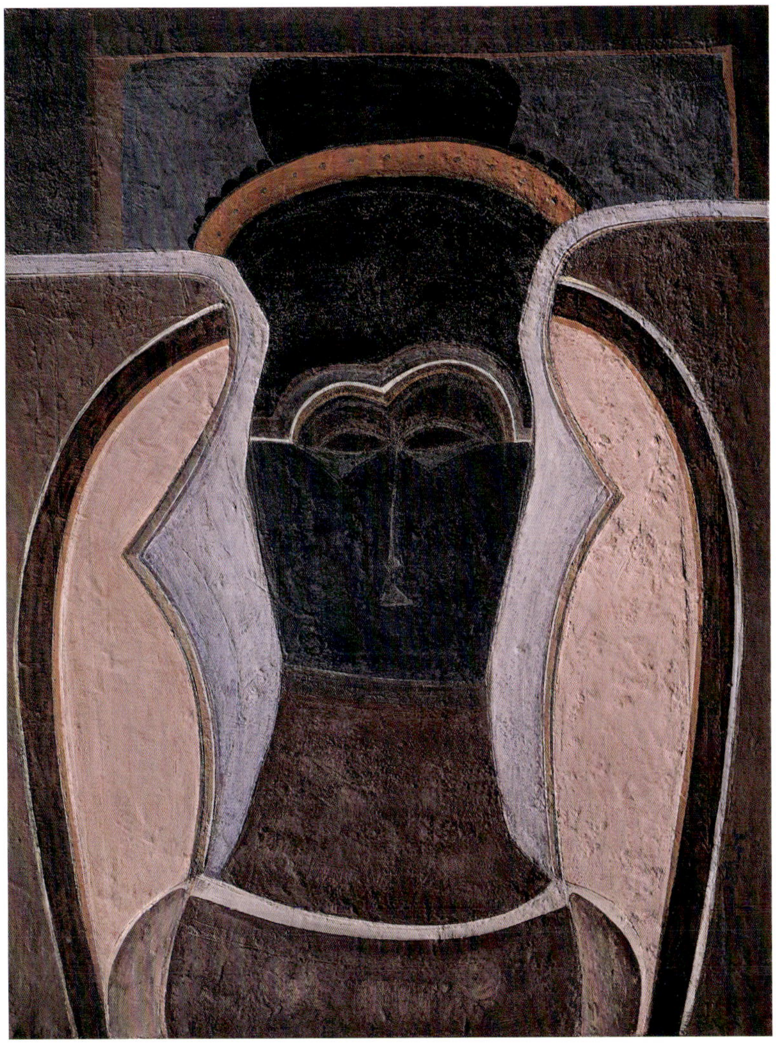

above
David, 1970
Tempera on board and paper
81 x 56 cm
© Shvartsman Heritage Art Foundation
Shvartsman Collection
Courtesy of Shvartsman Heritage
Art Foundation

left
Filial Hierarchy, 1960s
Oil on canvas
130 x 100 cm
© Shvartsman Heritage Art Foundation
State Russian Museum, St Petersburg
Courtesy of Shvartsman Heritage
Art Foundation

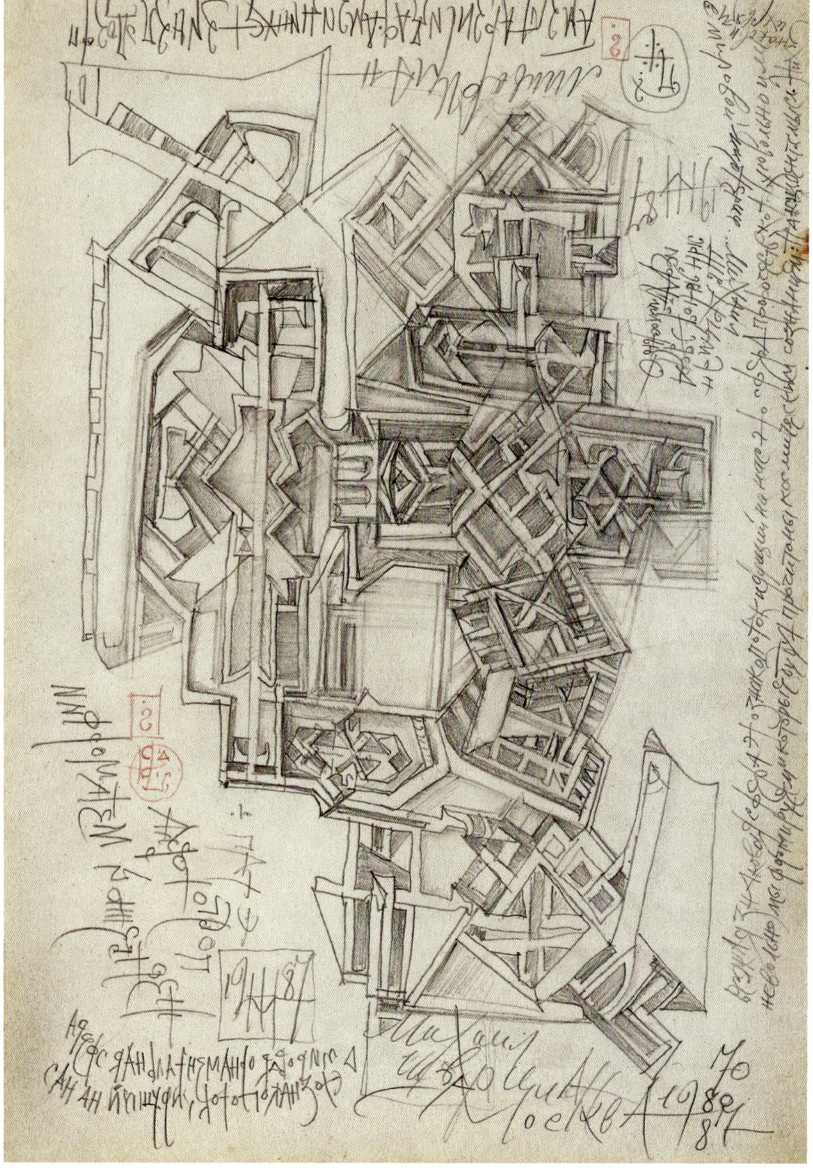

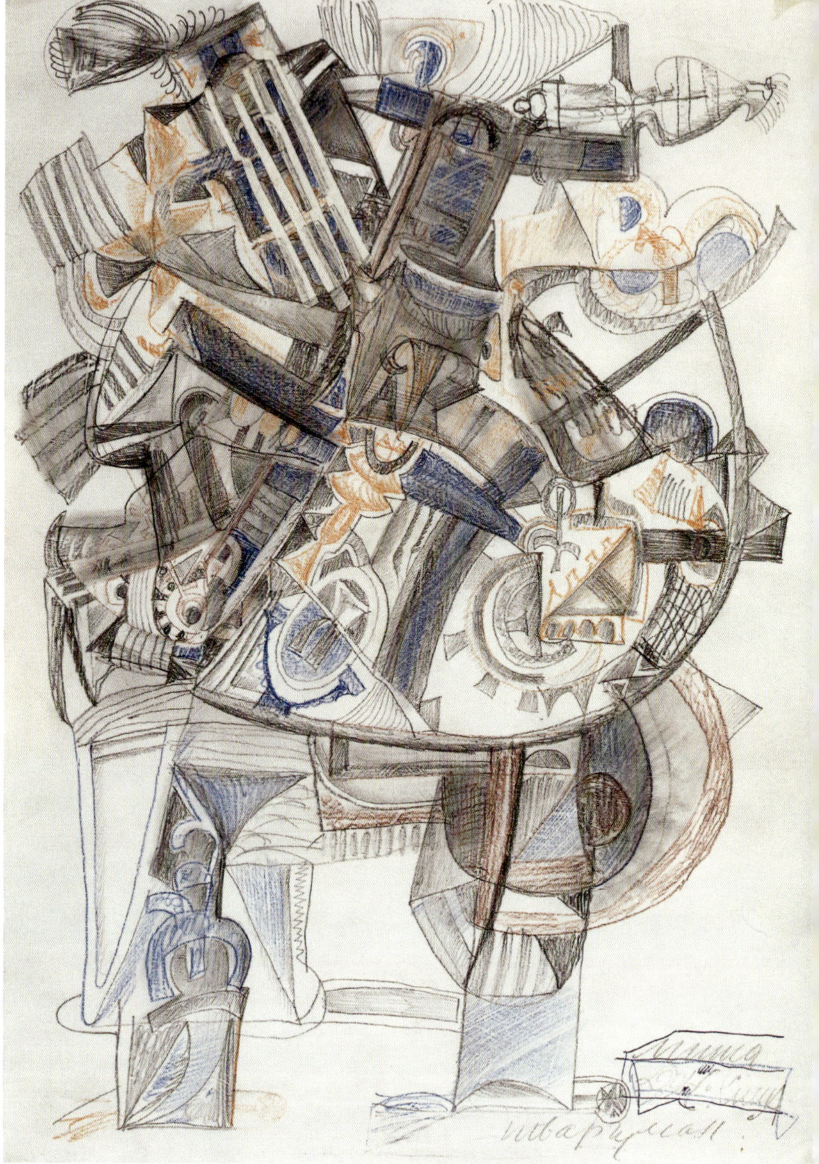

above left
Insights Cycle: No. 2: Coming at Us ..., 1987
Graphite and coloured pencil on paper
29.8 x 20.8 cm
© Shvartsman Heritage Art Foundation
Shvartsman Collection
Courtesy of Shvartsman Heritage
Art Foundation

above
Metamorphoses Cycle: No. 31, 1975
Graphite and coloured pencil on paper
30 x 21 cm
© Shvartsman Heritage Art Foundation
Shvartsman Collection
Courtesy of Shvartsman Heritage
Art Foundation

facing page
Bitter Grasses, 1977–86
Levkas and tempera on board and canvas
100 x 100 cm
© Shvartsman Heritage Art Foundation
Shvartsman Collection
Courtesy of Shvartsman Heritage
Art Foundation

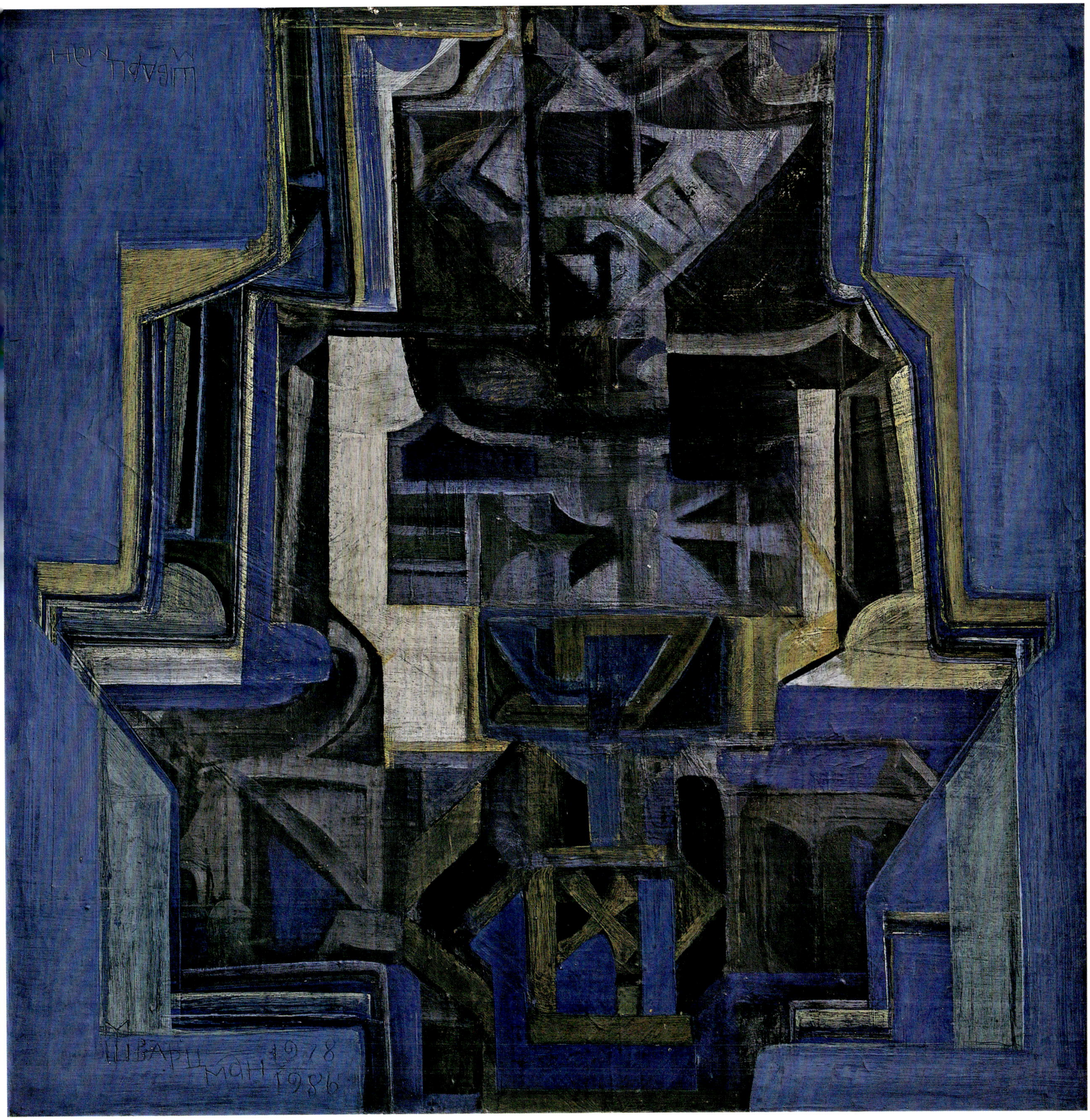
М
ШВАРЦ
МАН
1978
1986

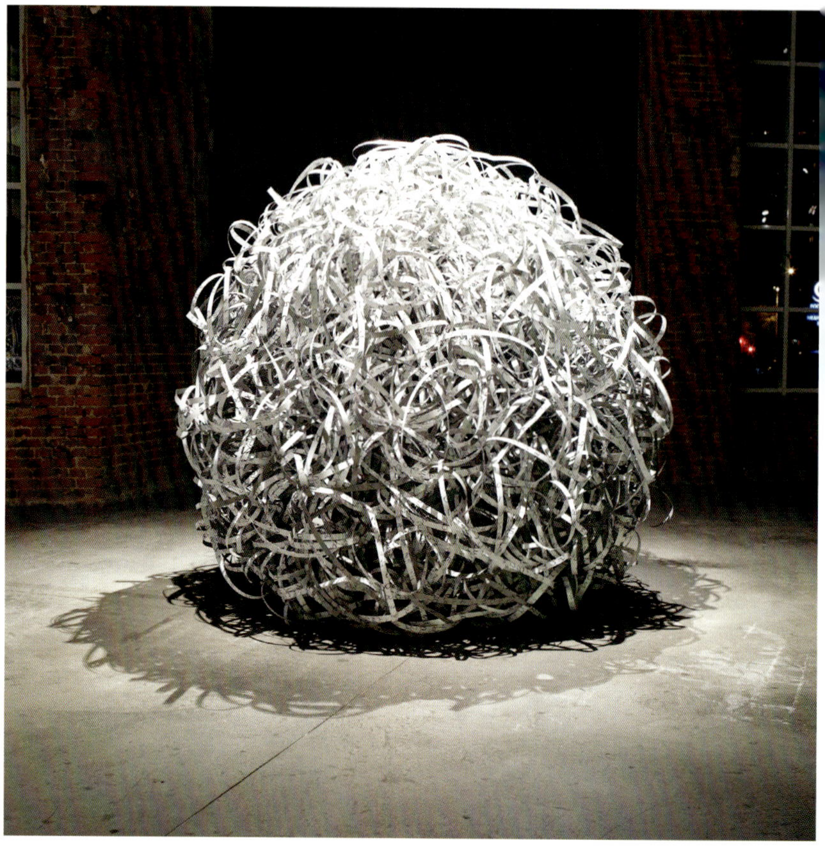

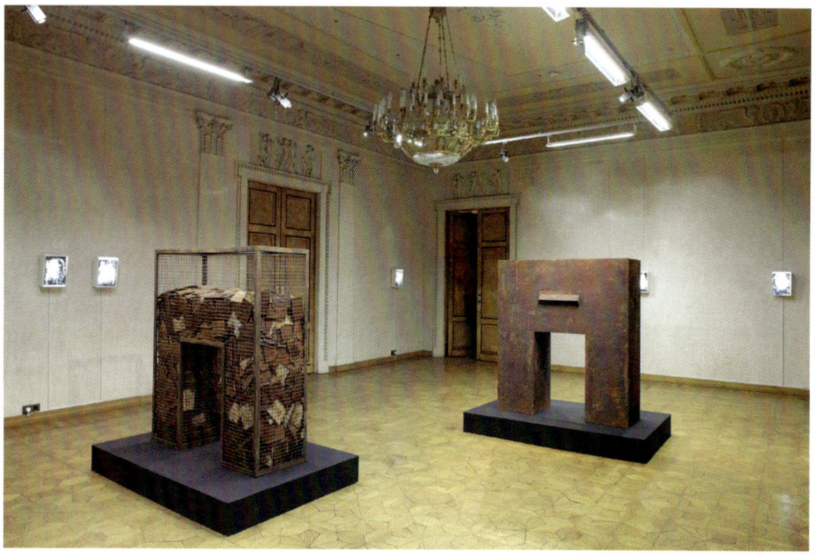

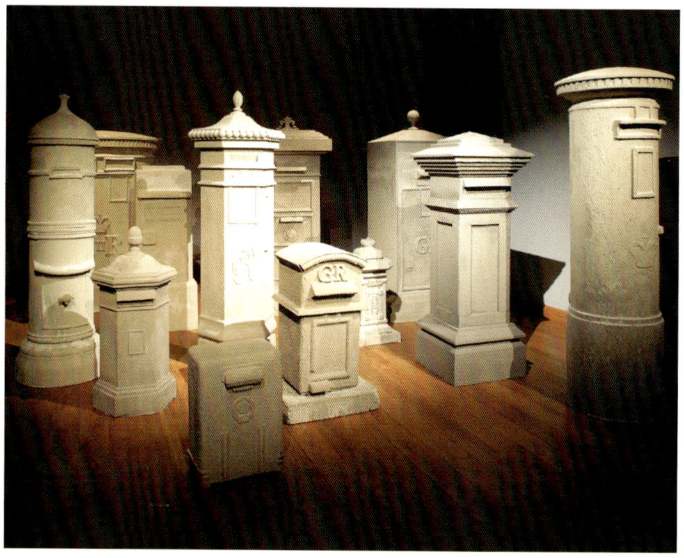

Born in Arkhangelsk, Haim Sokol has a distinct dual identity; he relocated to Jerusalem to pursue his studies in Hebrew linguistics and Jewish literature before returning to Russia and graduating from the Institute of Contemporary Art in Moscow. Sokol creates small sculptures, large installations and graphic works from the detritus of everyday life, which he finds strewn across rubbish dumps and on the street in both Moscow and Jerusalem, between which he now divides his time. Recognisable for his use of banal, everyday, ready-made objects – discarded photographs, brooms, dirty rags, discoloured, rusted metal – and his sombre palette, Sokol's works 'embody ... oblivion, which means they also belong to a suppressed world of poverty, injustice and unhappiness'. His goal is 'to reactivate the work of memory in order to discover the historical nature of our subjectivity'. Sokol has exhibited widely in Russia and abroad, and has participated in biennales in Moscow and Thessaloniki. In 2008 he was the recipient of the New Generation Prize at 'Innovation', the All-Russian Contemporary Art Competition organised by the National Centre for Contemporary Arts, Moscow.

Sokol prioritises aesthetics and poetics to create existential commentaries on the individual's position in contemporary society. Time and communication between past and present are recurrent themes. *Poste Restante* (2010) consists of twelve life-size concrete sculptures of urban mailboxes from different countries. Grouped together, they can be thought of as resembling anonymous city towers or tombstones. As symbols and facilitators of communication, here the mailboxes represent its death. In the artist's words, 'I create obsessive work of remembering (which usually fails), pseudo-archaeology and false memories ... The connection to our past [that] we feel creates the resonance between the individual past and the historical, collective one.'

top
Tumbleweed (Rhizome), 2009
Sculpture, painted steel, paint-marker, texts
250 cm (diam.)
Photo: Roman Suslov
© Roman Suslov
Courtesy of Moscow Biennale Art Foundation, Moscow, Russia

above left
Arches, 2010
Installation, metal
154 x 135 x 47.5 cm
Photo: Nadezhda Serebrykova
© Nadezhda Serebrykova
Courtesy of Triumph Gallery, Moscow, Russia

above
Poste Restante (study for outdoor installation), 2010
Sculpture, foam plastic, machine cutting, concrete
Dimensions variable
Photo: Nadezhda Serebrykova
© Nadezhda Serebrykova
Courtesy of Triumph Gallery, Moscow, Russia

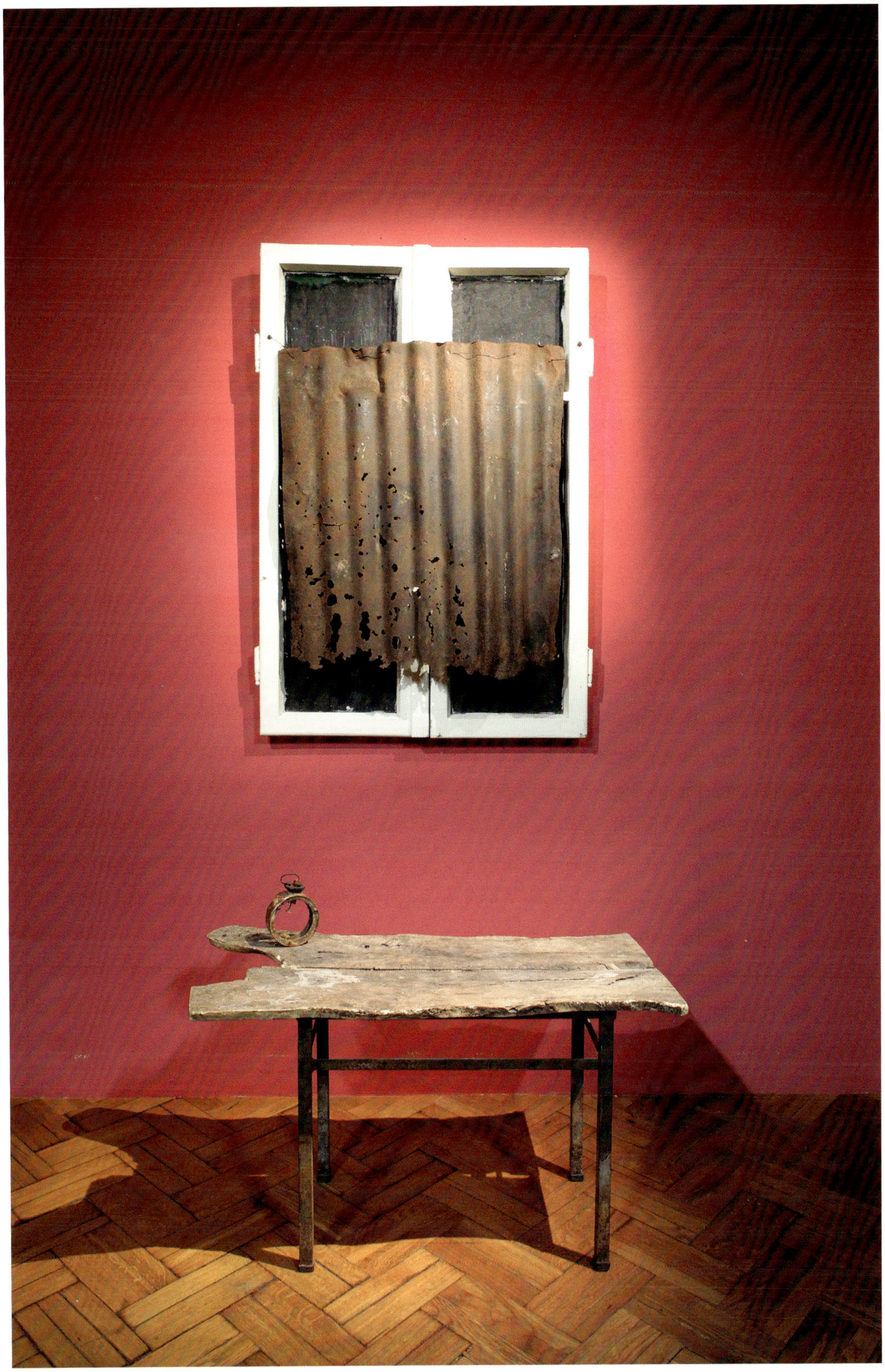

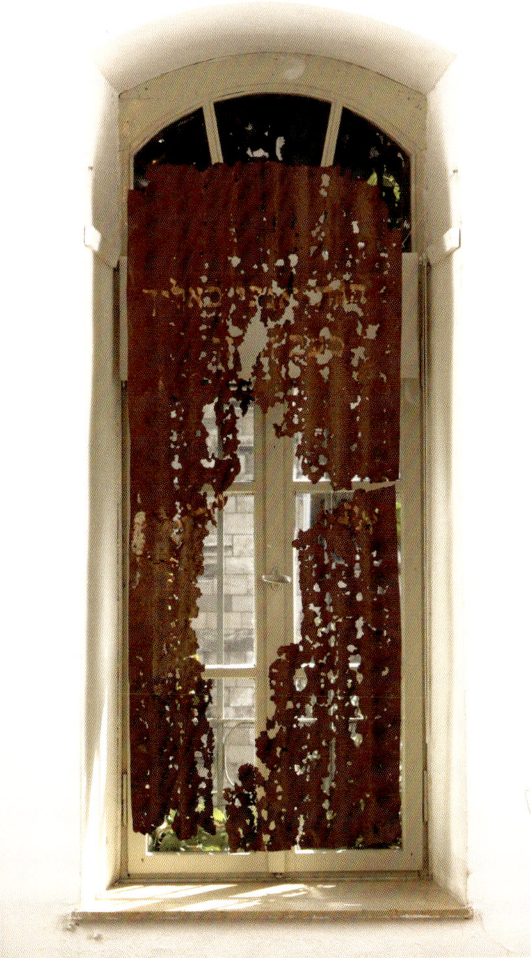

left
Parochet (Jewish ritual ornamental curtain covering the front of the holy ark in the synagogue), 2006
Time, iron, paint
70 x 170 cm
Photo: Masha Duchovny
© Masha Duchovny
Collection of Chava and Daniel Boyarin, Berkeley

above
Invisible, 2007–10
Installation, time, metal, wood, windows
Photo: Nadezhda Serebryakova
© Nadezhda Serebrykova
Courtesy of Triumph Gallery, Moscow

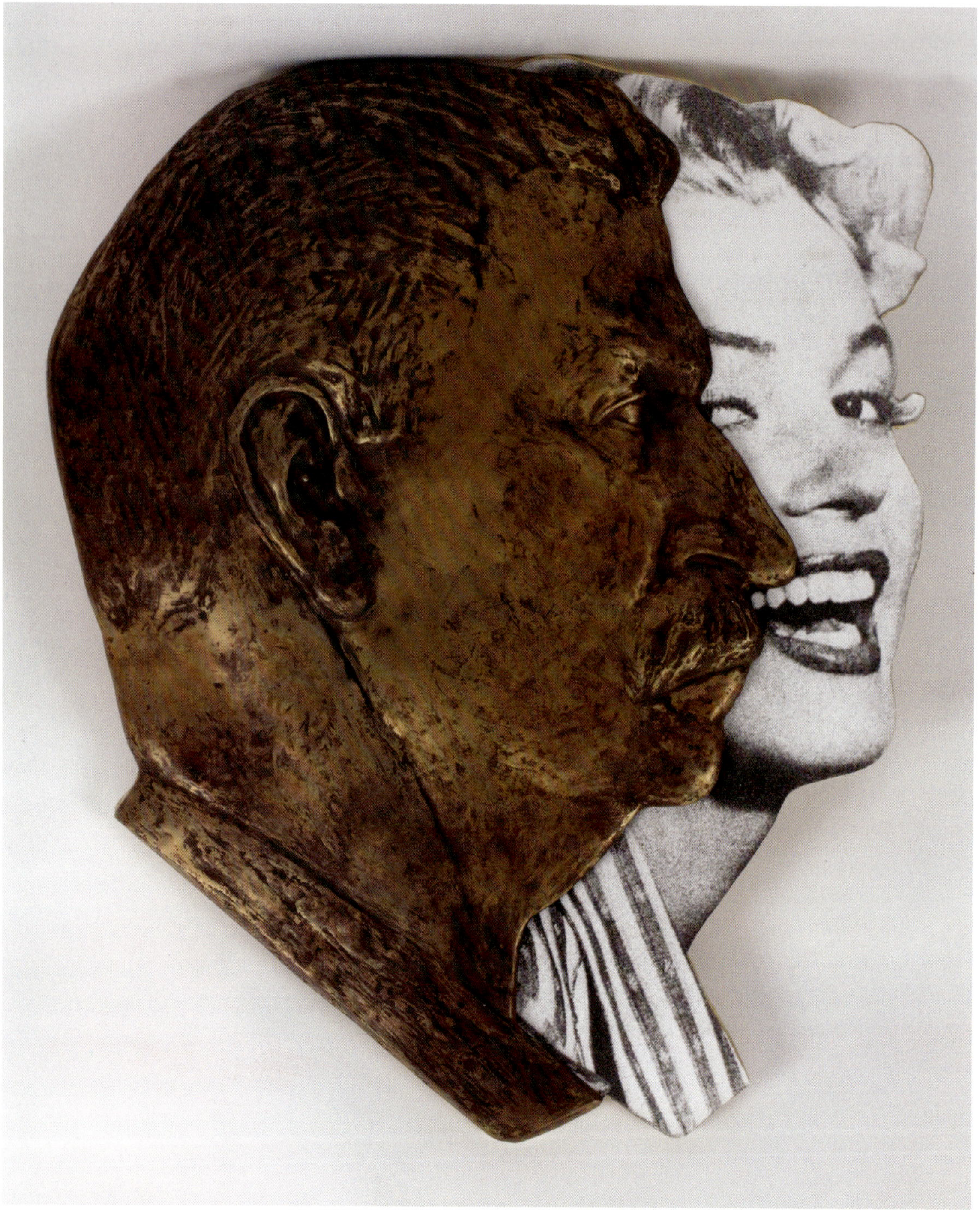

Sculptor Leonid Sokov, born in the village of Mikhalevo in 1941, lives and works in New York. When he was thirteen, he received a grant to enter the elite Moscow Secondary Art School (MSKhSh), where he received classical training in painting, sculpture and drawing. After three years of compulsory service in the Soviet Army, he attended the Stroganov Higher College of Art (1964–9), graduating as a sculptor. After graduation he undertook official commissions, mainly for children's playgrounds. Throughout the 1970s Sokov mixed in Moscow underground circles, in 1976 organising an independent exhibition of his own unofficial work, influenced in part by his association with Sots artists Komar and Melamid. This show brought him to the attention of the American collector Norton Dodge, who bought up the entire exhibition. In 1979 Sokov emigrated to New York. His work can be found in many Russian and Western collections, including the Metropolitan Museum of Art, New York; the Centre Pompidou, Paris; the State Tretyakov Gallery, Moscow; and the National Gallery of Australia, Sydney.

Sokov has said that he is 'interested in the problems of contemporary myth'. His art explores Russian, Soviet and American mythologies; he finds new modes of expression by combining contemporary cultural icons. A fascination with Soviet–American political competition during the Cold War finds expression in many of his works, in particular his startling juxtapositions of Marilyn Monroe and Josef Stalin. As cultural polarities and potent icons, Monroe symbolises the extremes of the capitalist culture industry while Stalin embodies the extremes of Soviet political power. Many of Sokov's works depict bears, such as his life-size painted wooden sculpture *Soviet-Russian Bear*, which holds a hammer and sickle (1984). He has explored the bear as an ancient awe-inspiring archetype, seeing in Russian bear festivals a parallel with Soviet society's veneration of Stalin and the trappings of State power.

Despite his traditional training and his close study of Henry Moore's sculpture while he was still in the Soviet Union, Sokov views himself outside of the tradition of European modernism, more as a shaman or cultural blacksmith hoping to heal people by means of his creative powers. He explores the mythology of official Soviet and European modernist sculpture, producing powerful works which unite these two apparently incongruous disciplines. His most important work on this theme, *The Meeting of Two Sculptures*, was first conceived in 1984 and has been reworked over several decades. Open to different interpretations, it combines a familiar image of Lenin, cast from a 1940s monument, with Giacometti's iconic sculpture of a walking man, symbol of existential angst. Thus existentialism is confronted by political ideology. Other pieces in the same series show Lenin's sculpture juxtaposed with iconic works by the modernist sculptors Brancusi and Calder. In Sokov's installation *The Shadows of Twentieth-century Sculpture* (2001), shown at the Venice Biennale, he takes this theme a step further with a large display of miniature replicas of modernist sculptures which rotate and cast shadows on the wall, casting doubt over society's veneration of some of Western Europe's most familiar twentieth-century icons.

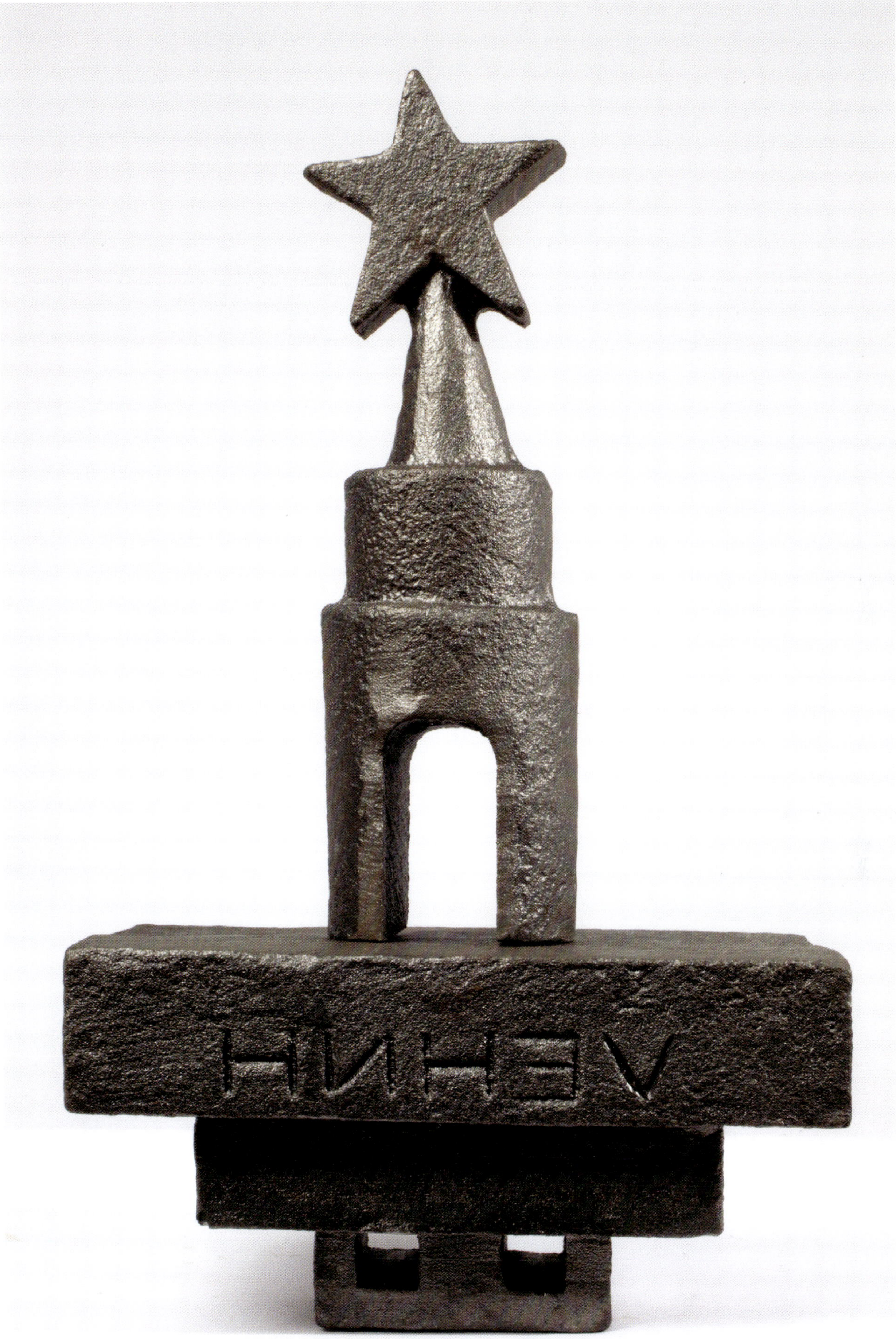

facing page
Two Profiles, 1989
Bronze, poster
86.4 x 72.4 x 7.6 cm
© Leonid Sokov
Courtesy of the artist

right
Inverted Mausoleum and Kremlin, 1990
Cast iron
39.4 x 22.9 x 14 cm
© Leonid Sokov
Courtesy of the artist

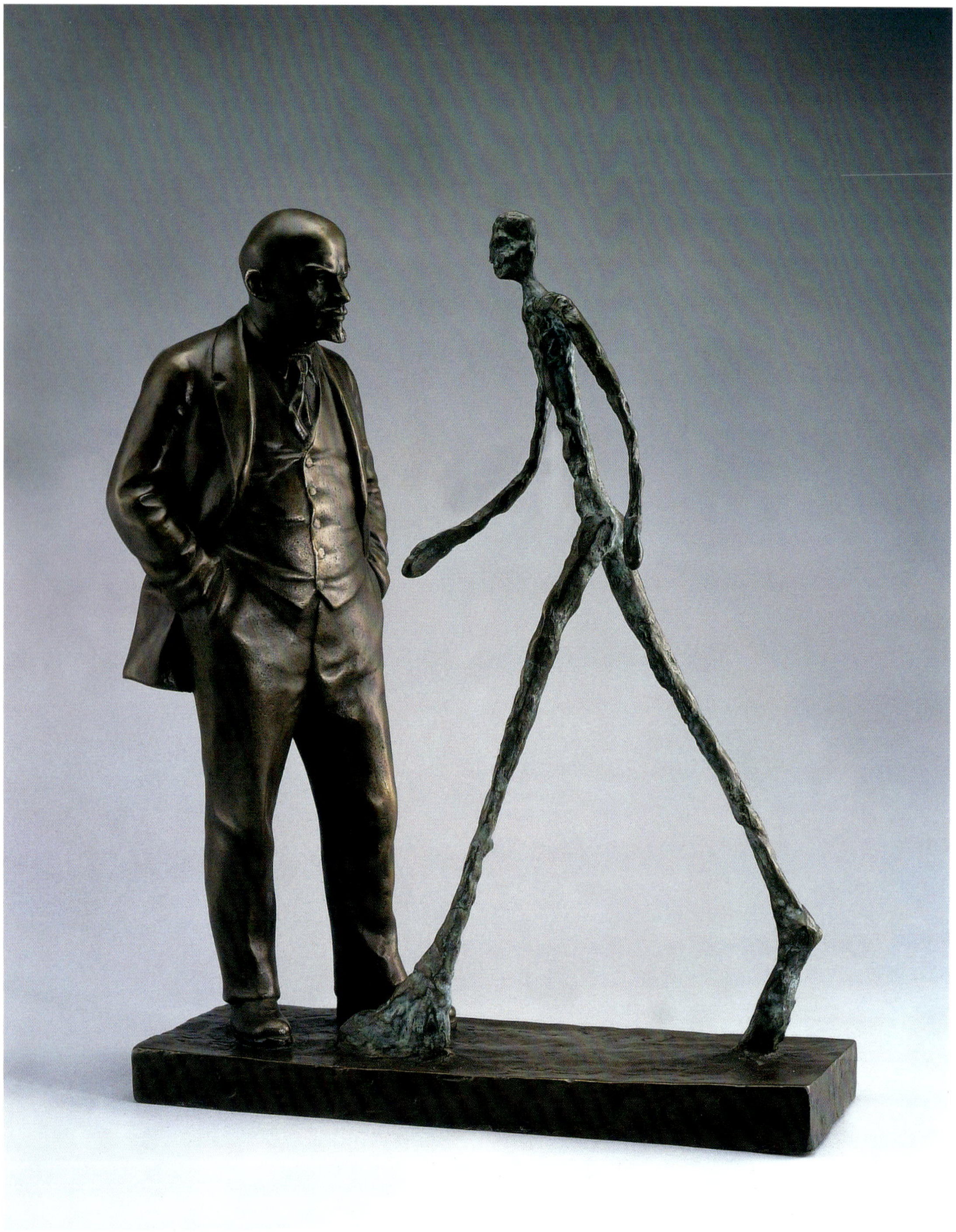

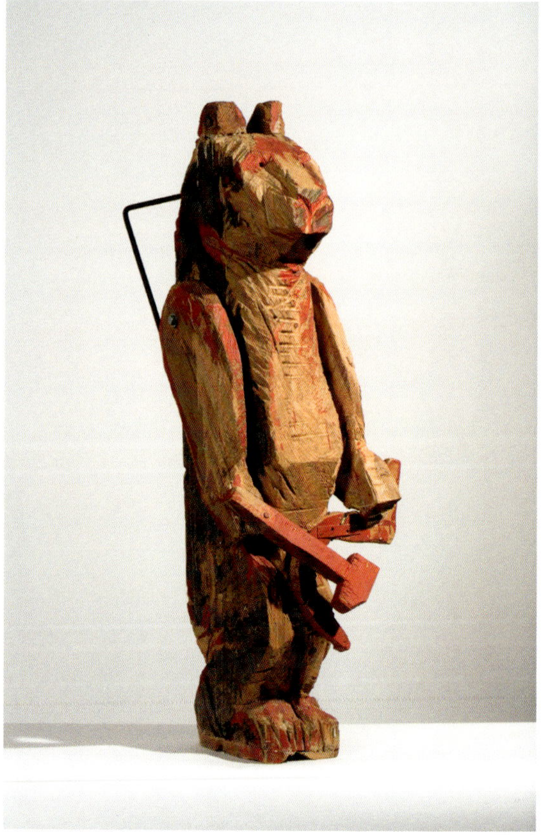

above
The Meeting of Two Sculptures: Lenin and Giacometti, 1989
Bronze, patina
48.3 x 38 x 23 cm
© Leonid Sokov
Collection of the artist
Courtesy of the artist

right
Soviet-Russian Bear, 1984
Oil, wood
172.7 x 40.6 x 48.3 cm
© Leonid Sokov
Courtesy of the artist

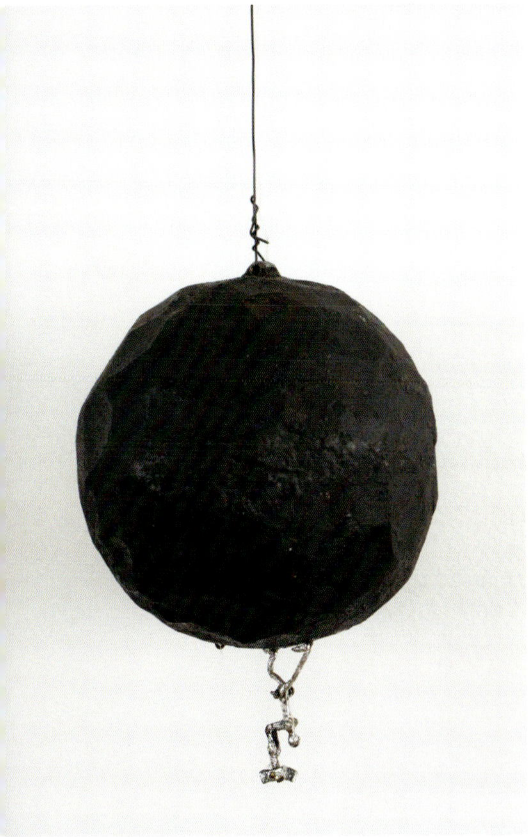

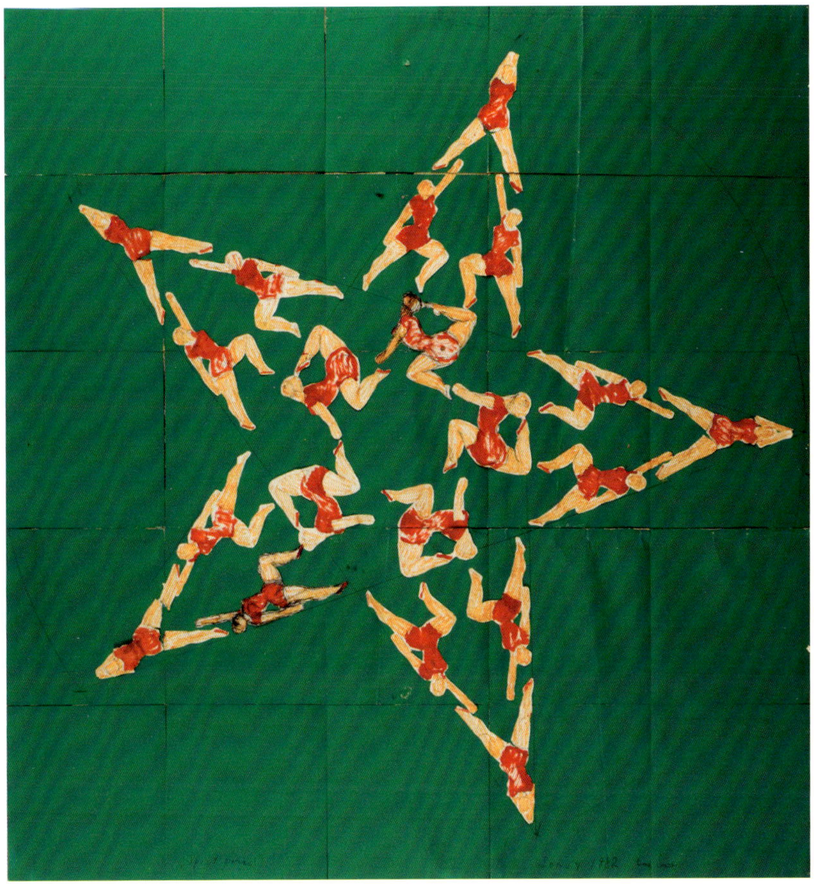

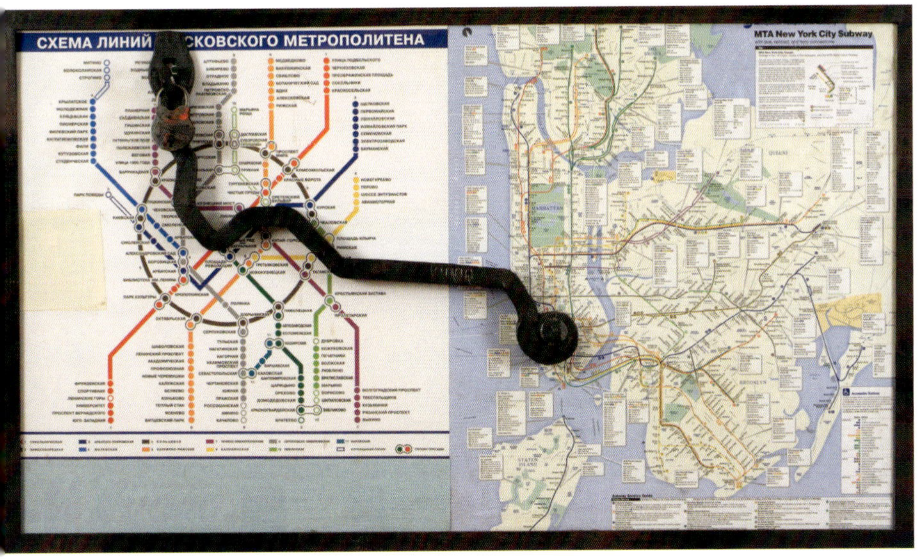

top
Three Hanging Bells, 1999 (1 of 3)
Cast iron, wire, rope
12.7 x 10.2 x 10.2 cm
© Leonid Sokov
Courtesy of the artist

above
Parade, 1982
Mixed media on canvas
132 x 127 cm
© Leonid Sokov
Courtesy of the artist

left
My Subway Map, 2000
Cast iron, subway maps
67 x 117 cm
© Leonid Sokov
Courtesy of the artist

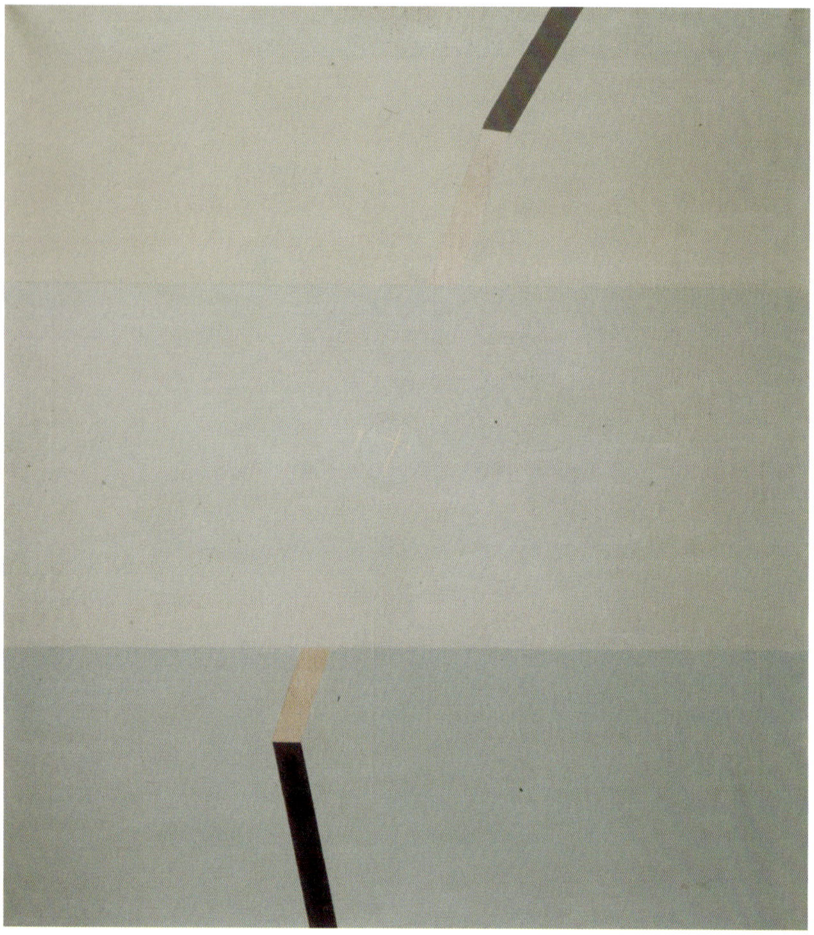

Eduard Steinberg

Born in Moscow in 1937, Eduard Steinberg was a member of the '60s generation that came of age in the exuberant and optimistic era of Khrushchev's Thaw. His work is deeply rooted in Russia's rich cultural traditions, from icon painting to early twentieth-century Symbolism to the radical abstraction of the avant-garde. By engaging with the long history of Russian culture, Steinberg's abstract geometries sought to reinvigorate painting with the spiritual values that had been long suppressed in the Soviet Union.

Steinberg's father was a poet, translator and artist who had trained at Moscow's Higher Art and Technical Studios (Vkhutemas) in the 1920s. After serving in World War II, he was arrested and sent to the gulag. On his return, Arkady Akimovich Steinberg settled in Tarusa, a town in the Oka countryside long associated with the creative intelligentsia. It was there, under his father's guidance and in the company of the many artists and poets who visited or lived in Tarusa, that the younger Steinberg undertook a course of self-education to become an artist. In 1961, he moved back to Moscow to join the ranks of the underground, exhibiting his canvases in such important shows as *Exhibition of Twelve Artists*, organised by Alexander Glezer at the Druzhba Club, Shosse Entuziastov (1967); the Beekeeping Pavilion exhibition at VDNKh (1975); and the 1977 Venice Biennale; as well as in the Union of Graphic Artists exhibition hall on Malaya Gruzinskaya in Moscow (1978).

Steinberg's work is associated with the metaphysical trend of unofficial painting, which also includes Mikhail Shvartsman, Vladimir Weisberg, Dmitry Krasnopevtsev, Ülo Sooster, Vladimir Yankilevsky and Dmitry Plavinsky. Despite their stylistic differences, these artists all sought to escape the constraints of the present – the politicised atmosphere of official art or the pursuit of ever newer tendencies required by modernism – by developing personal visions with the potential to reveal profound truths hidden below the surface. Steinberg's early landscapes and still lifes reveal a world of organic objects imbued with symbolic beauty, or a mystical world of heaven and earth. In his white geometric period of the 1960s and '70s, he used a spare pictorial language that embraced subtle colour harmony, minimal geometric forms and luminous, otherworldly space to tap into art's spiritual potential. One of Steinberg's major touchstones was the Suprematist painter Kazimir Malevich, whose *Black Square* shocked audiences in 1915. In a letter to the long-departed painter, Steinberg wrote, 'It seems to me that the human mind will always return to such a language in moments of mystical suffering at the tragedy of God's abandonment.' In this sense, Steinberg saw his own work as an attempt at resurrection.

above left
Composition (January), 1976
Oil on canvas
100 x 90 cm

Ekaterina and Vladimir Semenikhin Collection

above
Composition (February), 1976
Oil on canvas
99.5 x 90.5 cm

Ekaterina and Vladimir Semenikhin Collection

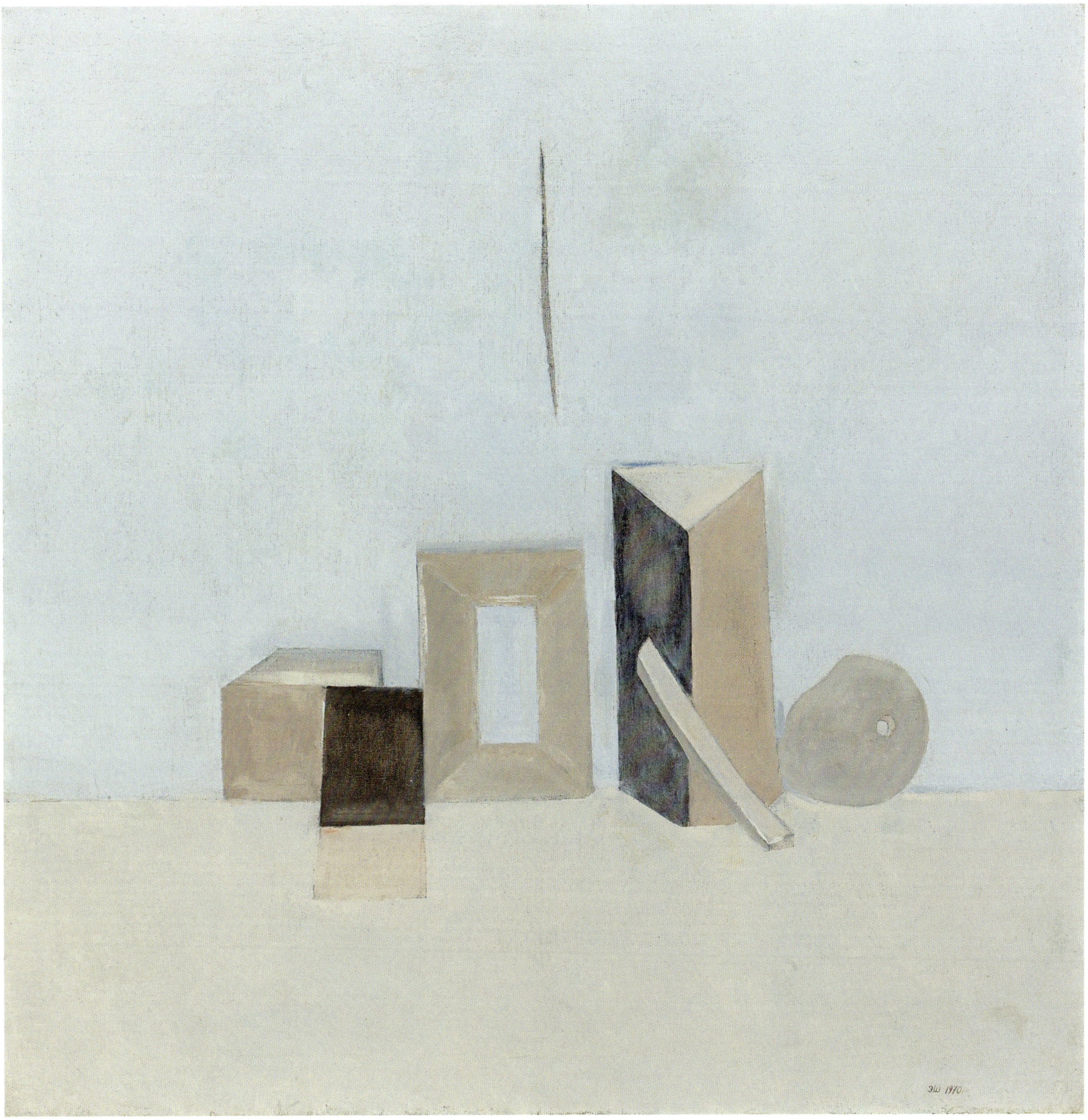

above
Composition, 1970
Oil on canvas
90.2 x 90.2 cm

Courtesy of Tsukanov Art Collection

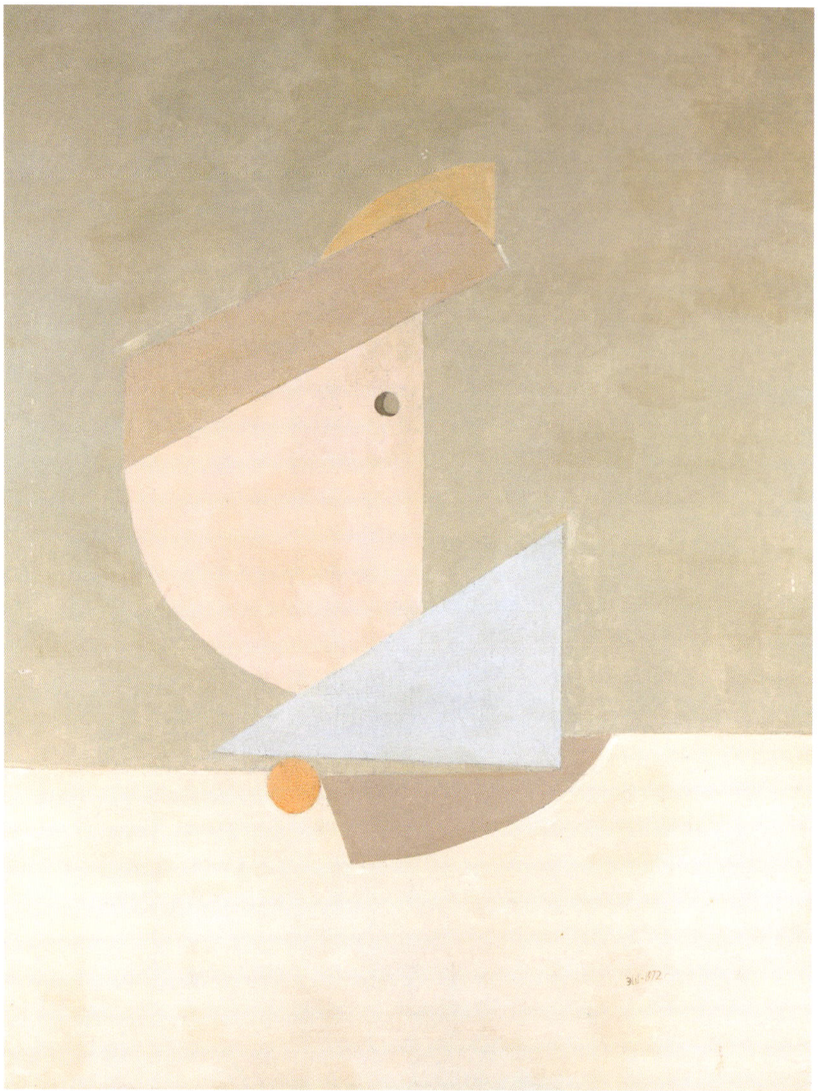

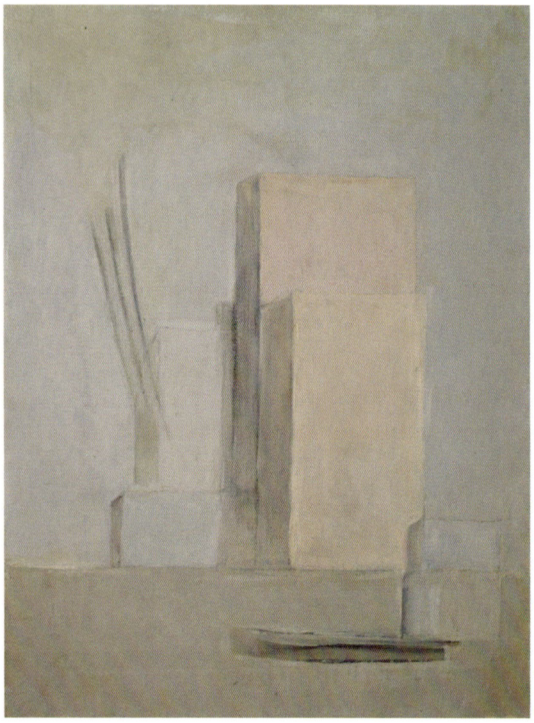

above
Cityscape (October), 1968
Oil on canvas
88 x 67 cm
© Eduard Steinberg
Ekaterina and Vladimir Semenikhin Collection

top
Composition – Blue Triangle, 1972
Oil on canvas
90 x 70 cm
© Eduard Steinberg
Courtesy of Tsukanov Art Collection

right
Composition with Fish, 1967
Oil on canvas
100.1 x 100.1 cm
© Eduard Steinberg
Courtesy of Sotheby's

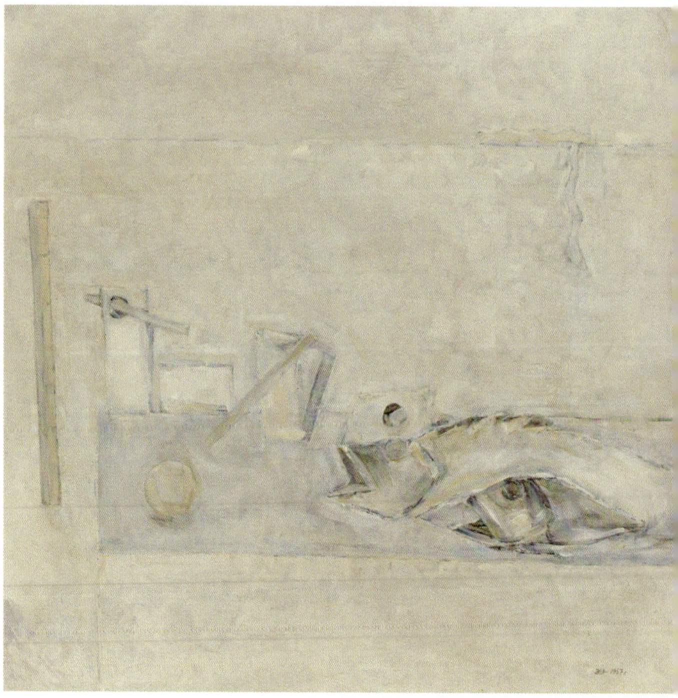

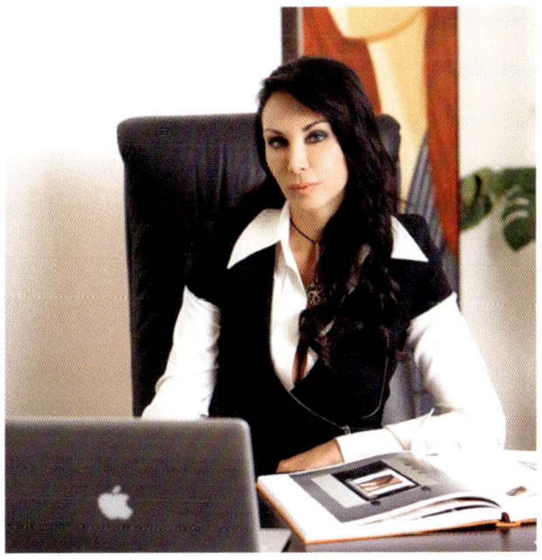

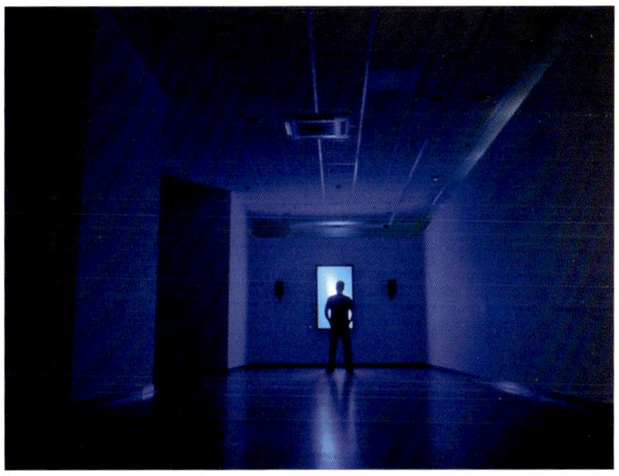

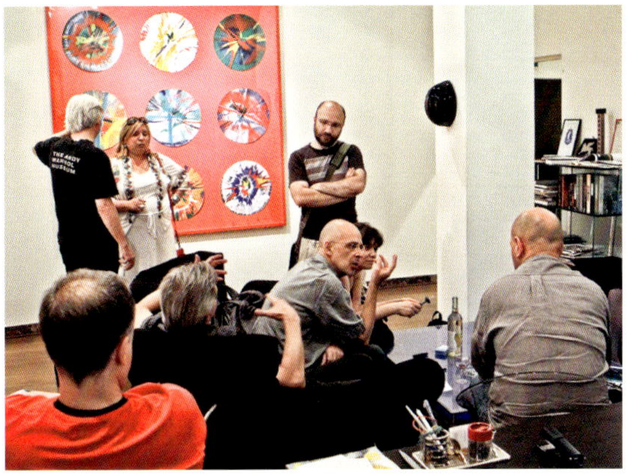

The Stella Art Foundation was established in Moscow in 2003 by the collector and philanthropist Stella Kesaeva. Born in 1965, Kesaeva is married to the entrepreneur Igor Kesaev, founder of the Mercury Group. The Mercury Group, involved in mining, oil, real estate and retail trade, is one of the foundation's main supporters. Distressed by the fact that in Russia contemporary culture was not being promoted in the same way as it was in Western Europe, Kesaeva was inspired to try and change things. She started by opening a commercial gallery in Moscow, shortly thereafter setting up her not-for-profit foundation as a springboard for building and promoting contemporary art and culture in Russia. Her stated aim was to 'bridge a cultural gap between the East and West inherited during the totalitarian rule in the Soviet Union and its former satellites'.

Based in the centre of Moscow on Skaryatinsky Lane, ten minutes' walk from the Kremlin, the Stella Art Foundation's goals are both promotional and educational. It organises exhibitions of contemporary art both at home and abroad, and promotes cultural exchange between Russian and international artists. Kesaeva is assembling a major collection of contemporary art with a strong focus on Moscow Conceptualism and Sots Art, as well as diverse international names including the likes of Andy Warhol, Joseph Kosuth, Marc Quinn and Yves Klein. Her holdings number around 600 works. In 2009 Kesaeva produced a catalogue of Russian highlights entitled *The Obscure Object of Art: Contemporary Russian Art 1975–2007*. A selection of items featured in the catalogue was shown at the Arsenale in Venice during the 53rd Biennale and at the Kunsthistorisches Museum, Vienna, in 2009. Kesaeva advocates the integration of Russian and international practitioners, observing that although artists who emigrated such as Komar and Melamid, the Kabakovs and Eric Bulatov are known abroad, established artists of the post-perestroika generation continue to languish in relative obscurity outside of Russia.

One of the foundation's main goals is to foster new and emerging talent. In 2006 it established a new award category, the 'New Generation', as part of the National Centre for Contemporary Art's Innovation Prize. Kesaeva considers the exhibitions she stages of work by young artists to be one of the pillars of the organisation's activities. She is also particularly interested in the multidisciplinary character of contemporary culture, which she sees in Russia as having originated with the avant-garde. In 2008 she organised the Moscow Poets' Club for meetings, debates, readings and performances, and to explore the boundaries between art and poetry. And in 2010 she appointed poet Lev Rubinstein to run a project called 'Evenings at Skaryatinsky'.

Stella Kesaeva was nominated by the Russian Ministry of Culture as commissioner of the Russian pavilion at the Venice Biennale in 2011 (and for 2013 and 2015). In 2011 she selected Andrei Monastyrsky and the group Collective Actions to be featured. This presentation, curated by Boris Groys, was intended to introduce an international audience to a staple of Russian Conceptual art from the 1970s.

Looking to the future, Kesaeva hopes to establish a major contemporary art museum in Moscow within the next decade. 'It is embarrassing,' she has said, 'that such a rich and large country as Russia does not yet have a museum the likes of the Pompidou Centre or MoMA.' Plans are underway to regenerate a space in Moscow designed by the Constructivist architect Konstantin Melnikov and convert it into a world-class museum. Kesaeva has secured the support of the Ministry of Culture, and the project will be funded by a State-private partnership.

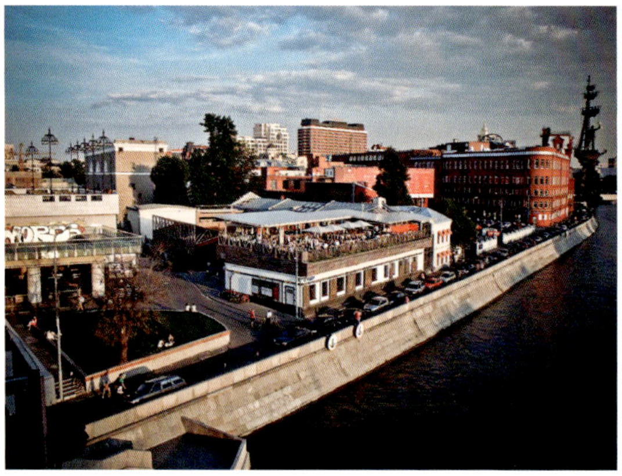

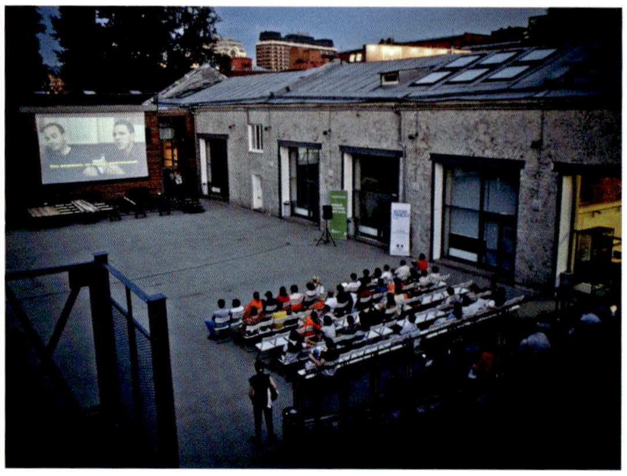

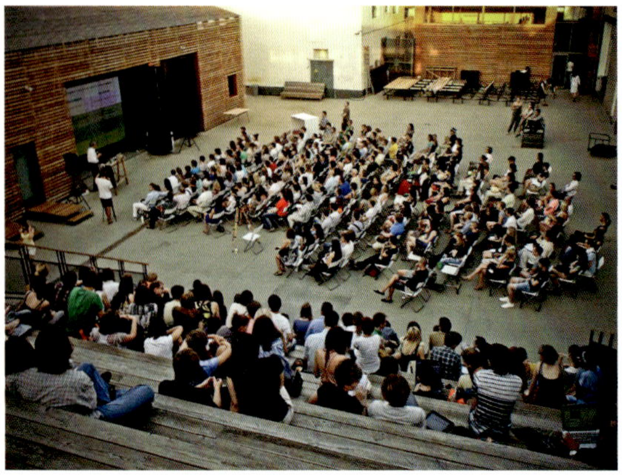

The pioneering Strelka Institute for Media, Architecture and Design is an independent, not-for-profit post-graduate institute dedicated to developing innovative perspectives on critical issues in Russia today. The institute provides tuition-free education in English to between twenty and forty-five students from Russia and abroad. It was in 2009 that a group of successful media professionals decided to create a new educational platform in Russia; they included Ilya Oskolkov-Tsentsiper, Sergey Adonyev, Alexander Mamut, Dmitry Likin and Oleg Shapiro. The institute opened the following year with Oskolkov-Tsentsiper as president and Dutch architect Rem Kolhaas as dean. Among the international student body are architects, graphic designers, economists and journalists.

Located in the grounds of the former Red October Chocolate Factory on Moscow's arrow-shaped Bolotny Island (*strelka* means 'arrow' in Russian), the institute overlooks the Kremlin and the Pushkin Museum of Fine Arts. Red October has become one of Moscow's premier destinations for contemporary culture, its galleries and photography studios, design bureaus and architectural workshops, bars and clubs attracting the city's trendy crowds. The institute itself comprises four studios, a lecture hall, a media library, a large courtyard-amphitheatre and Bar Strelka with its rooftop terrace.

The international architectural bureau OMA/AMO, of which Koolhaas is a partner, has helped to develop the institute's educational programme. The curriculum's foundation is a series of research projects organised into three parts over the course of a year. All new students start by participating in a two-month conference, structured as a programme of lectures, workshops and salons, thus exposing them to international educational and professional thinking. Then the students are introduced to the different areas of study. Following a winter recess, they are divided up according to their research themes; for the 2010/11 academic year these were Preservation, Energy, Public Space, Design and Thinning (the disappearance of small cities and emptying of rural areas). Over the course of six months, researchers explore these themes through academic and field investigations, interviews, consultations and analysis under the guidance of theme Initiators, project Supervisors and local Mentors. At the end of the term the institute releases the results of the research themes over the course of its summer programme. In addition to the presentation of research results, summer programmes include cultural and educational events dedicated to the future of the media, architecture and design, as well as lectures, workshops, film screenings, concerts and theatre performances. Most workshops are targeted at solving real problems in real spaces, for example the renovation of Gorky Park. The institute collaborates with universities in Europe, Asia and the US, including the Royal College of Art, the Hong Kong Design Institute and Massachusetts Institute of Technology.

In May 2011, the Strelka Institute became the first Russian organisation to receive the Vitality leaf Eco-office environmental certificate, developed by the Saint-Petersburg Ecological Union. The institute aims to function in as environmentally friendly a manner as possible, applying the latest technologies in order to save on energy, water and paper and for waste disposal, and using only recycled and non-toxic materials. Meanwhile all of the profits from the popular Bar Strelka go to support the institute. The bar hosts installations of artwork as well as Strelka Sound, a festival that brings international performers together with young Russian musicians.

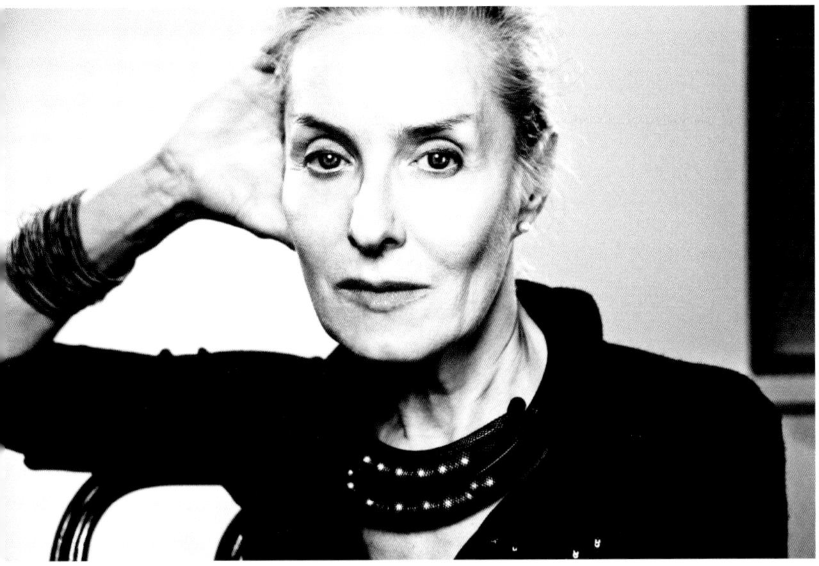

Olga Sviblova, founder and director of the Moscow House of Photography (now the Multimedia Art Museum), was born in 1953, and lives and works in Moscow and Paris. Having graduated from the Psychology Faculty of Moscow State University in 1978, she completed a PhD in Psychology in 1987. Already in the early 1980s she was known as a curator and critic of Russian underground art. 'I showed,' she says humorously, 'the people with strange eyes and long hair.'

Between 1984 and 1995, Sviblova curated exhibitions both at home and abroad, as well as directing several important documentary films including *The Black Square*, whose subject was Russian avant-garde art from 1953 to 1988. *The Black Square* won Sviblova a critics' award at Cannes, as well as a number of other prestigious prizes. She has organised several festivals focusing on photography and the other visual arts, among them the First Festival of Russian Underground Art (Finland) and the First International Month of Photography (Moscow).

Sviblova has presided over the Moscow House of Photography – the first Russian museum to implement a multivalent programme intended to develop photographic art – since its founding in 1996 under the auspices of the Moscow municipal government; it was renamed in 2002. Since the beginning she has organised and directed both the Photobiennale and Fashion and Style in Photography, as well as assembling or overseeing more than 500 exhibitions of Russian photography. Subjects have included contemporary art from Moscow, Soviet photography of the 1920s, the work of Dmitri Baltermants, Russian pictorial photography and the avant-garde photographer Alexander Rodchenko. In 2007 and 2009 Sviblova was curator of the Russian Pavilion at the Venice Biennale. Among her numerous honours are the Medal of the City of Moscow (1997) and the *Légion d'Honneur* (2008).

Although best known as the saviour of Russian photography, Sviblova continues to promote her country's art in all its guises. It may come as a surprise that this esteemed member of the Russian Academy of Arts worked as a street sweeper for six years while in her twenties. 'It wasn't out of heroism,' she has said, 'but so I could do what I wanted in the mornings and the evenings. I consider it the happiest time of my life. It was like a childhood that lasted until I was thirty. I was so fit I didn't need to go to the gym. And I didn't have any social obligations.' Sviblova was among the first Russian arts professionals to embrace the creative aspects of curatorship, citing the 1988 Sotheby's auction, which she attended, as a moment of radical change in Russia's artistic landscape. It was, she says, the 'first time I saw the really positive influence of the market'. Expanding on this theme, she explains her 'strange relationship' with commercialism: 'We had a big battle, not just Russia but all of the socialist countries ... without a market we received very bad results. Art is part of human activity. Without a market it couldn't exist.' Growing up during the Soviet period, 'money was nothing. To think about money was awful. So we were thinking about God, we were thinking about metaphysical ideas ... we were living in a completely constructed paradise. That was like [being given] an injection; you couldn't change your mind.' Nevertheless, Sviblova was able to envision other possibilities: 'I was sure that we might be better ... my perception was all the time to be independent and like what I like.' Her interest in art 'at first ... was completely [based on] love and curiosity, because I grew up in the galleries of the Pushkin Museum. It was ... a magical school where our teachers taught us to see the work ... so we knew history ... we visited museums to understand what human nature means'.

'I don't like power,' this extremely powerful woman asserts. 'I think it spoils our character, and to have even the smallest power is very dangerous. So every day you need to look in the mirror.' Sviblova also insists that she never wanted to be a public figure. What she does is follow her instinct: 'If I like something, I want to talk to other people. I want to share ... If I read something interesting, immediately all the city knows. If I find a good wine from an Italian man, half of Moscow knows, and everybody buys this wine.' Contemporary art in Russia, she firmly believes, 'is completely the same' in its dependence on word of mouth: 'There is a very small public that understands contemporary art. It is enough, it is normal.'

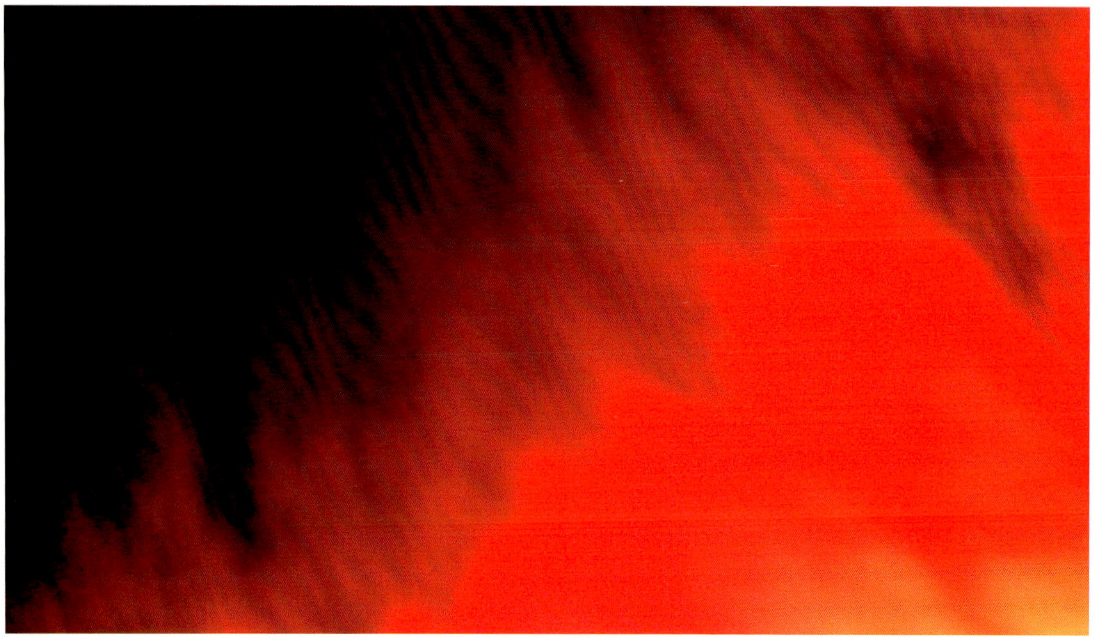

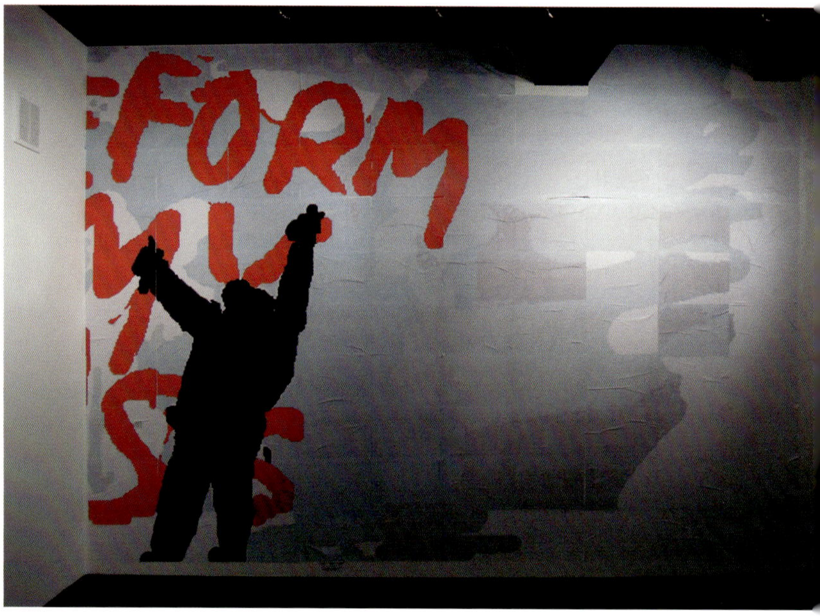

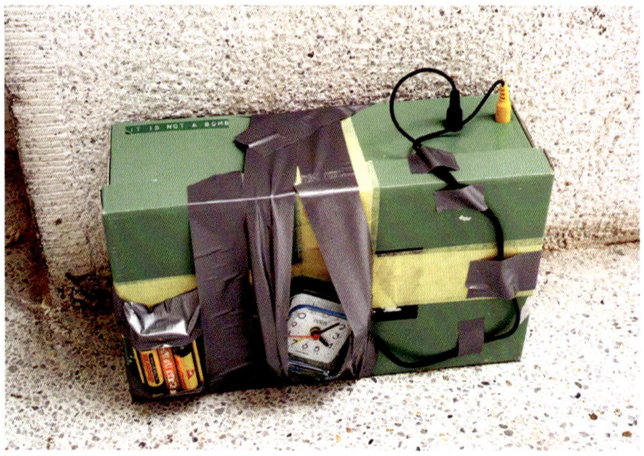

Avdei Ter-Oganyan was born in Rostov-on-Don in 1961 and studied art, first formally and then, after being expelled for 'avant-gardist propaganda', independently, reading and copying such modernist masters as Klee, Picasso and Matisse. Though known today as an *artiste provocateur*, Ter-Oganyan's first interests were painting and pictorial space. His experiments with modernist styles allowed him to master the variety of twentieth-century art and develop the precision and astuteness of his later projects outside of painting.

At the start of perestroika, Ter-Oganyan and a cohort of young avant-garde artists from the Grekov School of Art in Rostov founded the group Art or Death, which staged a number of provocative exhibitions between 1987 and 1990. One such show, *Provincial Avant-Garde*, was held in a public toilet and contained a work entitled *Brick in a Urinal*, a response to a critic who had mockingly described a Duchampian earlier work by Ter-Oganyan as a ready-made lacking a urinal.

In 1989, Ter-Oganyan moved to Moscow with fellow Art or Death member Valery Koshlyakov. Two years later, along with Konstantin Reunov, he founded a gallery on Tryokhprudny Pereulok that became an important site for innovative exhibitions and post-Conceptual curatorial projects. Ter-Oganyan's best-known action, however, took place in 1998 at Moscow's Manege, where he used an axe to chop up photographs of Russian Orthodox icons in a biting parody of iconoclasm. The action, entitled *Desecration of Holy Objects*, touched a nerve and provoked a criminal case against him for inciting national and religious hatred. In 1998 Ter-Oganyan emigrated to the Czech Republic, where he was granted political asylum.

Ter-Oganyan's son David is a Moscow-based Conceptual artist whose works employ semi-abstract modernist language to subtly reflect on such diverse issues as terrorism, colonialism and the possibility of creating politically engaged art within the context of a capitalist art market.

top
Color of My Blood, 2010
Photoprint
75 x 95 cm
© David Ter-Oganyan
Courtesy of the artist

above
Frafitist, 2011
Print on paper (mosaic)
320 x 600 cm
© David Ter-Oganyan
Smirnov & Sorokin Collection

left
Not a Bomb, 1997–2011
Mixed media
Photo. Ivars Gravlejs
© David Ter-Oganyan
Courtesy of the artist

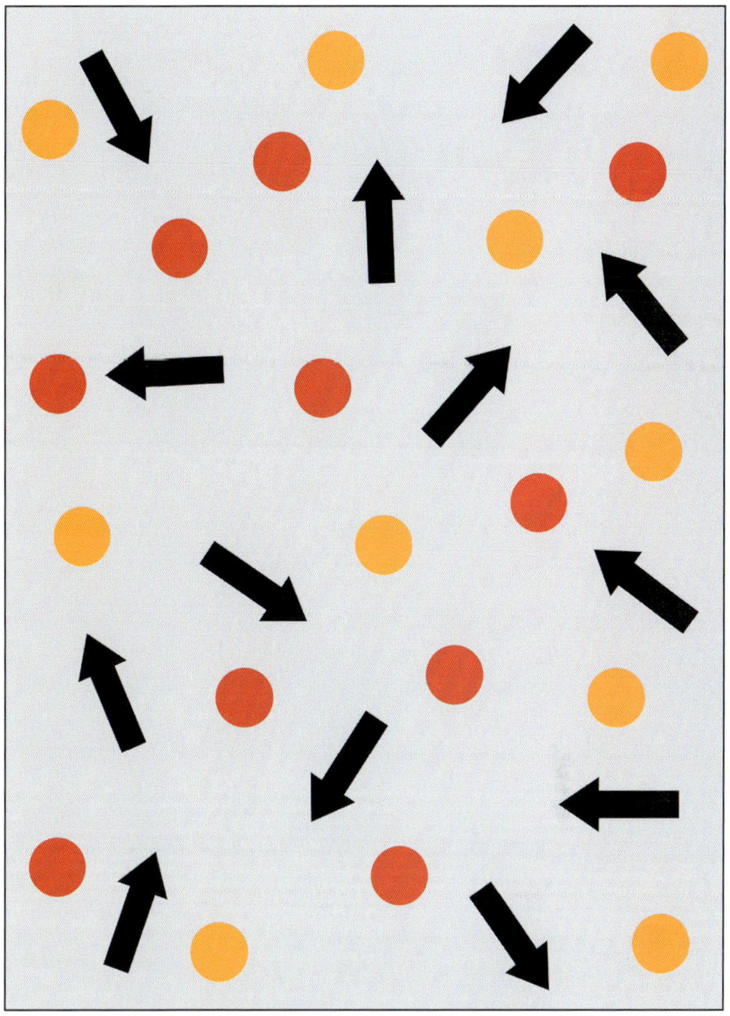

Это произведение создано для получения эстетического удовольствия.

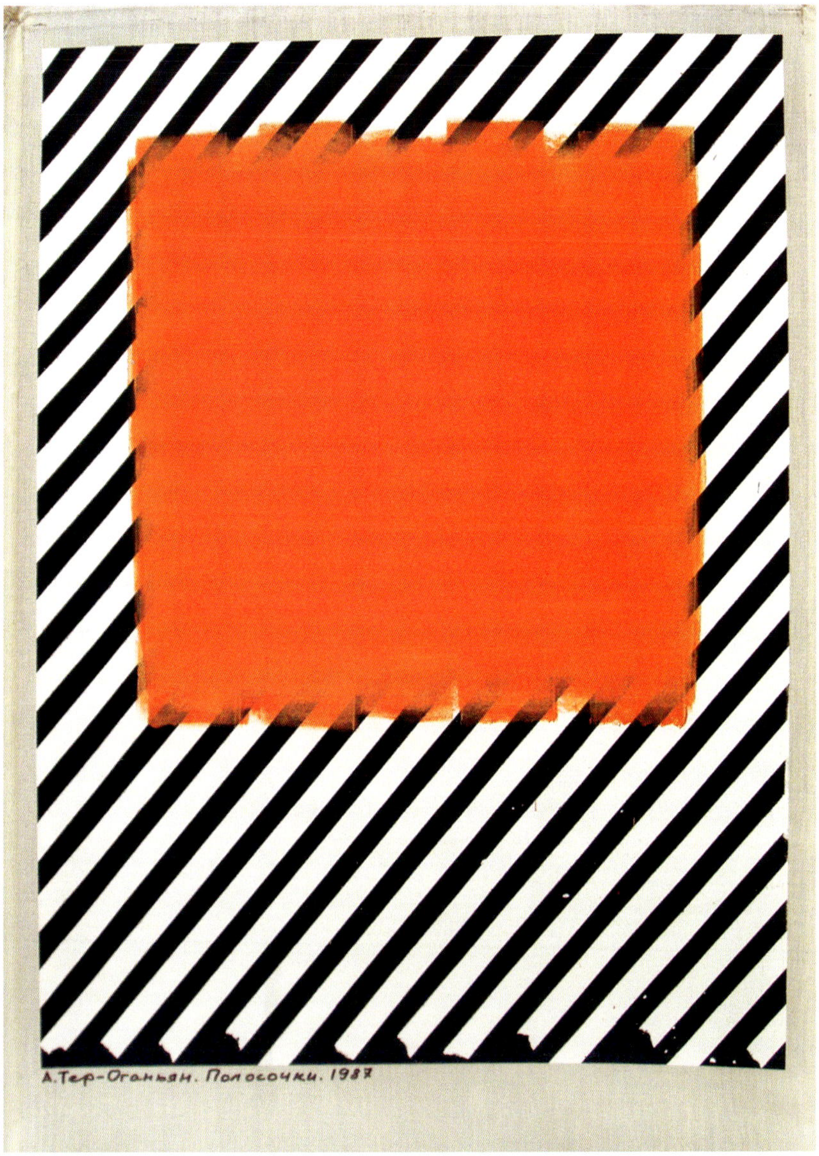

top right
This work is created to provide aesthetic enjoyment, from the series Radical Abstraction, 2004
© Avdei Ter-Oganyan

above
Strips, 2004
Canvas, oil
145 x 100 cm
© Avdei Ter-Oganyan
Courtesy of Guelman Gallery, Moscow

right
Explosion No.5, 2003
Oil on canvas
145 x 100 cm
© Avdei Ter-Oganyan
Courtesy of Guelman Gallery, Moscow

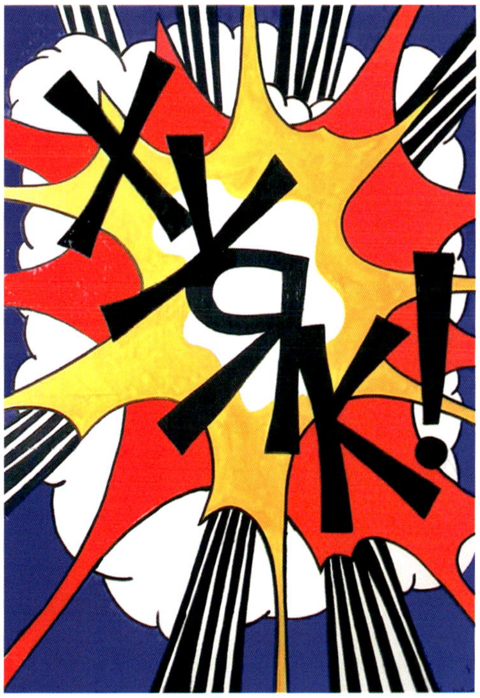

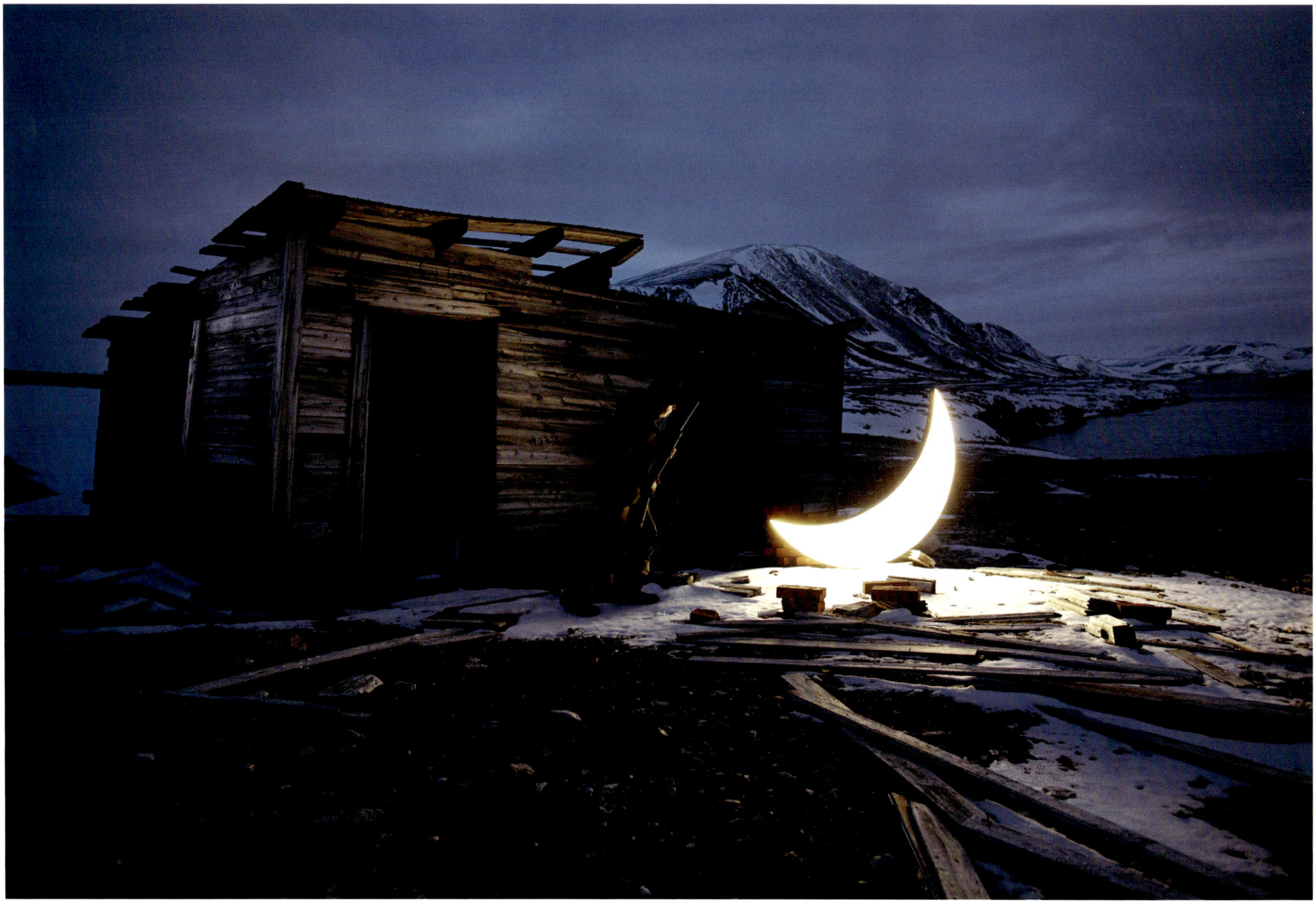

Leonid Tishkov was born in 1953 in a small town close to the Ural Mountains; his parents were both schoolteachers. He went to medical school in Moscow and graduated as a clinical therapist, but in his spare time wrote poetry, drew caricatures and illustrated medical encyclopaedias. During the Brezhnev era, Tishkov took part in an exhibition of caricatures in West Berlin, after which he was banned from publishing his graphic work. He began to work independently, combining drawings and text and creating albums and comic books. From the late 1970s on, he was a member of the Union of Graphic Artists and showed his caricatures in the liberal Malaya Gruzinskaya Street studios. At the end of the Brezhnev era, Tishkov began to work officially as an illustrator, winning a prestigious prize in 1988 for his illustrations to Yevgeny Zamyatin's novel *We*. Tishkov, who lives and works in Moscow, has exhibited widely throughout Europe and Russia, taking part in biennales in Moscow, Singapore and Ekaterinburg. There was a major retrospective of his work at the Moscow Museum of Modern Art in 2009.

Tishkov's practice embraces a wide range of traditional and new media, including installation, sculpture, video, photography, graphic art and book illustration. Using these diverse forms, he relies on narrative to explore childhood memories and Russian folklore, building a world of semi-real characters who can be seen as representatives of his own divided self. His use of text and image identify him as a peripheral figure of the Moscow underground of the 1980s. Tishkov's art draws on Surrealism and the absurd as he voyages through the subconscious, inventing dream symbols which accrue in a constantly evolving personal mythology. He views life as an existential journey, with the surrounding environment providing raw material. Among his most popular mythological figures are deep-sea divers – seamen, like aviators, were popular Soviet-era heroes – as explorers of the subconscious. He also has invented a character called the Dabloid, a heart-shaped organism with metamorphic properties about which he writes stories. One of his most popular series of photographic works, Private Moon (2003–), is an evolving collaboration with photographer Boris Bendikov. The series comprises documentary 'self-portraits' of the artist travelling the world with a large sculpture of the crescent moon as his imaginary soulmate. Having taken its inspiration from a painting by René Magritte, *The 16th September, Tree with Crescent Moon* (c. 1955), this work is both a personal homage to the Belgian Surrealist and a visual poem about loneliness.

above
Private Moon, The Arctic, 2010
Color photograph
Edition of 10
75 x 110 cm

Courtesy of Krokin Gallery

Leonid Tishkov

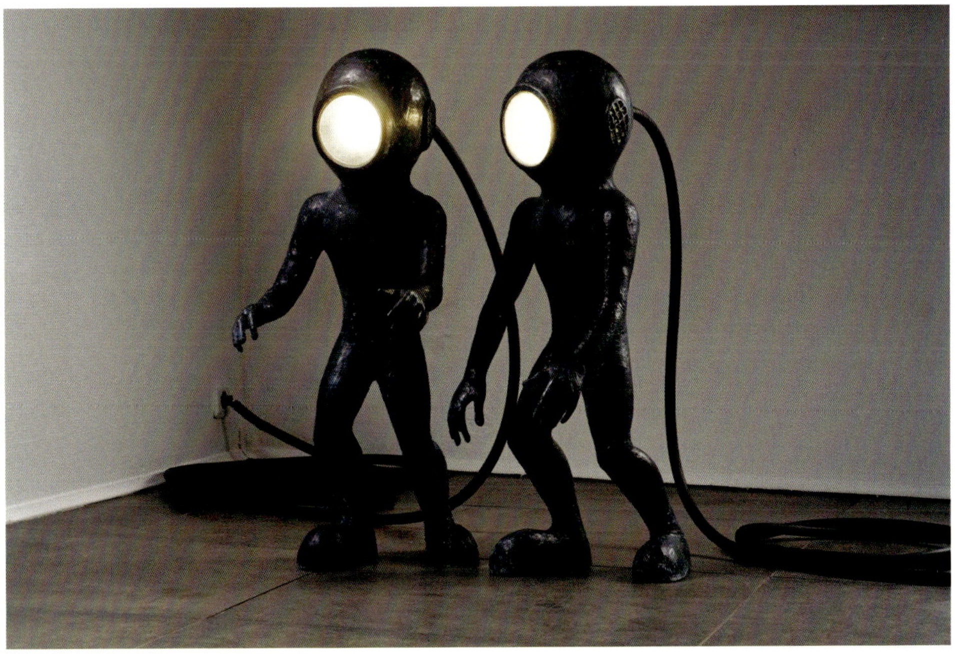

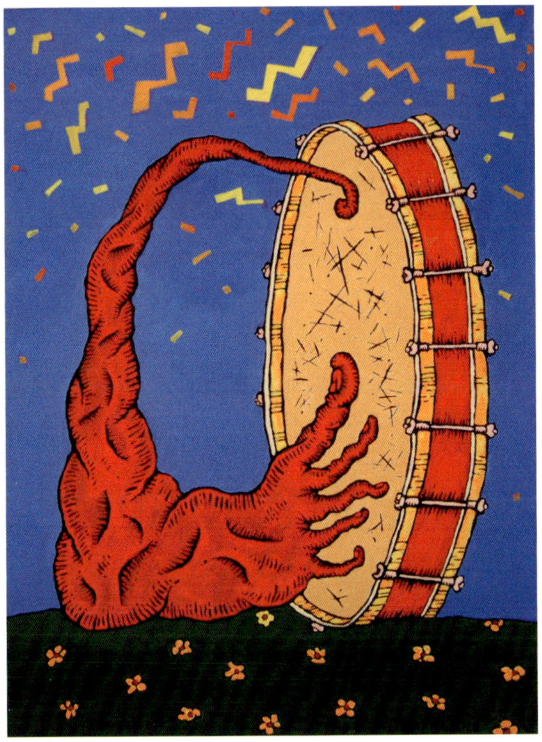

above
Dabloid Plays the Drum, 2007
Acrylic on canvas
60 x 45 cm
© Leonid Tishkov
Private collection

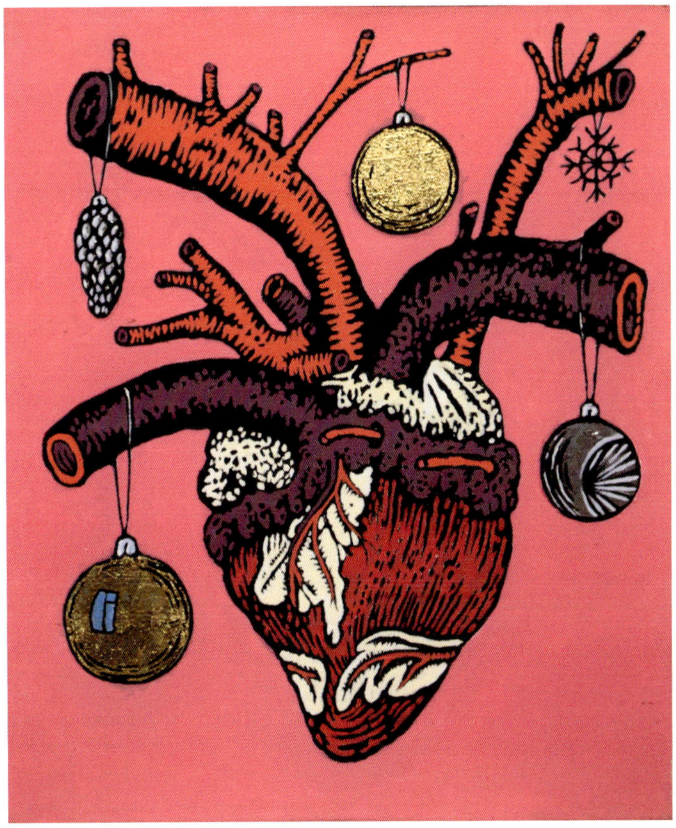

top
Deep-sea Divers, 2009
Bronze, rubber hose, electric lamps
Edition of 3
80 x 45 x 100 cm
© Leonid Tishkov
Private collection

left
Christmas Heart, 1997
Oil on canvas
80 x 60 cm
© Leonid Tishkov
Courtesy of Maxim Bokser

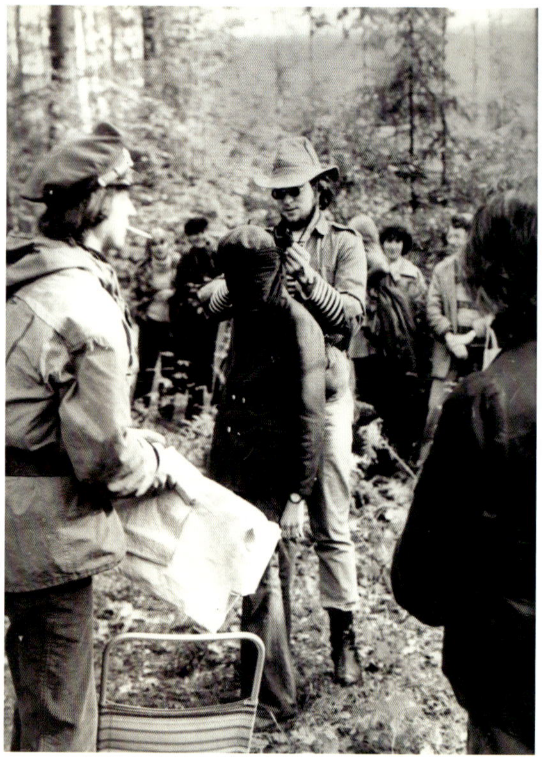

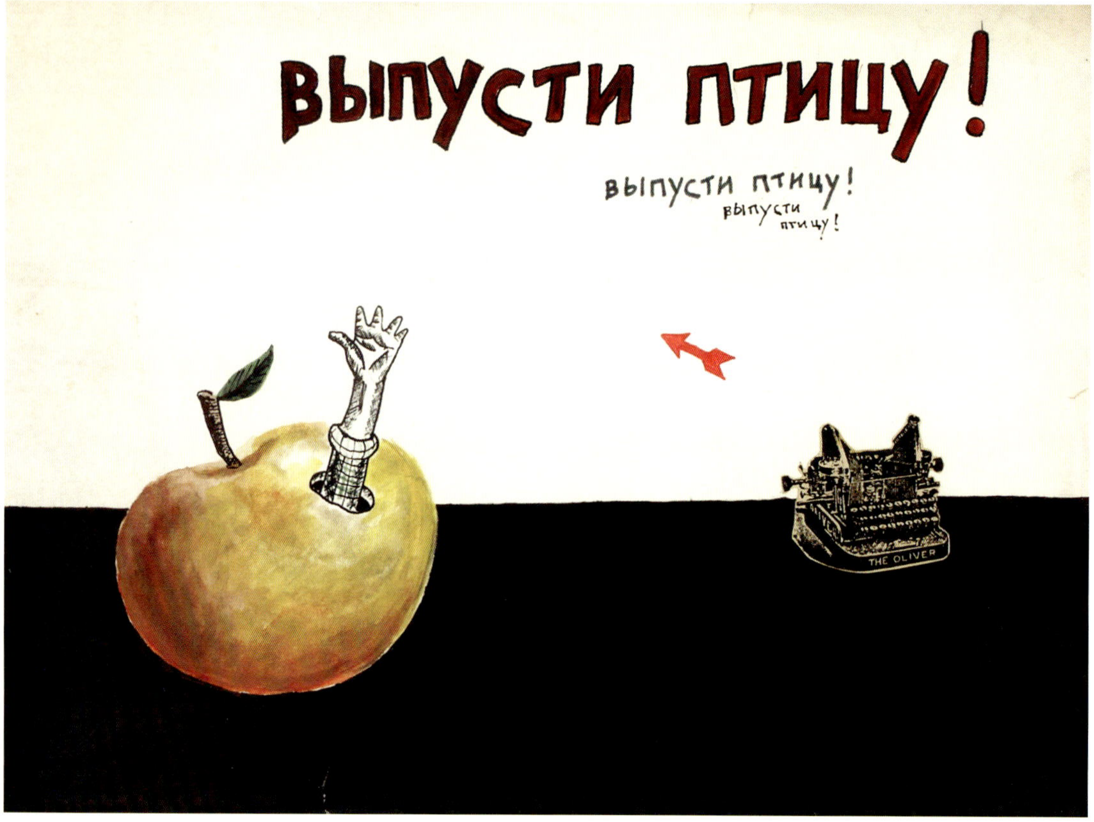

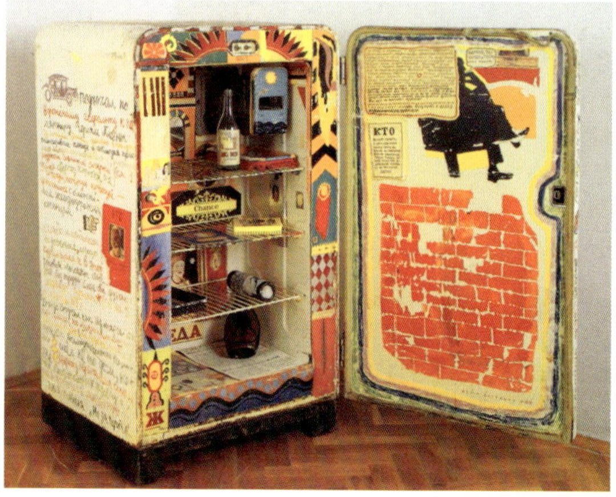

The Toadstools (Mukhomors) were an important Conceptual and performance group on the Moscow underground scene between 1978 and 1984. Its members were Konstantin Zvezdochetov (born 1958), Sven Gundlach (born 1959), the brothers Sergei and Vladimir Mironenko (both born 1959) and Alexei Kamensky (born 1955). Zvezdochetov and the Mironenkos studied stage design at the Moscow Art Theatre School (MKHaT) , graduating in 1982; Gundlach and Kamensky studied at the Moscow Polygraphic Institute; and Gundlach graduated from the Leningrad Academy of Arts in Theory and History of Art in 1984. The group dissolved in 1984 after the authorities banned their activities and three members were sent to remote army postings.

The Toadstools was one of several Conceptual groups in Moscow in the 1970s. Toadstool antics were loud, bawdy and anarchic, and often politically and socially engaged. Named after poisonous mushrooms, the group consciously styled itself in opposition to official culture. As the art historian Alexandra Danilova explains, 'The brightly coloured mushroom that attracts attention to itself is childlike and from the world of the fairy-tale; youth culture used it as a kind of drug.' Another important influence was the Russian avant-garde Futurist group OBERIU (Union of Real Art), a Dadaist group of Leftist writers, musicians and artists in the 1920s and '30s who staged provocative performances, stunts and readings of absurdist verse. Toadstool art embraced diverse practices, breaking down boundaries between media to combine painting, poetry, music and sound. They often worked with found objects which they decorated or defaced with texts and images, an example being *Fridge Novel* (1982). Their paintings were collaborative efforts. Hallmarks of typical Toadstool style are a bright palette, expressive brushstrokes, the use of felt-tip markers, and black outlines reminiscent of comic-book design, street art and graffiti. Zvezdochetov painted a series of portraits of the group's members dressed as world emperors in a naive style that loosely references the Sots Art practice of subverting Soviet official portraiture.

The group's performances were documented both while they were occurring and afterwards. They diarised, photographed and recorded in visual and textual formats or a combination of the two, typically on small scraps of paper, whether handwritten or typed. In *Metro* (1979) they spent a day touring several stations on the Moscow Underground and made a felt-tip-and-ink facsimile of the metro map to record the action. Imitating the Beatles, who were popular in the Soviet Union in the 1970s, they also created an album of photographs in which they masqueraded as members of the cult music group, sabotaging not only official culture but also pop icons.

top
Photo-documentation of The Shooting, Moscow Region, September, 1979
© The Toadstools
Courtesy Sergei Mironenko

above
Fridge Novel, 1982
Mixed media
104 x 60 x 57 cm
© The Toadstools
Collection Elena Kuprina-Lyakhovich and Maxim Lyakhovich
Courtesy E.K.ArtBureau

above left
Free the Bird, n.d.
Watercolour, highlighter and Indian ink on paper
30.6 x 43 cm
© The Toadstools
Collection Vladimir Mironenko
Courtesy E.K.ArtBureau

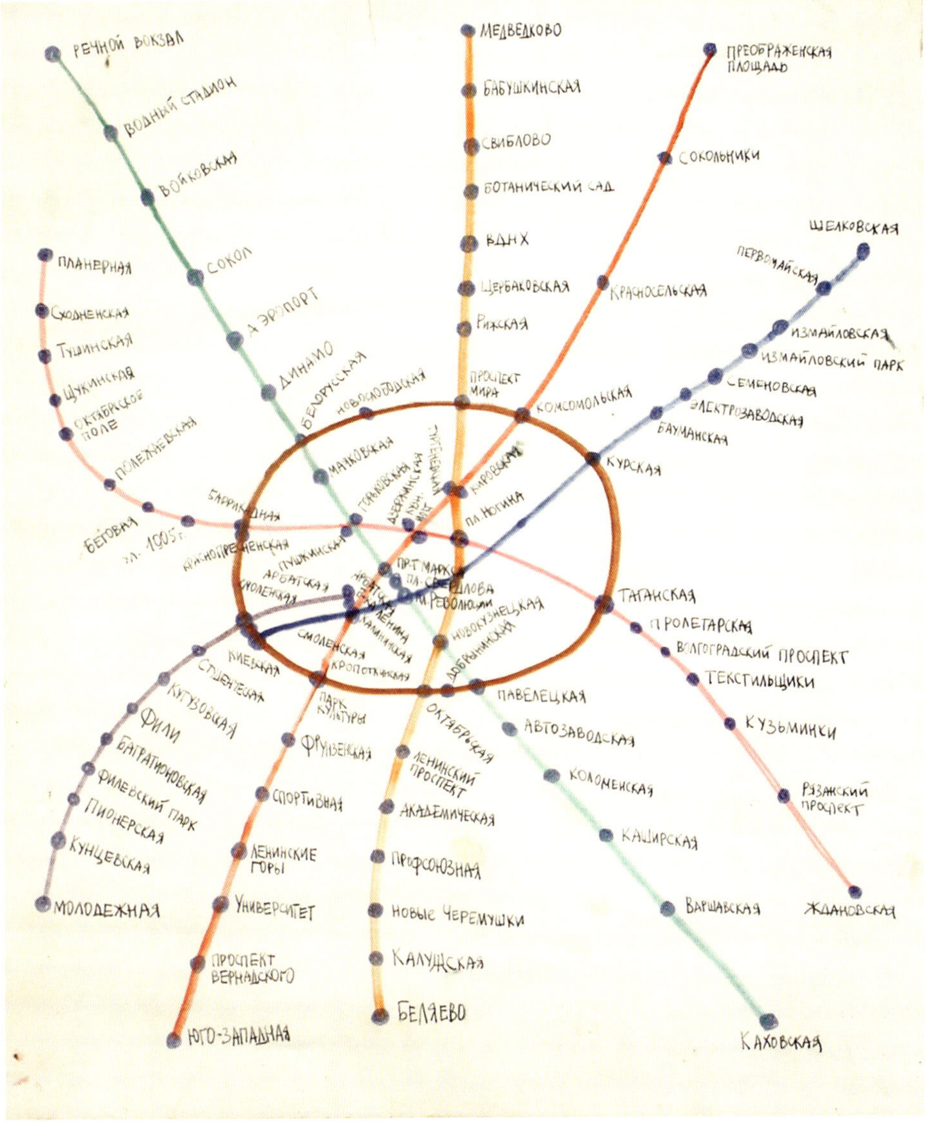

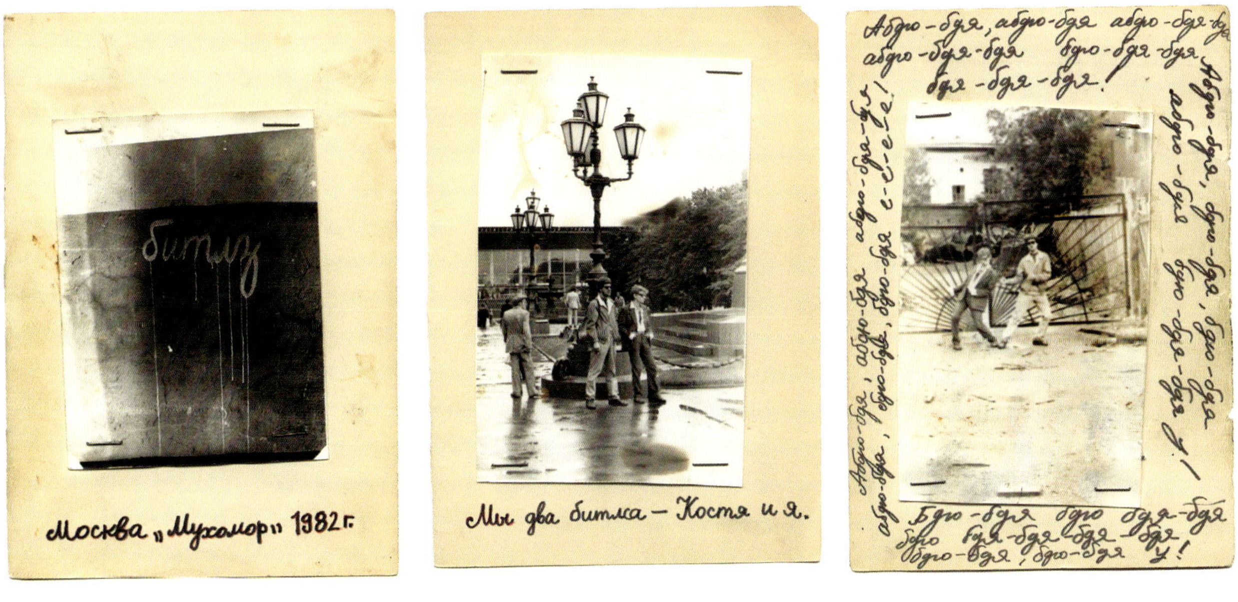

above
Documentation of the action Metro, 28 October 1979
Metro map, highlighter and ink on paper
43 x 36.5 cm
© The Toadstools
Collection Vladimir Mironenko
Courtesy E.K.ArtBureau

left
From The Beatles Album, 1982
Photograph, clip art and Indian ink on cardboard
29.5 x 21 cm (each)
© The Toadstools
Collection Elena Kuprina-Lyakhovich
and Maxim Lyakhovich
Courtesy E.K.ArtBureau

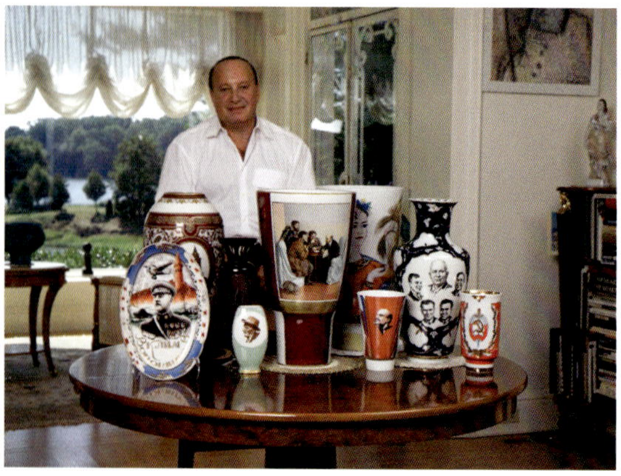

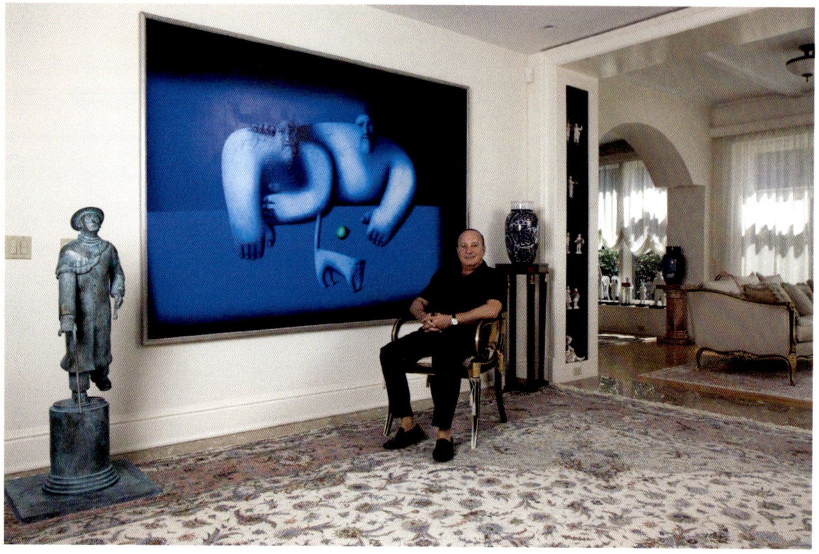

Collector Yuri Traisman was born in Moscow in 1948. He was surrounded by art from early childhood as his father Arkady was a graphic artist and his mother was a champion gymnast who taught at the Bolshoi Theatre, Moscow. Traisman studied engineering at the Moscow Institute of Construction and Engineering; after graduation his father found him a position in the restoration department of the Moscow Patriarchate. Although this was an administrative post, Traisman learned how to clean and restore icons. It was during this time that he began to collect them, especially discarded icons which he would restore. When he was twenty-six, his family emigrated to Italy, finally settling in the US in 1974. In America Traisman painted his own icons. When, in 1975, there was an exhibition of his work in Washington, DC, his icons were acquired by a Greek Orthodox church.

On arriving in the US, Traisman's father had opened Graphic Industry, a small studio that developed into a highly successful business employing over 150 people, many of them family members. The firm designed advertising products for large supermarkets using traditional print techniques Arkady Traisman had learned in the Soviet Union. By chance Yuri met the gallerist and art dealer Eva Glimcher, co-founder of PaceWildenstein, New York. Through Glimcher, he became acquainted with many American contemporary artists, including Robert Rauschenberg, Louise Nevelson and Andy Warhol. A number of them, such as Mark Rothko and Nevelson, had Russian heritage; Nevelson had been born in the Ukraine, and she and Traisman spoke Russian together. It was during this period that Traisman started to collect American Pop art, amassing an important collection which he later sold at auction.

By the late 1970s and early 1980s, unofficial artists were beginning to leave the Soviet Union to settle in the US, France or Israel. Traisman got to know the sculptor Ernst Neizvestny and bought a piece by him, the collector's first acquisition of Soviet underground art. Neizvestny had been asked to design Nikita Khrushchev's mausoleum, an ironic gesture since his work had been denounced in public by Khrushchev at the *Manege* show in Moscow in 1962. Traisman went on to purchase work by all of the major artists who emigrated to America, including Sots artists Alexander Kosolapov, Leonid Sokov, Grisha Bruskin, the Conceptualists Rimma and Valery Gerlovin, and Komar and Melamid. Having been introduced to emigré circles in Paris, he met and bought work by Oleg Tselkov, Oscar Rabin, Mikhail Roginsky and the Lianozovo painter Lev Kropivnitsky.

Although Traisman's collection is in part driven by nostalgia for his homeland, he is a pragmatic collector who seeks out works which fit into his collection as a whole, preferably career highlights by important names. As well as collecting, he has acted as a patron, having bronze sculptures by Bruskin and Neizvestny (among others) made in a workshop in Pennsylvania.

Traisman has exhibited his collection of unofficial art throughout the US and in Russia. In 1998 he published a catalogue of highlights entitled *Forbidden Art: The Postwar Avant-garde*. The accompanying show was on view in twelve American cities, including Los Angeles, Miami and Boston, and at the State Russian Museum, St Petersburg, and the State Tretyakov Gallery, Moscow. He has said that educating others about the history of art during the Soviet period is part of his mission.

Today Traisman divides his time between his homes in Connecticut and Moscow. He is involved with several foundations, as well as being a lecturer and book publisher. He was made an honorary member of the Russian Academy of Arts for his work in promoting Russian art throughout the world and, since 2006, has been vice-president of the Russian-Jewish Congress. Aside from his collection of Russian contemporary art, Traisman also has a large collection of vintage photography and Soviet Revolutionary porcelain, which he began to assemble in 1990, and which was exhibited in Russia and Washington, DC, in 2008–9.

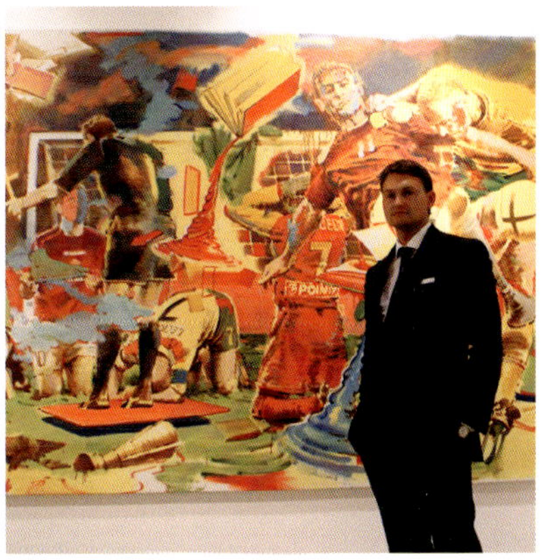

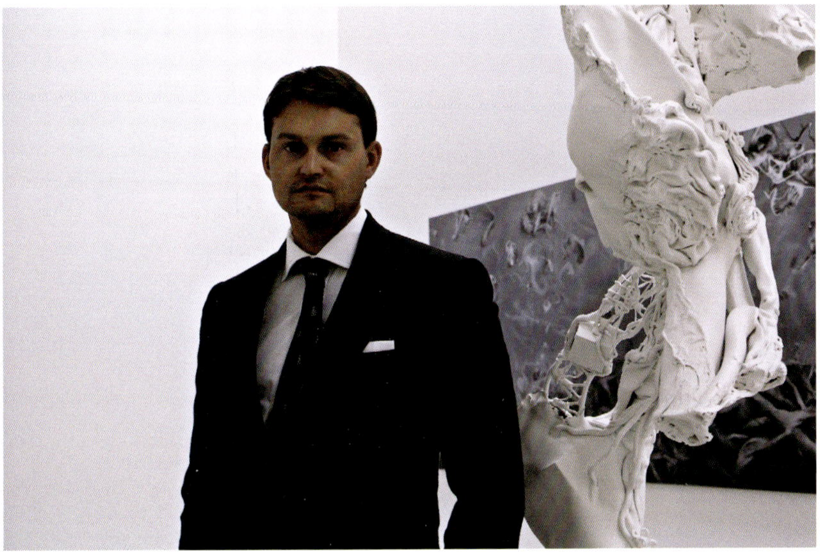

Andrei Tretyakov was born in Ekibastuz, Kazakhstan, in 1978. In 1995 his family moved to Moscow, where he finished high school. After moving to the US, he studied Finance and International Business at Pennsylvania State University. After graduation Tretyakov relocated to the UK, putting in a further year of academic study in Manchester. Of Russian parentage, he has close political and business ties with Kazakhstan through his father. Tretyakov started working for the mining company Kazakhmys as a trader in London, later becoming responsible for strategy and business development.

In Russia Tretyakov's family name is synonymous with collecting. In the mid-nineteenth century, Pavel Tretyakov founded what later became the State Tretyakov Gallery, one of the country's greatest national museums. Andrei's father has done genealogical research into the family's history, a daunting task as the Soviets destroyed most of the pre-Revolutionary archives. As a teenager, Andrei and his father visited open-air markets in Moscow where painters sold their work. He began to take a more serious interest in contemporary art around 2007 when he met Andrei Molodkin, of whose work he is a passionate supporter. Tretyakov admires art with a socio-political message, ascribing this preference to his upbringing as the child of a politician. Molodkin's sculpture using blood and oil addresses issues of power and business. 'I fell in love with it,' Tretyakov says. 'At the same time, I met new artists and my collection began to grow into other directions.'

When he first began collecting, Tretyakov became friends with the Paris gallerist Ilona Orel, who specialises in Russian contemporary art. This led to collaboration on a new gallery space in London. The pair went separate ways in 2009, at which point the gallery changed its name to Art Sensus. Although a public space, it reflects its owner's personal tastes: '*Sensus* means "feeling" or "appreciation" in Latin, so the gallery can be seen as a combination of art vision and appreciation, but it reflects my own vision.'

Ultimately Tretyakov sees himself as more of a collector than a gallerist. In fact his gallery is part commercial and part not-for-profit. At Art Sensus he organises numerous projects with educational rather than financial aims, one example being an exhibition focusing on Necrorealism. He has also on occasion broadened his brief to exhibit early twentieth-century art. Tretyakov now represents contemporary artists from other countries as well, saying, 'I like to work with art where the boundaries are non-existent. I don't want to see artists I support being known as Russian artists. I want them to be international, and I want them to work outside national boundaries.' As regards the marginalisation of Russian contemporary artists vis-à-vis others on the global stage, Tretyakov feels that Russians do not necessarily court full acceptance: 'I think you need to go back to understand Russian heritage, roots and character. Some artists actually like to be marginalised. They like to be seen as "Russian". They don't want to mix, they don't want to be international and cosmopolitan. They see it as decadent, bourgeois. They want to work without all the commercial pretence.' However, Tretyakov believes that becoming part of the international community is unavoidable.

Regarding the responsibility of curators to foster the art scene, he sees that responsibility as lying squarely with the government, and the main reason for a lack of infrastructure today as a holdover from Soviet times. 'The last seventy years of Soviet Russia [were] simply a big black hole ... if you look into the era of Soviet Realist art, everything was run by official commissions, and although there was an underground movement, it was not really enough. Now the government needs to nurture and foster a new generation of art critics and free artists with new creative ideas. We need a time machine to bridge the gap,' he jokes. A workable combination of private patronage and State sponsorship is essential, with the government creating a firm foundation upon which private patrons can build. 'You can't be a modern and contemporary society without embracing contemporary culture,' Tretyakov observes. 'We have lots of intellectual artists. Let's put them on the world stage and create an environment in which they can thrive.'

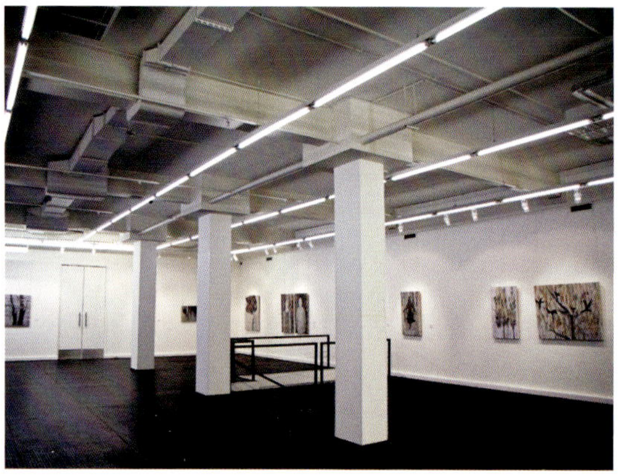

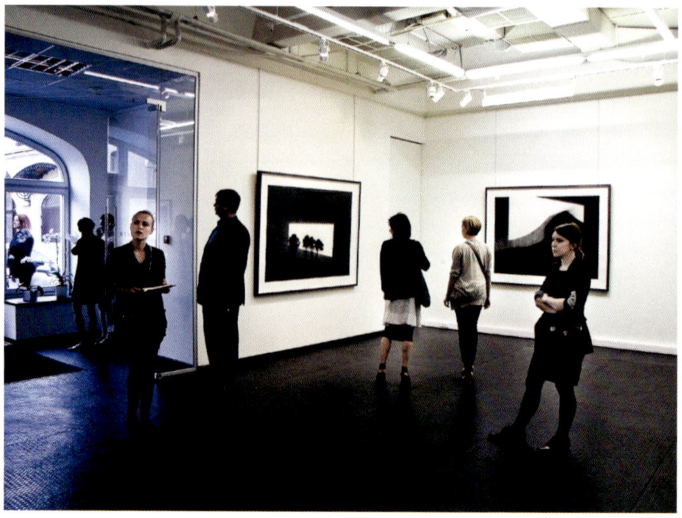

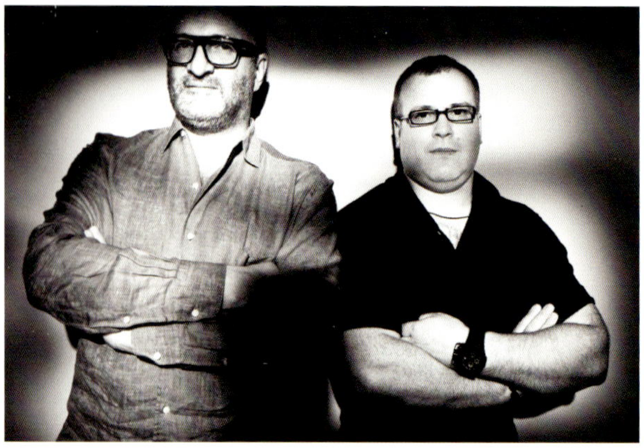

The Triumph Gallery was set up in Moscow in 2005 by Emelyan Zakharov and Dmitry Khankin. Both were born in 1966; they met at university. The gallery's first space was in an historic nineteenth-century Baroque-style mansion which belonged at the time to the oligarch Boris Berezovsky. Berezovsky let the duo use the building on condition that their new gallery would be named after the prestigious Triumph Award, a national prize for outstanding achievement in the field of culture. Since 2011 the gallery has been located on Ilyinka Street in a two-storey, 500-square-metre showroom close to the centre of Moscow. Triumph represents both Russian and international contemporary art. In 2007 the two gallerists temporarily merged their business with that of the artist and gallerist Alexander Yakut, whom they continue to represent today.

It was after Zakharov and Khankin left university that a passion for the commercial side of the art world inspired their shared life course. Zakharov's family has collected art for several generations; his father is director of the Moscow Conservatory, and his mother is a documentary film maker. Khankin's parents were both teachers. He started to earn money during the perestroika years by dealing in antique books; at the same time Zakharov was trading in furniture. The two combined forces and set up a gallery selling Old Master paintings. Zakharov is the 'bombardier' to Khankin's 'navigator'. Although they argue constantly, their collaboration is undeniably a productive one.

The duo shy away from collecting despite the fact that Zakharov at one time had a large collection, which he sold when a serious spinal injury left him fighting for his life. As Khankin says, 'You have to decide: are you selling art or are you collecting it? It's not interesting to do both. We do not use the word *collection*; we use the word *stock*. If you have stock you are a tsar; if you have no stock you are nothing.' The pair consider their gallery's particular strength to be their technical team, which stages ultra-lavish, ambitious installations. They concede that the local contemporary art market lacks strength and stability, and see as aspects of their role the introduction of a wider context as well as the providing of both entertainment and education.

One of Triumph's professional successes has been offering support to the leading contemporary group AES+F. The pair invest heavily in AES+F's grand-scale multimedia projects, publishing catalogues as well. Zakharov and Khankin are no strangers to controversy. They brought the work of Damien Hirst to Moscow for the first time in 1996 with the show *New Religion*, which portrayed science as a new spiritual system. The exhibition provoked heated debate among the Russian public and in the press. In 2008, one of the gallery's other artists, the ultra-nationalist Alexei Belyaev-Guintovt, whose art resurrects Soviet and Communist aesthetics, was awarded the Kandinsky Prize. The speech he gave at the prize ceremony was booed by rival artists due to his extreme right-wing views.

Khankin is concerned about the state of contemporary art in Russia, which he believes to be 'in a very deep crisis'. This he attributes to a lack of strong national identity and a systemic inability to think and reflect. Zakharov believes that the problem lies with the educational system: 'In the West, skills are not taught any more, which is bad, but [people] are taught how to think and question. Here we have the opposite problem.' Despite Moscow's strong tradition as a centre for Conceptual art, neither gallerist likes it. As Khankin says, 'Art must be beautiful first. Interpretation comes later.'

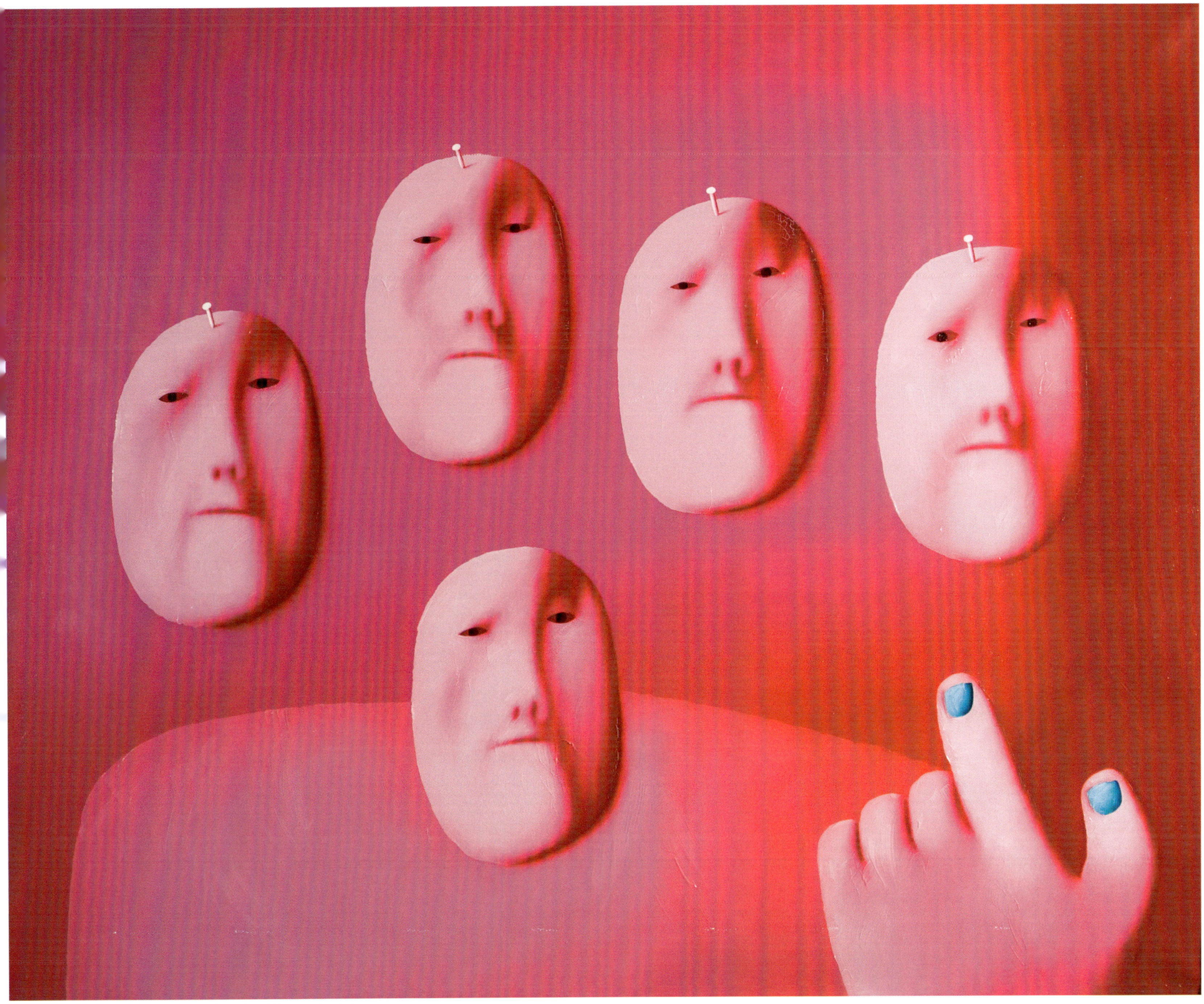

above
Five Faces with Hand
Oil on canvas
199.9 x 300 cm

Painter Oleg Tselkov was born in 1934 in Moscow. As a student he was expelled from several arts institutions for refusing to paint in the official style of Soviet Realism. He graduated from the more liberal Leningrad Theatre Institute in 1958 and was a member of the Union of Artists until forced to leave in 1970. In 1977 Tselkov emigrated to Paris, where he still lives and works, exhibiting in commercial galleries throughout Europe and the US. He had a major retrospective at the State Russian Museum, St Petersburg, and the State Tretyakov Gallery in 2004. His works can be found in the Jane Voorhees Zimmerli Art Museum, New Brunswick; Duke University Museum of Art, Durham; Stedelijk Museum, Amsterdam; and State Museum of Contemporary Art, Costakis Collection, Thessaloniki.

Tselkov seeks to express an image of fallen humanity in an approach that subverts the tradition of icon painting. Instead of painting saints as a 'window' onto a higher spiritual plane, his heroes are shown as naked human beings coloured by earthly pleasures and sin. Using semi-abstract forms, simplification and the grotesque, Tselkov shows the human condition as incomplete and the herd instinct as destructive. 'As an artist,' he has said, 'I create a human being, not God, but a human being that I can see. I have created a portrait of the crowd. Because in a crowd humans lose their image. If you look at the history of humanity, it is not the history of the individual but a history of the masses, and it is all soaked in blood, hate and deception.' He describes his palette this way: 'My colours must hit you in the head; they are not harmonious. I use colour as a force.'

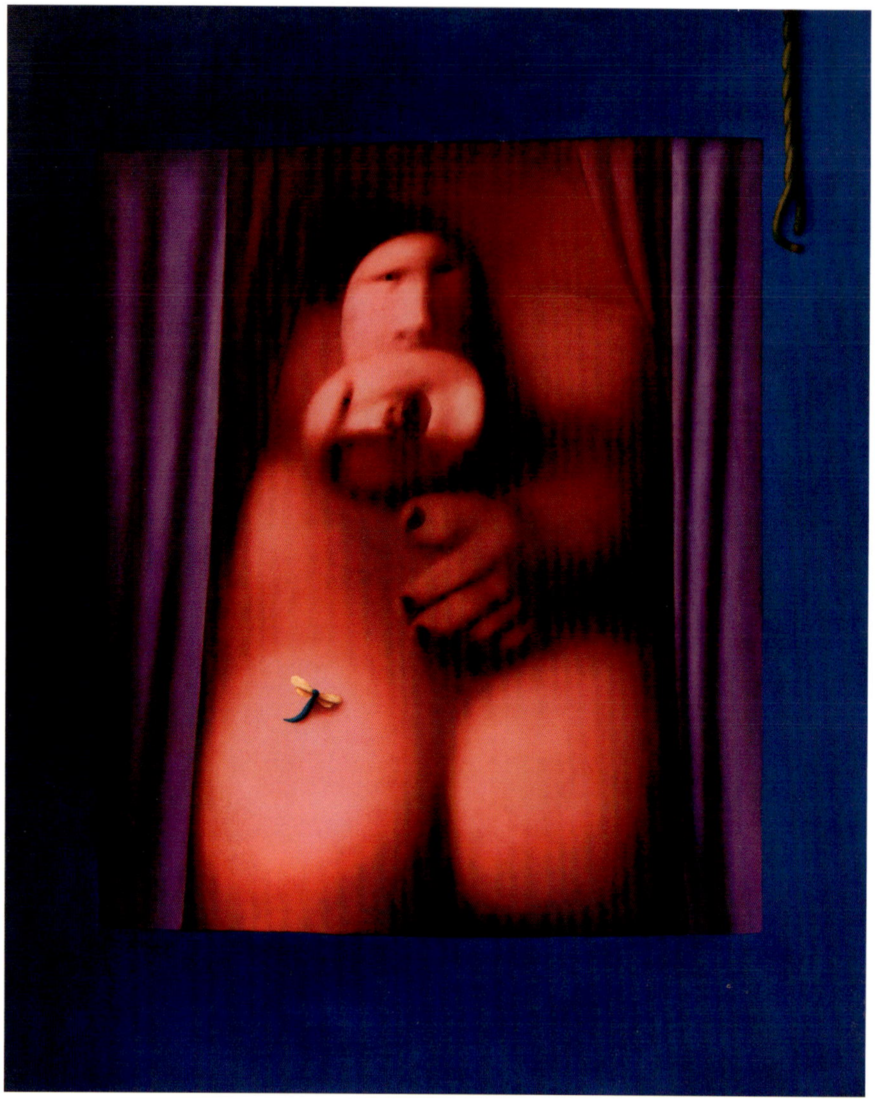

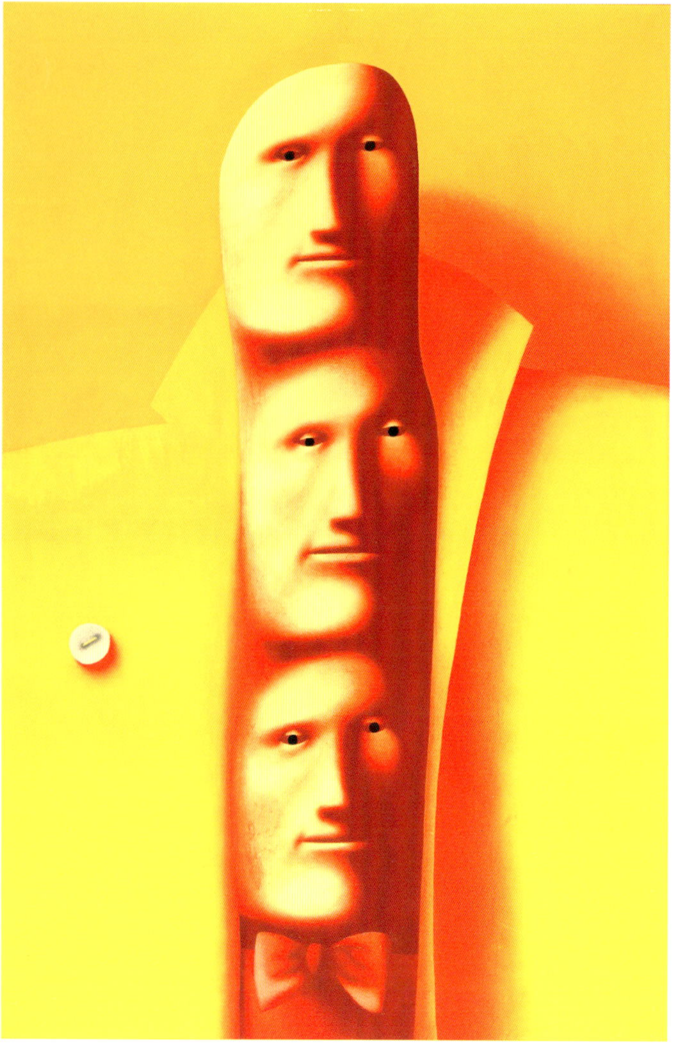

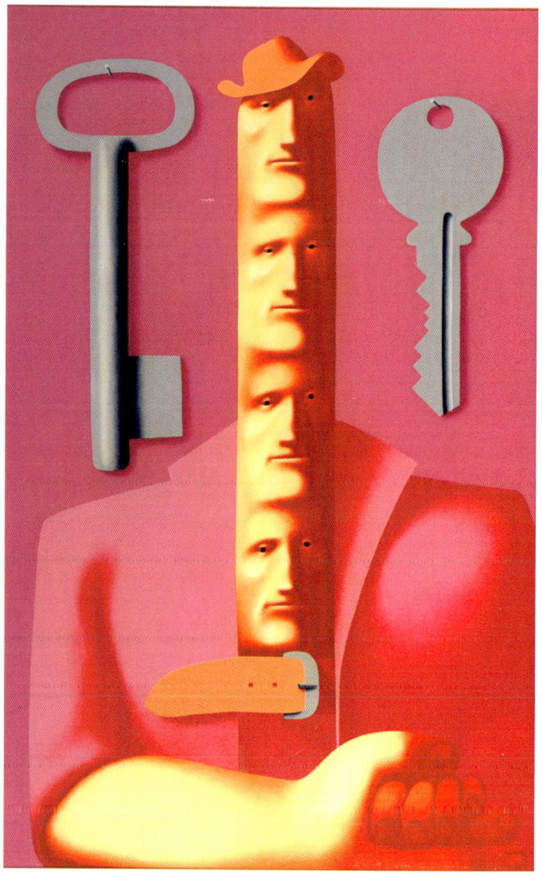

top
Two Persons, 1979
Oil on canvas
235 x 190 cm
© Oleg Tselkov
Courtesy of Vladimir Berschader

left
Three-faced Person, 1980
Oil on canvas
146 x 97 cm
© Oleg Tselkov
Courtesy of Vladimir Berschader

right
Four-headed with Keys, 1981
Oil on canvas
235 x 150 cm
© Oleg Tselkov
Courtesy of Vladimir Berschader

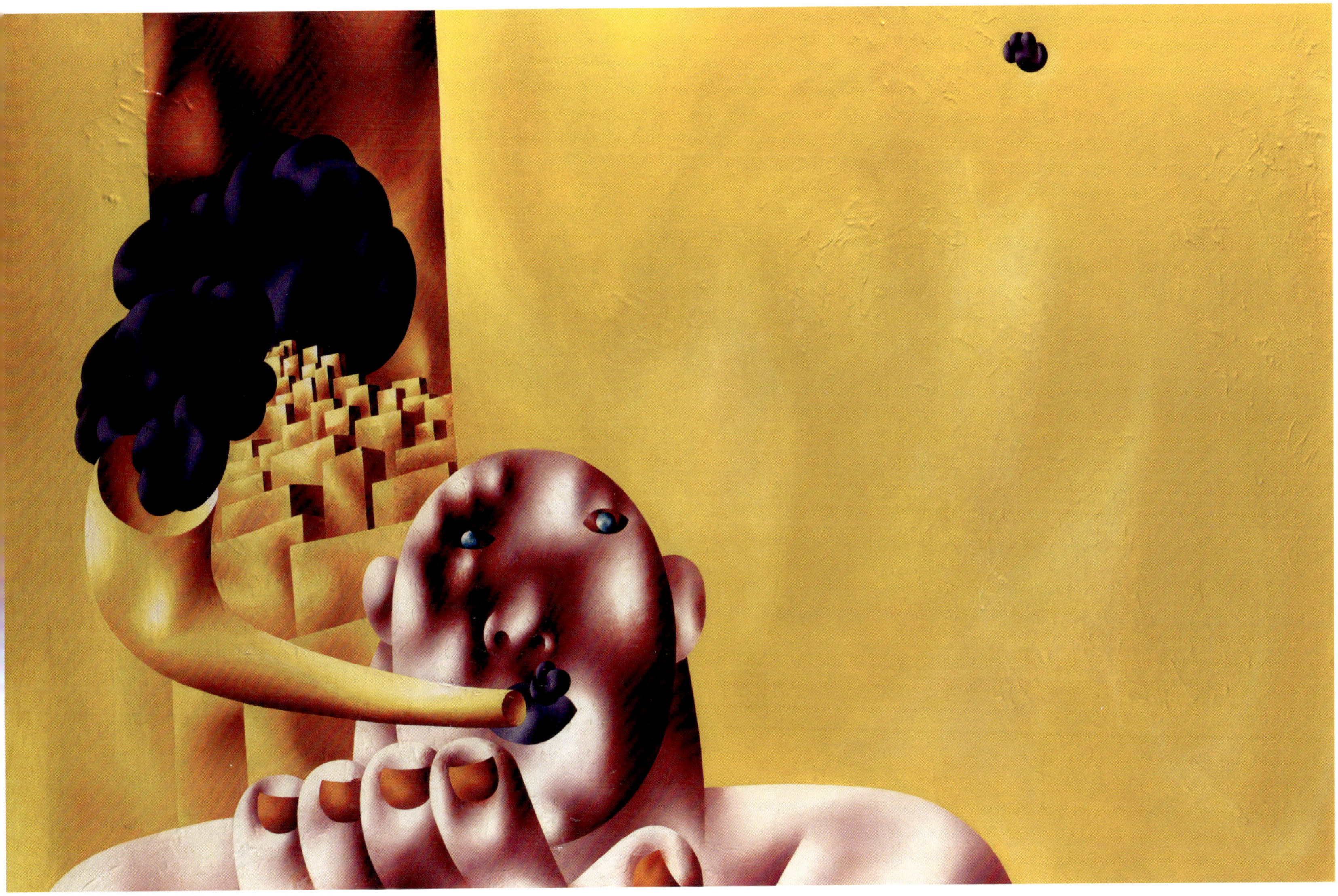

above
The Smoker, 1969
Oil on panel
100 x 152.5 cm
© Oleg Tselkov
Courtesy of Tsukanov Art Collection

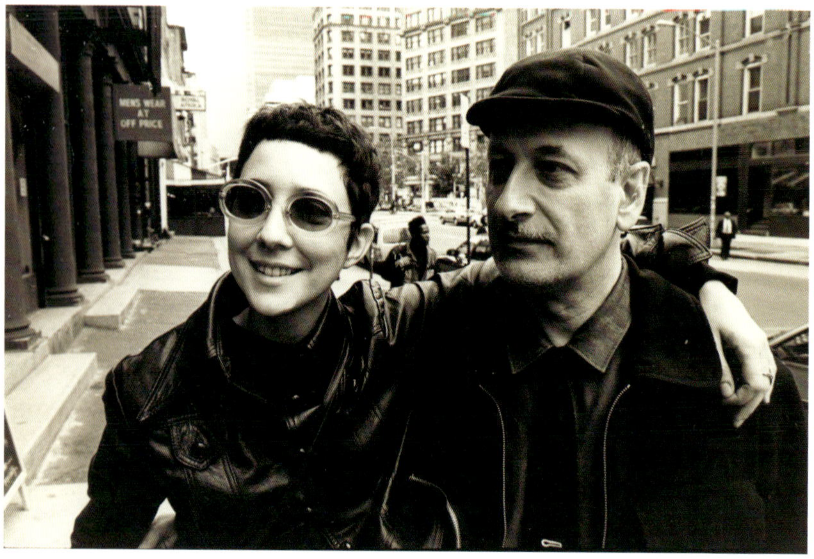

Victor & Margarita Tupitsyn

Freelance art historians, cultural theorists and curators Victor and Margarita Tupitsyn divide their time mainly between Paris and New York but have a peripatetic lifestyle. 'We are both interested in politics, and if we stay in one country too long we become dispirited by the local political situation, so we move elsewhere for a while,' they have said. The Tupitsyns write about and curate shows which focus on the Conceptual art of the Soviet underground. Margarita, who also writes about the historic avant-garde, was born in Moscow and brought up by artists Lydia Masterkova and Vladimir Nemukhin; even as a small child she felt encouraged to be part of their artistic milieu. Victor, whose main preoccupation is writing, was close to the network of poets and artists in Moscow's unofficial circles. Having met in 1973, the couple married within five months. They work and live in a spirit of supportive yet incisive professional debate.

Victor (born in 1945) received a Master's Degree from Moscow State University in Mathematics, although he also studied philosophy and was already a recognised poet and theorist. In 1974 the Tupitsyns took part in the 'Bulldozer Exhibition'; the authorities broke up the exhibition, and several artists were arrested. Victor was arrested as well and then forced to leave his job. Shortly thereafter, he and Margarita emigrated to the US. Victor defended his PhD thesis in 1976, and from 1980 on the couple were based in New York, where Victor taught at Pace University and Margarita received a PhD in Art History from the City University of New York (she studied with Rosalind Krauss). It was at this point that the Tupitsyns began to write about and curate shows of Russian underground art in America. Margarita's first show in New York was *Russian New Wave* (1981), and in 1986 she curated an exhibition of Sots Art at the New Museum of Contemporary Art.

The Tupitsyns speak of the 1980s as a time of receptivity to Russian Conceptual art because modernist painting was thought of as outmoded in the US. As Margarita has said, 'When Russian post-modernist art was shown in the West in the time of perestroika, many artists were quickly signed up by major Western galleries and exhibited in important art spaces.' Today the Tupitsyns believe that the shortage of contemporary Russian art being shown in Western galleries is due to its lack of a strong message and formal innovation, the result of the sudden socio-cultural vacuum of the 1990s. It is also the case that in Russia today artists lack a sense of milieu and a rigorous interpretation of theory. The Tupitsyns work closely only with selected artists such as Boris Mikhailov and Andrei Molodkin.

The Tupitsyns have both published widely on twentieth-century Russian art. An early collaboration was the Russian edition of *Flash Art* (1989); Victor edited a key anthology of contemporary Russian theory and philosophy of art, *Post Soviet Russia* (2003). Other books by Victor include *Communal (Post) Modernism* (1998), *The Museological Unconscious* (2009) and, together with Margarita, *Verbal Photography: Ilya Kabakov, Boris Mikhailov, and the Moscow Archive of New Art* (2004). As art historians and critics, the Tupitsyns believe that it is important to support contemporary cultural life by engaging with collectors. In particular they mention how in the 1980s they supported Norton Dodge in major acquisitions for his collection of works of the Russian Conceptual school, as well as the acquisition of key Sots Art pieces which are now in the Jane Voorhees Zimmerli Art Museum, New Brunswick.

Margarita, who in 1989 published *Margins of Soviet Art: Socialist Realism to the Present* and who is writing a book on Moscow Vanguard art, sees her role as narrowing 'the great divide' between West and East, specifically between Russian and American culture. She believes that her and Victor's achievement is closely linked to the period when post-war Russian art was taken most seriously in the West. She also feels that twentieth-century Russian art history has something to teach contemporary culture, citing the late 1930s as an example of a decisive moment when the Socialist Realist culture industry took over in the Soviet Union.

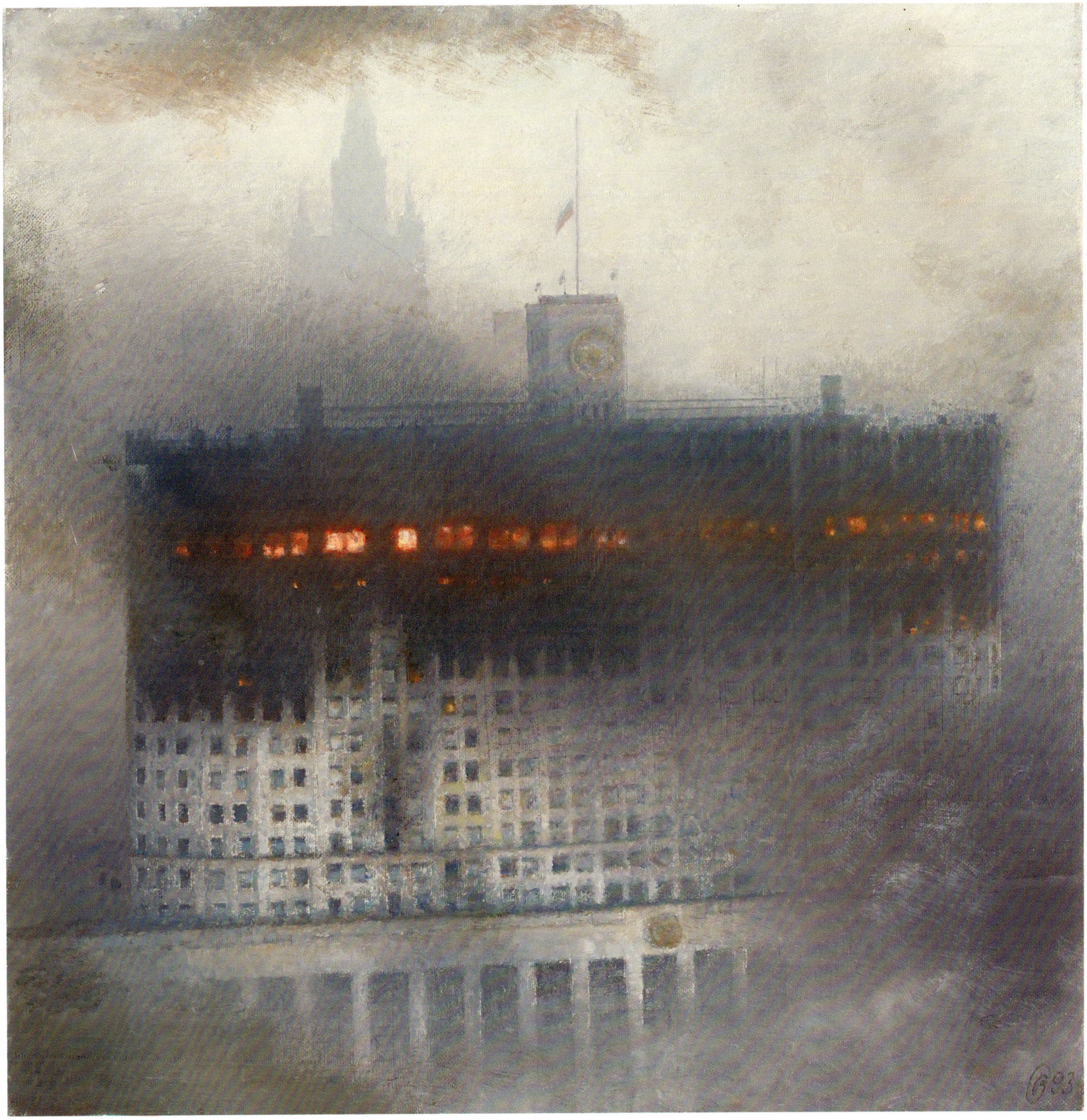

Born in 1931, Oleg Vassiliev attended the Surikov Institute until 1958. After graduating, he worked as a printmaker before gaining regular employment as a children's book illustrator under the auspices of the Union of Artists. In this capacity he shared a studio with his former classmate and close friend Eric Bulatov. For the next three decades the pair collaborated on professional illustration projects, often signing their joint products with a single name. Concurrently, Vassiliev pursued his own unofficial artistic work.

Vassiliev's approach was conditioned by intense intellectual exchanges with Bulatov. Both artists wished to recover the repressed historical memory of the Soviet avant-garde and its nineteenth-century forebears, a gap which had been apparent in the Surikov's curriculum. To further this goal, they sought out, as unofficial teachers, artists from the older generation with living memories of the period, such as Vladimir Favorsky and Robert Falk. The partial rehabilitation of Malevich's Suprematist paintings, by way of brief exhibitions in the 1960s, also inspired Vassiliev: 'A star shone and I felt how the rays were flying to reach me from distant space, touching and stimulating my consciousness,' he wrote in 1983. Despite being from the 'comparatively recent past', the avant-garde, he asserted, had been 'transformed into legend' as soon as he had become aware of them himself. Their inspiration precipitated him to adopt stylistic devices officially designated as formalist, and inspired an abiding concern for the relationship between 'the lateral expanse of the picture plane [and] a representation of the world beyond the canvas'. Throughout such investigations, the key intellectual problem was a reappraisal of the 'real'.

Vassiliev's unofficial art was exhibited in private settings to like-minded friends including the Conceptualist artists Ilya Kabakov and Ivan Chuikov and the poet Vsevolod Nekrasov. He sought no greater public recognition, choosing not to participate in the 'Bulldozer Exhibition' of 1974. Unlike others who did take part, Vassiliev would remain little known abroad until some years later, when *A-Ya* – a review of Soviet unofficial art published in the West by the émigré Igor Shelkovsky – featured his work. Taking advantage of political reforms a decade later, Vassiliev emigrated to the US in 1989 along with many of his peers. Unlike them, however, he eschewed the siren call of artistic life in New York, settling in rural Minnesota.

Vassiliev's recent painterly oeuvre has embraced both landscape and historical subject matter. In the former case, depictions of snowy forests and the rural geography of the American Midwest bear uncanny similarity to the fringes of his native Moscow. Though painted from life, the sites – muddy paths and truck stops, for example – are clearly chosen by the self-reflective logic and nostalgia of an émigré Likewise, his key cycle of drawings – the album *On Black Paper* (1994–7) – records a halcyon youth spent walking in the countryside with his friends Bulatov and Kabakov. The retrospective mood of such mature work is reinforced by a visual style in debt to nineteenth-century Realist painting. Having emigrated to the West, Vassiliev's search for the real now takes place in the fields of memory.

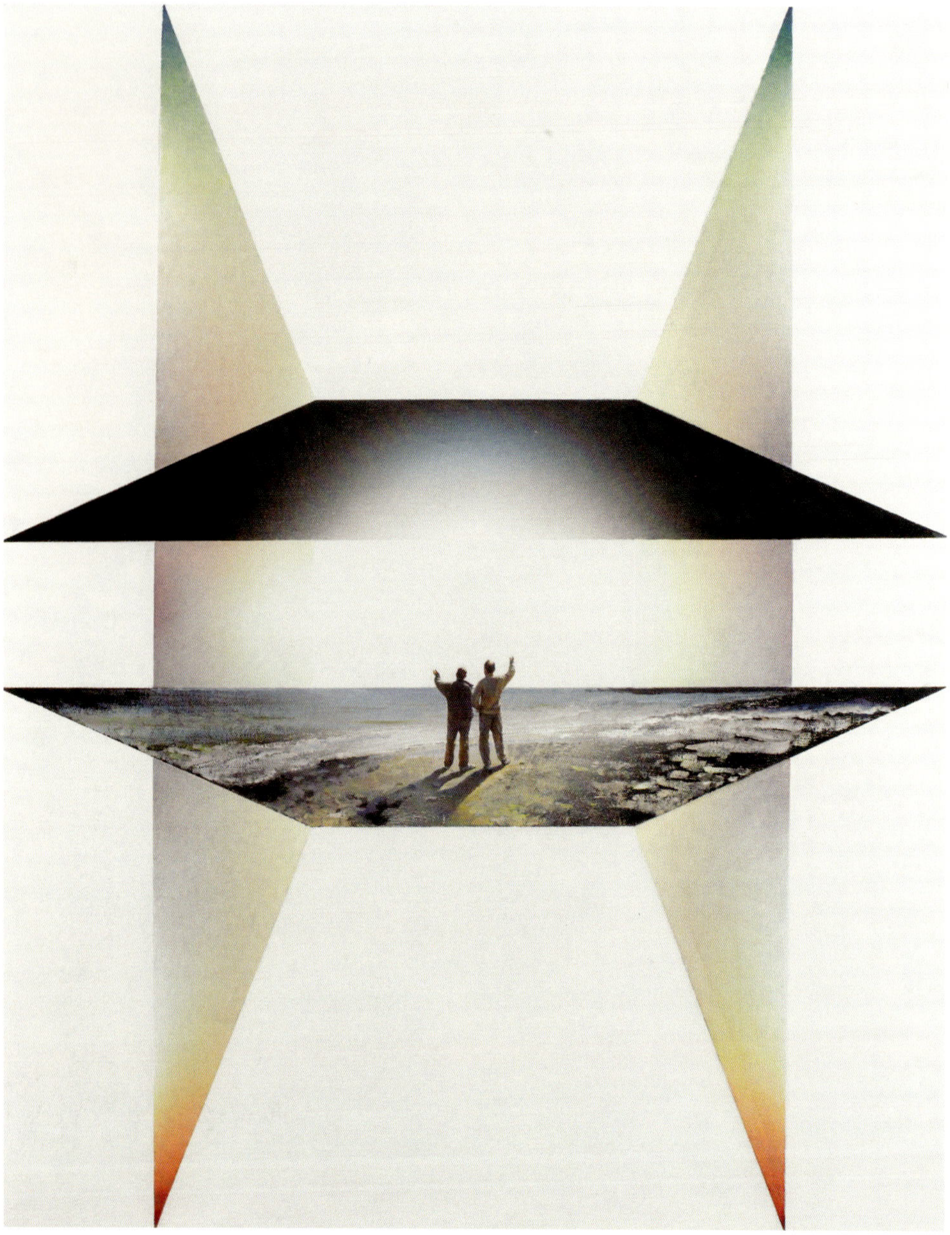

previous page
Home II, from the series White House, 1993
Oil on canvas
39.6 x 39.1 cm
© Oleg Vassiliev
Courtesy of Sotheby's

above
At the Seaside, 1989
Oil on canvas
153.4 x 119.9 cm
© Oleg Vassiliev
Collection of DES

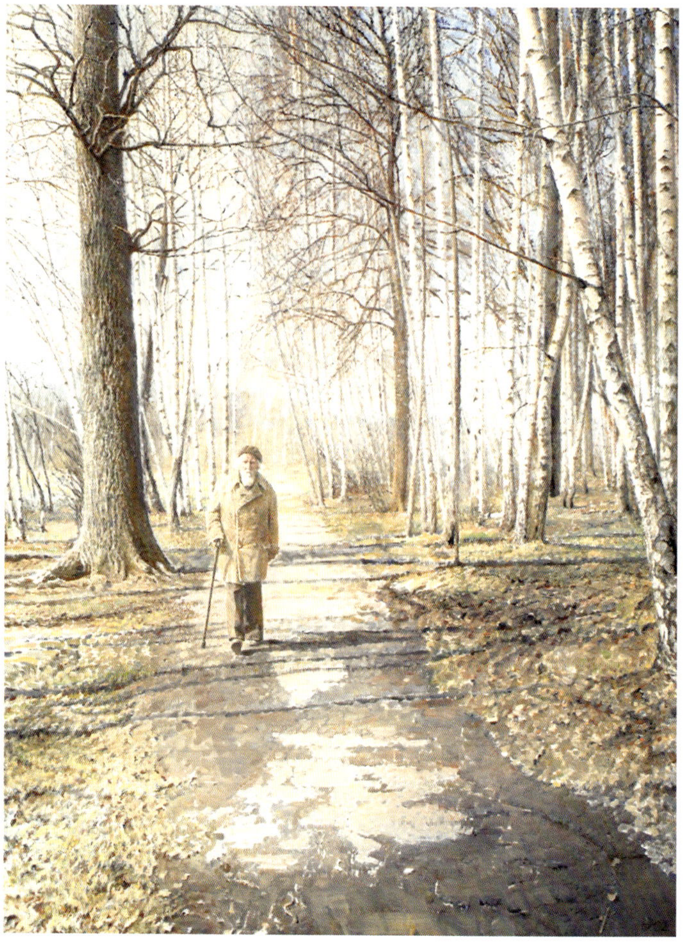

right
Return Home, 2002
122 x 89 cm
© Oleg Vassiliev
Collection of Neil Rector, US

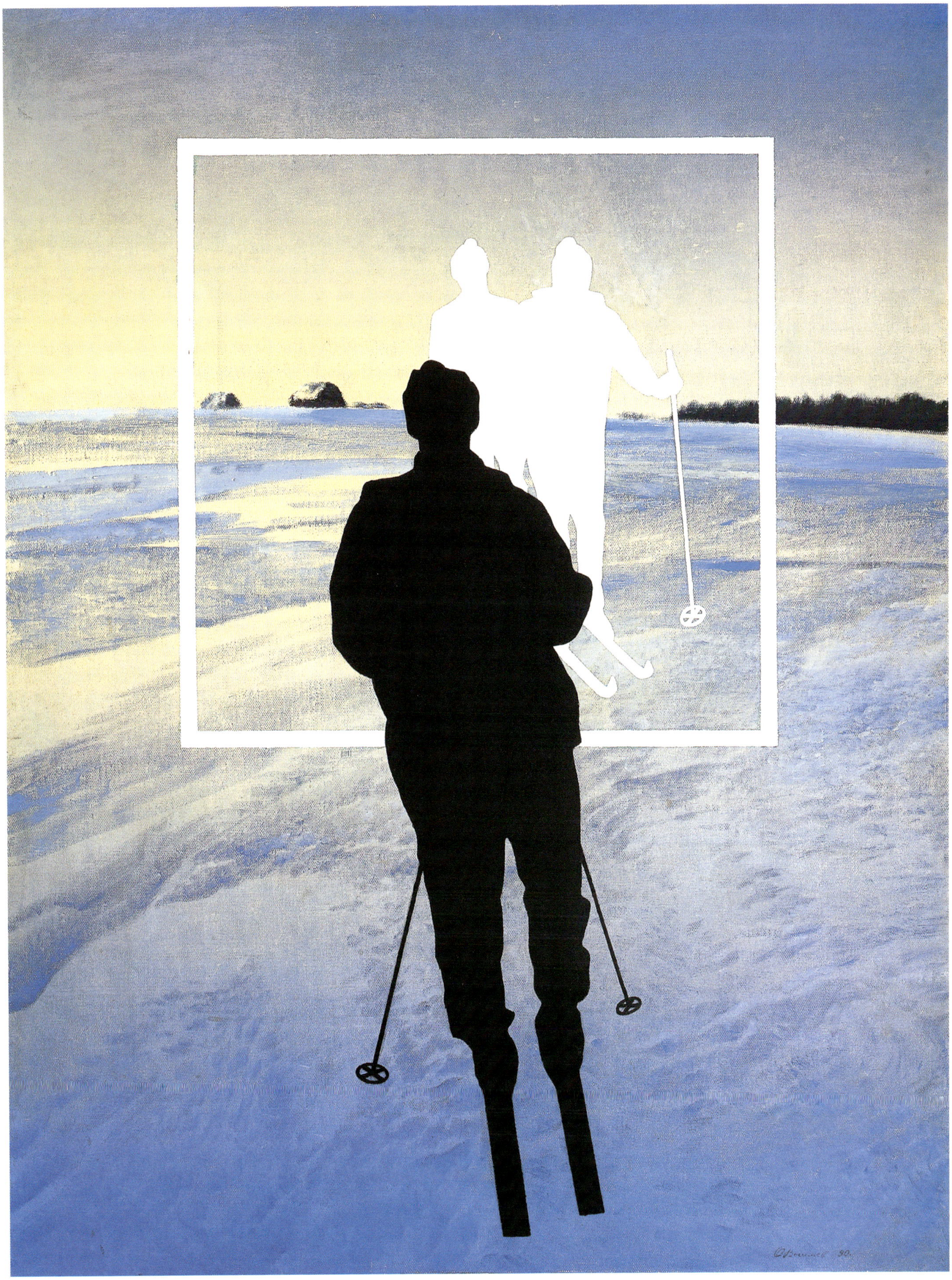

right
White Skiers, 1990
Oil on canvas
129.5 x 99.7 cm

Courtesy of Kolodzei Collection of Russian and Eastern European Art, Kolodzei Art Foundation

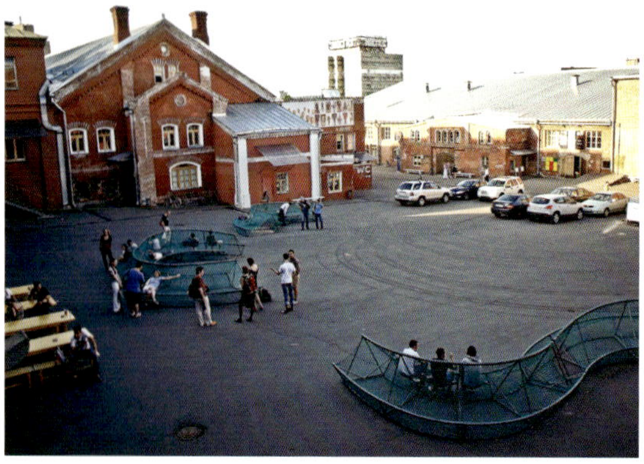

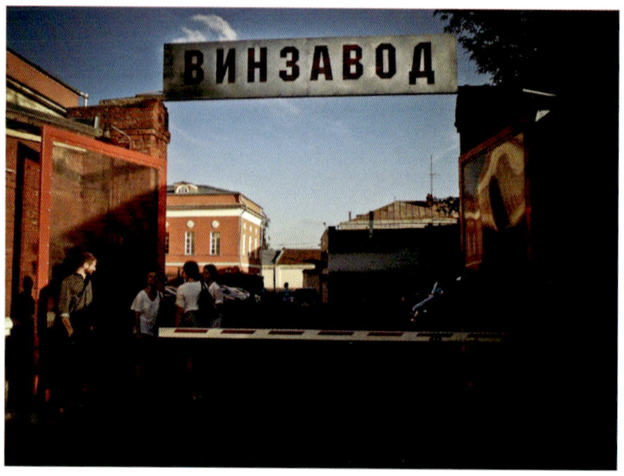

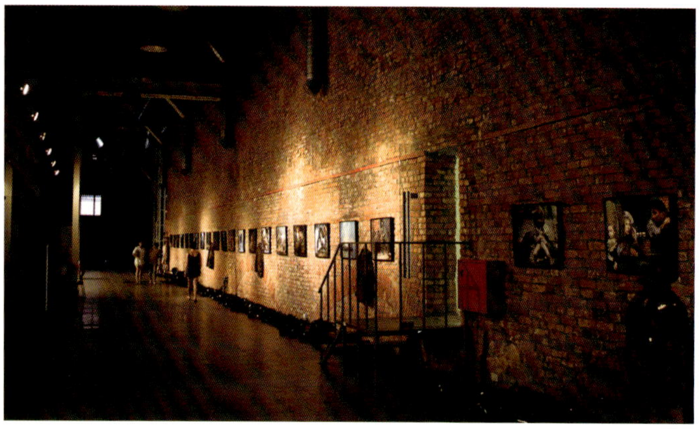

Vinzavod Centre for Contemporary Art, which opened in 2007, is Moscow's first contemporary arts centre. Consisting of seven buildings over a total of 20,000 square metres, it is home to some of Russia's most prestigious galleries including XL, Aidan, M&J Guelman, Regina Gallery and Proun, studios, exhibition spaces, a photography studio, clothing shops, art-supply and bookshops, various arts organisations and a café.

Vinzavod is located behind Kursk train station close to the city centre, its founders having been inspired by the reclaiming of former warehouses, factories and industrial areas and their transformation into cultural platforms. In the words of the centre's president Sofia Trotsenko, 'Just about everywhere in the world, some of the best spaces for contemporary art are former industrial sites that artists turn into studios. This has led to once abandoned neighbourhoods becoming new urban centres, which in turn leads to myriad other improvements: neighbourhoods become safer and more attractive, tourists come in droves, and real estate gains in value. In many major cities in Europe and the USA these centres are now an established part of local culture ... Inspired by this example, we decided to turn an old industrial site in Moscow into the city's first centre for contemporary art, where we could concentrate the best art resources ... and bring together in one space all the people who are determining the development of contemporary art as a whole.' The name *Vinzavod*, which means 'wine factory', refers to the centre's location in an old wine factory, with its workshops, tasting halls and cellars. In transforming this space, the emphasis was on preserving as much as possible of the original buildings and accentuating their nineteenth-century industrial beauty, which has otherwise almost disappeared from central Moscow.

Vinzavod has a unique atmosphere, and each space possesses a character all of its own. Besides the galleries, there are three main exhibition halls: the White Hall (770 square metres; the premier space for showing painting, installations and photography), the Red Hall (770 square metres; suited for performances and photo and video installations) and the Arched Hall (2,500 square metres; used for large-scale projects, video art and installations). The exhibition halls and other areas accommodate not only art shows but also diverse cultural events. The centre hosted the Second Moscow Biennale (2007); the 2007 Kandinsky Prize exhibition and award ceremony; Oleg Kulik's *I Believe* (2007); World Press Photo (2008); International Festival Design Art (2010); lectures by British architect Norman Foster and artists such as Robert Wilson and Frances Morris, and London Design Museum director Deyan Sudjic.

'The Vinzavod mission is to support contemporary art and artists, to introduce contemporary art to the widest possible audience, and to make art an integral part of contemporary life,' says Trotsenko. The centre's priorities include arranging and presenting exhibitions, curatorial projects, and educational and charitable programmes. In 2008 Vinzavod also founded, with the support of the Ministry of Culture, Best of Russia, a national photography contest that is open to anyone; and the START programme, which supports and promotes young Russian artists with no exhibition experience. The *Vinzavod Art Review*, Russia's first monthly newspaper focusing on the country's contemporary scene, chronicles life at the centre and includes contributions from acclaimed artists, curators and gallery owners.

Innovative projects, a non-stop exhibition schedule, and an outreach policy that embraces different communities, generations and styles all have made Vinzavod one of the best-known and -attended art centres in Moscow; since its opening it has had over a million visitors. And the entire neighbourhood around it has been transformed into a vibrant arts district.

Painter Vladimir Weisberg (1924–1985) was born, and lived and worked in, Moscow. Having started to draw at the age of six, he attended lectures at the Surikov Institute. Weisberg also trained under Sergei Musatov and, for a time, with the Moscow painter Alexander Osmerkin. As with many of the underground painters of his generation, he held an official but peripheral post, from 1964 to 1984 working as a painting tutor to architectural students. He met with some controversy in 1962 when one of his nudes shown in an important exhibition of Russian art at the Manege in Moscow was deemed to be pornography. Weisberg became a member of the Soviet Union of Artists in 1961. A large collection of his works is held in the Pushkin Museum of Fine Arts, Moscow, and he is represented in several other important public and private collections, including the State Tretyakov Gallery, Moscow; the State Russian Museum, St Petersburg; and the Jane Voorhees Zimmerli Art Museum, New Brunswick. Two major retrospectives of Weisberg's art have been held in Russia (1994 and 2006).

Executed in oils and watercolours, Weisberg's oeuvre consists of portraiture, still life and female nudes. Stylistically it can be divided into two phases. His works of the 1950s were influenced by the Moscow modernists who followed Cézanne. This can be seen in the criss-crossing of Weisberg's brushwork and his preoccupation with colour. His approach changed through the 1960s, when his use of white backgrounds and a pared-down colour palette became prevalent. In 1962 he published a treatise on his experiments with colour, 'Classification of the Main Forms of Colourist Perception', which coincided with a new emphasis in his art on semitones. Weisberg's paintings are commonly referred to as 'white on white', a term taken from Malevich's post-Suprematist period, when the avant-gardist himself rejected colour. Each of Weisberg's canvases were painstakingly built up using several layers of colour painted on a specially primed surface, a unique practice which he developed. Once he was satisfied with the colour, he would begin to pare it back, a process which he described as 'decolourisation'. Calling the overall process 'invisible painting', the artist's ultimate goal was harmony between objects and their environments.

It was in his still lives that Weisberg found the greatest resolution to his aesthetic strivings throughout the last two decades of his life. During the early 1960s he painted several apparently abstract compositions of crumpled newspapers and sheets. Later still lives are carefully constructed compositions using studio objects: three-dimensional geometric forms, especially cylinders which echo classical columns, classical busts, shells and coral, which he saw as an ideal natural construction. His works are rarely large in scale, and as a mature painter he preferred a square format. Compositions typically are arranged around a central white cube. In this preference for geometry and emphasis on the square, a link can be seen with the works of Malevich and the Russian avant-garde, although Weisberg's pictures are nearly always figurative. Ultimately they are metaphysical exercises in which form and colour create a palpable sensation of light and harmony.

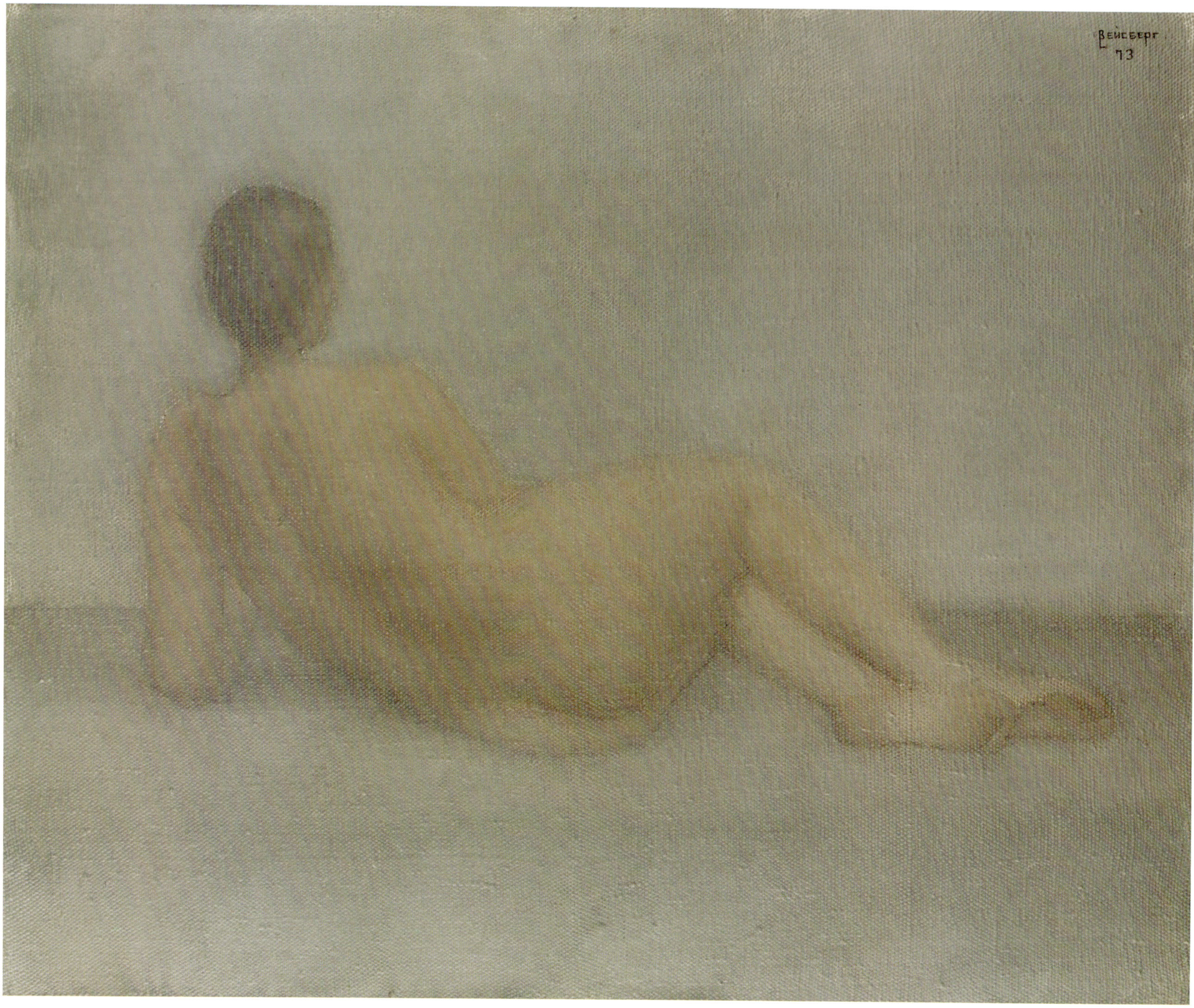

previous page
Geometrical Figures, 1975
Oil on canvas
61 x 64 cm
© Vladimir Weisberg
Private collector

above
Nude, 1973
Oil on canvas
48 x 58 cm
© Vladimir Weisberg
Courtesy of private collector

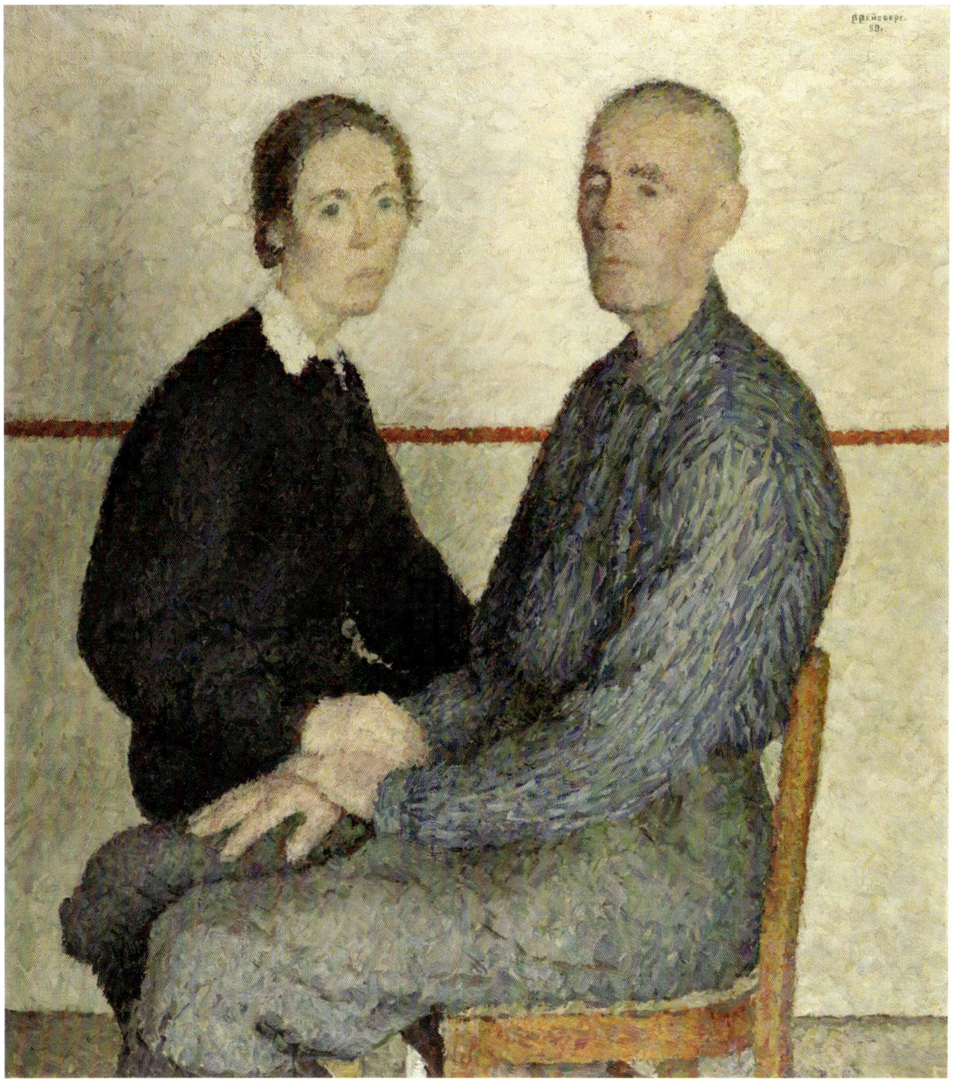

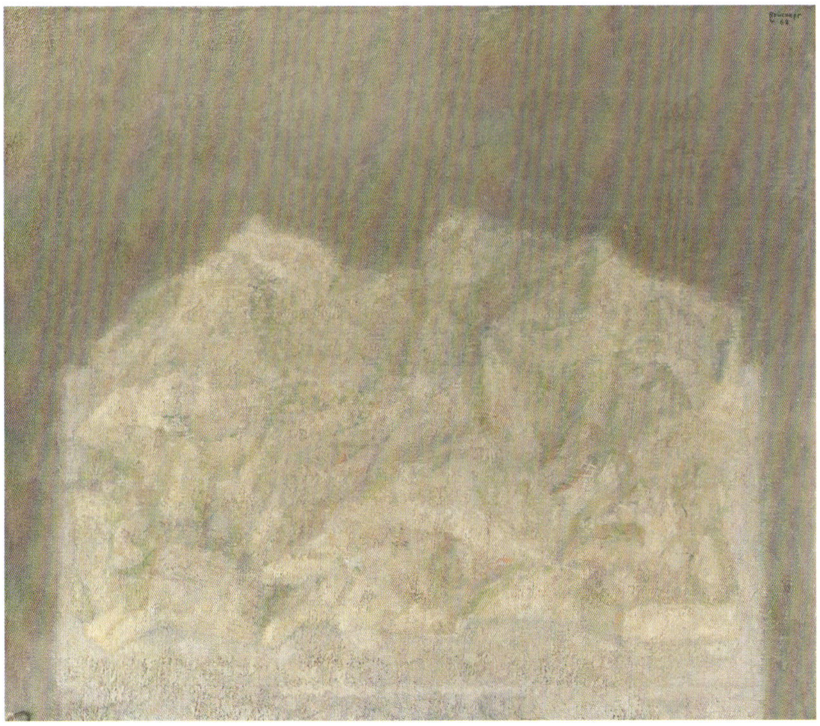

left
Composition with Gauze, 1968
Oil on canvas
65 x 75.4 cm
Private collection
Courtesy of Sotheby's

above
Family, 1959
Oil on canvas
111 x 110 cm
© Vladimir Weisberg
Courtesy of The State Pushkin Museum
of Fine Arts, Moscow

above
Cubes and Pyramid, 1975
Oil on canvas
45 x 55 cm
© Vladimir Weisberg
Private collection

facing page
Little Black Vase, 1976
Oil on canvas
48 x 53.5 cm
© Vladimir Weisberg
Private collection

Vladimir Weisberg

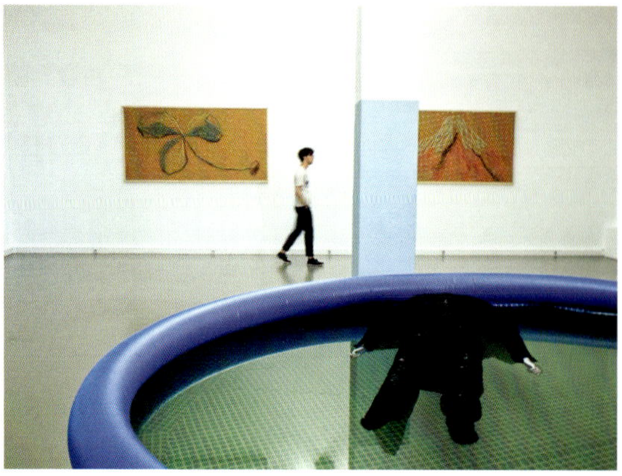

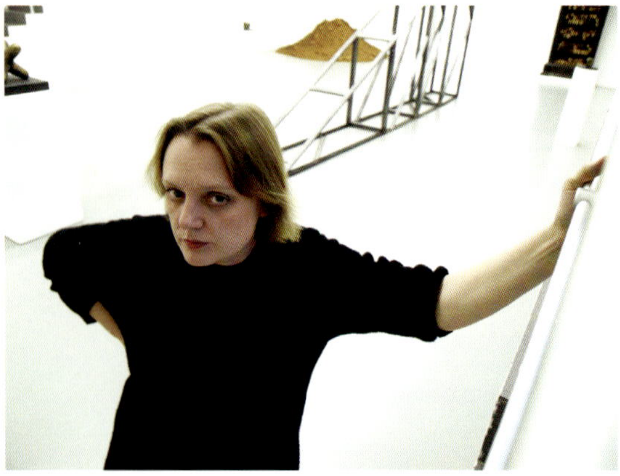

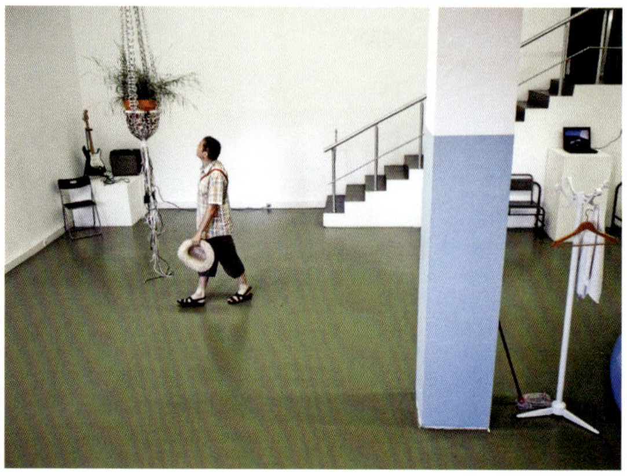

Established in 1993, XL Gallery is a commercial contemporary art gallery located in the Vinzavod Centre for Contemporary Art in Moscow's industrial district. Elena Selina, XL's founder and owner, was born in Moscow, the daughter of a mathematician and an economist. She studied art history, specialising in early twentieth-century Russian art and graduating in 1986. She then found a job in exhibitions management for the Soviet Union of Artists. This experience taught her how to curate, a skill for which she has a natural affinity and which she enjoys. After leaving this official post in the wake of perestroika, Selina set up her first independent gallery together with curator Elena Romanova in 1991, but they went their separate ways after a year because Selina did not wish to confine herself to working with the Moscow Conceptualists.

Selina sees the uniqueness of her gallery in its project-based approach, one reason why installation art is a particularly strong medium there. The gallery opened as a platform for making art, she has said, describing the early years as being a 'live journal with every show being a kind of new statement'. Selina looks for art that challenges new boundaries and takes risks. The name XL highlights her one-size-fits-all concept.

Selina describes the 1990s as a most interesting and professionally fulfilling decade. She backed the careers of painters Dubossarsky and Vinogradov at this time, and helped to promote Oleg Kulik, one of the most successful performance artists and photographers of that decade. It was an era when Russian art began to attract more attention from Western Europe; horizons were widened, and collectors came from abroad. Journalists writing about shows attended private views before they received official press releases, there was real sense of excitement about shows and new work, and there was also a sense of community. In Selina's opinion this atmosphere changed quickly after the art market began to grow fast around 2000, in part fuelled by the Western auction houses and by the increasing demand for traditional Russian art and plethora of new collectors in that field. Suddenly artists started to demand speculative prices for their work, but the domestic market was not ready; there were simply not enough collectors.

The opening up of the market changed not only the atmosphere but the roots of Moscow's creative life. Selina identifies 2006 as a watershed in this process, a time when people lost their ability to exercise independent judgement. It was also a moment of personal crisis for Selina: 'Art has to be pioneering, not something that just brings in money, so that time was hard for me.' Ironically it has been in the West, taking part in contemporary art fairs, that she has consistently found her most receptive audience. Most of her best works are bought by Western collectors who do not necessarily understand their context or know much about her gallery but who buy artworks because they like them.

If Selina is wholly positive about the globalisation of art, she is concerned about issues closer to home, specifically the state of contemporary criticism and of arts education. She laments critics' overemphasis on market-related journalism where the first question is always 'How much does this artist cost?' rather than 'What has he or she made?' Selina sees a flood of critics following fashion rather than engaging in rigorous debate and analysis, and her concern is that this can have a negative effect on the artists themselves. This in turn makes them harder for her to manage as a gallerist. And there is also the question of how to ensure that her exhibitions continue to make money so that the gallery can continue to exist. The paucity of good arts education is in part a result of the vacuum left in the wake of the Soviet Union: 'In terms of legal status, contemporary art has existed in Russia since the '90s. Before that it was underground, no less art, but it existed hermetically ... Everything changes when it is allowed to emerge and enter the market, and this period of legality [in Russia] has been very short.'

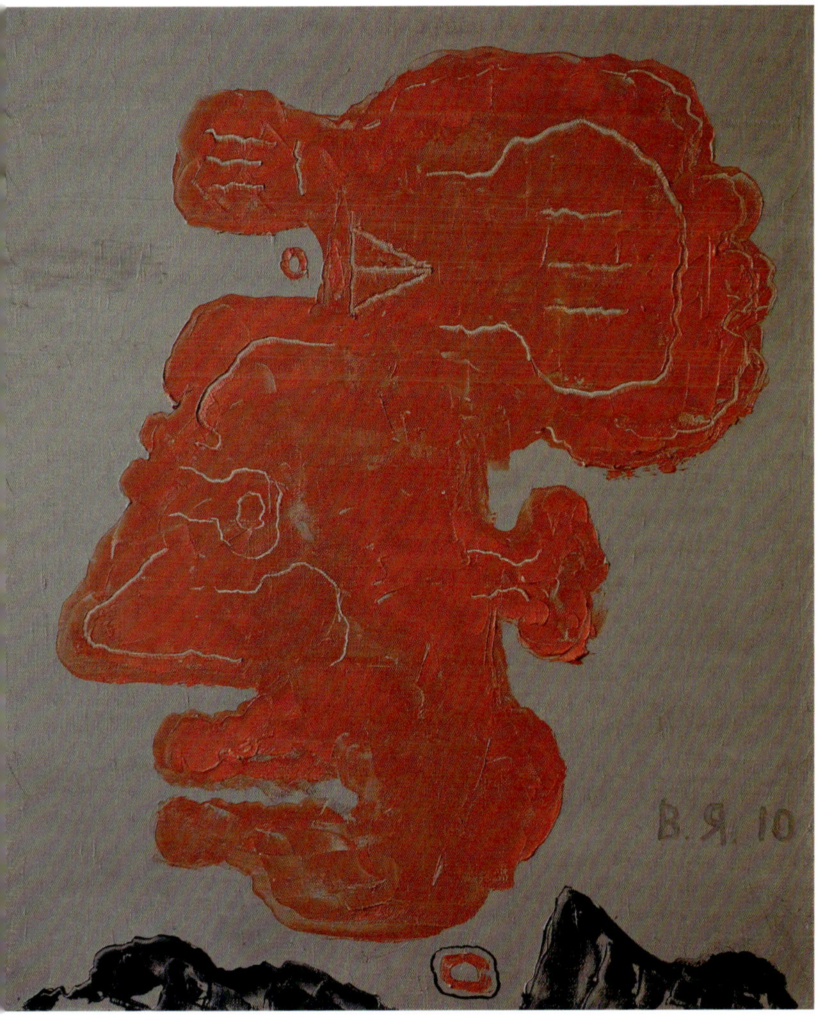

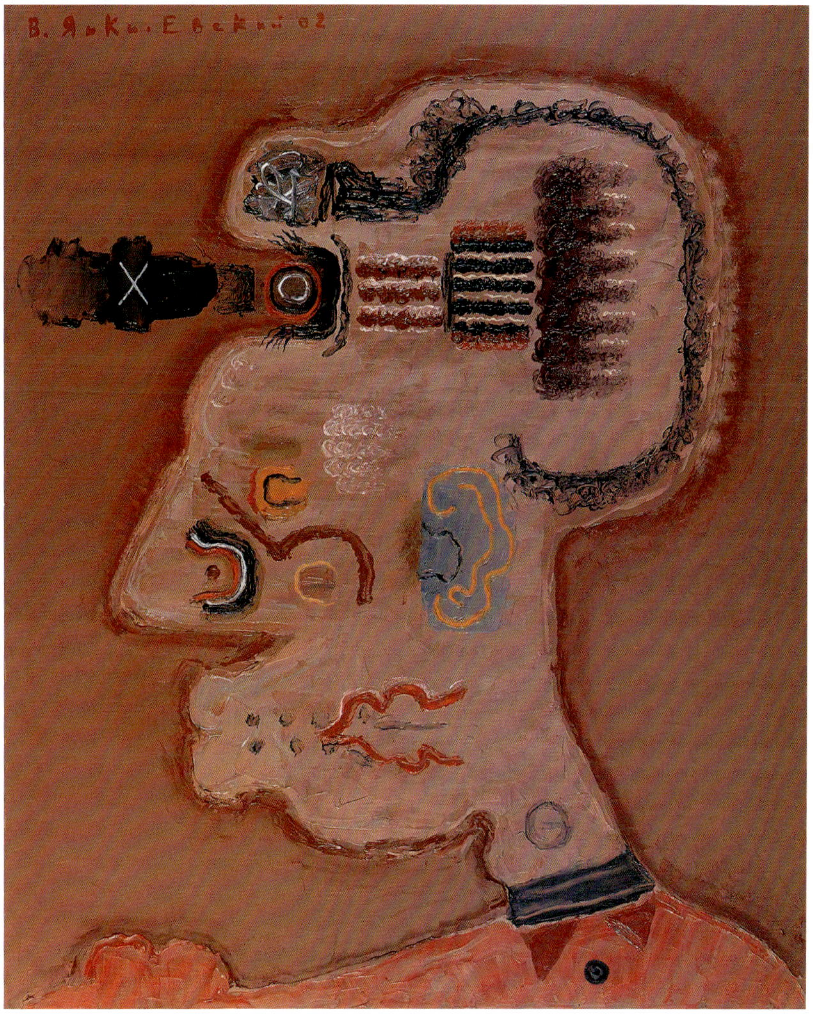

above
Portrait of a Man, 2010
Oil on canvas
60.5 × 50 cm
© Vladimir Yankilevsky
Collection of the artist

above right
Portrait of a Man, 2002
Oil on canvas
78 × 60 cm
© Vladimir Yankilevsky
Collection of the artist

Paris-based Vladimir Yankilevsky, born in Moscow in 1938, graduated from the Moscow Institute of Printed Arts and, like many of artists of his generation, found work as a book illustrator. Since the beginning, his career has been defined by an interest in abstract, anthropomorphic forms in paintings that reflect human anxieties and explore the conflict between individual and society. He creates triptychs and pentaptychs whose forms evoke the depths of metaphysical thought. Having moved to New York in 1990, two years later Yankilevsky settled in Paris, where he lives and works. He has exhibited widely in Moscow, St Petersburg, Paris, New York, Berlin and Bilbao.

The metaphysical content of Yankilevsky's paintings is a result of the artist's burning desire 'to illustrate emotion'. As he explains, 'I am trying to find the reflection of the system of human interactions in the bigger picture of what is happening around us in the universe. This is the theme of my large works.' Human relationships and the emotional experiences that they engender are themes that unite Yankilevsky's oeuvre, as is apparent, for example, in *Triptych No. 3: Exodus (Dedicated to R.S.)* (1963) or *Triptych No. 21: Adam and Eve. V* (2005). The reappearance of familiar topics throughout the artist's work is testament to his belief in an artistic 'idée fixe that follows you throughout your life ... a uniform link; it changes, transforms, but you sense it. It is genetic'.

Yankilevsky's works are marked by an idiosyncratic aesthetic that is, at times, reminiscent of science fiction but which distinguishes him from many of his peers. This innate strangeness, however, is welcomed by him as, in his own words, 'I've always been a stranger in Moscow; my ideas and thoughts were foreign to society. And when I came here [Paris], I was foreign. Here everything was already formed, and I didn't fit in. I still don't fit in.'

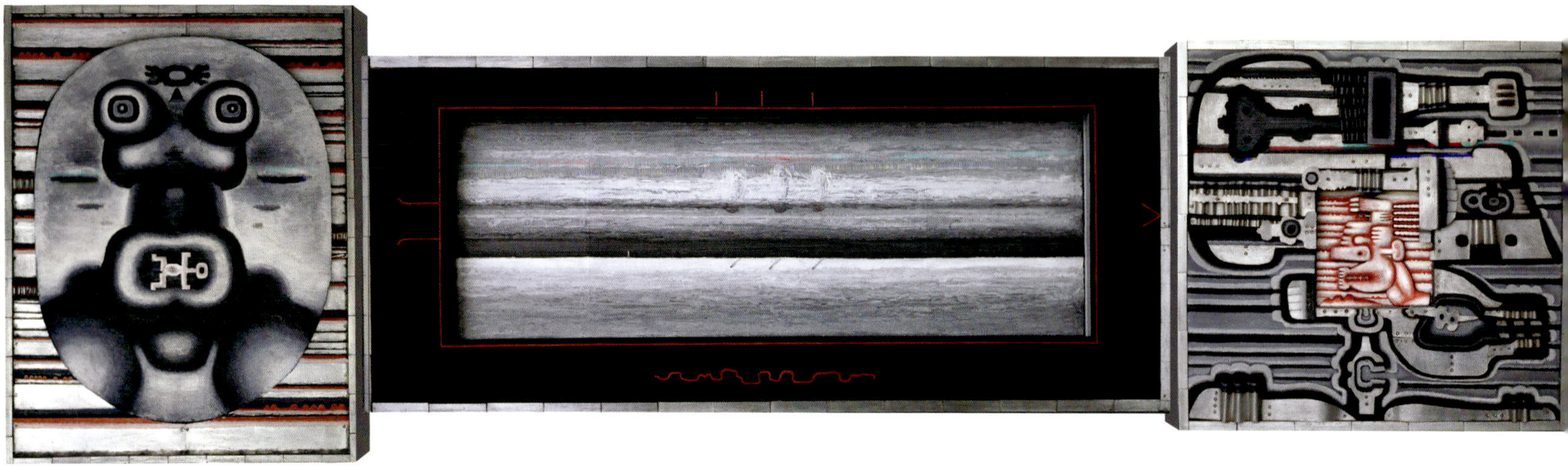

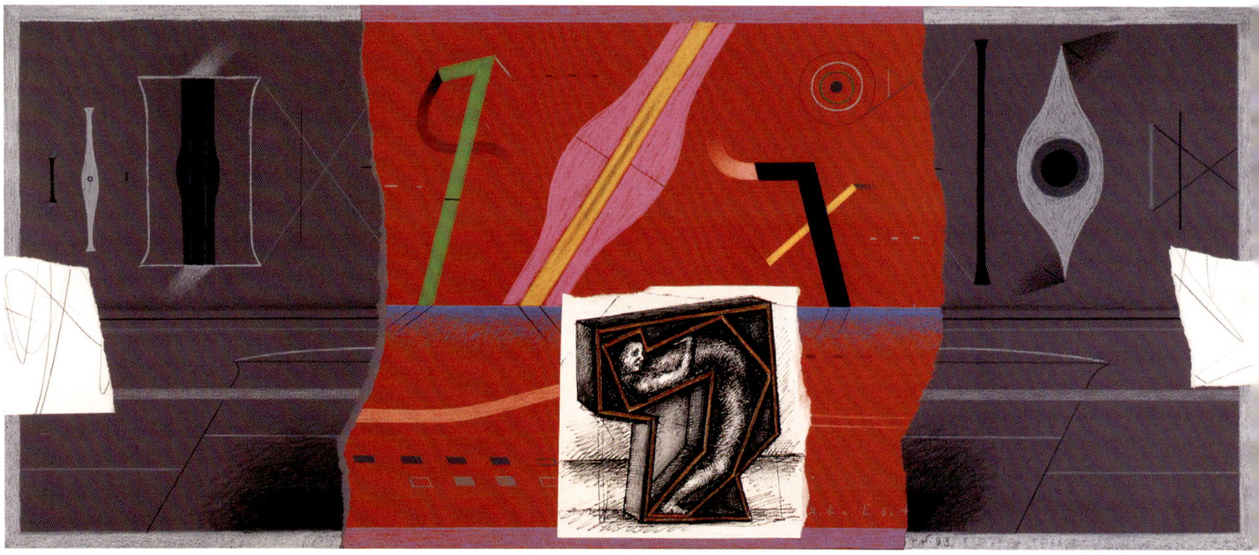

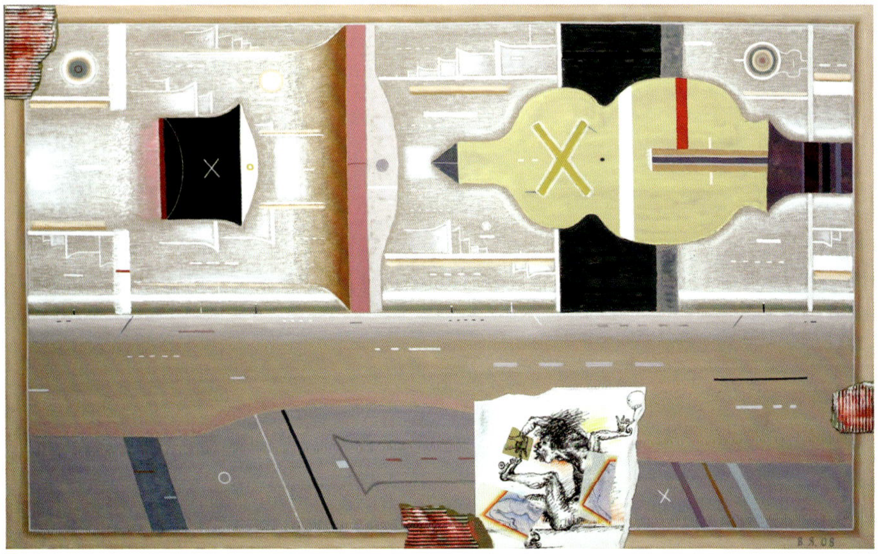

top
Triptych No. 4: A Being in the Universe (Dedicated to D. Shostakovich), 1964
Oil on metal and fibreboard
118 x 409.5 x 22 cm
(118 x 92.5 x 22; 91 x 213.5 x 9; 100 x 103.5 x 16.5)
© Vladimir Yankilevsky
Collection of the artist

left
Ghost Town, 2008
Oil on canvas
120 x 200 cm
© Vladimir Yankilevsky
Collection of the artist

above
From the cycle People in Boxes: At Home, 1993
Pastel on colored paper, collage,
50 x 118.2 cm
© Vladimir Yankilevsky
Collection of the Artist

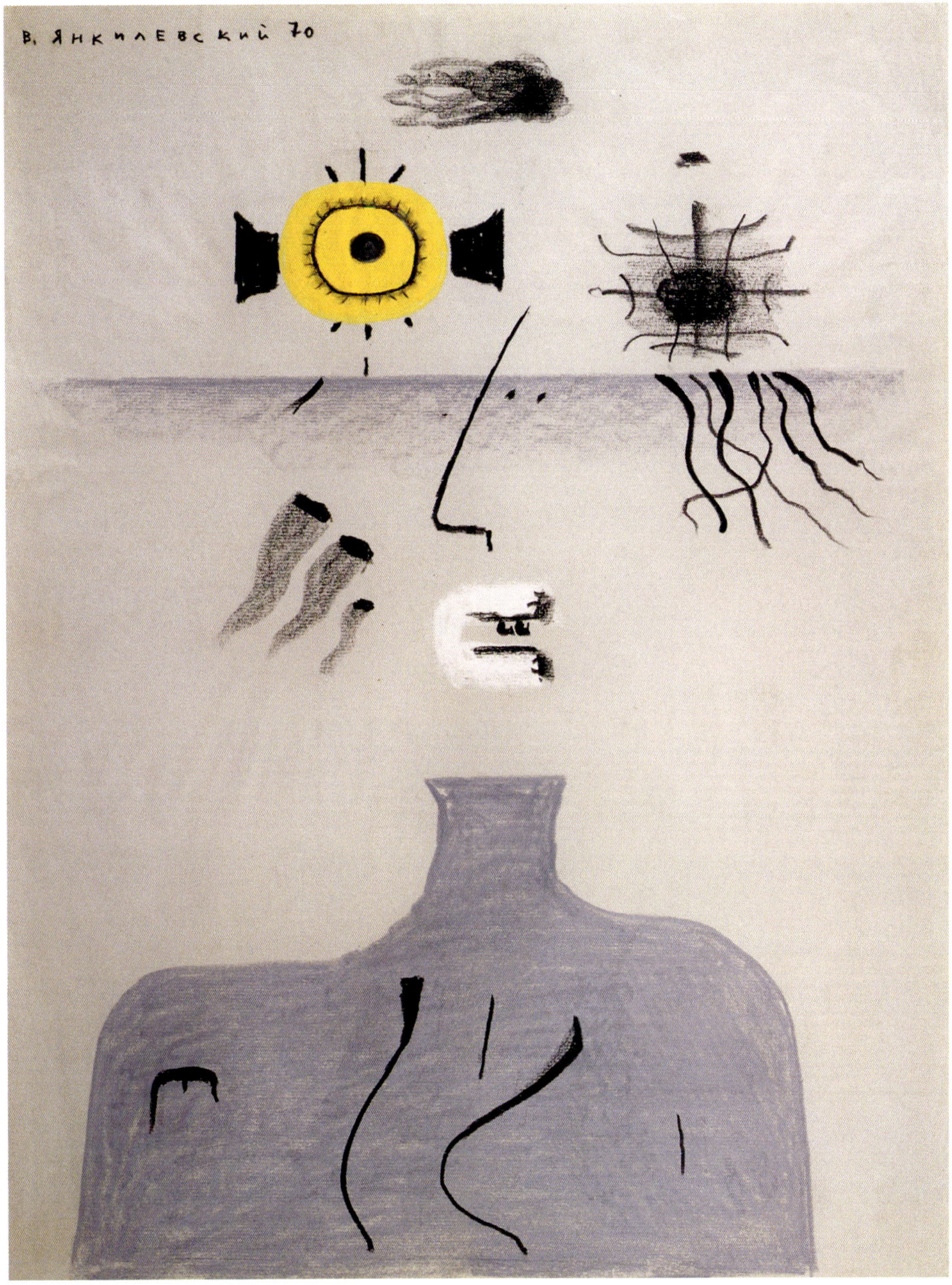

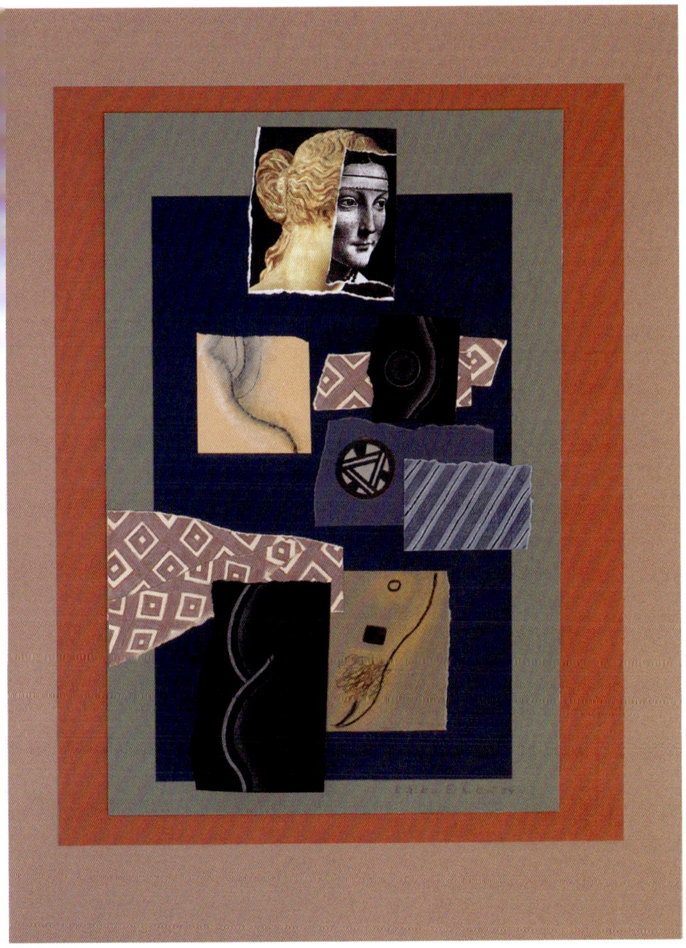

above
From the series Women's Faces, 1970
Pastel on paper
63.5 × 49 cm
© Vladimir Yankilevsky
Collection of the Artist

left
From the series Images of Women, 2004
Collage on cardboard
80 × 60 cm
© Vladimir Yankilevsky
Private Collection, London

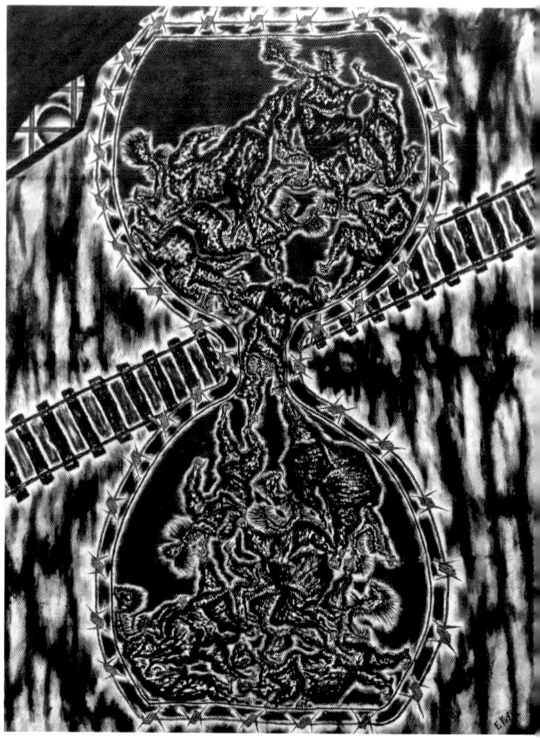

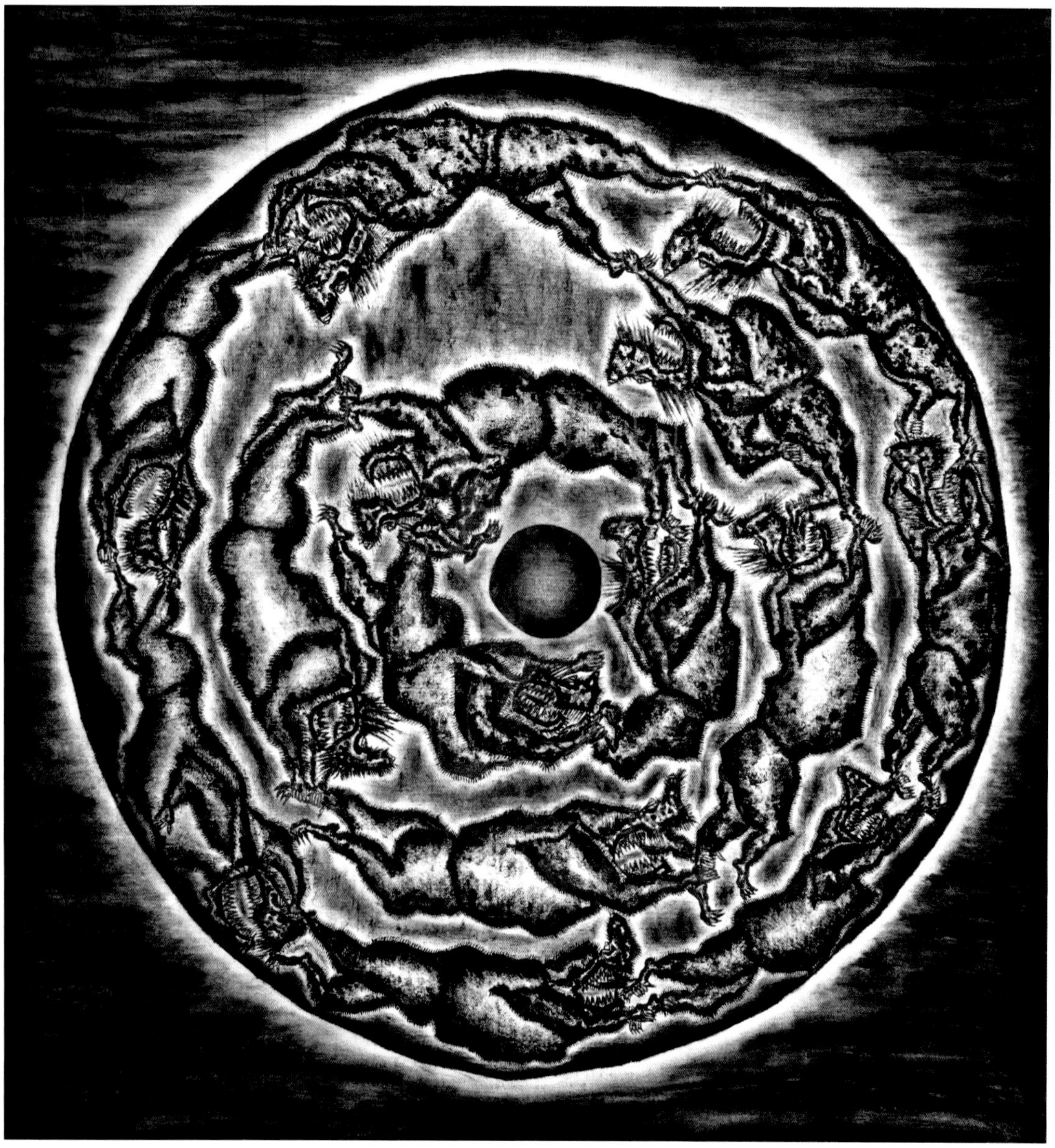

The work of avant-garde performance artist, photographer and film maker Evgeny Yufit is best undersood within the Necrorealist aesthetic, which he first promulgated in 1984. Born in 1961 in St Petersburg, where he continues to live and work, Yufit was the leader of the Necrorealists, whose members included Andrei Mertvyi, Oleg Kotelnikov and Evgeny Kondratyev. Working exclusively with 16-millimetre black-and-white film, Yufit's silent moving images set the tone for the movement, which focused on extremely formal cinematographic experimentation.

Although lacking a formal film education, Yufit's large body of work continuously develops a single conceptual thread, intermixing images of life and death that acquire an existential character. He blends boundaries to such an extent that his characters inhabit a no-man's-land between death and life. Films like *Werewolf Orderlies* (1984), *Spring* (1987) and *Daddy, Father Frost Is Dead* (1991) initially seem to take their inspiration from horror movies populated by zombies and featuring senseless violence and chase scenes. Yet Necrorealism, despite the morbid associations of its name, is founded on philosophical musings and games of free association. Yufit may mask his zombies and vampires in plaster casts and fake blood, but the effect is to enhance his exploration of humanity's unconscious, primeval, animalistic nature.

In 1985, Yufit set up the first independent film studio in Russia, Mzhalalafilm, a hotbed of radical experimentation where he produced his own first works. His artistic output extends to photography, which, like his films, demonstrates the influence of German Expressionism, French Surrealism and the silent movies of the 1920s. In fact, many of his photographs are often film stills which he turns upside down, enhancing their lack of focus to create organic-seeming masses. In both of his chosen media, Yufit avoids a clear narrative trajectory or structure, instead privileging the workings of the subconscious and of absurdism. In making these formal decisions, he also references the visual and literary traditions and contemporary reality of St Petersburg, a city that thrives on the dialectics of officialdom and underground culture.

Yufit's dark avant-garde films have attained international success at festivals in Locarno, Toronto, Montreal and Moscow. They form part of the permanent collections of the Film Institute Netherlands, Amsterdam; the Museum of Modern Art, New York; and the State Russian Museum, St Petersburg.

top
Time, 2009
Oil on canvas (central part of a triptych)
150 x 200 cm
© Evgeny Yufit
Courtesy of the artist

above left
Tired Sun, 2011
Oil on canvas
150 x 150 cm
© Evgeny Yufit
Courtesy of the artist

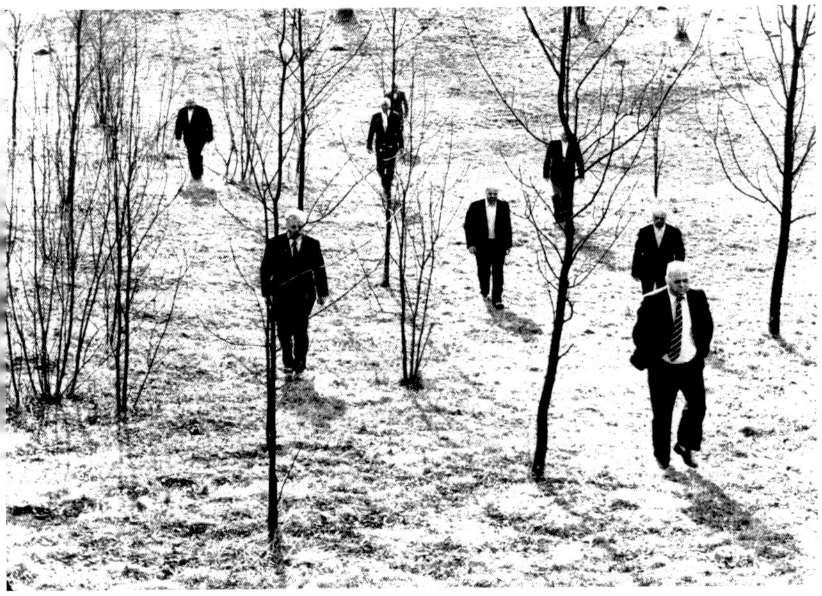

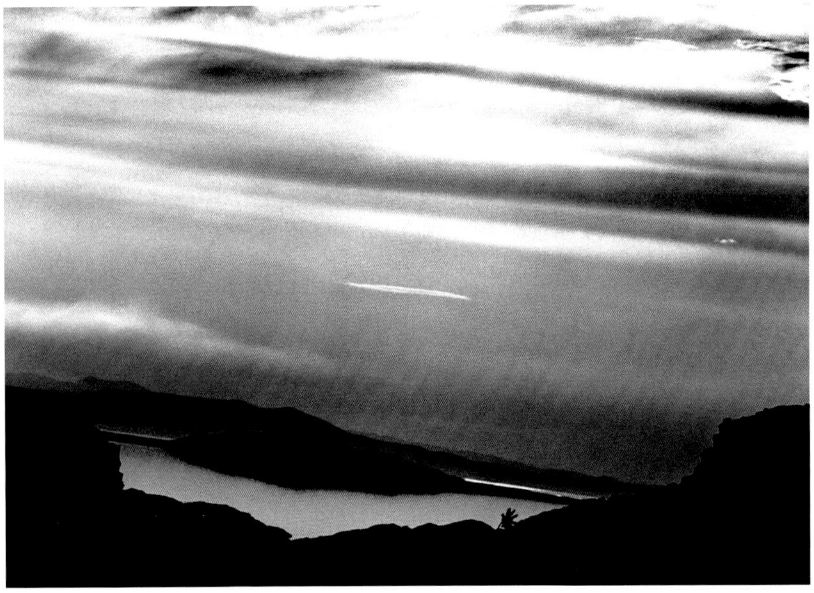

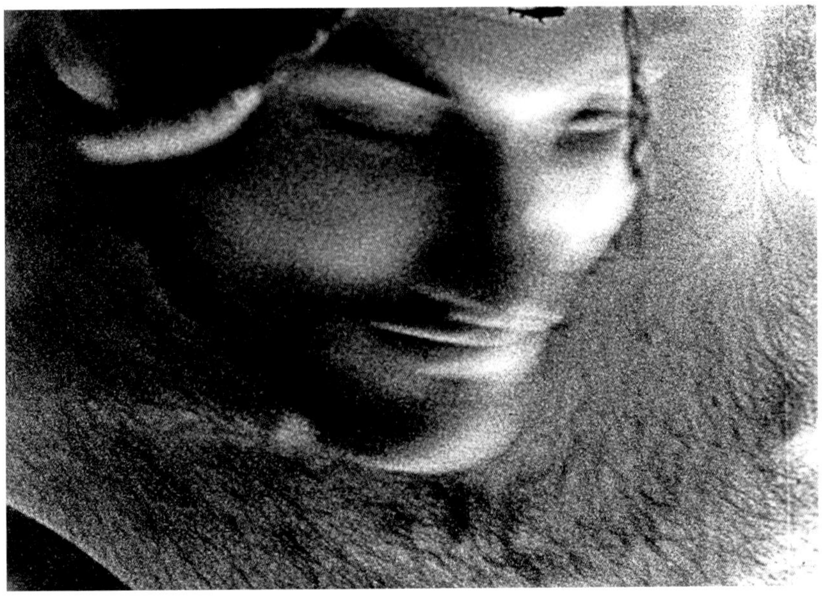

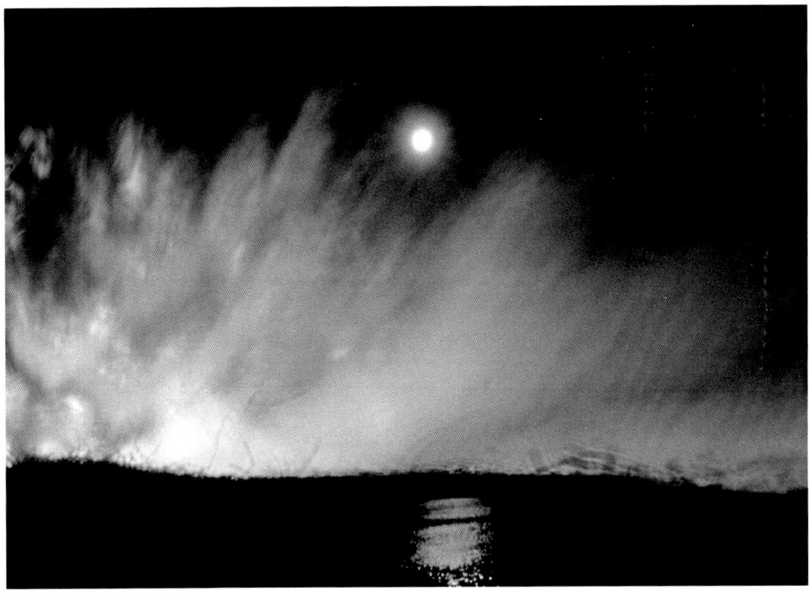

top
Transparent Grove, 1992
Black and white photograph
(central part of a triptych)
100 x 140 cm
© Evgeny Yufit
State Russian Museum, St Petersburg
Courtesy of the artist

above
Rustle, 1996
Black and white photograph
(part of a triptych)
100 x 140 cm
© Evgeny Yufit
Courtesy of the artist

top
From the series Longliver, 1997
Black and white photograph
100 x 140 cm
© Evgeny Yufit
Courtesy of the artist

above
From the series Silent Horizon, 2008
Black and white photograph
100 x 140 cm
© Evgeny Yufit
Courtesy of the artist

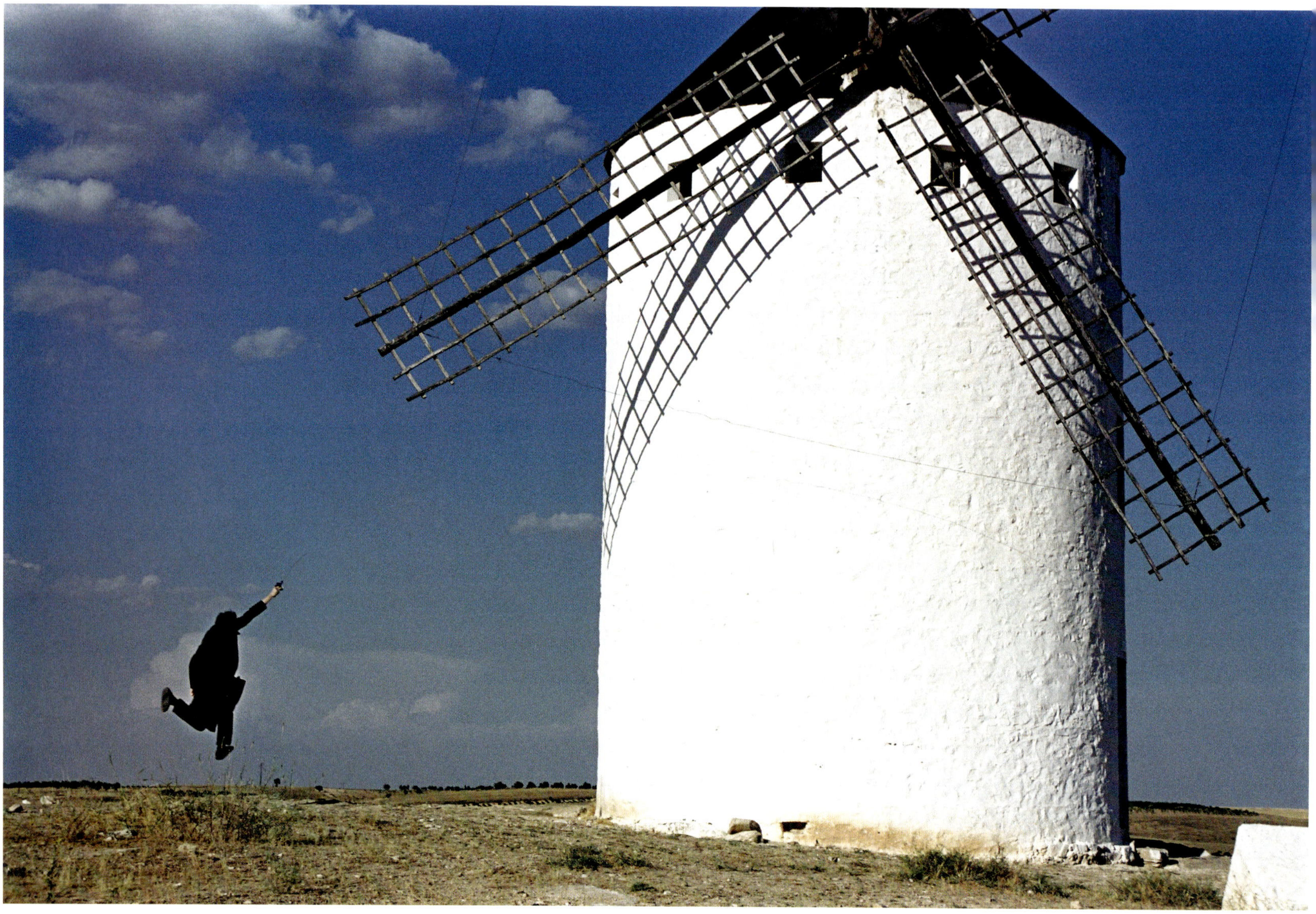

Born in 1959 in Dushanbe, Tajikistan, Vadim Zakharov graduated from the Moscow State Pedagogical University; today he lives and works in Berlin and Moscow. An artist, editor, archivist and collector of the Moscow Conceptualist circle since the late 1970s, Zakharov's oeuvre investigates art and culture in order to reveal his own critical, mystical and reflective roles within them. Zakharov won the Kandinsky Prize in 2009.

Zakharov's projects and actions are often humorous with a touch of the absurd. In his earliest actions, such as *I Made Enemies* (1982) and *The Eye Patch* (1983), he tried to cause a shift in habitual ways of seeing by challenging a number of older underground artists about their artistic convictions or changing his own physical perceptions by wearing an eye patch. Beginning in 1996, Zakharov undertook a series of tongue-in-cheek pilgrimages around Europe, Russia and Japan entitled *The Funny and Sad Adventures of the Foolish Pastor*. These performances approached the idea of utopia with an attitude of childish glee and mock ignorance, chasing windmills, fighting sumo wrestlers, and coming into contact with the 'huge, terrifying and inhuman' apparatus of governments and institutions.

As a Moscow Conceptualist, Zakharov comments on culture by reflecting it back on itself as if in a crooked mirror. *Russian Porcelain* (2004), for example, displays fragments of porcelain statuettes one might find in any petit-bourgeois apartment but in depraved configurations. In *Saint Sebastian Suite* (2009), the mystical reverse perspective of icons is made literal in furniture decorated with the radical geometry of the Russian avant-garde.

above
The Funny and Sad Adventures of the Foolish Pastor, Adventure 3: In Search of the Knight of the Rueful Countenance, 1996–2007
Campo de Criptana, Spain, 1996
Photo. Maria Porudominskaja

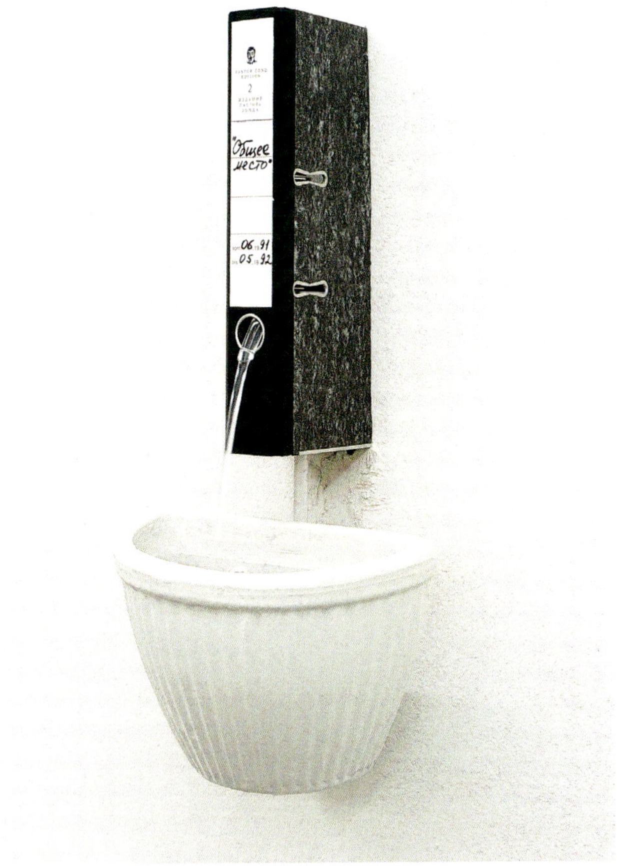

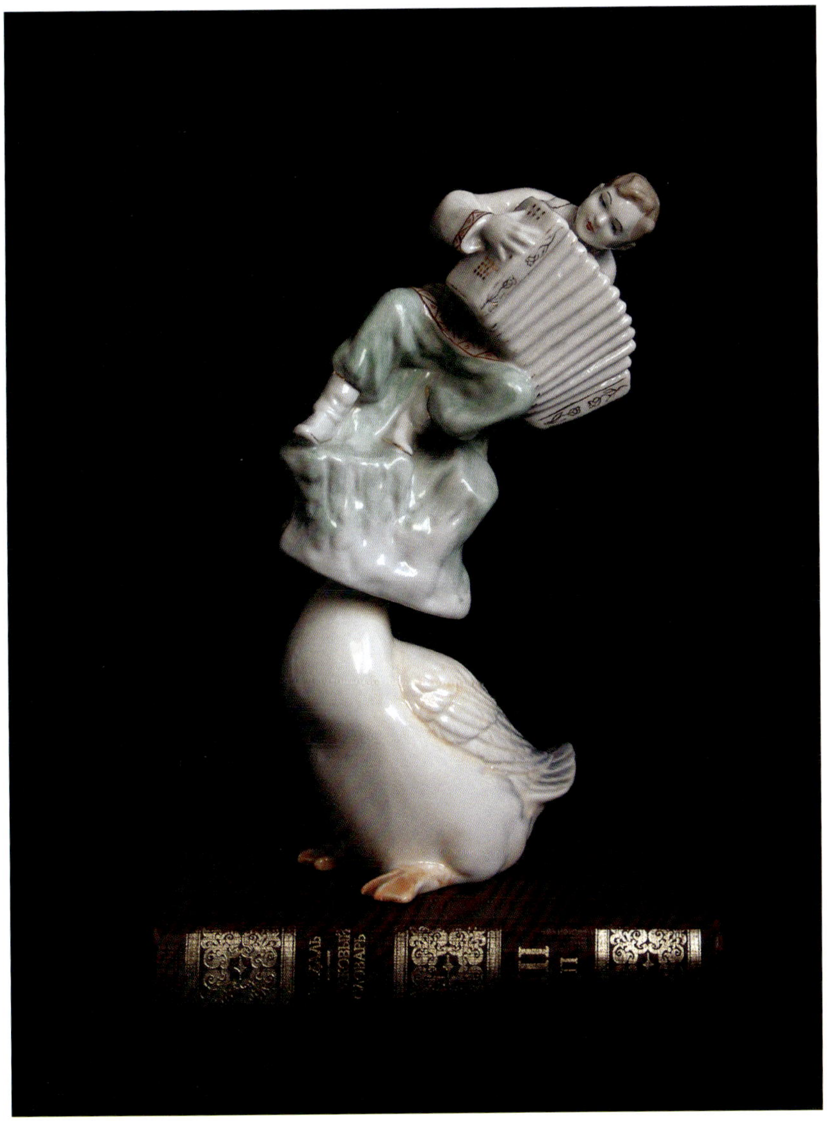

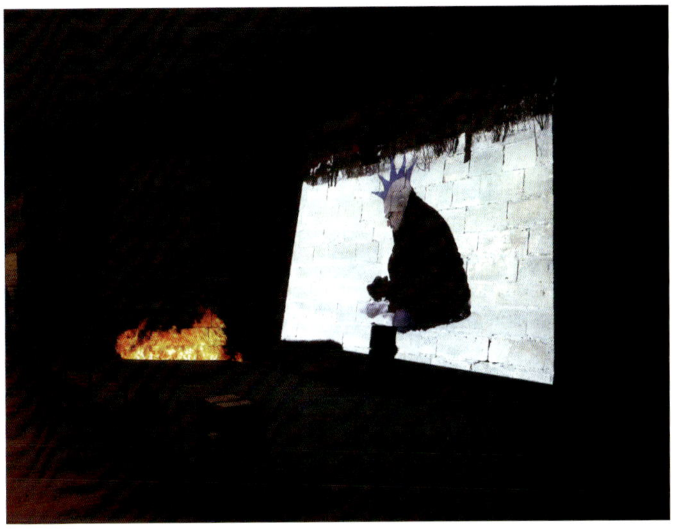

top
Fountain – Aqua Sacra, 1992
Mixed media
60 x 30 x 12 cm
Photo: Vadim Zakharov
© Vadim Zakharov
Courtesy of the artist

left
Russian Porcelain,
Dictionary of Dal, Volume 3, 2008
Porcelain, book
30 x 26 x 16 cm
Photo: Vadim Zakharov
© Vadim Zakharov
Courtesy of the artist

above
The End: Confession of a Contemporary Artist, 2010
3 video projections
Photo: Vadim Zakharov
© Vadim Zakharov
Courtesy of the artist

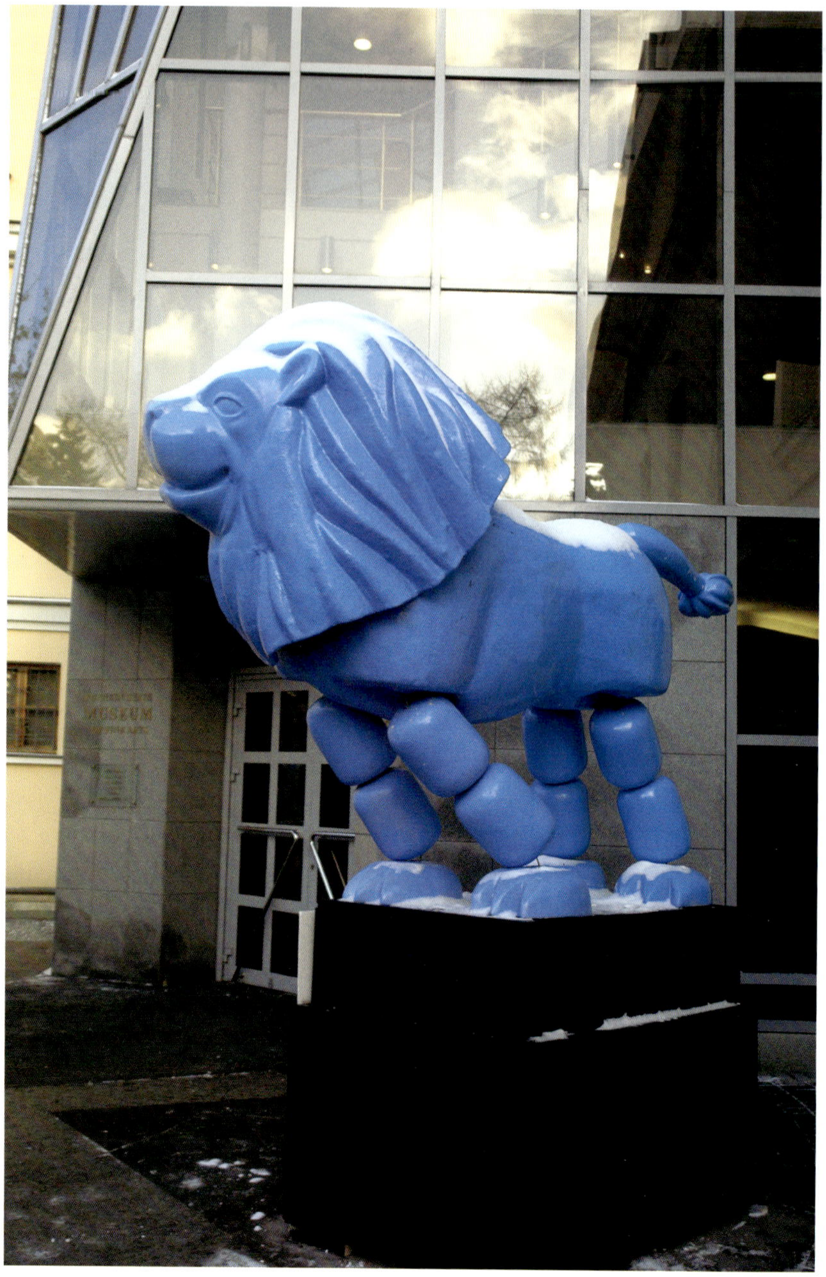

above
Author – monument of Utopie. Hommage to Pavel Filonov's exhibition – Witness of the Unseen, 2006
The State Russian Museum, St. Petersburg,
Museum of Privat Collection, Moscow
Photo: Vadim Zakharov
© Vadim Zakharov
Courtesy of the artist

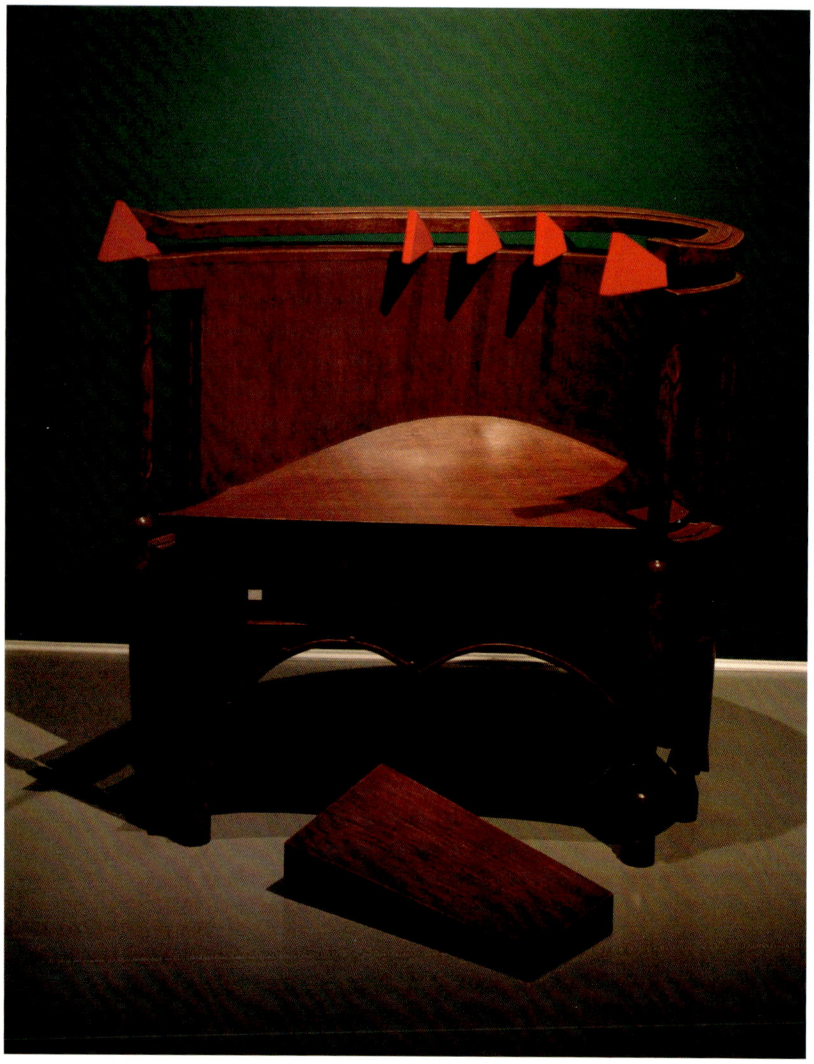

left
Saint Sebastian Suite, 2008
Wood
Photo: Vadim Zakharov
© Vadim Zakharov
Private collection

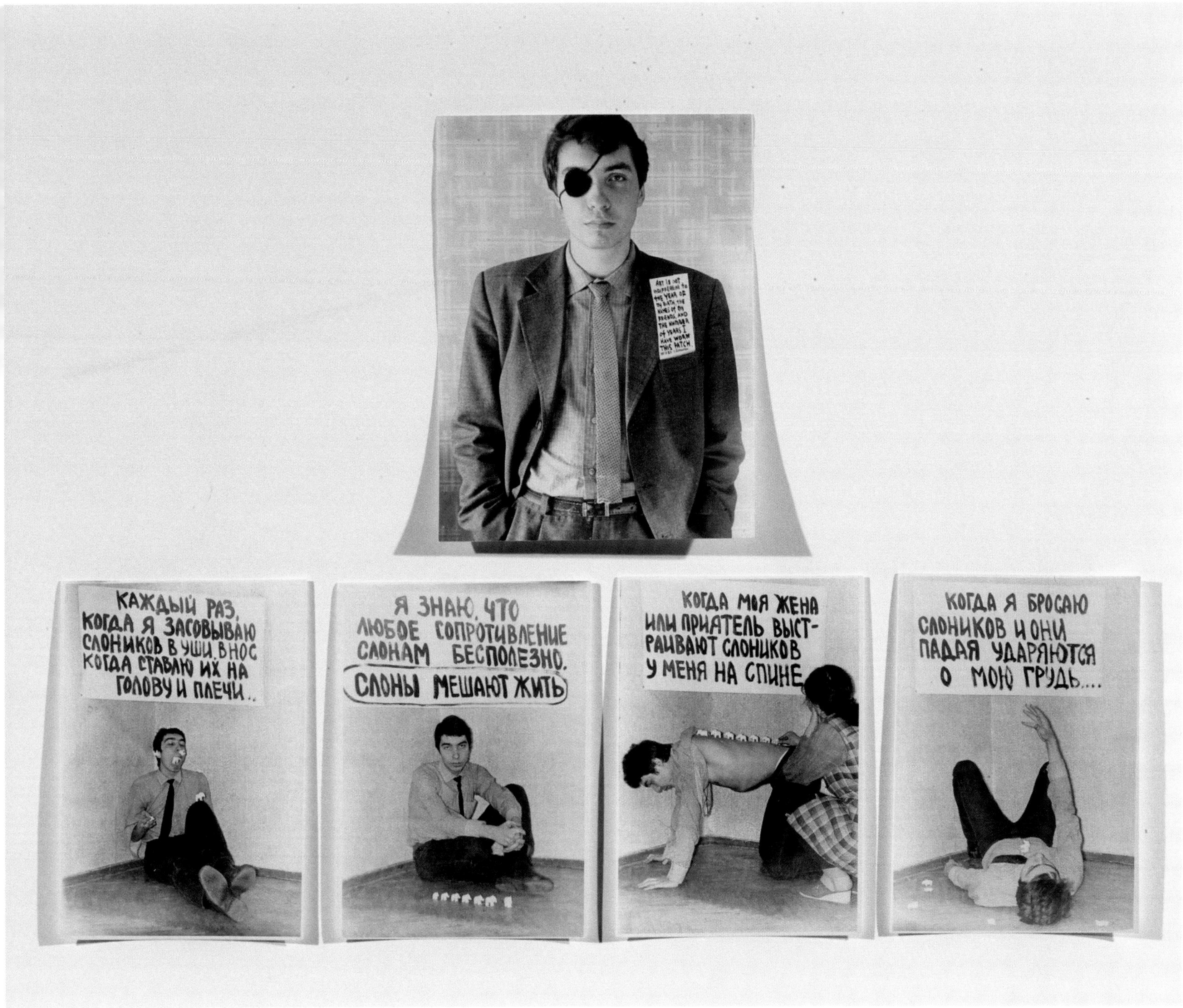

above
Eye-patch, 1983
Photographs
Varying dimensions
© Vadim Zakharov
Courtesy of the artist

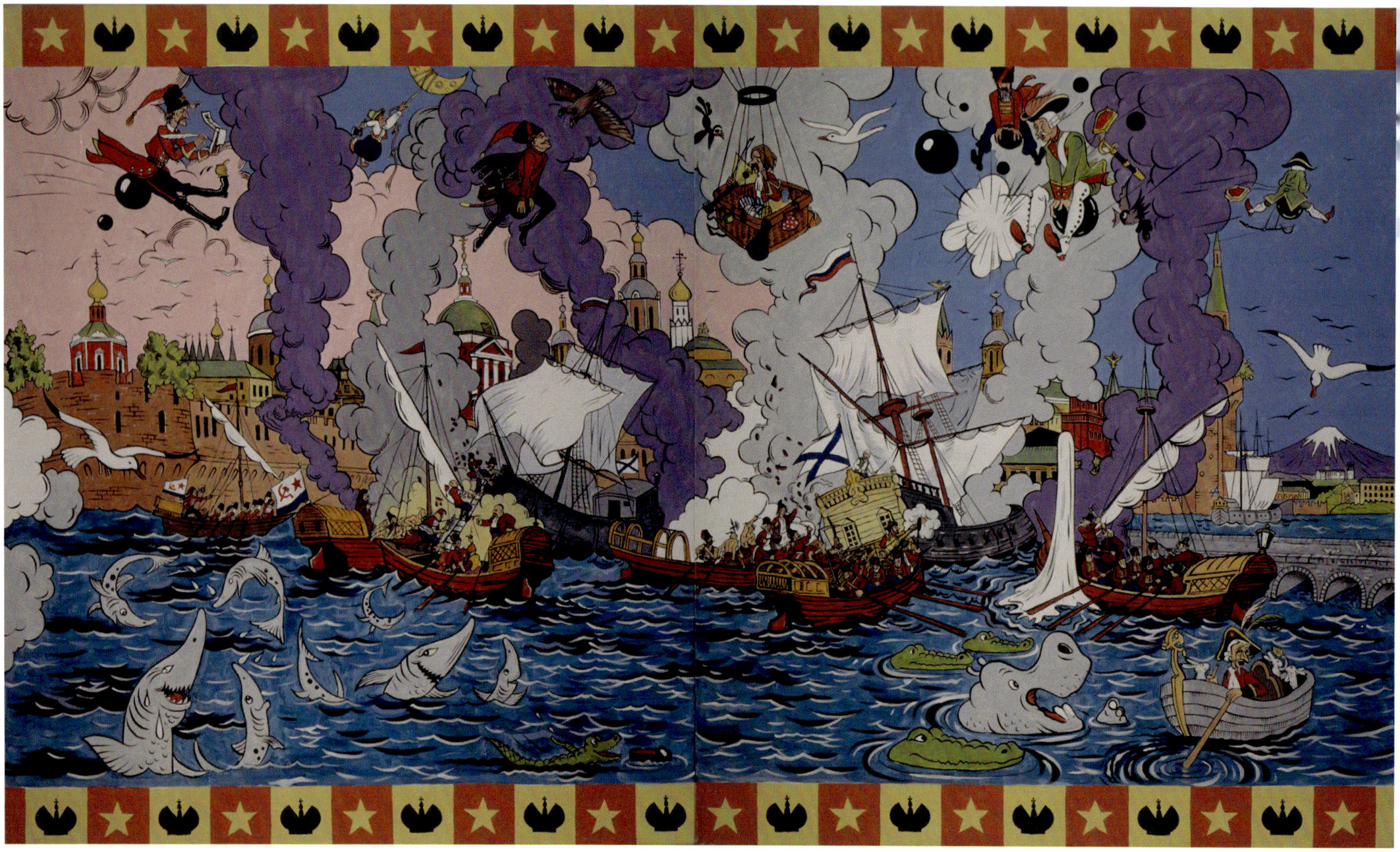

Konstantin Zvezdochetov

Painter, graphic artist and Conceptualist Konstantin Zvezdochetov was born in 1958 in Moscow, where he lives and works. He studied stage design at the Moscow Art Theatre School between 1976 and 1981. During the 1980s he was involved with a number of important Conceptual groups of the Moscow underground, whether as a member of the Toadstools group (1978–84), among the organisers of the first APTART exhibitions (1982) or as a founder member of Champions of the World (1986–8); he also participated in the Avantgardist Club. Zvezdochetov has shown work in numerous group and solo exhibitions throughout Russia and Europe. He is represented in museums in Italy, Hungary and the US, and in private collections such as the Ekaterina Cultural Foundation, Moscow. Using caricature and imitating comic-book illustration, Zvezdochetov's paintings explore the stereotypes and myths of contemporary culture.

above
Battle of Russians and Soviets,
2004
Acrylic on canvas
200 x 340 cm
© Konstantin Zvezdochetov
Ekaterina and Vladimir Semenikhin Collection

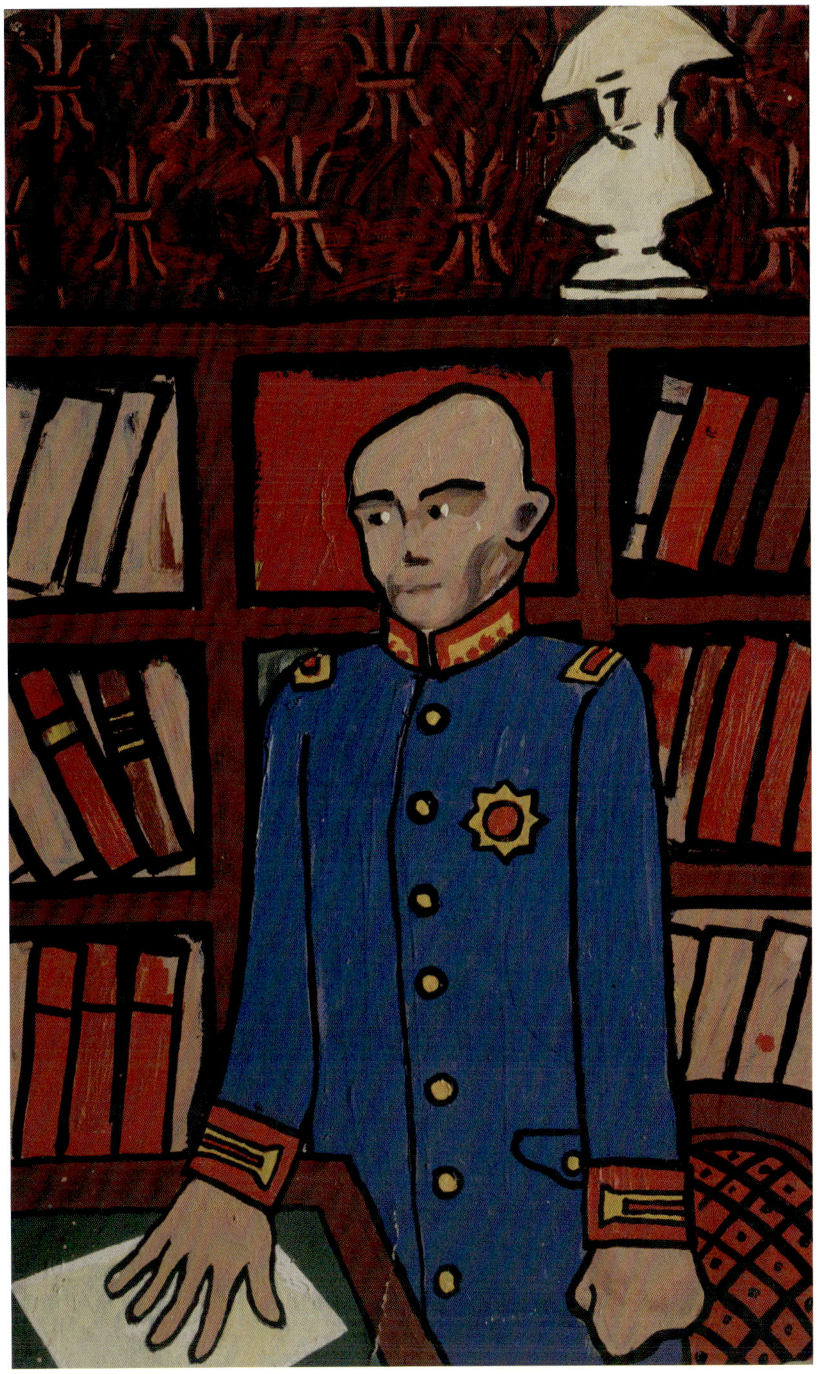

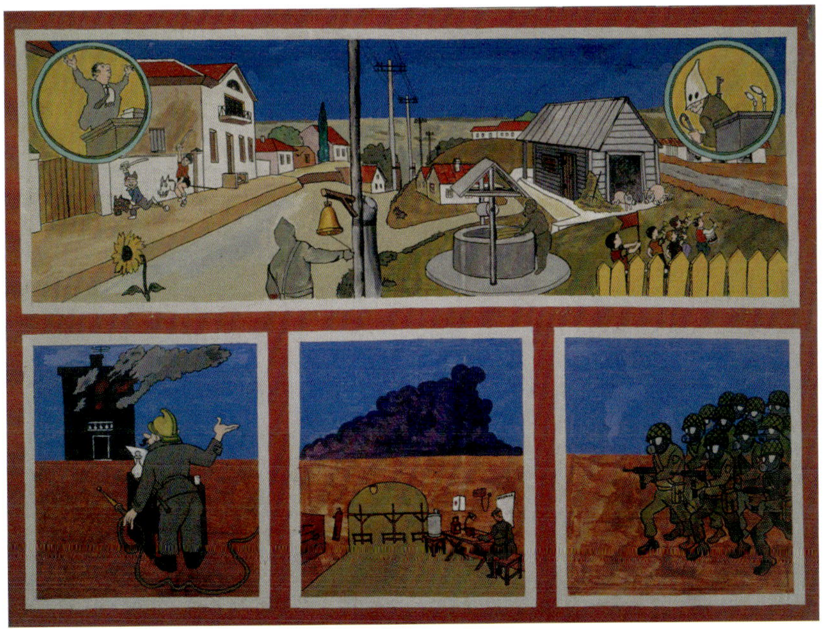

above
Civil Servant, 1983
Oil on fibreboard
80 x 50 cm
© Konstantin Zvezdochetov
Ekaterina and Vladimir
Semenikhin Collection

left
Maneuvers, 1999
Acrylic on canvas
145 x 194 cm
© Konstantin Zvezdochetov
Ekaterina and Vladimir
Semenikhin Collection

1953
- Death of Joseph Stalin
- Nikita Khrushchev becomes First Secretary of the Communist Party
- The Western Art exhibition rooms at the Pushkin Museum of Fine Arts, Moscow, are restored, the Soviet government having closed them in 1948 in an attempt to isolate Soviet art from the rest of the world

1955
- Signing of the Warsaw Pact

1955
- XX Party Congress at which Khrushchev officially denounces Stalin in the first step in the de-Stalinisation of the Soviet Union and the beginning of the Thaw

1957
- Sputnik space programme is started
- The International Festival of Youth is held in Moscow, the first time that Russian artists have the opportunity to see works by leading modern artists from the West
- During the mid-1950s, a group of unofficial painters and poets meets in Lianozovo to form an artistic community of the same name; they include Oscar Rabin, Vladimir Nemukhin, Lydia Masterkova and Lev Kropivnitsky, among others

1958
- Khrushchev becomes Premier of the Soviet Union
- Writer Boris Pasternak is awarded the Nobel Prize for Literature, but controversy forces him to reject it

1959
- American National Exhibition is staged in Sokolniki Park, Moscow, showing works by contemporary American abstract painters such as Pollock and Rauschenberg for the first time in Russia

1961
- Yuri Gagarin becomes the first man to orbit the Earth

1962
- Cuban Missile Crisis
- *One Day in the Life of Ivan Denisovich* by Alexander Solzhenitsyn is published in a Soviet magazine
- Vladimir Weisberg publishes a treatise on his experiments with colour and paints *White on White*, influenced by Malevich's post-Suprematist period
- Lev Nussberg establishes a group of Russian Kinetic artists, Dvizheniye, including Franciso Infante
- *Thirty Years of the Moscow Union of Artists* exhibition at the Manege, Moscow, shows the work of many nonconformist painters. Also on show is *New Reality*, including work by Beliutin's school of abstraction. The exhibition is publicly condemned by Khrushchev, thus marking an end to the Thaw

1963
- Vladimir Nemukhin paints his first work with playing cards

1964
- Khrushchev is deposed by Leonid Brezhnev

1967
- Collector Alexander Glezer organises an unofficial exhibition at the Druzhba Club, Moscow, entitled *Exhibition of Twelve Artists* and including work by Eduard Steinberg

1968
- Francisco Infante creates *Suprematist Games*, which marks the beginning of his Artifacts series

1971
- Khrushchev dies. His tomb is designed by nonconformist artist Ernst Neizvestny
- Eric Bulatov paints *Red Horizon* (1971–2), a radical work combining traditional landscape painting with Soviet official imagery, and questioning the existence of freedom and the infiltration of official ideology into private life

1972
- Soviet Union and US sign the SALT 1 Strategic Arms Limitation Treaty, ushering in a period of détente
- Komar and Melamid found the Sots Art movement; early works include *Double Self-Portrait as Lenin and Stalin*, which is destroyed during the 'Bulldozer Exhibition'

1973
- Dina Vierny presents an exhibition of Soviet unofficial artists, *Avant-garde russe*, in her Paris gallery; the show includes work by Eric Bulatov and Vladimir Yankilevsky

1974
- An open-air exhibition of unofficial art, known as the 'Bulldozer Exhibition', shows work by Vladimir Nemukhin, Oscar Rabin, Lydia Masterkova, and Komar and Melamid. The government orders a crackdown, with many works destroyed by bulldozers. This sparks an international scandal focusing on the lack of artistic freedom in the Soviet Union
- *Izmailovo Exhibition* – an officially sanctioned open-air exhibition – is mounted as a consequence of international pressure following the 'Bulldozer Exhibition'

1975
- Ilya Kabakov and Victor Pivovarov create a new artistic genre, the album, which combines text and image and has a wide-ranging influence on other contemporary artists
- Radical, short-lived artists' group The Nest stage a performance at VDNKh during which members hatch eggs in a giant nest, thus parodying Soviet agricultural shows

1976
- Komar and Melamid hold their first international exhibition at the Ronald Feldman Gallery, New York, though the duo continue to reside in Moscow
- Conceptual group Collective Actions is founded
- Leonid Sokov organises an exhibition of his unofficial work in his own apartment, bringing him to the attention of American collector Norton Dodge
- Painter Evgeny Rukhin dies in a studio fire rumoured to have been set at the behest of the KGB, though this is never proven

1977
- Venice Biennale of Dissent, staged during the gap year between two biennales, presents the work of dissident artists from the Communist bloc in a gesture of solidarity

1978
- Collector George Costakis, following mounting pressure from the KGB, emigrates to Greece
- While on a trip to Paris, Oscar Rabin is permanently stripped of his Soviet citizenship and refused entry back into the USSR
- Toadstools (Mukhomor) group is founded, lasting until 1984, when several members are made to enlist in the army

1979
- Soviet invasion of Afghanistan
- First dual-language magazine dedicated to Russian unofficial art, *A-Ya*, is published in Paris by Igor Shelkovsky. The debut issue includes an article by Boris Groys, 'Moscow Romantic Conceptualism', defining the movement that goes on to become known as 'Moscow Conceptualism'

1980
- Viktor Skersis and Vadim Zakharov begin collaborating under the title 'SZ'

1981
- Margarita Tupitsyn curates the *New Wave* exhibition at the Contemporary Russian Art Center of America, New York, thus bringing Russian Conceptual art to an international audience
- Underground rock band Kino is formed in St Petersburg, its front man being Viktor Tsoi. Closely intertwined with the city's unofficial artistic life, it later features artist George Gurianov as its drummer (1983–90)

1982
- Brezhnev dies
- First APTART exhibition is staged in artist Nikita Alexeev's Moscow apartment

1984
- Semyon Faibisovich begins his popular series The Moscow Underground (1984–8)
- Leonid Sokov creates *Meeting of Two Sculptors*, combining models of Lenin and Giacometti
- Artistic and literary group Mitki is founded by Vladimir Shinkarev and Dmitry Shagin, among others, and mounts its first collective exhibition

1985
- Mikhail Gorbachev becomes General Secretary of the Communist Party and attempts to improve the faltering economy by means of glasnost and perestroika reforms
- Evgeny Yufit invents Necrorealism, creating independent short films in his own studio, Mzhalalafilm, and inspiring a new movement

1986
- Artists' group Champions of the World is founded in Moscow, exhibiting in a show entitled *Art Against Commerce* at Bitsa Park

1987
- Group AES is formed, including Tatiana Aramazova, Lev Evzovich and Evgeney Svyatsky (Vladmir Fridkes joins in 1995)
- Group Inspection Medical Hermeneutics is founded by Pavel Pepperstein, Yuri Liederman and Sergei Anufriev in Moscow
- House on Furmanny is founded in Moscow's Furmanny Lane, a hub of the underground community
- The influential film *ASSA* is made, charting the life of the avant-garde, underground music scene in St Petersburg. Sergei Bugaev (Afrika) stars as the main character, Bananan. Timur Novikov, Sergei Shutov and others are also involved
- Immediate Photography group is founded by Alexei Shulgin, including Boris Mikhailov and Igor Moukhin

1988
- Singing Revolution in the Baltics (1988–91) results in independence for Estonia, Latvia and Lithuania
- Sotheby's legendary auction of modern and contemporary Russian art is held in Moscow. The star lot is Grisha Bruskin's *Fundamental Lexicon*, estimated at £18,000 and selling for £220,000
- Ilya Kabakov shows *Ten Characters* at the Ronald Feldman Gallery, New York, bringing his 'total installation' art to the West for the first time
- Museum of Non-Conformist Art opens in St Petersburg on the territory of the Pushkinskaya-10 Art-Center. Over the course of its existence, it expands to include exhibition, research and archive spaces, and becomes home to a collection of nonconformist artworks from the second half of the twentieth century

1989
- Velvet Revolution in Czechoslovakia sees the overthrow of the Soviet government
- In Leningrad, Timur Novikov founds the New Academy of Fine Arts, whose purpose is to promote underground Neo-Academicism. He also sets up the independent television station Piratskoye TV (1989–92) with Yuris Lesnik and Vladislav Mamyshev-Monroe
- Anatoly Osmolovsky founds the ETI (Art Territory Expropriation) movement to directly engage with and challenge contemporary Russian politics
- Curator Andrei Erofeev starts a collection of Russian contemporary unofficial art at the Tsaritsino Museum

1990
- Declaration of State Sovereignty of the Russian Soviet Federative Socialist Republic marks the beginning of constitutional reform in Russia
- Exhibition *Between Spring and Summer: Soviet Conceptual Art*, co-curated by Joseph Backstein, is shown at the Institute of Contemporary Art, Boston
- Lead singer of Kino, Viktor Tsoi, dies in an automobile accident in Latvia, aged twenty-eight

1991
- Soviet Union is finally dismantled with the creation of the Russian Federation, and Boris Yeltsin becomes its first President
- Collector Norton Dodge enters into an agreement with the Jane Voorhees Zimmerli Art Museum, New Brunswick, for the donation of a core group of works from his collection
- Institute of Contemporary Art, Moscow, is opened by Joseph Backstein. The aim of this independent, not-for-profit organisation is to bring fresh impetus to the Russian contemporary art world
- Painter Eric Bulatov emigrates to Paris

1992
- National Centre for Contemporary Arts, Moscow, is founded under State sponsorship to develop and promote contemporary Russian art at home and abroad
- Ilya and Emilia Kabakov settle in New York

1993
- Russian constitutional crisis results in the creation of the 5th Constitution of Russia, giving greater power to the presidency
- Ilya Kabakov represents Russia at the 45th Venice Biennale

1994
- Russian troops invade Chechnya

1995
- Chechen artist Alexei Kallima moves to Moscow

1996
- In presidential elections, Yeltsin narrowly defeats his Communist challenger, Gennady Zhyuganov
- *Interpol* exhibition in Stockholm, meant as an historic encounter between Western artists and artists from the former Communist states, achieves notoriety. Oleg Kulik is arrested for biting a member of the public during his performance *Dog House*
- Art Moscow, an annual international contemporary art fair, is launched at the Central House of Artists
- Moscow House of Photography is founded by Olga Sviblova
- First international Photobiennale is organised by the Moscow House of Photography
- Art Manege, an annual international fair of contemporary art, is established

1997
- Statue to Peter the Great by Zurab Tseretelli is erected in Moscow
- Maxim Kantor represents Russia at the 47th Venice Biennale with an exhibition entitled *Criminal Chronicles*
- Artists' group RADEK is founded by Anatoly Osmolovsky. Other members include Alexei Kallima, Alexei Buldakov and David Ter-Oganyan
- Boris Mikhailov begins his series Case History (1997–8) following his return to Kharkov after a DAAD residency in Berlin
- Performance artist Alexander Brener is jailed for painting a green dollar sign on a Suprematist work by Kazimir Malevich in the Stedelijk Museum, Amsterdam

1998
- Artist Avdei Ter-Oganyan destroys Orthodox icons with an axe and is later exiled to Prague after the Church initiates criminal proceedings against him

1999
- Vladimir Putin becomes Prime Minister of Russia
- Boris Yeltsin abdicates and Putin becomes acting President
- *ArtChronika*, Russia's first independent, privately owned popular art journal, is published
- Moscow Museum of Modern Art is opened by Zurab Tseretelli

2000
- Vladimir Putin is elected President of the Russian Federation
- Other Art Museum opens at the State University for Humanities, Moscow. Growing out of the collection of Leonid Talochkin (1936–2002), it is the largest museum of unofficial Russian art of the 1950s–80s, containing over 2,000 works

2001
- The sinking of the nuclear submarine *Kursk* in August 2000 prompts photographer Sergei Bratkov to create his series Sailors

2002
- Nord-Ost siege during which armed Chechens seize a crowded Moscow theatre, resulting in many deaths
- Timur Novikov dies prematurely of pneumonia. A posthumous exhibition of his work is held at the State Russian Museum, St Petersburg
- First ArtKlyazma (2002–5) contemporary Land art and open-air festival is held at Klyazma Reservoir on the outskirts of Moscow

2003
- Artist and architect Yuri Avvakumov sets up the Utopia Foundation to collect designs for unrealised architectural projects in Russia over the past 300 years
- Stella Kesaeva sets up the non-commercial Stella Art Foundation to facilitate cultural exchange, support Russian artists, and offer exhibition space in Moscow and a forum for creative disciplines extending beyond the visual arts to include poetry

2004
- Vladimir Putin is re-elected President
- In Beslan, a group of Chechen terrorists take a school hostage
- Avdei Ter-Oganyan creates his controversial Radical Abstractionism series
- Ilya Kabakov has a solo exhibition at the State Hermitage Museum, St Petersburg, the first exhibition of a living artist
- Unofficial artist Mikhail Roginsky dies in Paris, aged 73

2005
- Joseph Backstein organises the first International Moscow Biennale
- Innovation Award is launched by the National Centre for Contemporary Arts, Moscow, to reward outstanding achievements in the visual arts. The first winner is Alexei Kallima, for *Chelsea-Terek*
- Semyon Faibisovich returns to oil painting after a decade

2006
- Artist and writer Maxim Kantor publishes *The Drawing Textbook* describing the evolution of society through the example of art history, including a critique of the contemporary art scene

2007
- Foundation of the Kandinsky Prize. Artist Anatoly Osmolovsky is the first recipient
- Vinzavod Centre of Contemporary Art opens in Moscow
- Collector Igor Markin opens Art4.ru, Russia's first completely private museum for post-war, unofficial and contemporary art, in Moscow
- Ekaterina Cultural Foundation (founded 2002) opens a dedicated exhibition space in the centre of Moscow
- Curator Andrei Erofeev stages an exhibition of previously censored Russian contemporary art, *Forbidden Art*, at the Andrei Sakharov Museum, Moscow. He is later charged with inciting religious hostilities
- Sotheby's stages the first-ever auction dedicated to Russian modern and contemporary art in London
- Phillips de Pury and Co sell the John L. Stewart Collection of Russian Contemporary Art in London for a record total
- Death of Dmitry Prigov, aged 67

2008
- Dmitry Medvedev is elected President
- Russia defeats Georgia and recognises South Ossetia and Abkhazia as independent states
- Opening of the Garage Centre for Contemporary Culture in the former Bakhmetevsky Bus Garage, Moscow (designed by Konstantin Melnikov), with an exhibition of works by Ilya and Emilia Kabakov
- Painter Alexei Belyaev-Gvintovt wins the Kandinsky Prize. His acceptance speech is booed by members of the audience because of his ultra-nationalist views
- Baibakov Art Projects is founded by Maria Baibakova
- Perm Museum of Modern Art opens
- Phillips de Pury and Co sell Ilya Kabakov's *Beetle* (1982) for £2.9 million
- Painter Vladimir Nemukhin is made an honorary member of the Russian Academy of Arts
- Unofficial artist Lydia Masterkova dies in Saint-Laurent-sur-Othain, aged 82

2009
- Joseph Backstein invites Jean-Hubert Martin to curate a groundbreaking show at the Garage Centre for Contemporary Culture as part of the 3rd Moscow Biennale; *Against Exclusion* attracts unprecedented visitor numbers for a contemporary art exhibition in Moscow
- Strelka Institute for Media, Architecture and Design is founded in the Red October chocolate factory, Moscow
- Vadim Zakharov wins the Kandinsky Prize

2010
- Aslan Chekhoev opens Novy Museum, the first private museum dedicated to Russian contemporary art in St Petersburg
- First Ural Industrial Biennial of Contemporary Art is staged in Ekaterinburg
- Alexander Brodsky wins the Kandinsky Prize

2011
- Andrei Monastyrsky and Collective Actions represent Russia at the 54th Venice Biennale; the show is curated by Boris Groys
- The Garage Centre for Contemporary Culture closes at the Bakhmetevsky Bus Garage, relocating to Gorky Park

Additional photo credits
Page 30 © Epsilon, Getty Images
Page 280 © Tatiana Lieberman

Endpapers:
Haim Sokol
Palimpsests, 2007–10
Drawings on carbon paper, 10 light boxes
65 x 93 x 10 cm (each)
© Haim Sokol
Courtesy Anna Nova Gallery,
St Petersburg

Acknowledgements

Frozen Dreams: Contemporary Art from Russia is another cultural project in the long series that I have created, more as a result of a triumph of good intentions than due to the vagaries of commercial publishing. For all that, it is a superb product, if I may say so myself.

The book owes a debt of gratitude to Joanna Vickery, the executive editor, for her dedication in bringing the variegated pieces of this art puzzle together. Not an easy task by any standard, given the dearth of available research and the complexities of working in Russia.

Frozen Dreams can lay claim to being one of the best designed of TransGlobe's contemporary art books, all of which have been produced under the creative direction of Roger Fawcett-Tang. His skills are outpaced only by his patience, no mean feat when having to work under hands-on design direction. Caroline Campkin and the team at CS Graphics are to be thanked for their superb printing and flexible production scheduling, while my co-publisher Thames & Hudson deserve mention.

Andrea Belloli, the book's managing editor, has been instrumental in bringing all of the disparate forces and editorial resources necessary together under one roof. *Frozen Dreams* is indebted to Andrea for her professionalism and timely execution under testing schedules.

The book has benefited from many intellectual and organisational resources on several continents, from minor image contributions to more important editorial reviews. The essays by Eleanor Heartney, Alexandra Danilova and Ekaterina Bobrinskaia piece together, for the first time on behalf of an international audience, critical, art-historical, easily readable referential timelines for Russia's modern and contemporary art.

The book has also benefited from the work of three project assistants: Xenia Eriksson, Anya Harrison and Anna Glovatskaya. Xenia has been notable in her performance as the project's Moscow coordinator. The Moscow photographers, Maria Ionova-Gribina and Artyom Goloschapov, have produced some interesting portraiture for the profiles, while Rudi Amirkhani and Yuri Zekster deserve thanks for their assistance on the ground. Moscow arts figures such as Olga Sviblova, Aidan Salakhova and Joseph Backstein are among many who merit mention for their enthusiasm and support for the project.

The publishers also wish to thank Ruth Addison and Triumph Gallery, Ageytomesh Publishing: Andrey Trofimov and Dmitry Biryukov, Diliara Allakhverdova, ArtChronika Archive, Reto Barmettler, Svetlana Baskova, Vladimir Berschader, Erica Boginsky, Maxim Bokser, Catherine Borissoff, Matthew Bown, Aliki Costakis, Marina Dashevskaya, Anna Egorova and Art4.ru, Ekaterina Cultural Foundation: Alekandra Kharitonova, Alexandra Guseynova, Vera Gluschenko, Vera Essaian, Nina Feygina, Garage Centre for Contemporary Culture: Darya Kotova and Kirsty Wallace, Steve Gater, Greek State Museum of Contemporary Art – Costakis Collection: Maria Tsantsanoglou and Angelica Charistou, Guelman Gallery: Anja Luneva and Elena Akulova, Aleksey Gushchin, Mike Hawkman and Aidan Gallery, Urs Haener, Eleanore Hopper and Feldman Gallery, Maria Ionova-Gribina, Michèle and Marc Ivasilievitch, Yelena Kalinsky, Mark Kelner, Galina Khorkova and Kournikova Gallery, Emily Kodama, Natalia Kolodzei and Kolodzei Art Foundation, Ekaterina Kondranina and Multimedia Art Museum, Moscow, Tatiana Krol, Alexandra Kosheleva and E.K.ArtBureau, Elena Kuprina-Lyakhovich, Alex Lachmann, Anna Laks, Tatiana Lieberman, MacDougalls Fine Art Auctioneers, Mediatheque at NCCA, Tatyana Merzlikina, Elizaveta Meshkvicheva, Vita Mikhailova, Moscow Museum of Modern Art: Natalia Panyushkina and Kirill Rostov, Ivgenia Naiman, Xenia Novikova, Ilona Orel and the Orel Art Gallery, Perm Museum of Modern Art: Anastasia Serebrennekova, Ekaterina Goldobina and Elena Tararukhina, Alexandra Perovskaya and XL Gallery, Phillips de Pury and Co., Maria Plavinskaya, Sergey Popov and pop/off/art, Andrey Prigov, Philippe Pumain, Regina Gallery: Nadia Totskaya and Romilly Eveleigh, Dr Alla Rosenfeld, Pierre Rouart, Masha Sabsay and Korban Art Foundation, Nadim Samman, Julia Saraeva, Rodion Savkin and National Center of Contemporary Art, Iraida Shvartsman, Valery Sorokin, Sotheby's and Jonathan Massey, Patrick Masson, Patrick van Maris, Alina Davey, Yulia Kunze, Nat Madden and Roxane Zand , State Hermitage Museum: Dmitry Ozerkov, Darya Gorlenkova, Anastasia Mikliaeva and Elena Obukhovich, Stella Art Foundation: Anna Svergun, Nikolai Molok, Anya Stonelake and Whitespace Gallery, Kirill Svetlyakov, Susan Swenson, Daria Syuzeva and Strelka Institute, Igor Tsukanov, Natalia Tumanyan and State Pushkin Museum of Fine Arts, Moscow, Dr Margarita Tupitsyna, Elena Uspenskaya, Mikhail Vilkovsky, Vinzavod: Galima Akhmadullina and Julia Avseneva, Yelena Walker, Carol Warner, Dr Sarah Wilson, Natalia Zakharova and Anna Zelenova.

Hossein Amirsadeghi
1 September 2011

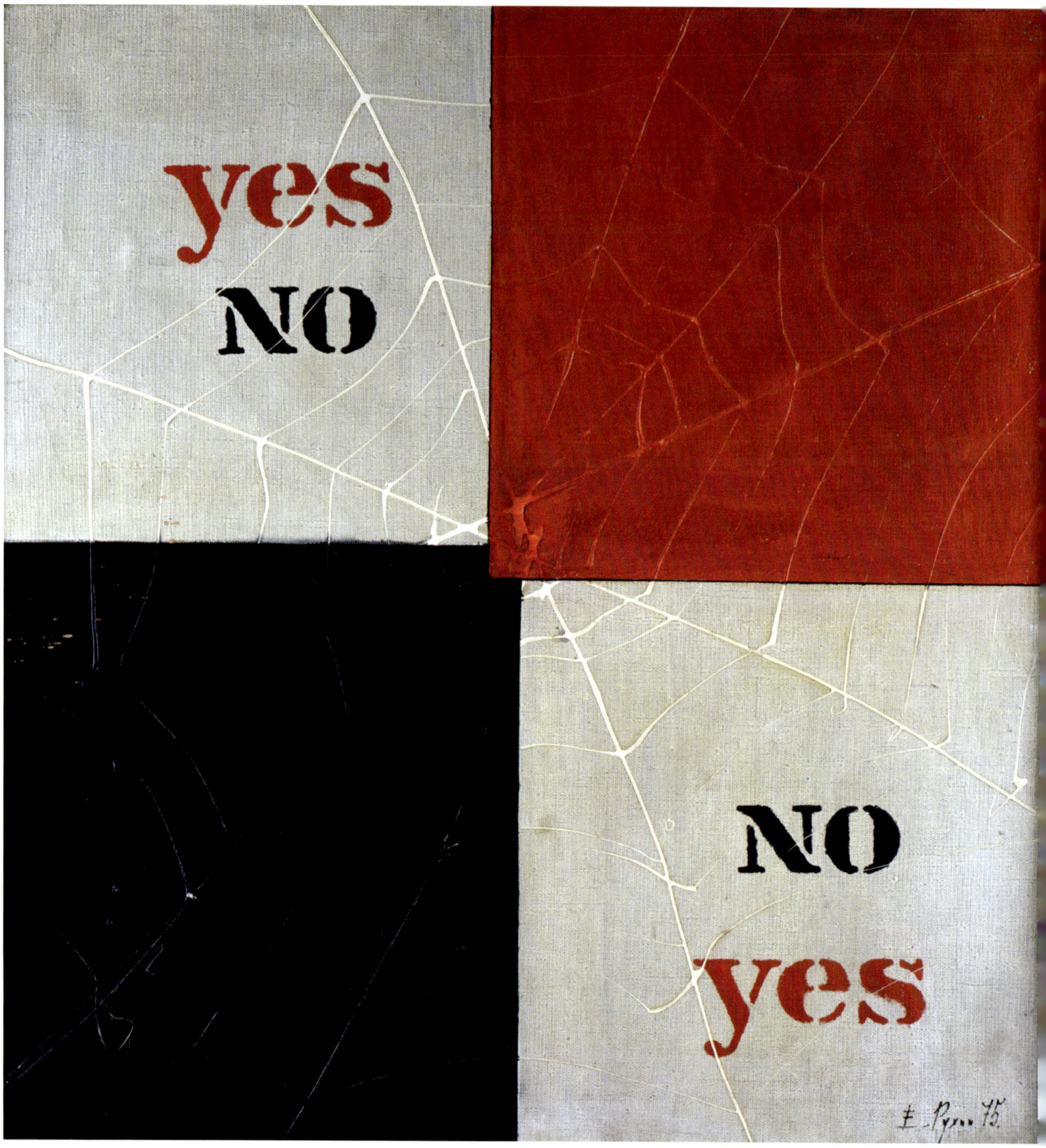

Evgeny Rukhin
Untitled, 1975
Oil on canvas
70 x 65.5 cm
© The Yevgeny Rukhin Foundation
Courtesy of Sotheby's

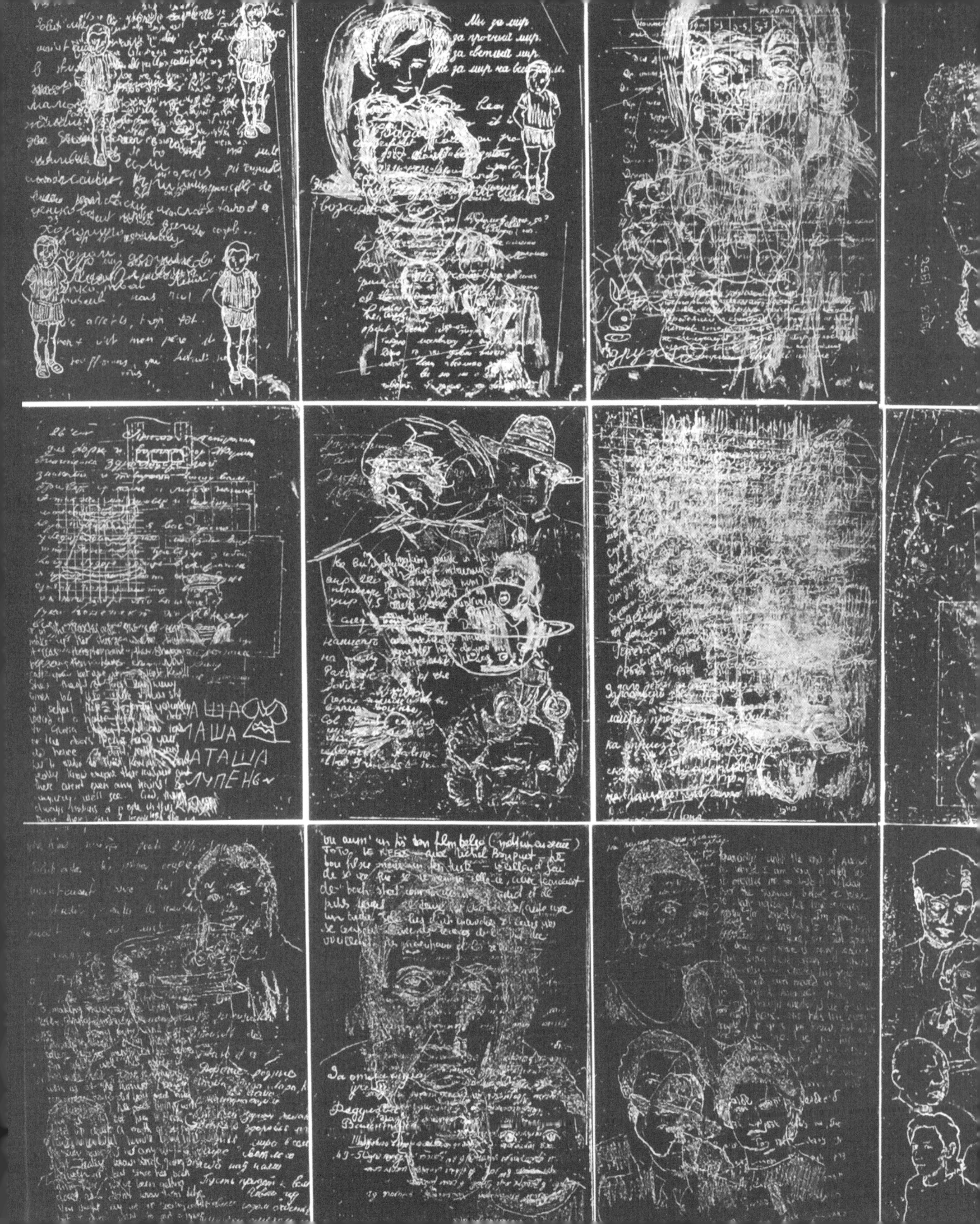
Ми за мир
за прочный мир
за светлый мир
МАША